SECOND EDITION

Assembler Language with ASSIST

ROSS A. OVERBEEK
W. E. SINGLETARY

Northern Illinois University

 SCIENCE RESEARCH ASSOCIATES, INC.
Chicago, Henley-on-Thames, Sydney, Toronto

A Subsidiary of IBM

This volume is respectfully dedicated to Professor William W. Boone of the University of Illinois, Urbana. Bill was the grandfather and father, respectively, of the authors in the field of mathematical logic. We welcome this opportunity to express our appreciation for the influence that he has had on our professional careers.

Ross A. Overbeek
W. E. Singletary

Acquisition Editor	Alan W. Lowe
Project Editor	Gretchen Hargis
Compositor	Graphic Typesetting Service
Cover Designer	Alex Teshin
Cover Art by	Edith Ge

Library of Congress Cataloging in Publication Data

Overbeek, Ross A.
  Assembler language with ASSIST.

  Includes index.
  I. Singletary, W. E. (Wilson E.) II. Title.
III. Title: Assembler language with A.S.S.I.S.T.
QA76.73.A8093 1983   001.64'24   82-16921
ISBN 0-574-21435-6

10 9 8 7 6 5 4 3

Contents

Preface

The objective of this text is the systematic introduction of a completely operational subset of assembler language. Elements of the language are introduced without the complications inherent in any attempt to cover file manipulation and data processing concepts in a first assembler language course. Concentration on the language alone permits a more thorough and comprehensive initial treatment.

Prior knowledge of flowcharting (including structured flowcharts) and a higher-level language provides a useful background for the material presented in this text but is not essential. No specific knowledge beyond a familiarity with ordinary arithmetic operations is presumed (although an ability to read with comprehension is helpful).

The authors are convinced that any programming language is most effectively taught by doing both of the following:

1. introducing complete programs in a simple subset of the language as early as possible
2. building upon that subset in an orderly and logical manner with the introduction of complete sample programs and exercises at manageable intervals

In order to achieve the text's goal most effectively, it was necessary to choose a method of initially bypassing the complicated I/O features of the language, as well as furnishing more comprehensible debugging tools than those available on production assemblers. The ASSIST student assembler was chosen for the following reasons:

1. ASSIST, at this writing, is the most widely used student assembler. This software package is now being used at more than 350 installations.
2. Only the five pseudo-instructions of ASSIST (XREAD, XPRNT, XDECI, XDECO, and XDUMP) are necessary to achieve the stated objectives. The macros that implement these instructions are included in the ASSIST package and may be used independently with any assembler.
3. Experience has shown that, under ASSIST, student jobs run in about one-fourth the time that these same jobs require under the vendor-supplied, assemble-and-go procedures.

4. Both OS and DOS versions of ASSIST are available to educational and commercial computer installations. An ASSIST software request form is available in the back of the *Instructor's Guide*.

It is the opinion of the authors that, to present a working knowledge of assembler language adequately in a first course, an aid such as ASSIST is an absolute necessity.

Preprints of the original version of this text were classroom-tested in introductory courses at various universities for three years, and the first edition itself has been generally available for more than six years. This experience has shown that the first nine chapters can be adequately covered in a fifteen-week semester. The assigned exercises for such courses have included a selection of nonprogramming assignments and an assigned program from each of the exercise sets in Chapters 2–9. The exercises are an integral part of any formal or self-study course, since programming is a skill that can be acquired only through practice.

This text is not intended to supplant the use of manuals. Many details of assembler language have been omitted to facilitate the exposition and to conserve space. It is highly recommended that the following manuals be used in conjunction with the text:

• IBM System/370 Principles of Operation (GA22-7000)
• Assembler Language (GC33-4010)
• System/370 Reference Summary (GX20-1850)

The reader should be aware that each of these publications has gone through several editions, and care should be exercised to assure that the latest edition of each has been obtained.

The authors acknowledge the many useful suggestions and advice received from Graham M. Campbell and John Mashey, the creators of ASSIST, during the writing of the original text. In addition, the authors are indebted to Charles Hughes, Frank Cable, and Walter Sillars for their careful reading of that text and the many useful suggestions that they offered.

Our editor, Alan W. Lowe of SRA, solicited suggestions and reviews from a dozen or more users of the text when this second edition was contemplated:

Paul Abrahams (Deerfield, Mass.)
Myron Greene (Georgia State University)
Thomas S. Heines (Cleveland State University)
Charles E. Hughes (University of Central Florida)
Roger Jones (DePaul University)
Luis Kramarz (Emory University)
John B. Lane (Edinboro State College)

R. Jeffrey Leake (University of Notre Dame)
Charles Pfleeger (University of Tennessee)
Shashi Sathaye (University of Kentucky)
David Straight (University of Tennessee)
A. J. Turner (Clemson University)
Gene R. Waters (Arizona State University)

The authors attempted to incorporate the suggestions on which there was a general consensus. In addition, the afterthoughts that the authors had since the publication of the original text are incorporated in this edition. We acknowledge our debt to Mr. Lowe and the reviewers for their frank, useful, and sometimes painful criticism and suggestions. It is our hope that they will not be disappointed with the result.

The major differences between this edition and the first one are as follows:

1. The EQU instruction and extended mnemonics have been moved forward to Chapter 2 as an aid in the documentation of later programs.

2. The chapter on decimal arithmetic has been moved forward and is now Chapter 5. This chapter has been updated to reflect the addition of instructions that first became available with the introduction of the 370s.

3. The chapter on external subroutines and linkage conventions has likewise been moved ahead and is now Chapter 6. This chapter has been revised rather extensively (the earlier material on internal subroutines has also been revised). It is hoped that these changes will provide a clearer and smoother presentation of this material. A section dealing with invoking subroutines written in other languages has been added to this chapter.

4. The chapter on input/output has been moved ahead and is now Chapter 7. A section dealing with the use of QSAM under DOS has been added to this chapter, to increase the flexibility of the text. This chapter utilizes features that are not available with ASSIST; for this reason, this material is normally omitted from our first course.

5. Chapter 8 now contains most of the material that was in Chapters 5, 6, and 10 of the original text.

6. A complete chapter on floating-point arithmetic has been added as Chapter 10.

7. Chapter 11 now deals with debugging. This material is new to this edition of the text.

8. A chapter on structured programming has been added. This is the current Chapter 12. In conjunction with the addition of this material, most of the programming examples in this version of the text are structured. The only exceptions are those examples dealing explicitly with the looping instructions.

9. Appendices F and G are additions. Appendix F provides source listings of the structured macros developed at Northern Illinois University, and Appendix G provides answers to the nonprogramming exercises in the text.

The authors take full responsibility for any errors present in this text. We invite suggestions, comments, and corrections from all readers of this work.

1

Number Systems and Computer Storage

1.1 NUMBER SYSTEMS

The system commonly used for representing numbers is the decimal number system. This is the familiar positional number system in which any natural number may be uniquely represented by use of the ten symbols 0, 1, 2, . . . , 9. In this system these ten symbols, also referred to as decimal digits, represent the numbers zero, one, two, . . . , nine, respectively. A unique representation of any natural number m can be given in the form

$$d_n d_{n-1} d_{n-2} \ldots d_1 d_0$$

where $m \geq 0$. The same natural number m can also be represented in the form

$$d_n \times 10^n + d_{n-1} \times 10^{n-1} + d_{n-2} \times 10^{n-2} + \ldots + d_1 \times 10^1 + d_0 \times 10^0$$

For example, the number one hundred twenty-three may be represented by

$$123$$

or by

$$1 \times 10^2 + 2 \times 10^1 + 3 \times 10^0$$

The decimal number system is also called the base ten system since ten digits are utilized in the number representations in this system. There is, however, nothing sacred about the base ten since the notion of a positional number system can be easily generalized to any given base b where b is a natural number greater than or equal to two. Consider the following examples:

- *Example 1.* The number one hundred twenty-three is to be represented in the base two or binary number system. The symbols 0 and 1 are chosen to represent zero and one, just as ten symbols were selected in the base ten system to represent zero, one, two, . . . , nine. Then, since

$$123 = 1 \times 2^6 + 1 \times 2^5 + 1 \times 2^4 + 1 \times 2^3 + 0 \times 2^2 + 1 \times 2^1 + 1 \times 2^0$$

the number one hundred twenty-three would be represented in the binary system by

$$1111011$$

- *Example 2.* The number one hundred twenty-three is to be represented in the base sixteen, or hexadecimal, number system. The symbols 0, 1, 2, . . . , 9, A, B, C, D, E, F are chosen to represent the numbers zero, one, two, . . . , nine, ten, . . . , fifteen. Then, since

$$123 = 7 \times 16^1 + 11 \times 16^0$$

the number one hundred twenty-three would be represented in the hexadecimal system by 7B.

Table 1-1 gives the representations of the numbers zero through thirty-two in each of these three number systems.

Table 1-1

Decimal	Hexa-decimal	Binary	Decimal	Hexa-decimal	Binary
0	0	0	17	11	10001
1	1	1	18	12	10010
2	2	10	19	13	10011
3	3	11	20	14	10100
4	4	100	21	15	10101
5	5	101	22	16	10110
6	6	110	23	17	10111
7	7	111	24	18	11000
8	8	1000	25	19	11001
9	9	1001	26	1A	11010
10	A	1010	27	1B	11011
11	B	1011	28	1C	11100
12	C	1100	29	1D	11101
13	D	1101	30	1E	11110
14	E	1110	31	1F	11111
15	F	1111	32	20	100000
16	10	10000			

The decimal, hexadecimal, and binary number systems have particular significance to an assembler language programmer. It is essential, for reasons that will become apparent later, that the programmer have the ability to convert a representation of a number given in any one of these three systems to a representation in either of the other two systems. Sections 1.2, 1.3, and 1.4 are devoted to a presentation of algorithms that may be used to perform these conversions.

In the remainder of this book, wherever a number representation appears and it would not otherwise be clear from the context which of the three number systems is intended, a subscript will be appended to the representation to indicate the appropriate base. As an example, consider 1011, which could represent eleven, one thousand eleven, or four thousand one hundred thirteen, depending upon the choice of the number base.

The following expressions should be clear to the reader:

$$1011_2 = 11_{10}$$
$$1011_{16} = 4113_{10}$$

1.2 BINARY- OR HEXADECIMAL-TO-DECIMAL CONVERSION

Let

$$a_n a_{n-1} \ldots a_2 a_1 a_0$$

be the representation of a number m in base b. Then, the decimal representation of m is given by the sum

$$d_n b^n + d_{n-1} b^{n-1} + \ldots d_2 b^2 + d_1 b^1 + d_0 b^0$$

where each d_i is the decimal equivalent of the corresponding a_i.

The following examples illustrate the effect of applying the above algorithm to number representations in the binary system:

a. 1011011_2 $= 1 \times 2^0 + 1 \times 2^1 + 0 \times 2^2 + 1 \times 2^3 + 1 \times 2^4$
$+ 0 \times 2^5 + 1 \times 2^6$
$= 1 \times 1 + 1 \times 2 + 0 \times 4 + 1 \times 8 + 1 \times 16$
$+ 0 \times 32 + 1 \times 64$
$= 91$

b. 1011_2 $= 1 \times 2^0 + 1 \times 2^1 + 0 \times 2^2 + 1 \times 2^3$
$= 11$

c. 110_2 $= 0 \times 2^0 + 1 \times 2^1 + 1 \times 2^2$
$= 6$

d. 10110111_2 $= 1 \times 2^0 + 1 \times 2^1 + 1 \times 2^2 + 0 \times 2^3 + 1 \times 2^4 + 1 \times 2^5$
$+ 0 \times 2^6 + 1 \times 2^7$
$= 183$

Exercise ————————————————————————————

Convert the following numbers in binary representations to their equivalent decimal representations.

a. 11   **c** 11110   **e.** 111   **g.** 101110111
b. 10111   **d.** 111011   **f.** 1111   **h.** 0111

The following examples illustrate the effect of applying the conversion algorithm to number representations in the hexadecimal system:

a. 613_{16} $= 3 \times 16^0 + 1 \times 16^1 + 6 \times 16^2$
$= 3 \times 1 + 1 \times 16 + 6 \times 256$
$= 1555$

b. A61 $= 1 \times 16^0 + 6 \times 16^1 + A \times 16^2$
$= 1 \times 1 + 6 \times 16 + 10 \times 256$
$= 2657$

c. BE $= E \times 16^0 + B \times 16^1$
$= 14 \times 1 + 11 \times 16$
$= 190$

Exercise ————————————————————————————

Convert the following hexadecimal representations to decimal representations.

a. F   **c.** BD2   **e.** CEF   **g.** F1
b. A1   **d.** 1000   **f.** EF   **h.** 126

1.3 DECIMAL-TO-BINARY OR -HEXADECIMAL CONVERSION

To obtain the representation of a number n in a given base b from the representation of n in the decimal system, the following algorithm may be applied:

Step 1. Divide n by b, giving a quotient q and remainder r.
Step 2. Write the representation of r in the base b as the rightmost digit or as the digit to the immediate left of the one last written.
Step 3. If q is zero, stop. Otherwise set n equal to q and go to Step 1.

The following example illustrates the effect of applying this algorithm to convert decimal to hexadecimal representations:

Assume that the given decimal representation is 123.

Step 1. Divide 123 by 16, giving $q = 7$ and $r = 11$.

Step 2. Since $r = 11 = B_{16}$, B is written as the rightmost digit in the hexadecimal representation.

Step 3. Since $q = 7$, set $n = 7$ and proceed to Step 1.

Step 1. Divide 7 by 16, giving $q = 0$ and $r = 7$.

Step 2. Since $r = 7 = 7_{16}$, write 7 to the immediate left of the digit previously written, giving 7B.

Step 3. Since $q = 0$, stop. The desired hexadecimal representation is 7B.

Figure 1-1 graphically illustrates the application of the conversion algorithm in the example just given.

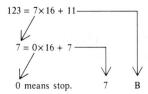

Figure 1-1

Hence $123 = 7B_{16}$

In a similar way the calculations performed in converting the decimal representation 123 to binary representation are illustrated in Figure 1-2.

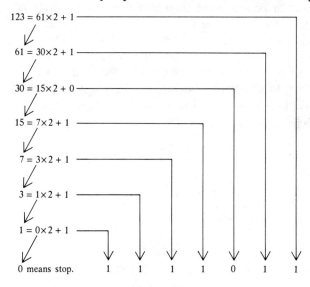

Figure 1-2

Hence $123 = 1111011_2$

Appendix C provides a convenient table to assist in conversions between the decimal and hexadecimal number systems.

Exercises

1. Convert the following decimal representations to hexadecimal representations.

a. 124   **b.** 42   **c.** 4000   **d.** 432

2. Convert the representations given above to binary representations.

1.4 CONVERSIONS BETWEEN BINARY AND HEXADECIMAL REPRESENTATIONS

Because 16 digits are required in the hexadecimal system and $16 = 2^4$, a very simple algorithm exists for converting binary representations to hexadecimal representations, and vice versa.

The algorithm for converting from binary to hexadecimal may be stated as follows:

Step 1. Starting at the right of a binary representation n, separate the digits into groups of four. If there are fewer than four digits in the last (leftmost) group, add as many zeros as may be necessary to the left of the leftmost digit to fill out the group. For example, if $n = 101101$, the digits should be separated into two groups depicted as follows: 10   1101. Since the leftmost group does not contain four digits, two leading zeros are added to give 0010   1101.

Step 2. Convert each group of four binary digits to a hexadecimal digit. The result is the hexadecimal representation of n.

The following examples should serve to clarify the use of this algorithm:

- *Example 1.* $n = 101101$

$$10 \quad 1101$$

Adding zeros to fill out the leftmost group yields

$$0010 \quad 1101$$

Then converting these groups of binary digits to hexadecimal representation yields

$$2 \quad D$$

Hence $101101_2 = 2D_{16}$

• *Example 2.* $n = 101011101$

The algorithmic process may be represented as follows:

$$
\begin{array}{ccc}
1 & 0101 & 1101 \\
0001 & 0101 & 1101 \\
1 & 5 & D
\end{array}
$$

Hence $101011101_2 = 15D_{16}$

• *Example 3.* $n = 111111$

This yields

$$
\begin{array}{cc}
11 & 1111 \\
0011 & 1111 \\
3 & F
\end{array}
$$

Hence $111111_2 = 3F_{16}$

To convert from hexadecimal representations to binary, the above algorithm is simply reversed; that is, each hexadecimal digit is represented by a group of four binary digits and then any leading zeros are dropped.

Consider the following examples of this process:

• *Example 1.* $n = 12BC$

The conversion process is illustrated as follows:

$$
\begin{array}{cccc}
1 & 2 & B & C \\
0001 & 0010 & 1011 & 1100
\end{array}
$$

Hence $12BC_{16} = 1001010111100_2$

• *Example 2.* $n = FB2$

This yields

$$
\begin{array}{ccc}
F & B & 2 \\
1111 & 1011 & 0010
\end{array}
$$

Hence $FB2_{16} = 111110110010_2$

• *Example 3.* $n = 1080$

This yields

$$
\begin{array}{cccc}
1 & 0 & 8 & 0 \\
0001 & 0000 & 1000 & 0000
\end{array}
$$

Hence $1080_{16} = 1000010000000_2$

Exercises

1. Convert the following hexadecimal representations to corresponding binary representations.

a. E   **c.** B976   **e.** FFAB
b. 10CD   **d.** 4210   **f.** ABCD

2. Convert the following binary representations to corresponding hexadecimal representations.

a. 101101111   **c.** 1010   **e.** 10111101111
b. 101010101   **d.** 11110001   **f.** 1011110011100010

In the remainder of this text, we shall follow the convention of referring to representations of numbers in the binary, decimal, and hexadecimal systems simply as binary, decimal, or hexadecimal numbers.

1.5 ADDITION AND SUBTRACTION OF BINARY AND HEXADECIMAL NUMBERS

The algorithms for the addition and subtraction of integer numbers in positional number systems are independent of the base in which the numbers are represented. These algorithms do, however, require that the table for addition of digits in the appropriate base be known. You are, no doubt, so familiar with the addition table for decimal digits that you automatically think of 8 plus 8 as 16, or 6 plus a carry (which we will write as 6 + c).

The algorithm for the addition of integer numbers, assuming that both addends are positive, is as follows:

Step 1. Write the two addends one above the other with the rightmost digits of these numbers aligned.

Step 2. Add the two rightmost digits; if a 1 appears above these digits, indicating a carry, add 1 to the result. Write the integer portion of this result to the immediate left of the last recorded digit in the sum; if a carry is part of the result, write a 1 above the next higher order pair of digits. (If one or both of the digits do not exist, assume a value of 0 for the missing digits.)

Step 3. Delete the rightmost digits of the two addends. If the digits of the addends are exhausted, stop; otherwise, go to Step 2.

To illustrate the use of this algorithm, suppose that the numbers 743 and 864 in the familiar decimal number system are to be added. The result of applying the algorithm is graphically depicted in Figure 1-3.

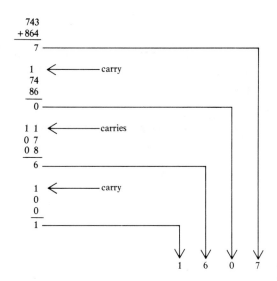

Figure 1-3

Collecting the results yields

$$
\begin{array}{r}
11 \quad \longleftarrow \text{ carries} \\
743 \\
+864 \\
\hline
1607
\end{array}
$$

Table 1-2 presents the addition of binary digits. This table is easy to remember since there are only two digits involved.

Table 1-2

+	0	1
0	0	1
1	1	0+c

The result of using this table and the addition algorithm to find the sum of 10110 and 1011 is graphically depicted in Figure 1-4.

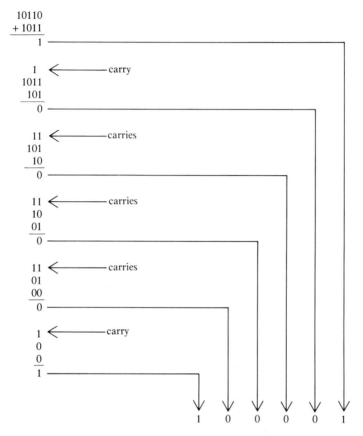

Figure 1-4

Collecting these results, we have

$$
\begin{array}{r}
1111 \quad\longleftarrow \text{ carries}\\
10110\\
+\,1011\\
\hline
100001
\end{array}
$$

With little or no practice you should easily master the art of adding binary numbers as indicated in the collected result without writing down the intermediate steps. This is the same way that you add decimal numbers. More practice is required in the case of hexadecimal numbers because the addition table (Table 1-3) is much more complex. Figure 1-5 graphically depicts the addition of the hexadecimal numbers 9A05 and FCDE.

Table 1-3

+	0	1	2	3	4	5	6	7	8	9	A	B	C	D	E	F
0	0	1	2	3	4	5	6	7	8	9	A	B	C	D	E	F
1	1	2	3	4	5	6	7	8	9	A	B	C	D	E	F	0+c
2	2	3	4	5	6	7	8	9	A	B	C	D	E	F	0+c	1+c
3	3	4	5	6	7	8	9	A	B	C	D	E	F	0+c	1+c	2+c
4	4	5	6	7	8	9	A	B	C	D	E	F	0+c	1+c	2+c	3+c
5	5	6	7	8	9	A	B	C	D	E	F	0+c	1+c	2+c	3+c	4+c
6	6	7	8	9	A	B	C	D	E	F	0+c	1+c	2+c	3+c	4+c	5+c
7	7	8	9	A	B	C	D	E	F	0+c	1+c	2+c	3+c	4+c	5+c	6+c
8	8	9	A	B	C	D	E	F	0+c	1+c	2+c	3+c	4+c	5+c	6+c	7+c
9	9	A	B	C	D	E	F	0+c	1+c	2+c	3+c	4+c	5+c	6+c	7+c	8+c
A	A	B	C	D	E	F	0+c	1+c	2+c	3+c	4+c	5+c	6+c	7+c	8+c	9+c
B	B	C	D	E	F	0+c	1+c	2+c	3+c	4+c	5+c	6+c	7+c	8+c	9+c	A+c
C	C	D	E	F	0+c	1+c	2+c	3+c	4+c	5+c	6+c	7+c	8+c	9+c	A+c	B+c
D	D	E	F	0+c	1+c	2+c	3+c	4+c	5+c	6+c	7+c	8+c	9+c	A+c	B+c	C+c
E	E	F	0+c	1+c	2+c	3+c	4+c	5+c	6+c	7+c	8+c	9+c	A+c	B+c	C+c	D+c
F	F	0+c	1+c	2+c	3+c	4+c	5+c	6+c	7+c	8+c	9+c	A+c	B+c	C+c	D+c	E+c

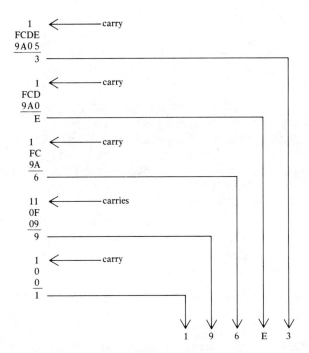

Figure 1-5

Collecting the results yields

$$
\begin{array}{r}
11\ \ 1 \quad \longleftarrow \ \text{carries} \\
\text{FCDE} \\
\underline{9\,\text{A}\,0\,5} \\
19\,6\,\text{E}\,3
\end{array}
$$

Subtraction is the inverse of addition. The addition tables given may, therefore, be utilized in performing subtraction. In the subtraction algorithm presented below it will be assumed that the subtrahend (the number to be subtracted) is less than or equal to the minuend (the number from which the subtrahend is to be subtracted), and, further, that both of these numbers are positive. (These should prove to be nonessential restrictions when a programmer is required, in practice, to perform subtraction on binary or hexadecimal numbers.)

The subtraction algorithm is as follows:

Step 1. Write the minuend above the subtrahend with the rightmost digits of these numbers aligned.

Step 2. *(a)* If the rightmost digit in the minuend is greater than or equal to the corresponding digit in the subtrahend, subtract the digit in the subtrahend from the corresponding digit in the minuend and write the result to the immediate left of the last recorded digit in the difference; otherwise

(b) If the rightmost digit d in the minuend is less than the corresponding digit in the subtrahend, replace d by $d + c$, decrease the next-higher-order nonzero digit in the minuend by 1, replace any intervening zero digits in the minuend by the digit corresponding in value to the base minus 1. Then subtract the rightmost digit in the subtrahend from $d + c$ and write the result to the immediate left of the last recorded digit in the difference.

Step 3. Delete the rightmost digits in the minuend and subtrahend. If the digits of these two numbers are exhausted, stop; otherwise, go to Step 2.

To use the addition table for the subtraction of two digits, first locate the digit in the subtrahend in the column of digits to the left of the table. Then locate the digit d in the minuend (or $d + c$) in the row corresponding to this digit. Finally, proceed vertically up the corresponding column to find the difference in the row of digits at the top of the table.

The result of using this algorithm to subtract 10011 from 111000 is graphically depicted in Figure 1-6.

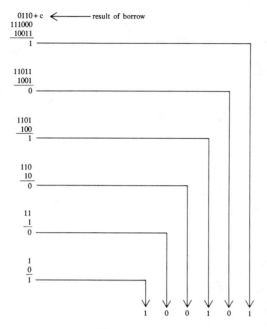

Figure 1-6

Collecting the results yields

$$0110 + c \longleftarrow \text{result of borrow}$$
$$111000$$
$$\underline{10011}$$
$$100101$$

Using the algorithm to subtract 9AE5 from FCDE results in Figure 1-7.

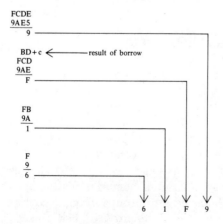

Figure 1-7

Collecting the results yields

$$BD + c \longleftarrow \text{result of borrow}$$
$$\begin{array}{r} FCDE \\ 9\,AE\,5 \\ \hline 6\,1\,F\,9 \end{array}$$

As in the case of addition, you should find that you can easily perform subtraction as indicated in the collected results without actually carrying out the intermediate steps.

Exercises

1. Add the following binary numbers.

a.		**b.**		**c.**	
	10110		110011		10110
+	1101	+	100111	+	10110

2. Subtract the following binary numbers.

a.		**b.**		**c.**	
	11101		10011		110001
−	1001	−	1011	−	10010

3. Add the following hexadecimal numbers.

a.		**b.**		**c.**		**d.**	
	FB28		82CD		E2C		1423
+	3254	+	1982	+	A31	+	19A0

4. Subtract the following hexadecimal numbers.

a.		**b.**		**c.**		**d.**	
	FCDE		89A3		642E		FFFF
−	985A	−	6494	−	150F	−	EADF

1.6 MAIN STORAGE ORGANIZATION

A computer is a high-speed electronic machine designed to store, manipulate, and retrieve data. The area in which data is stored is called the *main storage* of the computer. To understand how data is manipulated by a computer, it is first necessary to understand the manner in which this data is represented in storage. The following discussion deals with the representation of numeric data in the main storage of the computer.

Storage may be thought of as a long sequence of on-off switches called *binary digits* or *bits*. Typical current computer memories contain between 2^{14} and 2^{24} bits. These bits are organized into groups of eight contiguous bits, and each such group is called a *byte*. Bytes are assigned consecutive increasing hexadecimal numbers starting with the number 0. Thus, storage may be pictorially represented as

bbbbbbbb	bbbbbbbb	bbbbbbbb	. . .
byte 0	byte 1	byte 2	. . .

where each of the b's represents a bit and the number assigned to a given byte is called the absolute *address* of that byte. In order to relate the on-off switches to binary digits, it is standard convention to represent a switch that is on by a 1 and a switch that is off by a 0. Hence, the condition of each byte may be identified with an eight-digit binary number at any given moment. For example, if it is assumed that all of the switches in the first two bytes of storage are on, the condition of storage may be pictorially represented as

11111111	11111111	. . .
byte 0	byte 1	. . .

where byte 0 and byte 1 each contain the binary number corresponding to the decimal number 255. Because of the natural correspondence between binary and hexadecimal numbers, the condition of a byte can be represented by a two-digit hexadecimal number. Hence, the condition of storage given in the last example may be represented as

FF	FF	. . .
byte 0	byte 1	. . .

The byte is the fundamental unit of main storage in the sense that any position or address in storage which it is possible to specify is referred to by the address of the byte at that position. It is often necessary to reference *fields* that contain several bytes. The address of such a field is considered to be the address of the first (pictorially, the leftmost) byte in the field.

Aside from the bits and bytes there are several other units of storage which are of particular importance. If all of the bytes in storage are thought of as being grouped into consecutive nonoverlapping pairs beginning with byte zero, the resulting pairs of bytes are referred to as *halfwords*. This relationship of the bytes in storage to halfwords may be pictorially represented as follows:

B0 B1	B2 B3	B4 B5	B6 B7	B8 B9	etc.
H	H	H	H	H	

From the above discussion, it should be particularly noted that each address that is an even number is the address of a halfword, and only even numbers are halfword addresses. For this reason, each even address is called a *half-*

word boundary. Thus, it is valid to speak of the halfword beginning at address A8, but it is incorrect to speak of the halfword beginning at address A9.

In a manner analogous to that which pertains to halfwords, storage is also thought of as being organized into groups of four bytes, called *fullwords*, and groups of eight bytes, called *doublewords*. By analogy, each fullword must begin at an address that is evenly divisible by four, and each double-word must begin at an address that is evenly divisible by eight.

This relationship between bytes, halfwords, fullwords, and doublewords may be pictorially represented as shown in Figure 1-8.

byte 0	byte 1	byte 2	byte 3	byte 4	byte 5	byte 6	byte 7
HALFWORD beginning at 0		HALFWORD beginning at 2		HALFWORD beginning at 4		HALFWORD beginning at 6	
FULLWORD beginning at 0				FULLWORD beginning at 4			
DOUBLEWORD beginning at 0							

Figure 1-8

1.7 BINARY REPRESENTATION OF INTEGER NUMBERS

The capacity to perform integer arithmetic is a requirement common to all high-speed electronic digital computers. This requirement imposes the need to devise a method for representing both positive and negative integers in binary form. Several preliminary concepts must be introduced before the representation of integers in binary form in the computer is discussed.

Let n be the binary representation of any integer. Then the *one's complement* of n is the result of replacing each 0 in this representation with a 1 and replacing each 1 with a 0. For example, the binary representation of 9 is

$$1001$$

and the one's complement of this representation is

$$0110$$

If n is the binary representation of any integer, then the *two's complement* of n is formed by doing both of the following:

1. Find the one's complement of n.
2. Add 1 to this result.

For example, if the integer representations are in four digits, the two's complement of 5 may be found as follows:

> 0101   binary representation of 5
> 1010   one's complement of 5
> +1
> 1011   two's complement of 5

The 32-bit fullword is the unit of storage that was chosen in IBM computers for representing integer numbers. The fullword is, therefore, a particularly important unit of storage, since most arithmetic operations performed in these machines involve fullword operands. The method used for encoding integer numbers in fullwords is as follows:

1. Any integer in the range 0 to $2^{31} - 1$ (that is, 0 to 2,147,483,647) is represented in a fullword in its exact binary representation. Note that each 32-bit binary number in this range has a value of 0 in the leftmost bit position. This bit is called the *sign bit*, and all positive integer representations are characterized by having a sign bit value of 0.

2. Any integer in the range -1 to $-2^{31} + 1$ is encoded by taking the two's complement of the encoded form of its absolute value. A representation of -2^{31} is also allowed, but this representation (a 1 followed by 31 0's) is not the two's complement of the representation of any positive integer. The sign bit in the encoded form of each negative integer has a value of 1.

As an example, the encoded form of $+1$ is

> 00000000   00000000   00000000   00000001

The reader should verify that the encoded form of -1 is

> 11111111   11111111   11111111   11111111

There are two integers with encoded forms that are identical to their two's complements. These integers are 0 and -2^{31}.

Some rather remarkable things are true of the binary representations of integers in this scheme:

- The two's complement of the representation of a negative integer (with the exception of -2^{31}) is the representation of the absolute value of that integer.

- When binary addition is performed on the representations of integer numbers (whether the signs are mixed or not), the result has the correct value in the sign bit (provided that the result is in the range -2^{31} to $2^{31} - 1$).

Integer addition is performed by simply performing the usual binary addition. Integer subtraction is performed by first taking the two's complement of the subtrahend and then adding the result to the minuend. There is no need for the sign bits of the integer representations of the numbers involved in these operations to be checked before the operations are performed, for the sign bit of the result will be correct as noted above.

To conserve space and since 32-bit binary numbers are all but impossible to read at a glance, the printouts of the conditions of memory locations are always given in hexadecimal form. (Remember that one hexadecimal digit represents four binary digits.) The printed forms of the representations of 1 and -1 are, therefore,

$$00000001$$

and

$$FFFFFFFF$$

In the rest of this text, the conditions of storage locations will be indicated by the hexadecimal representations of the existing binary conditions.

Exercise

Give the fullword representations of the following numbers (as eight-digit hexadecimal numbers).

a. 1   **c.** -1 **e.** 8412
b. 248   **d.** -10 **f.** -8412

1.8 OVERFLOW

Overflow occurs when operations are performed on the representations of integer numbers with the effect that the carry into the sign bit of the result differs from the carry out of that position. As examples, consider the following addition operations on integers coded in five-bit binary numbers:

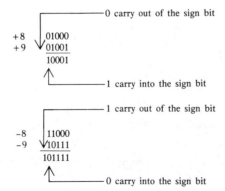

Note that in each case the result exceeds the range of numbers that can be encoded in five binary bits. The reader should verify that only numbers in the range -2^4 to $2^4 - 1$ can be encoded in five binary bits and that both 17 and -17 are out of this range.

In essence, overflow occurs when the result is outside the range that can be accommodated by the encoding scheme being used. The possibility of overflow in other situations will be covered when these situations are discussed.

Exercise

Which of the following operations will result in overflow (assuming the result is to be stored in a fullword)?

a. complement 42_{16}

b. complement 0

c. complement -80000000_{16}

d. add 4 to 75800000_{16}

e. subtract $7FFFFFFF_{16}$ from -4

f. add C to $7FFFFFF4_{16}$

g. subtract 4 from $-7FFFFFF0_{16}$

1.9 GENERAL-PURPOSE REGISTERS AND RELATIVE ADDRESSING

In Section 1.6, main storage was introduced as a hardware unit into which data could be stored in the form of binary numbers. Modern IBM computers also contain 16 general-purpose registers as units for storing and manipulating data. Each register is a 32-bit storage unit whose contents can be altered or accessed in much less time than it would take to alter or access a field in main storage. The relatively slow speed of accessing and altering storage, as compared to the extremely fast access time for the registers, is a result of the cost involved. Because of the difference in response time, the registers are often used as storage for frequently referenced data items or as operands in arithmetic operations.

In Section 2.2, we will describe the ways of doing arithmetic on numbers stored in registers and also the facilities for causing 32-bit words to be transferred to a register from a field in storage or vice versa. The 16 registers are numbered 0, 1, 2, . . . , 15 and will be referred to as R0, R1, . . . , R15 throughout this text.

One particularly important use of registers involves the concept of addressing. As previously stated, every byte of storage has associated with it an absolute address, and every field is addressed by the address of its leftmost byte. Whenever a program is run, it must be stored somewhere in main storage. Thus each instruction and each item of data in the program will have an absolute address. When, in a program, reference is made to a data item or to an instruction, the computer must have an absolute address to find what is referred to.

A difficulty arises immediately: The writer of a program does not know where in storage his program will be stored when it is run and therefore does not know any of the relevant absolute addresses. Some other means has to be provided for referring to data or instructions within the program.

The means that is provided is called *base-displacement addressing* or *explicit addressing*. The idea is that within a program the relative positions of any two statements are fixed, such that if the absolute address of any one statement in the program were known, then the address of any other statement could be calculated. To do this, one would compute the distance between the statement whose absolute address is known and the one whose address is to be found. Such a distance, measured as a number of bytes, is called a *displacement*.

But how, you ask, can the absolute address of even one statement in the program be known? The way this comes about will be covered in later chapters. For now, it is sufficient to know that, when a program is executed (not before), such an address will be contained in at least one of the general-purpose registers. A register that holds an absolute address, from which the addresses of other statements can be calculated, is called a *base register*.

The standard way, then, to refer to any data item or instruction in a program is to specify a base register and a displacement. When the instruction containing the reference is executed, the sum of the displacement and the absolute address in the base register will be calculated to obtain the absolute address of the item or instruction. For example, if the displacement specified were 4, the base register specified were R1, and R1 contained 0000007C, the absolute address formed would be 000080. (The 32-bit contents of a register will always be shown in their hexadecimal representation.)

Base-displacement addresses are often specified in the format

$$D(B)$$

where   D   is the displacement, expressed as a decimal number in the range 0 to 4095

        B   is the number of the base register

For example,

$$4(1) \qquad 20(13) \qquad 0(11)$$

are base-displacement addresses. In the first example, $4_{10} = 4_{16}$ is added to the contents of R1. In the second example, 20_{10} is converted to 14_{16} and added to the contents of R13. In the third example, the contents of R11 give the desired address without modification.

Occasionally, it is convenient to express an address as the sum of a displacement, the contents of a base register, and the contents of a second register as well. The additional register is called an *index register;* the format for an address that includes an index register is

D(X,B)

where   D and B   have the same meaning as above
           X   is the number of the index register

For example,

4(7,1)

is a D(X,B) address, using R7 as the index register, R1 as the base register, and 4 as the displacement. If R1 contains 0000007C and R7 contains 00000010, the address calculated will be the sum of the contents of the two registers plus the displacement, or 000090.

In the next chapter, we will introduce the machine instructions in which D(B) or D(X,B) addresses may be used. Such an address is always used as part of a particular instruction; it never stands alone. Moreover, the rules for the particular instruction always specify which of the two addressing formats should be used.

There are three details that qualify the above remarks:

1. When the contents of an index register or a base register are used to calculate an address, only the value represented by the rightmost 24 bits of the register is used in the calculation. Thus, for the purpose of calculating an address, the value added from a register must always be in the range 000000 to FFFFFF. As an example, suppose that R1 contained FFFFFFFF (the encoding of -1). Then the effective address derived from 0(R1) is not negative; rather it is FFFFFF, an extremely large absolute address.

2. In either the D(B) or the D(X,B) address format, the registers may be omitted. This means that when a D(B) address is required, the programmer may use either of the following forms:

Form	*Example*
D(B)	42(15)
D	42

Similarly, when a D(X,B) address is required, the programmer may use:

Form	*Example*
D(X,B)	42(1,14)
D(X)	42(1)
D(,B)	42(,14)
D	42

Note that if only one register is specified in the D(X,B) address format, the presence or absence of a comma determines whether the register given is considered an index register or a base register.

When registers are omitted from a D(B) or D(X,B) address, the calculation of the corresponding absolute address is performed by using 0 in place of the contents of the omitted registers. Thus, either 42(14) or 42(,14) is converted to an absolute address by adding the binary equivalent of decimal 42 to the binary number represented by the rightmost three bytes of the contents of R14.

3. R0 should not ordinarily be used as an index register or as a base register. If R0 is specified in an address, it will be taken to mean that the corresponding register has been omitted. (As an example, both 4(,15) and 4(0,15) refer to the same absolute address.)

Exercises

For the following two exercises, assume

0008AB40	is in R0
0000004C	is in R1
FC08AB44	is in R2

1. Determine which of the following are valid addresses of the form D(B). For those that are valid, calculate the corresponding absolute address.

a. 404(1)	**c.** 16(1)	**e.** 18(0)	**g.** 13(1,2)
b. 404(2)	**d.** 16(,1)	**f.** 18	**h.** 13(2,1)

2. Determine which of the following are valid relative addresses of the form D(X,B). For those that are valid, calculate the corresponding absolute address.

a. 64(1,2)	**c.** 2(,0)	**e.** 13(,1)	**g.** 13(1,2)
b. 64(1,0)	**d.** 13(1,)	**f.** 48(0,2,1)	**h.** 13(2,1)

2

Basic Concepts

2.1 THE FUNCTION OF A PROGRAM

The modern electronic digital computer is a remarkable device; it can perform literally millions of operations per second. If these operations occur in the proper sequence, meaningful results will be obtained that might have been totally inaccessible otherwise. The function of a program is to direct the order in which operations are executed within the computer. The creation of programs that correctly direct the sequence of operations is, therefore, of fundamental importance if computers are to be successfully utilized. Most of the remainder of this text will be devoted to a detailed description of the process of producing such programs.

The language described in this text is a symbolic language called *Basic Assembler Language*; this is the assembler language developed for use on IBM mainframe computers, beginning with the Model 360 class of machines. The task of the programmer is to produce a source program written in this language. The computer cannot directly carry out or execute assembler-language instructions. Each of these instructions must be translated into a machine-language instruction before the computer can begin to perform the task that the program was intended to accomplish. The machine-language instructions that the computer can execute directly are strings of binary digits that are difficult for a human to decipher. A program consisting entirely of machine-language instructions is called an *object program*.

After an assembler-language program has been prepared, a few additional instructions in *Job Control Language (JCL)* are added to the program, and the resulting program is presented to the computer through an input device, such as a card reader or a terminal. The JCL instructions invoke a program called an *assembler*, which translates the source program instructions into machine-language instructions and thus produces an object program.

During the translation, or assembly, of the source program, a listing is produced that displays the source-language instructions along with the machine-language instructions that are generated. If incorrectly formatted assembler-language instructions are encountered in the assembly process, error messages are printed in the listing and execution of the program is aborted after the assembly process is completed. However, if no syntax errors are detected, the object program is loaded into the main storage of the computer and execution of the program begins.

The fact that a source program contains no syntax errors is certainly no guarantee that the resulting object program will perform the task for which it was intended. The program may still contain logical errors that the assembler had no means of detecting. To correct such errors, the programmer must understand exactly what is involved in encoding assembler-language instructions into machine language. The rules for performing this translation are covered in succeeding chapters; for now, all that must be grasped is that the assembler will produce an object program.

Suppose that a program has been successfully assembled and loaded in storage. The actual execution of the program is sketchily depicted by the following algorithm:

Step 1. Initially, the absolute address of the first instruction of the program to be executed is inserted into a special pointer called the *Program Status Word (PSW)*.

Step 2. The machine retrieves from storage the instruction that is pointed to by the PSW.

Step 3. The machine then updates the contents of the PSW to point to the next instruction.

Step 4. The machine executes the operation indicated by the previously retrieved instruction. If the instruction did not cause a branch to occur (a branch is caused by a basic operation analogous to a GO TO statement in a higher-level language), then go to Step 2. Otherwise, put the absolute address that is to be branched to into the PSW, and go to Step 2.

The above procedure leaves a variety of questions unanswered. (For example, how does the machine halt?) It does, however, capture the essence of the way in which a program governs the operations of a machine. Later you will be able to visualize the details of the process more clearly.

2.2 RR INSTRUCTIONS

The process of encoding instructions can be clarified by considering some specific instructions in their symbolic and encoded forms. Instructions are encoded according to five distinct formats—RR, RX, RS, SI, and SS. The set of instructions encoded in the RR format is referred to as the RR *instructions*. In this section, the RR format will be covered in detail; discussions of the other formats will be deferred to later sections.

An RR instruction is most often used to cause an operation involving two registers. As a concrete example, consider the format of the Add Register instruction:

AR   r1,r2   (Add Register)

Execution of this instruction causes the contents of r2 to be added to the contents of r1; the contents of r2 are unaltered, unless r2 is r1. If an overflow occurs in the process of addition, a fixed-point overflow condition will exist; this will normally cause termination of the program, and a message will be printed indicating that an error has occurred.

For example, execution of the instruction

AR   14,0

causes the number contained in R0 (the number may be positive or negative) to be added to the contents of R14, with the result replacing the original contents of R14.

In the preceding discussion of the symbolic format of the AR instruction, the form that would be used by a programmer was presented. As previously mentioned, the symbolic form must be translated into an encoded form before the instruction is actually executed. The encoded form of any RR instruction is a 16-bit binary number that will occupy a halfword of storage in the machine when the program is executed. The encoded instruction can, therefore, be represented as a four-digit hexadecimal number. The precise format of an encoded RR instruction is

$h_0 h_0 h_{r1} h_{r2}$*

where $h_0 h_0$ is a two-digit operation code specifying the purpose of the instruction

   h_{r1} is the number of the register (0-F) that is to be used as the first operand

   h_{r2} is the number of the register that is to be used as the second operand

The operation code (op code) for an AR instruction is 1A. Therefore, the encoding of

AR   14,0

is 1AE0. The 1A means that the encoded instruction is an AR, the E indicates that the first operand is R14, and the 0 indicates that R0 is the second operand.

---

*Here, as in all instruction formats displayed in this work, each h represents one hexadecimal digit. Thus, $h_0 h_0$ is a one-byte operation code.

Before ending this discussion of RR instructions, we shall introduce the Subtract Register and Load Register instructions.

SR   r1,r2   (*Subtract Register*)

Execution of this instruction causes the number represented by the contents of r2 to be subtracted from the number represented by the contents of r1. Just as for an AR, the result replaces the contents of r1; r2 is unaltered, unless r2 is r1. Fixed-point overflow can occur.

LR   r1,r2   (*Load Register*)

Execution of this instruction causes the replacement of the original contents of r1 by the contents of r2, while the contents of r2 remain unaltered. Thus, execution of the instruction

LR   5,10

causes the contents of R10 to be copied into R5.

Additional RR instructions will be introduced throughout the remainder of this text. However, the first few examples will employ only these three RR instructions and several RX instructions, which are introduced in Section 2.3.

Exercises

1. Utilize the table of op codes in Appendix C to encode the following RR instructions.

a. AR	1,15	**c.** AR	14,3	**e.** AR	15,14
b. SR	2,10	**d.** SR	0,0		

2. Write the symbolic equivalent of the following encoded RR instructions.

a. 1820   **b.** 1AFE   **c.** 1BCC   **d.** 1834

3. Suppose that

R0 contains 001A2F0B
R1 contains FFFFA21C
R6 contains 000019EF

Then show the contents of all three registers after each of the following instructions.

a. LR	6,0	**c.** AR	1,6	**e.** SR	1,1
b. SR	6,0	**d.** SR	1,6		

2.3 RX INSTRUCTIONS

RX instructions usually cause an operation that involves a register and main storage to be performed. For example, consider the Load instruction:

$$L \qquad r,D(X,B) \qquad\qquad (Load)$$

Execution of this instruction causes the fullword in storage starting at the effective address derived from D(X,B) to be loaded into r. The original contents of r are replaced, while the fullword in storage remains unaltered. Three errors might occur during the execution of a Load instruction:*

1. If the absolute address calculated from D(X,B) is not a multiple of 4 (not a fullword boundary), a *specification exception* occurs.
2. If D(X,B) is an address greater than any actual storage address, an *addressing exception* will occur. This exception can happen only if either the X or the B register contains an excessively large number.
3. If D(X,B) is the actual address of an area, but the address is not within the area of storage allocated to the program, a *protection error* will occur.

The encoded form of an RX instruction occupies two halfwords and conforms to the following format:

$$h_0 h_0 h_r h_X \qquad h_B h_D h_D h_D$$

where $h_0 h_0$ is the op code indicating the particular instruction
h_r is the number of the register used as the first operand
h_X is the number of the index register (0 if omitted)
h_B is the number of the base register (0 if omitted)
$h_D h_D h_D$ is the displacement

Thus, since the op code of L is 58,

$$L \qquad 2,12(1,10)$$

is encoded as 5821 A00C. Note that the displacement used in a relative address must be in the range 0 to 4095 simply because $FFF_{16} = 4095_{10}$ is the largest three-digit hexadecimal number (and only three digits are provided in the encoded form of the instruction).

The ST instruction performs the inverse of the operation of the L instruction:

$$ST \qquad r,D(X,B) \qquad\qquad (Store)$$

---

*The discussion of errors here, as elsewhere in this text, has been kept to a minimum to avoid detracting from the essentials. A more comprehensive summary of the errors and their causes is included in Appendix D.

Execution of this instruction causes the contents of r to replace the fullword at the location determined by D(X,B); the condition of r remains unaltered. The absolute address corresponding to D(X,B) must, therefore, be on a fullword boundary. The same exceptions (errors) that can occur for an L instruction can also occur for an ST instruction.

Exercises

1. Utilize the table of operation codes presented in Appendix C to encode the following RX instructions.

a. L	15,0(3,2)	**c.** L	15,0(2)	**e.** L	15,24
b. L	15,0(,2)	**d.** ST	2,20(14,13)	**f.** ST	6,4(8)

2. Decode the following RX instructions.

a. 5801	500C	**c.** 5811	801C	**e.** 5023	D00C
b. 5010	0004	**d.** 5845	E004		

3. Suppose that

R2 contains 000ABC10
R3 contains 0000000B
R4 contains 000C1F11

Calculate the absolute address of areas in storage that would be referenced by the execution of each of the following instructions and determine whether a specification error would result.

a. L	0,16(2)	**c.** ST	15,20(3,4)
b. ST	1,16(4)	**d.** L	8,0(2,4)

2.4 A COMPLETE PROGRAM

In previous sections, the distinction between the symbolic and encoded (or machine) forms of instructions was presented. For example, 1A32 is the encoded form of the symbolic instruction

AR   3,2

Given a choice, a programmer would naturally choose to write programs using the symbolic instructions. The role of an *assembler program* is to accept as input a source program punched into cards using symbolic notations and to encode the instructions into *executable format*. The precise format used to punch a symbolic instruction into a card that can be submitted to the assembler is as follows:

1. A label may be punched into the card starting in column 1. A label is a string of from one to eight characters such that:

   a. The first character is either a letter from A to Z, a $, a #, or an @.

   b. Each of the characters following the first character may be any of the above or any one of the decimal digits (0, 1, 2, . . . , 9).

   Thus,

   > WORD1
   > LOOP
   > MYROUTNE
   > BRANCH01

   are valid labels. (The uses of labels will be introduced in Section 2.5.)

2. A mnemonic for the operation code, such as AR for Add Register, is punched starting in column 10. (Appendix C contains a list of valid op codes and the corresponding mnemonics.)

3. The operands are punched starting in column 16.

4. Any comment that the user wishes to append to the instruction can be punched after allowing at least one blank following the last character of the operands. The only restriction on the comment is that it cannot extend past column 71 of the card.

The following example of a symbolic instruction, with indications of where the fields would appear on a card, illustrates the above points:

```
1          10    16
LOADUP     L     1,0(2,3)    LOAD THE WORD INTO R1
```

Up to this point, the only symbolic instructions that have been discussed are those that are to be encoded into executable instructions. There are, however, several instructions, called *assembler instructions*, that are not used to generate machine instructions. Rather, these instructions are used to communicate to the assembler information about how the user's program is to be processed and to direct the generation of constants and storage areas. The following assembler instructions are of particular importance:

1. The CSECT instruction is used to begin a program and must appear before any executable instructions in the program. The format of the CSECT instruction is

   > label   CSECT

2. The end of a program is signified by an END statement. The END statement has as an operand the label of the place in the program where execution of the program should begin. Normally this label is the label of the CSECT statement. For example, the CSECT and END statements would typically occur as

```
MYPROG    CSECT
          .
          .
          .
          END   MYPROG
```

3. A DC statement is used to define constants. The only form of a DC statement that is needed at this point is

       label   DC   mF'n'

where   m   is a nonnegative decimal integer (duplication factor)
        n   is a decimal integer

If m is omitted, it is assumed to be 1. The effect of this DC statement is to cause m consecutive fullwords, each containing the number n, to be generated. Thus,

       TWO   DC   F'2'

causes one fullword containing 00000002 to be generated and makes it accessible to the program by its symbolic name TWO. DC statements can appear anywhere between the CSECT and END statements in the program. The fullwords that are generated as the result of such DC statements will always begin on fullword boundaries.

4. A DS statement is used to set aside areas of storage for fullwords that require no initial values. The format of the DS statement is

       label   DS   mF

The above statement causes the assembler to set aside the next m fullwords as a storage area. An area of n bytes, which may or may not begin on a fullword boundary, can be set aside by use of a DS statement in the following format:

       label   DS   CLn

Here, CLn stands for Character,Length n. Again, if more than one such area is required, a duplication factor can be used. For example, the statement

       label   DS   mCLn

causes m fields, each of which has a length of n bytes, to be set aside.

Before looking at a sample program, two additional details should be mentioned:

• When execution of a program begins, R15 will always contain the absolute address of the beginning of the program. For now, this can be assumed to mean that R15 contains the address of the first generated instruction in the program. This fact is significant since it allows all relative addresses to be created using R15 as a base register.

- When execution of a program begins, R14 contains the absolute address of the routine that should be branched to when execution of the program has been completed. That is, when execution of a program terminates, a branch to the address in R14 should be effected. This is referred to as *exiting* from the program. Although branching instructions are not covered until later in this text, the format of the branch instruction that causes the exit is

> label BCR B'1111',14

The reader should now be capable of understanding Program 2-1. Since input and output of data and branching have not yet been discussed, this program necessarily performs an extremely simple task. It does, however, illustrate many of the points we have covered and deserves careful consideration.

Program 2-1

```
ADD2      CSECT
* THIS PROGRAM ADDS TWO NUMBERS TOGETHER THAT ARE TAKEN
* FROM THE 5TH AND 6TH WORDS OF THE PROGRAM.   THE SUM
* IS STORED IN THE 7TH WORD OF THE PROGRAM.
          L      1,16(,15)      LOAD 1ST NUMBER INTO R1
          L      2,20(15)       LOAD 2ND NUMBER INTO R2
          AR     1,2            ADD R2 TO R1
          ST     1,24(15)       STORE RESULT FROM R1 INTO
                                   7TH WORD IN PROGRAM
*
          BCR    B'1111',14     EXIT FROM PROGRAM
          DC     F'4'
          DC     F'6'
          DS     F
          END    ADD2
```

Since this is the first program presented in this text, it seems appropriate to cover aspects of it in detail.

- The statement ADD2 CSECT is an example of how a program should begin. The name ADD2 is arbitrary; however, it is a good idea to choose a name related to the purpose of the program.
- The next three statements are comments. Any card with an asterisk in column 1 is a comment card and does not generate any code. The comment itself can be anywhere on the card from column 2 through column 71. A paragraph giving the purpose of the program and any general information that a reviewing programmer might find helpful should always preface a program.

- The actual instructions in this program that will be translated into executable code are

L	1,16(,15)
L	2,20(15)
AR	1,2
ST	1,24(15)
BCR	B'1111',14

The assembler will convert these into machine code and produce a listing of the following form:

LOC	OBJ CODE	SOURCE	STATEMENT
000000	5810 F010	L	1,16(,15)
000004	582F 0014	L	2,20(15)
000008	1A12	AR	1,2
00000A	501F 0018	ST	1,24(15)
00000E	07FE	BCR	B'1111',14

In the first instruction, R15 is used as a base register. In the other RX instructions no base register is used, and R15 is used as an index register. When only one of the two registers is specified in a D(X,B) address, it makes no operational difference in the execution of the program whether it is used as the X or the B register.

- The constants are generated starting at location 000010 and the listing produced from the DC and DS statements is

000010	00000004	DC	F'4'
000014	00000006	DC	F'6'
000018		DS	F

Note that the DS statement generates no object code.

- The END statement marks the end of the program and contains the label of the starting point as the operand. Normally, this is the label that is used in the CSECT statement.

2.5 XDUMP AND IMPLICIT ADDRESSES

Several improvements could be made in the program presented in Section 2.4 (Program 2-1). The most obvious one is that the result of the addition should be displayed. The techniques for handling input/output (I/O) will, for the most part, be deferred to later sections of this chapter. Until that material is covered, the XDUMP instruction will be used to display answers.

The XDUMP statement is a *pseudo-instruction* that may be utilized when the ASSIST assembler is used to perform the encoding of symbolic instructions. The format of the XDUMP instruction is

> label   XDUMP   area,length

The first operand must be the D(X,B) address of an area to be displayed on the printed output. The second operand indicates the number of bytes of storage to be displayed. The execution of an XDUMP instruction will normally cause the contents of the indicated area, along with some explanatory information, to be displayed in the printed output.* If the two operands are omitted, however, the contents of the 16 registers will be displayed rather than the contents of an area in storage. Thus, the instruction

> XDUMP   12(15),4

will cause a four-byte area in storage, starting at the address given by 12(15), to be displayed in the printed output. On the other hand, the instruction

> XDUMP

causes the contents of the registers to be printed out.

The main use of the XDUMP instruction is as a debugging tool, to locate errors in a program. The reader will quickly learn the utility of this tool as a mechanism for tracing the progress of execution through a program and for verifying the results produced by sections of a program. For now it may also be used to display the final output of programs.

In Program 2-1, it was necessary that the programmer calculate all of the relative addresses used in the program. In a large program, it would be extremely tedious to perform these calculations. This motivates the use of a different form of relative addressing, called implicit addressing. An *implicit address* is an address that the assembler will be required to convert to an explicit address.

The two most common forms of implicit addresses used with RX instructions are

> label

and

> label(r)

where   label   is the label of a field in the program
           r   is a register number

---

*Actually, an XDUMP instruction with an operand will cause a number of 32-byte lines of storage to be printed. Each of these lines will begin with an address that is a multiple of 32 (20_{16}). The number of lines printed will be the least number that contains all of the bytes specified by the operand.

When only a label is used, the implicit address refers to the field with the given label. Thus, the code

         L   1,WORD
                .
                .
                .
    WORD   DS   F

illustrates the use of the first form of an implicit address. If a register is used in an implicit address, the effective address is the address calculated by adding the contents of the register to the address of the indicated field. Hence, assuming that R10 contains one of the eight values 0, 4, 8, . . . , 28, the code

         L   1,WORDS(10)
                .
                .
                .
    WORDS   DS   8F

causes one of the eight words generated by the instruction

    WORDS   DS   8F

to be loaded into R1; which word is determined by the contents of R10. In this case, R10 plays the role of an index register (i.e., it is used as an index into a sequence of fields).

Implicit addresses of the following forms may also be used:

$$label \pm n$$
$$label \pm n(r)$$

where   n   is a decimal integer
         r   is the number of a register

For example,

$$AREA + 10(2)$$

represents the address found by adding the contents of R2 to the address of the tenth byte past AREA.

As previously mentioned, when an implicit address is used, the assembler must convert it to the corresponding explicit address. Thus, the following information must be available to the assembler:

1. which register should be used as a base register
2. what absolute address will be in the base register

For example, in Program 2-1 the fact that R15 contains the absolute address of ADD2 when program execution begins must be available to the assembler. This information can be conveyed to the assembler by the USING statement, which is of the form

USING   label,reg

where   label   is the label of a field

   reg   is the number of a register which may be assumed to contain the absolute address of that field during the execution of the program

These concepts are far from trivial. The reader is urged to consider Program 2-2 carefully. This rewritten version of ADD2 utilizes both XDUMP and implicit addressing and presents a significant enhancement of the version given in Program 2-1.

Program 2-2

```
ADD2      CSECT
          USING ADD2,15
          L     1,WORD1      LOAD THE CONTENTS OF WORD1 INTO R1
          L     2,WORD2      LOAD THE CONTENTS OF WORD2 INTO R2
          AR    1,2          GET THE SUM OF THE TWO WORDS; AND
          ST    1,WORD3      STORE THE SUM INTO WORD3
          XDUMP WORD3,4      DUMP OUT THE ANSWER
          BCR   B'1111',14   EXIT FROM THE PROGRAM
WORD1     DC    F'4'
WORD2     DC    F'6'
WORD3     DS    F
          END   ADD2
```

Note the following two improvements:

- The USING statement tells the assembler that, when it converts implicit addresses (labels) to explicit base-displacement form, it may use R15 as the base register and it may assume that, when the program is executed, R15 will contain the absolute address of ADD2.
- XDUMP causes the sum stored in WORD3 to be displayed in the printed output.

Exercises

1. Keypunch the latest version of ADD2 and run it. Carefully examine the output (both the assembler listing and the printing caused by the XDUMP).

Remove the BCR instruction, which caused the exit from the program. Rerun the program and note the following: After executing XDUMP, an attempt was made to execute the instruction represented by WORD1. Since the first byte of WORD1 is 00, an error occurred (00 is not a valid op code). This caused a "dump." A dump gives a portrayal of storage as it was when the error occurred. You should become familiar with the contents of a dump, since dumps will recur throughout your experience as a programmer.

2. Write a program containing two constants, one equal to 10 and one equal to 20. The program should calculate 10 minus 20 and XDUMP the answer. Run the program and verify the results.

2.6 THE CONDITION CODE AND BRANCHING

Of the executable instructions covered so far (ST, L, AR, SR, LR, XDUMP), AR and SR are unique in that they alter the setting of the condition code (CC). The condition code is a two-bit number. Certain instructions set the value of the CC to particular values, reflecting the outcome of the instructions. For example, the execution of an AR or SR instruction will set the CC as depicted in the following table:

CC	Meaning
0	The result of the operation was 0.
1	The result was < 0.
2	The result was > 0.
3	Overflow occurred.

Thus, if R1 contained 00001AFC and R2 contained 001247AE, execution of the instruction

$$\text{AR} \qquad 1,2$$

would cause the CC to be set to 2, indicating a positive result in R1.

The CC is actually part of a 64-bit unit called the Program Status Word (PSW). In Section 2.1, we pointed out that the PSW always contains the address of the next instruction to be executed. An examination of the format of the PSW (see Appendix C) will reveal that the CC occupies bits 34 and 35 (counting from the left, starting with 0) and that the address of the next instruction is kept in bits 40–63.

A programmer may take advantage of the CC by using it to determine the flow of execution through the program. This facility is brought about through the use of the Branch on Condition (BC) instruction, which causes a branch to be taken or not taken depending on the value of the CC. If the branch is taken, the next instruction executed will be at the address to be branched to, *not* the instruction immediately following the BC instruction. Otherwise, the BC instruction has no effect, and the instruction immediately following it will be the next instruction executed. The format of the BC instruction is

> label BC B'mask',addr

The second operand gives the address, in D(X,B)* form, where execution is continued if the branch is taken. The first operand is used to designate the settings of the CC that will cause the branch to occur. There are four possible settings of the CC—0,1,2, and 3. The mask is a four-bit binary number; each bit starting from the left corresponds to one of the possible values of the CC. When a BC instruction is executed, the branch will be taken only if a 1-bit number in the mask corresponds to the current setting of the CC. Thus, execution of the instruction

> BC B'1011',LOOP

will cause a branch to LOOP, if the setting of the CC is 0, 2, or 3. Note that a mask of 1111 will cause the branch to occur under all conditions. For example, execution of the instruction

> BC B'1111',READ

would cause an unconditional branch to the instruction with the label READ.
    The encoded format of the BC instruction is

> $h_0 h_0 h_m h_X$ $h_B h_D h_D h_D$

where $h_0 h_0$ is the op code 47
 h_m is the mask
 $h_X h_B h_D h_D h_D$ is the normal encoding of a D(X,B) address for
 an RX instruction

Thus, the instruction

> BC B'0001',12(3,4)

would be encoded as 4713 400C by the assembler. Program 2-3 illustrates the use of the BC instruction. It is assumed that the programmer will fill in his own values for W1 and W2 if he should choose to keypunch and run this program.

---

*Whenever a D(X,B) or D(B) address is specified as an operand, an implicit address may be used instead of the explicit form.

Program 2-3

```
* THIS PROGRAM PRINTS THE LARGER OF TWO NUMBERS.
* THE NUMBERS ARE IN W1 and W2.
MAX       CSECT
          USING MAX,15       R15 POINTS TO HEAD OF PROG
          L     1,W1          LOAD THE FIRST WORD
          L     2,W2          GET THE SECOND WORD INTO R2
          SR    1,2           R1 WILL NOW BE POS IF W1 IS HIGH
          BC    B'0010',ONE   BRANCH IF W1 IS HIGH
          XDUMP W2,4          PRINT OUT W2
          BC    B'1111',GO    BRANCH TO EXIT
ONE       XDUMP W1,4          PRINT OUT W1
GO        BCR   B'1111',14    EXIT
W1        DC    F'any value'
W2        DC    F'any value'
          END   MAX
```

In Program 2-3, a branch to ONE will be taken if the CC is 2 after the execution of the SR instruction. Hence, the branch to ONE will occur only if the result of the subtraction is positive, which corresponds to the case in which the word W1 contains a number greater than the number stored in W2.

Like many RX instructions, the BC instruction has an RR counterpart. The BCR (Branch on Condition Register) is coded as follows:

$$BCR \qquad B'mask',r$$

where   mask   is the same as in the BC instruction
        r   is the number of the register that contains the address to be branched to

Thus,

$$BCR \qquad B'1111',14$$

is an unconditional branch to the address in R14. Since R14 always contains the exit address when a program begins execution, the

$$BCR \qquad B'1111',14$$

instruction is used to cause the normal termination of a program.

Exercise

Write a program similar to Program 2-3 in which the user puts any desired value into the three words W1, W2, and W3; the program finds the smallest of the three words and utilizes an XDUMP instruction to display the result.

2.7 THE XREAD AND XDECI INSTRUCTIONS

In the following discussion, we assume that the maximum length of an input record to be entered by the XREAD is 80 characters. Therefore, this discussion is framed in terms of card images, but it should be equally applicable to input records accepted from other media.

A punched card used as input contains up to 80 characters of data. When these characters are read into storage, each will occupy one byte. There are 256 legitimate values that can be punched into a single column of a card. Each of these possible values for the column of a card is converted to a unique image when it is read into storage. A complete table listing the possible ways to punch a value into the column of a card and the image of each possible combination of punches is given in Appendix C. A small part of that table is given in Table 2-1.

Table 2-1

Punches	Representing	Image in Storage
none	blank	40
11-4	*	5C
12-1	A	C1
12-2	B	C2
0	0	F0
1	1	F1
2	2	F2
3	3	F3
4	4	F4
5	5	F5
6	6	F6
7	7	F7
8	8	F8
9	9	F9

- *Example.* If a card containing 1234 punched into the first four columns is read into an area called CARD, what would be in the first four bytes of CARD?

  The first byte of CARD will contain the value that corresponds to a 1. Since that is F1, the first byte of CARD is F1. The second will be F2; the third, F3; and the fourth, F4. Thus, the first four bytes of CARD would contain F1F2F3F4.

Exercises

1. If a card containing **122A3 in the first seven columns is read into an area called INPUT, what will the first seven bytes of INPUT look like after the card is read in?

2. Using Appendix C, determine what the following characters would look like in storage:

$$\$ \quad @ \quad \# \quad X \quad and \quad Z$$

The XREAD instruction is a pseudo-instruction that can be used to read the contents of a punched card into an area of storage. The format of the XREAD instruction is

label   XREAD   area,length

where   area   is the address, in D(X,B) form, of the area into which the card should be read

length   is the number of columns to be read. The length should be 80 or less. If it is less than 80, the remaining columns of the data card will be ignored.

The settings of the CC after the execution of an XREAD instruction convey the following information:

CC	Meaning
0	The card was read successfully.
1	No card could be read. This is called an end-of-file or EOF condition.
2	— (The CC is never set to this value.)*
3	—

Exercise

The following program reads in a deck of cards. After each card is read, the area containing the image of the card is XDUMPed. When EOF occurs, an exit is taken. Comment, punch, and run the program. Use two or more data cards as input, and punch a variety of characters into each card. Carefully study the XDUMPs to verify that the images are what you would expect.

```
READ    CSECT
        USING   READ,15
LOOP    XREAD   IN,80
        BCR     B'0100',14
        XDUMP   IN,80
        BC      B'1111',LOOP
IN      DS      CL80
        END     READ
```

---

*A dash is used consistently throughout this text to indicate condition code settings that cannot occur.

The data that is punched into a card and read into storage appears in what is called *character format*. In particular, the character representations of the decimal digits are F0, F1, F2, . . . , F9. Suppose that a card containing 4 in column 1, 3 in column 3, and blanks elsewhere has been read into storage. In storage the image of the card would be

$$F440F3404040 . . .$$

Suppose further that it is required to add the numbers represented by the first and third bytes of the card image. There are two immediate problems:

- F4 and F3 cannot be added together in their character representations. They must first be converted to the corresponding binary numbers.

- The binary numbers must be inserted into registers, since the addition is to be done with an AR instruction.

The XDECI is a pseudo-instruction provided for converting numbers in their character representation in storage to their corresponding binary representation in a register. The format for the XDECI instruction is

label   XDECI   r,addr

where   r   is the number of the register into which the binary form of the number will be inserted
        addr is the D(X,B) address of the number in its character format

Execution of an XDECI instruction has the following effects:

1. Beginning at the location given by addr, memory is scanned for the first character that is not a blank.

2. If the first character found is anything other than a decimal digit or a plus or minus sign, R1 is set to the address of that character and the condition code is set to 3 (overflow) to show that no decimal number could be converted. The contents of r are not changed, and nothing more is done.

3. If the first character is a plus or minus sign or a decimal digit, from one to nine decimal digits are scanned, and the number is converted to binary and placed in r.

4. R1 is set to the address of the first nondigit after the string of decimal digits. Thus, r should not usually be 1. This permits the user to scan across a card image for any number of decimal values. The values should be separated by blanks.

5. If ten or more decimal digits are found before a blank separator, R1 is set to the address of the first character that is not a decimal digit, the CC is set to 3, and r is left unchanged. A plus or minus sign alone causes a similar action, with R1 set to the address of the character following the sign character.

Note that execution of the XDECI alters R1. Therefore, a programmer cannot expect to save a value in R1 if he issues an XDECI.

The CC is set by XDECI as follows:

CC	Meaning
0	The number converted was 0.
1	The number converted was < 0.
2	The number converted was > 0.
3	An attempt was made to convert an invalid number.

It should be pointed out that the scan performed by the execution of an XDECI instruction will continue, perhaps beyond the field to be scanned, until a nonblank character is encountered. Thus, if a card image is to be scanned, it is advisable to mark the end of the card image with a nonblank character other than a decimal digit, so that the condition code may be checked to determine when the end of the card image has been reached. For example, this could be done as follows:

```
CARD       DS        CL80
           DC        C'*'
```

Program 2-4 reads in data cards with two numbers on each card. The difference between the numbers is calculated and XDUMPed.

Program 2-4

```
**********************************************************************
*
* THIS PROGRAM READS NUMBERS (TWO PER CARD) AND XDUMPS OUT THE
* DIFFERENCE OF THE TWO NUMBERS.
*
**********************************************************************
*
DIFF       CSECT
           USING DIFF,15
*
           XREAD CARD,80              READ THE FIRST CARD
*
LOOP       BC        B'0100',EXIT     BRANCH IF EOF HAS OCCURRED
*
           XDECI 2,CARD               GET THE FIRST NUMBER ON THE CARD
           BC        B'0001',GETNXT   SKIP THIS CARD ON A BAD VALUE
           XDECI 3,0(1)               NOW GET THE SECOND NUMBER
           BC        B'0001',GETNXT   SKIP THIS CARD ON A BAD VALUE
*
```

Program 2-4 (continued)

```
*         SR    2,3               GET THE DIFFERENCE
          ST    2,WORD            SAVE AND XDUMP THE DIFFERENCE
          XDUMP WORD,4
*
GETNXT    XREAD CARD,80           TRY TO READ THE NEXT CARD
          BC    B'1111',LOOP      GO BACK UP TO TEST FOR EOF
*
EXIT      BCR   B'1111',14        EXIT FROM THE PROGRAM
*
CARD      DS    CL80              CARD INPUT AREA
WORD      DS    F                 PUT THE DIFFERENCE HERE
          END   DIFF
```

Exercise

Write a program to sum a set of numbers. The program is to read cards and take one number from each card. When end-of-file occurs, the program should XDUMP the answer and then terminate.

2.8 THE XPRNT AND XDECO INSTRUCTIONS

In Section 2.7, the character format of data was introduced. The DC statement, which has been used previously to generate fullword binary constants, can also be used to generate character constants. The format of the appropriate DC statement is

> label   DC   mCLn'character string'

where m   is a duplication factor (a nonnegative integer)
       Ln   gives the length of the constant to be generated
       character string   is a string of characters

For example, the instruction

> F1   DC   2CL3'A B'

causes two consecutive three-byte fields to be generated, each containing C140C2 (the hexadecimal representation). The following additional rules apply to this use of the DC statement:

1. If the duplication factor is omitted, it is assumed to be 1. Hence,

> DC   1CL3'*A*'

and

> DC   CL3'*A*'

generate the same thing.

2. If the length that is specified is greater than that required to hold the character string, blanks will be padded on the right. Thus,

DC   CL6'*A*'

would generate 5CC15C404040. If the specified length does not allow enough bytes to represent all of the characters in the character string, the rightmost characters will be truncated. For example,

DC   CL2'*A*'

would generate the two-byte field 5CC1. If the length is unspecified, a field just large enough to represent the character string will be generated. Therefore,

DC   2C'ABC'

and

DC   2CL3'ABC'

each generate two three-byte fields.

3. There are two special characters, ' and &, that are unique in the following respect: To generate a string containing either an ' or an &, two adjacent occurrences of the character must occur in the character string, rather than a single occurrence. Thus,

DC   C' A' 'B'

generates the three-byte field C17DC2, and

DC   C'&&'

generates just one byte containing 50.

The following examples should help to clarify the above comments:

Coded	Generated
DC CL1'0'	F0
DC CL2'0'	F040
DC 2CL2'89'	F8F9F8F9
DC C'WORD'	E6D6D9C4
DC C'&&AB"C'	50C1C27DC3
DC CL3'ABCD'	C1C2C3

Exercise ───

Show what the following DC statements generate. (Use the hexadecimal representation of the contents of the generated fields.)

```
F1          DC      CL5'A'
            DC      2C'A'
            DC      3CL2'B'
            DC      C'1'''
F49         DC      C'&&0'
            DC      CL4'$$WORD'
```

Just as data that is read in from a card is stored in character format, so too is data that is to be printed. There are two steps involved in printing a line:

1. The line to be printed must be constructed in an area of storage. The actual characters that will appear in the printed line begin in the second byte of the area. The initial byte is reserved for a carriage control character, a byte that controls the positioning of the printed line on a page. The codes that can be used in the first byte and their meanings are

blank	Single-space before printing.
0	Double-space before printing.
1	Skip to the head of the next page before printing.

    The entire print line (including the carriage control byte) must contain 133 characters or less, because there are only 132 print positions on most printers.

2. After the print line has been constructed, an XPRNT instruction can be used to print the line. The format of the XPRNT instruction is

    label   XPRNT addr,length

where	addr	is the D(X,B) address of the print line in storage
	length	is the number of bytes to be taken from storage in constructing the record to be sent to the printer

    Program 2-5 illustrates the use of the XPRNT instruction. The program reads any number of cards, printing one line per card. The first line will be printed at the top of a page, and all successive lines will be double-spaced.

Program 2-5

```
**********************************************************************
*
* THIS PROGRAM SIMPLY READS AND PRINTS CARDS UNTIL EOF OCCURS.
*
**********************************************************************
*
PRINT     CSECT
          USING PRINT,15
*
*         XREAD CARD1,80           READ THE FIRST CARD
*
*         BC    B'0100',EXIT       EXIT ON EMPTY FILE
*
*         XPRNT CC1,81             PRINT THE FIRST CARD
*
*         XREAD CARD2,80           NOW READ THE SECOND CARD
*
LOOP      BC    B'0100',EXIT       BRANCH ON EOF
*
          XPRNT CC2,81             PRINT THE CARD
*
          XREAD CARD2,80           TRY TO READ THE NEXT CARD
          BC    B'1111',LOOP       GO BACK TO TEST FOR EOF
*
EXIT      BCR   B'1111',14         LEAVE THE PROGRAM
*
* IT'S A GOOD PRACTICE TO HAVE JUST 1 EXIT POINT FROM A PROGRAM.
* THAT'S WHY WE ALWAYS BRANCH TO EXIT.
*
CC1       DC    C'1'               CAUSE SKIP TO TOP OF PAGE
CARD1     DS    CL80               INPUT AREA FOR FIRST CARD
*
CC2       DC    C'0'               DOUBLE SPACE THE REST
CARD2     DS    CL80               ALL BUT FIRST CARD GET READ HERE
*
          END   PRINT
```

Simply knowing how to print strings of characters is not enough to permit the results of computations to be displayed. Previously, the problem of converting numbers from character to binary format was solved by the introduction of the XDECI instruction. The inverse problem must now be addressed.

Suppose that a result has been developed in a register and one wishes to display this result on a printer. This involves taking the number from the register, converting it from its binary representation to its character representation, and placing the result into the storage area of the print line. All of this can be done quite simply by use of the XDECO instruction

label   XDECO reg,addr

Execution of this pseudo-instruction causes the number in the register given as the first operand to be converted to a 12-byte character representation and stored at the D(X,B) address given by the second operand. The contents of the register are unaltered. For example, execution of the instruction

XDECO 10,ANSWER

causes the binary number in R10 to be converted to its character format and the result to be stored in 12 bytes of storage, starting at ANSWER. The contents of R10 are unaltered.

The number will be right-justified in the 12-byte field, with leading blanks. A minus sign will be printed to the left of the first significant digit if the number is negative. Program 2-6 illustrates the use of XDECO. It reads two numbers from each card and prints the sum of those two numbers.

Program 2-6

```
***********************************************************************
*
* THIS PROGRAM READS DATA CARDS, EACH OF WHICH CONTAINS TWO
* NUMBERS.  THE SUM OF THE TWO NUMBERS IS PRINTED.
*
***********************************************************************
*
SUMUP      CSECT
           USING SUMUP,15
*
           XPRNT HEADING,28         PRINT A PAGE HEADING
*
           XREAD CARD,80            READ THE FIRST CARD
*
CHECKEOF BC   B'0100',EXIT          BRANCH ON EOF
*
           XDECI 2,CARD             WE ASSUME THAT BOTH NUMBERS
           XDECI 3,0(1)             ARE VALID
*
           AR    2,3                CALCULATE THE SUM
*
           XDECO 2,OUTPUT           PUT PRINTABLE FORM INTO PRINT LINE
*
           XPRNT CRG,13             PRINT THE SUM (SINGLE SPACED)
*
           XREAD CARD,80            TRY TO READ THE NEXT CARD
           BC    B'1111',CHECKEOF   GO CHECK FOR EOF
*
EXIT     BCR   B'1111',14           LEAVE THE PROGRAM
*
CARD     DS    CL80                 CARD INPUT AREA
*
CRG      DC    C' '                 SINGLE SPACE CARRIAGE CONTROL
OUTPUT   DS    CL12                 OUTPUT THE SUM HERE
*
HEADING  DC    C'1THIS IS THE OUTPUT OF SUMUP'
         END   SUMUP
```

Exercises

1. Write a program to read in a set of numbers (one number per card) and print the sum of the numbers. A header should be printed at the top of the page, each number should be printed (one per line), and the result should be printed on the last line.

2. Write a program similar to the one described in the previous exercise. The only difference should be that the first data card contains the number of data cards that follow it. For example, if

$$\left.\begin{array}{r} 4 \\ \end{array}\right. \text{ Number of data cards}$$

$$\left.\begin{array}{r} 2 \\ -4 \\ 8 \\ 1 \end{array}\right\} \text{ Data cards}$$

were the input, the answer would be 7.

3. Write a program to compute the alternating sum/difference of an arbitrary number of values, where termination of data is indicated by an input value less than 0. Do not include the value of this trailer in your computation. For example, if the input data were

$$\left.\begin{array}{r} 26 \\ 43 \\ 71 \\ 122 \end{array}\right\} \text{ Data cards}$$

$$\left.\begin{array}{r} -6 \end{array}\right. \text{ Sentinel (trailer) card}$$

the answer would be $26 - 43 + 71 - 122 = -68$.

4. Write a program to find the total gross weight of a set of trucks. The program should read a deck of any number of cards, each of which contains the gross weight of one truck. The cards should be echo checked (XPRNTed) as they are read. The total gross weight should be printed with an appropriate label.

2.9 MORE INSTRUCTIONS AND EXAMPLES

Many RR instructions have RX counterparts that execute equivalent operations except that they require a word in main storage as the second operand. For example, the LR and L instructions perform similar tasks: The LR causes the second operand to be taken from a register, while the L accesses a fullword from storage.

The RX counterpart of AR is

$$\text{A} \qquad \text{r,D(X,B)} \qquad\qquad (Add)$$

Execution of this instruction causes the fullword starting at the address given by D(X,B) to be added to the contents of the register given by r. The contents of the fullword in storage are unaltered, and the result replaces the contents of r. For example, execution of the instruction

$$A \qquad 2,WORD$$

causes the contents of WORD to be added to the contents of R2. If D(X,B) resolves to other than a multiple of 4 (i.e., a fullword boundary), a specification error may result. If D(X,B) indicates a word outside the boundaries of the program, either a protection or addressing error may occur. If the result of the addition is too large or small to fit into r, a fixed-point overflow occurs.

The S instruction

$$S \qquad r,D(X,B) \qquad \qquad (Subtract)$$

corresponds to the SR instruction, just as the A instruction corresponds to the AR instruction. The description of the S is the same as for the A except that the second operand is subtracted from the contents of r.

The next two instructions to be discussed, the CR and C instructions, can be used to compare two numbers. The effect of either of these instructions is limited to the setting of the condition code.

$$CR \qquad r1,r2 \qquad \qquad (Compare\ Register)$$

As a consequence of the execution of this instruction, the condition code is set according to the following rules:

CC	Meaning
0	The contents of r1 and r2 are equal.
1	The number in r1 < the number in r2.
2	The number in r1 > the number in r2.
3	—

No errors can occur.

$$C \qquad r,D(X,B) \qquad \qquad (Compare)$$

This RX instruction has the same function as the CR instruction except that the fullword starting at D(X,B) is used for the second operand. Protection, addressing, or specification errors can occur, as in the other RX instructions.

Program 2-7 illustrates the use of the A and CR instructions. The program reads a set of numbers and prints the following:

- the number of numbers read
- the smallest number read
- the largest number read

Program 2-7

```
************************************************************************
*
*  THIS PROGRAM READS AN INPUT STREAM OF CARDS, EACH OF WHICH
*  CONTAINS A SINGLE NUMBER.  THE PROGRAM PRINTS THE SMALLEST VALUE,
*  THE LARGEST VALUE, AND THE NUMBER OF VALUES IN THE STREAM.  IF
*  THERE ARE NO INPUT CARDS, OR IF THE FIRST CARD DOESN'T HAVE A
*  VALID NUMBER ON IT, AN ERROR MESSAGE IS PRINTED AND THE PROGRAM
*  EXITS.  THE LOGIC IS AS FOLLOWS:
*
*    STEP 1.  TRY TO READ THE FIRST CARD.  IF SUCCESSFUL, GO TO STEP 3.
*
*    STEP 2.  PRINT AN "EMPTY INPUT" MESSAGE AND GO TO STEP 12
*             TO EXIT FROM THE PROGRAM.
*
*    STEP 3.  TRY TO GET THE NUMBER OFF THE CARD.  IF SUCCESSFUL,
*             GO TO STEP 5.
*
*    STEP 4.  PRINT "INVALID 1ST NUMBER" MESSAGE AND GO TO STEP 12
*             TO EXIT FROM THE PROGRAM.
*
*    STEP 5.  USE THE FIRST VALUE AS THE INITIAL "SMALLEST SO FAR"
*             AND THE INITIAL "LARGEST SO FAR" VALUES.  ALSO, SET
*             THE COUNT OF VALUES READ TO 1.
*
*    STEP 6.  READ THE SECOND CARD.
*
*    STEP 7.  TEST FOR EOF (END CONDITION FOR THE LOOP).  WHEN EOF
*             OCCURS, BRANCH TO STEP 11 TO PRINT THE RESULTS.
*
*    STEP 8.  TRY TO GET THE NUMBER FROM THE CARD.  IF YOU CAN,
*             COUNT IT, AND PROCEED TO STEP 9.  ELSE, GO TO
*             STEP 10 TO READ THE NEXT CARD.
*
*    STEP 9.  IF THE VALUE IS LOWER THAN THE "SMALLEST SO FAR",
*             USE IT AS THE NEW VALUE FOR "SMALLEST SO FAR".
*             SIMILARLY, IF IT'S LARGER THAN THE "LARGEST SO
*             FAR", IT IS USED AS THE NEW VALUE.
*
*    STEP 10. TRY TO READ THE NEXT CARD AND GO BACK TO THE
*             TOP OF THE LOOP (STEP 7).
*
*    STEP 11. PRINT THE 3 VALUES (COUNT, SMALLEST, AND LARGEST).
*
*    STEP 12. EXIT FROM THE PROGRAM.
*
************************************************************************
*
MIN@MAX   CSECT
          USING MIN@MAX,15
*
***<STEP 1>     READ THE FIRST CARD
*
          XREAD CARD,80
          BC    B'1011',GOTCARD     BRANCH IF THERE WAS A CARD
*
***<STEP 2>     PRINT "EMPTY INPUT" MESSAGE
*
          XPRNT EMPTYMSG,16
          BC    B'1111',EXIT
*
***<STEP 3>     TRY TO GET THE NUMBER OFF THE FIRST CARD
*
GOTCARD   XDECI 2,CARD
          BC    B'1110',GOT1ST      BRANCH IF IT WAS VALID
*
***<STEP 4>     PRINT "INVALID 1ST NUMBER" MESSAGE
*
          XPRNT BAD1ST,23
          BC    B'1111',EXIT
```

Program 2-7 (continued)

```
*
***<STEP 5>   INITIALIZE MIN, MAX, AND COUNT
*
GOT1ST   LR     3,2             R3 WILL HOLD MAXIMUM VALUE SO FAR
         LR     4,2             R4 WILL HOLD MINIMUM VALUE SO FAR
         L      5,ONE           R5 COUNTS THE NUMBER VALID CARDS
*
***<STEP 6>   READ THE SECOND CARD
*
         XREAD  CARD,80
*
***<STEP 7>   LOOP UNTIL EOF OCCURS
*
CHKEOF   BC     B'0100',EOF
*
***<STEP 8>   IF THE NUMBER IS INVALID, JUST SKIP IT; ELSE, COUNT IT
*
         XDECI  2,CARD
         BC     B'0001',READNXT
         A      5,ONE           COUNT IT (SINCE IT WAS VALID)
*
***<STEP 9>   SET NEW MAX OR MIN, IF NECESSARY
*
         CR     2,3             CHECK FOR NEW MAX
         BC     B'1100',CHKMIN  BRANCH IF <= OLD MAX
*
         LR     3,2             ELSE, SET NEW MAX
         BC     B'1111',READNXT AND GO READ NEXT VALUE
*
CHKMIN   CR     2,4             CHECK FOR NEW MIN
         BC     B'1010',READNXT BRANCH IF NOT < OLD MIN
*
         LR     4,2
*
***<STEP 10>  TRY TO READ THE NEXT CARD
*
READNXT  XREAD  CARD,80
         BC     B'1111',CHKEOF  BRANCH BACK TO CHECK EOF
*
***<STEP 11>  PRINT THE RESULTS
*
EOF      XDECO  5,#READ         PUT # READ INTO PRINT LINE
         XPRNT  LINE1,28        AND PRINT IT
*
         XDECO  3,SMALLEST      PUT MINIMUM INTO PRINT LINE
         XPRNT  LINE2,29        AND PRINT IT
*
         XDECO  4,LARGEST       PUT MAXIMUM INTO PRINT LINE
         XPRNT  LINE3,28        AND PRINT IT
*
***<STEP 12>  EXIT
*
EXIT     BCR    B'1111',14
*
*********************************************************************
*
CARD     DS     CL80            CARD INPUT AREA
*
EMPTYMSG DC     C'1*** EMPTY INPUT'
*
BAD1ST   DC     C'1*** INVALID 1ST NUMBER'
*
ONE      DC     F'1'
*
LINE1    DC     C'1# OF CARDS READ'
#READ    DS     CL12
*
LINE2    DC     C'0SMALLEST VALUE ='
SMALLEST DS     CL12
*
LINE3    DC     C'0LARGEST VALUE ='
LARGEST  DS     CL12
*
         END    MIN@MAX
```

The following instructions (LCR, LNR, LPR, and LTR) are similar to the LR instruction. Of these four instructions, the LTR will probably prove most useful.

Execution of the instruction

LCR   r1,r2   *(Load Complement)*

causes the complement of r2 to be loaded into r1. If r2 contains the number n before the instruction is executed, r2 will remain unchanged (unless r2 and r1 are the same register) and r1 will contain $-n$ after execution. The CC is set as follows:

CC	Meaning
0	r1 contains 0.
1	r1 contains a negative number.
2	r1 contains a positive number.
3	Overflow occurred.

Execution of the RR instruction

LNR   r1,r2   *(Load Negative)*

causes the negative of the absolute value of the contents of r2 to replace the contents of r1. The contents of r2 are unaltered (unless r1 is r2). The CC is set as follows:

CC	Meaning
0	r1 contains 0.
1	r1 contains a negative number.
2	—
3	—

Execution of the RR instruction

LPR   r1,r2   *(Load Positive)*

causes the absolute value of the contents of r2 to replace the contents of r1. The contents of r2 are unaltered (unless r1 is r2). Fixed-point overflow will occur if r2 contains the maximum negative number (80000000). The CC is set as follows:

CC	Meaning
0	r1 contains 0.
1	—
2	r1 contains a positive number.
3	Overflow occurred.

Execution of the RR instruction

$$\text{LTR} \qquad \text{r1,r2} \qquad\qquad (Load\ and\ Test)$$

causes the contents of r2 to be loaded into r1 and sets the condition code. The contents of r2 are unaltered. Thus, this instruction is the same as LR except for the setting of the CC. The CC is set as follows:

CC	Meaning
0	r1 contains 0.
1	r1 contains a negative number.
2	r1 contains a positive number.
3	—

LTR is the instruction that should be used to check whether a register contains zero. For example, in order to branch to a routine called ZERO in the case where R12 contains zero, the following two instructions should be used:

```
LTR     12,12        SET THE CC
BC      B'1000',ZERO
```

Since R12 is loaded into itself, the only effect of the LTR is to set the CC.

Program 2-8 utilizes the LPR instruction to take the absolute value of a number. It reads in a set of numbers (one number per card) and computes three sums—the sum of the absolute values of all the numbers, the sum of the positive numbers, and the sum of the negative numbers.

Program 2-8

```
**********************************************************************
*
* THIS PROGRAM READS IN A DECK OF CARDS, EACH OF WHICH CONTAINS
* A VALID NUMBER.  THE PROGRAM ACCUMULATES THE SUM OF
*
*     THE POSITIVE NUMBERS
*
*     THE NEGATIVE NUMBERS
*
* AND THE ABSOLUTE VALUES OF THE NUMBERS
*
*
* WHEN EOF IS DETECTED, THE PROGRAM PRINTS A SINGLE LINE
* DISPLAYING THE THREE SUMS.  THE LOGIC IS AS FOLLOWS:
*
*    STEP 1.   SET THE THREE ACCUMULATORS (POSITIVE, NEGATIVE,
*              AND ABSOLUTE VALUES) TO 0.
*
*    STEP 2.   TRY TO READ THE FIRST CARD.
*
*    STEP 3.   CHECK FOR END OF THE LOOP (EOF).  WHEN IT OCCURS
*              BRANCH TO STEP 6 TO PRINT THE RESULTS.
*
*    STEP 4.   ADD THE NUMBER OFF THE CARD TO THE APPROPRIATE
*              ACCUMULATORS.
```

Program 2-8 (continued)

```
*
*    STEP 5.   TRY TO READ THE NEXT CARD AND GO BACK TO THE TOP
*              OF THE LOOP (STEP 3).
*
*    STEP 6.   PRINT THE RESULTS.
*
*    STEP 7. EXIT FROM THE PROGRAM.
*
************************************************************************
*
SUM3      CSECT
          USING SUM3,15
*
***<STEP 1>     ZERO THE ACCUMULATORS
*
          SR    3,3               R3 ACCUMULATES SUM OF POSITIVE #S
          SR    4,4               R4 ACCUMULATES SUM OF NEGATIVE #S
          SR    5,5               R5 ACCUMULATES ABSOLUTE VALUES
*
***<STEP 2>     TRY TO READ THE FIRST CARD
*
          XREAD CARD,80
*
***<STEP 3>     TEST FOR EOF (EXIT CONDITION FOR THE LOOP)
CHKEOF    BC    B'0100',EOF
*
***<STEP 4>     ACCUMULATE VALUES (ASSUME # ON CARD IS VALID)
*
          XDECI 2,CARD
          BC    B'0100',NEG       BRANCH IF VALUE IS NEGATIVE
*
          AR    3,2               ADD TO SUM OF POSITIVE VALUES
          BC    B'1111',ADDABS    GO ADD IT TO ABSOLUTE VALUES
*
NEG       AR    4,2               ADD IT TO SUM OF NEGATIVE VALUES
          LPR   2,2               SET VALUE TO POSITIVE
*
ADDABS    AR    5,2               ACCUMULATE ABSOLUTE VALUES
*
***<STEP 5>     TRY TO READ THE NEXT CARD AND GO BACK TO HEAD OF LOOP
*
          XREAD CARD,80
          BC    B'1111',CHKEOF
*
***<STEP 6>     PRINT THE RESULTS
*
EOF       XDECO 3,SUMPOS          PUT SUM OF POSITIVE VALUES INTO LINE
          XDECO 4,SUMNEG          PUT SUM OF NEGATIVE VALUES INTO LINE
          XDECO 5,SUMABS          PUT SUM OF ABSOLUTE VALUES INTO LINE
          XPRNT ANSWER,132        PRINT THE LINE
*
***<STEP 7>     EXIT
*
          BCR   B'1111',14
*
************************************************************************
*
ANSWER    DC    C'1THE SUM OF THE POS. NUMBERS = '
SUMPOS    DS    CL12
          DC    C' THE SUM OF THE NEG. NUMBERS = '
SUMNEG    DS    CL12
          DC    C' THE SUM OF THE ABSOLUTE VALUES = '
SUMABS    DS    CL12
*
CARD      DS    CL80              CARD INPUT AREA
*
          END   SUM3
```

2.10 MULTIPLICATION AND DIVISION

There are two quite similar instructions that can be utilized to create the product of two fullwords whose values are in binary integer format. These are the MR and M instructions.

In the instruction

MR   r1,r2   (*Multiply Register*)

the first operand, r1, must be an even register and will designate an even/odd pair of registers. The multiplicand (the number to be multiplied) is taken from the odd register of the even/odd pair. Thus, if r1 were 4, the multiplicand would be taken from R5. The multiplier is taken from r2. The execution of this instruction causes the product of the multiplicand and the multiplier to be formed as a 64-bit signed integer, which replaces the original contents of the even/odd pair of registers designated by r1. The contents of r2 are unaltered unless r2 is one of the registers of the even/odd pair designated by r1.

An example may help to clarify the use of the MR instruction. Suppose that

R1 contains 00000004
R2 contains 0000FFFF
R3 contains 00000005

Then if

MR   2,1

is executed, the multiplicand in R3 will be multiplied by the multiplier from R1. The result will replace the R2-R3 pair, giving

R1: unchanged
R2-R3: 00000000 00000014 ($4 \times 5 = 14_{16}$)

Two points are worth noting:

- The product would have to be very large (greater than 7FFFFFFF) or very small (less than -80000000) before the even register of the pair would contain anything but an extension of the sign bit. Thus, if the result were positive, the even register would normally contain 00000000; if the result were negative (and not $< -2^{31}$), the even register would contain FFFFFFFF.

- r2 can be the number of either register in the pair designated by r1. For example, execution of the instruction

MR   0,1

causes the square of the number in R1 to replace the contents of the even/odd pair R0-R1.

Now consider the RX counterpart of the MR instruction:

M   r,D(X,B)   (*Multiply*)

This instruction is like the MR except that the multiplier is taken from the fullword of storage beginning at the address given by D(X,B). Hence, if R1 contained 00000001, then execution of the instructions

M   R0,TWO

.

.

.

TWO   DC   F'2'

would cause the product to replace the contents of the pair R0-R1. (R0 would be set to 00000000, and R1 would be set to 00000002.) Addressing, protection, and specification exceptions can occur, just as with other RX instructions, if the resolution of D(X,B) produces an erroneous effective address.

Exercise

Assume that

R0 contains F01821F0
R1 contains FFFFFFFF
R2 contains 00000003
R3 contains 00000004

Show what would be in the registers after execution of each of the following instructions:

a. MR 2,1   **b.** MR 0,2   **c.** MR 2,3   **d.** MR 2,2

Assume further that WORD1 and WORD2 are defined by

WORD1   DC   F'10'
WORD2   DC   F'–2'

Show what would be in the registers after execution of each of the following instructions:

e. M 0,WORD1   **g.** M 2,WORD1
f. M 0,WORD2   **h.** M 2,WORD2

Division of binary integer numbers is performed by using either a DR or a D instruction. The description of the DR instruction is

DR   r1,r2   (*Divide Register*)

The first operand, r1, designates an even/odd pair of registers containing the dividend (the number to be divided). The second operand, r2, is the number of a register containing the divisor. The execution of the instruction causes the quotient result of the division to replace the contents of the odd register of the even/odd pair. The sign of the quotient is determined by normal algebraic rules. The remainder, which always has the same sign as the dividend, replaces the contents of the even register of the pair. If the quotient cannot be represented as a 32-bit signed integer, fixed-point overflow will occur.

The use of a DR instruction requires that care be exercised with respect to the contents of the even register of the even/odd pair, since the dividend is considered to be the entire 64-bit number contained in the linked pair of registers. If the dividend is small enough to be contained in only the odd register of the pair, one of two things must be done to initialize the contents of the even register:

- If the dividend is positive (i.e., the odd register contains a positive number), then the even register must be set to all zeros.
- If the dividend is negative, the even register must be set to FFFFFFFF.

The action in either case is to extend the sign bit of the odd register through the even register. As an example of the effects of executing a DR instruction, suppose that

> R2 contains 00000000
> R3 contains 00000007
> R4 contains FFFFFFFE (-2)

Then, execution of the instruction

> DR   2,4

would leave the registers as follows:

- R2 would contain the remainder signed consistent with the dividend: 00000001.
- R3 would contain the quotient with the correct sign: FFFFFFFD (-3).
- The contents of R4 would remain unchanged.

The RX counterpart of DR is D:

> D   r,D(X,B)   (*Divide*)

The D instruction functions just like the DR instruction except that the divisor is taken from the fullword beginning at D(X,B). Thus,

> D   2,MINUS2
> .
> .
> .
> MINUS2 DC   F'-2'

would have produced the same results in R2 and R3 as the preceding example.

As mentioned earlier, the even register of the even/odd pair used in a divide operation must be set carefully. There is a simple way to handle the problem. Suppose that R3 contains the dividend and that R2 must be set to the correct sign extension. Then,

```
            M         2,ONE
            .
            .
            .

ONE         DC        F'1'
```

accomplishes this (since multiplication by 1 just converts the 32-bit value in R3 to a 64-bit value in R2-R3). This technique is used in several of the sample programs.

Exercise

Suppose that

```
            R1  contains 00000003
            R2  contains 00000000
            R3  contains 00000014
            R4  contains FFFFFFFF
            R5  contains FFFFFF10
```

Show what would be in the registers after execution of each of the following instructions:

a. DR 2,1   **b.** DR 2,4   **c.** DR 2,5   **d.** DR 4,1

Further suppose that WORD1 and WORD2 are defined as follows:

```
    WORD1    DC      F'-4'
    WORD2    DC      F'14'
```

Show the results of executing each of the following instructions:

e. D 2,WORD1   **g.** D 4,WORD1
f. D 2,WORD2   **h.** D 4,WORD2

Program 2-9 illustrates the use of the multiply and divide instructions. It reads two numbers from each card; it multiplies the two numbers and also divides the second number into the first. Both results are then printed.

Program 2-9

```
*****************************************************************************
*
* THIS PROGRAM IS USED TO ILLUSTRATE THE MULTIPLY AND DIVIDE
* INSTRUCTIONS.  IT READS CARDS, EACH OF WHICH CONTAINS TWO NUMBERS.
* THE PRODUCT OF THE TWO NUMBERS IS CALCULATED, AND THE RESULT OF
* DIVIDING THE SECOND NUMBER INTO THE FIRST IS FOUND.  BOTH RESULTS
* ARE PRINTED FOR EACH INPUT CARD.  THE LOGIC IS AS FOLLOWS:
*
*    STEP 1.   READ THE FIRST CARD.
*
*    STEP 2.   IF EOF HAS OCCURRED, GO TO STEP 6 TO EXIT.
*
*    STEP 3.   GET THE TWO NUMBERS OFF THE CARD (WE ASSUME THAT THEY
*              ARE VALID) AND COMPUTE THE PRODUCT AND QUOTIENT.
*
*    STEP 4.   PRINT THE PRODUCT AND QUOTIENT.
*
*    STEP 5.   READ THE NEXT CARD AND GO BACK TO STEP 2.
*
*    STEP 6.   EXIT.
*
*****************************************************************************
*
MULTDIV  CSECT
         USING MULTDIV,15
*
***<STEP 1>    READ THE FIRST CARD.
*
         XREAD CARD,80
*
***<STEP 2>    IF EOF HAS OCCURRED, GO TO STEP 6.
*
TESTEOF  BC    B'0100',EXIT
*
***<STEP 3>    CALCULATE PRODUCT AND QUOTIENT.
*
         XDECI 3,CARD            GET THE FIRST NUMBER
*
         XDECI 4,0(1)            AND NOW THE SECOND
*
         LR    7,3
         MR    6,4               PUT THE PRODUCT IN R6-R7
*
* NOTE THAT IN ALMOST ALL CASES ONE MAY ASSUME THAT THE RESULT
* WILL FIT INTO THE ODD REGISTER OF THE PAIR.  THIS PROGRAM
* WILL WORK PROPERLY ONLY IF THAT ASSUMPTION IS MADE.
*
         LR    9,3
         M     8,ONE             THIS PUTS THE CORRECT VALUE IN R8
*
* THE MULTIPLY PROPAGATES THE SIGN BIT THRU R8.  THUS, IF THE NUMBER
* IN R3 IS POSITIVE, R8 WILL GET SET TO 00000000.  IF IT'S NEGATIVE,
* R8 GETS SET TO FFFFFFFF.
*
         DR    8,4               R9 NOW HAS THE QUOTIENT
*
***<STEP 4>    PRINT THE COMPUTED VALUES.
*
         XDECO 7,PROD
         XDECO 9,QUOT            PUT THE VALUES INTO PRINT LINE
*
         XPRNT PLINE,54          PRINT THE LINE
*
***<STEP 5>    TRY TO READ THE NEXT CARD.
*
         XREAD CARD,80
         BC    B'1111',TESTEOF   AND GO BACK TO TEST FOR EOF
*
```

Program 2-9 (continued)

```
***<STEP 6>    EXIT.
*
EXIT    BCR    B'1111',14
*
*********************************************************************
*
ONE     DC     F'1'                  USED TO SET UP SIGN IN EVEN REG FOR
*                                    THE DIVIDE
PLINE   DC     C'0'                  CARRIAGE CONTROL FOR DOUBLE-SPACING
        DC     C'PRODUCT IS '
PROD    DS     CL12                  PUT THE PRODUCT HERE
        DC     C'   THE QUOTIENT IS '
QUOT    DS     CL12                  PUT THE QUOTIENT HERE
*
CARD    DS     CL80                  CARD INPUT AREA
        END    MULTDIV
```

2.11 REGISTER EQUATES AND EXTENDED MNEMONICS

The EQU is an assembler instruction that causes no machine code to be generated. The instruction is used simply to establish a correspondence between a label and an expression. For now, we shall consider only EQUates of the form

label   EQU   expression

where expression is an integer. The effect of the instruction is to establish a correspondence between label and expression so that any occurrence of label in the program will be treated in the same manner as an occurrence of expression.

The following EQU statements should occur in every program:

```
R0          EQU     0
R1          EQU     1
             .
             .
             .
R15         EQU     15
```

Then, wherever a reference is made to a register in the program, the appropriate label should be used. For example, the statement

L   R1,WORD

should be used rather than the statement

L   1,WORD

The reason for using these EQU statements is that most assemblers produce a cross-reference table with the program listing. This table lists, for each label, the number of the instruction in which the label was defined and the numbers of all instructions in which the label is used. Thus, a ready reference to the use of each of the registers is provided. When macros are discussed in Chapter 9, a technique for eliminating the drudgery of inserting these 16 statements in each program will be presented.

The extended mnemonics are a convenience, provided by the assembler, that allows the coding of many of the conditional branches without the necessity of explicitly specifying the masks. Since this feature provides a facility for specifying branch conditions through the use of mnemonics, it simplifies the task of coding programs. The readability of assembler listings is also greatly enhanced through the use of extended mnemonics, because the tedious chore of continually checking the meanings of particular masks in BC and BCR instructions is eliminated. The following two sets of instructions illustrate the use of this option:

1. Using the BC instruction:

```
        CR        3,4
        BC        B'1000',ADDR
```

2. Using an extended mnemonic:

```
        CR        3,4
        BE        ADDR
```

The same code is generated for each of these sets of instructions. That is, the

```
        BE        address
```

is just an alternative to

```
        BC        B'1000',address
```

Appendix B contains a table of the extended mnemonics, together with the corresponding BC and BCR instructions. Note that each extended mnemonic is intended to be used with a particular class of instructions that sets the condition code. Thus, both

```
        BZ        LOOP
```

and

```
        BE        LOOP
```

are equivalent to

```
        BC        B'1000',LOOP
```

However, the BZ (Branch Zero) mnemonic is intended to be used following an arithmetic operation, while BE (Branch Equal) should be used following a compare instruction.

A discussion of the use of the NOP and NOPR instructions is deferred to Section 8.2. Though these instructions may seem pointless, since they generate branches with masks of B'0000', the reader is asked to accept on faith at this point that they do have important uses.

It is unfortunate but true that, with most assemblers, only the NOPR and BR mnemonics can be used as alternatives for BCR instructions. However, since by far the most common use of the BCR instruction is to effect an unconditional branch, the BR mnemonic provides an alternative to most uses of the BCR instruction.

The programming examples in the remainder of this text will utilize both register EQUates and extended mnemonics.

2.12 LITERALS

It will frequently be necessary to use constants that are not altered by the program. For example, if 4 were to be added to the contents of R1, the following instructions could be used:

```
        A       R1,FOUR
        .
        .
        .
FOUR    DC      F'4'
```

In this case FOUR is a constant that is never altered. As a convenience, the two instructions above could be replaced by the single instruction

```
        A       R1, =F'4'
```

In this case, the second operand is a *literal*, which is simply a constant specification preceded by an equality symbol. If a literal is used, the assembler will automatically generate the constant and use the address of the generated constant in the encoding of the instruction. For example,

```
        D       R2, =F'10'
```

will cause the assembler to generate a fullword containing 0000000A and to use the address of that generated constant in the encoding of the Divide instruction.

Literals may be used for character constants as well. For example, the instruction

```
        XPRNT   =C'1THIS PRINTS A HEADER',21
```

will cause a character string to be printed at the top of a page. This technique is particularly convenient for printing error messages and output headings.

Unless the user specifies otherwise, the assembler will store the generated constants used as literals immediately following the end of a program.

The user may specify exactly where the literals are to be generated by using a

LTORG

command. The LTORG instructs the assembler to store at this point in the program all literals that have been generated but have not been stored as the result of any previous LTORG. Normally, the LTORG is placed before the user-defined constants in a program but after the last instruction in the program.

The reader is urged to utilize both literals and the LTORG command in future programs.

Program 2-10 illustrates the use of both character and fullword literals.

Program 2-10

```
**********************************************************************
*
* THIS PROGRAM READS A SERIES OF CARDS, EACH OF WHICH CONTAINS
* TWO NUMBERS.  FOR EACH CARD THE PROGRAM PRINTS THE TWO NUMBERS AND
* THEIR AVERAGE.   THE LOGIC IS:
*
*   STEP 1.   PRINT A HEADER.
*
*   STEP 2.   TRY TO READ THE FIRST CARD.
*
*   STEP 3.   IF EOF HAS OCCURRED, GO TO STEP 7.
*
*   STEP 4.   GET THE 2 NUMBERS OFF THE CARD AND COMPUTE
*             THEIR AVERAGE.
*
*   STEP 5.   PRINT THE TWO NUMBERS AND THE AVERAGE.
*
*   STEP 6.   READ THE NEXT CARD AND GO BACK TO STEP 3.
*
*   STEP 7.   PRINT "END OF REPORT" MESSAGE AND EXIT.
*
**********************************************************************
*
AVERAGE   CSECT
          USING AVERAGE,R15
*
***<STEP 1>    PRINT THE HEADER
*
          XPRNT =C'1AVERAGES REPORT',16
*
***<STEP 2>    READ THE FIRST CARD
*
          XREAD CARD,80
*
***<STEP 3>    LOOP UNTIL END-OF-FILE
*
LOOP      BC    B'0100',EXIT
*
***<STEP 4>    GET THE NUMBERS AND THEIR AVERAGE
*
          XDECI R2,CARD             GET 1ST NUMBER
          XDECI R3,0(R1)            AND THE SECOND
*
          LR    R5,R3
          AR    R5,R2               R5 NOW HAS THE SUM OF THE NUMBERS
*
```

Program 2-10 (continued)

```
*         M      R4,=F'1'              THIS PUTS THE CORRECT SIGN
*                                      EXTENSION INTO R4
          D      R4,=F'2'              R5 NOW HAS THE AVERAGE
*
***<STEP 5>      PRINT THE NUMBERS AND THEIR AVERAGE
*
          XDECO R2,NUMBER1             PUT 1ST NUMBER INTO CHARACTER FORM
          XDECO R3,NUMBER2             PUT 2ND NUMBER INTO CHARACTER FORM
          XDECO R5,AVG                 PUT AVERAGE INTO CHARACTER FORM
*
          XPRNT PRNTLINE,93            PRINT THE RESULTS
*
***<STEP 6>      READ THE NEXT CARD AND GO BACK TO STEP 3.
*
          XREAD CARD,80
          B     LOOP
*
***<STEP 7>      PRINT "END OF REPORT" MESSAGE AND EXIT.
*
EXIT      XPRNT =C'0END OF REPORT',14
          BR    R14                    EXIT
*
*****************************************************************
*
          LTORG
*
CARD      DS    CL80                   CARD INPUT AREA
*
PRNTLINE DC     C'0THE FIRST NUMBER WAS'
NUMBER1  DS     CL12                   PUT THE 1ST NUMBER HERE
         DC     C'   THE SECOND NUMBER WAS'
NUMBER2  DS     CL12                   PUT 2ND NUMBER HERE
         DC     C'   AVERAGE ='
AVG      DS     CL12                   PUT AVERAGE HERE
*
R0       EQU    0
R1       EQU    1
R2       EQU    2
R3       EQU    3
R4       EQU    4
R5       EQU    5
R6       EQU    6
R7       EQU    7
R8       EQU    8
R9       EQU    9
R10      EQU    10
R11      EQU    11
R12      EQU    12
R13      EQU    13
R14      EQU    14
R15      EQU    15
         END    AVERAGE
```

2.13 THE LA INSTRUCTION

The LA instruction, the last instruction to be covered in this chapter, performs a simple operation but proves to be a very useful instruction:

$$LA \qquad r,D(X,B) \qquad\qquad (Load\ Address)$$

Execution of an LA instruction will cause the effective address given by
D(X,B) to be resolved and the address itself to be inserted into the register
designated by r. (Since the calculated address is only 24 bits long, it will

occupy only the rightmost three bytes of r; the left byte of r will be set to zero.) Thus, execution of the instruction

           LA   R1,WORD

puts the address of WORD into R1.
   Carefully note the difference between

           LA   R1,WORD

and

           L   R1,WORD

The first instruction—the LA—"points" R1 at WORD (i.e., puts the address of WORD into R1), while the second actually loads the contents at the address of WORD into R1. Hence, the instruction

           L   R1,WORD

has exactly the same effect as the pair of instructions

           LA   R1,WORD
           L   R1,0(R1)

   Two special* but very common uses for the LA instruction should be emphasized.

1. A value n in the range $0 \leq n \leq 4095$ may be loaded into a register r by executing an instruction of the form

           LA   r,n

   In this case the value n is an example of a D(X,B) address in which X and B are omitted. For example, execution of the instruction

           LA   R2,20

   resolves the storage address into the value 20 and puts this value into R2 (setting R2 to 00000014). This is usually the most efficient way of loading small, positive-constant values in binary integer form into a register.

2. Suppose that a register r contains a nonnegative number. To add an increment n less than 4096 to r, an instruction of the following form could be used:

           LA   r,n(r)

   For example, execution of the instruction

---

*These are special only in the sense that the value being loaded into r is not an "address" as implied by the instruction's name.

LA   R14,32(R14)

adds 32 to R14 and puts the result into R14. Note that this will work only if the sum can be represented as a 24-bit binary number. This is usually the most efficient way of incrementing registers by small, positive-integer values.

In later sections of this text, many examples will deal with manipulating tables of numbers. In such programs, LA instructions frequently appear. Program 2-11 simply builds a table of numbers and then XDUMPs the completed table. Study carefully both the logic of the program and the uses of the LA instruction.

Program 2-11

```
*******************************************************************
*
* THE FOLLOWING PROGRAM BUILDS A TABLE OF FULLWORDS, AND THEN XDUMPS
* THE COMPLETED TABLE.  IT READS ONE NUMBER OFF EACH INPUT CARD,
* RECOGNIZING THE END OF INPUT WHEN A TRAILER CARD CONTAINING
* 999999 IS ENCOUNTERED.  THE LOGIC OF THE PROGRAM IS:
*
*    STEP 1.  INITIALIZE R3 TO POINT TO THE FIRST ENTRY IN THE TABLE.
*             R4, WHICH IS USED TO COUNT THE ENTRIES IN THE TABLE, IS
*             INITIALLY SET TO 0.
*
*    STEP 2.  READ THE FIRST CARD.
*
*    STEP 3.  CHECK FOR THE TRAILER. IF IT IS THE TRAILER, GO TO STEP 6
*             TO XDUMP THE TABLE.
*
*    STEP 4.  PUT THE NUMBER INTO THE TABLE (ADDING 1 TO THE COUNT OF
*             ENTRIES AND INCREMENTING THE POINTER TO THE NEXT ENTRY).
*
*    STEP 5.  READ THE NEXT CARD AND GO BACK TO STEP 3.
*
*    STEP 6.  XDUMP OUT THE CONTENTS OF THE TABLE AND EXIT.
*
*******************************************************************
*
TABUILD  CSECT
         USING TABUILD,R15
*
***<STEP 1>    INITIALIZE COUNTER AND POINTER TO NEXT ENTRY
*
         SR    R4,R4         SET COUNT OF ENTRIES TO 0
         LA    R3,TABLE      POINT AT FIRST ENTRY (NEXT ENTRY TO FILL)
*
***<STEP 2>    READ THE FIRST CARD
*
         XREAD CARD,80       IT IS ASSUMED THAT THERE IS A CARD AND
*                            THAT IT CONTAINS A NUMBER
         XDECI R2,CARD
*
***<STEP 3>    CHECK FOR TRAILER
*
TRAILCHK C     R2,=F'999999' CHECK FOR TRAILER
         BE    ENDINPUT
*
***<STEP 4>    ADD THE NUMBER TO THE TABLE
*
         ST    R2,0(R3)      PUT NUMBER INTO NEXT SLOT IN THE TABLE
         LA    R4,1(R4)      ADD 1 TO COUNT OF ENTRIES IN THE TABLE
         LA    R3,4(R3)      MOVE "NEXT ENTRY" POINTER FORWARD 1 ENTRY
```

Program 2-11 (continued)

```
*
***<STEP 5>    READ THE NEXT CARD AND GET THE NUMBER INTO R2
*
        XREAD CARD,80
        XDECI R2,CARD          THE NEXT NUMBER IS NOW IN R2
*
        B     TRAILCHK
*
***<STEP 6>    XDUMP THE COMPLETED TABLE
*
ENDINPUT XDUMP TABLE,200
        XDUMP
*
* THE SECOND XDUMP IS TO DISPLAY R4, WHICH HAS THE COUNT OF THE NUMBER
* OF ENTRIES IN THE TABLE.
*
        BR    R14              EXIT FROM THE PROGRAM
*
        LTORG
CARD    DS    CL80             CARD INPUT AREA
TABLE   DS    50F              ROOM FOR 50 ENTRIES
R0      EQU   0
R1      EQU   1
R2      EQU   2
R3      EQU   3
R4      EQU   4
R5      EQU   5
R6      EQU   6
R7      EQU   7
R8      EQU   8
R9      EQU   9
R10     EQU   10
R11     EQU   11
R12     EQU   12
R13     EQU   13
R14     EQU   14
R15     EQU   15
        END   TABUILD
```

Exercises

1. Write a program that can be used to calculate the cost per square foot of a plot of land. The program should accept as input one or more cards, each of which will contain three values for the plot of land: its length, width, and total cost. The program should print the three input values, as well as the calculated cost per square foot. For example, suppose that the following two cards were used as input:

250	75	2678
100	50	6754

The program should produce the following output:

LENGTH	WIDTH	COST IN DOLLARS	COST/SQUARE FOOT IN CENTS
250	75	2678	14
100	50	6754	135

2. Write a program that can be used to balance a checkbook. The program should accept as input a sequence of cards such that:

a. The first card will contain a single value, the beginning balance.
b. Each of the remaining cards will contain two numbers. The first number will be a 0 or a 1, indicating that the second number represents either a deposit or a withdrawal, respectively.

The program should print the input values, as well as a remaining balance, following the processing of each card. After all input cards have been processed, the program should print

a. the total number of withdrawals
b. the total number of deposits
c. the average amount per withdrawal
d. the average amount per deposit

For example, if

```
4295
0 5210
1 1011
1 1246
0 1000
```

were the input values, the program should print

CHECK/DEPOSIT CODE	AMOUNT (IN CENTS)	BALANCE (IN CENTS)
		4295
0	5210	9505
1	1011	8494
1	1246	7248
0	1000	8248

```
        # CHECKS          =    2
        # DEPOSITS        =    2
        AVG. AMT./CHECK   = 1128
        AVG. AMT./DEPOSIT = 3105
```

3. Write a program to tabulate test scores. As input, the program should read a sequence of cards, each of which will contain a test score in the range 0 to 100. Output similar to the following should be produced by the program:

TEST SCORE SUMMARY

RANGE	# SCORES	% OF TOTAL
91–100	13	18
81–90	24	34
71–80	16	22
61–70	10	14
0–60	7	10

TOTAL # OF TEST SCORES =   70

4. Suppose that a person invested a specified sum of money at a known interest rate. Write a program to calculate the amount of money represented by the investment after n years. (Assume that the interest is compounded annually.) Specifically, the program should accept as input a single card containing three values—the amount of the original investment, the interest rate, and the number of years for which the money is to be invested. The program should produce output similar to the following:

INVESTMENT SUMMARY

ORIGINAL AMOUNT	=	50000 (IN CENTS)
PER CENT	=	7
# YEARS	=	4

# YEARS	AMOUNT
1	53500
2	57245
3	61252
4	65540

AVERAGE INTEREST EARNED PER YEAR =   3884

5. Write a program that can be used to calculate the capacity of a series of swimming pools and the amount of water required to fill each pool to 80 percent of its capacity. As input, the program should accept parameter cards containing three values—the length, width, and depth of a particular design of swimming pool. As output, a report similar to the following should be produced:

CAPACITY REPORT

LENGTH	WIDTH	DEPTH	VOLUME	80% FILLED
20	60	6	7200	5760
15	25	4	1500	1200
60	40	8	19200	15360

6. A grocery firm has commissioned you to do a study on customer purchases. Your first task is to read in a set of cards, each containing two values: the quantity of an item purchased and the cost of the item in cents.

You must find the following:

a. the total cost of each set of items
b. the average number of items per purchase
c. the average cost per item (of all items sold)

Your output should consist of one line per input card (containing the quantity, the cost per item, and the total cost) and one summary line (containing the average number of items per purchase and the average cost per item). All output should be suitably labeled.

The input cards contain two values, separated by one or more blanks. They may be located anywhere on the card. Do not worry about rounding the averages.

3

Looping, Subroutines, and More Instructions

3.1 THE STC AND IC INSTRUCTIONS

The STC and IC instructions are quite similar to the ST and L instructions. The main difference is that characters instead of fullwords are stored or loaded.

Execution of the instruction

$$\text{STC} \qquad \text{r,D(X,B)} \qquad\qquad (\textit{Store Character})$$

will cause the rightmost byte of r (bits 24–31) to be stored into the byte of memory indicated by D(X,B). Since D(X,B) does not have to be on a fullword boundary, a specification error cannot occur. However, if D(X,B) is outside the boundaries of the program containing the STC instruction, a protection exception or an addressing exception might occur. The condition code is not altered.

For example, execution of the instructions

$$\text{LA} \qquad \text{R2,64} \qquad 64 = \text{X'40'} = \text{C' '}$$
$$\text{STC} \qquad \text{R2,BLANK}$$

causes a blank to be stored into the first byte of the field labeled BLANK.

The instruction

$$\text{IC} \qquad \text{r,D(X,B)} \qquad\qquad (\textit{Insert Character})$$

can be used to transfer a single byte from memory into the rightmost byte of a register. The register to be altered is designated by the first operand, and the address of the byte in memory is specified by the second operand. The condition code is not altered, and the only errors that can occur are protection and addressing exceptions. Note that the left three bytes of r are not altered by the execution of the instruction.

Thus, execution of the instruction

$$\text{IC} \qquad \text{R14,FLAG}$$

causes the rightmost byte of R14 to be replaced by the contents of FLAG.

3.2 LOOPING USING THE BCT AND BCTR INSTRUCTIONS

The construction of loops is one of an assembly-language programmer's most important tasks. The recognition that efficient looping is critical to the performance of many programs led to the creation of several instructions designed specifically to facilitate looping. In this section, two such instructions, BCT and BCTR, are described.

One common type of loop is encountered whenever a particular routine is to be executed a known number of times—say, n times. The general form of this type of loop is as follows:

Step 1. Set I equal to n.
Step 2. Execute the body of the loop.
Step 3. Set I equal to $I - 1$.
Step 4. If I is not equal to 0, go to Step 2.
Step 5. Continue with the rest of the program.

A flowchart of this type of loop is given in Figure 3-1.

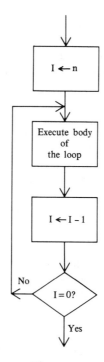

Figure 3-1

This type of loop is best implemented through use of either the BCT or the BCTR instruction. The format of the BCT is

BCT   r,D(X,B)   (*Branch on Count*)

Execution of this instruction causes the contents of r to be decremented by 1. If r does not then contain 0, a branch to the address given by D(X,B) is taken. If r does contain 0, then the instruction following the BCT instruction will be executed next. The setting of the CC is not altered.

The format of the BCTR is

BCTR   r1,r2   (*Branch on Count Register*)

This instruction performs the same task as the BCT except that the address to be branched to is contained in r2. However, there is one important point: If r2 is R0, 1 is subtracted from r1, but no branch is taken.

It should be clear at this point how the general form of the loop given in Figure 3-1 can be implemented. Assume that the register r is not used in the body of the loop and that the loop is to be executed n times. Then, the following code could be used:

```
              LA      r,n        PUT N INTO R
label         .
              .
              (body of loop)
              .
              .
              BCT     r,label    BRANCH BACK N – 1 TIMES
```

An alternative method to illustrate the use of the BCTR would be

```
              LA      r1,n
              LA      r2,label
label         .
              .
              body of loop
              .
              .
              BCTR    r1,r2
```

Actually, the BCTR is utilized for looping far less frequently than the BCT. Its main use is simply to decrement a register by 1. For example, execution of the instruction

BCTR   R11,0

subtracts 1 from R11. Since the second operand is 0, no branch is ever taken.

This entire discussion may be made more concrete with some examples.

• *Example 1.* It is often required to have a program reuse the storage reserved for a print line. In this case, blanks are usually written over the line before refilling it. Although a more efficient way to clear a print line will be discussed in Section 4.4, the following small loop would achieve this purpose:

```
           IC    R1,=C' '          PUT BLANK INTO R1
           LA    R3,133            BLANK OUT 133 CHARACTERS
BLANK1     STC   R1,PLINE-1(R3)    PUT IN ONE BLANK
           BCT   R3,BLANK1         BRANCH BACK 132 TIMES
             .
             .
             .
PLINE      DS    CL133
```

Note the following about this loop:

a. IC   R1,=C' ' uses a character literal. The effect is to set the rightmost byte of R1 to the character representation of the code for a blank.

b. PLINE−1(R3) is an implicit address that uses an index register (it specifies the address of PLINE−1 offset by the contents of R3). The first time through the loop R3 will contain 133 and PLINE−1(R3) will equal PLINE+132, the last character of the print line. When R3 contains 1 on the last time through the loop, PLINE−1(R3) will be equal to PLINE. Thus, the entire print line is blanked out by the loop.

• *Example 2.* A program that reads in five numbers (one number per card) and finds their sum is to be written. The BCT could be used for this purpose as in Program 3-1.

Program 3-1

```
************************************************************************
*
* THE FOLLOWING PROGRAM SUMS 5 INPUT NUMBERS AND PRINTS THE RESULT.
* THE LOGIC IS AS FOLLOWS:
*
*    STEP 1. SET TOTAL TO 0.  SET UP THE LOOP COUNTER WITH A
*            VALUE OF 5 (THE NUMBER OF TIMES THE LOOP WILL BE
*            EXECUTED).
*
*    STEP 2. READ A CARD AND ADD THE VALUE ON THE CARD TO THE
*            TOTAL.
*
*    STEP 3. DECREMENT THE LOOP COUNTER.  IF IT'S > 0, GO
*            BACK TO STEP 2.
*
*    STEP 4. PRINT THE TOTAL.
*
*    STEP 5. EXIT.
*
************************************************************************
```

Program 3-1 (continued)

```
*
SUM5     CSECT
         USING SUM5,R15
*
***<STEP 1>   INITIALIZE TOTAL AND LOOP COUNTER
*
         SR    R4,R4              SET TOTAL TO 0
         LA    R2,5               SET LOOP COUNTER TO 5
*
***<STEP 2>   READ A CARD AND ADD THE VALUE ON IT TO TOTAL.
*
READNXT  XREAD CARD,80
         XDECI R3,CARD            GET THE VALUE
         AR    R4,R3              AND ADD IT TO TOTAL
*
***<STEP 3>   TEST FOR TIME TO STOP.
*
         BCT   R2,READNXT         BRANCH IF MORE CARDS TO PROCESS
*
***<STEP 4>   PRINT THE RESULT
*
         XDECO 4,TOTAL
         XPRNT CRG,13             PRINT THE RESULT
*
***<STEP 5>   EXIT.
*
         BR    R14
*
*****************************************************************
*
CARD     DS    CL80               CARD INPUT AREA
*
CRG      DC    C'1'               CARRIAGE CONTROL - TOP-OF-PAGE
TOTAL    DS    CL12               PUT THE TOTAL HERE
*
         LTORG
*
R0       EQU   0
R1       EQU   1
R2       EQU   2
R3       EQU   3
R4       EQU   4
R5       EQU   5
R6       EQU   6
R7       EQU   7
R8       EQU   8
R9       EQU   9
R10      EQU   10
R11      EQU   11
R12      EQU   12
R13      EQU   13
R14      EQU   14
R15      EQU   15
         END   SUM5
```

- *Example 3.* Program 3-2 reads in two positive numbers, x and y, from a single data card. It then prints out the expansion of x/y to 50 decimal places except in the case where $x \geq y$.

Note the following about Program 3-2:

a. The routine ERROR is branched to if either x or y fails to be positive or if x is not less than y.

b. After execution of the instruction

DR   R2,R4

R3 contains the digit that should be printed. That digit, however, is in binary. 240 decimal is added to convert the binary digit to a character digit. (This would convert 00 to F0, 01 to F1, etc.) Remember that a binary number cannot be printed without first converting it to character format.

Program 3-2

```
***********************************************************************
*
* THIS PROGRAM READS TWO POSITIVE NUMBERS, X AND Y.  IT THEN CALCULATES
* X/Y TO 50 PLACES PAST THE DECIMAL AND PRINTS THE RESULT.  IT
* IS ASSUMED THAT X < Y.  THE LOGIC IS AS FOLLOWS:
*
*    STEP 1.   READ THE INPUT CARD AND GET X AND Y.  IF EOF OCCURS,
*              OR IF EITHER NUMBER IS INVALID, GO TO STEP 2; ELSE
*              GO TO STEP 3.
*
*    STEP 2.   PRINT AN ERROR MESSAGE AND GO TO STEP 7 TO EXIT.
*
*    STEP 3.   SET THE LOOP COUNTER (NUMBER OF TIMES TO EXECUTE
*              THE LOOP) TO 50.  SET A POINTER TO WHERE THE FIRST
*              DIGIT GOES IN THE PRINT LINE (INCREMENTED ONE
*              POSITION EACH TIME THRU THE LOOP).
*
*    STEP 4.   CALCULATE THE NEXT DIGIT IN THE EXPANSION AND PUT
*              IT INTO THE PRINT LINE.
*
*    STEP 5.   INCREMENT THE POINTER TO THE NEXT POSITION IN THE
*              PRINT LINE.  THEN DECREMENT THE LOOP COUNTER;
*              IF IT HASN'T REACHED 0, GO BACK TO STEP 4.
*
*    STEP 6.   PRINT THE CONSTRUCTED LINE.
*
*    STEP 7.   EXIT.
*
***********************************************************************
*
EXPAND    CSECT
          USING EXPAND,R15
*
***<STEP 1>    GET THE INPUT VALUES.  IF OK, GO TO STEP 3.
*
          XREAD CARD,80
          BC    B'0100',ERROR     EOF IS AN ERROR
*
          XDECI R3,CARD           GET X
          BNP   ERROR             IT MUST BE POSITIVE
*
          XDECI R4,0(R1)          GET Y
          BNP   ERROR             Y MUST BE POSITIVE TOO
*
          CR    R3,R4             X MUST BE LESS THAN Y
          BL    OK                BRANCH IF EVERYTHING IS OK
*
***<STEP 2>    PRINT AN ERROR MESSAGE AND GO EXIT.
*
          XPRNT =C'1ERROR IN INPUT',15
          B     EXIT
*
***<STEP 3>    SET UP LOOP COUNTER AND POSITION FOR RESULTS.
*
OK        LA    R5,50             SET LOOP COUNTER TO 50
          LA    R6,EXOUT          SET POINTER TO FIRST DIGIT
*
***<STEP 4>    PRODUCE THE NEXT DIGIT IN THE EXPANSION.
```

Program 3-2 (continued)

```
*
LOOP       M     R2,=F'10'        MULTIPLY DIVIDEND BY 10
           DR    R2,R4            THE DIGIT TO PRINT IS THE QUOTIENT
           LA    R3,240(R3)       CONVERT IT TO PRINTABLE CHARACTER
           STC   R3,0(R6)         PUT IT IN THE PRINT LINE
           LR    R3,R2            PUT REMAINDER BACK FOR NEXT DIVIDE
*
***<STEP 5>   INCREMENT POSITION IN RESULT AND CHECK FOR END OF LOOP.
*
           LA    R6,1(R6)         INCREMENT POSITION FOR NEXT DIGIT
           BCT   R5,LOOP
*
***<STEP 6>   PRINT THE RESULT.
*
           XPRNT CRG,52
*
***<STEP 7>   EXIT.
*
EXIT       BR    R14
*
********************************************************************
*
CARD       DS    CL80             CARD INPUT AREA
*
CRG        DC    C'1.'            CARRIAGE CONTROL AND DECIMAL POINT
EXOUT      DS    CL50             DECIMAL EXPANSION GOES HERE
*
           LTORG
*
R0         EQU   0
R1         EQU   1
R2         EQU   2
R3         EQU   3
R4         EQU   4
R5         EQU   5
R6         EQU   6
R7         EQU   7
R8         EQU   8
R9         EQU   9
R10        EQU   10
R11        EQU   11
R12        EQU   12
R13        EQU   13
R14        EQU   14
R15        EQU   15
           END   EXPAND
```

3.3 THE BXLE AND BXH INSTRUCTIONS

In constructing complex programs, it is common to manipulate data in tables. In such cases, loops utilizing the logic shown in Figure 3-2 frequently arise. Such a loop can certainly be implemented with the repertoire of instructions introduced so far. However, since this pattern of logic is so common, a specific instruction was introduced to facilitate its implementation:

BXLE   r1,r2,D(B)   *(Branch on Index Low or Equal)*

To describe the actions resulting from the execution of a BXLE instruction, we will refer to the index register, the increment register, and the limit register. These registers are determined as follows:

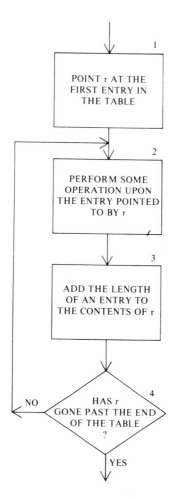

r is any register other than 0, which is used here as an index into the table.

Figure 3-2

- r1 is the index register.
- If r2 is an even register, it represents an even/odd pair. In this case, the even register is the increment register, and the odd register is the limit register.
- If r2 is an odd register, then r2 is both the increment register and the limit register.

The actions caused by the execution of the BXLE are then:

1. The contents of the increment register are added to the contents of the index register.
2. If the new contents of the index register are less than or equal to the limit register, a branch to D(B) takes place. Otherwise, execution continues, with the instruction immediately following the BXLE instruction.

If the contents of the index, increment, and limit registers are represented by

<r(index)>
<r(incr)>
<r(limit)>

respectively, the effects of the BXLE can be portrayed in a flowchart as in Figure 3-3.

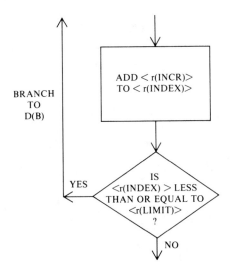

Figure 3-3

It should now be clear that the BXLE instruction alone can be used to implement blocks 3 and 4 of Figure 3-2.

An example of the use of the BXLE will illustrate its power. Suppose that a table of fullwords, TABLE, exists and that R3 contains the address of the last entry in the table. Each of the two sections of code at the top of page 80 scans TABLE for the smallest integer in the table. In the first case, no BXLE is employed; in the second, a BXLE is used.

The use of the BXLE clearly results in a shorter sequence of instructions in the loop itself. The execution time of the program using the BXLE is considerably less also. In fact, in most programs where a table must be searched, the BXLE should be used.

The perceptive reader will have noted that the format of the BXLE does not conform to the normal RX format. In fact, the BXLE is an RS instruction, not an RX instruction. The symbolic form for an RS instruction is

label   mnemonic   r1,r2,D(B)

```
* IT IS ASSUMED THAT THE TABLE CONTAINS AT LEAST 2 ENTRIES AND
* THAT R3 CONTAINS THE ADDRESS OF THE LAST ENTRY.
          L     R4,TABLE         GET 1ST ENTRY - SMALLEST-SO-FAR
          LA    R5,TABLE+4       POINTS TO NEXT ENTRY TO LOOK AT
LOOP      C     R4,0(R5)         COMPARE SMALLEST-SO-FAR AND CURRENT
          BNH   CHKEND
          L     R4,0(R5)         WE HAVE A NEW SMALLEST-SO-FAR
CHKEND    LA    R5,4(R5)         GO TO NEXT ENTRY
          CR    R5,R3            CHECK FOR END OF TABLE
          BNH   LOOP             BRANCH IF NOT PAST END


* THE SAME LOOP USING A BXLE.
          LA    R2,4             GET THE LENGTH OF A TABLE ENTRY
          L     R4,TABLE         GET 1ST ENTRY - SMALLEST-SO-FAR
          LA    R5,TABLE+4       POINTS TO NEXT ENTRY TO LOOK AT
LOOP      C     R4,0(R5)         COMPARE SMALLEST-SO-FAR AND CURRENT
          BNH   CHKEND
          L     R4,0(R5)         WE HAVE A NEW SMALLEST-SO-FAR
CHKEND    BXLE  R5,R2,LOOP       BRANCH IF MORE ENTRIES TO SCAN
```

where   r1 and r2   are register numbers

D(B)   is an address (no index register can be used)

The format for the generated machine instruction is

$$h_0 h_0 h_{r1} h_{r2} h_B h_D h_D h_D$$

where $h_0 h_0$ is the op code

h_{r1} is r1

h_{r2} is r2

h_B is the base register

$h_D h_D h_D$ is the 12-bit displacement

There are two main differences between the RX and the RS formats:

- There are three operands in an RS instruction and only two in an RX instruction.
- An index register may be used in an RX instruction, but not in an RS instruction.

The instruction

BXH   r1,r2,D(B)   (*Branch on Index High*)

is another RS instruction closely related to the BXLE instruction. It can be used to implement the pattern of logic in Figure 3-4.

The function of the BXH is identical to the function of the BXLE except that the branch to D(B) will occur only when the addition of the increment makes the index register greater than the limit register. The actions caused by the execution of a BXH are visually depicted in Figure 3-5.

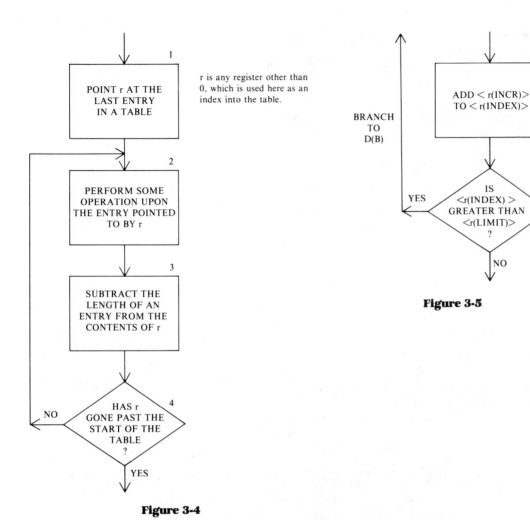

r is any register other than
0, which is used here as an
index into the table.

Figure 3-5

Figure 3-4

The key to scanning through a table with a BXH is to put a negative value
in the increment register. Thus, our previous example, in which a table was
scanned for its least integer, could have been coded as

```
* IT IS ASSUMED THAT THE TABLE CONTAINS AT LEAST 2 ENTRIES AND THAT
* R3 CONTAINS THE ADDRESS OF THE LAST ENTRY.
          L     R4, =F'-4'      PUT IN MINUS THE LENGTH OF AN ENTRY
          LR    R6,R3           R6 <-ADDRESS OF LAST ENTRY
          L     R2,TABLE        R2 <-SMALLEST-SO-FAR
          LA    R5,TABLE        SET POINTER TO FIRST ENTRY
```

```
LOOP      C     R2,0(R6)          CHECK FOR NEW SMALLEST
          BNH   CHKEND
          L     R2,0(R6)          NEW SMALLEST-SO-FAR
CHKEND    BXH   R6,R4,LOOP
```

In the above example, it was again assumed that R3 pointed to the last entry in the table.

The reader might at this point wonder why a programmer would ever choose to make the second operand in a BXLE or BXH an odd register. By being reasonably clever, it is often possible to implement a loop with one less register by making the increment register the limit register as well. For example, the section of code presented above need not have required the use of R4. Instead, the following code could have been used:

```
          L     R5,=F'−4'         INCREMENT AND LIMIT REG ARE  −4
          LR    R6,R3             R6 <− ADDRESS OF LAST ENTRY
          LA    R2,TABLE+4        NOW CONVERT R6 FROM A POINTER TO
*                                 A DISPLACEMENT
          SR    R6,R2
          L     R2,TABLE          R2 <− SMALLEST-SO-FAR
LOOP      C     R2,TABLE+4(R6)    CHECK FOR A SMALLER VALUE
          BNH   CHKEND
          L     R2,TABLE+4(R6)
CHKEND    BXH   R6,R5,LOOP        BRANCH IF MORE TO SCAN
```

There may be a question about how to recognize when to use a BXLE or BXH. In a loop where a fixed increment is to be added to a pointer each time through the loop, either a BXLE or BXH should probably be used. A few extra instructions will be required for initialization of the loop variables before entering the loop, but the execution time will be more than compensated for if the program executes the instructions in the loop more than just once or twice.

Another question that often arises is: Why worry about saving a few microseconds here and there? It is true that too much programmer time can be spent in an attempt to determine how to minimize the execution time of a program. However, a major part of the execution time of many programs is spent in processing loops; therefore, it is definitely important to try to optimize code within these loops. The efficient coding of loops may often speed up the execution of a program by 100 percent or more. A small amount of time spent now learning how to code loops efficiently will make the task far easier in the future.

Exercises

1. For each of the following loops, indicate the number of times the body of the loop will be executed.

a.

	LA	R8,12
LOOP	·	
	·	
	BCT	R8,LOOP

b.

	LA	R5,TABEND − 10
	L	R6, = F′ − 10′
	LA	R7,TABLE − 10
LOOP	·	
	·	
	BXH	R5,R6,LOOP
	·	
	·	
TABLE	DS	8CL10
TABEND	DS	0C

c.

	SR	R1,R1
LOOP	·	
	·	
	BCT	R1,LOOP

d.

	LA	R3,TABLE + 20
	L	R4, = F′ − 5′
	LA	R5,TABLE
LOOP	·	
	·	
	BXH	R3,R4,LOOP
	·	
TABLE	DS	10CL5

e.

	LA	R5,40
	L	R7, = F′ − 10′
LOOP	LA	R2,TABLE(R5)
	·	
	·	
	BXH	R5,R7,LOOP

f.

	LA	R3,TABLE
	LA	R4,5
	LA	R5,TABLE + 20
LOOP	·	
	·	
	BXLE	R3,R4,LOOP

g.

```
                   L      R7, = A(TABLE)
                   LA     R8,4
                   L      R9, = A(TEND)
        LOOP       .
                   .
        BXLE              R7,R8,LOOP
        TABLE      DS     5F
        TEND       DS     0F
```

2. Write a program to build a table of not more than 50 fullword integers. Having built the table, the program should print out the values in the table, n per line, where n is an input value. The input of the program should consist of a sequence of cards characterized by the following:

- The first card contains n (which will be less than or equal to 8), the number of integers to be displayed on each print line.
- The remaining cards each contain a single integer to be stored in the table.

After building the table, the program should XDUMP the contents of the table before printing them n per line. The following programming considerations should be noted:

a. In building and printing the table, it is often convenient to use an index register to address a fullword or a 12-byte field in the print line.
b. To build a table, a loop containing a BXH with an odd increment register should be used.
c. Avoid sequences of instructions of the type

```
            LA     R3,4(R3)
            CR     R3,R5
            BNH    LOOP
```

and use a BXLE or perhaps a BCT instead.

3. Write a program to perform the following operations:

a. Read a sequence of cards, each of which will contain a single integer, and build a table of up to 50 words from the values on the cards. While storing the values into the table, the program should accumulate their sum.
b. The program should then calculate the average value of the entries in the table and XDUMP the contents of the table, the sum, and the average.
c. Finally, the program should calculate and print out the number of values in the table that are greater than the average, the number of values equal to the average, and the number of values less than the average.

4. Suppose that a bank has recorded for a particular day the number of customers who entered the bank during every half-hour that the bank was open. Furthermore, suppose that the bank was open a total of seven hours, so that there were 14 time periods for which numbers were recorded. Write a program to read 14 cards, each of which contains the number of people who entered the bank during the corresponding half-hour, and print a report conforming to the following format:

BANK ACTIVITY REPORT

PERIOD	# OF CUSTOMERS	% OF TOTAL	CUMULATIVE %
1	8	2	2
2	13	4	7
3	12	4	11
4	18	6	17
5	24	8	25
6	23	8	33
7	37	12	46
8	33	11	57
9	29	9	67
10	18	6	73
11	19	6	80
12	17	5	85
13	21	7	93
14	20	6	100

TOTAL # CUSTOMERS = 292

5. Suppose that a company maintains a master deck of cards containing information detailing how many units of each item that the company sells are in stock. Specifically, each card in the deck contains two nonnegative integers: an item number (a unique item number is assigned to each product that the company sells) and the number of units in stock. Furthermore, the cards in the deck occur in ascending order, based on the item number. Write a program to process requests for information about how much stock is in store. The program should accept as input

- the master deck
- a single card containing -1, which marks the end of the master cards
- a set of request cards, each of which contains a single item number

The program should first read in the master deck and build a table. Each entry in the table should contain two fullwords, the first containing the item number and the second the number of units of that item that are in stock. After the card containing -1 has been read, the program should XDUMP the constructed table so that the contents can be verified. Then, as the request cards are read, a report similar to the following should be produced:

INVENTORY INFORMATION REPORT

ITEM #	UNITS IN STOCK
234	842
421	0
24	NO ENTRY IN MASTER DECK
1840	13

6. Write a program to do the following tasks:

a. First the program should read a sequence of cards, each of which contains two integers, and store the values into two separate tables. There will be at most 50 input cards. The program should XDUMP the contents of the two tables.

b. The program should construct a third table by adding corresponding entries in the existing tables. Thus, if -5 and 24 were the fourth elements in the first and second tables, respectively, 19 would be the resulting element that should be stored as the fourth element in the third table.

c. Finally, the program should print out the contents of the third table, printing one number per print line.

7. Write a program that (1) reads in a table of integers (and XDUMPs it), (2) compacts the table by removing duplicate entries, and (3) prints out the resulting table.

Each input card contains a single integer. There will be at most 30 input values. (Assume that the values occur in ascending order.)

One way to compact the table is as follows:

a. Set two pointers to point at the first table entry. The first pointer gives the next entry to look at, and the second pointer gives the position of the next-kept value.

b. Now move the first pointer through all the entries in the table except the last. Whenever a value is not equal to its successor, move it to the position given by the second pointer (and update the second pointer).

c. Finally, move over the last entry.

Make sure that your program will work if the table contains fewer than two values.

Print the values one per line, after printing a suitable heading.

8. This problem differs from Exercise 7 in two ways:

a. The values do not necessarily occur in ascending order. (Think your algorithm out carefully before coding.)
b. Each input card can contain any number of values.

To set the values of an input card, define the CARD input area as follows:

```
CARD     DS      CL80
         DC      C'*'
```

Then, use repeated XDECIs until a condition code of 3 (invalid value) results.

3.4 BAL, BALR, AND SUBROUTINES

A standard technique employed in the design of complex programs involves partitioning a program into smaller *subroutines*. The logic of each subroutine is far simpler than that of the whole program. To implement this technique, it is first helpful to draw a *block diagram*, which pictorially represents the segmentation of the given program. Flowcharts of the individual subroutines are then constructed to complete the description of the logic of the program. Occasionally, a subroutine itself will be complex enough to warrant a block diagram. In this case, the entire process is carried one step further by breaking the subroutine down into "lower-level" subroutines.

As an illustration of this process, consider the problem of creating a program to accomplish the following tasks:

1. Read a set of numbers arranged in ascending order into a table.
2. Print out the numbers in the table.
3. Read in a second table.
4. Print out the second table.
5. Merge the two tables.
6. Print out the one large table.

A detailed flowchart of a program to perform these six tasks without utilizing subroutines would be large and complex. If instead the program were broken down into subroutines, the overall logic could be represented by Figure 3-6.

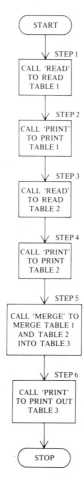

Figure 3-6

Since the flowcharts of the subroutines would divert attention from this discussion, they have been relegated to Appendix A.

Now that the logic required to perform the desired functions has been described, the job of implementing it in an actual program remains to be done. The BAL instruction can be used to facilitate this process.

BAL   r,D(X,B)   *(Branch and Link)*

Execution of this instruction causes the following actions to occur:

- The right 32 bits of the Program Status Word (PSW) are stored in r. This means that, after the execution of the BAL, r will contain the address of the instruction immediately following the BAL (since the PSW contains that address in bits 40–63).

• A branch to D(X,B) is taken.

Thus, execution of the instruction

    BAL   R10,SORT

causes a branch to SORT. Furthermore, to cause a return to the instruction following the BAL, the instruction

    BR   R10

could be used.

Program 3-3 utilizes the BAL instruction to implement the logic depicted in Figure 3-6. The code for the subroutines has been included in Appendix A, along with the detailed flowcharts. The reader should finish this section and Section 3.5 before carefully examining the program in the appendix.

Program 3-3

```
***********************************************************************
*
* THIS PROGRAM ILLUSTRATES THE USE OF SUBROUTINES.  THE PROGRAM
*
*          1) READS A SET OF NUMBERS INTO 'TABLE1'.  IT IS
*             ASSUMED THAT THE INPUT VALUES HAVE BEEN SORTED INTO
*             ASCENDING ORDER.
*
*          2) PRINTS OUT THE NUMBERS IN 'TABLE1'.
*
*          3) READS IN A SECOND SET OF NUMBERS INTO 'TABLE2'.
*
*          4) PRINTS OUT THE NUMBERS IN 'TABLE2'.
*
*          5) MERGES THE NUMBERS IN THE TWO TABLES INTO 'TABLE3'.
*
*          6) PRINTS OUT THE NUMBERS IN 'TABLE3'.
*
* THE LOGIC OF THE PROGRAM IS AS FOLLOWS:
*
*          STEP 1.  CALL 'READ' TO READ IN THE FIRST TABLE.  THIS WILL
*                   REQUIRE PASSING TO 'READ' THE ADDRESS OF THE TABLE
*                   TO FILL.   THE 'READ' ROUTINE WILL RETURN THE ADDRESS
*                   OF THE LAST ENTRY, WHICH IS STORED IN 'ENDT1'.
*
*          STEP 2.  CALL 'PRINT' TO PRINT OUT THE VALUES IN 'TABLE1'.
*
*          STEP 3.  CALL 'READ' TO READ IN THE VALUES FOR 'TABLE2', AND
*                   SAVE THE ADDRESS OF THE LAST ENTRY IN 'ENDT2'.
*
*          STEP 4.  CALL 'PRINT' TO DISPLAY THE VALUES IN 'TABLE2'.
*
*          STEP 5.  CALL 'MERGE' TO MERGE THE VALUES IN 'TABLE1' AND
*                   'TABLE2' INTO 'TABLE3'.
*
*          STEP 6.  CALL 'PRINT' TO DISPLAY THE VALUES IN 'TABLE3'.
*
*          STEP 7.  EXIT.
*
***********************************************************************
```

Program 3-3 (continued)

```
MAINPROG CSECT
         USING MAINPROG,R15
*
***<STEP 1>    READ IN THE VALUES FOR 'TABLE1'.
*
*
         LA    R2,TABLE1           R2 IS USED TO PASS THE ADDRESS OF
                                   WHERE THE VALUES ARE TO BE STORED
         BAL   R10,READ            READ IN 'TABLE1'
         ST    R3,ENDT1            SAVE THE ADDRESS OF THE LAST VALUE
*
***<STEP 2>    PRINT OUT THE VALUES IN 'TABLE1'.
*
         BAL   R10,PRINT           R2 MUST HAVE ADDRESS OF 'TABLE1' AND
*                                  R3 MUST HAVE ADDRESS OF LAST ENTRY
*
***<STEP 3>    READ IN THE VALUES FOR 'TABLE2'.
*
         LA    R2,TABLE2           POINT TO THE SECOND TABLE
         BAL   R10,READ            READ IN THE VALUES
         ST    R3,ENDT2            SAVE ADDRESS OF LAST ENTRY
*
***<STEP 4>    PRINT OUT THE VALUES IN 'TABLE2'.
*
         BAL   R10,PRINT
*
***<STEP 5>    NOW MERGE THE TWO TABLES INTO 'TABLE3'.
*
         LA    R2,TABLE1           R2 <- ADDRESS OF FIRST TABLE
         LA    R3,TABLE2           R3 <- ADDRESS OF SECOND TABLE
         LA    R4,TABLE3           R4 <- ADDRESS OF TABLE TO BUILD
*
         L     R5,ENDT1            R5 <- ADDRESS OF LAST ENTRY IN TABLE1
         L     R6,ENDT2            R6 <- ADDRESS OF LAST ENTRY IN TABLE2
*
         BAL   R10,MERGE           NOW MERGE THE TWO TABLES
*
***<STEP 6>    PRINT OUT THE CONTENTS OF 'TABLE3'.
*
         LA    R2,TABLE3
         LR    R3,R7               'MERGE' PUT ADDRESS OF LAST ENTRY
*                                  INTO R7
         BAL   R10,PRINT           NOW PRINT THE MERGED TABLE
*
***<STEP 7>    EXIT.
*
         BR    R14
*
*********************************************************************
*
*              STORAGE AREAS FOR THE MAIN ROUTINE
*
*********************************************************************
*
         LTORG
ENDT1    DS    F                   ADDRESS OF LAST ENTRY IN TABLE1
ENDT2    DS    F                   ADDRESS OF LAST ENTRY IN TABLE2
TABLE1   DS    50F                 BUILD THE FIRST TABLE HERE
TABLE2   DS    50F                 AND THE SECOND TABLE HERE
TABLE3   DS    100F                AND THE MERGED TABLE HERE
*
*********************************************************************
*
*                    READ ROUTINE
*
* THIS IS THE READ ROUTINE.  WHEN IT IS ENTERED, R2 CONTAINS THE
* ADDRESS OF THE TABLE TO BE FILLED.  EACH DATA CARD CONTAINS ONE
* NUMBER.  END OF THE TABLE IS DESIGNATED BY A CARD CONTAINING
* 999999.  UPON EXITING, R3 CONTAINS THE ADDRESS OF THE LAST ENTRY
* OF THE TABLE.  NO OTHER REGISTERS ARE ALTERED.  R10 IS THE LINK
* REGISTER.
*
*********************************************************************
         the READ routine
```

Program 3-3 (continued)

```
************************************************************************
*
*                     PRINT ROUTINE
*
* THIS ROUTINE PRINTS OUT THE VALUES IN THE TABLE POINTED TO BY
* R2.   R3 MUST CONTAIN THE ADDRESS OF THE LAST ENTRY IN THE TABLE.
* R10 IS THE LINK REGISTER.   ENTRIES ARE PRINTED OUT 1 PER LINE.
* NO REGISTERS ARE ALTERED BY A CALL TO THIS ROUTINE.
* THE LOGIC IS AS FOLLOWS:
*
************************************************************************


        the PRINT routine


************************************************************************
*
*                     MERGE ROUTINE
*
* THIS ROUTINE MERGES THE TWO SORTED TABLES INTO A THIRD TABLE.   UPON
* ENTRANCE
*
*        R2 = ADDRESS OF FIRST TABLE
*        R3 = ADDRESS OF SECOND TABLE
*        R4 = ADDRESS OF THIRD TABLE
*        R5 = ADDRESS OF LAST ENTRY IN FIRST TABLE
*        R6 = ADDRESS OF LAST ENTRY IN SECOND TABLE
*
* THE ROUTINE WILL SET R7 TO THE ADDRESS OF THE LAST ENTRY IN THE
* THIRD TABLE, WHICH IS PRODUCED BY MERGING THE FIRST TWO TABLES.
* R10 IS THE LINK REGISTER.   ONLY R7 IS ALTERED BY A CALL TO THIS
* ROUTINE.
*
************************************************************************


        the MERGE routine


        LTORG
R0      EQU   0
R1      EQU   1
R2      EQU   2
R3      EQU   3
R4      EQU   4
R5      EQU   5
R6      EQU   6
R7      EQU   7
R8      EQU   8
R9      EQU   9
R10     EQU   10
R11     EQU   11
R12     EQU   12
R13     EQU   13
R14     EQU   14
R15     EQU   15
        END   MAINPROG
```

There are at least two good reasons why subroutines should be used:

- They save a considerable amount of code. READ, for example, was coded only once in the sample program, although it was invoked from two separate points in the program.

- Subroutines make the logical structure of a program more obvious. Thus, although MERGE was called only once, it performed a logically distinct task and was, therefore, coded as a separate subroutine.

Remember these points when defining a subroutine:

* All *input conventions* should be clearly stated in the comment statements and should be such that the routine can be called from any point in the program.
* Anything that is altered by the subroutine should be noted clearly in the comments. Registers that are altered for reasons other than to return information to the calling program are usually restored to their original contents before exiting from the subroutine.

There is an RR counterpart of the BAL instruction:

$$\text{BALR} \qquad \text{r1,r2} \qquad \textit{(Branch and Link Register)}$$

This instruction is similar to BAL except that the branch address is taken from r2. Thus, execution of the instructions

```
LA      R9,ROUTINE
BALR    R10,R9
```

is equivalent to execution of the instruction

```
BAL     R10,ROUTINE
```

The main use of the BALR will be with external subroutines, which are covered in Section 6.2. There is one special rule concerning the BALR: If r2 is 0, then no branch is taken. Hence,

```
            BALR    R12,0
            USING   BASEAD,R12
BASEAD      instruction
```

could be used to establish R12 as a base register. The BALR will just cause the address of BASEAD to be put into R12, and the USING statement notifies the assembler of that fact.

3.5 STM AND LM INSTRUCTIONS

The two instructions STM and LM can be used for storing and restoring the contents of registers, several at a time.

Execution of the RS-type instruction

$$\text{STM} \qquad \text{r1,r2,D(B)} \qquad \textit{(Store Multiple)}$$

causes all registers from r1 through r2 to be stored in contiguous fullwords of storage, starting at the address given by D(B). Thus, execution of the instruction

```
STM     R4,R8,SAVE
```

will cause the contents of R4, R5, R6, R7, and R8 to be stored into five fullwords starting at SAVE. If r2 is less than r1, then r1 through R15 followed by R0 through r2 are stored. For example, execution of the instruction

        STM   R14,R1,SAVE

will cause the contents of four registers, R14, R15, R0, and R1, to be stored.
  The instruction

        LM   r1,r2,D(B)   *(Load Multiple)*

is similar to STM except that the registers are loaded rather than stored. Hence, execution of the instruction

        LM   R12,R2,REGSAVE

loads R12 through R15, and R0 through R2, from the seven fullwords starting at REGSAVE.
  In Section 3.4, we emphasized that a subroutine should restore the contents of registers that are altered in the execution of the subroutine. This can be very easily implemented with the STM and LM instructions. For example, the code

```
ROUTINE   STM   R0,R15,SAVE   STORE CALLER'S REGISTERS
          .
          .
          body of routine
          .
          .
          LM    R0,R15,SAVE   RELOAD THE CALLER'S REGISTERS
          BR    R10           RETURN TO CALLER
SAVE      DS    16F           STORE REGISTERS HERE
```

would allow any register other than the base register to be altered in the routine. (Note that this technique is used in the subroutines contained in Appendix A.)

3.6 A-TYPE ADDRESS CONSTANTS

We shall conclude this chapter with a discussion of another form of the DC statement:

      label   DC   A(exp)

In this form of the DC statement, the operand is referred to as an *A-type address constant*. The statement generates a fullword, according to the following rules:

- If exp is a nonnegative integer, the generated fullword will contain the binary representation of the integer (i.e., F'exp' could have been used instead of A(exp)).

- If exp is a label or is of the form label ± n, the generated fullword will contain the appropriate address.

Thus, the statement

           DC   A(5)

generates 00000005, and

           DC   A(SAVE)

generates a fullword containing the address of SAVE. Several expressions can be included in one statement. For example, the statement

           DC   A(L1,20,L2)

generates three words: the first word contains the address of L1; the second, the value 20; and the third, the address of L2.

A-type constants can also be used in literals. Frequently, this feature is utilized to load registers with input parameters before a call is issued to a subroutine. For example, in Step 5 of Program 3-3, the instructions

```
      LA   R2,TABLE1    R2 <- ADDRESS OF FIRST TABLE
      LA   R3,TABLE2    R3 <- ADDRESS OF SECOND TABLE
      LA   R4,TABLE3    R4 <- ADDRESS OF TABLE TO BUILD
*
      L    R5,ENDT1     R5 <- ADDRESS OF LAST ENTRY IN TABLE1
      L    R6,ENDT2     R6 <- ADDRESS OF LAST ENTRY IN TABLE2
```

could have been replaced with

```
      LM        R2,R4, = A(TABLE1,TABLE2, TABLE3)
      LM        R5,R6,ENDT1
```

A-type constants can be particularly useful when dealing with several large tables in the same program. Normally, the instructions

           LA   R1,TABLE

and

           L   R1, = A(TABLE)

would have the same effect. The major difference, however, is that to use the LA, TABLE must be addressable as a displacement of the contents of the base register. Since the maximum allowable displacement is 4095, this means that TABLE must be within 4095 bytes of the address in the active base register. On the other hand, use of the instruction

$$\text{L} \qquad \text{R1}, = \text{A(TABLE)}$$

requires only that the literal itself be addressable. As an example, in Program 3-3, suppose that TABLE1 and TABLE2 had each contained 500 fullwords rather than 50. In that case, use of the instruction

$$\text{LA} \qquad \text{R4,TABLE3}$$

would have caused an addressability error (since the start of TABLE3 is more than 4095 bytes past the address in the base register), while use of the instruction

$$\text{L} \qquad \text{R4}, = \text{A(TABLE3)}$$

would have been acceptable.

Exercises

1. Write a program to perform the following tasks:

a. Read in a sequence of cards, each of which contains a single integer. Store the integers in a table of fullwords. You may assume that the cards were arranged so that each integer is at least as large as the one that preceded it.
b. Print the contents of the table.
c. Remove duplicate numbers from the table. Thus, if three consecutive words each contain the integer 4, the resulting table will contain only one word with the value 4.
d. Print the "compressed" table.

Your program should utilize three subroutines—one to read in a table of integers, one to print a table of integers, and one to compress a table of integers. The subroutines should be coded so that they could be used to read, print, or compress any table—not just the table in the program. This means that the address of this particular table must be an input parameter to each of the subroutines.

2. Write a program to perform the following tasks:

a. Read in a sequence of cards, each of which contains a single positive integer, and store the values in a table of fullwords. The end of the sequence is determined when a card containing 0 is read. The 0 should not be entered in the table.

b. Display the contents of the table.

c. Read in a sequence of cards containing values that are to be stored in a second table. Again, the end of the input sequence is detected when a card containing 0 is read.

d. Display the contents of the second table.

e. Build a third table containing only those values that occur in both of the tables previously constructed.

f. Display the contents of the third table.

Your program should contain three subroutines—one to read in a sequence of integers and construct a table, one to print the values stored in a table, and one to build a table of integers that occur in both of two specified tables. You may assume that neither of the tables read from cards contains two identical entries.

3. This exercise is identical to the preceding exercise except that here you may assume that the integers on the input cards for each table have been arranged in ascending order. In this case, you should again have three subroutines, but the subroutine that can be called to extract matching entries should utilize a more efficient algorithm. The recommended logic for this subroutine is as follows:

Assume that PTR1 points to the first entry in the first table, PTR2 points to the first entry in the second table, and PTR3 points to the first entry in the table to be constructed.

Step 1. Compare the entry in the first table pointed to by PTR1 with the entry in the second table pointed to by PTR2. If the entry in the first table is higher, go to Step 5. If the entry in the second table is higher, go to Step 6.

Step 2. Move the entry pointed to by PTR1 to the entry in the third table given by PTR3.

Step 3. Increment PTR3 to point to the next entry in the third table.

Step 4. Increment PTR1 to the next entry in the first table. If PTR1 has been moved past the end of the first table, stop. (The matching entries have all been added to the third table.)

Step 5. Increment PTR2 to the next entry in the second table. If PTR2 has been moved past the end of the second table, stop. Otherwise, go to Step 1.

Step 6. Increment PTR1 to the next entry in the first table. If PTR1 has been moved past the end of the first table, stop. Otherwise, go to Step 1.

Although details have been omitted from the previous algorithm, the reader should be able to grasp the basic process that should be used to construct the third table.

4. Write a program to perform the following tasks:

a. Read in a sequence of cards, each of which contains a single test score in the range 0 to 100. The scores should then be stored in a table of fullwords.
b. Display the scores stored in the table.
c. Rearrange the scores in the table so that they occur in descending order. This process is usually referred to as *sorting* a table.
d. Display the contents of the table again.

Your program should utilize three internal subroutines—one to read the test scores, one to display the test scores, and one to sort the scores.
   A variety of algorithms can be used to sort a table. One of the simplest can be described as follows:

Step 1. Find the largest number in the table.
Step 2. Swap the first entry in the table with the largest entry.
Step 3. If more than one entry remains to the right of the largest number (in the unsorted section of the table), repeat the procedure for the remaining unsorted section of the table.

For example, if

$$4 \qquad -5 \qquad 20 \qquad -10$$

were to be sorted, the following events would occur:

• Since 20 is the largest number, 20 and 4 will be swapped. This gives

$$20 \qquad -5 \qquad 4 \qquad -10$$

• Since 4 is the largest of the right three numbers, it will be swapped with -5. This gives

$$20 \qquad 4 \qquad -5 \qquad -10$$

• Since -5 is the larger of the right two entries, it will be swapped with itself (which leaves the table unaltered).
• Since only one entry remains in the unsorted section of the table (-10), the sort has been completed.

5. This exercise is identical to the preceding exercise except that a different algorithm should be used to sort the table. The algorithm for this exercise can be briefly described as follows:

For each element in the table except the leftmost, starting from the left, repeat the following step as often as possible: *If the element to the left of the given element is less than the given element, swap the two elements.*

For example, if

$$-1 \qquad 0 \qquad 32 \qquad -10 \qquad 5 \qquad 0$$

were to be sorted, the following steps would occur:

- Since -1 is less than 0, swap the two numbers. This gives

$$0 \qquad -1 \qquad 32 \qquad -10 \qquad 5 \qquad 0$$

- Since 32 is greater than both 0 and -1, it gets swapped twice. This gives

$$32 \qquad 0 \qquad -1 \qquad -10 \qquad 5 \qquad 0$$

- Since -1 is greater than -10, no swaps are necessary to move -10 to its proper spot in the sorted section of the table.
- Since 5 is greater than -10, -1, and 0, three swaps are necessary to move 5 to its correct location. This gives

$$32 \qquad 5 \qquad 0 \qquad -1 \qquad -10 \qquad 0$$

- Finally, two swaps are needed to move the rightmost 0 to its proper location. The result is

$$32 \qquad 5 \qquad 0 \qquad 0 \qquad -1 \qquad -10$$

6. Suppose that we agree to encode characters, punctuation, and the like as integers, using the following correspondence:

Character	Value
A	1
B	2
C	3
.	.
.	.
Z	26
blank	27
,	28
.	29
0	30
1	31
2	32
.	.
.	.
9	39

Thus, "SEE YOU AT 2." would be encoded as

19 5 5 27 25 15 21 27 1 20 27 32 29

Write the following subroutines:

- READSTR reads an encoded string into a table. Upon entrance, R2 must have the address of the table. Each input card will contain one integer. The routine should stop reading when it encounters a 0. (0 marks the end of a string.) R3 is the only altered register; it is set to the length of the string (the number of integers in it). If end-of-file occurs before reaching a 0, R3 should be set to 0.

- COMPSTR compares two strings. Upon entrance, R2 points to one string and R4 points to a second string. R3 contains the number of characters to compare. R6 is the only altered register. It is set to 0 if the strings match. Otherwise, it is set to 1.

- FINDSTR searches through a string, looking for a given substring. Upon entrance, R2 contains the address of the string and R3 contains the length of the string. R4 contains the address of the substring and R5 contains its length. R6 is the only altered register; it is set to the address of the first occurrence of the substring in a given string (or to 0, if there are no such occurrences).

Now write a program that performs the following actions until end-of-file occurs:

a. Read in a string (call this the "message").
b. Read in a second string (call this the "word").
c. XDUMP both the message and the word.
d. Find the first occurrence of the word in the message.
e. XDUMP the address.

When you have finished, take time to reflect. You could now write routines to encode/decode messages using complex arithmetic functions (for security purposes). By constructing a library of routines, you could build up all of the functions required for "text processing." If you became worried about memory space, you could store each integer in a single byte.

4

Rounding Out the Essentials

4.1 THE SPACE, EJECT, AND TITLE INSTRUCTIONS

There are several assembler instructions that the programmer should make frequent use of to improve the readability of a program listing. SPACE, EJECT, and TITLE are instructions that generate no object code, and so in no way affect the execution of the program. They do, however, alter the format of the printed listing that the assembler produces.

The SPACE instruction

> SPACE   n

causes n blank lines to be inserted into the assembler listing at that point in the source code. If n is omitted, it is assumed to be 1. If there are fewer than n lines left on a page of the listing, it will cause a skip to the top of the next page.

The EJECT instruction

> EJECT

skips the assembler listing to the top of the next page.

The TITLE instruction

> TITLE   'header'

causes the following to happen:

1. The assembler listing skips to the top of the next page.

2. The "header" prints at the top of the new page as well as at the top of all following pages until another TITLE command is encountered. Apostrophes and ampersands may be used in the header by following the same convention as for a DC statement: To have one apostrophe or ampersand printed, code two of them adjacent in the header.

Every assembler program should contain at least one TITLE instruction, make frequent use of the SPACE instruction to accent breaks in logic, and contain occasional instances of the EJECT instruction to indicate major breaks in logic. The short time required to insert these instructions will be more than offset by the increased readability of the program listing.

Program 4-1 is intended to illustrate the techniques discussed in this section. This program is a recoded version of the program that appears in Appendix A. A listing of the source program has been included along with the actual program listing so that the positions of the SPACE, TITLE, and EJECT cards may be observed. Carefully examine both of these listings and observe the improvements that have been obtained through the use of these simple techniques.

Program 4-1

```
          TITLE 'PROGRAM ILLUSTRATING SUBROUTINES - MAIN PROGRAM'
*****************************************************************************
*
* THIS PROGRAM ILLUSTRATES THE USE OF SUBROUTINES.  THE PROGRAM
*
*         1) READS A SET OF NUMBERS INTO 'TABLE1'.  IT IS
*            ASSUMED THAT THE INPUT VALUES HAVE BEEN SORTED INTO
*            ASCENDING ORDER.
*
*         2) PRINTS OUT THE NUMBERS IN 'TABLE1'.
*
*         3) READS IN A SECOND SET OF NUMBERS INTO 'TABLE2'.
*
*         4) PRINTS OUT THE NUMBERS IN 'TABLE2'.
*
*         5) MERGES THE NUMBERS IN THE TWO TABLES INTO 'TABLE3'.
*
*         6) PRINTS OUT THE NUMBERS IN 'TABLE3'.
*
* THE LOGIC OF THE PROGRAM IS AS FOLLOWS:
*
*         STEP 1.   CALL 'READ' TO READ IN THE FIRST TABLE.  THIS WILL
*                   REQUIRE PASSING TO 'READ' THE ADDRESS OF THE TABLE
*                   TO FILL.  THE 'READ' ROUTINE WILL RETURN THE ADDRESS
*                   OF THE LAST ENTRY, WHICH IS STORED IN 'ENDT1'.
*
*         STEP 2.   CALL 'PRINT' TO PRINT OUT THE VALUES IN 'TABLE1'.
*
*         STEP 3.   CALL 'READ' TO READ IN THE VALUES FOR 'TABLE2', AND
*                   SAVE THE ADDRESS OF THE LAST ENTRY IN 'ENDT2'.
*
*         STEP 4.   CALL 'PRINT' TO DISPLAY THE VALUES IN 'TABLE2'.
*
*         STEP 5.   CALL 'MERGE' TO MERGE THE VALUES IN 'TABLE1' AND
*                   'TABLE2' INTO 'TABLE3'.
*
*         STEP 6.   CALL 'PRINT' TO DISPLAY THE VALUES IN 'TABLE3'.
*
*         STEP 7.   EXIT.
*
*****************************************************************************
          SPACE 3
MAINPROG  CSECT
          USING MAINPROG,R15
*
***<STEP 1>     READ IN THE VALUES FOR 'TABLE1'.
*
          LA    R2,TABLE1          R2 IS USED TO PASS THE ADDRESS OF
*                                  WHERE THE VALUES ARE TO BE STORED
```

Program 4-1 (continued)

```
        BAL   R10,READ          READ IN 'TABLE1'
        ST    R3,ENDT1          SAVE THE ADDRESS OF THE LAST VALUE
*
***<STEP 2>    PRINT OUT THE VALUES IN 'TABLE1'.
*
        BAL   R10,PRINT         R2 MUST HAVE ADDRESS OF 'TABLE1' AND
*                               R3 MUST HAVE ADDRESS OF LAST ENTRY

        SPACE 2
*
***<STEP 3>    READ IN THE VALUES FOR 'TABLE2'.
*
        LA    R2,TABLE2         POINT TO THE SECOND TABLE
        BAL   R10,READ          READ IN THE VALUES
        ST    R3,ENDT2          SAVE ADDRESS OF LAST ENTRY
*
***<STEP 4>    PRINT OUT THE VALUES IN 'TABLE2'.
*
        BAL   R10,PRINT
        SPACE 2
*
***<STEP 5>    NOW MERGE THE TWO TABLES INTO 'TABLE3'.
*
        LA    R2,TABLE1         R2 <- ADDRESS OF FIRST TABLE
        LA    R3,TABLE2         R3 <- ADDRESS OF SECOND TABLE
        LA    R4,TABLE3         R4 <- ADDRESS OF TABLE TO BUILD
*
        L     R5,ENDT1          R5 <- ADDRESS OF LAST ENTRY IN TABLE1
        L     R6,ENDT2          R6 <- ADDRESS OF LAST ENTRY IN TABLE2
*
        BAL   R10,MERGE         NOW MERGE THE TWO TABLES
*
***<STEP 6>    PRINT OUT THE CONTENTS OF 'TABLE3'.
*
        LA    R2,TABLE3
        LR    R3,R7             'MERGE' PUT ADDRESS OF LAST ENTRY
*                               INTO R7
        BAL   R10,PRINT         NOW PRINT THE MERGED TABLE
*
***<STEP 7>    EXIT.
*
        BR    R14
*
        SPACE 5
*********************************************************************
*
*              STORAGE AREAS FOR THE MAIN ROUTINE
*
*********************************************************************
*
        LTORG
ENDT1   DS    F                 ADDRESS OF LAST ENTRY IN TABLE1
ENDT2   DS    F                 ADDRESS OF LAST ENTRY IN TABLE2
TABLE1  DS    50F               BUILD THE FIRST TABLE HERE
TABLE2  DS    50F               AND THE SECOND TABLE HERE
TABLE3  DS    100F              AND THE MERGED TABLE HERE
*
```

Program 4-1 (continued)

```
        TITLE 'SUBROUTINES - READ, PRINT, AND MERGE'
*****************************************************************************
*
*                      READ ROUTINE
*
* THIS IS THE READ ROUTINE.  WHEN IT IS ENTERED, R2 CONTAINS THE
* ADDRESS OF THE TABLE TO BE FILLED.  EACH DATA CARD CONTAINS ONE
* NUMBER. END OF THE TABLE IS DESIGNATED BY A CARD CONTAINING
* 999999.  UPON EXITING, R3 CONTAINS THE ADDRESS OF THE LAST ENTRY
* OF THE TABLE.  NO OTHER REGISTERS ARE ALTERED.  R10 IS THE LINK
* REGISTER.
*
*
* THE LOGIC IS AS FOLLOWS:
*
*        STEP 1.  READ THE NEXT CARD AND GET THE VALUE OFF IT.
*
*        STEP 2.  IF THE VALUE ON THE CARD IS 999999, GO TO STEP 5.
*
*        STEP 3.  STORE THE VALUE INTO THE TABLE BEING BUILT.
*                 INCREMENT THE POINTER TO WHERE THE NEXT VALUE GOES.
*
*        STEP 4.  READ THE NEXT CARD, GET THE VALUE OFF IT, AND GO
*                 BACK TO STEP 2.
*
*        STEP 5.  SET R3 TO POINT TO THE LAST ENTRY.
*
*        STEP 6.  EXIT.
*
*****************************************************************************
         SPACE 3
READ     STM   R4,R2,READSAVE    SAVE ALL REGS EXCEPT R3
*
***<STEP 1>   READ THE NEXT CARD AND GET THE VALUE OFF IT.
*
         XREAD CARD,80           IT IS ASSUMED THAT THERE IS A CARD
         XDECI R4,CARD           AND THAT THE NUMBER IS VALID
*
***<STEP 2>   TEST FOR END OF LOOP (VALUE OF 999999).
*
READLOOP C     R4,=F'999999'
         BE    SETLAST           BRANCH IF END OF INPUT VALUES
*
***<STEP 3>   STORE VALUE INTO TABLE AND INCREMENT NEXT ENTRY POINTER.
*
         ST    R4,0(R2)          STORE ENTRY
         LA    R2,4(R2)          POINT TO NEXT ENTRY
*
***<STEP 4>   READ THE NEXT CARD, GET VALUE, AND GO TO STEP 2.
*
         XREAD CARD,80           READ THE CARD
         XDECI 4,CARD            AND GET THE VALUE
         B     READLOOP
```

Program 4-1 (continued)

```
*
***<STEP 5>    SET POINTER TO LAST ENTRY.
*
SETLAST  LR    R3,R2              R2 HAS ADDRESS OF "NEXT ENTRY"
         S     R3,=F'4'           R3 NOW POINTS TO LAST ENTRY
*
***<STEP 6>    RETURN TO CALLER.
*
         LM    R4,R2,READSAVE     RESTORE ALL REGISTERS BUT R3
         BR    R10                AND RETURN
*
         LTORG
*
CARD     DS    CL80               CARD INPUT AREA
*
READSAVE DS    15F                ROOM FOR ALL REGISTERS, EXCEPT R3
*
         SPACE 5
************************************************************************
*
*                   PRINT ROUTINE
*
* THIS ROUTINE PRINTS OUT THE VALUES IN THE TABLE POINTED TO BY
* R2.  R3 MUST CONTAIN THE ADDRESS OF THE LAST ENTRY IN THE TABLE.
* R10 IS THE LINK REGISTER.  ENTRIES ARE PRINTED OUT 1 PER LINE.
* NO REGISTERS ARE ALTERED BY A CALL TO THIS ROUTINE.
* THE LOGIC IS AS FOLLOWS:
*
*        STEP 1.  PRINT A HEADING.
*
*        STEP 2.  IF ALL OF THE ENTRIES HAVE BEEN PRINTED, GO
*                 TO STEP 4.
*
*        STEP 3.  PRINT ONE ENTRY, INCREMENT POINTER TO NEXT ENTRY,
*                 AND GO BACK TO STEP 2.
*
*        STEP 4.  PRINT "END OF TABLE" MESSAGE.
*
*        STEP 5.  EXIT.
*
************************************************************************
         SPACE 3
PRINT    STM   R0,R15,PRINTSAV    SAVE ALL OF THE REGISTERS
*
***<STEP 1>    PRINT A HEADING.
*
         XPRNT =C'0*** START OF TABLE ***',23
*
***<STEP 2>    CHECK FOR END OF TABLE.
*
PRINTLP  CR    R2,R3              COMPARE CURRENT AGAINST LAST
         BH    PRINTEND           BRANCH IF PAST LAST ENTRY
*
***<STEP 3>    PRINT ONE ENTRY AND GO BACK TO STEP 2.
*
         L     R4,0(R2)           GET A VALUE FROM THE TABLE
         XDECO R4,OUTVAL          CONVERT TO PRINTABLE FORMAT
         XPRNT PRNTLINE,13        PRINT IT
*
         LA    R2,4(R2)           INCREMENT POINTER TO NEXT ENTRY
         B     PRINTLP
*
***<STEP 4>    PRINT "END OF TABLE" MESSAGE.
*
PRINTEND XPRNT =C'0*** END OF TABLE ***',21
*
```

Program 4-1 (continued)

```
***<STEP 5>    EXIT.
*
         LM      R0,R15,PRINTSAV    RESTORE ALL REGISTERS
         BR      R10                EXIT
*
         LTORG
*
PRNTLINE DC      C' '               CARRIAGE CONTROL
OUTVAL   DS      CL12               OUTPUT THE VALUES HERE
*
PRINTSAV DS      16F                SAVE REGISTERS HERE
         EJECT
*******************************************************************
*
*                   MERGE ROUTINE
*
* THIS ROUTINE MERGES THE TWO SORTED TABLES INTO A THIRD TABLE.  UPON
* ENTRANCE
*
*        R2 = ADDRESS OF FIRST TABLE
*        R3 = ADDRESS OF SECOND TABLE
*        R4 = ADDRESS OF THIRD TABLE
*        R5 = ADDRESS OF LAST ENTRY IN FIRST TABLE
*        R6 = ADDRESS OF LAST ENTRY IN SECOND TABLE
*
* THE ROUTINE WILL SET R7 TO THE ADDRESS OF THE LAST ENTRY IN THE
* THIRD TABLE, WHICH IS PRODUCED BY MERGING THE FIRST TWO TABLES.
* R10 IS THE LINK REGISTER.  ONLY R7 IS ALTERED BY A CALL TO THIS
* ROUTINE.
*
* THE LOGIC IS AS FOLLOWS:
*
*        STEP 1.  IF ALL VALUES FROM BOTH TABLES ARE IN THE THIRD
*                 TABLE, GO TO STEP 6.
*
*        STEP 2.  IF (ALL VALUES IN TABLE2 ARE ALREADY IN TABLE3 OR
*                 (SOME VALUES IN TABLE1 HAVE NOT YET BEEN
*                 MOVED AND THE NEXT ONE FROM TABLE1 IS LESS
*                 THAN THE NEXT ONE FROM TABLE2)), GO TO STEP 3.
*                 ELSE, GO TO STEP 4.
*
*        STEP 3.  MOVE A VALUE FROM TABLE1 TO TABLE3, UPDATING THE
*                 POINTER TO THE NEXT ENTRY IN TABLE1.  GO TO STEP 5.
*
*        STEP 4.  MOVE A VALUE FROM TABLE2 TO TABLE3, UPDATING THE
*                 POINTER TO THE NEXT ENTRY IN TABLE2.
*
*        STEP 5.  UPDATE THE POINTER TO THE NEXT ENTRY IN TABLE3 AND
*                 GO BACK TO STEP 1.
*
*        STEP 6.  SET R7 TO POINT TO THE LAST ENTRY IN TABLE3.
*
*        STEP 7.  EXIT.
*
*******************************************************************
         SPACE 3
MERGE    STM     R8,R6,MERGESAV     SAVE ALL REGS, EXCEPT R7
*
***<STEP 1>    BRANCH TO STEP 6, IF ALL ENTRIES HAVE BEEN MOVED.
*
MERGELP  CR      R2,R5
         BNH     SOMELEFT           BRANCH IF NOT ALL OF TABLE1 HAS
*                                   BEEN MOVED
         CR      R3,R6
         BH      POINTR7            BRANCH IF ALL ENTRIES HAVE BEEN
*                                   MOVED TO TABLE3
         SPACE 2
```

Program 4-1 (continued)

```
*
***<STEP 2>     FIGURE OUT WHICH TABLE THE NEXT ENTRY COMES FROM.
*
SOMELEFT CR      R3,R6
         BH      FROMT1            BRANCH IF TABLE2 EXHAUSTED
*
         CR      R2,R5
         BH      FROMT2            BRANCH IF TABLE1 EXHAUSTED
*
         L       R8,0(R2)          R8 <- NEXT ENTRY FROM TABLE1
         C       R8,0(R3)
         BH      FROMT2            BRANCH IF T1'S ENTRY IS HIGH
         SPACE 2
*
***<STEP 3>     MOVE ENTRY FROM TABLE1 TO TABLE3.
*
FROMT1   L       R8,0(R2)          LOAD ENTRY FROM TABLE1
         ST      R8,0(R4)          STORE INTO TABLE3
         LA      R2,4(R2)          INCREMENT POINTER INTO TABLE1
         B       INCRT3            GO INCREMENT TABLE3'S POINTER
*
***<STEP 4>     MOVE ENTRY FROM TABLE2 TO TABLE3.
*
FROMT2   L       R8,0(R3)          LOAD ENTRY FROM TABLE2
         ST      R8,0(R4)          AND PUT IT INTO TABLE3
         LA      R3,4(R3)          INCREMENT POINTER INTO TABLE2
*
***<STEP 5>     INCREMENT TABLE3'S POINTER AND GO BACK TO STEP 1.
*
INCRT3   LA      R4,4(R4)          INCREMENT POINTER TO NEXT ENTRY
*                                  FOR TABLE3
         B       MERGELP
*
***<STEP 6>     POINT R7 AT LAST ENTRY IN TABLE3.
*
POINTR7  LR      R7,R4             R4 POINTS JUST PAST LAST ENTRY
         S       R7,=F'4'          NOW R7 POINTS AT LAST ENTRY
*
***<STEP 7>     EXIT.
*
         LM      R8,R6,MERGESAV    RESTORE ALL REGISTERS BUT R7
         BR      R10               AND RETURN
*
MERGESAV DS      15F               REGISTER SAVEAREA
         SPACE 5
         LTORG
R0       EQU     0
R1       EQU     1
R2       EQU     2
R3       EQU     3
R4       EQU     4
R5       EQU     5
R6       EQU     6
R7       EQU     7
R8       EQU     8
R9       EQU     9
R10      EQU     10
R11      EQU     11
R12      EQU     12
R13      EQU     13
R14      EQU     14
R15      EQU     15
         END     MAINPROG
```

Program 4-1 (Second version)

```
LOC   OBJECT CODE   ADDR1 ADDR2  STMT   SOURCE STATEMENT
                                    2   ******************************************************************
                                    3   *
                                    4   *    THIS PROGRAM ILLUSTRATES THE USE OF SUBROUTINES.   THE PROGRAM
                                    5   *
                                    6   *        1) READS A SET OF NUMBERS INTO 'TABLE1'.   IT IS
                                    7   *           ASSUMED THAT THE INPUT VALUES HAVE BEEN SORTED INTO
                                    8   *           ASCENDING ORDER.
                                    9   *
                                   10   *        2) PRINTS OUT THE NUMBERS IN 'TABLE1'.
                                   11   *
                                   12   *        3) READS IN A SECOND SET OF NUMBERS INTO 'TABLE2'.
                                   13   *
                                   14   *        4) PRINTS OUT THE NUMBERS IN 'TABLE2'.
                                   15   *
                                   16   *        5) MERGES THE NUMBERS IN THE TWO TABLES INTO 'TABLE3'.
                                   17   *
                                   18   *        6) PRINTS OUT THE NUMBERS IN 'TABLE3'.
                                   19   *
                                   20   *    THE LOGIC OF THE PROGRAM IS AS FOLLOWS:
                                   21   *
                                   22   *        STEP 1.   CALL 'READ' TO READ IN THE FIRST TABLE.   THIS WILL
                                   23   *                  REQUIRE PASSING TO 'READ' THE ADDRESS OF THE TABLE
                                   24   *                  TO FILL.   THE 'READ' ROUTINE WILL RETURN THE ADDRESS
                                   25   *                  OF THE LAST ENTRY, WHICH IS STORED IN 'ENDT1'.
                                   26   *
                                   27   *        STEP 2.   CALL 'PRINT' TO PRINT OUT THE VALUES IN 'TABLE1'.
                                   28   *
                                   29   *        STEP 3.   CALL 'READ' TO READ IN THE VALUES FOR 'TABLE2', AND
                                   30   *                  SAVE THE ADDRESS OF THE LAST ENTRY IN 'ENDT2'.
                                   31   *
                                   32   *        STEP 4.   CALL 'PRINT' TO DISPLAY THE VALUES IN 'TABLE2'.
                                   33   *
                                   34   *        STEP 5.   CALL 'MERGE' TO MERGE THE VALUES IN 'TABLE1' AND
                                   35   *                  'TABLE2' INTO 'TABLE3'.
                                   36   *
                                   37   *        STEP 6.   CALL 'PRINT' TO DISPLAY THE VALUES IN 'TABLE3'.
                                   38   *
                                   39   *        STEP 7.   EXIT.
                                   40   *
                                   41   ******************************************************************

000000                             43   MAINPROG CSECT
000000                             44            USING MAINPROG,R15
                                   45   *
```

```
                                    46 ***<STEP 1>    READ IN THE VALUES FOR 'TABLE1'.
                                    47 *
000000 4120 F050    00050          48         LA   R2,TABLE1    R2 IS USED TO PASS THE ADDRESS OF
                                    49 *                         WHERE THE VALUES ARE TO BE STORED
000004 45A0 F370    00370          50         BAL  R10,READ     READ IN 'TABLE1'
LOC    OBJECT CODE  ADDR1 ADDR2  STMT  SOURCE STATEMENT
                          00050
000008 5030 F048          00048   51         ST   R3,ENDT1     SAVE THE ADDRESS OF THE LAST VALUE
                                    52 *
                                    53 ***<STEP 2>    PRINT OUT THE VALUES IN 'TABLE1'.
                                    54 *
00000C 45A0 F43C    0043C          55         BAL  R10,PRINT    R2 MUST HAVE ADDRESS OF 'TABLE1' AND
                                    56 *                         R3 MUST HAVE ADDRESS OF LAST ENTRY

                                    58 *
                                    59 ***<STEP 3>    READ IN THE VALUES FOR 'TABLE2'.
                                    60 *
000010 4120 F118    00118          61         LA   R2,TABLE2    POINT TO THE SECOND TABLE
000014 45A0 F370    00370          62         BAL  R10,READ     READ IN THE VALUES
000018 5030 F04C    0004C          63         ST   R3,ENDT2     SAVE ADDRESS OF LAST ENTRY
                                    64 *
                                    65 ***<STEP 4>    PRINT OUT THE VALUES IN 'TABLE2'.
                                    66 *
00001C 45A0 F43C    0043C          67         BAL  R10,PRINT

                                    69 *
                                    70 ***<STEP 5>    NOW MERGE THE TWO TABLES INTO 'TABLE3'.
                                    71 *
000020 4120 F050    00050          72         LA   R2,TABLE1    R2 <- ADDRESS OF FIRST TABLE
000024 4130 F118    00118          73         LA   R3,TABLE2    R3 <- ADDRESS OF SECOND TABLE
000028 4140 F1E0    001E0          74         LA   R4,TABLE3    R4 <- ADDRESS OF TABLE TO BUILD
                                    75 *
00002C 5350 F048    00048          76         L    R5,ENDT1     R5 <- ADDRESS OF LAST ENTRY IN TABLE1
000030 5860 F04C    0004C          77         L    R6,ENDT2     R6 <- ADDRESS OF LAST ENTRY IN TABLE2
                                    78 *
000034 45A0 F4EC    004EC          79         BAL  R10,MERGE    NOW MERGE THE TWO TABLES
                                    80 *
                                    81 ***<STEP 6>    PRINT OUT THE CONTENTS OF 'TABLE3'.
                                    82 *
000038 4120 F1E0    001E0          83         LA   R2,TABLE3    'MERGE' PUT ADDRESS OF LAST ENTRY
00003C 1837                        84         LR   R3,R7         INTO R7
                                    85 *
00003E 45A0 F43C    0043C          86         BAL  R10,PRINT    NOW PRINT THE MERGED TABLE
                                    87 *
                                    88 ***<STEP 7>    EXIT.
                                    89 *
000042 07FE                        90         BR   R14
                                    91 *
```

PROGRAM ILLUSTRATING SUBROUTINES - MAIN PROGRAM   PAGE   3

          93 ***
          94 *
          95 *   STORAGE AREAS FOR THE MAIN ROUTINE
          96 *
          97 ***
          98 *
          99   LTORG

LOC   OBJECT CODE   ADDR1 ADDR2   STMT   SOURCE STATEMENT
000048   100 ENDT1   DS   F   ADDRESS OF LAST ENTRY IN TABLE1
00004C   101 ENDT2   DS   F   ADDRESS OF LAST ENTRY IN TABLE2
000050   102 TABLE1   DS   50F   BUILD THE FIRST TABLE HERE
000118   103 TABLE2   DS   50F   AND THE SECOND TABLE HERE
0001E0   104 TABLE3   DS   100F   AND THE MERGED TABLE HERE
                                     105 *

LOC	OBJECT CODE	ADDR1	ADDR2	STMT	SOURCE STATEMENT			
				107	***			
				108	*			
				109	*			
				110	* READ ROUTINE			
				111	* THIS IS THE READ ROUTINE. WHEN IT IS ENTERED, R2 CONTAINS THE			
				112	* ADDRESS OF THE TABLE TO BE FILLED. EACH DATA CARD CONTAINS ONE			
				113	* NUMBER. END OF THE TABLE IS DESIGNATED BY A CARD CONTAINING			
				114	* 999999. UPON EXITING, R3 CONTAINS THE ADDRESS OF THE LAST ENTRY			
				115	* OF THE TABLE. NO OTHER REGISTERS ARE ALTERED. R10 IS THE LINK			
				116	* REGISTER.			
				117	*			
				118	*			
				119	* THE LOGIC IS AS FOLLOWS:			
				120	*			
				121	* STEP 1. READ THE NEXT CARD AND GET THE VALUE OFF IT.			
				122	*			
				123	* STEP 2. IF THE VALUE ON THE CARD IS 999999, GO TO STEP 5.			
				124	*			
				125	* STEP 3. STORE THE VALUE INTO THE TABLE BEING BUILT.			
				126	* INCREMENT THE POINTER TO WHERE THE NEXT VALUE GOES.			
				127	*			
				128	* STEP 4. READ THE NEXT CARD, GET THE VALUE OFF IT, AND GO			
				129	* BACK TO STEP 2.			
				130	*			
				131	* STEP 5. SET R3 TO POINT TO THE LAST ENTRY.			
				132	*			
				133	* STEP 6. EXIT.			
				134	*			
				135	***			

```
000370  9042 F400          00400            137  READ      STM   R4,R2,READSAVE      SAVE ALL REGS EXCEPT R3
                                            138  *
                                            139  ***<STEP 1>        READ THE NEXT CARD AND GET THE VALUE OFF IT.
                                            140  *
000374  E000 F3B0 0050 003B0  003B0         141            XREAD CARD,80              IT IS ASSUMED THAT THERE IS A CARD
00037A  5340 F3B0                           142            XDECI R4,CARD              AND THAT THE NUMBER IS VALID
                                            143  *
                                            144  ***<STEP 2>        TEST FOR END OF LOOP (VALUE OF 999999).
                                            145  *
00037E  5940 F3A8          003A8            146  READLOOP  C     R4,=F'999999'
000382  4780 F39C          0039C            147            BE    SETLAST             BRANCH IF END OF INPUT VALUES
                                            148  *
                                            149  ***<STEP 3>        STORE VALUE INTO TABLE AND INCREMENT NEXT ENTRY POINTER.
                                            150  *
000386  5042 0000          00000            151            ST    R4,0(R2)            STORE ENTRY
00038A  4122 0004          00004            152            LA    R2,4(R2)            POINT TO NEXT ENTRY
                                            153  *
                                            154  ***<STEP 4>        READ THE NEXT CARD, GET VALUE, AND GO TO STEP 2.
                                            155  *
00038E  E000 F3B0 0050 003B0  003B0         156            XREAD CARD,80              READ THE CARD
000394  5340 F3B0                           157            XDECI 4,CARD               AND GET THE VALUE
000398  47F0 F37E          0037E            158            B     READLOOP
                                            159  *
```

```
LOC     OBJECT CODE       ADDR1 ADDR2  STMT  SOURCE STATEMENT

                                       160   ***<STEP 5>      SET POINTER TO LAST ENTRY.
                                       161   *
00039C  1832                           162   SETLAST   LR    R3,R2            R2 HAS ADDRESS OF "NEXT ENTRY"
00039E  5B30 F3AC         003AC        163             S     R3,=F'4'         R3 NOW POINTS TO LAST ENTRY
                                       164   *
                                       165   ***<STEP 6>      RETURN TO CALLER.
                                       166   *
0003A2  9842 F400         00400        167             LM    R4,R2,READSAVE   RESTORE ALL REGISTERS BUT R3
0003A6  07FA                           168             BR    R10              AND RETURN
                                       169   *
                                       170             LTORG
0003A8  000F423F                       171                   =F'999999'
0003AC  00000004                       172                   =F'4'
                                       173   *
0003B0                                 174   CARD      DS    CL80             CARD INPUT AREA
                                       175   *
000400                                 176   READSAVE  DS    15F              ROOM FOR ALL REGISTERS, EXCEPT R3
                                       177   *


                                       179   ******************************************************************
                                       180   *                                                                *
                                       181   *                          PRINT ROUTINE                          *
                                       182   *                                                                *
                                       183   * THIS ROUTINE PRINTS OUT THE VALUES IN THE TABLE POINTED TO BY   *
                                       184   * R2.  R3 MUST CONTAIN THE ADDRESS OF THE LAST ENTRY IN THE TABLE.*
                                       185   * R10 IS THE LINK REGISTER.  ENTRIES ARE PRINTED OUT 1 PER LINE.  *
                                       186   * NO REGISTERS ARE ALTERED BY A CALL TO THIS ROUTINE.            *
                                       187   * THE LOGIC IS AS FOLLOWS:                                        *
                                       188   *                                                                *
                                       189   *         STEP 1.   PRINT A HEADING.                              *
                                       190   *                                                                *
                                       191   *         STEP 2.   IF ALL OF THE ENTRIES HAVE BEEN PRINTED, GO   *
                                       192   *                   TO STEP 4.                                    *
                                       193   *                                                                *
                                       194   *         STEP 3.   PRINT ONE ENTRY, INCREMENT POINTER TO NEXT ENTRY, *
                                       195   *                   AND GO BACK TO STEP 2.                        *
                                       196   *                                                                *
                                       197   *         STEP 4.   PRINT "END OF TABLE" MESSAGE.                 *
                                       198   *                                                                *
                                       199   *         STEP 5.   EXIT.                                         *
                                       200   *                                                                *
                                       201   ******************************************************************

004AC                                  203   PRINT     STM   R0,R15,PRINTSAV  SAVE ALL OF THE REGISTERS
                                       204   *
                                       205   ***<STEP 1>      PRINT A HEADING.
                                       206   *
00043C  900F F4AC                      207             XPRNT =C'0*** START OF TABLE ***',23
000440  E020 F470 0017 00470           208   *
```

```
       SUBROUTINES - READ, PRINT, AND MERGE

LOC    OBJECT CODE    ADDR1 ADDR2   STMT   SOURCE STATEMENT
                                    209  ***<STEP 2>    CHECK FOR END OF TABLE.
                                    210  *
000446 1923                         211  PRINTLP  CR   R2,R3             COMPARE CURRENT AGAINST LAST
000448 4720 F462            00462   212           BH   PRINTEND          BRANCH IF PAST LAST ENTRY
                                    213  *
                                    214  ***<STEP 3>    PRINT ONE ENTRY AND GO BACK TO STEP 2.
                                    215  *
00044C 5842 0000            00000   216           L    R4,0(R2)          GET A VALUE FROM THE TABLE
000450 5240 F49D            0049D   217           XDECO R4,OUTVAL        CONVERT TO PRINTABLE FORMAT
000454 E020 F49C 000D 0049C 218           XPRNT PRNTLINE,13             PRINT IT
                                    219  *
00045A 4122 0004            00004   220           LA   R2,4(R2)          INCREMENT POINTER TO NEXT ENTRY
00045E 47F0 F446            00446   221           B    PRINTLP
                                    222  *
                                    223  ***<STEP 4>    PRINT "END OF TABLE" MESSAGE.
                                    224  *
000462 E020 F487 0015 00487 225  PRINTEND XPRNT =C'0*** END OF TABLE ***',21
                                    226  *
                                    227  ***<STEP 5>    EXIT.
                                    228  *
000468 980F F4AC            004AC   229           LM   R0,R15,PRINTSAV   RESTORE ALL REGISTERS
00046C 07FA                         230           BR   R10               EXIT
                                    231  *
                                    232           LTORG
000470 F05C5C5C40E2E3C1            233  =C'0*** START OF TABLE ***'
000487 F05C5C5C40C5D5C4            234  =C'0*** END OF TABLE ***'
                                    235  *
00049C 40                          236  PRNTLINE DC   C' '              CARRIAGE CONTROL
00049D                             237  OUTVAL   DS   CL12              OUTPUT THE VALUES HERE
                                    238  *
0004AC                             239  PRINTSAV DS   16F               SAVE REGISTERS HERE
```

LOC   OBJECT CODE   ADDR1 ADDR2 STMT   SOURCE STATEMENT

```
241  *****************************************************************
242  *
243  *                        MERGE ROUTINE
244  *
245  *  THIS ROUTINE MERGES THE TWO SORTED TABLES INTO A THIRD TABLE.  UPON
246  *  ENTRANCE
247  *
248  *           R2 = ADDRESS OF FIRST TABLE
249  *           R3 = ADDRESS OF SECOND TABLE
250  *           R4 = ADDRESS OF THIRD TABLE
251  *           R5 = ADDRESS OF LAST ENTRY IN FIRST TABLE
252  *           R6 = ADDRESS OF LAST ENTRY IN SECOND TABLE
253  *
254  *  THE ROUTINE WILL SET R7 TO THE ADDRESS OF THE LAST ENTRY IN THE
255  *  THIRD TABLE, WHICH IS PRODUCED BY MERGING THE FIRST TWO TABLES.
256  *  R10 IS THE LINK REGISTER.  ONLY R7 IS ALTERED BY A CALL TO THIS
257  *  ROUTINE.
258  *
259  *  THE LOGIC IS AS FOLLOWS:
260  *
261  *     STEP 1.  IF ALL VALUES FROM BOTH TABLES ARE IN THE THIRD
262  *              TABLE, GO TO STEP 6.
263  *
264  *     STEP 2.  IF (ALL VALUES IN TABLE2 ARE ALREADY IN TABLE3 OR
265  *              (SOME VALUES IN TABLE1 HAVE NOT YET BEEN
266  *              MOVED AND THE NEXT ONE FROM TABLE1 IS LESS
267  *              THAN THE NEXT ONE FROM TABLE2)), GO TO STEP 3.
268  *              ELSE, GO TO STEP 4.
269  *
270  *     STEP 3.  MOVE A VALUE FROM TABLE1 TO TABLE3, UPDATING THE
271  *              POINTER TO THE NEXT ENTRY IN TABLE1.  GO TO STEP 5.
272  *
273  *     STEP 4.  MOVE A VALUE FROM TABLE2 TO TABLE3, UPDATING THE
274  *              POINTER TO THE NEXT ENTRY IN TABLE2.
275  *
276  *     STEP 5.  UPDATE THE POINTER TO THE NEXT ENTRY IN TABLE3 AND
277  *              GO BACK TO STEP 1.
278  *
279  *     STEP 6.  SET R7 TO POINT TO THE LAST ENTRY IN TABLE3.
280  *
281  *     STEP 7.  EXIT.
282  *
283  *****************************************************************
```

```
00544                    285  MERGE     STM   R8,R6,MERGESAV      SAVE ALL REGS, EXCEPT R7
                         286  ***<STEP 1>          BRANCH TO STEP 6, IF ALL ENTRIES HAVE BEEN MOVED.
                         287
                         288
0004EC  9086 F544
0004F0  1925            289  MERGELP   CR    R2,R5
0004F2  47D0 F4FC       290            BNH   SOMELEFT           BRANCH IF NOT ALL OF TABLE1 HAS
0004FC                  291  *                                    BEEN MOVED
```

SUBROUTINES - READ, PRINT, AND MERGE

```
 LOC    OBJECT CODE  ADDR1 ADDR2  STMT  SOURCE STATEMENT
0004F6  1936                       292        CR   R3,R6
0004F8  4720 F538          00538   293        BH   POINTR7      BRANCH IF ALL ENTRIES HAVE BEEN
                                   294  *                        MOVED TO TABLE3

                                   296  *
                                   297        ***<STEP 2>       FIGURE OUT WHICH TABLE THE NEXT ENTRY COMES FROM.
                                   298  *
0004FC  1936                       299  SOMELEFT CR  R3,R6
0004FE  4720 F514          00514   300        BH   FROMT1       BRANCH IF TABLE2 EXHAUSTED
                                   301  *
000502  1925                       302        CR   R2,R5
000504  4720 F524          00524   303        BH   FROMT2       BRANCH IF TABLE1 EXHAUSTED
                                   304  *
000508  5882 0000          00000   305        L    R8,0(R2)     R8 <- NEXT ENTRY FROM TABLE1
00050C  5983 0000          00000   306        C    R8,0(R3)
000510  4720 F524          00524   307        BH   FROMT2       BRANCH IF T1'S ENTRY IS HIGH

                                   309  *
                                   310        ***<STEP 3>       MOVE ENTRY FROM TABLE1 TO TABLE3.
                                   311  *
000514  5882 0000          00000   312  FROMT1   L   R8,0(R2)   LOAD ENTRY FROM TABLE1
000518  5084 0000          00000   313        ST   R8,0(R4)     STORE INTO TABLE3
00051C  4122 0004          00004   314        LA   R2,4(R2)     INCREMENT POINTER INTO TABLE1
000520  47F0 F530          00530   315        B    INCRT3       GO INCREMENT TABLE3'S POINTER

                                   317  *
                                   318        ***<STEP 4>       MOVE ENTRY FROM TABLE2 TO TABLE3.
000524  5883 0000          00000   319  FROMT2   L   R8,0(R3)   LOAD ENTRY FROM TABLE2
000528  5084 0000          00000   320        ST   R8,0(R4)     AND PUT IT INTO TABLE3
00052C  4133 0004          00004   321        LA   R3,4(R3)     INCREMENT POINTER INTO TABLE2

                                   322  *
                                   323        ***<STEP 5>       INCREMENT TABLE3'S POINTER AND GO BACK TO STEP 1.
                                   324  *
000530  4144 0004          00004   325  INCRT3   LA  R4,4(R4)   INCREMENT POINTER TO NEXT ENTRY
                                   326  *                        FOR TABLE3
000534  47F0 F4F0          004F0   327        B    MERGELP

                                   328  *
                                   329        ***<STEP 6>       POINT R7 AT LAST ENTRY IN TABLE3.
                                   330  *
000538  1874                       331  POINTR7  LR  R7,R4      R4 POINTS JUST PAST LAST ENTRY
00053A  5B70 F580          00580   332        S    R7,=F'4'     NOW R7 POINTS AT LAST ENTRY
                                   333  *
                                   334        ***<STEP 7>       EXIT.
                                   335  *
00053E  9886 F544          00544   336        LM   R8,R6,MERGESAV  RESTORE ALL REGISTERS BUT R7
000542  07FA                       337        BR   R10             AND RETURN
                                   338  *
000544                             339  MERGESAV DS  15F         REGISTER SAVEAREA
```

```
SUBROUTINES - READ, PRINT, AND MERGE

LOC    OBJECT CODE    ADDR1 ADDR2    STMT    SOURCE STATEMENT
                                     341             LTORG
000580 00000004                      342                     =F'4'
000000                               343     R0      EQU     0
000001                               344     R1      EQU     1
000002                               345     R2      EQU     2
000003                               346     R3      EQU     3
000004                               347     R4      EQU     4
000005                               348     R5      EQU     5
000006                               349     R6      EQU     6
000007                               350     R7      EQU     7
000008                               351     R8      EQU     8
000009                               352     R9      EQU     9
00000A                               353     R10     EQU     10
00000B                               354     R11     EQU     11
00000C                               355     R12     EQU     12
00000D                               356     R13     EQU     13
00000E                               357     R14     EQU     14
00000F                               358     R15     EQU     15
                                     359             END     MAINPROG
```

*** NO   STATEMENTS FLAGGED - NO   WARNINGS, NO   ERRORS

*** DYNAMIC CORE AREA USED: LOW: 14432 HIGH: 1168 LEAVING: 107280 FREE BYTES. AVERAGE: 43 BYTES/STMT ***

*** ASSEMBLY TIME =   0.283 SECS,   1272 STATEMENTS/SEC ***

*** PROGRAM EXECUTION BEGINNING - ANY OUTPUT BEFORE EXECUTION TIME MESSAGE IS PRODUCED BY USER PROGRAM ***

*** START OF TABLE ***
        1
        2
        3
       10
       11
       14

*** END OF TABLE ***

```
*** START OF TABLE ***
    -20
      1
      4
      5
     12
     16

*** END OF TABLE ***
*** START OF TABLE ***
    -20
      1
      1
      2
      3
      4
      5
     10
     11
     12
     14
     16

*** END OF TABLE ***
*** EXECUTION TIME =    0.023 SECS.          491 INSTRUCTIONS EXECUTED -     21347 INSTRUCTIONS/SEC ***

*** AM004 - NORMAL USER TERMINATION BY RETURN ***

*** TOTAL RUN TIME UNDER ASSIST =     0.000 SECS ***
```

4.2 DOCUMENTATION STANDARDS

The aspect of the function of a programmer that has been most liberally abused is that of providing adequate documentation of the programs produced. The fact that a programmer has prepared a sequence of optimally coded instructions that produces correct results when tested against trial data hardly means he has adequately fulfilled his function. The job of preparing a production program cannot be considered complete unless the program is supported by (1) a complete, detailed, and concise description of the function that the program is to perform, (2) a complete set of block diagrams and flowcharts that portray the logic of the program, (3) a step algorithm that is detailed in the program listing and relates individual sections of code to the blocks of the flowcharts, and (4) an adequate set of comments to explain the function of individual instructions within the program.

During the past decade, there has been a constant shift from assembler-language programs to programs written in higher-level languages. This conversion has taken place even though assembler-language programs are usually more efficient in the use of storage and time. One of the major causes of this shift is that programs coded in assembler language are characteristically more difficult to use, maintain, and alter. The difficulties encountered with the assembler-language programs result primarily from the fact that most of these programs are inadequately documented. There is no accurate estimate of the millions of dollars that could have been saved out of the vast sums spent on the use, maintenance, alteration, and recoding of assembler-language programs, had these programs been adequately documented when they were first written.

Although it is certainly true that many programs should be written in higher-level languages rather than in assembler language, the use of assembler language has been unnecessarily curtailed by the failure to adhere to adequate standards of documentation. The following minimal documentation standards are proposed for all assembler-language programs:

1. For each program, a block diagram and a set of flowcharts presenting a visual description of the logic of the program should be prepared. These diagrams should be neatly drawn and should conform to normal flowcharting practices. If the program includes subroutines, a separate set of diagrams should be included for each routine.

2. At the beginning of each routine of a program, comments conveying the following information should appear:

   a. A description of the function of the routine. This description should be complete enough to enable any qualified programmer to ascertain quickly the purpose of the routine.

b. A description of the entry conditions. For example, if particular registers are assumed to contain specific parameters when the routine is entered, these assumptions should be stated.

c. A description of the exit conditions. For example, if any of the registers are altered by the routine, these alterations should be stated.

d. A step algorithm. The steps should be related to the blocks in the block diagram. Each step should completely describe, in readable English, the purpose of the related section of code.

3. Between the instructions for a routine, the steps of the step algorithm should be delimited by some appropriate comment cards. In this text, cards of the form

   ***<STEP n>

will be used for this purpose.

4. Every statement defining a storage area should be followed by a comment containing a description of the use of that area.

5. Individual statements should be commented wherever appropriate. Each such comment should convey information that cannot be deduced from the instruction itself. For example the line

   AR   R3,R4   ADD R4 TO R3

gives the reader no more information than the instruction itself. However, the line

   AR   R3,R4   ADD AMOUNT TO TOTAL

conveys useful information that is not deducible from the instruction.

Compliance with these documentation standards may seem to introduce an unnecessary amount of effort into the production of a program. This is true if only the time spent by a programmer in completing a program is taken into account. However, consideration should be given to the fact that a program may be used frequently over a period of five or more years, requiring constant maintenance and, more often than not, periodic alterations. Clearly, adherence to strict documentation standards results in minimizing the time spent on these operations. Thus, in most cases, the proper documentation of a program will result in a net savings of programmer time.

4.3 TWO SI INSTRUCTIONS: MVI AND CLI

In this section, an instruction format—the SI format—which has not previously been discussed, and two instructions encoded in this format—MVI and CLI—will be introduced. The SI format is utilized for the encoding of instructions involving an area in storage and a single known byte. This known byte, which is referred to as the *immediate byte,* is actually generated in the encoded instruction itself. The symbolic form of an SI instruction is

> label   mnemonic   address, byte

The format for encoded SI instructions is

$$h_0 h_0 h_I h_I \quad h_B h_D h_D h_D$$

where $h_0 h_0$ is the op code
        $h_I h_I$ is the immediate byte
        h_B is the number of the base register
        $h_D h_D h_D$ is the displacement

Note that the encoded form of the address must be D(B); no index register may be specified. As an example, the instruction

> MVI   42(R15),C'$'

is encoded as 925B F02A.

The immediate byte of an SI instruction is almost invariably specified in one of three ways:

1. If the immediate byte is to be interpreted as a character, it should be specified by a single character enclosed within single quotes and preceded by the letter C. In the example,

> MVI   42(R15),C'$'

the immediate byte is specified as the character $.

2. The immediate byte can be specified as a two-digit hexadecimal constant. This may be done by enclosing the hexadecimal digits within single quotes and preceding them with the letter X. Thus, the instruction

> MVI   42(R15),X'5B'

generates exactly the same code as the instruction

> MVI   42(R15),C'$'

3. This way of specifying the immediate byte emphasizes the values of the bits in that byte. The method is to specify the immediate byte as an eight-digit binary number enclosed within single quotes and preceded by the letter B. In this form, the instruction generating the same code as do the previous examples is

> MVI   42(R15),B'01011011'

Of the SI instructions, MVI and CLI are perhaps the most useful and the most frequently used.

MVI   D(B),byte   *(Move Immediate)*

Execution of this instruction results in the replacement of the contents of the byte at the address D(B) with a copy of the immediate byte. For example, the instruction

MVI   PRNTLINE,C' '

has the effect of moving a blank to the first character of PRNTLINE.

CLI   D(B),byte   *(Compare Logical Immediate)*

Execution of this instruction effects a comparison of the immediate byte with the byte at the address D(B). The condition code is set to reflect the outcome of this comparison. In the comparison, both operands are treated as unsigned binary numbers (i.e., $X'00'$ is the lowest value, and $X'FF'$ is the highest possible value). Such a comparison is called a *logical compare*. The condition code is set as follows:

CC	Meaning
0	The operands are equal.
1	The first operand is low.
2	The first operand is high.
3	—

As an illustration of the use of these two instructions, consider the following section of code:

```
               LA    R4,CARD        LOAD THE ADDRESS OF A CARD
*                                   WHICH HAS BEEN READ
               LA    R2,1           R2 IS THE INCREMENT REGISTER
*                                   FOR BXLE
               LA    R3,CARD+79     END MARKER FOR THE BXLE
*
SCAN           CLI   0(R4),C' '     LOOK FOR BLANKS
               BNE   BUMPINDX       REPLACE ONLY BLANKS
               MVI   0(R4),C'0'     REPLACE BLANKS WITH ZEROS
BUMPINDX       BXLE  R4,R2,SCAN
```

This section of code simply has the effect of replacing every occurrence of a blank in CARD with a 0.

4.4 MVC AND CLC: THE SS COUNTERPARTS OF MVI AND CLI

In this section, another instruction format, the SS format, is introduced. The SS format is used to encode instructions involving two operands that are both fields in storage. The two SS instructions discussed here, MVC and CLC, are the SS counterparts of the MVI and CLI instructions discussed in Section 4.3.

There are two forms of the SS format. One is used when the operands are assumed to be of the same length, and the other is used when the two operands differ in length. For the purpose of this discussion, only the first form is introduced. This symbolic form of the SS format is

> label   mnemonic   D1(L,B1),D2(B2)

where   D1(B1) is the address of the first operand
        D2(B2) is the address of the second operand
        L   is the length of each operand

The corresponding encoded format has the form

> $h_0 h_0 h_L h_L$ $h_{B1} h_{D1} h_{D1} h_{D1}$ $h_{B2} h_{D2} h_{D2} h_{D2}$

where $h_0 h_0$ is the op code
        $h_L h_L$ is the length less one
        $h_{B1} h_{D1} h_{D1} h_{D1}$ specifies the address of the first operand
        $h_{B2} h_{D2} h_{D2} h_{D2}$ specifies the address of the second operand

Note that the length specification in the encoded format is one less than the actual length of the operands. This encoded length is referred to as the *length code*. Since the length code is one less than the length of the operands, lengths from 1 to 256 may be specified. This is an important point to remember when working with SS instructions.

As a specific example, the SS instruction

> MVC   14(8,R12),0(R1)

generates

$$\overset{L-1}{D2\overset{\frown}{07}} \quad C00E \quad 1000$$

Implicit addresses may be used with the SS instructions. Here, as in the case of RS and SI instructions, no index register can be specified in the implicit address. When an implicit address is used to specify the first operand, the length is specified by enclosing it within parentheses immediately following the implicit address. This is a possible source of confusion. For example, the instruction

MVC   FIELD1(15),FIELD2

specifies that the length of the operands is 15 and the address of the first operand is FIELD1 (not FIELD1 offset by the contents of R15).

It is permissible to specify a length of 0 in an SS instruction. If this is done, the length code generated is 00. Thus, a length specification of 0 causes the same code to be generated as does a length specification of 1. The conditions under which it might be desirable to specify a length of 0 are covered in Section 8.6.

A length attribute is associated with each label in a program. If no length is specified in an SS instruction, the length attribute of the label used to specify the first operand is taken to be the length by default. For example, if the statements

MVC   FWORD,0(R2)

.

.

.

FWORD   DS   F

are used in a program, the code generated by the MVC statement would indicate a length of 4. The rules governing which length attributes are assigned to various fields are covered in Section 8.1. Until you are familiar with these rules, a length should be explicitly assigned for each occurrence of an SS instruction.

Execution of the instruction

MVC   D1(L,B1),D2(B2)   *(Move Character)*

has the effect of replacing the contents of the L bytes beginning at D1(B1) with a copy of the contents of the L bytes beginning at D2(B2). The contents of these bytes are altered one at a time, starting from the left. This fact is unimportant if the fields do not overlap, but it is extremely important when the fields do overlap. The condition code is not altered by execution of the instruction.

The MVC is an extremely useful instruction. The following examples illustrate two of its most common uses.

It is common practice for a program to utilize a single storage area for the accumulation of information to be printed. During different phases of the execution of the program a variety of types of information may occupy such an area. This is most often accomplished by moving various fields into this area through the use of MVC statements. For example, execution of the statements

```
MVC     PRNTLINE(13), = C'0THE TOTAL IS'
XDECO   R2,PRNTLINE + 13
XPRNT   PRNTLINE,25
```

causes the total from R2 to be printed, preceded by an appropriate character string.

The contents of a storage area may be altered so that each byte represents a blank. This is done by a single MVC instruction such as

```
MVC     PLINE, = CL133' '
```

Execution of this instruction, however, requires the generation of 133 bytes of blanks. A truly elegant method of accomplishing the same result involves the use of an MVC instruction with overlapping operands. This method is illustrated by the two following instructions:

```
MVI     PLINE,C' '
MVC     PLINE + 1(132),PLINE
```

Execution of the MVI instruction alters the contents of the first byte of PLINE to 40 (a blank). Figure 4-1 depicts the sequence of actions effected by execution of the MVC instruction.

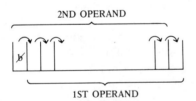

Figure 4-1

This process may be described as follows:

1. A copy of the first byte of the second operand is moved to the first byte of the first operand. That is, a copy of the blank in PLINE + 0 is moved to PLINE + 1.
2. A copy of the second byte of the second operand, PLINE + 1 (now a blank), is moved to the second byte of the first operand, PLINE + 2.
3. The process continues, with one byte being moved at a time, until PLINE contains only blanks.

This is a standard technique for blanking out a print line; you should become familiar with it.

Execution of the instruction

$$\text{CLC} \qquad \text{D1(L,B1),D2(B2).} \qquad (Compare\ Logical)$$

causes a logical comparison of the two operands to be made. (Recall that, in a logical comparison, both operands are treated as unsigned binary numbers.) Based on the result of this comparison, the condition code is set, with the following interpretation:

CC	Meaning
0	The operands are equal.
1	The first operand is low.
2	The first operand is high.
3	—

4.5 REFERENCING THE LOCATION COUNTER

At this point the reader is, of course, well aware that the general function of an assembler is the conversion of source statements into executable form. This process involves, among other things, a determination of the relative address of all instructions, constants, storage areas, and literals. These relative addresses are calculated by controlling the value of a location counter—an integral part of the assembler.

Before the processing of the set of source statements in any given assembly begins, the value in the location counter is initialized to 0. Then, after each successive instruction is processed, the value in the location counter is incremented by the length of the object code generated by that instruction. The value that the location counter contained when an instruction was encountered is displayed to the left of each instruction in the listing produced by the assembler. The location counter would be of little interest to the programmer if a facility did not exist for referencing the value of the location counter.

To reference the value of the location counter within a source code instruction, an asterisk is used. The value assigned to the asterisk in a given instruction will be the value that the location counter contained when the instruction was being assembled. Thus, the statements

```
          B        *+8
          L        R1,0(R2)
```

are equivalent to

```
          B        PASTLOAD
          L        R1,0(R2)
PASTLOAD  DS       0H
```

since $*+8$ is interpreted as the value of the location counter before generation of the branch instruction, incremented by 8. The use of

```
PASTLOAD        DS        0H
```

just establishes a position in the code. It does not generate any object code. Exactly why this works will be clarified in Chapter 8. Similarly, the instructions

```
                CLI       0(R1),C' '
                BE        *+12
                LA        R1,1(R1)
                B         *-12
```

are equivalent to

```
LOOP            CLI       0(R1),C' '
                BE        HIT
                LA        R1,1(R1)
                B         LOOP
HIT             DS        0H
```

The principal advantage of using references to the location counter is to avoid cluttering a listing with unnecessary labels. The use of such references can, however, lead to errors if instructions are later added to the program. For example, the instructions

```
                CLI       0(R1),C' '
                BE        *+12
                LA        R1,1(R1)
                LA        R2,1(R2)
                B         *-12
```

are definitely not equivalent to

```
LOOP            CLI       0(R1),C' '
                BE        HIT
                LA        R1,1(R1)
                LA        R2,1(R2)
                B         LOOP
HIT             DS        0H
```

To avoid such errors, extreme caution should be exercised whenever references to the location counter are made and programs containing such references are altered. A good rule-of-thumb limit is $*+12$ or $*-12$.

4.6 USES OF THE ORG INSTRUCTION

An ORG instruction actually alters the value in the location counter. The format for this instruction is

ORG   [address]

The brackets are used to indicate that the operand is optional. If the operand is specified, the value in the location counter is reset to the value associated with this address. If the operand is not specified, the value in the location counter is set to the address of the first available location in the CSECT that contains the ORG instruction. For example, the code

```
HDR1        DC    C'1'                CARRIAGE CONTROL
            DC    CL38' '             WE'LL ORG IN THE CONSTANTS
            ORG   HDR1 + 15
            DC    C'CLASS LIST FOR'
HDRDEPT     DS    CL4                 PUT DEPT HERE
            DC    C' '
HDRCOURS    DS    CL4                 PUT COURSE HERE
            ORG
```

may be used to define a particular set of column headers. Note that the ORG instruction is used to position a constant as well as the areas for the department and course codes. This technique is especially useful, because changing the spacing of the headers requires only that the ORG statements be changed.

The following example illustrates how the ORG instruction may be used to assign several alternative labels to the same area in storage:

```
CARD        DS    CL80
            ORG   CARD
SOCSEC#     DS    CL9
NAME        DS    CL20
SAMPLE#     DS    CL4
SEX         DS    CL1
HAIR        DS    CL2
EYES        DS    CL2
            ORG   CARD
SAMPLE      DS    CL9
#MALES      DS    CL4
#FEMALES    DS    CL4
            ORG
```

In this case, three alternative definitions of a single 80-byte area are specified. Thus, NAME and #MALES refer to exactly the same storage locations. In each case, the field being referenced is located at CARD + 9.

The program presented in Figure 4-2 and Program 4-2 illustrates the use of the instructions presented in this chapter. The purpose of this program is to produce a "class list" for each of the classes taught in a given school. The input to the program is assumed to be a set of cards punched to conform to the format on page 129.

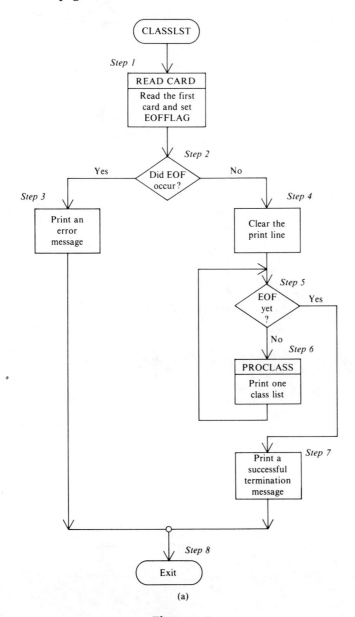

(a)

Figure 4-2

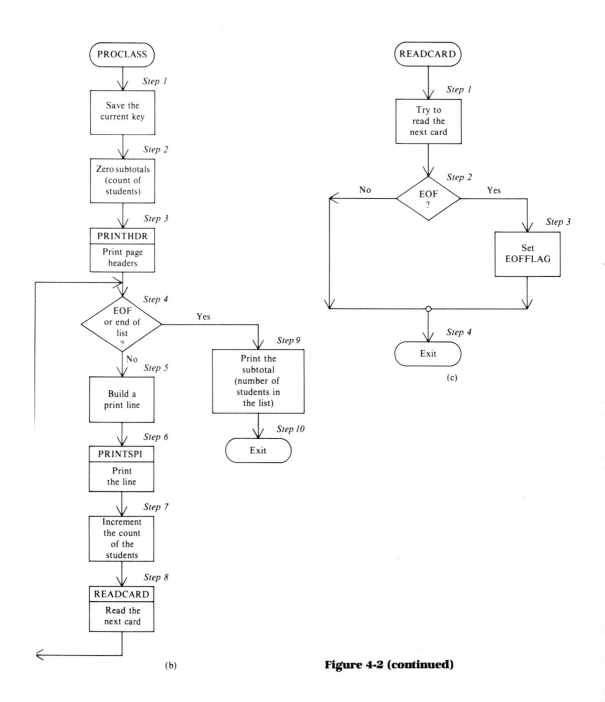

(b)

(c)

Figure 4-2 (continued)

Card Column	Contents
1–4	Department offering the course
5–8	Course number
9–18	Last name of student
19–28	First name of student
29–80	Unused

It is further assumed that this card file has been sorted in ascending order, based on the first 28 columns of the cards. The program produces a class list for each class, including the total number of students registered in the class.

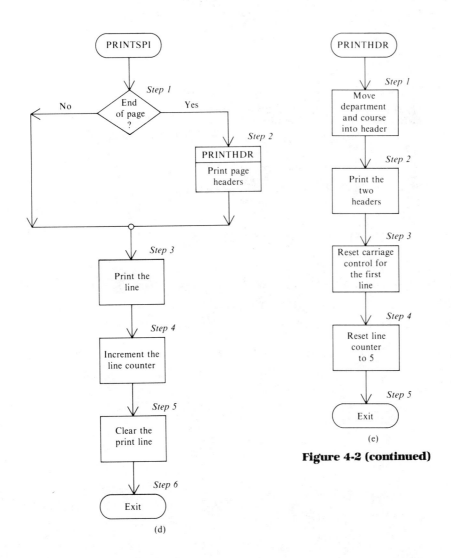

Figure 4-2 (continued)

Program 4-2

```
            TITLE 'A PROGRAM TO PRODUCE CLASS LISTS'
***********************************************************************
*
* THE FOLLOWING PROGRAM CAN BE USED TO PRODUCE CLASS LISTS.  AS
* INPUT THE PROGRAM ACCEPTS CARDS PUNCHED ACCORDING TO THE FOLLOWING
* FORMAT:
*
*       1 - 4    DEPARTMENT OFFERING THE COURSE
*       5 - 8    COURSE NUMBER
*       9 - 18   LAST NAME
*      19 - 28   FIRST NAME OF THE STUDENT
*      29 - 80   UNUSED
*
* IT IS ASSUMED THAT THE CARDS HAVE BEEN SORTED INTO ASCENDING ORDER
* BASED ON THE FIRST 28 COLUMNS.  THE PROGRAM PRODUCES A SEPARATE
* LIST (BEGINNING ON A NEW PAGE) FOR EACH CLASS.  EACH LIST IS
* TERMINATED WITH A LINE GIVING THE NUMBER OF STUDENTS ENROLLED IN
* THAT CLASS.  THE LOGIC OF THE PROGRAM IS AS FOLLOWS:
*
*        STEP 1. CALL READCARD TO READ THE FIRST CARD AND SET
*                EOFFLAG TO SHOW WHETHER OR NOT EOF OCCURRED.
*
*        STEP 2. IF EOF DID NOT OCCUR, GO TO STEP 4.
*
*        STEP 3. PRINT AN ERROR MESSAGE (NO INPUT).  GO TO STEP 8.
*
*        STEP 4. CLEAR THE PRINT LINE.  AFTER THIS THE LINE IS
*                CLEARED IMMEDIATELY AFTER EACH NEW LINE IS PRINTED.
*
*        STEP 5. IF EOF HAS OCCURRED (NO MORE LISTS TO PRINT), GO TO
*                STEP 7.
*
*        STEP 6.  CALL PROCLASS TO PRINT ONE CLASS LIST.
*
*        STEP 7. PRINT A "SUCCESSFUL TERMINATION" MESSAGE.
*
*        STEP 8. EXIT.
*
*
***********************************************************************
*
CLASSLST CSECT
         USING CLASSLST,R15
*
***<STEP 1>     READ THE FIRST CARD AND SET EOFFLAG
*
         BAL   R11,READCARD       READ THE 1ST CARD
*
***<STEP 2>     IF THERE INPUT, GO TO STEP 4 TO PRINT THE LISTS.
*
         CLI   EOFFLAG,C'Y'
         BNE   CLEARLN            BRANCH IF EOF WAS NOT DETECTED
*
***<STEP 3>     PRINT A "NO INPUT" ERROR MESSAGE AND EXIT
*
         XPRNT =C'1*** NO INPUT ***',17
         B     EXIT
```

Program 4-2 (continued)

```
*
***<STEP 3>    CLEAR THE PRINT LINE TO ALL BLANKS
*
CLEARLN MVI    PRNTLINE,C' '      CLEAR THE PRINT LINE
        MVC    PRNTLINE+1(132),PRNTLINE
*
***<STEP 4>    CALL PROCLASS REPEATEDLY UNTIL EOF OCCURS
*
PROCLOOP CLI   EOFFLAG,C'Y'       CONTINUE LOOPING UNTIL EOF
        BE     PRINTEND
*
        BAL    R11,PROCLASS       PRINT 1 CLASS LIST
*
        B      PROCLOOP
*
***<STEP 5>    PRINT "SUCCESSFUL TERMINATION" MESSAGE
*
PRINTEND XPRNT =C'1*** SUCCESSFUL TERMINATION ***',31
*
***<STEP 6>    LEAVE THE PROGRAM
*
EXIT    BR     R14                LEAVE THE PROGRAM
*
*********************************************************************
*
* THE READCARD ROUTINE ATTEMPTS TO READ A CARD.  IF END-OF-FILE
* OCCURS, EOFFLAG WILL BE SET TO 'Y' (IT IS INITIALIZED TO 'N',
* SO IT WILL REMAIN 'N' UNTIL EOF OCCURS).
*
*        STEP 1. TRY TO READ THE NEXT CARD.
*
*        STEP 2. IF EOF OCURRED, SET EOFFLAG TO 'Y' (IT IS ASSUMED
*                THAT EOFFLAG WAS INITIALIZED TO 'N').
*
*        STEP 3. RETURN TO CALLER.
*
*********************************************************************
*
READCARD STM   R0,R15,READSAVE    SAVE CALLER'S REGISTERS
*
***<STEP 1>    TRY TO READ THE NEXT CARD.
*
        XREAD  CARD,80            TRY TO READ THE NEXT CARD
*
***<STEP 2>    IF EOF OCCURRED, SET EOFFLAG TO 'Y'
*
        BC     B'1011',READEXIT   BRANCH IF NOT EOF
*
        MVI    EOFFLAG,C'Y'       SET EOF INDICATOR
*
***<STEP 3>    RETURN TO CALLER
*
READEXIT LM    R0,R15,READSAVE    RESTORE CALLER'S REGISTERS
        BR     R11                RETURN TO CALLER
*
READSAVE DS    16F                REGISTER SAVE AREA
*
```

Program 4-2 (continued)

```
*************************************************************************
*
* PROCLASS PRODUCES 1 CLASS LIST.  WHEN IT COMPLETES, EITHER
* EOF HAS OCCURRED (EOFFLAG WILL BE Y) OR THE FIRST CARD FOR THE
* NEXT CLASS LIST HAS BEEN READ.  THE LOGIC IS AS FOLLOWS:
*
*        STEP 1. SAVE THE DEPT AND COURSE FROM THE CARD.  THESE TWO
*                FIELDS REPRESENT THE "CURRENT KEY" - THEY
*                IDENTIFY THE COURSE FOR WHICH THE CURRENT LIST IS
*                TO BE PRINTED.  THE CURRENT LIST WILL INCLUDE ALL
*                CARDS UP TO THE POINT WHERE A NEW KEY OCCURS.
*
*        STEP 2. SET THE COUNT OF STUDENTS IN THE LIST TO 0.
*
*        STEP 3. CALL PRINTHDR TO PRINT PAGE AND COLUMN HEADERS FOR
*                THE FIRST PAGE OF THE CLASS LIST
*
*        STEP 4. CHECK TO SEE IF EOF HAS OCCURRED, OR IF A CARD FOR
*                THE NEXT CLASS LIST HAS BEEN READ.  IF EITHER EVENT
*                HAS OCCURRED, IT'S TIME TO END THIS LIST (SO GO TO
*                STEP 9).
*
*        STEP 5. BUILD A PRINT LINE FROM THE DATA ON THE CARD.
*
*        STEP 6. CALL PRINTSP1 TO PRINT THE LINE (AND HEADERS, IF
*                NECESSARY).  THE PRINT LINE WILL BE CLEARED AFTER
*                THE LINE IS PRINTED.
*
*        STEP 7. ADD 1 TO THE COUNT OF STUDENTS PRINTED IN THE LIST.
*
*        STEP 8. CALL READCARD TO TRY TO READ THE NEXT CARD.  THEN
*                GO BACK TO STEP 4 TO CHECK FOR END OF THE LOOP.
*
*        STEP 9. PRINT THE LAST LINE OF THE CLASS LIST, THE LINE
*                THAT GIVES THE TOTAL NUMBER OF STUDENTS IN THE CLASS.
*
*        STEP 10.RETURN TO CALLER.
*
*
*************************************************************************
PROCLASS STM   R0,R15,PRCLSAVE     SAVE CALLER'S REGISTERS
*
***<STEP 1>    SAVE KEY FOR THE CURRENT CLASS LIST
*
         MVC   CURRKEY,CARD        SAVE THE KEY (DEPT,COURSE)
*
***<STEP 2>    SET COUNT OF STUDENTS IN CLASS TO 0
*
         SR    R2,R2               SET COUNT OF STUDENTS IN THE
*                                  LIST TO 0
*
***<STEP 3>    PRINT THE HEADERS FOR THE FIRST PAGE OF THE LIST
*
         BAL   R11,PRINTHDR        PRINT THE PAGE HEADERS
*
***<STEP 4>    CHECK FOR END OF LIST (EOF OR NEXT KEY)
*
PROCCARD CLI   EOFFLAG,C'Y'        END LOOP ON EOF OR NEW KEY
         BE    PRINTTOT
         CLC   CURRKEY,CARD
         BNE   PRINTTOT            MISMATCH MEANS NEW KEY
*
***<STEP 5>    CONSTRUCT A PRINT LINE
*
         MVC   DEPTOUT,DEPTIN      NOW MOVE DATA FIELDS
         MVC   COURSOUT,COURSIN    THE PRINT LINE
         MVC   LNAMEOUT,LNAMEIN
         MVC   FNAMEOUT,FNAMEIN
*
```

Program 4-2 (continued)

```
***<STEP 6>     CALL PRINTSP1 TO PRINT THE LINE
*
        BAL     R11,PRINTSP1        PRINT THE LINE (AND HEADERS,
*                                   IF NECESSARY)
*
*
***<STEP 7>     ADD 1 TO COUNT OF STUDENTS IN THE LIST
*
        LA      R2,1(R2)            ADD 1 TO COUNT OF STUDENTS
*
***<STEP 8>     TRY TO READ THE NEXT CARD
*
        BAL     R11,READCARD        TRY TO READ THE NEXT CARD
*
        B       PROCCARD
*
***<STEP 9>     PRINT THE LAST LINE (TOTAL # STUDENTS) IN LIST
*
PRINTTOT XDECO  R2,PRNTLINE+25      PUT TOTAL INTO PRINT LINE
        MVC     PRNTLINE+7(18),=C'TOTAL # STUDENTS ='
        MVI     PRNTLINE,C'0'       SET CARRIAGE CONTROL FOR
*                                   DOUBLE-SPACE
        XPRNT   PRNTLINE,133        PRINT LAST LINE FOR LIST
        MVI     PRNTLINE,C' '       CLEAR THE PRINT LINE
        MVC     PRNTLINE+1(132),PRNTLINE
*
***<STEP 10>    RETURN TO CALLER
*
        LM      R0,R15,PRCLSAVE     RESTORE CALLER'S REGISTERS
        BR      R11
*
PRCLSAVE DS     16F                 REGISTER SAVE AREA
*
*******************************************************************
*
*
* THE PRINTHDR ROUTINE PRINTS PAGE AND COLUMN HEADERS AND THEN RESETS
* THE LINECTR TO 5 (THE NEXT LINE IS LINE 5 OF THE PAGE).
*
*       STEP 1.   PUT DEPT AND COURSE INTO HEADER LINE
*
*       STEP 2.   PRINT THE TWO HEADER LINES.
*
*       STEP 3.   RESET THE CARRIAGE CONTROL TO DOUBLE-SPACE FOR THE
*                 FIRST LINE OF THE PAGE.
*
*       STEP 4.   RESET THE LINE COUNTER TO 5 (THE FIFTH LINE OF THE
*                 PAGE IS THE "NEXT LINE").
*
*       STEP 5.   RETURN TO CALLER.
*
*******************************************************************
*
PRINTHDR STM    R0,R15,HDRSAVE      SAVE THE CALLER'S REGISTERS
*
***<STEP 1>     MOVE DEPT AND COURSE INTO PAGE HEADER
*
        MVC     HDRDEPT,CURRKEY     TAKE DEPT AND COURSE
        MVC     HDRCOURS,CURRKEY+4     FROM CURRKEY
*
***<STEP 2>     PRINT THE PAGE AND COLUMN HEADERS
*
        XPRNT   HDR1,39
        XPRNT   HDR2,43
*
***<STEP 3>     SET CARRIAGE CONTROL FOR FIRST LINE OF PAGE
*
        MVI     PRNTLINE,C'0'       SET CC FOR DOUBLE-SPACE
*
***<STEP 4>     RESET LINE COUNTER TO 5 (NEXT LINE IS 5TH OF PAGE)
*
```

Program 4-2 (continued)

```
         MVC    LINECTR,=F'5'        SET LINE COUNTER TO 5
*
***<STEP 5>    RETURN TO CALLER
*
         LM     R0,R15,HDRSAVE       RESTORE CALLER'S REGISTERS
         BR     R11                  RETURN TO CALLER
*
HDRSAVE  DS     16F                  REGISTER SAVE AREA
*
*
HDR1     DC     C'1'                 CARRIAGE CONTROL
         DC     CL38' '              WE'LL ORG IN THE CONSTANTS
         ORG    HDR1+15
         DC     C'CLASS LIST FOR '
HDRDEPT  DS     CL4                  PUT DEPT HERE
         DC     C' '
HDRCOURS DS     CL4                  PUT COURSE HERE
         ORG
*
*
HDR2     DC     C'0'                 CARRIAGE CONTROL
         DC     CL42' '              AGAIN, WE'LL ORG IN THE VALUES
         ORG    HDR2+4
         DC     C'DEPT'
         ORG    HDR2+9
         DC     C'COURSE'
         ORG    HDR2+19
         DC     C'LAST NAME'
         ORG    HDR2+33
         DC     C'FIRST NAME'
         ORG
*
*******************************************************************
*
*
* PRINTSP1 IS CALLED TO PRINT A LINE AFTER SINGLE-SPACING.  IF THE
* LINE WOULD OCCUR AFTER LINE 50 ON THE PAGE, HEADERS ARE PRINTED
* FIRST (AND THE FIRST LINE AFTER THE HEADER GETS DOUBLE-SPACED).
*
*         STEP 1.  IF THE LINE COUNTER SHOWS THE CURRENT LINE TO BE
*                  LESS THAN OR EQUAL TO FIFTY, GO TO STEP 3.
*
*         STEP 2.  CALL PRINTHDR TO ADVANCE TO THE NEXT PAGE, PRINTING
*                  PAGE AND COLUMN HEADERS.
*
*         STEP 3.  PRINT THE LINE.
*
*         STEP 4.  INCREMENT THE LINE COUNTER BY 1.
*
*         STEP 5.  CLEAR THE PRINT LINE.
*
*         STEP 6.  RETURN TO CALLER.
*
*******************************************************************
*
PRINTSP1 STM    R0,R15,PRSPSAVE      SAVE CALLER'S REGISTERS
*
***<STEP 1>    CHECK TO SEE IF IT'S TIME FOR A NEW PAGE
*
         CLC    LINECTR,=F'50'
         BNH    NOWPRINT             BRANCH IF HEADERS AREN'T
*                                    NECESSARY
*
***<STEP 2>    CALL PRINTHDR TO PRINT HEADERS ON THE NEXT PAGE
*
         BAL    R11,PRINTHDR         PRINT HEADERS
*
***<STEP 3>    PRINT THE LINE
*
NOWPRINT XPRNT  PRNTLINE,133         PRINT THE LINE
```

Program 4-2 (continued)

```
*
***<STEP 4>      INCREMENT THE LINE COUNTER
*
        L       R3,LINECTR          INCREMENT THE LINECTR
        LA      R3,1(R3)
        ST      R3,LINECTR
*
***<STEP 5>      CLEAR THE PRINT LINE
*
        MVI     PRNTLINE,C' '       CLEAR THE PRINT LINE
        MVC     PRNTLINE+1(132),PRNTLINE
*
***<STEP 6>      RETURN TO CALLER
*
        LM      R0,R15,PRSPSAVE     RESTORE CALLER'S REGISTERS
        BR      R11
*
PRSPSAVE DS     16F                 REGISTER SAVE AREA
*
***********************************************************************
*
CURRKEY DS      CL8                 CURRENT DEPT AND COURSE
*
CARD    DS      0CL80               CURRENT CARD
DEPTIN  DS      CL4                 DEPT OFFERING THE COURSE
COURSIN DS      CL4                 COURSE #
LNAMEIN DS      CL10                LAST NAME OF STUDENT
FNAMEIN DS      CL10                FIRST NAME OF STUDENT
        DS      CL52
*
*
EOFFLAG DC      C'N'                EOF INDICATOR (Y MEANS EOF)
*
LINECTR DS      F                   LINE COUNTER (CURRENT LINE ON PAGE)
*
PRNTLINE DS     CL133               THE PRINT LINE
        ORG     PRNTLINE+4          WE ORG TO COLUMNS
DEPTOUT DS      CL4                 DEPT OFFERING THE COURSE
        ORG     PRNTLINE+10
COURSOUT DS     CL4                 COURSE #
        ORG     PRNTLINE+19
LNAMEOUT DS     CL10                STUDENT'S LAST NAME
        ORG     PRNTLINE+33
FNAMEOUT DS     CL10                STUDENT'S FIRST NAME
        ORG
*
        LTORG
R0      EQU     0
R1      EQU     1
R2      EQU     2
R3      EQU     3
R4      EQU     4
R5      EQU     5
R6      EQU     6
R7      EQU     7
R8      EQU     8
R9      EQU     9
R10     EQU     10
R11     EQU     11
R12     EQU     12
R13     EQU     13
R14     EQU     14
R15     EQU     15
*
        END     CLASSLST
```

Particular attention should be given to the following sequence of statements from Program 4-2:

```
CARD      DS  0CL80   CURRENT CARD
DEPTIN    DS  CL4     DEPT OFFERING THE COURSE
COURSIN   DS  CL4     COURSE #
LNAMEIN   DS  CL10    LAST NAME OF STUDENT
FNAMEIN   DS  CL10    FIRST NAME OF STUDENT
          DS  CL52
```

The statement defining CARD reserves no storage, since the duplication factor is 0. The purpose of this statement is to signify that the next 80 bytes together give a more detailed description of the single field CARD. This technique is also used for reserving storage for the print line. In both cases, the advantage gained is the ability to reference subfields by meaningful labels. For example, CARD+8 and LNAMEIN refer to exactly the same address.

4.7 LOGICAL ARITHMETIC AND COMPARISON INSTRUCTIONS

To understand the significance of the instructions that will be introduced in this section, it is necessary first to understand exactly how addition and subtraction are executed on a computer. To illustrate the procedures involved, it will be helpful to consider specific examples. In these examples, four-bit instead of 32-bit signed binary integers will be used. The motivation for this simplication will be obvious if the reader takes the time to try the algorithms on 32-bit integers.

To add two signed binary integers, one can proceed as follows:

1. Set the carry digit for the rightmost position to 0.

2. Starting from the rightmost digits, add the two corresponding digits and the carry digit to determine which digit is assigned to the result. If a 0 or a 1 results from the addition, this becomes the corresponding bit in the result, and the carry digit for the next position to the left is set to 0. If a 10 or an 11 results from the addition, a 0 or a 1 is written as the corresponding digit of the result, and the next carry digit is set to 1.

3. The carry digit resulting from the addition performed on the leftmost bits does not alter the result. However, if it differs from the digit carried into the leftmost position, overflow is recognized.

Thus, to add 1011 and 0010, the following steps are executed:

$$
\begin{array}{rl}
\text{carry} & 0010 \\
 & 1011 \\
+ & 0010 \\
\hline
\text{result} & 1101
\end{array}
$$

In this case, 2 was added to -5, giving -3. Since the two leftmost carry digits agree, no overflow occurred.

The following examples illustrate the process more completely:

overflow	yes	no	yes	no
carry	1000	1111	0110	0001
	1111	1101	0111	0101
	1000	1111	0010	0001
result	0111	1100	1001	0110

Subtraction can be explained quite easily in terms of addition. To subtract a number n from a number m, add $-n$ to m. To understand this process, the reader must be completely familiar with the method of representing negative numbers introduced in Section 1.5. For example, to subtract 1101 from 0010:

- Convert 1101 to its complement, 0011.
- Add 0010 and 0011, giving 0101.

If overflow occurs when $-n$ and m are added together, then overflow for the subtraction is recognized.

Now the AL, ALR, SL, SLR, CL, and CLR instructions can be discussed. Each of these instructions has a counterpart among the instructions that have already been covered. This correspondence is presented in the following list:

Instruction	*Format*	
Add	A	r,D(X,B)
Add Logical	AL	r,D(X,B)
Add Register	AR	r1,r2
Add Logical Register	ALR	r1,r2
Subtract	S	r,D(X,B)
Subtract Logical	SL	r,D(X,B)
Subtract Register	SR	r1,r2
Subtract Logical Register	SLR	r1,r2
Compare	C	r,D(X,B)
Compare Logical	CL	r,D(X,B)
Compare Register	CR	r1,r2
Compare Logical Register	CLR	r1,r2

The only differences between the AL and ALR instructions and their counterparts are:

* If overflow occurs as a result of the execution of an AL or an ALR instruction, the overflow does not cause termination of the program.
* The condition code is set as follows:

CC	Meaning
0	The result is 0 and the leftmost carry digit was 0.
1	The result is not 0 and the leftmost carry digit was 0.
2	The result is 0 and the leftmost carry digit was 1.
3	The result is not 0 and the leftmost carry digit was 1.

The only differences between the SL and SLR instructions and their counterparts are:

* Just as for AL and ALR, overflow is ignored.
* The condition code is set as follows:

CC	Meaning
0	—
1	The result is not 0 and the leftmost carry digit was 0.
2	The result is 0.
3	The result is not 0 and the leftmost carry digit was 1.

The CL and CLR instructions perform exactly like C and CR, except that the operands are treated as 32-bit unsigned integers.

Although the logical arithmetic and comparison instructions are used occasionally when no indication of overflow is desired, their main use is in the construction of extended-precision operations. That is, one can build routines to add, subtract, or compare arbitrarily large integers using these instructions. As an example, routines to add, subtract and compare 64-bit signed integers are presented in Program 4-3. Note that similar routines could be contructed to manipulate integers of any size.

Program 4-3

```
* THE FOLLOWING ROUTINE ADDS THE DOUBLEWORD POINTED TO BY R3 TO
* THE DOUBLEWORD POINTED TO BY R4.  R10 IS USED AS THE LINK REGISTER.
*
ADDRT     LM    R0,R1,0(R3)         LOAD OPERAND1
          AL    R1,4(R4)            ADD RIGHT WORDS
          BC    B'1100',ADDLEFT     BRANCH IF NO CARRY RESULTED
          A     R0,=F'1'            ADD 1 IF CARRY OCCURRED
*
ADDLEFT   A     R0,0(R4)            ADD LEFT WORDS
          STM   R0,R1,0(R3)         STORE RESULT INTO OPERAND1
          BR    R10
```

Program 4-3 (continued)

```
* THIS ROUTINE CALCULATES THE DIFFERENCE OF THE TWO DOUBLEWORDS
* POINTED TO BY R3 AND R4.  THE RESULT IS STORED INTO THE FIRST
* OPERAND.  R10 IS ASSUMED TO CONTAIN THE EXIT ADDRESS.
*
SUBRT     LM     R0,R1,0(R3)         LOAD THE FIRST OPERAND
          SL     R1,4(R4)            SUBTRACT RIGHT WORD
          BC     B'0011',SUBLEFT     BRANCH IF CARRY OCCURRED
          BCTR   R0,0
SUBLEFT   S      R0,0(R4)            SUBTRACT LEFT WORDS
          STM    R0,R1,0(R3)         STORE BACK INTO OPERAND 1
          BR     R10


* THE FOLLOWING ROUTINE COMPARES TWO 64-BIT SIGNED INTEGERS
* WHICH ARE POINTED TO BY R3 AND R4.  R10 IS ASSUMED TO CONTAIN
* THE EXIT ADDRESS.
*
COMPRT    LM     R0,R1,0(R3)         LOAD FIRST OPERAND
          C      R0,0(R4)            COMPARE LEFT WORDS
          BCR    B'0110',R10         EXIT IF THEY AREN'T EQUAL
          CL     R1,4(R4)            ELSE, USE RIGHT WORDS
          BR     R10
```

Exercises

1. Write a program to read in two lists of words and then merge them into one list. Each list will contain at most 50 English words in alphabetical order, and each word will consist of at most eight letters. The words should be read off cards conforming to the following specifications:

a. There will be two sets of cards, one for each list. (The cards for the second list immediately follow the cards for the first list.)
b. Each card in a set, except perhaps the last card, will contain exactly five words, starting in columns 10, 20, 30, 40, and 50.
c. The last card in a set can contain one to five words.
d. A $ immediately follows the last word in a set (i.e., in either column 18, 28, 38, 48, or 58).

Your program should contain three subroutines—one to read in a set of cards and build a table of words, one to display the entries in a table of words, and one to merge two tables into a third table.

The actual steps in the program should be as follows:

Step 1. Read in the first list.
Step 2. Display the first list.
Step 3. Read in the second list.
Step 4. Display the second list.
Step 5. Merge the two lists.
Step 6. Display the merged lists.

Assume that neither of the first two lists contains duplicate entries. If a word were to occur in both of the two input lists, your program should insert only one copy of the word into the merged table.

2. Write a program to perform the following tasks:

a. Read in a set of cards, each of which will contain from zero to six English words. Each word will contain up to 10 characters and will begin in either column 1, 11, 21, 31, 41, or 51. Thus, each card will contain six 10-character fields. Any field containing a blank in the leftmost position can be ignored. Store the words into a table.

b. Display the contents of the constructed table.

c. Sort the words in the table into alphabetical order.

d. Display the contents of the sorted table.

To sort the table, use an algorithm similar to the one discussed in Exercise 4 at the end of Section 3.6. In that case, however, entries in a table were to be sorted into descending order. To sort a table into ascending order, the following technique can be used:

Step 1. Find the "smallest" entry in the table (i.e., the word that should appear first).

Step 2. Swap the first entry in the table with the smallest entry.

Step 3. If more than one entry remains in the unsorted section of the table, repeat the procedure for that section of the table.

For example, if

| ZOO | MOUSE | CAT | APPLE |

were to be sorted, the following events would occur:

• Since APPLE should appear at the head of the list, APPLE and ZOO are swapped, giving

| APPLE | MOUSE | CAT | ZOO |

The unsorted section of the table is then composed of all words to the right of APPLE. Since three entries remain, more exchanges are necessary.

• Since CAT should appear at the head of the remainder of the list (i.e., the right three words), CAT and MOUSE are swapped, giving

| APPLE | CAT | MOUSE | ZOO |

• Since MOUSE should appear at the head of the remainder of the list, it is swapped with itself (which leaves the table unaltered). Since only one word remains to the right of MOUSE, the process has been completed.

3. This exercise is similar to the preceding exercise, except that a sort algorithm similar to the one discussed in Exercise 5 at the end of Section 3.6 should be used to sort the table. This algorithm can be described briefly as follows:

For each element in the table except the leftmost, starting from the left, repeat the following operation as often as possible: *If the element to the left of the given element should appear to the right of the given element, swap the two elements.*

For example, to sort

      ZOO   MOUSE   CAT   APPLE

using this algorithm, the following events would occur:

- Since ZOO should occur to the right of MOUSE, the two words are swapped, giving

      MOUSE   ZOO   CAT   APPLE

- Two swaps are then required for CAT, which gives

      CAT   MOUSE   ZOO   APPLE

- Since all three words to the left of APPLE should occur to the right of APPLE, three swaps occur, leaving

      APPLE   CAT   MOUSE   ZOO

4. Suppose that all of the students in a class have punched personal information cards in the following format:

Columns	Contents
1–20	Student's name
21	A code giving the student's standing: 1—freshman 2—sophomore 3—junior 4—senior
22–25	Student's major
26	If a nonblank value occurs here, the student is auditing the class.

Write a program to read the cards and produce the following report:

CLASS REPORT

FRESHMEN		SOPHOMORES		JUNIORS		SENIORS	
NAME	MAJOR	NAME	MAJOR	NAME	MAJOR	NAME	MAJOR
JOHN DORN	ENGL						
		ELIZABETH DOE	PSYC				
				MARY CALLEY	MATH		
.		.		.		.	
.		.		.		.	
.		.		.		.	

The following should be noted on the report:

a. One student name is printed per line under the appropriate column (given by his or her standing).
b. If a student is auditing the course, an asterisk should be printed immediately to the left of his or her name.
c. Information about 50 students should be printed on each page. Headers should appear on each page. Thus, if there were 80 students, two pages would be printed; both pages would contain page headers.

You may find it convenient to use a subroutine to print a line. The subroutine would use a variable LINECNT initially containing 51, and utilize the following logic:

Step 1. If LINECNT is less than or equal to 50, go to Step 3.
Step 2. Print page headers. Set LINECNT to 1. Print the line of the report, using a carriage control of 0 to cause double-spacing. Exit.
Step 3. Print the line of the report, using a blank as the carriage control character. Add 1 to LINECNT. Exit.

5. Many stores prepare invoices for their sales. Such an invoice might appear as follows:

Item	# Units	Cost/Unit	Cost
0421	2	1.14	2.28
3841	1	14.00	14.00

Total $= 16.28$

Suppose that a store wished to have a computer verify the calculations on each invoice. Write such a program. The program should accept cards conforming to the following specifications:

a. There will be a set of cards for each invoice. This set will be composed of one card for each "line item" and one card containing the total.
b. All of the line item cards for an invoice will occur before the total card and will conform to the following format:

Columns	Contents
1	1
2–5	Item number
6–8	Number of units
10–15	Cost per unit
17–23	Cost

c. The total card for an invoice will follow the item cards and will conform to the following format:

Columns	Contents
1	2
2–10	Total cost

For each invoice, print the following:

LINE ITEMS	1421	4	100	400
	2981	2	109	216*
	0410	1	19100	19100
			TOTAL =	19716

If any field in a line item card contains only blanks or if the cost is incorrect, an asterisk should be printed to the right of the cost. Similarly, if the total is not accurate, print an asterisk to the right of it.

6. Write a program to perform the following tasks:

a. Read in a sequence of cards, each of which will contain from zero to six English words of up to 10 characters in length. The words can begin in columns 1, 11, 21, 31, 41, or 51. Thus, each card will contain six 10-character fields. If the left character of a field is a blank, the field should be ignored. Construct a table from the words on the cards. When a card containing END in columns 1–3 is read, all the cards containing words to be put into the first table have been processed.
b. Display the contents of the table.
c. Read in a second sequence of cards and construct a second table.
d. Display the second table.
e. Build a third table containing only those values that occur in both of the tables previously constructed.
f. Display the contents of the third table.

Assume that neither of the two original tables will contain more than 30 words and that neither table contains duplicate entries.

7. This exercise is identical to the preceding exercise except that you may assume that the words in each of the two original tables occur in alphabetical order. See the discussion in Exercise 3 at the end of Section 3.6 for an algorithm to extract the appropriate words efficiently.

8. Write a program to print names and addresses "four up." The program should read cards, each containing a single name and address. Each line of the name and address is 15 characters in length. Each card will contain from three to five lines. (The last five columns on each card are ignored.) For example, the following are all valid data cards:

JOHN ANDERSON	1527 STATE ST.	MORGANTOWN	OHIO	
ROBIN BENNIT	P.O. BOX 156	KINROSS	MICHIGAN	
J. D. DORSCH	GODFREY LANE	JASPER, ILL.		
MARY LARSON	375 R.RT. 18	BAKER	ARKANSAS	
BOB SMITH	3155 FIRST ST	APT 3B	JACKSON	FLA

The program should print the data from four cards simultaneously, single-spacing between lines. The first line of each set of four should be double-spaced. Do not print any blank lines. (If all cards in a set have four or less lines, do not print a fifth line.) For this input, the following lines would be printed:

JOHN ANDERSON	ROBIN BENNIT	J. D. DORSCH
1527 STATE ST.	P.O. BOX 156	GODFREY LANE
MORGANTOWN	KINROSS	JASPER, ILL.
OHIO	MICHIGAN	

MARY LARSON	BOB SMITH
375 R.RT. 18	3155 FIRST ST
BAKER	APT 3B
ARKANSAS	JACKSON
	FLA

Your program should use at least the following subroutines:

- READSET reads a set of up to four cards into a designated area. It returns the number of cards read (which may be zero).
- PRINTSET prints a set of cards. It uses the routine FILLUP.
- FILLUP constructs one print line. It takes as input the array of cards and the line number (1 to 5).

5

Decimal Arithmetic

5.1 ZONED AND PACKED DECIMAL FORMATS

The decimal instruction set provides facilities for (1) performing arithmetic operations on integers represented in the familiar decimal system and (2) editing data (preparing data in readable form before printing). Two distinct formats, *zoned decimal* and *packed decimal*, are utilized for the representation of decimal numbers. The particular instruction used dictates which of these formats is required. Generally, the packed decimal format is required for arithmetic operations, while the zoned decimal format is utilized for input/output operations.

The decimal instruction set provides several advantages or conveniences over the binary instruction set in addition to the facility for performing operations on decimal numbers. All the decimal instructions are of the SS (storage to storage) type and allow operations to be performed on fields of varying lengths. This provides some added precision over binary arithmetic, since decimal numbers from one to 31 digits in length may be represented in the packed decimal format. Because the arithmetic operations are performed in storage, the operations generally require only a single instruction. For example, it requires only a single instruction to add two decimal fields in storage, but it would require an L, A, ST sequence to add the corresponding binary numbers. In addition, there is a convenient means for rounding decimal numbers, which some applications absolutely require.

In discussing either the zoned or packed decimal format, we will refer to the left hexadecimal digit of a byte as the *zone digit* and to the right digit as the *numeric digit*. A number may be represented in zoned decimal format according to the following rules:

- One decimal digit is represented per byte. The zone digit of all but the rightmost byte must be F. The numeric digit in each (including the rightmost byte) is the numeric digit represented by that byte.

- The zone digit of the rightmost byte is used to represent the sign of the number. A, C, E, and F are valid zone digits for the sign of a positive number; a zone digit of B or D in the rightmost byte represents a negative number.

As an example,

F1F2F3F4

is a zoned decimal representation of $+1234$, and

F1F2F3D4

is a representation of -1234.

Note that a zoned decimal representation of a number can differ from the character representation of that number only in the zone digit of the rightmost byte. Note also that the character representation of a positive number is a valid zoned decimal representation of that number. For example,

DC   C'012'

generates F0F1F2, which is a zoned decimal representation for $+012$.

Zoned decimal numbers can be generated by the use of Z-type DC statements. The general format for this statement is

label   DC   mZLn'p'

where   m   is a valid duplication factor
        Z   specifies zoned decimal
        Ln specifies a length
        p   is the decimal representation of the number to be generated

If m is omitted, a duplication factor of 1 is assumed. If Ln is omitted, the length of the field generated will equal the number of digits in p. If Ln specifies a length greater than the number of digits in p, zeros (F0) are added on the left. Optionally, p may contain a sign and a decimal point. If the sign is omitted, the number is assumed to be positive. A plus sign will generate a sign zone of C, and a minus sign will result in a sign zone of D. If a decimal point is included, there is no resulting effect on what is generated. The sole purpose of the decimal point is to remind anyone who may read the assembler listing that an assumed decimal point was intended.

The following list of examples should help to clarify these points:

Coded	*Generated*
DC 2Z'-1'	D1D1
DC Z'$+.2$'	C2
DC Z'2'	C2
DC ZL3'4'	F0F0C4
DC 2ZL2'$-.1$'	F0D1F0D1
DC Z'1.10'	F1F1C0

In contrast to zoned decimal representations of numbers, each byte of a packed decimal representation except the rightmost represents two decimal digits. A number n may be represented in packed decimal format by execution of the following steps:

1. Move the sign of n to the right of a decimal representation of n.
2. If n has an even number of digits, add a zero as the leftmost digit.
3. Pair the digits of n starting from the left. This leaves the rightmost digit and the sign as the rightmost pair.
4. Each pair represents a byte, with the digits represented by four bits each. The valid signs are the same as for zoned decimal representations.

As an example, -1234 may be represented in packed decimal format as follows:

1. Move the sign to the right, giving $1234-$.
2. Add a zero to the left, since there are an even number of digits. This gives $01234-$.
3. Pair the digits from the left, giving 01 23 4 $-$.
4. Encode each pair in a byte, using a valid sign. This gives 01234D or 01234B as a three-byte representation of -1234.

Packed decimal numbers may be generated by means of the P-type DC statement. The general format for this statement is

> label   DC   mPLn′p′

where   m   is a valid duplication factor
         P   specifies packed decimal
        Ln   specifies a length (in bytes)
        p   is a decimal representation of the number to be generated

If m is omitted, a duplication factor of 1 is assumed. If Ln is omitted, the smallest field in which the number can be represented is used. A decimal point may be used in p with the same result as in the Z-type constant. (The decimal point does not affect what is generated.) C is generated for a plus sign, and D is generated for a minus sign. These points are illustrated by the following list of examples.

Coded		Generated
DC	2P′ − 1′	1D1D
DC	P′ + .2′	2C
DC	P′2′	2C
DC	PL3′4′	00004C
DC	2PL2′ − .12′	012D012D

5.2 THE PACK AND UNPK INSTRUCTIONS

The instructions for converting numbers between zoned and packed decimal representations are SS instructions with two lengths specified. The general format for this type of instruction, called *SS decimal*, is

> label   mnemonic   D1(L1,B1),D2(L2,B2)

If implicit addressing is used, the following format applies:

> label   mnemonic   field1(L1),field2(L2)

The generated instruction is of the form

$$h_0 h_0 h_{L1} h_{L2} \qquad h_{B1} h_{D1} h_{D1} h_{D1} \qquad h_{B2} h_{D2} h_{D2} h_{D2}$$

where $h_0 h_0$ specifies the op code
        h_{L1} is the length code of the first operand
        h_{L2} is the length code of the second operand
        $h_{B1} h_{D1} h_{D1} h_{D1}$ specifies the address of the first operand
        $h_{B2} h_{D2} h_{D2} h_{D2}$ specifies the address of the second operand

Note that each length code occupies four bits. This, of course, means that 15 is the largest possible length code and 16 is the largest valid length of either operand. Thus, decimal numbers with from one to 16 digits may be represented in zoned decimal format, while decimal numbers with from one to 31 digits may be represented in packed decimal format. Another point worth noting is that if an implicit address with an unspecified length is utilized as either operand, the length attribute of the symbol will be used as an assumed length.

The instruction for converting a number from its zoned to its packed decimal representation is

$$\text{PACK} \qquad \text{D1(L1,B1),D2(L2,B2)} \qquad \qquad (Pack)$$

The address of the zoned decimal number to be converted is specified by the second operand, and the result is placed in the field whose address is specified by the first operand. Execution of this statement has the following effects:

- The rightmost byte of the second operand is placed in the rightmost byte of the first operand, with the zone and numeric digits reversed.

- The remaining numeric digits from the second operand are moved to the first operand, proceeding from right to left. If there are more digits in the second operand than the first operand will accommodate, the remaining leftmost digits are ignored. If the second operand has fewer numeric digits than necessary to fill the first operand, the remaining digit positions of the first operand are filled with zeros.

As an example, suppose F1 and F2 are as shown:

F1 | 00 | 00 | 00 | 00 |
F2 | F9 | F8 | F7 | F6 | F5 | F4 | F3 |

Then, if the instruction

         PACK   F1(4),F2(7)

is executed, F1 is set to 9876543F. Figure 5-1 illustrates the process.

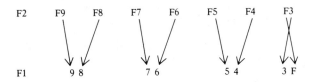

Figure 5-1

In a similar way, the instruction

         PACK   F1(3),F2(7)

sets F1 to 76543F00, and the instruction

         PACK   F1(4),F2(5)

sets F1 to 0098765F.

Note that the execution of a PACK instruction does not depend upon the second operand's being a valid zoned decimal number. For example, if F1 were as above and F2 contained

         C1C2C3C4D8F101

then execution of the statement

         PACK   F1(4),F2(7)

would set F1 to 12348110.

It is important to remember that the execution of a PACK instruction does not validate the number to be packed. Because of this, the hexadecimal digits in any byte may be easily swapped simply by packing the byte into itself. For example, the instruction

         PACK   BYTE(1),BYTE(1)

reverses the zone and numeric digits in BYTE.

The format of the instruction for performing the reverse process (converting a packed decimal number to a zoned decimal representation) is

UNPK   D1(L1,B1),D2(L2,B2)   (*Unpack*)

Execution of an UNPK instruction results in the following action:

- The rightmost byte of the second operand is placed in the rightmost byte of the first operand, with the zone and numeric digits reversed.

- The four-bit hexadecimal digits of the second operand are placed in the numeric digits of the first operand. The zone digits of all but the rightmost byte of the first operand are set to F. If there are more digits in the second operand than the first operand will accommodate, the remaining leftmost digits of the second operand are ignored. If there are fewer digits in the second operand, the remaining leftmost digits of the first operand are set to F0.

For example, suppose F1 and F2 are as shown:

F1	00	00	00	00	00
F2	12	34	5C		

Then, the instruction

UNPK   F1(5),F2(3)

sets F1 to F1F2F3F4C5. In a similar way, execution of the instruction

UNPK   F1(1),F2(3)

sets F1 to C500000000, and execution of the instruction

UNPK   F1(5),F2(2)

sets F1 to F0F0F1F243.

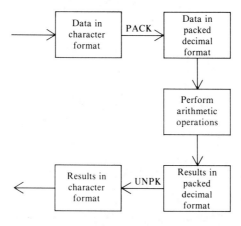

Figure 5-2

The principal use of the PACK and UNPK instructions occurs in situations where numeric data is to be used in decimal arithmetic operations and later printed or displayed in character format. The PACK instruction is used to convert such data into packed decimal format. In this format, the decimal instructions may be used to perform arithmetic operations on the data. The UNPK instruction may then be used to convert the results to character format for printing purposes. This process may be represented as in Figure 5-2.

Care must be exercised, however, when unpacking a numeric data item, to assure that F results as the sign digit (since F must be the zone digit of any printable numeric character). The sign may be set by using an OI instruction. This technique is discussed in Section 8.2.

As will be indicated later, the PACK and UNPK instructions may also be used in conjunction with the instructions for converting packed decimal numbers to binary numbers (and vice versa) to perform the operations for which the ASSIST instructions XDECI and XDECO were designed.

Exercises

For each of the following exercises, show the value that would be in FLD1 after execution of the instruction.

	FLD1	FLD2	Instruction	FLD1 after Execution
1.	01234F	F0F1F2	PACK FLD1,FLD2	_____
2.	AB		PACK FLD1,FLD1	_____
3.	F1F2F3F4		PACK FLD1,FLD1	_____
4.	000000	ABCDEF	PACK FLD1,FLD2	_____
5.	000000	123F	UNPK FLD1,FLD2	_____
6.	1234567D	026C	UNPK FLD1,FLD2	_____
7.	ABCDEF		UNPK FLD1,FLD1	_____
8.	40404040	4D	UNPK FLD1,FLD2	_____

5.3 THE DECIMAL INSTRUCTIONS AP, SP, AND ZAP

In Sections 5.1 and 5.2, the packed decimal format was introduced. In this section, some of the instructions available for performing arithmetic operations on packed decimal numbers will be discussed. However, before we proceed with this discussion, consideration should be given to the desirability of using packed decimal numbers rather than binary numbers. The principal advantage of packed decimal numbers over binary numbers is that the values represented by packed decimal numbers are more readily recognizable. Thus, when a scan of a storage dump must be made to determine the value represented by a given field, the task is much simpler if that value is represented by a packed decimal number. For example,

0123C

is a more readily distinguishable representation of $+123$ than is

007B

The facility gained in the debugging of programs through the use of packed decimal numbers should be obvious. Another advantage gained by the use of the arithmetic instructions for packed decimal numbers is that there is no need to convert numbers from packed decimal to binary format and back again.

The disadvantage of working with packed decimal numbers is that the execution times for the instructions for performing arithmetic operations are much greater than the execution times for the binary counterparts of these instructions. The programmer should carefully weigh this disadvantage against the advantages gained by the use of packed decimal numbers before deciding which format to employ. In general, the use of packed decimal instructions should be avoided in the coding of loops and other frequently executed sections of code. Finally, it should be noted that the use of both types of arithmetic instructions in the same program is not uncommon.

The instructions for addition, subtraction, and movement of packed decimal numbers are the AP, SP, and ZAP instructions. When these instructions are used, an error we have not previously discussed, the *data exception*, may be encountered. This error occurs when a field that is not in packed decimal format is specified as an operand of one of these instructions. Other causes of data exception errors will be noted in the discussions of individual instructions.

Another error not previously discussed that may occur with the use of these instructions is *decimal overflow*. This error has a fixed-point counterpart (the error that occurs with an A or S instruction). Here, as in the case of fixed-point overflow, a bit in the PSW determines whether or not overflow results in termination of the execution of a program; just as in the other case, an SPM instruction may be used to set that bit (bit 37) on or off. A technique for doing this will be discussed in Chapter 8.

Execution of the instruction

AP D1(L1,B1),D2(L2,B2)   (*Add Decimal*)

causes the sum of the two numbers designated by D1(L1,B1) and D2(L2,B2) to be formed. This sum then replaces the first operand. If the storage occupied by the first operand is insufficient to accommodate all nonzero digits of the result, overflow occurs. The condition code is set as follows:

CC	Meaning
0	The result is 0.
1	The result is < 0.
2	The result is > 0.
3	Overflow occurred.

Note that overflow does not necessarily occur if the length of the second operand is greater than the length of the first operand. Overflow occurs only if the length of the first operand is less than that required to represent all of the nonzero digits of the result.

Execution of the instruction

> SP   D1(L1,B1),D2(L2,B2)   *(Subtract Decimal)*

is analogous to the execution of AP. In this case, the difference of two numbers (rather than their sum) is calculated. For example,

> SP   FLD1, = P '4'

subtracts 4 from the contents of FLD1 and puts the result into FLD1.

Execution of the instruction

> ZAP   D1(L1,B1),D2(L2,B2)   *(Zero and Add Decimal)*

causes the first operand to be set to zero. The second operand is then added to it and the result replaces the first operand. Thus, the net result of executing a ZAP instruction is the movement of the second operand into the location originally occupied by the first operand. The condition code is set to the same value that would result from the execution of an AP or SP instruction. A data exception will occur only if the second operand is not a valid packed decimal number. The ZAP instruction is most frequently used for either of the following two purposes:

1. To set a field to zero. For example,

> ZAP   F1, = P'0'

sets F1 to zero.

2. To move a packed decimal number from one field to another. Note that the condition code is set and may be used to determine whether the second operand is positive, negative, or zero.

The following examples should help to clarify the use of the AP, SP, and ZAP instructions. Suppose that F1, F2, and F3 have the indicated values:

F1	01128C	(+1128)
F2	001D	(−1)
F3	00054F	(+54)

The execution of the following instructions would produce the indicated results:

Instruction		Result		CC
AP	F1,F2	01127C	(in F1)	2
AP	F3,F2	00053C	(in F3)	2
AP	F3, $=P'-100'$	00046D	(in F3)	1
AP	F2, $=P'-999'$	000D	(in F2)	3
SP	F1, $=P'1'$	01127C	(in F1)	2
SP	F2,F2	000C	(in F2)	0
SP	F2,F3	055D	(in F2)	1
SP	F2, $=P'999'$	000D	(in F2)	3
ZAP	F1, $=P'0'$	00000C	(in F1)	0
ZAP	F3,F2	00001D	(in F3)	1
ZAP	F2,F1	128C	(in F2)	3

Exercises

For each of the following exercises, show the value that would be in FLD1 after execution of the instruction.

	FLD1	FLD2	Instruction		FLD1 after Execution
1.	01234F	001D	AP	FLD1,FLD2	_____
2.	01234F	00001D	SP	FLD1,FLD2	_____
3.	FFFF	021F	ZAP	FLD1,FLD2	_____
4.	00200D	100F	AP	FLD1,FLD2	_____
5.	00100D	020D	SP	FLD1,FLD2	_____
6.	40404040	000C	ZAP	FLD1,FLD2	_____

5.4 THE DECIMAL INSTRUCTIONS MP, DP, AND CP

In this section, the repertoire of decimal arithmetic instructions is rounded out with a discussion of the decimal multiply, divide, and compare instructions. A sample program is included to illustrate the use of decimal arithmetic. The rules governing the use of the decimal multiply and divide instructions are somewhat complex and require careful examination.

Execution of the instruction

MP   D1(L1,B1),D2(L2,B2)   (*Multiply Decimal*)

causes the product of the two operands to be formed. The result then replaced the first operand. The condition code is unaltered. A specification exception will occur if L2 is greater than 8 or if L2 is greater than or equal to L1. If the first L2 bytes of the first operand are not all zeros, a data exception occurs. A data exception will also occur if either of the operands is not in valid packed decimal format.

To illustrate the use of the MP instruction, suppose that F1 contains 00015C. Then the instruction

> MP   F1, = PL1'5'

would leave 00075C in F1. However, the instruction

> MP   F1, = PL2'5'

would cause a data exception, since the first two bytes of F1 are not 0000. A specification exception would result from execution of the instruction

> MP   F1, = PL3'5'

since F1 is only three bytes in length.

Execution of the statement

> DP $D_1(L_1,B_1),D_2(L_2,B_2)$ (*Divide Decimal*)

results in the formation of a quotient and remainder determined by division of the first operand by the second. The first operand is then replaced by this quotient and remainder. The quotient is left in D1(L3,B1), where $L3 = L1 - L2$. The remainder is left in D3(L2,B1), where $D3 = D1 + (L1 - L2)$. That is, the remainder is on the right and is exactly as long as the divisor, and the quotient occupies the remaining bytes on the left. A specification exception occurs if L2 is greater than 8 or if L2 is greater than or equal to L1. If the quotient will not fit into $L1 - L2$ bytes, a decimal divide exception occurs. If either of the operands is not in valid packed decimal format, a data exception error occurs.

For purposes of illustration, suppose that F1 contains 01500C. Then, execution of the instruction

> DP   F1, = PL2'298'

would leave 5C010C in F1. The quotient (5C) is on the left, and the remainder (010C) is on the right. On the other hand, execution of the instruction

> DP   F1, = PL3'298'

would result in a specification exception, and an attempt to execute

> DP   F1, = PL2'15'

would cause a decimal divide exception (since 100C will not fit into one byte).

Execution of the statement

> CP   D1(L1,B1),D2(L2,B2)   (*Compare Decimal*)

causes a numeric comparison of the two operands to be made, and the condition code is set as follows, to reflect the outcome of this comparison:

CC	Meaning
0	The operands are equal.
1	The first operand is low.
2	The first operand is high.
3	—

Exercises

For each of the following exercises, show the value that would be in FLD1 after execution of the instruction.

	FLD1	FLD2		Instruction	FLD1 after Execution
1.	00004F	020F	MP	FLD1,FLD2	_____
2.	00013D	9C	MP	FLD1,FLD2	_____
3.	0000200D	150D	MP	FLD1,FLD2	_____
4.	01000F	500C	DP	FLD1,FLD2	_____
5.	02010D	5D	DP	FLD1,FLD2	_____
6.	0000100C	020C	DP	FLD1,FLD2	_____

5.5 X-TYPE CONSTANTS

To specify the patterns associated with the use of the EDit instruction, it is convenient to have a facility for generating arbitrary hexadecimal constants. This facility is provided by the following form of the DC statement:

            label   DC   nXLm'p'

where   n   is the duplication factor
        m   is the length
        p   is a hexadecimal constant

Thus, the statement

            DC   3XL2'A2F1'

will cause a six-byte field containing A2F1A2F1A2F1 to be generated. If the duplication factor is omitted, it is assumed to be 1. Therefore, the two statements

            DC   XL3'12A1BF'

and

DC   1XL3'12A1BF'

generate identical strings. If the indicated length of the field is more than sufficient to accommodate the digits of p, zeros are added on the left. For example, the statement

DC   XL3'ABC'

will cause 000ABC to be generated. On the other hand, if the indicated length is insufficient to accommodate the digits in p, digits are dropped from the left. Thus, the statement

DC   XL2'12345'

causes 2345 to be generated. The following examples should reinforce the preceding remarks.

Statement	*Generated String*
DC X'FFD1'	FFD1
DC X'A'	0A
DC XL2'1'	0001
DC 3X'5'	050505
DC 2XL1'F12'	1212

Generation of an X-type constant, unlike the F-type, does not cause an automatic boundary alignment. For example, the statement

TWELVE   DC   XL4'C'

does not necessarily generate a fullword containing a value of 12 (as DC F'12' would). The constant may or may not be generated on a fullword boundary. To force TWELVE to be generated on a fullword boundary, either of these pairs of statements could be used:

TWELVE   DS   OF
          DC   XL4'C'

or

          DS   OF
TWELVE   DC   XL4'C'

The X-type constants, like the other types, may be used in literals. When they are so used, a special rule governing the generation of literals may be taken advantage of. This rule states that all literals of length 4 are generated on fullword boundaries. Hence, instructions such as

A   R1, = XL4'1'

and

$$\text{L} \qquad \text{R2,} = \text{X}'\text{FF0000FF}'$$

may be used without fear of causing a specification error to occur.

5.6 THE ED INSTRUCTION

The EDit instruction is used to convert a packed decimal number (or a contiguous sequence of packed decimal numbers) into a form properly formatted for printed output. It provides facilities for suppressing leading zeros, inserting commas and decimal points, appending algebraic signs, and inserting text. Since so many variations are allowed, the algorithm governing the execution of this instruction is quite complex.

The format of the ED instruction is

> label ED D1(L,B1),D2(B2)

where D1(L,B1) designates the address and length of the field that is to contain the formatted result after execution of the instruction

D2(B2)   gives the address of one or more contiguous packed decimal numbers

Before the editing process can be discussed, however, some terminology must be introduced.

1. The first operand is called the *pattern*. The characters in the pattern determine the format of the edited result that will replace it. The characters in the pattern are classified as follows:

   a. 20 (that is, X'20') is called a *digit selector*.
   b. 21 is called a *significance starter*.
   c. 22 is called a *field separator*.
   d. Any other character is called a *message character*.

2. The second operand is called the *source field*, and its hexadecimal digits are called *source digits*. The source field may contain one or more packed decimal numbers. The number of source digits involved in the editing process (i.e., the length of the source field) is determined by the contents of the pattern.

3. There is a switch called the *significance indicator*, which will be either on or off. The function of this switch will become clear after the following discussion.

4. The first character of the pattern is called the *fill character*. When leading zeros or message characters are to be suppressed, they are replaced in the pattern by the fill character.

The pattern and the source field are both processed from left to right. The pattern is processed one character at a time, while the source field is processed one hexadecimal digit at a time. At the beginning of execution, the significance indicator is off. The first character of the pattern is examined and becomes the fill character. If this character is other than a digit selector or a significance starter, it is left unchanged and the next character of the pattern is examined. From this point, execution proceeds as follows:

1. If the character from the pattern is a digit selector, a digit from the source field is examined.

   a. If the significance indicator is off, and

      i) if this digit is a zero, the character in the pattern is replaced by the fill character. On the other hand,
      ii) if this digit represents a nonzero decimal digit, it is converted to zoned format by appending a leading zone digit, and the result replaces the character in the pattern. If this occurs, the significance indicator is turned on.

   b. If the significance indicator is on, this digit is converted to zoned format and replaces the character in the pattern.

2. If the character from the pattern is a significance starter, the result is the same as in the case of a digit selector except that the significance indicator is always turned on after the character in the pattern is replaced.

3. If the character from the pattern is a field separator, it is replaced by the fill character and the significance indicator is turned off.

4. If the character from the pattern is a message character, and

   a. the significance indicator is off, this character is replaced in the pattern by the fill character.
   b. the significance indicator is on, the message character in the pattern is left unchanged.

The next character in the pattern is then selected and the process is repeated until the pattern is completely processed. Each character in the pattern and each hexadecimal digit in the source field is examined only once.

In this discussion, it has been assumed that the source field is correctly formatted. An invalid packed decimal number in the source field could lead to a data exception. Of course, incorrect addresses in the instruction could cause protection or addressing errors. The condition code is set as follows:

CC	Meaning
0	The source inspected for the last field is 0.
1	The source inspected for the last field < 0.
2	The source inspected for the last field > 0.

The following progressively more complex examples illustrate the operation of the editing algorithm:

- *Example 1.*   Suppose that F1 contains 40202020 and F2 contains 123C. Then, execution of the instruction

  ED   F1(4),F2

  would leave 40F1F2F3 (the same as C' 123') in F1. To see this in detail, go through the algorithm carefully and note the following:

  1. Since 40 (a blank) is the first character of the pattern, it becomes the fill character.
  2. As each successive character of the pattern is examined, each is replaced by the character form of the corresponding source digit (since the last three pattern characters are digit selectors).

  Therefore, if a three-digit decimal number is to be edited from F2 into the third through fifth bytes of PLINE, the following code could be used:

  MVC   PLINE + 1(4), = X'40202020'
  ED   PLINE + 1(4),F2

- *Example 2.*   There is only one problem with Example 1; if F2 contains a zero (000C), only blanks would be put into PLINE. This would occur because the algorithm replaces leading zeros with the fill character (in this case, a blank). To remedy that problem, a significance starter should be used as follows:

  MVC   PLINE + 1(4), = X'40202120'
  ED   PLINE + 1(4),F2

  In any case other than the one in which F2 contains a zero, this pattern produces exactly the same result as 40202020. However, if F2 does contain 000C, a zero is printed rather than all blanks. Note that only one zero would be printed. The significance starter will not cause the zero in its corresponding digit position to print, but subsequent zeros are printed.

- *Example 3.*   Suppose that the number in F2 is to be interpreted as a number of the form X.XX. In this case, a decimal point (X'4B') should be inserted into the pattern, giving

  MVC   PLINE + 1(5), = X'40204B2020'
  ED   PLINE + 1(5),F2

  Note, however, that this will not produce the desired result, if the first digit is zero; in that case, the 4B will be replaced by the fill character, 40. So again a significance starter is needed:

  MVC   PLINE + 1(5), = X'40214B2020'
  ED   PLINE + 1(5),F2

Thus, if F2 contained 012C, this last edit would cause .12 (X'40404BF1F2') to be put into PLINE.

• *Example 4.* Suppose that F2 is two bytes long but always contains at most a two-digit number. Would

$$
\begin{array}{ll}
\text{MVC} & \text{PLINE} + 1(3), = \text{X}'402120' \\
\text{ED} & \text{PLINE} + 1(3), \text{F2}
\end{array}
$$

put the desired value into PLINE? The answer is no, but this is a mistake that programmers often make. Any field containing a single packed decimal number contains an odd number of numeric digits. The sum, therefore, of the number of digit selectors and significance starters in a pattern should probably be odd. For example, if F2 contains 010C,

$$
\begin{array}{ll}
\text{MVC} & \text{PLINE} + 1(3), = \text{X}'402120' \\
\text{ED} & \text{PLINE} + 1(3), \text{F2}
\end{array}
$$

causes just 1 to be put into PLINE, while

$$
\begin{array}{ll}
\text{MVC} & \text{PLINE} + 1(4), = \text{X}'40202120' \\
\text{ED} & \text{PLINE} + 1(4), \text{F2}
\end{array}
$$

causes 10 to be put into PLINE. Occasionally, only the leading digits are wanted, and so an even number of 20's and 21's may be legitimate. The point here is that the source digits should be carefully matched with the characters in the pattern when the pattern is constructed.

• *Example 5.* Suppose that F2 is a five-byte field containing a number to be printed in the form

$$\text{X,XXX,XXX.XX}$$

Naturally, leading zeros and commas should be suppressed (e.g., 000000000C should cause .00 to be put into PLINE). The pattern for this would be

$$
\begin{array}{ll}
\text{MVC} & \text{PLINE} + 1(13) = \text{X}'40206B2020206B2020214B2020' \\
\text{ED} & \text{PLINE} + 1(13), \text{F2}
\end{array}
$$

Note that a significance starter is used.

• *Example 6.* Suppose that F2 contains a five-digit number (F2 is three bytes long) of the form

$$\text{XXX.XX}$$

where the number represents an amount of money to be printed on a check. It is often desirable that an amount such as 1.23 be printed as

$$\text{**1.23}$$

In this case, leading zeros should be replaced with asterisks rather than with blanks. This is done by specifying an asterisk as the fill character, as follows:

$$\text{MVC} \quad \text{PLINE} + 1(7), = X'5C2020214B2020'$$
$$\text{ED} \quad \text{PLINE} + 1(7), F2$$

- *Example 7.* Suppose that F2 contains a three-digit number that may be negative. The easiest way to print an indication of the sign is to use the form

$$\text{XXX}$$

for a positive number and

$$\text{XXX} -$$

for a negative number. This can be done by using

$$\text{MVC} \quad \text{PLINE} + 1(5), = X'4020212060'$$
$$\text{ED} \quad \text{PLINE} + 1(5), F2$$

Here the 60 $(-)$ is a message character. When a byte whose rightmost character indicates a positive number (A, C, E, or F) is processed, the significance indicator is turned off. Hence, any message character or characters immediately following in the pattern are replaced by the fill character. If a character indicating a negative number (B or D) is encountered under the same conditions, however, the significance indicator is left on, and any message characters immediately following in the pattern are printed. These details are covered in the complete algorithm at the end of this chapter. Occasionally, the form

$$\text{XXX CR}$$

is preferred for a negative number. In this case, the pattern would be

$$\text{MVC} \quad \text{PLINE} + 1(7), = X'4020212040C3D9'$$
$$\text{ED} \quad \text{PLINE} + 1(7), F2$$

- *Example 8.* Suppose that F2 and F3 are contiguous two-byte fields, each containing a number of the form

$$\text{X.XX}$$

To print both numbers with one intervening blank, a field separator could be used. For example,

$$\text{MVC} \quad \text{PLINE} + 1(10), = X'40214B202022214B2020'$$
$$\text{ED} \quad \text{PLINE} + 1(10), F2$$

puts both numbers into PLINE in the format

$$\text{X.XX} \quad \text{X.XX}$$

- *Example 9.* Suppose that F2 and F3 contain two-digit numbers to be printed in the format

XX XX

Note that

```
MVC      PLINE + 1(4), = X'40202120'
ED       PLINE + 1(4),F2
MVC      PLINE + 4(4), = X'40202120'
ED       PLINE + 4(4),F3
```

does not produce the desired result; the pattern for F3 causes the last digit of the first number to be erased. Instead, the following code should be used:

```
MVC      PLINE + 4(4), = X'40202120'
ED       PLINE + 4(4),F3
MVC      PLINE + 1(4), = X'40202120'
ED       PLINE + 1(4),F2
```

In general, problems can be avoided by editing fields to be printed on the same line from right to left (instead of the more natural left to right).

Program 5-1 illustrates the use of the instructions introduced to this point.

Program 5-1

```
          TITLE 'PAYROLL EXAMPLE UTILIZING PACKED DECIMAL INSTRUCTIONS'
*****************************************************************************
*
* THIS PROGRAM CALCULATES EMPLOYEES' PAY.  THE INPUT CARDS MUST
* CONFORM TO THE FOLLOWING FORMAT:
*
*         1-20  EMPLOYEE'S NAME
*         21-22 # OF HOURS WORKED
*         23-26 WAGE RATE AS $XX.XX WHERE THE '$' AND '.' DO
*               NOT APPEAR ON THE INPUT CARD
*         27-80 UNUSED
*
* IF AN EMPLOYEE WORKS OVER 40 HOURS, HE WILL BE PAID TIME
* AND A HALF ON ALL OF THE OVERTIME.  THE LOGIC OF THE
* PROGRAM IS AS FOLLOWS:
*
*   STEP 1.   CALL PRNTHDR TO PRINT THE PAGE HEADER FOR THE
*             FIRST PAGE.
*
*   STEP 2.   READ THE FIRST INPUT CARD.
*
*   STEP 3.   IF END-OF-FILE HAS OCCURRED, GO TO STEP 11.
*
*   STEP 4.   CONVERT THE FIELDS ON THE CARD TO PACKED DECIMAL.
*
*   STEP 5.   IF THE EMPLOYEE WORKED OVER 40 HOURS, GO TO STEP 7.
*
*   STEP 6.   CALCULATE THE PAY = RATE * (# HOURS WORKED).  GO
*             TO STEP 8.
*
*   STEP 7.   CALCULATE THE PAY = (RATE * 40) +
*                                 ((RATE * 1.5) * (# HOURS - 40))
*
*   STEP 8.   CONSTRUCT THE PRINT LINE.
*
*   STEP 9.   CALL PRNTLINE TO PRINT THE LINE (AND A NEW HEADER, IF
*             NECESSARY).
*
*   STEP 10.  READ THE NEXT INPUT CARD.  GO TO STEP 3.
*
*   STEP 11. EXIT.
*
*****************************************************************************
*
PAYROLL   CSECT
          USING PAYROLL,R15
*
```

Program 5-1 (continued)

```
***<STEP 1>    PRINT THE PAGE HEADER FOR THE FIRST PAGE
*
        BAL    R12,PRNTHDR
***<STEP 2>    READ THE FIRST CARD
*
        XREAD  CARD,80
*
***<STEP 3>    IF END-OF-FILE, GO TO STEP 11.
*
TESTEND BC     B'0100',EXIT
***<STEP 4>    CONVERT FIELDS TO PACKED DECIMAL
*
        PACK   HOURS,HOURSIN  PACK # HOURS WORKED
        PACK   RATE,RATEIN    PACK THE PAY RATE
*
***<STEP 5>    IF OVERTIME, GO TO STEP 7.
*
        CP     HOURS,=P'40'   OVER 40 HOURS REQUIRES OVERTIME
        BH     OVERTIME
*
***<STEP 6>    CALCULATE PAY = (HOURS WORKED) * (PAY RATE)
*
        ZAP    PAY,RATE
        MP     PAY,HOURS
        B      BLDPRNT          GO BUILD THE PRINT LINE
*
***<STEP 7>    PAY = (RATE * 40) + ((RATE * 1.5) + (HOURS - 40))
*
OVERTIME ZAP   PAY,RATE
        MP     PAY,=P'40'     GET PAY FOR THE 1ST 40 HOURS
        ZAP    OVTIME,RATE    SAVE THE RATE
        MP     OVTIME,=P'15'  GET 1.5 * RATE
        DP     OVTIME,=P'10'
        ZAP    OVHRS,HOURS     CALCULATE # HOURS OF OVERTIME
        SP     OVHRS,=P'40'    OVHRS <- # HOURS OVERTIME
        MP     OVTIME(6),OVHRS
        AP     PAY,OVTIME(6)  PAY NOW CONTAINS THE TOTAL
*
***<STEP 8>    CONSTRUCT THE PRINT LINE
*
BLDPRNT MVC    NAMEOUT,NAMEIN
        MVC    RATEOUT,=X'402020214B2020'
        ED     RATEOUT,RATE
*
        MVC    HOURSOUT,=X'40202120'
        ED     HOURSOUT,HOURS
*
        MVC    PAYOUT,=X'4020206B2020214B2020'
        ED     PAYOUT,PAY+1
*
*
***<STEP 9>    CALL PRNTLINE TO PRINT THE LINE
*
        BAL    R12,PRNTLINE
*
***<STEP 10>   READ THE NEXT CARD AND GO BACK TO STEP 3.
*
        XREAD  CARD,80
        B      TESTEND
*
***<STEP 11>   EXIT.
*
EXIT    BR     R14
*
******************************************************************
* THIS ROUTINE IS CALLED TO PRINT A LINE.  IF NECESSARY, PRNTHDR
* WILL BE CALLED TO START A NEW PAGE.  THE LOGIC IS
*
*   STEP 1.  IF THE LINECTR IS LESS THAN OR EQUAL TO 50, GO TO STEP 3.
*
*   STEP 2.  CALL PRNTHDR TO PRINT PAGE HEADERS AND RESET THE LINECTR.
*
*   STEP 3.  PRINT THE LINE (AND SET CARRIAGE CONTROL TO ' ' FOR THE
*            NEXT LINE).
*
*   STEP 4.  EXIT.
*
******************************************************************
```

Program 5-1 (continued)

```
*
PRNTLINE STM    R0,R15,PRNTSAVE    SAVE CALLER'S REGISTERS
***<STEP 1>     CHECK LINECTR TO SEE IF HEADERS ARE REQUIRED
*
         CP     LINECTR,=P'50'
         BNH    PRINTNOW           BRANCH IF ROOM ON PAGE
*
***<STEP 2>     CALL PRNTHDR TO PRINT PAGE HEADERS
*
         BAL    R12,PRNTHDR
***<STEP 3>     NOW PRINT THE LINE & INCREMENT THE LINECTR
*
PRINTNOW XPRNT  PLINE,133
         AP     LINECTR,=P'1'      INCR LINECTR
         MVI    PLINE,C' '         SET CC FOR NEXT LINE
*
***<STEP 4>     EXIT
*
         LM     R0,R15,PRNTSAVE    RESTORE CALLER'S REGISTERS
         BR     R12                RETURN
PRNTSAVE DS     16F                SAVE CALLER'S REGISTERS HERE
*
****************************************************************************
*
* THIS ROUTINE JUST PRINTS THE PAGE HEADER, RESETS THE LINECTR,
* AND SETS THE CARRIAGE CONTROL IN PLINE TO CAUSE THE NEXT LINE
* TO BE DOUBLE-SPACED.   THE LOGIC IS
*
*   STEP 1.  PRINT THE HEADER.
*
*   STEP 2.  RESET THE LINECTR TO 3 (NEXT LINE PRINTED IS 3TH OF PAGE)
*
*   STEP 3.  SET CARRIAGE CONTROL TO DOUBLE-SPACE.
*
*   STEP 3.  EXIT.
*
****************************************************************************
*
***<STEP 1>     PRINT THE HEADERS
*
PRNTHDR  XPRNT  COLHDR,133
*
***<STEP 2>     RESET THE LINECTR
*
         ZAP    LINECTR,=P'3'
*
***<STEP 3>     SET CARRIAGE CONTROL FOR DOUBLE-SPACE
*
         MVI    PLINE,C'0'
*
***<STEP 4>     EXIT
*
         BR     R12
*
****************************************************************************
*
         LTORG
CARD     DS     CL80               IO AREA FOR THE INPUT CARD
         ORG    CARD
NAMEIN   DS     CL20               EMPLOYEE'S NAME
HOURSIN  DS     CL3                HOURS WORKED
RATEIN   DS     CL4                PAY RATE (XX.XX)
         ORG
*
COLHDR   DC     CL133'1'           PAGE HEADER
         ORG    COLHDR+4
         DC     C'NAME'
         ORG    COLHDR+23
         DC     C'HRS.'
         ORG    COLHDR+31
         DC     C'RATE'
         ORG    COLHDR+38
         DC     C'TOTAL PAY'
         ORG
```

Program 5-1 (continued)

```
*
PLINE     DC    CL133' '          PRINT LINE
          ORG   PLINE+1
NAMEOUT   DS    CL20              EMPLOYEE'S NAME
          ORG   PLINE+22
HOURSOUT  DS    CL4               HOURS WORKED
          ORG   PLINE+28
RATEOUT   DS    CL7               PAY RATE
          ORG   PLINE+35
PAYOUT    DS    CL10              CALCULATED PAY FOR THIS WEEK
          ORG
*
LINECTR   DS    PL2                   NEXT LINE OF PAGE
*
HOURS     DS    PL2               HOURS WORKED
OVHRS     DS    PL2               OVERTIME HOURS
RATE      DS    PL3               RATE OF PAY (XXX.XX)
PAY       DS    PL5               TOTAL PAY FOR THE WEEK
OVTIME    DS    PL8               OVERTIME PAY
*
R0        EQU   0
R1        EQU   1
R2        EQU   2
R3        EQU   3
R4        EQU   4
R5        EQU   5
R6        EQU   6
R7        EQU   7
R8        EQU   8
R9        EQU   9
R10       EQU   10
R11       EQU   11
R12       EQU   12
R13       EQU   13
R14       EQU   14
R15       EQU   15
          END   PAYROLL
```

Exercises

Examine the following patterns and source fields. Then fill in the values that are left blank. The first line has been completed as an illustration.

Patterns		Numbers	
P1:	40 20 20 20	F1:	12 3C
P2:	40 20 21 20	F2:	00 0C
P3:	5C 20 21 20	F3:	01 2C
P4:	40 20 4B 20 20	F4:	12 34 56 7C
P5:	40 21 4B 20 20	F5:	00 00 12 3C
P6:	40 20 20 6B 20 20 21 4B 20 20	F6:	00 00 00 0C
P7:	40 20 20 6B 20 20 21 4B 20 20 40 C3 D9	F7:	00 01 23 4D

Instruction	Resulting Pattern Value	Character String
ED P1(4),F1	40 F1 F2 F3	123
1. ED P1(4),F2	__ __ __ __	_____
2. ED P1(4),F3	__ __ __ __	_____
3. ED P2(4),F1	__ __ __ __	_____
4. ED P2(4),F2	__ __ __ __	_____
5. ED P2(4),F3	__ __ __ __	_____

6.	ED	P3(4),F1	— — — —	————
7.	ED	P3(4),F2	— — — —	————
8.	ED	P3(4),F3	— — — —	————
9.	ED	P4(5),F1	— — — — —	————
10.	ED	P4(5),F2	— — — — —	————
11.	ED	P4(5),F3	— — — — —	————
12.	ED	P5(5),F1	— — — — —	————
13.	ED	P5(5),F2	— — — — —	————
14.	ED	P5(5),F3	— — — — —	————
15.	ED	P6(10),F4	— — — — — — — — — —	————
16.	ED	P6(10),F5	— — — — — — — — — —	————
17.	ED	P6(10),F6	— — — — — — — — — —	————
18.	ED	P7(13),F4	— — — — — — — — — — — — —	————
19.	ED	P7(13),F5	— — — — — — — — — — — — —	————
20.	ED	P7(13),F6	— — — — — — — — — — — — —	————
21.	ED	P7(13),F7	— — — — — — — — — — — — —	————

5.7 THE SRP INSTRUCTION

The SRP instruction can be used to shift a packed decimal number. A left shift is equivalent to multiplying by a power of 10, and a right shift can be used to calculate the result of dividing by a power of 10. Furthermore, the SRP can be used to round off the result on a right shift. To understand the operation performed by this instruction, it is necessary to know how the direction and number of digits involved in a shift are encoded in a six-bit binary number. This encoding is done as follows:

- A left shift of up to 31 positions is represented by a binary number that designates the number of positions. For example, a left shift of 10 digits is encoded as 001010.

- A right shift of from 1 to 32 positions is specified by subtracting the number of positions from 64 and representing the result as a six-bit binary number. For example, a right shift of 1 may be encoded as

$$\begin{array}{r} 64 \\ \underline{-1} \\ 63 = 111111 \end{array}$$

With this in mind, the following detailed description of the SRP instruction should be clear.

Execution of the instruction

SRP D1(L,B1),D2(B2),i   (Shift and Round Decimal)

causes the contents of the field designated by the first operand to be shifted. The direction and number of positions involved in the shift are determined by doing the following:

- Calculate the address represented by D2(B2).
- Use the rightmost six bits of this address as the encoded form described above.

The sign is not altered unless the result is zero; in this case, the sign is always made positive. If the shift is to the right, the value i (which should be in the range 0 to 9) is used as a rounding factor. That is, i is added to the leftmost digit shifted off the right and, if the result is greater than 9, 1 is added to the result after the shift. If a left shift occurs and nonzero digits are lost, a decimal overflow occurs (which normally causes termination of program execution). The condition code is set as follows:

CC	*Meaning*
0	The result is 0.
1	The result is negative.
2	The result is positive.
3	Overflow occurred.

Thus, execution of the instruction

        SRP   RATE,B′000100′,0

would result in a left shift of four positions, and execution of the instruction

        SRP   TIME,B′111111′,5

would result in a right shift of one position, with a rounding factor of 5. Execution of the instruction

        SRP   WAGE,0(R2),0

can cause a shift right or left (depending on the contents of the rightmost six bits of R2).

When the second operand does not involve a register, a decimal value can be specified. In this case, the decimal value is converted to the binary equivalent by the assembler. This leads to the following conventions:

- A left shift of n positions is represented by n.
- A right shift of n positions is represented by $(64 - n)$.

Thus, the first two SRP examples cited earlier could have been coded as follows:

        SRP   RATE,4,0

and

$$SRP \qquad TIME,(64-1),5$$

Exercises

For each of the following exercises, show the value that would be in FLD1 after execution of the instruction.

FLD1	Instruction	FLD1 after Execution
1. 00004F	SRP FLD1,4,0	_____
2. 00013D	SRP FLD1,2,0	_____
3. 0000262C	SRP FLD1,(64−2),5	_____
4. 01925F	SRP FLD1,(64−3),0	_____
5. 02654C	SRP FLD1,(64−2),5	_____
6. 0000168C	SRP FLD1,2,5	_____
7. 0000168D	SRP FLD1,(64−4),5	_____

5.8 THE CVB AND CVD INSTRUCTIONS

In the examples given in the text so far, the pseudo-instructions XDECI and XDECO have been used to convert numbers in character format to binary representations and vice versa. These pseudo-instructions are not available on most assemblers. In this section, the instructions for converting numbers in packed decimal format to their binary representations and for converting from binary to packed decimal format are introduced. Then, the standard methods for converting between binary and character representations of numbers are indicated.

Execution of the instruction

$$CVB \qquad r,D(X,B) \qquad\qquad (Convert\ to\ Binary)$$

causes the contents of r to be replaced by the binary representation of the packed decimal number at the address D(X,B). If D(X,B) is not the address of a doubleword (i.e., is not a multiple of 8), a specification exception occurs. If D(X,B) is the address of a doubleword that does not contain a valid packed decimal number, a data exception occurs. Finally, if the packed decimal number at D(X,B) is too large to be represented in 32 bits, a fixed-point divide exception occurs.

Assume, for example, that DWORD is a doubleword whose contents are 000000000000010F. The execution of the instruction

$$CVB \qquad R1,DWORD$$

will cause the contents of R1 to be replaced by 0000000A.

Execution of the instruction

CVD   r,D(X,B)   (*Convert to Decimal*)

causes the contents of the doubleword at D(X,B) to be replaced by the packed decimal representation of the binary number in r. If D(X,B) is not the address of a doubleword, a specification exception will occur.

Thus, if R1 contains FFFFFFFF, execution of the instruction

CVD   R1,DWORD

replaces the contents of D(X,B) with 000000000000001D. (Actually, a determination of which valid negative sign is to be used must be made. It is sufficient, however, for the reader to assume only that some valid negative sign is used.)

The standard technique for converting the character representation of a number to the binary representation of that number is first to convert the number to packed decimal format by use of a PACK instruction and then to convert the resulting packed decimal number to binary by use of a CVB instruction. Essentially the reverse of this process—utilizing a CVD instruction and then an UNPK instruction—is used to convert from binary to character representations. These processes are illustrated in Figure 5-3.

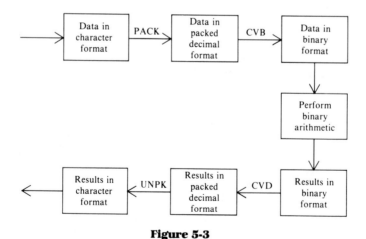

Figure 5-3

The reader is again cautioned that the UNPK instruction actually converts a number to zoned decimal representation and that an OI instruction should be used to assure that the sign digit is F if character format is desired.

5.9 THE EDMK INSTRUCTION

The EDMK instruction provides all of the facilities provided by the ED instruction and, in addition, sets a pointer to the first nonzero digit of an edited number string under the proper conditions. The general format of this instruction is

$$\text{EDMK} \qquad \text{D1(L,B1), D2(B2)} \qquad\qquad (Edit\ and\ Mark)$$

Execution of this instruction has precisely the same effect on the first operand as does the execution of the corresponding ED instruction. Further, let x be the last character of the result such that the following conditions are met:

- x was formed by the replacement of a 20 or 21 by a source digit.
- The significance indicator was off before the replacement occurred (i.e., the significance indicator was turned from off to on with the creation of x).

In this case, the rightmost three bytes of R1 are set to the address of x. If no such x exists, R1 is left unaltered. Normally, since there will be at most one character that fulfills the above conditions, the last such character is usually the first such character as well.

To illustrate the effect of the execution of an EDMK instruction, suppose that

$$\text{F1 contains } 402020214B2020$$
$$\text{F2 contains } 01230F$$
$$\text{F3 contains } 00097F$$

Then, execution of the instruction

$$\text{EDMK} \qquad \text{F1,F2}$$

sets the contents of F1 to 4040F1F24BF3F0 and places the address of F1 + 2 in the rightmost three bytes of R1. The leftmost byte of R1 is unaltered. On the other hand, execution of the instruction

$$\text{EDMK} \qquad \text{F1,F3}$$

replaces the contents of F1 with 404040404BF9F7 and R1 is unaltered. In this case, the significance indicator is turned on because of the presence of the 21 (the significance starter).

The two most common uses of the EDMK are to insert a dollar sign in front of a number representing a cash amount and to insert a minus sign in front of a negative number. As a specific example, suppose that F2 is a three-byte field containing a valid positive packed decimal number and that F1 contains the same pattern as in the previous example. Then, if the packed decimal number in F2 has three or more significant digits (i.e., has fewer than three leading zeros), execution of the instruction

EDMK   F1,F2

leaves the address of the first nonblank in the right three bytes of R1. What is really necessary, however, is that R1 point to the first nonblank character under all conditions. This may be accomplished by means of the following two instructions:

LA   R1,F1+4
EDMK   F1,F2

Execution of the first of these instructions puts the eventual address of the period into R1. If R1 is not altered by execution of the EDMK instruction, the period is the first nonblank character in F1. A complete sequence of instructions to put the number and the dollar sign into F1 is as follows:

LA   R1,F1+4
EDMK   F1,F2
BCTR   R1,R0   SUBTRACT 1 FROM R1
MVI   0(R1),C'$'   PUT IN THE $

Although numbers are sometimes converted to printable form through the use of an UNPK and an OI instruction, an ED or an EDMK instruction should be used in most cases. This concludes the discussion on the subject of editing output. It will be assumed from this point on that you are equipped to edit all of your output.

Program 5-2 illustrates a variety of the techniques discussed up to this point. You should study it carefully, along with the sample output in Table 5-1, before continuing.

Table 5-1 is an example of the output of GROWTH, given an initial balance of $10,000, a target balance of $20,000, an interest rate of 10 percent, and four interest periods per year.

Table 5-1

INTEREST PERIOD	BEGINNING BALANCE	INTEREST	END BALANCE
1	10,000.00	250.00	10,250.00
2	10,250.00	256.25	10,506.25
3	10,506.25	262.66	10,768.91
4	10,768.91	269.22	11,038.13
5	11,038.13	275.95	11,314.08
6	11,314.08	282.85	11,596.93
7	11,596.93	289.92	11,886.85

Table 5-1 (continued)

INTEREST PERIOD	BEGINNING BALANCE	INTEREST	END BALANCE
8	11,886.85	297.17	12,184.02
9	12,184.02	304.60	12,488.62
10	12,488.62	312.22	12,800.84
11	12,800.84	320.02	13,120.86
12	13,120.86	328.02	13,448.88
13	13,448.88	336.22	13,785.10
14	13,785.10	344.63	14,129.73
15	14,129.73	353.24	14,482.97
16	14,482.97	362.07	14,845.04
17	14,845.04	371.13	15,216.17
18	15,216.17	380.40	15,596.57
19	15,596.57	389.91	15,986.48
20	15,986.48	399.66	16,386.14
21	16,386.14	409.65	16,795.79
22	16,795.79	419.89	17,215.68
23	17,215.68	430.39	17,646.07
24	17,646.07	441.15	18,087.22
25	18,087.22	452.18	18,539.40
26	18,539.40	463.49	19,002.89
27	19,002.89	475.07	19,477.96
28	19,477.96	486.95	19,964.91
29	19,964.91	499.12	20,464.03

AVG INTEREST = $360.83

Program 5-2

```
            TITLE 'A PROGRAM TO SHOW THE GROWTH OF AN INVESTMENT'
*****************************************************************************
*
* THIS PROGRAM PRODUCES A TABLE WHICH SHOWS THE GROWTH OF A PRINCIPLE
* AMOUNT OF MONEY WHICH IS INVESTED AT A FIXED RATE OF INTEREST.  THE
* INPUT WILL INDICATE THE BEGINNING PRINCIPLE, THE TARGET AMOUNT, THE
* INTEREST RATE, AND THE NUMBER OF PERIODS FOR WHICH THE INTEREST IS
* COMPOUNDED EACH YEAR.  THE OUTPUT WILL BE A TABLE WHICH WILL INDICATE
* FOR EACH PERIOD
*
*           THE BEGINNING BALANCE
*           THE INTEREST FOR THE PERIOD
*           THE FINAL BALANCE FOR THE PERIOD
*
* THE CALCULATION IS TERMINATED WHEN THE PRINCIPLE AT THE END OF A
* PERIOD EQUALS OR EXCEEDS THE TARGET AMOUNT.
*
* THE PROGRAM ACCEPTS A SINGLE INPUT CARD CONFORMING TO THE FOLLOWING
* FORMAT:
*
*           COLUMNS           CONTENTS
*
*            1-7              BEGINNING PRINCIPLE (IN CENTS)
*            9-15             TARGET AMOUNT (IN CENTS)
*            17-22            ANNUAL INTEREST RATE (TO FOUR DECIMAL PLACES)
*            24-25            THE # OF INTEREST PERIODS PER YEAR
*
```

Program 5-2 (continued)

```
* THE LOGIC OF THE PROGRAM IS AS FOLLOWS:
*
*    STEP 1.  READ THE INPUT CARD AND GET THE VALUES OFF IT.
*
*    STEP 2.  CALL PRNTHDRS TO PRINT THE HEADERS FOR THE FIRST PAGE.
*
*    STEP 3.  IF THE CURRENT PRINCIPLE HAS REACHED THE TARGET AMOUNT,
*             GO TO STEP 8.
*
*    STEP 4.  CALCULATE THE VALUES FOR THE NEXT INTEREST PERIOD.
*
*    STEP 5.  CALL PRNTLINE TO PRINT THE LINE FOR THE NEXT PERIOD.
*
*    STEP 6.  ADD THE INTEREST FOR THE PERIOD TO THE TOTAL INTEREST.
*
*    STEP 7.  ADD THE INTEREST FOR THE PERIOD TO THE CURRENT PRINCIPLE
*             AND GO BACK TO STEP 3.
*
*    STEP 8.  CALCULATE THE AVERAGE INTEREST PER PERIOD.
*
*    STEP 9.  PRINT THE FINAL LINE.
*
*    STEP 10. EXIT.
*
*******************************************************************
*
GROWTH   CSECT
         USING  GROWTH,R15
*
***<STEP 1>      READ THE INPUT AND GET THE STARTING VALUES
*
         XREAD  CARD,80              READ THE CARD
         PACK   CURPRIN,BEGPRIN      GET THE 1ST PRINCIPLE
         PACK   TARGPRIN,TARGAMNT    AND THE TARGET AMOUNT
*
         PACK   WORK,ANNULINT        CALCULATE INTEREST PER PERIOD
         SRP    WORK,3,0             ANNUAL RATE * 1000
         PACK   NUMPERYR,INTPERDS
         DP     WORK,NUMPERYR        DIVIDED BY # PERIODS PER YEAR
         SRP    WORK(6),(64-3),5     DIVIDED BY 1000, ROUNDED
         ZAP    INTPER,WORK(6)       THE INTEREST PER PERIOD
*
***<STEP 2>      PRINT HEADERS FOR THE FIRST PAGE
*
         BAL    R12,PRNTHDRS
*
***<STEP 3>      TEST FOR END OF THE CALCULATION
*
CALCLOOP CP     CURPRIN,TARGPRIN     HAS PRINCIPLE REACHED TARGET?
         BNL    PRNTLAST             YES -> BRANCH
*
***<STEP 4>      CALCULATE THE INTEREST FOR THE NEXT PERIOD & BUILD LI
*
         ZAP    WORK,CURPRIN
         MP     WORK,INTPER          PRINCIPLE * INTEREST
         SRP    WORK,(64-6),5        GET IT IN CENTS ROUNDED
         ZAP    CURINT,WORK
*
         ZAP    NEWPRIN,CURPRIN      BAL AT END OF PERIOD = STARTING BA
         AP     NEWPRIN,CURINT                           + INTEREST
*
         AP     PERIOD,=P'1'
         MVC    OINTPER,=X'40202120'
         ED     OINTPER,PERIOD       PUT IN THE NUMBER OF THE PERIOD
*
         MVC    OBEGBAL,=X'4020206B2020214B2020'
         ED     OBEGBAL,CURPRIN      PUT IN THE BEGINNING BALANCE
*
         MVC    OINTERST,=X'4020206B2020214B2020'
         ED     OINTERST,CURINT      PUT IN THE INTEREST FOR THE PERIOD
*
         MVC    OENDBAL,=X'4020206B2020214B2020'
         ED     OENDBAL,NEWPRIN      PUT IN THE NEW PRINCIPLE
*
***<STEP 5>      CALL PRNTLINE TO PRINT THE LINE
*
         BAL    R12,PRNTLINE
*
***<STEP 6>      ACCUMULATE TOTAL INTEREST
*
         AP     TOTINT,CURINT
*
***<STEP 7>      RESET CURRENT PRINCIPLE TO NEW VALUE (ADD IN INTEREST)
*
         ZAP    CURPRIN,NEWPRIN
         B      CALCLOOP
```

Program 5-2 (continued)

```
*
***<STEP 8>      CALCULATE AVERAGE INTEREST PER PERIOD
*
PRNTLAST SRP     TOTINT,1,0          MULT TOTAL INT * 10
         DP      TOTINT,PERIOD
         SRP     TOTINT(6),(64-1),5 GET AVG PER PERIOD
*
         LA      R1,AVGINT+7
         MVC     AVGINT,=X'4020206B2020214B2020'
         EDMK    AVGINT,TOTINT+2
         BCTR    R1,0
         MVI     0(R1),C'$'          R1 POINTS JUST TO LEFT OF 1ST DIGIT
*
***<STEP 9>      PRINT FINAL LINE
*
         XPRNT   LASTLINE,35
*
***<STEP 10>     EXIT
*
         BR      R14
*
**************************************************************************
* THIS ROUTINE IS CALLED TO PRINT A LINE.  IF NECESSARY, PRNTHDRS
* WILL BE CALLED TO START A NEW PAGE.  THE LOGIC IS
*
*   STEP 1.  IF THE LINECTR IS LESS THAN OR EQUAL TO 50, GO TO STEP 3.
*
*   STEP 2.  CALL PRNTHDRS TO PRINT PAGE HEADERS AND RESET THE LINECTR.
*
*   STEP 3.  PRINT THE LINE (AND SET CARRIAGE CONTROL TO ' ' FOR THE
*            NEXT LINE).
*
*   STEP 4.  EXIT.
*
**************************************************************************
PRNTLINE STM     R0,R15,PRNTSAVE    SAVE CALLER'S REGISTERS
*
***<STEP 1>      CHECK LINECTR TO SEE IF HEADERS ARE REQUIRED
*
         CP      LINECTR,=P'50'
         BNH     PRINTNOW           BRANCH IF ROOM ON PAGE
*
***<STEP 2>      CALL PRNTHDRS TO PRINT PAGE HEADERS
*
         BAL     R12,PRNTHDRS
*
***<STEP 3>      NOW PRINT THE LINE & INCREMENT THE LINECTR
*
PRINTNOW XPRNT   PLINE,133
         AP      LINECTR,=P'1'      INCR LINECTR
         MVI     PLINE,C' '         SET CC FOR NEXT LINE
*
***<STEP 4>      EXIT
*
         LM      R0,R15,PRNTSAVE    RESTORE CALLER'S REGISTERS
         BR      R12                RETURN
PRNTSAVE DS      16F                SAVE CALLER'S REGISTERS HERE
*
**************************************************************************
* THIS ROUTINE JUST PRINTS THE PAGE HEADERS, RESETS THE LINECTR,
* AND SETS THE CARRIAGE CONTROL IN PLINE TO CAUSE THE NEXT LINE
* TO BE DOUBLE-SPACED.  THE LOGIC IS
*
*   STEP 1.  PRINT THE 2 HEADERS.
*
*   STEP 2.  RESET THE LINECTR TO 4 (NEXT LINE PRINTED IS 4TH OF PAGE)
*
*   STEP 3.  SET CARRIAGE CONTROL TO DOUBLE-SPACE.
*
*   STEP 4.  EXIT.
*
**************************************************************************
***<STEP 1>      PRINT THE HEADERS
*
PRNTHDRS XPRNT   COLHDR1,133
         XPRNT   COLHDR2,133
*
***<STEP 2>      RESET THE LINECTR
*
         ZAP     LINECTR,=P'4'
*
```

```
***<STEP 3>      SET CARRIAGE CONTROL FOR DOUBLE-SPACE
*
         MVI     PLINE,C'0'
*
***<STEP 4>      EXIT
*
         BR      R12
*
******************************************************************
*
         LTORG
*
CARD     DS      CL80                  IO AREA FOR THE INPUT CARD
         ORG     CARD
BEGPRIN  DS      CL7                   BEGINNING PRINCIPLE IN CENTS
         ORG     CARD+8
TARGAMNT DS      CL7                   END WHEN THIS VALUE IS REACHED
         ORG     CARD+16
ANNULINT DS      CL6                   ANNUAL INTEREST TO 4 DEC PLACES
         ORG     CARD+23
INTPERDS DS      CL2                   INTEREST PERIODS PER YEAR
         ORG
*
COLHDR1  DC      CL133'1'              FIRST PAGE HEADER
         ORG     COLHDR1+2
         DC      C'INTEREST'
         ORG     COLHDR1+25
         DC      C'BEGINNING'
         ORG     COLHDR1+40
         DC      C'INTEREST'
         ORG     COLHDR1+55
         DC      C'END BALANCE'
         ORG
*
COLHDR2  DC      CL133' '
         ORG     COLHDR2+2
         DC      C'PERIOD'
         ORG     COLHDR2+26
         DC      C'BALANCE'
         ORG
*
PLINE    DC      CL133' '              PRINT LINE
         ORG     PLINE+1
OINTPER  DS      CL4                   INTEREST PERIOD
         ORG     PLINE+23
OBEGBAL  DS      CL10                  STARTING BALANCE
         ORG     PLINE+38
OINTERST DS      CL10                  INTEREST FOR PERIOD
         ORG     PLINE+53
OENDBAL  DS      CL10                  NEW BALANCE
         ORG
*
LASTLINE DC      C'0'
         DC      CL10' '
         DC      C'AVG INTEREST ='
AVGINT   DS      CL10
*
CURINT   DS      PL4                   INTEREST FOR PERIOD
CURPRIN  DS      PL4                   CURRENT PRINCIPLE
NEWPRIN  DS      PL4                   NEW PRINCIPLE
TARGPRIN DS      PL4                   TARGET PRINCIPLE
*
INTPER   DS      PL4                   INTEREST PER PERIOD (TO 4 DEC PLACES)
PERIOD   DC      PL2'0'                INTEREST PERIOD (FROM 1)
NUMPERYR DS      PL2                   INTEREST PERIODS PER YEAR
*
TOTINT   DC      PL8'0'                TOTAL INTEREST
*
WORK     DS      PL8                   A WORK AREA
LINECTR  DS      PL2                   NEXT LINE OF PAGE
*
R0       EQU     0
R1       EQU     1
R2       EQU     2
R3       EQU     3
R4       EQU     4
R5       EQU     5
R6       EQU     6
R7       EQU     7
R8       EQU     8
R9       EQU     9
R10      EQU     10
R11      EQU     11
R12      EQU     12
R13      EQU     13
R14      EQU     14
R15      EQU     15
         END     GROWTH
```

Exercises

At this point, you should be capable of obtaining input values without using XDECI and converting output values to character format without using XDECO. Therefore, neither of these instructions should be utilized in the following exercises.

1. Write a program to calculate the average cost per square foot of a plot of land. Specifically, your program should perform the following tasks:

a. The program should read in a set of cards in the following format:

Columns	Contents
1–4	Width (in feet) of a plot of land
5–8	Length (in feet) of the plot
9–15	Price (in dollars) of the plot

As the cards are read, a report similar to the following should be produced:

WIDTH	LENGTH	AREA	COST	COST/SQ. FT.
100	50	5000	9,000	1.80
150	200	30000	6,000	.20
.	.	.	.	.
.	.	.	.	.
.	.	.	.	.

b. At end-of-file, a single line conforming to the following format should be produced:

TOTAL AREA =   84,000   TOTAL COST = $202,000   AVG. COST/SQ. FT. = $2.40

All arithmetic operations should be done with decimal arithmetic instructions.

2. Write a program that will produce an amortization table for an installment loan. The input will indicate the principal of the loan, the nominal annual interest rate, and the monthly payment. The output from your program will be a table that will indicate, for each month of the life of the loan, the payment number, the payment, the portion of the payment applied to principal repayment, and the outstanding principal at the end of the month. All arithmetic operations should be done with decimal instructions.

Your program should read a single input card conforming to the following format:

Columns	Contents
1–7	The principal (in cents)
10–15	The nominal annual interest rate (to four decimal places)
20–25	Monthly payment

For example, a loan of $1000.00 at an annual interest rate of 6 percent (.5 percent per month) with monthly payments of $100.00 would be represented as follows:

```
Col.   12345678901234567890123456789012345678901234567890123456789012345. . .
       0100000  060000      010000
```

The table produced should contain five columns as follows:

Col. 1: The payment number, beginning with zero

Col. 2: The payment (in the last period, the payment required may be less than a full regular payment)

Col. 3: The interest for the month, computed as principal at the beginning of the month multiplied by one-twelfth the annual interest rate, rounded to the nearest cent

Col. 4: The portion of the monthly payment applied to the repayment of the principal, computed as the difference between the monthly payment and the interest

Col. 5: The principal outstanding at the end of the month after suitable adjustment for the monthly payment transaction, obtained by subtraction

For example, the output produced for the loan described as sample input might be:

PAYMENT NUMBER	PAYMENT	INTEREST	PRINCIPAL REPAYMENT	OUTSTANDING PRINCIPAL
0				1,000.00
1	100.00	5.00	95.00	905.00
2	100.00	4.53	95.47	809.53
3	100.00	4.05	95.95	713.58
4	100.00	3.57	96.43	617.15
5	100.00	3.09	96.91	520.24
6	100.00	2.60	97.40	422.84
7	100.00	2.11	97.89	324.95
8	100.00	1.62	98.38	226.57
9	100.00	1.13	98.87	127.70
10	100.00	.64	99.36	28.34
11	28.48	.14	28.34	0.00

3. Write a program to maintain the balance for a savings account. The program should accept as input a deck of cards, each of which will conform to one of the following four formats:

Card Type	Columns	Contents
Initial balance card	1	0
	2–10	Amount (in cents)
Deposit card	1	1
	2–10	Amount
Withdrawal card	1	2
	2–10	Amount
Interest calculation card	1	3
	2–4	Interest rate (e.g., 550 would represent a rate of 5.50%)

The program should produce a report similar to the following:

	SAVINGS	ACCOUNT	REPORT	
TRAN. CODE	AMOUNT	RATE	CURRENT BALANCE	
0	212.14		212.14
1	110.00		322.14
2	42.00		280.14
3		4.00	288.63
.	.	.	.
.	.	.	.
.	.	.	.

```
#  DEPOSITS   =  14
TOTAL  AMOUNT  OF  DEPOSITS =  $1,420.00
AVG.  AMOUNT/DEPOSIT        =    $101.43


#  WITHDRAWALS  =  42
TOTAL  AMOUNT  OF  WITHDRAWALS   =  $1,380.06
AVG.  AMOUNT/WITHDRAWAL          =    $32.86
                CURRENT  BALANCE  =    $252.08
```

When an interest calculation card is encountered, the program should calculate the amount of interest as

rate * (minimum balance since last interest calculation card)

This amount should then be added to the current balance.

4. Frequently, it is necessary to store information into a table so that it can be retrieved and possibly altered at a later time. For example, an automobile parts supply firm might keep a table of parts. Each table entry would contain a parts number and the number of units in stock. In this case, as in many other common cases, the information in one entry of the table is composed of two parts, a key (the part number) and data associated with the key (the number of units in stock).

A variety of efficient techniques can be used to store and retrieve information based on a key. This exercise requires the implementation of one of the more unusual (but highly efficient) of these techniques.

The basic idea of *hashing* is to take a key and convert it through some fixed process to a number in the range from 0 to n − 1. The resulting number can then be used to determine which entry in a table should be used to store the data item associated with the key.

In particular, given a key KEY, we compute a hash function HASH(KEY) = X (a number) and use this value as the index into the table where the search is to begin. We shall assume a table with n locations or entries for storing "key-data" pairs. These table entries will be numbered, 0, 1, 2, . . . , $n − 1$. Hash addressing, then, consists of arithmetically converting the KEY of a key-data pair to a number X = HASH(KEY) where $0 \leq X \leq n − 1$. This number is used as an index into the table where the key and the data are to be stored. The number X is said to be obtained by "hashing" the key.

As long as no two keys hash to the same number, the time involved to search for a particular key is the time spent doing the hashing. To enter data having a particular key, the hash function is evaluated and the data is stored in the appropriate table entry. To search the table, the hash function is again evaluated and the computed index indicates the location of the sought data item in the table. Trouble occurs, however, when two keys hash to the same table entry. This situation is called *collision*. Since only one key-data pair may be stored in an entry of the table, it is necessary to find another location for the second (or subsequent) key-data pairs hashing to a particular entry.

Collision problems can be handled by means of the *linear probe*. If upon attempting to enter the key and data into the table, it is found that a collision occurs at an entry X, consecutive entries X + 1, X + 2, . . . , down the table are searched until an empty entry is found, and the key and data are entered there. If an empty entry is not found before the end of the table is reached, the search is continued at the top of the table.

It should now be clear how a table is searched for a particular key. The key is hashed to obtain the index of the entry X where the key-data should appear in the table. Then the given key is compared with the keys in the table at consecutive entries X, X + 1, X + 2, . . . , until a match is established. If an empty entry is found before a match is established, the given key is not in the table.

In this exercise, you are to construct a table for looking up the number of units of automobile parts in stock. Use the hash addressing technique discussed above to construct a table of 50 entries, each containing

- a five-digit part number (three bytes)
- a five-digit number giving the number of units in stock (three bytes)

The number of units in stock can be negative, indicating that orders have been accepted even though the part is not currently in stock.

The program should accept, as input, three types of cards:

Card Type	Columns	Contents
Part definition card	1–5	Part number
	6–10	Number of units in stock
	11	'P'
	12–80	Unused
Order card	1–5	Part number
	6–10	Number to subtract from units in stock
	11	'O'
	12–80	Unused
New stock card	1–5	Part number
	6–10	Number to add to units in stock
	11	'S'

When a part definition card is processed, the program should attempt to make a new entry in the hash table. If the part number already exists in the table, an error message should be printed.

When an order card or a shipment card is processed, the program should access the appropriate entry in the hash table. If there is no entry for the part, an error message should be printed. Otherwise, the units in stock should be altered and the new value displayed.

When end-of-file occurs, the following summary lines should be printed:

TOTAL NUMBER OF PARTS = 32
TOTAL NUMBER WITH NEGATIVE NUMBER OF UNITS IN STOCK = 8
% WITH NEGATIVE NUMBER OF UNITS IN STOCK = 24%

5. In the first paragraph of Exercise 4, a table containing keyed entries was introduced. Read that paragraph before reading the rest of this exercise.

One of the more efficient ways to access information stored in a table involves a technique referred to as a *binary search*. To use a binary search to retrieve information in a table, the entries in the table must be sorted into either ascending or descending order, based on the keys in the entries. Since the table that will be constructed by the program described in this exercise will contain entries in ascending order, the following discussion will presume such an ordering.

Assume that a table exists such that all of the entries in the table occur in ascending order, based on their keys. The following procedure can be used to locate the entry with a designated key, K:

- Compare K with the key in the middle entry in the table. It is then possible to determine whether the desired entry is in the upper half or the lower half of the table. Thus, with a single comparison, half of the entries in the table can be eliminated as possibilities for the desired match.
- Repeat the above step for that half of the table where the desired key must occur, if it is in the table. By continuing this process, either the desired entry will be found or it will be determined that the entry is not in the table.

This technique for searching a table is surprisingly efficient. For example, to search for an entry with a given key in a table of 1000 entries will require at most 11 comparisons.

Suppose that an automobile parts supply firm wishes to maintain records of parts that have been ordered but not shipped. Code a program that could be used by the company to perform the required calculations. The input to the program will be as follows:

- First, a master deck of cards should be read, with one card per part sold by the company. Each of these cards will conform to the following format:

Columns	Contents
1–5	Part number
6–25	Description of the part
26–32	Price of the part

The end of the master deck can be detected by checking for a card with a % in column 1. The cards in the master deck will be arranged in ascending order, based on the part number field (columns 1–5). You may assume that no more than 100 cards will occur in the master deck.

- Following the master deck will be a set of intermixed order and shipment cards. The formats of these cards are as follows:

Card Type	Columns	Contents
Order card	1–5	Part number
	6–10	Number of units
	11	O
Shipment card	1–5	Part number
	6–10	Number of units
	11	S

Your program should perform the following tasks:

a. Read in the master deck and store the entries in a table. The format of each entry in the table will be

3 bytes	Part number in packed decimal
5 bytes	Number of outstanding orders (also in packed decimal)
4 bytes	Price per unit
20 bytes	Description of the part

b. After you have read in the master deck, the program should read and process the order and shipment cards. If an order card or shipment card contains a part number not contained in the table, an error message should be printed. When an order card is processed, the "number of outstanding orders" field must be incremented, and a line similar to the following should be printed:

PART # = 59321   ORDERS = 520   AMOUNT = $52.00   WING NUT

When a shipment card is processed, the "number of outstanding orders" should be decremented and a line similar to the one above should be printed. You may assume that this number will never be negative. Whenever an entry in the table must be located, a binary search should be used.

c. When end-of-file occurs, lines similar to the following should be printed:

```
TOTAL  NUMBER  OF  PARTS  ORDERED  =  123
TOTAL  NUMBER  SHIPPED  =  98
TOTAL  AMOUNT  OF  OUTSTANDING  ORDERS  =  $5,423.00
TOTAL  AMOUNT  OF  SHIPPED  ORDERS  =  $28,416.46
%  OF  ORDERS  STILL  OUTSTANDING  =  20.3%
```

5.10 THE EDIT ALGORITHM

For completeness, an overview flowchart (Figure 5-4), a detailed flowchart (Figure 5-5), and a step algorithm for the edit process are included here. These should be comprehensible to the reader who has a thorough understanding of the material covered in Section 5.6.

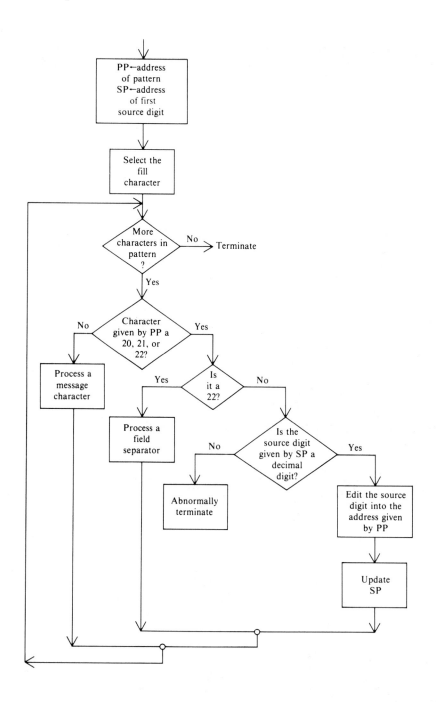

Figure 5-4

185

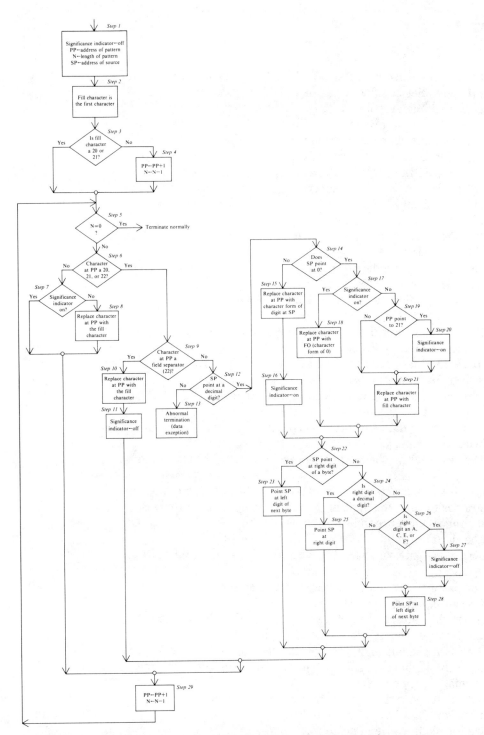

Figure 5-5

Step 1. Set the significance indicator off. Point PP at the leftmost byte of the pattern. Set N equal to the length of the pattern.

Step 2. Call the character pointed at by PP (the first character in the pattern) the *fill character*. The fill character is determined just once; it will not change throughout the execution of the algorithm.

Step 3. If the fill character is 20 or 21, go to Step 5.

Step 4. Move PP past the fill character (add 1 to PP), and decrement the count of characters in the pattern that have not been processed. (Subtract 1 from N.)

Step 5. If N is 0, terminate normally.

Step 6. If the next character in the pattern (pointed to by PP) is a 20, 21, or 22, go to Step 9.

Step 7. If the significance indicator is on, go to Step 29 (leaving the character in the result).

Step 8. Since the significance indicator is off, replace the character in the pattern with the fill character. Go to Step 29.

Step 9. If the next character in the pattern (pointed to by PP) is not a field separator (22), go to Step 12.

Step 10. Replace the character in the pattern with the fill character.

Step 11. Set the significance indicator off. Go to Step 29.

Step 12. If the next character in the source field (pointed to by SP) is a decimal digit, go to Step 14.

Step 13. At this point, a data exception has occurred, so the algorithm terminates abnormally.

Step 14. If the next digit in the source field (pointed to by SP) is a 0, go to Step 17.

Step 15. Replace the character in the pattern (the line 20 or 21) with the character form of the digit in the source field (pointed to by SP).

Step 16. Turn the significance indicator on. Go to Step 22.

Step 17. If the significance indicator is off, go to Step 19.

Step 18. Replace the pattern character with F0 (character form of 0). Go to Step 22.

Step 19. If the pattern character is not a 21, go to Step 21.

Step 20. Turn the significance indicator on.

Step 21. Replace the pattern character (the 21) with the fill character.

Step 22. If SP points at the left digit of a byte, go to Step 24.

Step 23. Point SP at the left digit of the next byte. Go to Step 29.

Step 24. If the right digit of the same byte in the source field does not contain a decimal digit, go to Step 26.

Step 25. Point SP at the right digit of the byte. Go to Step 29.

Step 26. If the right digit is B or D, go to Step 28.

Step 27. Turn the significance indicator off.

Step 28. Point SP at the left digit of the next byte.

Step 29. Move to the next character in the pattern. (Add 1 to PP, and subtract 1 from N.) Go back to Step 5.

6

External Subroutines
and DSECTs

6.1 FUNCTIONS OF THE ASSEMBLER
AND LOADER

The process normally utilized to convert an assembler-language program to executable (machine-language) code is depicted in Figure 6-1.

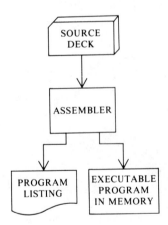

Figure 6-1

The *source deck*, the set of cards into which the assembler-language program has been punched, is translated by the assembler into an executable version of the program. If no errors are detected in the source deck during the process of assembly, execution of the translated form of the program may begin immediately. This is certainly the most direct approach to the execution of a program, and it is satisfactory for most short programs that are intended to be executed once or, at most, a few times. However, in a normal industrial environment, the typical program is intended to be executed many, many times. In such cases, it is essential to avoid the necessity of using the assembler to translate the source deck each time a particular program is to be executed. Thus, most industrial computing centers employ a procedure similar to the one illustrated in Figure 6-2.

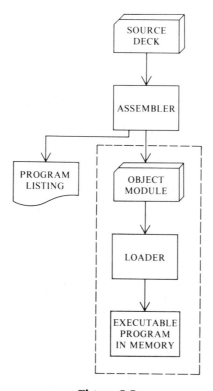

Figure 6-2

In this procedure, the output (an executable version of the program) from the assembler is retained in the form of an *object module*. The function of the *loader* is to copy the translated code from the object module into storage so that execution of the program can begin.

Thus, once a completely debugged source deck has been obtained, it is necessary to utilize the entire procedure depicted in Figure 6-2 only on the first occasion that the program is executed. On all subsequent occasions, execution of the program may be accomplished simply by utilizing the part of the procedure that is enclosed in broken lines. That is, once an object module has been created, the program may be readied for execution just by utilizing the loader to copy the translated code from the object module into storage.

To understand the discussion of external subroutines that begins in Section 6.2, it will be necessary for the reader to keep in mind the procedure represented by Figure 6-2.

6.2 AN INTRODUCTION TO EXTERNAL SUBROUTINES

The reader should, by this time, be well aware of the advantages that may be gained through the use of subroutines. The creation of general subroutines that can be invoked from any point in a program may serve to accomplish the following:

- simplify the logic of the program
- significantly reduce the amount of code required
- facilitate the task of debugging

The subroutines that have been considered to this point are called *internal subroutines*, because they are themselves part of the programs by which they are invoked. It is possible, however, to produce subroutines that may be invoked by any program. Such subroutines are called *external subroutines*, because they may be created and maintained separately from the programs by which they will be invoked.

Two important factors make the general use of external subroutines possible:

1. The source deck for an external subroutine may be assembled separately to produce an object module. The resulting object module may then be entered into an object module library, which is simply a collection of object modules residing on some mass storage device such as a disk pack.

2. The loader may accept as input not only an object module but an object module library as well. From this input, the loader will construct an executable program that employs any required external subroutines from the object module library.

The use of external subroutines leads to an extended version of the procedure presented in Figure 6-2. This extended procedure is illustrated in Figure 6-3.

Consideration of Figure 6-3 should indicate the complete independence of the external subroutine from the main program. Thus, external subroutines that perform commonly required tasks may be created and entered into the object module library and made available to any number of programmers. Just how useful it can be to a programmer to have a common set of thoroughly debugged subroutines available should become apparent when the specific examples presented in this chapter are considered.

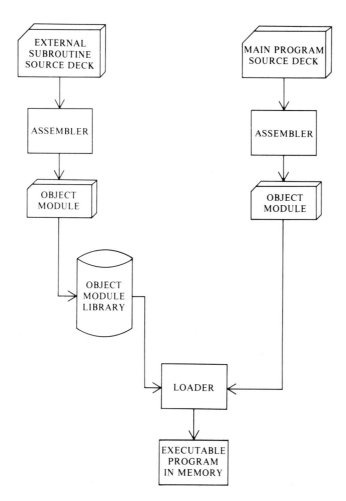

Figure 6-3

6.3 CODING AND INVOKING
EXTERNAL SUBROUTINES

In Section 6.2, we presented an overview of external subroutines. Here, we will discuss the details of the techniques used to code and invoke external subroutines.

Each external subroutine should begin with a statement of the form

        name   CSECT

where name is the label by which the subroutine will be called. The CSECT statement defines the beginning of a *control section*, which is a block of code that may be assembled and relocated independently of other blocks of code. For our present purpose, it will be useful to think of each control section as constituting a separate subroutine.

As discussed in Section 6.2, once a subroutine has been debugged it is usually assembled into a separate object module. In such cases, the source deck for the subroutine will resemble in most respects the source decks with which you are familiar. During debugging stages, however, several external subroutines are frequently included in the same source deck with a program by which they are called. Such a source deck has the following form:

```
MAINPROG     CSECT
             .
             .
             .
             LTORG
SUBRT1       CSECT
             .
             .
             .
             LTORG
SUBRT2       CSECT
             .
             .
             .
             LTORG
             END   MAINPROG
```

Here, the beginning of each subroutine is determined by the positioning of the CSECT statements. Each new control section will begin on a doubleword boundary. The LTORG statements should be included to ensure that the literals for each subroutine are not assembled as part of the first control section (in this case, MAINPROG) but, rather, are grouped with the subroutine of which they are intended to be a part.

The problem of invoking (or calling) an external subroutine from a main program or another external subroutine is slightly more complex than it may at first appear. For example, assume that SUBRTN is an external subroutine. If SUBRTN has been assembled separately from the calling routine, the statement

```
        BAL      R14,SUBRTN
```

will not suffice to invoke SUBRTN. When this statement is encountered by the assembler, SUBRTN will be identified as an undefined symbol. A similar comment applies to the statements

```
            L        R15, = A(SUBRTN)
            BALR     R14,R15
```

In this case, SUBRTN will again be declared an undefined symbol if SUBRTN has been assembled separately. The address of SUBRTN must be obtained before this subroutine can be invoked. This is accomplished through the use of a V-type constant. The format for specifying a V-type constant is

```
     label          DC       V(ext-symbol)
```

where ext-symbol is normally the label of a CSECT statement. The referenced CSECT may occur in the same source deck or it may be assembled separately. In either event, the actual value generated by this statement is a fullword containing 00000000. The address of the referenced subroutine is filled in by the loader when the executable program is constructed in storage. Thus, the statement

```
     SUBADDR    DC       V(SUBRTN)
```

will cause 00000000 to be generated when the program is assembled, but SUBADDR will contain the address of SUBRTN when execution of the program begins. From this discussion, it should be clear that the statements

```
            L        R15,SUBADDR
            BALR     R14,R15
                         .
                         .
                         .
     SUBADDR    DC       V(SUBRTN)
```

could be used to call SUBRTN. The call can be made more conveniently through the use of a V-type literal, as follows:

```
            L        R15, = V(SUBRTN)
            BALR     R14,R15
```

Consideration of the use of external subroutines should naturally give rise to the following questions:

- What registers may be altered by the subroutines?
- How should parameters be passed on to the subroutines?
- How should results be passed back to the calling routine?

Before a subroutine can be of use to a large number of programmers, answers to these questions must be carefully documented. To facilitate the creation of common subroutines, a set of basic, standardized linkage conventions have evolved. These are as follows:

1. When control is passed to an external subroutine, R15 should contain the address of the first instruction in the subroutine, and R14 should contain

the address in the calling routine to which control is to be returned. Hence, if the statements

```
L       R15, = V(SUBRTN)
BALR    R14,R15
```

were used to call SUBRTN, both R14 and R15 would contain the appropriate values.

2. Critical parameters to be passed to a subroutine are normally passed through a parameter list. A *parameter list* is a set of contiguous fullwords, each of which contains an address. Upon entry to the subroutine, R1 should contain the address of the parameter list. For example, to pass the address of a table to be sorted and the address of a field containing the number of entries in the table to an external subroutine called SORT-TAB, the following code could be used:

```
LA      R1,PARMLIST
L       R15, = V(SORTTAB)
BALR    R14,R15
        .
        .
        .

PARMLIST  DC    A(TABLE,NUM)
NUM       DC    F'20'
```

The exact format of the parameter list should be included in the documentation for the subroutine. If only a few parameters are to be passed to a subroutine, these may be passed through registers. For example, the statements

```
LM      R2,R3, = A(TABLE,20)
L       R15, = V(SORTTAB)
BALR    R14,R15
```

could be used to call the subroutine, if it is assumed that the parameters for SORTTAB would be extracted from R2 and R3 rather than from a parameter list. In cases where the number of words in the parameter list can vary, it is common practice to set the leftmost bit of the last word in the list to 1. This allows the called routine to easily determine the number of words in the list.

3. Values to be returned from the subroutine to the calling routine are normally stored in areas designated in the parameter list. However, if just a single value is to be returned, it is frequently passed back in R0.

4. It is the responsibility of the subroutine to store the contents of the registers upon entry to the subroutine and to restore these original values to the registers before returning control to the calling routine. It is the

responsibility of the calling program to place into R13 the address of an 18-fullword area, called a *register save area*, which the called subroutine may utilize to store the original contents of the registers. The format of the register save area is illustrated in Figure 6-4.

ignored
Backward pointer
Forward pointer
R14
R15
.
.
.
R12

Figure 6-4

The uses of the second and third words in the register save area will be discussed later in this section. Words 4 through 18 are used to store the original contents of registers 14, 15, 0, 1, . . . 12. Thus, the statement

        STM   R14,R12,12(R13)

should be the first instruction executed upon entry to a subroutine. The statements

        LM   R14,R12,12(R13)
        BR   R14

should be used to restore the original contents of the registers and to return control to the calling routine.

5. Because of the frequent use of R1, R14, and R15 in subroutine calls, these registers should not be used as base registers. For this reason, each external subroutine should contain a section of code that establishes a base register for use in calculating addresses within that routine. For example, the statements

        BALR   R12,0
        USING   BASEPT,R12
BASEPT DS   0H

could be used to establish R12 as a base register. The BALR statement simply causes the address of the next executable statement to be placed in R12. (No branch occurs, because the second operand is R0.) The DS statement serves only as a means of establishing an address corresponding to the label BASEPT. (No storage area is reserved, since none is requested.)

The details of the process by which the *operating system* initiates the execution of a program are well beyond the scope of this book. There is one point, however, that should be mentioned in this regard. A save area for utilization by the main program is provided and the register linkage conventions that apply to external subroutines are in effect. Thus, the convention that R15 should contain the address of the first executable instruction of the called routine upon entry to that routine should explain why it has been possible to assume that R15 was properly prepared for use as a base register in all of the examples presented to this point. Likewise, the convention pertaining to R14 should explain why those programs could be exited by branching to the address in R14.

To adhere to the linkage conventions that we have just outlined, each external subroutine (or main program) that calls no external subroutines should begin with a section of code similar to

```
ROUTINE    CSECT
           STM     R14,R12,12(R13)
           BALR    R12,0
           USING   BASEPT,R12
BASEPT     DS      0H
```

This causes the contents of the calling routine's registers to be saved in the save area provided by the calling routine (or operating system) and establishes R12 as the base register. In the interior of the routine, neither the base register nor R13 should be altered. The routine should exit with the instructions

```
           LM      R14,R12,12(R13)
           BR      R14
```

This restores the original contents of the calling routine's registers and returns control to that routine.

Program 6-1, which calls no external subroutines, illustrates the proper linkage to the calling program (or to the operating system).

Program 6-1

```
***********************************************************************
*
*  THIS PROGRAM READS DATA CARDS, EACH OF WHICH CONTAINS TWO
*  NUMBERS.  THE SUM OF THE TWO NUMBERS IS PRINTED.
*
***********************************************************************
*
SUMUP     CSECT
          STM    R14,R12,12(R13)      SAVE CALLER'S REGISTERS
          BALR   R12,0
          USING  BASEPT,R12
BASEPT    DS     0H
*
          XPRNT  HEADING,28           PRINT A PAGE HEADING
*
          XREAD  CARD,80              READ THE FIRST CARD
*
CHECKEOF  BC     B'0100',EXIT         BRANCH ON EOF
*
          XDECI  R2,CARD              WE ASSUME THAT BOTH NUMBERS
          XDECI  R3,0(R1)             ARE VALID
*
          AR     R2,R3                CALCULATE THE SUM
*
          XDECO  R2,OUTPUT            PUT PRINTABLE FORM INTO PRINT LINE
*
          XPRNT  CRG,13               PRINT THE SUM (SINGLE SPACED)
*
          XREAD  CARD,80              TRY TO READ THE NEXT CARD
          B      CHECKEOF             GO CHECK FOR EOF
*
EXIT      LM     R14,R12,12(R13)      RESTORE CALLER'S REGISTERS
          BR     R14                  EXIT
*
CARD      DS     CL80                 CARD INPUT AREA
*
CRG       DC     C' '                 SINGLE SPACE CARRIAGE CONTROL
OUTPUT    DS     CL12                 OUTPUT THE SUM HERE
*
HEADING   DC     C'1THIS IS THE OUTPUT OF SUMUP'
R0        EQU    0
R1        EQU    1
R2        EQU    2
R3        EQU    3
R4        EQU    4
R5        EQU    5
R6        EQU    6
R7        EQU    7
R8        EQU    8
R9        EQU    9
R10       EQU    10
R11       EQU    11
R12       EQU    12
R13       EQU    13
R14       EQU    14
R15       EQU    15
          END    SUMUP
```

The situation is somewhat more complex in the case of a main program or subroutine that calls an external subroutine. For purposes of illustration, suppose SUBRTN1 has called SUBRTN2 and that SUBRTN2 is to call SUBRTN3 in turn. Then SUBRTN2 should do the following:

- Establish a save area for use by SUBRTN3.
- Doubly link this save area to the save area provided by SUBRTN1.
- Place the address of this save area in R13.

This can be accomplished by a sequence of instructions similar to

```
          LA       R14,SAVEAREA
          ST       R14,8(R13)
          ST       R13,4(R14)
          LR       R13,R14
```

The first ST instruction fills in the forward pointer in the save area in SUBRTN1 with the address of the save area in SUBRTN2. The second ST instruction fills in the backward pointer in the save area in SUBRTN2 with the address of the save area in SUBRTN1. Finally, the LR instruction places the address of the save area in SUBRTN2 into R13.

Program 6-2 illustrates the use of these conventions. In this example, two subroutines, READTAB and SORTTAB, are called by MAIN. Study the listing of this program carefully before proceeding.

Program 6-2

```
          TITLE 'EXAMPLE OF A PROGRAM CALLING AN EXTERNAL SUBROUTINE'
**********************************************************************
*
*  THIS PROGRAM CALLS THE SUBROUTINE 'READTAB' TO READ IN A TABLE
*  OF INTEGERS, XDUMPS THE TABLE, CALLS 'SORTTAB' TO SORT THE
*  TABLE, AND THEN XDUMPS THE SORTED TABLE.  THE LOGIC IS AS FOLLOWS:
*
*     STEP 1.   CALL READTAB TO READ IN A TABLE OF INTEGERS.
*
*     STEP 2.   XDUMP THE TABLE OF UNSORTED INTEGERS
*
*     STEP 3.   CALL SORTTAB TO SORT THE TABLE.
*
*     STEP 4.   XDUMP THE TABLE OF SORTED INTEGERS.
*
*     STEP 5.   EXIT.
*
**********************************************************************
*
MAIN      CSECT
          STM    R14,R12,12(R13)      SAVE CALLER'S REGISTERS
          BALR   R12,0                ESTABLISH THE BASE REGISTER
          USING  BASEPT,R12
BASEPT    DS     0H
          LA     R14,SAVEAREA         NOW LINK UP THE SAVE AREAS
          ST     R14,8(R13)
          ST     R13,4(R14)
          LR     R13,R14              POINT R13 AT NEW SAVE AREA
*
***<STEP 1>     CALL READTAB TO READ IN A TABLE OF INTEGERS
*
          LA     R1,=A(TABLE,NUMENT)
          L      R15,=V(READTAB)
          BALR   R14,R15              CALL READTAB
*
***<STEP 2>     XDUMP THE UNSORTED TABLE
*
          XDUMP  TABLE,200
*
***<STEP 3>     CALL SORTTAB TO SORT THE TABLE
*
          LA     R1,=A(TABLE,NUMENT)
          L      R15,=V(SORTTAB)
          BALR   R14,R15
*
***<STEP 4>     XDUMP THE SORTED TABLE
*
          XDUMP  TABLE,200
```

```
*
***<STEP 5>     EXIT
*
          L     R13,4(R13)          R13 NOW POINTS AT OLD SAVE AREA
          LM    R14,R12,12(R13)     RESTORE CALLER'S REGISTERS
          BR    R14                 RETURN TO CALLER
*
          LTORG
*
SAVEAREA  DS    18F                 REGISTER SAVE AREA
TABLE     DS    50F                 TABLE TO HOLD THE INTEGERS
NUMENT    DS    F                   SET TO CONTAIN THE NUMBER
*                                   OF ENTRIES IN THE TABLE
*
*
*********************************************************************
*
* 'READTAB' IS AN EXTERNAL SUBROUTINE THAT READS IN A TABLE OF
* INTEGERS.  THE PARAMETER LIST TO READTAB MUST CONTAIN
*
*        THE ADDRESS OF THE TABLE
*        THE ADDRESS OF A WORD THAT GETS SET TO THE NUMBER OF
*            ENTRIES IN THE TABLE
*
* THE LOGIC OF READTAB IS AS FOLLOWS:
*
*   STEP 1.  SET A POINTER TO THE FIRST ENTRY IN THE TABLE.
*
*   STEP 2.  READ THE FIRST CARD.
*
*   STEP 3.  IF END-OF-FILE HAS OCCURRED, GO TO STEP 6.
*
*   STEP 4.  PUT THE NUMBER INTO THE TABLE.
*
*   STEP 5.  READ THE NEXT CARD AND GO TO STEP 3.
*
*   STEP 6.  CALCULATE THE NUMBER OF ENTRIES, STORE IT, AND
*            RETURN TO THE CALLER.
*
*********************************************************************
*
READTAB   CSECT
          STM   R14,R12,12(R13)     SAVE CALLER'S REGISTERS
          BALR  R12,0               SET UP A NEW BASE REGISTER
          USING READBASE,R12
READBASE  DS    0H
*
          LM    R2,R3,0(R1)         R2 <- A(TABLE)
*                                   R3 <- A(NUMBER OF ENTRIES)
***<STEP 1>     SET POINTER THAT ALWAYS POINTS TO NEXT ENTRY
*
          LR    R4,R2               R4 POINTS AT NEXT OPEN ENTRY
***<STEP 2>     READ THE FIRST CARD
*
          XREAD CARD,80
***<STEP 3>     IF ENF-OF-FILE HAS OCCURRED, GO TO STEP 6.
*
TESTEND   BC    B'0100',EXIT
***<STEP 4>     PUT THE NUMBER IN TO THE NEXT TABLE ENTRY
*
          XDECI R5,CARD
          ST    R5,0(R4)            STORE NUMBER INTO THE TABLE
          LA    R4,4(R4)            POINT TO NEXT TABLE ENTRY
*
***<STEP 5>     READ THE NEXT NUMBER AND GO BACK TO STEP 3.
*
          XREAD CARD,80
          B     TESTEND
***<STEP 6>     SAVE THE NUMBER OF TABLE ENTRIES AND RETURN
*
EXIT      SR    R4,R2
          SRA   R4,2                R4 HAS THE NUMBER OF ENTRIES
          ST    R4,0(R3)            RETURN ANSWER TO CALLER
*
          LM    R14,R12,12(R13)     RESTORE CALLER'S REGISTERS
          BR    R14                 RETURN TO CALLER
*
          LTORG
*
CARD      DS    CL80                CARD INPUT AREA
*
```

Program 6-2 (continued)

```
******************************************************************
*
* 'SORTTAB' CAN BE CALLED TO SORT A TABLE OF INTEGERS INTO
* ASCENDING ORDER.  THE PARAMETER LIST MUST CONTAIN
*
*         THE ADDRESS OF THE TABLE TO BE SORTED
*         THE ADDRESS OF A WORD CONTAINING THE NUMBER OF ENTRIES
*            IN THE TABLE
*
* TO SEE HOW THE ALGORITHM WORKS, THINK OF THE TABLE AS BEING
* DIVIDED INTO A SORTED PART (ON THE LEFT) AND AN UNSORTED
* PART.  THE NUMBERS IN THE SORTED PART ARE IN ASCENDING ORDER.
* INITIALLY, ONLY THE LEFTMOST NUMBER IS IN THE SORTED PART.
* NOW PICK UP THE FIRST UNSORTED NUMBER.  NOW SHIFT OVER ANY
* OF THE SORTED NUMBERS THAT ARE LARGER THAN IT, MAKING ROOM
* FOR THE NUMBER IN THE SORTED LIST.  PUT IT INTO THE LIST.
* THUS, WE MOVE ONE NUMBER AT A TIME INTO THE SORTED LIST.
* CONTINUE MOVING NUMBERS FROM THE UNSORTED SECTION INTO THE
* SORTED LIST UNTIL ALL THE NUMBERS HAVE BEEN MOVED.  THEN THE
* SORT IS COMPLETE.  THIS LOGIC GOES AS FOLLOWS:
*
*   STEP 1.   SET A POINTER TO THE SECOND WORD OF THE TABLE (FIRST
*             ELEMENT IN THE UNSORTED SECTION).  GET THE NUMBER
*             OF WORDS IN THE UNSORTED SECTION.
*
*   STEP 2.   IF THERE ARE NO MORE WORDS IN THE UNSORTED SECTION,
*             GO TO STEP 8.
*
*   STEP 3.   PICK UP THE FIRST WORD IN THE UNSORTED SECTION.
*
*   STEP 4.   IF THERE ARE NO MORE NUMBERS TO THE LEFT OF IT,
*             OR IF THE NUMBER JUST TO THE LEFT IS SMALLER, GO
*             TO STEP 6.
*
*   STEP 5.   MOVE ONE NUMBER IN THE SORTED SECTION TO THE RIGHT,
*             AND DECREMENT THE POINTER TO THE NEXT WORD TO LOOK
*             AT.  GO BACK TO STEP 4.
*
*   STEP 6.   STORE THE # AT THE CORRECT SPOT IN THE SORTED
*             LIST.
*
*   STEP 7.   MOVE THE POINTER TO THE FIRST UNSORTED NUMBER OVER
*             ONE POSITION TO THE RIGHT.  GO TO STEP 2.
*
*   STEP 8.   RETURN TO CALLER.
*
******************************************************************
*
SORTTAB  CSECT
         STM    R14,R12,12(R13)     STORE CALLER'S REGISTERS
         BALR   R12,0
         USING  SORTBASE,R12
SORTBASE DS     0H
*
***<STEP 1>   GET POINTER TO 1ST UNSORTED AND COUNT OF UNSORTED
*
         LM     R2,R3,0(R1)         R2 <- A(TABLE)
*                                   R3 <- A(# WORDS IN TABLE)
         LA     R4,4(R2)            R4 <- A(1ST UNSORTED)
         L      R5,0(R3)
         BCTR   R5,0                R5 <- # WORDS IN UNSORTED SECTION
*
***<STEP 2>   IF NO MORE UNSORTED, GO TO STEP 8
*
CHECKEND S      R5,=F'1'
         BM     SORTEXIT            BRANCH IF NO MORE UNSORTED
*
***<STEP 3>   PICK UP FIRST UNSORTED WORD
*
         L      R6,0(R4)            R6 <- FIRST UNSORTED WORD
*
         LR     R7,R4
         S      R7,=F'4'            R7 <- A(WORD TO LOOK AT NEXT)
***<STEP 4>   IF NO MORE WORDS SHOULD BE SHIFTED, GO TO STEP 6.
*
CHECK1   CR     R7,R2
         BL     GOTSPOT             BRANCH IF NO MORE WORDS
*
         C      R6,0(R7)
         BNL    GOTSPOT             BRANCH IF WORD DOESN'T GET SHIFTED
*
***<STEP 5>   SHIFT ONE OVER AND GO BACK TO STEP 4.
*
         MVC    4(4,R7),0(R7)
         S      R7,=F'4'
         B      CHECK1
```

Program 6-2 (continued)

```
*
***<STEP 6>    PUT THE NUMBER INTO ITS CORRECT SPOT
*
GOTSPOT   ST    R6,4(R7)
***<STEP 7>    INCREMENT POINTER INTO UNSORTED SECTION
*
          LA    R4,4(R4)
          B     CHECKEND
*
***<STEP 8>    RETURN TO CALLER
*
SORTEXIT  LM    R14,R12,12(R13)    RESTORE CALLER'S REGISTERS
          BR    R14                EXIT
*
          LTORG
R0        EQU   0
R1        EQU   1
R2        EQU   2
R3        EQU   3
R4        EQU   4
R5        EQU   5
R6        EQU   6
R7        EQU   7
R8        EQU   8
R9        EQU   9
R10       EQU   10
R11       EQU   11
R12       EQU   12
R13       EQU   13
R14       EQU   14
R15       EQU   15
          END   MAIN
```

The following facts are relevant to observance of the register linkage conventions and should be remembered:

- R13 should always contain the address of a register save area and, hence, should not be used for normal computations.

- R1, R14, and R15 should not be used as base registers and, because of their frequent use in subroutine calls, should never be loaded with values that are considered to be more or less permanent.

Although the register linkage conventions may seem complex, observance of them breaks down into two rather simple cases:

1. A routine that calls no external subroutines should begin with a section of code similar to

```
ROUTINE    CSECT
           STM     R14,R12,12(R13)
           BALR    R12,0
           USING   BASEPT,R12
BASEPT     DS      0H
```

This causes the original contents of the registers to be saved and establishes R12 has a base register. (Recall that a BALR instruction with R0 as second operand simply loads the link register with the address of the next instruction.) In the interior of the routine, neither the base register nor R13 should be altered. The routine should exit with the instructions

```
              LM        R14,R12,12(R13)
              BR        R14
```

2. A routine that may invoke one or more external subroutines should begin
   with a sequence of instructions similar to

```
ROUTINE       CSECT
              STM       R14,R12,12(R13)
              BALR      R12,0
              USING     BASEPT,R12
BASEPT        LA        R14,SAVEAREA
              ST        R14,8(R13)
              ST        R13,4(R14)
              LR        R13,R14
```

In this case, the routine should exit with the

```
              L         R13,4(R13)
              LM        R14,R12,12(R13)
              BR        R14
```

In concluding this section, it should be noted that it is possible to use R13
simultaneously as a save area pointer and a base register. This has the advantage of leaving an additional register free for computational uses. The following section of code accomplishes this purpose:

```
ROUTINE       CSECT
              STM       R14,R12,12(R13)
              BAL       R14,80(R15)
SAVEAREA      DS        18F
              ST        R13,4(R14)
              ST        R14,8(R13)
              LR        R13,R14
              USING     SAVEAREA,R13
```

This particular section of code should be studied carefully. It is not difficult
to comprehend how this code works, if one understands that the instruction

```
              BAL       R14,80(R15)
```

loads the address of SAVEAREA in R14 and causes a branch around
SAVEAREA to the instruction

```
              ST        R13,4(R14)
```

It must be remembered that, according to convention, R15 contains the
address of the first instruction of the routine at the time the routine is
entered.

Exercises

1.

a. Write a subroutine NEXTWORD to find the next "word" in a string. For the purposes of this exercise, you may consider any sequence of characters up to the next blank (or the end of the string) as a word. The parameter list to the subroutine should have the following format:

- address of a string of characters (delimited by a X'00')
- address of a fullword set to point to the first nonblank in the string (0, if there are no more nonblanks)
- address of a fullword set to the address of the first character past the word (the address of the delimiting character, which should be a space or a X'00')

b. Write a subroutine that counts the number of characters and words in a line. The routine should accept as input the following parameter list:

- address of a string (delimited by a X'00')
- address of a fullword that should be set to the number of characters in the line (do not include the 00)
- address of a fullword that should be set to the number of words in the line

2. Write a subroutine that removes the duplicates from a table of integers. The routine should accept as input the following parameter list:

- address of a table of integers
- address of a word that contains the number of entries in the table

The subroutine should remove duplicate values and reset the count to the updated value.

3. This is the same as Exercise 2, except that in this case you should assume that the values in the table occur in ascending order.

4. The SHELL sort algorithm is a more efficient sorting algorithm than the sort shown in Section 6.3. Code a subroutine, SHELL, that takes the following parameter list:

- address of a table of integers
- address of a word containing the number of entries in the table

Suppose that the table is called V and that N contains the number of entries in V. Then, SHELL should use the following sort algorithm to order the entries in V:

Step 1. Set GAP ← N/2, GAPDIS ← GAP*4, and ENDPT ← the address of the last entry in V.

Step 2. If GAP = 0, go to Step 11. (The table is sorted.)

Step 3. NEXTEL ← address of V+GAPDIS. NEXTEL references the (GAP+1)st entry in V.

Step 4. If NEXTEL > ENDPT, go to Step 10.

Step 5. SORTEL ← NEXTEL – GAPDIS

Step 6. If SORTEL < V, or the entry pointed to by SORTEL <= the entry at SORTEL+GAPDIS, go to Step 9.

Step 7. Exchange the entry at SORTEL with the entry at SORTEL+GAPDIS.

Step 8. SORTEL ← SORTEL – GAPDIS. Go to Step 6.

Step 9. NEXTEL ← NEXTEL + 4. Go to Step 4.

Step 10. GAP ← GAP/2. GAPDIS ← GAP*4. Go to Step 2.

Step 11. Exit.

The whole algorithm is much clearer if vector notation is used along with pseudo-code. In this case, the algorithm is as follows:

```
SHELL: PROCEDURE (V,N)
    GAP ← N/2
    Do while (GAP > 0)
        NEXTEL ← GAP + 1
        Do while (NEXTEL <= N)
            SORTEL ← NEXTEL − GAP
            Do while (SORTEL > 0 and V(SORTEL) > V(SORTEL+GAP))
                Exchange V(SORTEL) and V(SORTEL+GAP)
                SORTEL ← SORTEL − GAP
            Enddo
            NEXTEL ← NEXTEL + 1
        Enddo
        GAP ← GAP/2
    Enddo
Endproc
```

Write a program that reads in a table of integers, XDUMPs the table, calls SHELL to sort the table, and XDUMPs the sorted table.

6.4 LINKAGES BETWEEN BAL AND HIGH-LEVEL LANGUAGES

The facility to write subroutines that can be assembled and kept in a library is of fundamental importance. This facility allows the creation of powerful service routines that any other assembler program can conveniently invoke. Fortunately, assembler subroutines can be easily invoked from many high-level languages as well. In particular, the linkages between FORTRAN, COBOL, and assembler routines are all straightforward. To use a PL/I routine from any of these languages or to invoke a subroutine in these languages from PL/I is not quite as easy. The details for all of these interfaces can be found in the IBM manuals. (Normally, the programmer's guide for a high-level language discusses the interfaces to subroutines in other languages.) In this section, we give a brief overview of how assembler routines can be interfaced to FORTRAN and COBOL routines.

To invoke an assembler routine from COBOL or FORTRAN, the CALL statement is used. Thus, to invoke SORTTAB from FORTRAN

> CALL SORTTAB(V,N)

could be used, where V is assumed to be a vector of fullword integers and N is a single integer. This requires that V and N be declared as INTEGER*4. The exact storage format of the FORTRAN data types is given in the FORTRAN Programmer's Guide. To invoke SORTTAB from COBOL,

> CALL 'SORTTAB' USING V N

would be used, where V and N are declared in the data division of the program as

```
01 V.
   05    TABEL PIC S9(5)
         USAGE IS COMP OCCURS 50 TIMES.

01 N     PIC 9(5) USAGE IS COMP.
```

To allow SORTTAB to be called in this way from FORTRAN or COBOL programs, it must be modified to observe two linkage conventions required by these languages. These are:

1. R15 is used as a *return code*. Normally, it should be set to 0 by the subroutine. We recommend always setting R15 to 0 in subroutines called from high-level language programs.

2. Before exiting, the thirteenth byte of the save area (12(R13)) must be set to X'FF'.

Hence, SORTTAB would have to be modified to use the following code to exit:

```
EXIT    LM    R14,R12,12(R13)
        MVI   12(R13),X'FF'
        SR    R15,R15
        BR    R14
```

These slight changes are all that is required to make a subroutine accessible from either COBOL or FORTRAN.

Although it is common to invoke assembler routines from COBOL or FORTRAN, it is much less common to invoke a high-level language routine from assembler language. Occasionally, however, it is very convenient. For example, in Chapter 10, two COBOL service routines are used to perform floating-point conversions. Calling high-level language subroutines normally requires that a standard initialization subroutine be invoked before actually calling the service routines. (The name of the initialization module depends on the compiler.) The actual call to the subroutine follows standard linkage conventions. Thus, in the example presented in Chapter 10, the assembler program first uses

```
L       R15, = V(ILBOSTP0)
BALR    R14,R15
```

to initialize the variables used by the COBOL subroutines. Then, to invoke the COBOL service routine to convert a floating-point number from external to internal format,

```
LA      R1, = A(EXTNUM,INTNUM)
L       R15, = V(FLETOI)
BALR    R14,R15
```

is used.

The preceding discussion is necessarily brief. However, the interested reader can find a complete discussion of linkages between BAL and high-level languages in the language reference and programmer's guide manuals.

6.5 DUMMY SECTIONS (DSECTs)

A *dummy section*, or DSECT, begins with a statement of the form

```
label           DSECT
```

The end of the dummy section is delimited by the occurrence of a CSECT statement, another DSECT statement, or an END statement. The statements in the body of a dummy section specify a format, but these statements do not cause any object code to be generated. As an example, the following DSECT describes a three-word area:

```
PARMLIST    DSECT
TABLADDR    DS      A    ADDRESS OF THE TABLE
KEYADDR     DS      A    ADDRESS OF A KEY
NUMENT      DS      F    NUMBER OF ENTRIES
*                        IN THE TABLE
```

The format described by a DSECT may be associated with a particular area in storage. The labels on the DSECT statements may then be used to specify addresses in that area in assembler statements that cause object code to be generated. Therefore, the register that is to contain the address of the area must be specified before the assembler statements that use labels from the dummy section to reference fields in that area are assembled. Unexpected or erroneous results may still occur, if the specified register does not contain the correct address at execution time. A statement of the form

USING   dsect,r

indicates to the assembler that the area at the address specified by the contents of the register r conforms to the format specified by the dummy section designated by the first operand. The assembler utilizes the information from the USING statement to convert any addresses specified by labels from the dummy section to addresses specified by displacements from the address in register r. As an example, consider the following section of code:

```
USING   PARMLIST,R1
L       R2,NUMENT
L       R5,KEYADDR
```

Since the USING statement conveys that during execution R1 will contain the address of an area in storage that conforms to the format specified by the dummy section PARMLIST, the word to be loaded into R2 is located eight bytes from the address in R1. Thus, the first Load instruction is encoded as 5820 1008. Similarly, the reference to KEYADDR is converted to four bytes from the address in R1. The actual code generated by the previous example is displayed in the assembler listing presented in Program 6-3.

At least two significant advantages can be gained through the use of DSECTs:

- The readability of a program can be markedly improved. For example,

```
L       R2,NUMENT
```

is far clearer than

```
L       R2,8(R1)
```

- A program that employs a DSECT is more easily alterable than one in which explicit addresses are used exclusively.

To illustrate the second advantage, suppose that the program to invoke SEARCH has been coded with the parameters defined in a different order. This situation could be corrected in the subroutine containing the PARM-LIST dummy section by simply reordering the statements in the dummy section. Then, when SEARCH is reassembled, all of the addresses will be converted to the correct values. If, however, explicit addressing had been used, it would have been necessary to alter each statement that referenced a field in the parameter list, before reassembling the program.

Program 6-3

CSECT EXAMPLE - SUBROUTINE TO SEARCH TABLE

LOC	OBJECT CODE	ADDR1 ADDR2	STMT	SOURCE STATEMENT	
000000			34	PARMLIST DSECT	
			35	* THIS DSECT GIVES THE FORMAT OF THE INPUT PARAMETER LIST.	
000000			36	TABLADDR DS A	ADDRESS OF THE TABLE TO SEARCH
000004			37	KEYADDR DS A	ADDRESS OF THE KEY TO SEARCH FOR
000008			38	NUMENT DS F	NUMBER OF ENTRIES IN THE TABLE
000000			40	SEARCH CSECT	
			42	***<STEP 1>	SAVE REGS AND ESTABLISH A BASE REG
000000	90EC D00C	0000C	43	STM R14,R12,12(R13)	STORE CALLER'S REGISTERS
000004	05C0		44	BALR R12,R0	SET UP BASE REGISTER
000006			45	USING *,R12	
			47	***<STEP 2>	SCAN TABLE FOR DESIRED ENTRY
			48	USING PARMLIST,R1	R1 CONTAINS ADDRESS OF INPUT PARM.S
000000			49	L R2,NUMENT	LOAD # ENTRIES IN THE TABLE
0000C6	5820 1008	00008	50	L R3,KEYADDR	LOAD ADDRESS OF THE KEY
00000A	5850 1004	00004	51	L R3,TABLADDR	LOAD ADDRESS OF THE TABLE
00000E	5830 1000	00000			

In the previous example, the DSECT is used to describe the format of a single area. However, a DSECT may be used to reference more than one area in storage during the execution of a program. This is illustrated in the complete listing of SEARCH presented in Program 6-4. In this case, each individual area to be referenced must conform to the format described in the dummy section, and the register specified in the USING statement must be adjusted to contain the address of a specific area, before fields in that area are actually referenced. In SEARCH, the dummy section TABENTRY is used to specify the format of an entry in the table, and R3 is used as a pointer to the entry. Thus, by altering R3 (referred to as the base register for TABENTRY), the labels in the dummy section can be made to apply to any specific entry in the table.

One further aspect of the use of dummy sections requires examination: Different base registers may be used with a dummy section in different parts of a program. Thus, in one section of code, the statement

$$\text{USING} \qquad \text{AREA,R5}$$

could be used to indicate that R5 is to be the base register for AREA, while the statement

$$\text{USING} \qquad \text{AREA,R4}$$

could occur in another section of the same program. To make it clear which register the assembler is to use in converting implicit addresses to explicit addresses, the effect of one USING statement should be canceled before another is issued. This is accomplished through the use of the DROP statement, which has the following format:

$$\text{DROP} \qquad r_1, r_2, \ldots, r_n$$

This statement simply serves to inform the assembler that registers $r_1, r_2, \ldots, r_n$ are no longer to be used as base registers in calculating explicit addresses.

As an illustration, consider the following section of code:

```
AREA        DSECT
FIELD1      DS      CL10
FIELD2      DS      H
FIELD3      DS      F
MAIN        CSECT
              .
              .
              .
```

```
        USING  AREA,R5
        .
        .
        .
        USING  AREA,R4
        L      R1,FIELD3
        .
        .
        .
```

Here, it is not clear whether FIELD3 should be converted to 12(R5) or to 12(R4). However, if the statement

```
        DROP   R5
```

were inserted immediately preceding the second USING statement, R5 would not be used as a base register for AREA in any following statement unless so specified by another USING statement. Thus, FIELD3 could then be unambiguously converted to 12(R4). It is sound practice always to drop the base register of a given dummy section at the end of any sequence of code that references labels in that particular dummy section. This assures that the desired base register will be selected by the assembler when implicit addresses are to be converted to explicit addresses.

Program 6-4

```
    CSECT EXAMPLE - SUBROUTINE TO SEARCH TABLE

LOC     OBJECT CODE   ADDR1 ADDR2  STMT   SOURCE STATEMENT
                                    2   *  THE FOLLOWING SUBROUTINE CAN BE CALLED TO SEARCH A TABLE OF THE
                                    3   *  FOLLOWING FORMAT:
                                    4   *
                                    5   *        KEY    +0(6)        THE KEY UPON WHICH THE TABLE IS SEARCHED
                                    6   *        PROD#  +6(5)        THE PRODUCT NUMBER
                                    7   *        PRICE  +11(4)       THE PRICE WHICH IS STORED AS PACKED DECIMAL
                                    8   *                            IN THE FORM (XXXXX.XX)
                                    9   *        STOCK  +15(4)       THE NUMBER OF UNITS IN STOCK (PACKED DECIMAL)
                                   10   *
                                   11   *  THE INPUT TO THE SUBROUTINE IS A PARAMETER LIST SPECIFYING AN ENTRY
                                   12   *  WHICH SHOULD BE PRINTED.  THE FORMAT OF THE PARAMETER LIST IS:
                                   13   *
                                   14   *        TABLE  +0(4)        ADDRESS OF THE TABLE TO SEARCH (FORMATTED AS
                                   15   *                            SHOWN ABOVE)
                                   16   *        KEY    +4(4)        ADDRESS OF THE KEY TO USE IN THE SEARCH
                                   17   *        #      +8(4)        NUMBER OF ENTRIES IN THE TABLE
                                   18   *
                                   19   *  HERE +N(M) MEANS AN M-BYTE FIELD AT A DISPLACEMENT OF N BYTES.
                                   20   *
                                   21   *  THE LOGIC OF THE SUBROUTINE IS:
                                   22   *
                                   23   *  STEP 1.  SAVE CALLER'S REGISTERS AND SET UP A BASE REG.
                                   24   *
                                   25   *  STEP 2.  SEARCH TABLE FOR THE SOUGHT ENTRY.  IF IT'S FOUND, GO
                                   26   *           TO STEP 4.  ELSE, GO TO STEP 3.
                                   27   *
                                   28   *  STEP 3.  PRINT AN ERROR MESSAGE - ENTRY NOT IN TABLE.
                                   29   *           GO TO STEP 5.
                                   30   *
                                   31   *  STEP 4.  PRINT THE MATCHED ENTRY.
                                   32   *
                                   33   *  STEP 5.  EXIT.

000000                             35      PARMLIST DSECT
                                   36   *  THIS DSECT GIVES THE FORMAT OF THE INPUT PARAMETER LIST.
000000                             37      TABLADDR DS    A          ADDRESS OF THE TABLE TO SEARCH
000004                             38      KEYADDR  DS    A          ADDRESS OF THE KEY TO SEARCH FOR
000008                             39      NUMENT   DS    F          NUMBER OF ENTRIES IN THE TABLE

000000                             41      SEARCH   CSECT

000000  90EC D00C            0000C 43      ***<STEP 1>  SAVE REGS AND ESTABLISH A BASE REG
000004  05C0                       44               STM   R14,R12,12(R13)   STORE CALLER'S REGISTERS
000006                             45               BALR  R12,R0            SET UP BASE REGISTER
                                   46               USING *,R12

000000                             48      ***<STEP 2>  SCAN TABLE FOR DESIRED ENTRY
                                   49               USING PARMLIST,R1      R1 CONTAINS ADDRESS OF INPUT PARM.S
000000  5820 1008           00008  50               L     R2,NUMENT        LOAD # ENTRIES IN THE TABLE
000000A 5850 1004           00004  51               L     R5,KEYADDR       LOAD ADDRESS OF THE KEY
00000E  5830 1000           00000  52               L     R3,TABLADDR      LOAD ADDRESS OF THE TABLE
```

Program 6-4 (continued)

```
DSECT EXAMPLE - SUBROUTINE TO SEARCH TABLE

LOC     OBJECT CODE      ADDR1 ADDR2  STMT  SOURCE STATEMENT
                                       53        USING TABENTRY,R3
000012  D505 3000 5000   00000 00000   54  SRCHLP   CLC   TABKEY,0(R5)              COMPARE KEY WITH THE KEY IN 1 ENTRY
000018  4780 C02E                       55           BE    GOTENTRY
00001C  4130 3013              00013    56           LA    R3,TANXTENT              LOAD ADDRESS OF THE NEXT ENTRY
000020  4620 C00C              00012    57           BCT   R2,SRCHLP                BRANCH IF MORE ENTRIES TO TRY

                                        59  ***<STEP 3>   PRINT AN ERROR MESSAGE
000024  D205 C076 5000   0007C 00000    60           MVC   ERRKEY,0(R5)             MOVE KEY TO ERROR MESSAGE
00002A  E020 C073 0023   0007B          61           XPRNT ERRLINE,35               PRINT ERROR MESSAGE
000030  47F0 C058              0005E    62           B     LEAVE

                                        64  ***<STEP 4>   PRINT THE MATCHED ENTRY
000034  D205 C099 3000   0009F 00000    65  GOTENTRY MVC   PRNTKEY,TABKEY           MOVE KEY TO PRINT LINE
00003A  D204 C0A1 3006   000A7 00006    66           MVC   PRNTPROD,TABPROD#        MOVE PRODUCT NUMBER TO PRINT LINE
000040  C208 C0A8 C06C   000AE 00072    67           MVC   PRNTPRIC,=X'4020202021482020'   EDIT IN THE PRICE
000046  DE08 C0A8 C06C   000AE 00072    68           ED    PRNTPRIC,TABPRICE        EDIT IN THE PRICE
00004C  D209 C0B3 C062   000B9 00068    69           MVC   PRNTSTCK,=X'40206B2020206B202120'
000052  DE09 C0B3 300F   000B9 0009E    70           ED    PRNTSTCK,TABSTOCK        EDIT IN THE # OF UNITS OF STOCK
000058  E020 C098 0025   0009E          71           XPRNT PRNTLINE,37

                                        73  ***<STEP 5>   EXIT
00005E  98EC D00C              0000C    74  LEAVE    LM    R14,R12,12(R13)
000062  07FE                            75           BR    R14

                                        76           LTORG
000068  40206B2020206B2020              77           =X'40206B2020206B202120'
000072  4020202021482020                78           =X'4020202021482020'
000078  F0                              79  ERRLINE  DC    C'0'                     CARRIAGE CONTROL
00007C                                  80  ERRKEY   DS    CL6                      KEY VALUE WHICH WASN'T FOUND
000082  40604C5D5E3D9E8                 81           DC    C' - ENTRY IS NOT IN THE TABLE'
00009E  F0                              82  PRNTLINE DC    C'0'                     CARRIAGE CONTROL
0000A5  4040                            83  PRNTKEY  DS    CL6                      KEY OF MATCHED ENTRY
0000A7                                  84           DC    CL2' '
0000AC  4040                            85  PRNTPROD DS    CL5                      PRODUCT NUMBER OF MATCHED ENTRY
0000AE                                  86           DC    CL2' '
0000B7  4040                            87  PRNTPRIC DS    CL9                      PRICE OF MATCHED ENTRY
                                        88           DC    CL2' '
0000B9                                  89  PRNTSTCK DS    CL10                     NUMBER OF UNITS IN STOCK
000000                                  90  R0       EQU   0
000001                                  91  R1       EQU   1
000002                                  92  R2       EQU   2
000003                                  93  R3       EQU   3
000005                                  94  R5       EQU   5
00000C                                  95  R12      EQU   12
00000D                                  96  R13      EQU   13
00000E                                  97  R14      EQU   14
00000F                                  98  R15      EQU   15
000000                                  99  TABENTRY DSECT
                                       100  * THIS DSECT GIVES THE FORMAT OF AN ENTRY IN THE TABLE
000000                                 101  TABKEY   DS    CL6                      THE KEY
000006                                 102  TABPROD# DS    CL5                      PRODUCT NUMBER
000008                                 103  TABPRICE DS    PL4                      PRICE AS XXXXX.XX
00000F                                 104  TABSTOCK DS    PL4                      UNITS OF STOCK ON HAND
000013                                 105  TANXTENT DS    0X                       ADDRESS OF THE NEXT ENTRY
                                       107           END
```

7
Input/Output under OS and DOS

7.1 INTRODUCTION

Throughout Chapters 1–6, the tacit assumption was made that all input and output of data was to be accomplished using the pseudo-instructions XREAD and XPRNT. This approach offers the following major advantages over more conventional approaches:

1. The complexities involved in the standard techniques used for the input and output of data are avoided initially. Therefore:

   a. Complete programs can be introduced very early.
   b. Full concentration can be focused on the assembler-language instructions and their use in manipulating data.

2. Student programs may be processed under ASSIST. Therefore:

   a. As much as 75 percent of processing time can be saved.
   b. Abbreviated dumps with excellent diagnostics can save paper and time spent debugging programs.

There is a major disadvantage, of course, if the learning process stops here. The student might have gained a rather thorough knowledge of the assembler-language instruction set but still has no idea of how input and output are handled in a conventional setting.

The purpose of this chapter is to introduce some of the basic notions involved in data organization that are prerequisite to any discussion of input and output and then to introduce one of the widely used methods of handling the input and output of data.

7.2 SEQUENTIAL FILES

All electronic high-speed digital computers (the IBM machines are prime examples) can be thought of as devices used for the manipulation of data.

This data is normally stored on external storage media such as punched cards, magnetic tape, and magnetic disks. Data is transferred from these media to the main storage of the computer and from computer storage to these media by input and output (I/O) devices. The I/O devices that are relevant to this discussion include the card reader, printer, magnetic tape drive, and magnetic disk drive.

Areas in computer storage into which data is input from external media and from which data is output to external media are called *buffers*. The amount of data transferred in a single I/O operation is normally the amount required to fill a buffer and is referred to as a *physical record*. The *length* of a physical record is the number of bytes the record contains.

For data to be manipulated by the execution of a user program, the data must be passed from an input buffer to the program; likewise, data that is to be output must be passed from the user program to an output buffer. The amount of data passed from a buffer to a user program or from a user program to a buffer in a single operation is referred to as a *logical record*.

A *file* is an organized collection of related data records. In the case of the card and printer files with which the reader is familiar, the distinction between logical and physical records is not crucial, since in either case the length of a logical record and the length of a physical record are the same. Furthermore, the lengths of these records are fixed; for example, all records in a card file have a length of 80 bytes. In Sections 7.3 and 7.4, however, it will become apparent that these notions take on added significance when tape or disk files are under consideration.

A *sequential file* is made up of records that must be processed serially (one after another in some fixed order). Card files and printed files are excellent examples of sequential files. In each case, the ordering of the file is apparent. With a card file, each card in the file must be processed in the order in which it occurs; likewise, with a printed file, the lines directed to the printer must be printed in some fixed order.

Although file organizations other than sequential (for example, indexed sequential and random access) are commonly used on most modern data processing equipment, the discussion in this chapter will, for the sake of simplicity, be confined to the processing of sequential files.

As indicated earlier, the logical records in a card file or a printed file are all the same length. In general, however, when processing files that reside on magnetic tapes or magnetic disk packs, a programmer can choose either to force all the records in the file to be the same length or to allow the lengths of the individual records to vary. In the first case, the records in the file are said to conform to the *fixed-length format;* in the second case, the records are said to be in the *variable-length format*. The fixed-length format is particularly simple, since no control information must be added to a record to indicate the length of the record. Variable-length records, however, require a means of designating the length of each logical record.

The standard format for a variable-length logical record is

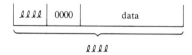

Here, the first two bytes are reserved for the length of the record; the third and fourth bytes are normally set to 0000. The four-byte field of control information is called the *Record Descriptor Word (RDW)* and must be included in each record in a file of variable-length logical records.

7.3 TAPE FILES

A magnetic tape drive is similar in several respects to a common tape recorder/player. In both cases, information can be stored on magnetic tapes for future retrieval and the tapes are normally rewound between uses. Of course, in one instance the data is a sound image, while in the other it consists of images of strings of binary bits.

The tapes utilized by magnetic tape drives are normally as long as 2400 feet, and the storage capacity of these tapes is, literally, enormous. A single reel of tape can be used to store several files, each containing thousands of records. It is not uncommon for one reel of tape to contain 30 million characters of data.

The files on a reel of tape are numbered, starting with 1. Several special records normally precede the data records in each file; these records, called *label records*, contain information about the file. For example, the format of the records in a file is a part of the information stored in the label records for that file. Thus, it is possible to determine the format of the records in a file as well as a variety of other information about the file by simply examining the label records in that file.

When data is stored on a magnetic tape, a gap is left between the individual data records. This gap, or empty space, is referred to as an *interrecord gap*. Although such a gap is only .60 to about .75 inches wide, this can exceed the length of tape necessary to store a 100-character record by a factor of as much as 10, because data is so densely packed on the tape. A typical density factor is 1600 characters per inch. In addition, each interrecord gap represents a place where the tape must be physically stopped and restarted. A typical time for starting and stopping a tape is approximately five times as long as the time required to read a 100-character record.

By applying a little arithmetic, the reader can easily determine that, if individual 100-character records were stored on a tape, the tape could be 90 percent blank spaces and the time occupied in starting and stopping this tape could be 80 percent of the time required to read the tape. To alleviate this situation, it is common to store more than one logical record between interrecord gaps. This technique is called *blocking*. The set of records stored between gaps is called a *block*, and the number of these records is called the *blocking factor*.

From this information the reader can easily calculate the effect that a blocking factor of 10 would have on the length of tape required to store and the length of time required to read a lengthy file of 100-character records. Assume, for example, that such a file contained 10,000 records. Blocking reduces the number of interrecord gaps from 10,000 to 1000. This effectively reduces the length of tape required to store the file by 5400 inches; the amount of time required to read the file is about one-sixth of what it would have been without blocking.

When magnetic tape drives are used for the input or output of data, a physical record (the amount of data transferred in a single I/O operation) is the data recorded between two adjacent interrecord gaps. Thus, a block and a physical record are the same. If a blocking factor of 1 is used, a logical record and a physical record have the same length. However, if, as in the previous example, 100-byte logical records are blocked using a blocking factor of 10, a logical record has a length of 100 bytes while a physical record has a length of 1000 bytes. The advantages gained by using a large blocking factor must always be weighed against the expense of the computer storage required to store large blocks of data.

Before we leave the topic of tape files, one more aspect of blocking must be discussed. When logical records in variable-length format are blocked, the lengths of the blocks may vary because of the variation in the lengths of the logical records. In this case, control information must be added to the beginning of each block of records to indicate the length of the block. The format of a block of variable-length records is

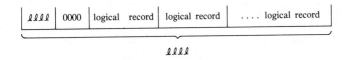

where the two bytes $\ell\ell\ell\ell$ indicate the length of the block.

7.4 DISK FILES

A *direct-access device* is an I/O device that permits any single physical record stored on the device to be accessed without having to access any other physical record stored on the device. There are a variety of direct-access devices in common use. However, in this section, only the magnetic moving-head disk drive will be considered. A typical moving-head disk pack (the recording medium for a disk drive) has six disks that are mounted on a vertical shaft. There are five movable arms, each controlling two read-write heads used to record or read information from the inside surfaces of the disks. These arms move in unison.

If the read-write heads are not moved during the time required for the disk pack to rotate once, each of the read-write heads will have moved past an area of a disk that forms a ring on the surface of that disk. There is a fixed number of positions—say, 200—to which the read-write heads can be moved. Thus, for each disk in the disk pack, there are 200 concentric rings that can be used to store data on each surface in contact with a read-write head. Each such ring is called a *track*. Each track has the same storage capacity, which is a function of the particular model or type of disk pack under consideration.

Suppose that as the disk pack revolves, the read-write heads are not moved. Then, the collection of tracks that passes under the individual read-write heads is called a *cylinder*. The tracks in a cylinder are naturally related, since data can be stored on or read from all the tracks in that cylinder without intermediate movement of the read-write heads.

One common moving-head disk drive in use at this writing has 30 recording surfaces. Such a disk pack is capable of storing more than 300 million characters of data.

This discussion of magnetic disk drives is confined to a consideration of sequential files. The following sequence describes the basic order in which physical records in a sequential file are stored on a disk pack.

1. The read-write heads are first positioned to the cylinder in which the file is to begin.
2. Physical records are stored in all the tracks in the current cylinder until this cylinder is filled. Then, all the read-write heads are moved to the next adjacent cylinder where storage is continued.

As in the case of files stored on magnetic tape, label records are normally associated with disk files. However, with disk files, these records are not stored at the beginning of the file to which they are related. Instead, for each file, the position of that file on the disk pack and the label records associated with the file are stored in the *volume table of contents (VTOC)*. There is one VTOC per pack, and it is used to store information pertinent to each file stored on that pack.

The records stored on a track of a disk pack resemble the records stored on a magnetic tape. In each case, relatively large gaps occur between physical records. For this reason, blocking is used with disk files just as with tape files. With a disk file, however, the size of the blocks should be chosen to conform to the storage capacity of a track: The block size should be chosen so as to avoid an unnecessarily large gap at the end of the track.

For example, if the storage capacity of a track were equal to two blocks of n characters each, it would be wasteful to choose a blocking factor resulting in a physical record size of $2n\text{-}n/2$ bytes, as this would result in a gap of $n/2$ bytes at the end of each track. For most types of disk packs, charts are available that give suggested block sizes. These charts should be consulted before the block size is selected for any disk file.

7.5 AN OVERVIEW OF THE QUEUED SEQUENTIAL ACCESS METHOD (QSAM)

The routines required to effect the reading of a card or the printing of a line are incredibly complex. The routines required to access records on tape or disk files are even more complex, because the logical records must be extracted from the physical records or blocks. Since the problems posed by accessing and creating files are so substantial, routines for performing these functions are available on most computer systems. These routines may be invoked by the application programmer through appropriate macro instructions.

The details concerning the definition of macros are deferred to Chapter 9. For now, the reader may think of a macro instruction simply as a single instruction that will cause a sequence of assembler instructions to be generated. Specifically, when a module is required to perform a given function, a macro instruction can be used to generate the instructions necessary to call the module.

A complete set of macros and modules for performing I/O functions is referred to as an *access method*. Only one such access method, the *queued sequential access method* (QSAM), will be considered here. The basic services provided by QSAM are presented in this section; the specific details of the macro instructions available to the application programmer for invoking the modules to perform these services are deferred to Section 7.6.

1. In the case of *output files* (files created by a user program), QSAM provides modules that can be invoked to do the following:

    a. Open the file. This service must be performed before any attempt is made to transfer a record to the file. Such a module performs initialization tasks, such as readying an output device to receive the file and inserting label records on a tape file.

    b. Transfer a record to a buffer. When a module of this type is invoked, a record is transferred from the application program to a buffer. When the last record in a block has been transferred to the buffer, the block is output to the appropriate recording medium through an I/O device. Thus, with a tape file that consists of fixed-length records grouped ten to a block, the module invoked will cause a physical record to be output every tenth time it is invoked. On the other hand, with an unblocked file (such as a printer file), a physical record is output each time the module is invoked.

c. Close the file. Such a module must be invoked after the last of the records in a file has been transferred to a buffer. This module causes the last block assembled to be output and a variety of necessary "clean-up" operations to be performed.

2. In the case of *input files*, QSAM provides modules that can be invoked to do the following:

a. Open the file. Such a module initiates the input of the first block of the file to a buffer so that it will be available when the application program makes a request for a record from the file.

b. Pass a record to the application program. When such a module is invoked, a record is made available to the user program from a buffer residing in memory. The buffer is automatically replenished with physical records. When an attempt is made to pass a record after the file has been exhausted, control is transferred to a routine in the application program that processes end-of-file.

c. Close the file. This routine is normally invoked by the user program before termination.

Before discussing QSAM macro instructions, we need to discuss a few details of the existing methods for passing records back and forth between the user program and buffers. Two basic methods are available in QSAM for accomplishing this. These are represented by the *move mode* and the *locate mode*.

When an input file is processed using QSAM in the move mode, one logical record is actually transferred from a buffer to an area specified by the user program whenever an input record is requested. However, when the locate mode is employed, the address of the record is returned in a register and no actual movement of data takes place. When an output file is processed using QSAM in the move mode, each output request causes a logical record to be transferred to a buffer. On the other hand, if the locate mode is specified, the address of the location to which the record should be moved is returned to the application program in a register and no actual movement of data takes place.

7.6 INVOKING QSAM SERVICES IN AN OS ENVIRONMENT

The services offered by QSAM are sketchily outlined in Section 7.5. In this section, the QSAM macro instructions used to invoke the routines that perform these services are discussed.

The DCB macro instruction is used to generate a storage area where information about the characteristics and status of a particular file is retained. Such a storage area is called a *data control block (DCB)*. There must be a DCB instruction for each file processed by a program. Since no executable statements are generated, the DCB instructions are normally placed at the end of a program, along with the DC and DS statements. The DCB macro instruction has numerous keyword operands. The following format contains the most commonly used operands:

label	DCB	DSORG = PS
		DDNAME = ddname
		RECFM = recfm
		LRECL = lrecl
		BLKSIZE = blksize
		EODAD = eodad
		MACRF = macrf

The meanings of these operands are as follows:

- DSORG = PS specifies that the file is a sequential file.
- DDNAME = ddname specifies the name by which the file will be described in the Job Control Language statements when the program is executed. Although this topic is beyond the scope of this text, we will give brief attention to it at the end of this chapter. Suffice it to say here that any symbol acceptable as a label for an assembler-language statement can be used.
- RECFM = recfm specifies the format of the records in the file. The most common specifications and formats are:

Recfm	Meaning
F	Fixed-length, unblocked records
V	Variable-length, unblocked records
FB	Fixed-length, blocked records
VB	Variable-length, blocked records
FA	Fixed-length records with a carriage control character in the first byte

The FA value is normally specified only for files that are to be printed.

- LRECL = lrecl specifies the length of logical records in the file. In the case of variable-length records, lrecl should be the maximum length of a record (including the Record Descriptor Word).
- BLKSIZE = blksize specifies the maximum size of a block in the file. For example, if LRECL = 80 and RECFM = FB were specified, BLKSIZE = 800 would be used to indicate that 10 logical records are included in each block.

With variable-length records, the block size must be at least 4 larger than lrecl, to allow for the Block Descriptor Word.

- EODAD = eodad specifies the label of a routine to which control is to be passed if a record is requested after the file has been exhausted. When the routine gains control, registers R2–R13 will contain the same values that they contained when the request was made.

- MACRF = macrf specifies whether the file is an input or an output file and whether locate or move mode will be used in processing the file. The normal values are:

Macrf	Meaning
GL	Input file using locate mode
GM	Input file using move mode
PL	Output file using locate mode
PM	Output file using move mode

The following examples should help to clarify the use of the DCB macro instruction:

- *Example 1.*   A DCB for a card input file might be specified as follows:

```
CARDIN    DCB  DSORG=PS,DDNAME=CARDFL,RECFM=F,        X
               LRECL=80,BLKSIZE=80,EODAD=EOF,          X
               MACRF=GM
```

In this case, move mode will be used and, when end-of-file occurs, control will be passed to the routine EOF.

- *Example 2.*   A DCB for a file that is to be printed could be specified as follows:

```
PRINTOUT DCB  DSORG=PS,DDNAME=REPORT,RECFM=FA,        X
              LRECL=133,BLKSIZE=133,MACRF=PM
```

In this case, move mode is specified. The first character of each record is to be interpreted as a carriage control character (just as the first character is used as a carriage control character when a line is printed using XPRNT). Note that every record in the file must be 133 bytes long; using XPRNT, the length can range from 1 to 133 bytes.

- *Example 3.*   A DCB for a payroll master file of variable-length records that will be read from a disk or tape using locate mode might be coded as follows:

```
PAYROLL   DCB  DSORG=PS,DDNAME=PAYMAST,RECFM=VB,       X
               LRECL=428,BLKSIZE=3520,                 X
               EODAD=PAYEOF,MACRF=GL
```

The OPEN macro instruction is used to invoke a routine that causes one or more files to be opened. The format for this instruction is

      label   OPEN   (entry1,entry2, . . .)

where each entry is of the form

            dcblabel,(INPUT)

or

            dcblabel,(OUTPUT)

For example, the macro instruction

           OPEN   (CARDIN,(INPUT),PRINTOUT,(OUTPUT))

could be used to initialize the processing of two files with DCBs labeled CARDIN and PRINTOUT.

The GET macro instruction is used to invoke a routine that will obtain a record from an open input file. The format for the GET macro instruction, using move mode, is

      label   GET   dcblabel,area

Execution of the called module will cause one record to be moved from the input file with the DCB labeled dcblabel to be moved to the area specified by the second operand. For example, the macro instruction

           GET   CARDIN,CARD

could be used to move the contents of a card into an area labeled CARD. If end-of-file occurs, the next instruction executed in the user program is determined by the label specified in the EODAD operand in the DCB CARDIN. If a file is to be accessed using locate mode, only the first operand of the GET macro instruction should be specified. As a result, the address of the desired record will be placed in R1. Thus, the macro instruction

           GET   PAYROLL

could be used to insert into R1 the address of the next record from the file with the DCB PAYROLL.

The PUT macro instruction is used to invoke a routine for passing records from the user program to an output file. The two alternate formats for the PUT macro instruction are

      label   PUT   dcblabel,area

and

      label   PUT   dcblabel

When the first format is used, the record is actually moved from the location designated by the second operand to an output buffer. When the second format is used, the address to which the record should be moved is returned in R1 and no data transfer occurs. The first format is far more common than the second.

The CLOSE macro instruction is used to invoke a routine that will cause the processing of one or more files to be terminated. The format for this instruction is

> label   CLOSE (entry1,entry2, . . .)

where each entry has the form

> dcblabel,,

Thus, the macro instruction

> CLOSE (CARDIN,,PRINTOUT,,PAYROLL)

could be used to close the three files with DCBs labeled CARDIN, PRINT-OUT, and PAYROLL. The adjacent commas are used to specify that a parameter designating possible options is omitted. The reader should consult the appropriate IBM manual to determine what options are available and when they should be used.

Two details concerning the use of IBM macros should be carefully noted before leaving this discussion of QSAM:

1. The use of almost any IBM-supplied macro can cause the destruction of the contents of R0, R1, R14, and R15.
2. A register save area should be established before any QSAM routine is invoked.

Programs 7-1 through 7-4 illustrate the use of the QSAM macro instructions. Study these examples carefully.

The reader should note that, although these examples illustrate I/O using QSAM services, the programs are certainly not structured. The main problem in writing a structured program that utilizes QSAM involves the EODAD address. When writing structured programs, the EODAD address should be set up as follows:

```
INFILE    DCB   ...EODAD=EODRTN,...
EODRTN    MVI   EOFFLAG,C'Y'      SET END-OF-FILE FLAG
          BR    R14               GO TO INSTRUCTION FOLLOWING GET
EOFFLAG   DC    C'N'              SET TO 'Y' AT END-OF-FILE
```

Program 7-1

HOW TO READ CARDS AND PRINT LINES WITH QSAM

```
LOC    OBJECT CODE  ADDR1 ADDR2  STMT  SOURCE STATEMENT

                                  2  * THIS SHORT PROGRAM IS DESIGNED TO ILLUSTRATE THE STEPS REQUIRED
                                  3  * TO READ CARDS AND/OR PRINT LINES USING QSAM.
                                  4  *
                                  5  * THE PROGRAM SIMPLY 80-80 LISTS A DECK OF CARDS, SKIPPING
                                  6  * TO THE TOP OF A PAGE AFTER EVERY 50 LINES.
                                  7  *
                                  8  * THE LOGIC IS AS FOLLOWS:
                                  9  *
                                 10  *    STEP 1.  OBSERVE NORMAL OS LINKAGE CONVENTIONS.
                                 11  *
                                 12  *    STEP 2.  OPEN THE DCBS.
                                 13  *
                                 14  *    STEP 3.  SET THE COUNTER OF LINES LEFT TO PRINT ON THE
                                 15  *             CURRENT PAGE TO 50.
                                 16  *
                                 17  *    STEP 4.  GET A CARD. IF END-OF-FILE OCCURS AN AUTOMATIC
                                 18  *             BRANCH TO STEP 8 WILL OCCUR.
                                 19  *
                                 20  *    STEP 5.  PRINT OUT THE CARD JUST READ.
                                 21  *
                                 22  *    STEP 6.  SET THE CARRIAGE CONTROL TO SINGLE SPACE, AND
                                 23  *             DECREMENT THE COUNT OF LINES LEFT FOR THIS PAGE.
                                 24  *             IF THE COUNT IS NOT 0, GO TO STEP 4.
                                 25  *
                                 26  *    STEP 7.  SET THE CARRIAGE CONTROL FOR SKIP TO TOP OF PAGE
                                 27  *             BEFORE PRINTING, AND GO BACK TO STEP 3.
                                 28  *
                                 29  *    STEP 8.  CLOSE THE DCBS, AND EXIT.
                                 30  *
000000                           31  LISTPROG CSECT
                                 32           PRINT NOGEN
                                 33  *
                                 34  ***<STEP 1>   FOLLOW NORMAL LINKAGE CONVENTIONS
000000 90EC 000C        0000C    35           STM   R14,R12,12(R13)    STORE CALLER'S REGISTERS
000004 45EF 0050        00050    36           BAL   R14,80(R15)        BRANCH AROUND THE SAVE AREA
000008                           37           DS    18F                REGISTER SAVE AREA
00005C 50ED 0008        00008    38           ST    R14,8(R13)         NOW LINK THE SAVE AREAS
000054 50DE 0004        00004    39           ST    R13,4(R14)
000058 18DE                      40           LR    R13,R14            R13 WILL BE THE BASE REGISTER
                                 41           USING LISTPROG+8,R13
                                 42  *
                                 43  *
                                 44  ***<STEP 2>   OPEN THE DCBS.
00005A                           45           OPEN  (CARDDCB,(INPUT),PRINTDCB,(OUTPUT))
                                 53  *
                                 54  ***<STEP 3>   SET THE COUNT OF LINES LEFT ON THE PAGE TO 50.
00006A 4120 0032        00032    55  STARTPG  LA    R2,50              R2 <- # LINES LEFT ON PAGE
                                 56  *
```

Program 7-1 (continued)

```
LCC  OBJECT CODE   ADDR1 ADDR2  STMT  SOURCE STATEMENT

                                 57  ***<STEP 4>  READ A CARD.
00006E                           58  READLOOP GET   CARDDCB,CARD        READ A CARD
                                 63  *
                                 64  ***<STEP 5>  PRINT IT.
00007C                           65           PUT   PRINTDCB,CARD-1     PRINT IT
                                 70  *
                                 71  ***<STEP 6>         SET CARRIAGE CONTROL TO SINGLE SPACE. IF MORE LINES LEFT
                                 72  *                   ON THE PAGE, GO BACK TO STEP 4.
00008A 9240 D0AC                 73           MVI   CARD-1,C' '         SET FOR SINGLE SPACING
00008E 4620 D06E   0006E         74           BCT   R2,READLOOP         BRANCH UNLESS PAGE BREAK OCCURS
                                 75  *
                                 76  ***<STEP 7>         SET CARRIAGE CONTROL TO SKIP TO TOP OF PAGE.
000092 92F1 D0AC                 77           MVI   CARD-1,C'1'         SET CARRIAGE CONTROL TO
                                 78  *                                  SKIP TO TOP OF PAGE BEFORE PRINTING
000096 47F0 D062   0006A         79           B     STARTPG            GO SET THE LINE COUNTER
                                 80  *
                                 81  ***<STEP 8>  CLOSE FILES AND EXIT.
00009A                           82  EOFRT CLOSE (CARDDCB,,PRINTDCB)    CLOSE THE FILES
0000AA 58DD 0004   00004         90           L     R13,4(R13)
0000AE 98EC D00C   0000C         91           LM    R14,R12,12(R13)    RESTORE CALLER'S REGISTER'S
0000B2 07FE                      92           BR    R14
                                 93  *
0000B4 F1                        94           DC    C'1'               CARRIAGE CONTROL
0000B5                           95  CARD     DS    CL80               CARDS ARE READ INTO THIS AREA
0000B5                           96  CARDDCB  DCB   DSORG=PS,DDNAME=INPUTFL,MACRF=GM,EODAD=EOFRT,    X
                                 97                 RECFM=F,BLKSIZE=80,LRECL=80
000105                          151  *
                                152  PRINTDCB DCB   DSORG=PS,DDNAME=OUTPUT,MACRF=PM,RECFM=FA,       X
                                               LRECL=81,BLKSIZE=81
000168                          206  *        LTORG
0001C0                          207           EQUREGS
000000                          208           END   LISTPROG
                                225
```

Program 7-2

COPYFILE - COPY AND DISPLAY A SEQUENTIAL FILE

PAGE 1

16 JUN 75

```
LOC    OBJECT CODE   ADDR1 ADDR2   STMT   SOURCE STATEMENT

                                    2 *   THIS PROGRAM ILLUSTRATES THE USE OF QSAM TO READ AND
                                    3 *   WRITE SEQUENTIAL FILES.  IN THIS PARTICULAR CASE A FILE
                                    4 *   OF 100-BYTE RECORDS IS COPIED.  THE RECORDS ARE BLOCKED
                                    5 *   INTO BLOCKS OF 1600 BYTES.  THE PROGRAM ALSO DISPLAYS THE
                                    6 *   CONTENTS OF EACH RECORD (IT IS ASSUMED THAT THE RECORDS
                                    7 *   CONTAIN DATA WHICH IS ALL IN CHARACTER FORMAT.)  THE
                                    8 *   INPUT FILE IS PROCESSED IN LOCATE MODE, WHILE BOTH OUPUT
                                    9 *   FILES UTILIZE MOVE MODE.  THE LOGIC OF COPYFILE IS AS FOLLOWS:
                                   10 *
                                   11 *   STEP 1.  OBSERVE NORMAL OS SAVE AREA LINKAGE CONVENTIONS.
                                   12 *
                                   13 *   STEP 2.  OPEN THE DCBS.
                                   14 *
                                   15 *   STEP 3.  SET THE COUNT OF LINES LEFT TO PRINT ON THE CURRENT
                                   16 *            PAGE TO 50.
                                   17 *
                                   18 *   STEP 4.  READ A RECORD FROM THE INPUT FILE.  SINCE PROCESSING
                                   19 *            IS BEING DONE USING LOCATE MODE, THE ADDRESS OF THE
                                   20 *            RECORD IS RETURNED IN R1 (RATHER THAN MOVING THE
                                   21 *            RECORD TO A WORK AREA IN THE USER'S ROUTINE).
                                   22 *
                                   23 *   STEP 5.  WRITE THE RECORD OUT TO THE NEW FILE USING MOVE MODE.
                                   24 *            NOTE THAT THE ADDRESS OF THE RECORD IS SPECIFIED AS
                                   25 *            THE VALUE IN A REGISTER.
                                   26 *
                                   27 *   STEP 6.  PRINT THE RECORD.  THIS REQUIRES FIRST MOVING IT TO
                                   28 *            A WORK AREA SO THAT CARRIAGE CONTROL CAN BE INSERTED.
                                   29 *
                                   30 *   STEP 7.  SET THE CARRIAGE CONTROL TO SINGLE SPACE.  IF THERE
                                   31 *            ARE MORE LINES LEFT TO PRINT ON THE CURRENT PAGE, GO
                                   32 *            BACK TO STEP 4.
                                   33 *
                                   34 *   STEP 7.  SET CARRIAGE CONTROL FOR SKIP TO 1 BEFORE PRINTING,
                                   35 *            AND RETURN TO STEP 3.
                                   36 *
                                   37 *   STEP 7.  PRINT END OF LIST MESSAGE, CLOSE THE FILES, AND EXIT.
                                   38 *
                                   39 *
000000                             40   COPYFILE CSECT
                                   41            PRINT NOGEN
                                   42   ***<STEP 1>  FOLLOW NORMAL LINKAGE CONVENTIONS
000000 90EC D00C        0000C      43            STM   R14,R12,12(R13)   STORE CALLER'S REGISTERS
000004 45EF D050        00050      44            BAL   R14,90(R15)       BRANCH AROUND THE SAVE AREA
000008                              45            DS    18F               REGISTER SAVE AREA
000050 50ED D008        00008      46            ST    R14,8(R13)        NOW LINK THE SAVE AREAS
000054 50DE D004        00004      47            ST    R13,4(R14)
000058 18DE                        48            LR    R13,R14           R13 WILL BE THE BASE REGISTER
                        00008      49            USING COPYFILE+8,R13
                                   50 *
                                   51 *
```

Program 7-2 (continued)

COPYFILE - COPY AND DISPLAY A SEQUENTIAL FILE

```
LOC      OBJECT CODE   ADDR1 ADDR2  STMT  SOURCE STATEMENT

00005A                               52  ***<STEP 2>  OPEN THE DCBS
                                     53            OPEN  (FILEIN,(INPUT),FILEOUT,(OUTPUT),LIST,(OUTPUT))
                                     63  *
00006E  4120 0032        00032       64  ***<STEP 3>  SET COUNT OF LINES LEFT ON PAGE TO 50.
                                     65  STARTPG  LA   R2,50           R2 <- # LINES LEFT ON PAGE
                                     66  *
000072                               67  ***<STEP 4>  READ A RECORD FROM THE INPUT FILE.
00007C  1831                         68  READLOOP GET  FILEIN          THIS RETURNS ADDRESS OF REC. IN R1
                                     72            LR   R3,R1           SAVE ADDRESS IN REGISTER WHICH
                                     73  *                             DOESN'T GET DESTROYED
                                     74  *
                                     75  ***<STEP 5>  WRITE THE RECORD OUT TO THE NEW FILE.
00007E                               76            PUT  FILEOUT,(3)
                                     81  * NOTE THAT THE SECOND OPERAND IS USED TO GIVE THE ADDRESS OF
                                     82  * THE RECORD TO WRITE OUT, AND THAT OPERAND MAY BE SPECIFIED AS
                                     83  * THE VALUE IN A REGISTER BY JUST ENCLOSING THE REGISTER NUMBER
                                     84  * WITH PARENTHESES.
                                     85  *
00008A  D263 D001 D000  00D9 00000   86  ***<STEP 6>  PRINT THE RECORD.
000090                               87            MVC  RECORD+1(100),0(R3)  MOVE RECORD TO WORK AREA
                                     88            PUT  LIST,RECORD    PRINT OUT THE RECORD
                                     93  *
                                     94  ***<STEP 7>  SET CARRIAGE CONTROL FOR SINGLE SPACE, AND
                                     95  *             TEST FOR MORE LINES LEFT ON PAGE.
00009E  9240 D000        00D8        96            MVI  RECORD,C' '    SET CARRIAGE CONTROL FOR SINGLE SPACE
0000A2  4620 D0A         00072       97            BCT  R2,READLOOP    BRANCH UNLESS PAGE BREAK OCCURS
                                     98  *
                                     99  ***<STEP 8>  SET CARRIAGE CONTROL FOR SKIP TO TOP OF PAGE.
0000A6  92F1 D000        00D8       100            MVI  RECORD,C'1'
0000AA  47F0 D066        0006E      101            B    STARTPG        BRANCH TO RESET LINE COUNTER
                                    102  *
                                    103  ***<STEP 9>  PRINT END OF LIST, CLOSE DCBS, AND EXIT.
0000AE                             104  EOFRT    PUT  LIST,ENDMESS
0000BC                             109            CLOSE (LIST,,FILEIN,,FILEOUT)
0000CE  58DD 0004        00004     119            L    R13,4(R13)
0000D2  98EC D00C        0000C     120            LM   R14,R12,12(R13)  RESTORE CALLER'S REGISTERS
0000D6  07FE                       121            BR   R14             EXIT
                                    122  *
0000D8  F1404040404040            123  RECORD   DC   CL101'1'        AREA FOR 1 RECORD AND CARR. CONTROL
0000E0  F05C5C5C5C5C40C5          124  ENDMESS  DC   CL101'0***** END OF LISTING ******'
                                    125  *
0001A2                             126  LIST     DCB  DDNAME=LIST,DSORG=PS,MACRF=PM,BLKSIZE=101,RECFM=FA,  X
                                                           LRECL=101
000204                             180  FILEIN   DCB  DSORG=PS,DDNAME=FILEIN,MACRF=GL,EODAD=EOFRT,RECFM=FB,  X
                                                           BLKSIZE=1600,LRECL=100
000264                             234  FILEOUT  DCB  DSORG=PS,DDNAME=FILEOUT,MACRF=PM,RECFM=FB,  X
                                                           BLKSIZE=1600,LRECL=100
                                    289  *
0002C8                             289            LTORG
                                    290            EQUREGS
0C0000                             307            END  COPYFILE
```

Program 7-3

VARBUILD - BUILD A FILE OF VARIABLE-LENGTH RECORDS

LCC	OBJECT CODE	ADDR1	ADDR2	STMT	SOURCE STATEMENT
				2 *	THIS SIMPLE PROGRAM IS DESIGNED TO ILLUSTRATE THE USE OF VARIABLE
				3 *	LENGTH RECORDS. THE PROGRAM READS CARDS, EACH OF WHICH CONTAINS
				4 *	
				5 *	A STUDENT'S SOCIAL SECURITY NUMBER IN COL.S 1-9 AND
				6 *	A TEST SCORE (0-100) IN COLUMNS 11-13.
				7 *	
				8 *	ALL OF THE CARDS FOR A GIVEN STUDENT OCCUR TOGETHER IN THE CARD
				9 *	INPUT FILE. THE PROGRAM CREATES 1 VARIABLE-LENGTH RECORD FOR
				10 *	EACH STUDENT; THE RECORD CONTAINS ALL OF THE STUDENT'S TEST
				11 *	SCORES IN PACKED DECIMAL FORMAT. THE PRECISE FORMAT OF THE
				12 *	GENERATED RECORDS IS
				13 *	
				14 *	+0(4) RDW (2 BYTES OF LENGTH, 2 BYTES OF 0000)
				15 *	+4(9) SOCIAL SECURITY NUMBER
				16 *	+13(UP TO 40) THE STUDENT'S SCORES
				17 *	EACH SCORE WILL BE IN A 2-BYTE PACKED DEC. FIELD
				18 *	
				19 *	THUS, THE MAXIMUM LENGTH OF ONE OF THE GENERATED RECORDS IS 53,
				20 *	AND THIS WOULD REQUIRE 20 CONSECUTIVE TEST SCORES FOR THE
				21 *	SAME STUDENT. THE LOGIC OF THE PROGRAM IS
				22 *	
				23 *	STEP 1. OBSERVE NORMAL OS LINKAGE CONVENTIONS.
				24 *	
				25 *	STEP 2. OPEN BOTH DCBS.
				26 *	
				27 *	STEP 3. READ THE FIRST RECORD AND SAVE ITS ADDRESS.
				28 *	
				29 *	STEP 4. PUT THE SOC. SEC. # INTO THE NEW RECORD. ALSO,
				30 *	PACK IN THE SCORE OFF THE 1ST CARD.
				31 *	
				32 *	STEP 5. READ CARDS, PACKING THE SCORES INTO THE DISK RECORD,
				33 *	UNTIL A CARD WITH A NEW SOC. SEC. # IS READ OR END-
				34 *	OF-FILE OCCURS. IF END-OF-FILE OCCURS, A BRANCH TO
				35 *	STEP 7 WILL TAKE PLACE AUTOMATICALLY.
				36 *	
				37 *	STEP 6. CALL 'PUTREC' TO PUT IN THE RDW AND WRITE OUT THE
				38 *	CONSTRUCTED RECORD. GO TO STEP 4 (SINCE THE 1ST
				39 *	RECORD FOR THE NEXT GUY HAS BEEN READ ALREADY).
				40 *	
				41 *	STEP 7. CALL 'PUTREC' TO WRITE OUT THE LAST RECORD.
				42 *	
				43 *	STEP 8. CLOSE THE FILES AND EXIT.
				44 *	
				45	PRINT NOGEN
000000				46	VARBUILD CSECT

Program 7-3 (continued)

```
LOC    OBJECT CODE       ADDR1 ADDR2 STMT  SOURCE STATEMENT

                                     47 ***<STEP 1>   OBSERVE NORMAL OS LINKAGE CONVENTIONS.
000000 90EC D00C          000C       48           STM   R14,R12,12(R13)        SAVE CALLER'S REGISTERS
000004 45EF 0050          0050       49           BAL   R14,80(R15)            BRANCH AROUND SAVE AREA
000008                               50           DS    18F                    REGISTER SAVE AREA
000050 50ED 0008          0008       51           ST    R14,8(R13)             SET FORWARD LINK
000054 50DE 0004          0004       52           ST    R13,4(R14)             SET BACK LINK
000058 18DE                          53           LR    R13,R14
                          00008      54           USING VARBUILD+8,R13         R13 IS THE BASE REGISTER

                                     55 *
00005A                               56 ***<STEP 2>   OPEN THE DCBS.
                                     57           OPEN  (CARDFL,(INPUT),VARFL,(OUTPUT))

                                     65 *
00006A                               66 ***<STEP 3>   READ THE 1ST RECORD.
                                     67           GET   CARDFL                 GET THE FIRST RECORD
000074 1831                          71           LR    R3,R1                  R3 <- ADDRESS OF FIRST RECORD

                                     72 *
                                     73 ***<STEP 4>   PUT IN THE SOC. SEC. # AND 1ST SCORE.
000076 D208 D0F4 3000     00FC 00000 74  MAINLOOP  MVC   SOCSEC#(9),0(R3)       MOVE IN SOC. SEC. # FOR NEW RECORD
00007C F212 D0FD 300A     00FD 00105 75           PACK  SCORES(2),10(3,R3)     PACK IN FIRST TEST SCORE
000082 4120 D0FF          00107      76           LA    R2,SCORES+2            R2 <- ADDRESS TO PACK NEXT SCORE

                                     77 *
000086                               78 ***<STEP 5>   PUT IN SCORES FOR CONSECUTIVE CARDS WITH THE SAME #.
                                     79  BUILDLP   GET   CARDFL                 GET THE NEXT CARD

                                     83 *
000090 D508 D0F4 1000     00FC 00000 84           CLC   SOCSEC#(9),0(R1)       SAME STUDENT?
000096 4770 D0A0          00A8       85           BNE   NEXTGUYS               NO -> BRANCH
00009A F212 2000 100A     0002 00000 86           PACK  0(2,R2),10(3,R1)       PACK IN THE TEST SCORE
0000A0 4122 0002          0002       87           LA    R2,2(R2)               INCREMENT THE POINTER TO NEXT SCORE
0000A4 47F0 D07E          007E       88           B     BUILDLP

                                     89 *
                                     90 ***<STEP 6>   CALL 'PUTREC' TO WRITE OUT THE RECORD.
0000A8 1831                          91  NEXTGUYS  LR    R3,R1                  SAVE ADDRESS OF LAST INPUT RECORD
0000AA 45A0 D0C8          00D0       92           BAL   R10,PUTREC             CALL A ROUTINE TO WRITE THE RECORD
0000AE 47F0 D076          0076       93           B     MAINLOOP               GO BACK TO PROCESS NEXT SET

                                     94 *
                                     95 ***<STEP 7>   EOF OCCURRED.  NOW WRITE THE LAST RECORD.
0000B2 45A0 D0C8          00D0       96  EOFRTN    BAL   R10,PUTREC             WRITE THE LAST RECORD
                                     97
```

Program 7-3 (continued)

```
     VARBUILD - BUILD A FILE OF VARIABLE-LENGTH RECORDS

LCC OBJECT CODE  ADDR1 ADDR2  STMT  SOURCE STATEMENT

0000B6                         98 ***<STEP 8>  CLOSE THE FILES AND EXIT.
                               99       CLOSE (CARDFL,,VARFL)
0000C6 58DD 0004        0004  107       L     R13,4(R13)       RESTORE CALLER'S REGISTERS
0000CA 98EC D00C        D00C  108       LM    R14,R12,12(R13)
0000CE 07FE                   109       BR    R14              EXIT
                              110 *
                              111 * PUTREC SIMPLY FILLS IN THE RDW AND ISSUES A PUT TO CAUSE THE
                              112 * RECORD TO BE WRITTEN TO THE DISK FILE (ACTUALLY, THE PUT
                              113 * CAUSES THE RECORD TO BE TRANSFERRED TO THE OUTPUT BUFFER).
                              114 *
0000D0 5B20 D0E8        D0E8  115 PUTREC  S    R2,=A(RDW)       R2 <- LENGTH OF RECORD
0000D4 4020 D0F0        D0F0  116       STH   R2,RDW           STORE INTO LEFT HALF OF RDW
0000D8 D201 D0F2 D0EC 000FA 000F4  117   MVC  RDW+2(2),=H'0'   ZERO RIGHT HALF
0000DE                        118       PUT   VARFL,RDW        WRITE 1 VARIABLE-LENGTH RECORD
0000EC 07FA                   123       BR    R10              RETURN
                              124 *
0000F0                        125       LTORG
0000F0 000000F8               126               =A(RDW)
0000F4 0000                   127               =H'0'
                              128 * THE VARIABLE-LENGTH RECORD IS CONSTRUCTED HERE.  THE
                              129 * THREE FIELDS — RDW, SOCSEC#, AND SCORES — ARE ALL PART
                              130 * OF THE RECORD.
                              131 *
0000F8                        132 *
0000F8                        133 RDW     DS   F               RECORD DESCRIPTOR WORD
0000FC                        134 SOCSEC# DS   CL9             SOCIAL SECURITY NUMBER
000105                        135 SCORES  DS   20PL2           MAXIMUM OF 20 SCORES IN THE RECORD
                              136 *
00012D                        137 CARDFL  DCB  DSORG=PS,DDNAME=INPUT,MACRF=GL,EODAD=EODRTN,     X
                                               RECFM=F,BLKSIZE=80,LRECL=80
                              191 *
                              192 * THE FOLLOWING DCB DEFINES THE PARAMETERS TO WRITE A FILE
                              193 * OF VARIABLE-LENGTH BLOCKED RECORDS USING MOVE-MODE.
                              194 *
000190                        195 VARFL   DCB  DSORG=PS,DDNAME=VARFILE,MACRF=PM,RECFM=VB,       X
                                               LRECL=53,BLKSIZE=3520
                              249 *
000000                        250       EQUREGS
                              267       END  VARBUILD
```

Program 7-4

VARLIST - HOW TO ACCESS VARIABLE-LENGTH RECORDS

LOC	OBJECT CODE	ADDR1	ADDR2	STMT	SOURCE STATEMENT
				2	* IN THIS EXAMPLE THE RECORDS PRODUCED BY 'VARBUILD' ARE
				3	* ACCESSED AND USED TO PRINT OUT THE TEST SCORES FOR ALL
				4	* THE STUDENTS. THE READER SHOULD STUDY VARBUILD CAREFULLY
				5	* BEFORE EXAMINING THIS EXAMPLE, SINCE THE FORMAT AND CONTENTS
				6	* OF THE RECORDS ARE DISCUSSED THERE.
				7	*
				8	* THE LOGIC OF VARLIST IS AS FOLLOWS:
				9	*
				10	* STEP 1. OBSERVE NORMAL OS LINKAGE CONVENTIONS.
				11	*
				12	* STEP 2. OPEN THE DCBS.
				13	*
				14	* STEP 3. READ A VARIABLE-LENGTH RECORD. ON EOF GO TO STEP 6.
				15	*
				16	* STEP 4. CONSTRUCT A PRINT LINE FROM THE DATA IN THE RECORD.
				17	*
				18	* STEP 5. PUT OUT THE PRINT LINE. GO TO STEP 3.
				19	*
				20	* STEP 6. CLOSE THE FILES AND EXIT.
				21	*
000000				22	VARLIST CSECT
				23	PRINT NOGEN
				24	*
				25	***<STEP 1> FOLLOW NORMAL LINKAGE CONVENTIONS
000000	90EC	000C		26	STM R14,R12,12(R13) STORE CALLER'S REGISTERS
000004	45EF	0050		27	BAL R14,80(R15) BRANCH AROUND THE SAVE AREA
000008				28	DS 18F REGISTER SAVE AREA
000050	50ED	0008		29	ST R14,8(R13) NOW LINK THE SAVE AREAS
000054	50DE	0004		30	ST R13,4(R14)
000058	18DE			31	LR R13,R14 R13 WILL BE THE BASE REGISTER
00005A		0008		32	USING VARLIST+8,R13
				33	*
				34	*
				35	***<STEP 2> OPEN THE DCBS.
00005A				36	OPEN (VARIN,(INPUT),OUTFL,(OUTPUT))
				44	*
				45	***<STEP 3> READ A RECORD. ON EOF GO TO STEP 6.
00006A				46	GETLOOP GET VARIN,RECORD GET A VARIABLE-LENGTH RECORD
				51	*

Program 7-4 (continued)

VARLIST - HOW TO ACCESS VARIABLE-LENGTH RECORDS

LOC	OBJECT CODE	ADDR1	ADDR2	STMT	SOURCE STATEMENT	
				52	***<STEP 4>	CONSTRUCT THE PRINT LINE.
000078	9240 D0D8	000E0		53	MVI PRNTLINE,C' '	CLEAR THE PRINT LINE
00007C	D283 D0D9 D0D8	000E1	000E0	54	MVC PRNTLINE+1(132),PRNTLINE	
				55	*	PUT SOC SEC # INTO PRINT LINE
00008C	D208 D0D9 D162	000E1	001EA	57	MVC PRNTLINE+1(9),RECORD+4	
000086	4120 D0E6	000EE		58	LA R2,PRNTLINE+14	R2 <- ADDRESS TO PUT NEXT SCORE
00008C	4130 D16B	00173		59	LA R3,RECORD+13	R3 <- ADDRESS OF NEXT SCORE TO EDIT
000090	4840 D15E	00166		60	LH R4,RECORD	R4 <- LENGTH OF RECORD
000094	5840 D258	00260		61	S R4,=F'13'	R4 <- LENGTH OF SCORES IN RECORD
000098	8A40 0001	00001		62	SRA R4,1	R4 <- # OF SCORES IN THE RECORD
				63	*	
00009C	D203 2000 D25C	00000	0025C	64 DUMP#S	MVC 0(4,R2),=X'40202120'	
0000A2	DE03 2000 3000	00000	00000	65	ED 0(4,R2),0(R3)	EDIT IN 1 SCORE
0000A8	4122 0005	00005		66	LA R2,5(R2)	POINT TO NEXT SCORE IN PRINT LINE
0000AC	4133 0002	00002		67	LA R3,2(R3)	POINT TO NEXT SCORE
0000B0	4640 D094	0009C		68	BCT R4,DUMP#S	GO BACK IF MORE TO PUT IN LINE
				69	*	
				70	***<STEP 5>	PRINT THE LINE AND GO BACK TO STEP 3.
				71	PUT OUTFL,PRNTLINE	PRINT A LINE
0000C2	47F0 D062	0006A		76	B GETLOOP	
				77	*	
				78	***<STEP 6>	CLOSE THE FILES AND EXIT.
0000C6				79 EOD	CLOSE (VARIN,OUTFL)	CLOSE THE FILES
0000D6	58DD 0004	00004		87	L R13,4(R13)	NOW EXIT
0000DA	98EC D00C	0000C		88	LM R14,R12,12(R13)	
0000DE	07FE			89	BR R14	
				90	*	
0000E0				91 PRNTLINE	DS CL133	PRINT LINE
				92	*	
000166				93	DS 0H	ALIGN RECORD ON A HALFWORD
				94	*	THIS ALLOWS LH OF THE RECORD LENGTH
000166				95 RECORD	DS CL53	
00019B				96 OUTFL	DCB DSORG=PS,DDNAME=PRINTOUT,MACRF=PM,RECFM=FA,	X
					LRECL=133,BLKSIZE=133	
				151	*	
0001FC				152 VARIN	DCB DSORG=PS,DDNAME=VARIN,MACRF=GM,RECFM=VB,EODAD=EOD,	X
					LRECL=53,BLKSIZE=3520	
				206	*	
				207	EQUREGS	
					LTORG	
000260	0000000D			224	=F'13'	
000260				225		
000264	40202120			226	=X'40202120'	
000000				227	END VARLIST	

This uses a feature that is not presented in the examples: at end-of-file, R14 contains the address of the instruction immediately following the GET. Thus

```
            GET   INFILE,CARD
LOOP        CLI   EOFFLAG,C'Y'          TEST FOR END-OF-FILE
            BE    EXITLOOP
            .
            .
            .
            GET   INFILE,CARD
            B     LOOP
```

illustrates the construction of structured loops, using an EODRTN that simply sets a flag when end-of-file occurs.

The preceding examples, although they are complete assembler-language programs, do not consider the required Job Control Language statements necessary to connect the programs logically with the files that they are to process. As we noted before, it is not our intent to present a detailed discussion of Job Control Language. The following short discussion of DD statements is included just to give the reader a brief introduction to their use.

For each file that you wish to process, you must specify a Job Control Language statement called a *DD statement*. The DD statement has the form

```
            //ddname       DD       operands
```

where the ddname is the same as that coded in the DDNAME operand of the DCB being used to process the file. The operands vary in accordance with the type of device on which the file is recorded and the services that you require of the operating system. Some simple examples of DD statements and brief explanations of their meanings follow:

- *Example 1.*   //INPUT DD   *

  This indicates that the data to be processed is coming from the same input medium (probably cards) as the DD statement. The DCB used to read this data will have as an operand DDNAME = INPUT.

- *Example 2.*   //OUTPUT DD SYSOUT = A

  This indicates that data will be written to a printer. The DCB used to write this data will have as an operand DDNAME = OUTPUT.

- *Example 3.*   //FILE DD UNIT = 2400,VOL = SER = MYTAPE,
  //   LABEL = (2,SL),DSN = MYFILE,DISP = OLD

  This indicates that data will be read from a nine-track tape that has been named MYTAPE. The data area used is the second file on the tape and has been named MYFILE. The DCB used to read this data will have as an operand DDNAME = FILE.

- *Example 4.* //DISK DD UNIT = 2314, VOL = SER = PACK01,
  DSN = DATASET, DISP = (NEW, KEEP),
  //   SPACE = (TRK,(2))

This indicates that data will be written onto a 2314 disk storage pack. This new file will be named DATASET and the system will reserve space for two tracks of data. The DCB used to write this data will have as an operand DDNAME = DISK.

The essential ideas necessary for utilization of the basic services offered by QSAM have been covered. The reader should be aware, however, that there are many available options, some of which are of considerable importance, to be considered if extensive use of QSAM is anticipated. For more details on the facilities offered by QSAM, refer to the appropriate IBM manual on data management services.

7.7 INVOKING QSAM SERVICES IN A DOS ENVIRONMENT

DOS is the operating system that IBM supports for many of its smaller machines. The services offered by DOS are more limited than those offered by OS. However, the basic I/O services, such as processing of sequential files, are almost identical under the two systems. In this section, we present the use of QSAM services under DOS.

Under OS, the DCB macro is used to generate a storage area for retaining information about the organization and status of a file. Under DOS, each file must also have such a storage area. However, in this case, the programmer must choose the macro based on the general type of device on which the file resides. For example,

- DTFCD is used for card files.
- DTFPR is used for printer files.
- DTFSD is used for sequential files on disk.

These are the only types of files that will be discussed in this section. The interested reader should consult the appropriate IBM reference manual for the full range of alternatives.

The DTFs, each of which represents a single file to be processed, are normally generated at the end of a program, along with the DS and DC statements. The label on a DTF must not be more than seven characters long. Following are the most commonly used formats:

1. *Processing a card file* (DTFCD).

```
label        DTFCD   DEVADDR = SYSIPT
                     RECFORM = FIXUNB
                     BLKSIZE = 80
                     TYPEFLE = INPUT
                     EOFADDR = eodad
                     IOAREA1 = io1
                     IOAREA2 = io2
                     WORKA = YES
                     DEVICE = device
```

a. DEVADDR = SYSIPT specifies that the file is a standard input file. SYSIPT is a symbolic reference that normally indicates a card input file.

b. RECFORM = FIXUNB specifies a file that has fixed-length, unblocked records.

c. BLKSIZE = 80 gives the length of each physical block. (For unblocked files, each physical block contains a single record.)

d. TYPEFLE = INPUT specifies that the records will be read. If OUTPUT were specified, the file could be used to punch cards.

e. EOFADDR = eodad specifies the address that control should pass to on end-of-file.

f. IOAREA1 = io1 specifies the name of an area that the system can use as an I/O buffer. One such area is required, but two should normally be used. (Two allow the system to read into one buffer while data is accessed in the other buffer.) The area io1 must be defined with a DS statement somewhere in the program, and the area must be long enough to hold a physical block. Normally, the I/O buffers are defined just before the END statement (since they do not have to be addressable).

g. IOAREA2 = io2 is optional but highly recommended.

h. WORKA = YES specifies move mode.

i. DEVICE = device must be used to specify the type of device used. In our examples, we specify 2540, which is one model of card reader. However, this parameter depends on the configuration being used.

2. *Processing a printed file* (DTFPR).

```
label        DTFPR   DEVADDR = SYSLST
                     RECFORM = FIXUNB
                     BLKSIZE = blksize
                     CTLCHR = ASA
                     IOAREA1 = io1
                     IOAREA2 = io2
                     WORKA = YES
                     DEVICE = device
```

The blksize is normally a value up to 133 (for most printers). CTLCHR = ASA is used to indicate that the first character of each line should be interpreted as a carriage control character. The other parameters are similar to those specified on the DTFCD.

3. *Processing a sequential disk file* (DTFSD).

```
label          DTFSD    DEVADDR = SYSddd
                        RECFORM = format
                        BLKSIZE = blksize
                        RECSIZE = recsize
                        TYPEFLE = access-type
                        EOFADDR = eodad
                        IOAREA1 = io1
                        IOAREA2 = io2
                        WORKA = YES
                        IOREG = (r)
                        DEVICE = device
```

a. The DEVADDR operand specifies a "logical address' for the device. Normally, the names are SYS001, SYS002, etc.—using a distinct value for each file in the program.

b. RECFORM gives the record format. The most common values are

Format	*Meaning*
FIXUNB	Fixed-length, unblocked records
FIXBLK	Fixed-length, blocked records
VARUNB	Variable-length, unblocked records
VARBLK	Variable-length, blocked records

c. BLKSIZE = blksize gives the size of a physical block. One peculiarity of this parameter is that output files require an extra eight bytes. Therefore, a RECFORM = FIXBLK, with TYPEFLE = OUTPUT, RECSIZE = 100, and 16 records per block requires BLKSIZE = 1608.

d. RECSIZE = recsize gives the length of a logical record. This parameter should not be used for variable-length records. (The RDW will be used to determine the length.)

e. TYPEFLE = access-type. Use INPUT or OUTPUT in most cases.

f. EOFADDR = eodad gives the end-of-file address. Use only on input files.

g. IOAREA1 = io1. Again, io1 must be defined in the program (normally at the end), and it must be large enough to hold a physical block.

h. IOAREA2 = io2. Again, this is optional but should normally be used. It can significantly reduce run time.

i. WORKA = YES specifies move mode. If locate model is desired, leave this parameter off and use the IOREG operand.

j. IOREG = (r) specifies locate mode. Under OS, the record address is always returned in R1; but under DOS, you specify the register number (2-12) to be used to locate the record. Thus, IOREG = (3) specifies R3 as the register used to reference a position in one of the buffers.

k. DEVICE = device specifies the type of disk on which the file resides.

The following examples should help to clarify use of the DTFs:

* *Example 1.* A card file.

```
CARDDTF    DTFCD    DVADDR = SYSIPT,BLKSIZE = 80,                        X
                    RECFORM = FIXUNB,TYPEFLE = INPUT,                    X
                    EOFADDR = EOFRT,WORKA = YES,IOAREA1 = CARDIO1,  X
                    IOAREA2 = CARDIO2,DEVICE = 2540
```

This could be used to read cards in move mode from a 2540 card reader. At end-of-file, a branch would automatically occur to EOFRT. CARDIO1 and CARDIO2 would be 80-byte areas defined toward the end of the program.

* *Example 2.* A printed file.

```
PRINTDTF    DTFPR    DEVADDR = SYSLST,BLKSIZE = 133,RECFORM = FIXUNB, X
                     WORK A = YES,CTLCHR = ASA,DEVICE = 3202,            X
                     IOAREA1 = PRINTIO1,IOAREA2 = PRINTIO2
```

This could be used to print records in move mode (with **carriage control** characters) on a 3202 printer.

* *Example 3.* A sequential disk file.

```
FILEIN      DTFSD    DEVADDR = SYS001,RECFORM = FIXBLK,BLKSIZE = 1600, X
                     RECSIZE = 100,EOFADDR = EOFRT,TYPEFLE = INPUT,     X
                     IOREG = (3),DEVICE = 3340,IOAREA1 = INIO1,         X
                     IOAREA2 = INIO2
```

This specifies an input file, processed in locate mode (with R3 as the locate register), from a 3340 disk drive.

The OPEN and CLOSE macros have a slightly different format under DOS. Use

OPEN   file1,file2,...

to open several files and

CLOSE   file1,file2,...

to close the files. Thus,

OPEN   CARDDTF,PRNTDTF

would open two files.

The GET and PUT macros are essentially identical to those used under OS. Use

GET   dtfname,area

for move mode access and

GET   dtfname

for locate mode access. (In this case, the IOREG is pointed at the record to be processed.) Use

PUT   dtfname,area

for move mode access. We do not recommend locate mode PUTs.

Before we end this discussion, two more points must be covered:

- The use of almost any IBM macro can cause the destruction of the contents of R0, R1, R14, and R15 (just as under OS).
- DOS does not invoke a user program in the same way as OS does. In particular, R13, R14, and R15 are no longer set up according to OS conventions. When you enter the main program, use

```
program    CSECT
           BALR  R12,0
           USING *,R12
```

to set up a base register. If you intend to call external subroutines, point R13 at an 18-word register save area. To leave the main program, use

EOJ

which causes an exit back to the operating system.

With these comments in mind, you should be able to understand Programs 7-5 through 7-8. They illustrate the use of cards, printers, and sequential disk files (for both fixed-length and variable-length records). These programs are rewritten versions of the programs presented in Section 7.6— Programs 7-1 through 7-4.

Program 7-5

```
LOC      OBJECT CODE   ADDR1 ADDR2   STMT   SOURCE STATEMENT

                                        2   *   THIS SHORT PROGRAM IS DESIGNED TO ILLUSTRATE THE STEPS REQUIRED
                                        3   *   TO READ CARDS AND/OR PRINT LINES USING QSAM UNDER DOS.
                                        4   *
                                        5   *   THE PROGRAM SIMPLY 80-80 LISTS A DECK OF CARDS, SKIPPING TO THE TOP
                                        6   *   OF A PAGE AFTER EVERY 50 LINES.
                                        7   *
                                        8   *   THE LOGIC IS AS FOLLOWS:
                                        9   *
                                       10   *     STEP 1.   NORMAL DOS LINKAGE CONVENTIONS ARE NOT THE SAME AS
                                       11   *               UNDER OS.  ALL THAT IS ACTUALLY REQUIRED IS TO SET
                                       12   *               UP A BASE REGISTER (DO NOT ASSUME THAT R13, R14, AND
                                       13   *               R15 ARE ESTABLISHED FOR YOU, AS UNDER OS).
                                       14   *
                                       15   *     STEP 2.   OPEN THE FILES.
                                       16   *
                                       17   *     STEP 3.   SET THE COUNTER OF THE LINES TO PRINT ON THE CURRENT
                                       18   *               PAGE TO 50.
                                       19   *
                                       20   *     STEP 4.   GET A CARD.  IF END-OF-FILE OCCURS, AN AUTOMATIC
                                       21   *               BRANCH TO STEP 8 WILL OCCUR.
                                       22   *
                                       23   *     STEP 5.   PRINT OUT THE CARD JUST READ.
                                       24   *
                                       25   *     STEP 6.   SET THE CARRIAGE CONTROL TO SINGLE SPACE, AND
                                       26   *               DECREMENT THE COUNT OF THE LINES LEFT FOR THIS PAGE.
                                       27   *
                                       28   *     STEP 7.   SET THE CARRIAGE CONTROL FOR SKIP TO TOP OF PAGE
                                       29   *               BEFORE PRINTING, AND GO BACK TO STEP 3.
                                       30   *
                                       31   *     STEP 8.   CLOSE THE FILES AND EXIT.  NOTE THAT TO EXIT A DOS
                                       32   *               PROGRAM THE "EOJ" MACRO IS USED.
                                       33   *
000000                                 34   LISTPROG CSECT
                                       35            PRINT NOGEN
                                       36   ***<STEP 1>       SET UP A BASE REGISTER
                                       37   *
                                       38   *
000000 05C0                            39            BALR  R12,0
                          00002        40            USING *,R12
                                       41   *
                                       42   ***<STEP 2>       OPEN THE FILES
                                       43   *
                                       44            OPEN  CARDDTF,PRNTDTF
                                       53   *
                                       54   ***<STEP 3>       SET THE COUNT OF LINES LEFT ON THE PAGE TO 50
                                       55   *
000016 4120 0032        00032          56   STARTPG  LA    R2,50          R2 <- # LINES LEFT ON THE PAGE
                                       57   *
                                       58   ***<STEP 4>       READ A CARD
                                       59   *
                                       60   READLOOP GET   CARDDTF,CARD    READ A CARD
```

```
          HOW TO READ CARDS AND PRINT LINES UNDER DOS                             DOS/VSE ASSEMBLER 15.41 82-05-03      PAGE    3

  LOC    OBJECT CODE    ADDR1 ADDR2   STMT   SOURCE STATEMENT

                                       66   *
                                       67   *** <STEP 5>    PRINT IT.
                                       68   *
  00003A 9240 C05E            00060    69       PUT   PRNTDTF,CARD-1     PRINT IT
                                       75   *** <STEP 6>
                                       76   *    SET THE CARRIAGE CONTROL TO SINGLE SPACE.   IF MORE LINES
                                       77   *    LEFT ON THE PAGE, GO TO STEP 4.
  00003E 4620 C018            0001A    78       MVI   CARD-1,C' '        SET CC TO BLANK
                                       79       BCT   R2,READLOOP
                                       80   *
                                       81   *** <STEP 7>    SET CC FOR TOP OF PAGE
                                       82   *
  000042 92F1 C05E            00060    83       MVI   CARD-1,C'1'
  000046 47F0 C014            00016    84       B     STARTPG           GO START A NEW PAGE
                                       85   *** <STEP 8>    CLOSE FILES AND EXIT
                                       86   *
                                       87       EOFRT CLOSE CARDDTF,PRNTDTF
                                       88             EOJ
                                       97   *
  000060 F1                           100   *                          CARRIAGE CONTROL BYTE
                                      101   CARD  DC    C'1'
  000061                             102         DS    CL80
                                      103   *
  000060                             104   CARDDTF DTFCD DEVADDR=SYSIPT,BLKSIZE=80,RECFORM=FIXUNB,TYPEFLE=INPUT,  X
                                                        WORKA=YES,IOAREA1=CARDIO1,IOAREA2=CARDIO2,               X
                                                        DEVICE=2540
                                      125   *
                                      126   PRNTDTF DTFPR DEVADDR=SYSLST,BLKSIZE=81,RECFORM=FIXUNB,WORKA=YES,     X
                                                        CTLCHR=ASA,IOAREA1=PRINTIO1,IOAREA2=PRINTIO2,            X
                                                        DEVICE=3203
                                      147   *
  000120                             148   CARDIO1  DS   CL80                    THE I/O BUFFER AREAS
  000170                             149   CARDIO2  DS   CL80
  0001C0                             150   PRINTIO1 DS   CL81
  000211                             151   PRINTIO2 DS   CL81
            0000C                    152   R12      EQU  12
            00002                    153   R2       EQU  2
                                     154            END
  000268 5B5BC2D6D7C5D540                  155   =C'$$BOPEN '
  000270 5B5BC2C3D3D6E2C5                  156   =C'$$BCLOSE'
  000278 000000B8                          157   =A(CARDDTF)
  00027C 00000061                          158   =A(CARD)
  000280 000000F0                          159   =A(PRNTDTF)
  000284 00000060                          160   =A(CARD-1)
```

Program 7-6

```
LOC     OBJECT CODE    ADDR1 ADDR2    STMT    SOURCE STATEMENT

                                        2  *    THIS PROGRAM ILLUSTRATES THE USE OF QSAM (UNDER DOS) TO READ
                                        3  *    AND WRITE SEQUENTIAL DISK FILES.  IN THIS PARTICULAR CASE
                                        4  *    A FILE OF 100-BYTE RECORDS IS COPIED.  THE RECORDS ARE
                                        5  *    GROUPED INTO PHYSICAL BLOCKS OF 1600 BYTES.  THE PROGRAM ALSO
                                        6  *    DISPLAYS THE CONTENT OF EACH RECORD (IT IS ASSUMED THAT THE
                                        7  *    RECORDS CONTAIN DATA WHICH IS ALL IN CHARACTER FORMAT).  THE
                                        8  *    INPUT FILE IS PROCESSED IN LOCATE MODE (USING R3 AS THE IO
                                        9  *    REGISTER SET TO POINT AT THE READ RECORD), WHILE BOTH OUTPUT
                                       10  *    FILES ARE PROCESSED IN MOVE MODE.  THE LOGIC IS AS FOLLOWS:
                                       11  *
                                       12  *    STEP 1.   SET UP A BASE REGISTER.
                                       13  *
                                       14  *    STEP 2.   OPEN THE FILES.
                                       15  *
                                       16  *    STEP 3.   SET THE COUNT OF LINES LEFT TO PRINT ON THE
                                       17  *              CURRENT PAGE TO 50.
                                       18  *
                                       19  *    STEP 4.   READ A RECORD FROM THE INPUT FILE.  SINCE
                                       20  *              PROCESSING IS BEING DONE USING LOCATE MODE,
                                       21  *              THE ADDRESS OF THE RECORD IS RETURNED IN THE
                                       22  *              IO REGISTER (R3 FOR THIS FILE).
                                       23  *
                                       24  *    STEP 5.   WRITE THE RECORD OUT TO THE NEW FILE USING
                                       25  *              MOVE MODE.  NOTE THAT THE ADDRESS OF THE
                                       26  *              RECORD CAN BE A VALUE IN A REGISTER.
                                       27  *
                                       28  *    STEP 6.   PRINT THE RECORD.  THIS REQUIRES FIRST MOVING
                                       29  *              IT TO A WORK AREA SO THAT CARRIAGE CONTROL
                                       30  *              CAN BE INSERTED.
                                       31  *
                                       32  *    STEP 7.   SET THE CARRIAGE CONTROL TO SINGLE SPACE.  IF
                                       33  *              THERE ARE MORE LINES LEFT TO PRINT ON THE
                                       34  *              CURRENT PAGE, GO BACK TO STEP 4.
                                       35  *
                                       36  *    STEP 8.   SET THE CARRIAGE CONTROL FOR SKIP TO 1 BEFORE
                                       37  *              PRINTING, AND RETURN TO STEP 3.
                                       38  *
                                       39  *    STEP 9.   PRINT THE END OF LIST MESSAGE, CLOSE THE FILES,
                                       40  *              AND EXIT.
                                       41  *
000000                                 42  COPYFILE CSECT
                                       43           PRINT NOGEN
                                       44  *
                                       45  ***<STEP 1>    SET UP A BASE REGISTER
                                       46  *
000000 05C0                            47           BALR  R12,0
                                00002  48           USING *,R12
                                       49  *
                                       50  ***<STEP 2>    OPEN THE FILES
                                       51  *
                                       52           OPEN  FILEIN,FILEOUT,LIST
```

Program 7-6 (continued)

```
LOC     OBJECT CODE        ADDR1 ADDR2  STMT  SOURCE STATEMENT

                                         62  *
                                         63  *  ***<STEP 3>    SET THE COUNT OF LINES LEFT ON THE PAGE TO 50
                                         64  *
00001A  4120 0032                  0032  65  STARTPG  LA    R2,50         R2 <- # LINES LEFT ON THE PAGE
                                         66  *
                                         67  *  ***<STEP 4>    READ A RECORD FROM THE INPUT FILE
                                         68  *
                                         69  READLOOP GET   FILEIN
                                         74  *
                                         75  *  ***<STEP 5>    WRITE THE RECORD OUT TO THE NEW FILE
                                         76  *
                                         77           PUT   FILEOUT,(3)       *** NOTE THAT THE SECOND OPERAND CAN
                                         83  *                                *** BE AN ADDRESS IN A REGISTER
                                         84  *
                                         85  *  ***<STEP 6>    PRINT THE RECORD
                                         86  *
000038  D263 C0AB 000AD 00000      87           MVC   RECORD+1(100),0(R3)   MOVE RECORD TO WORK AREA
                                         88           PUT   LIST,RECORD
                                         94  *
                                         95  *  ***<STEP 7>    SET CARRIAGE CONTROL FOR SINGLE SPACE, AND TEST
                                         96  *                 FOR MORE LINES LEFT ON THE PAGE
00004E  9240 C0AA         000AC     97           MVI   RECORD,C' '        SET CC TO BLANK
000052  4620 C01C         0001E     98           BCT   R2,READLOOP
                                         99  *
                                        100  *  ***<STEP 8>    SET CC FOR TOP OF PAGE
                                        101  *
000056  92F1 C0AA         000AC    102           MVI   RECORD,C'1'
00005A  47F0 C018         0001A    103           B     STARTPG            GO START A NEW PAGE
                                        104  *
                                        105  *  ***<STEP 9>    PRINT END-OF-LIST MESSAGE, CLOSE FILES, & EXIT
                                        106  EOFRT    PUT   LIST,ENDMESS
                                        112           CLOSE LIST,FILEIN,FILEOUT
                                        122           EOJ
                                        125  *
                                        126           LTORG
000088  5B5BC2D6D7C5D540           127           =C'$$BOPEN '
000090  5B5BC2C3D3D6E2C5           128           =C'$$BCLOSE'
000098  000001B0                   129           =A(FILEIN)
00009C  00000258                   130           =A(FILEOUT)
0000A0  00000178                   131           =A(LIST)
0000A4  000000AC                   132           =A(RECORD)
0000A8  00000111                   133           =A(ENDMESS)
                                        134  *
0000AC  F140404040404040           135  RECORD   DC    CL101'1'           ROOM FOR 1 RECORD WITH CC
000111  F05C5C5C40C5D5C4           136  ENDMESS  DC    CL101'0*** END OF LISTING ***'
                                        137  *
                                        138  LIST     DTFPR DEVADDR=SYSLST,BLKSIZE=101,RECFORM=FIXUNB,WORKA=YES,     X
                                                           CTLCHR=ASA,IOAREA1=PRINTIO1,IOAREA2=PRINTIO2,             X
                                                           DEVICE=3203
                                        159  *
                                        160  FILEIN   DTFSD DEVADDR=SYS001,BLKSIZE=1600,EOFADDR=EOFRT,               X
```

Program 7-6 (continued)

```
LOC     OBJECT CODE   ADDR1  ADDR2   STMT    SOURCE STATEMENT

                                             IOAREA1=INIO1,IOAREA2=INIO2,                                    X
                                             DEVICE=3340,IOREG=(3),RECFORM=FIXBLK,RECSIZE=100,               X
                                             TYPEFLE=INPUT
                                     220 *
                                     221 FILEOUT  DTFSD DEVADDR=SYS002,BLKSIZE=1608,DEVICE=3340,             X
                                                        IOAREA1=OUTIO1,IOAREA2=OUTIO2,WORKA=YES,             X
                                                        RECFORM=FIXBLK,RECSIZE=100,TYPEFLE=OUTPUT
                                     286 *
                                     287 PRINTIO1 DS    CL101
                                     288 PRINTIO2 DS    CL101
                                     289 INIO1    DS    CL1600
                                     290 INIO2    DS    CL1600
                                     291 OUTIO1   DS    CL1608
                                     292 OUTIO2   DS    CL1608
                                     293 *
00030C                               294 R3       EQU   3
000371                               295 R12      EQU   12
0003D6                               296 R2       EQU   2
000A16                    00003      297          END
001056                    0000C
00169E                    00002
```

Program 7-7

```
LOC     OBJECT CODE   ADDR1 ADDR2   STMT   SOURCE STATEMENT

                                      2  *  THIS PROGRAM ILLUSTRATES THE USE OF VARIABLE LENGTH RECORDS
                                      3  *  UNDER DOS.  THE PROGRAM READS CARDS, EACH OF WHICH CONTAINS
                                      4  *
                                      5  *      A STUDENT'S SOCIAL SECURITY NUMBER IN COL.S 1-9 AND
                                      6  *      A TEST SCORE (0-100) IN COLUMNS 11-13.
                                      7  *
                                      8  *  ALL OF THE CARDS FOR A GIVEN STUDENT OCCUR TOGETHER IN THE CARD INPUT
                                      9  *  FILE.  THE PROGRAM CREATES 1 VARIABLE-LENGTH RECORD FOR EACH STUDENT;
                                     10  *  THE RECORD CONTAINS ALL OF THE STUDENT'S TEST SCORES IN PACKED
                                     11  *  DECIMAL FORMAT.  THE PRECISE FORMAT OF THE GENERATED RECORDS IS
                                     12  *
                                     13  *      +0(4)   RDW (2 BYTES OF LENGTH, 2 BYTES OF 0000)
                                     14  *      +4(9)   SOCIAL SECURITY NUMBER
                                     15  *      +13(UP TO 40) THE STUDENT'S SCORES
                                     16  *            EACH SCORE WILL BE IN A 2-BYTE PACKED FIELD
                                     17  *
                                     18  *  THUS, THE MAXIMUM LENGTH OF ONE OF THE GENERATED RECORDS IS 53,
                                     19  *  AND THIS WOULD REQUIRE 20 CONSECUTIVE TEST SCORES FOR THE SAME
                                     20  *  STUDENT.  THE LOGIC OF THE PROGRAM IS
                                     21  *
                                     22  *      STEP 1.  SET UP A BASE REGISTER.
                                     23  *
                                     24  *      STEP 2.  OPEN THE FILES.
                                     25  *
                                     26  *      STEP 3.  READ THE FIRST RECORD AND SAVE ITS ADDRESS
                                     27  *
                                     28  *      STEP 4.  PUT THE SOC. SEC. # INTO THE NEW RECORD.  ALSO,
                                     29  *               PACK IN THE SCORE OFF THE FIRST CARD.
                                     30  *
                                     31  *      STEP 5.  READ CARDS, PACKING THE SCORES INTO THE DISK
                                     32  *               RECORD, UNTIL A CARD WITH A NEW SOC. SEC. #
                                     33  *               IS READ OR END-OF-FILE OCCURS.  IF END-OF-FILE
                                     34  *               OCCURS, A BRANCH TO STEP 7 WILL TAKE PLACE
                                     35  *               AUTOMATICALLY.
                                     36  *
                                     37  *      STEP 6.  CALL 'PUTREC' TO PUT IN THE RDW AND WRITE OUT
                                     38  *               THE CONSTRUCTED RECORD.  GO TO STEP 4 (SINCE
                                     39  *               THE FIRST RECORD FOR THE NEXT STUDENT HAS
                                     40  *               BEEN READ ALREADY).
                                     41  *
                                     42  *      STEP 7.  CALL 'PUTREC' TO WRITE OUT THE LAST RECORD.
                                     43  *
                                     44  *      STEP 8.  CLOSE THE FILES AND EXIT.
                                     45  *
000000                               46  VARBUILD CSECT
                                     47         PRINT NOGEN
                                     48  ***<STEP 1>   SET UP A BASE REGISTER
                                     49  *
                                     50  *
000000 05C0                          51         BALR  R12,0
00002                                52         USING *,R12
```

Program 7-7 (continued)

```
LOC     OBJECT CODE      ADDR1 ADDR2  STMT  SOURCE STATEMENT

                                       53  *
                                       54  *** <STEP 2>        OPEN THE FILES
                                       55  *
                                       56           OPEN   CARDFL,VARFL
                                       65  *
                                       66  *** <STEP 3>        READ THE FIRST RECORD
                                       67  *
                                       68           GET    CARDFL,CARD
                                       74  *
                                       75  *** <STEP 4>        PUT IN THE SOC. SEC. # AND THE FIRST SCORE
                                       76  *
000026 D208 C116 C0C0  00118 000CC     77  MAINLOOP MVC    SOCSEC#(9),CARD
00002C F212 C11F C0CA  00121 000CC     78           PACK   SCORES(2),CARD+10(3)  PACK IN FIRST TEST SCORE
000032 4120 C121        00123          79           LA     R2,SCORES+2      R2 <- ADDRESS TO PACK NEXT SCORE
                                       80  *
                                       81  *** <STEP 5>        PUT IN SCORES FOR CONSECUTIVE #S WITH THE SAME SSN
                                       82  *
000046 D508 C116 C0C0  00118 000C2     83  BUILDLP  GET    CARDFL,CARD      GET THE NEXT CARD
                                       89  *
00004C 4770 C05C        0005E          90           CLC    SOCSEC#(9),CARD  SAME STUDENT?
000050 F212 2000 C0CA  00000 000CC     91           BNE    NEXTGUYS         NO -> BRANCH
000056 4122 0002        0002           92           PACK   0(2,R2),CARD+10(3)  PACK IN THE TEST SCORE
00005A 47F0 C034        00036          93           LA     R2,2(R2)
                                       94           B      BUILDLP
                                       95  *
                                       96  *** <STEP 6>        CALL 'PUTREC' TO WRITE OUT THE RECORD
                                       97  *
00005E 45A0 C07E        00080          98  NEXTGUYS BAL    R10,PUTREC       WRITE THE RECORD
000062 47F0 C024        00026          99           B      MAINLOOP
                                      100  *
                                      101  *** <STEP 7>        EOF OCCURRED, SO WRITE THE LAST RECORD
                                      102  *
000066 45A0 C07E        00080         103  EOFRTN   BAL    R10,PUTREC       WRITE THE LAST RECORD
                                      104  *
                                      105  *** <STEP 8>        CLOSE THE FILES AND EXIT
                                      106  *
                                      107           CLOSE  CARDFL,VARFL
                                      116           EOJ
                                      119  *
                                      120  * PUTREC SIMPLY FILLS IN THE RDW AND ISSUES A PUT TO CAUSE THE
                                      121  * RECORD TO BE WRITTEN TO THE DISK (ACTUALLY, THE PUT CAUSES
                                      122  * THE RECORD TO BE TRANSFERRED TO THE OUTPUT BUFFER).
                                      123  *
000080 5B20 C0B6        000B8         124  PUTREC   S      R2,=A(RDW)       R2 <- LENGTH OF THE RECORD
000084 4020 C112        00114         125           STH    R2,RDW           STORE INTO LEFT HALF OF THE RDW
000088 D201 C114 C0BE  00116 000C0    126           MVC    RDW+2(2),=H'0'
                                      127           PUT    VARFL,RDW
00009E 07FA                           133           BR     R10              RETURN
                                      134  *
0000A0                                135           LTORG
0000A0 5B5BC2D6D7C5D540               136           =C'$$BOPEN '
```

Program 7-7 (continued)

```
LOC     OBJECT CODE      ADDR1 ADDR2  STMT  SOURCE STATEMENT

0000A8  5B5BC2C3D3D6E2C5               137              =C'$$BCLOSE'
0000B0  00000150                       138              =A(CARDFL)
0000B4  000000C2                       139              =A(CARD)
0000B8  00000114                       140              =A(RDW)
0000BC  00000190                       141              =A(VARFL)
0000C0  0000                           142              =H'0'
0000C2                                 143  CARD    DS  CL80
                                       144  *
                                       145  * THE VARIABLE-LENGTH RECORD IS BUILT HERE.   THE THREE FIELDS
                                       146  * ARE ALL PART OF THE RECORD.
                                       147  *
000114                                 148  RDW     DS  F               RECORD DESCRIPTOR WORD
000118                                 149  SOCSEC* DS  CL9             SOCIAL SECURITY NUMBER
000121                                 150  SCORES  DS  20PL2           MAX POF 20 SCORES IN THE RECORD
                                       151  *
                                       152  CARDFL  DTFCD DEVADDR=SYSIPT,BLKSIZE=80,RECFORM=FIXUNB,TYPEFLE=INPUT, X
                                                          EOFADDR=EOFRTN,WORKA=YES,IOAREA1=CARDIO1,                X
                                                          IOAREA2=CARDIO2,DEVICE=2540
                                       173  *
                                       174  VARFL   DTFSD DEVADDR=SYS001,BLKSIZE=3520,DEVICE=3340,                X
                                                          IOAREA1=OUTIO1,IOAREA2=OUTIO2,WORKA=YES,                X
                                                          RECFORM=VARBLK,TYPEFLE=OUTPUT
                                       242  *
000250                                 243  OUTIO1  DS  CL3520
001010                                 244  OUTIO2  DS  CL3520
001DD0                                 245  CARDIO1 DS  CL80
001E20                                 246  CARDIO2 DS  CL80
                                       247  *
                                0000A  248  R10     EQU 10
                                0000C  249  R12     EQU 12
                                00002  250  R2      EQU 2
                                00000  251          END VARBUILD
```

Program 7-8

```
LOC    OBJECT CODE    ADDR1 ADDR2  STMT  SOURCE STATEMENT

                                     2  * IN THIS EXAMPLE THE RECORDS PRODUCED BY 'VARBUILD' ARE
                                     3  * ACCESSED AND USED TO PRINT OUT THE TEST SCORES FOR ALL THE
                                     4  * STUDENTS.  THE READER SHOULD STUDY VARBUILD CAREFULLY BEFORE
                                     5  * EXAMINING THIS EXAMPLE, SINCE THE FORMAT AND CONTENTS OF THE
                                     6  * RECORDS ARE DISCUSSED THERE.
                                     7  *
                                     8  * THE LOGIC OF VARLIST IS AS FOLLOWS:
                                     9  *
                                    10  *      STEP 1.   SET UP A BASE REGISTER.
                                    11  *
                                    12  *      STEP 2.   OPEN THE FILES.
                                    13  *
                                    14  *      STEP 3.   READ THE FIRST RECORD ON EOF GO TO STEP 6.
                                    15  *
                                    16  *      STEP 4.   CONSTRUCT A PRINT LINE FROM THE RECORD
                                    17  *
                                    18  *      STEP 5.   PUT OUT THE PRINT LINE AND GO TO STEP 3.
                                    19  *
                                    20  *      STEP 6.   CLOSE THE FILES AND EXIT.
                                    21  *
000000                              22  VARLIST  CSECT
                                    23           PRINT NOGEN
                                    24  *
                                    25  ***<STEP 1>       SET UP A BASE REGISTER
                                    26  *
000000 05CØ                00002    27  .        BALR  R12,0
                                    28           USING *,R12
                                    29  *
                                    30  ***<STEP 2>       OPEN THE FILES
                                    31  *
                                    32           OPEN  VARIN,OUTFL
                                    41  *
                                    42  ***<STEP 3>       READ THE FIRST RECORD
                                    43  *
                                    44  GETLOOP  GET   VARIN,RECORD
                                    50  *
                                    51  ***<STEP 4>       CONSTRUCT THE PRINT LINE
                                    52  *
000026 9240 CØB6           000B8    53           MVI   PRNTLINE,C' '          CLEAR THE PRINT LINE
00002A D283 CØB7 CØB6 000B9 000B8   54           MVC   PRNTLINE+1(132),PRNTLINE
                                    55  *
                                    56  *  PUT THE SOC SEC # INTO THE PRINT LINE
                                    57  *
000030 D208 CØB7 C140 000B9 00142   58           MVC   PRNTLINE+1(9),RECORD+4
000036 4120 CØC6           000C6    59           LA    R2,PRNTLINE+14    R2 <-  ADDRESS TO PUT NEXT SCORE
00003A 4130 C149           0014B    60           LA    R3,RECORD+13      R3 <-  ADDRESS OF NEXT SCORE TO EDIT
00003E 4840 C13C           0013E    61           LH    R4,RECORD         R4 <-  LENGTH OF THE RECORD
000042 5B40 CØA6           000A6    62           S     R4,=F'13'         R4 <-  LENGTH OF SCORES IN THE RECORD
000046 8A40 0001           00001    63           SRA   R4,1              R4 <-  # OF SCORES IN THE RECORD
                                    64  *
00004A D203 2000 CØAA 00000 000AC   65  DUMPMS   MVC   0(4,R2),=X'40202120'
```

Program 7-8 (continued)

```
VARLIST - HOW TO ACCESS VARIABLE-LENGTH RECORDS                                    DOS/VSE ASSEMBLER 15.57  82-05-03

LOC     OBJECT CODE       ADDR1 ADDR2   STMT  SOURCE STATEMENT

000050  DE03 2000 3000    00000 00000    66           ED    0(4,R2),0(R3)          EDIT IN 1 SCORE
000056  4122 0005               00005    67           LA    R2,5(R2)
00005A  4133 0002               00002    68           LA    R3,2(R3)               POINT TO NEXT SCORE
00005E  4640 C048               0004A    69           BCT   R4,DUMPNS
                                         70     *
                                         71     ***<STEP 5>     PRINT THE LINE AND GO BACK TO STEP 3.
                                         72     *
000072  47F0 C014               00016    73           PUT   OUTFL,PRNTLINE         PRINT A LINE
                                         79           B     GETLOOP
                                         80     *
                                         81     ***<STEP 6>     CLOSE THE FILES AND EXIT
                                         82     *
                                         83     EOD   CLOSE VARIN,OUTFL
                                         92           EOJ
                                         95     *
                                         96           LTORG
000090  5B5BC2D6D7C5D540                 97                 =C'$$BOPEN '
000098  5B5BC2C3D3D6E2C5                 98                 =C'$$BCLOSE'
0000A0  00000180                         99                 =A(VARIN)
0000A4  0000013E                        100                 =A(RECORD)
0000A8  0000000D                        101                 =F'13'
0000AC  40202120                        102                 =X'40202120'
0000B0  00000230                        103                 =A(OUTFL)
0000B4  000000B8                        104                 =A(PRNTLINE)
0000B8                                  105     PRNTLINE DS   CL133                 THE PRINT LINE
                                        106     *
00013E                                  107           DS    0H                      ALIGN RECORD ON A HALFWORD BOUNDARY -
                                        108     *                                   THIS ALLOWS A LH OF THE RECORD LENGTH
00013E                                  109     RECORD DS    CL53
                                        110     *
                                        111     VARIN  DTFSD DEVADDR=SYS001,BLKSIZE=3520,DEVICE=3340,          X
                                                             IOAREA1=INIO1,IOAREA2=INIO2,WORKA=YES,            X
                                                             RECFORM=VARBLK,EOFADDR=EOD,TYPEFLE=INPUT
                                        173     *
                                        174     OUTFL  DTFPR DEVADDR=SYSLST,BLKSIZE=133,RECFORM=FIXUNB,WORKA=YES, X
                                                             CTLCHR=ASA,IOAREA1=PRINTIO1,IOAREA2=PRINTIO2,    X
                                                             DEVICE=3203
                                        195     *
000260                                  196     INIO1     DS   CL3520
001020                                  197     INIO2     DS   CL3520
001DE0                                  198     PRINTIO1  DS   CL80
001E30                                  199     PRINTIO2  DS   CL80
                                        200     *
        00002                           201     R2        EQU  2
        00003                           202     R3        EQU  3
        00004                           203     R4        EQU  4
        0000C                           204     R12       EQU  12
        00000                           205               END  VARLIST
```

8

Advanced Techniques

8.1 CONSTANTS, LITERALS, AND THE DC AND DS STATEMENTS

The DC and DS statements and literals have been touched upon in earlier sections. These areas will be covered here in considerably more depth. The reader is cautioned, however, that this presentation is not intended to be exhaustive. The intent here, as in all other sections of this text is to offer a clear working introduction to the subject. Detailed presentations of all the subjects covered are available in the manuals published by IBM.

To understand the general format of the DC statement, one must have a knowledge of the expressions and terms that may be used in defining constants. Terms are of two types, self-defining and relocatable.

A *self-defining term* is a term that has an inherent value, in contrast to a term that is assigned a value by the assembler. There are four types of self-defining terms:

* A *decimal self-defining term* is simply a string of decimal digits. For example, 0, 983, 08, and 48932 are decimal self-defining terms.

* A *character self-defining term* consists of from one to three characters enclosed within apostrophes and preceded by a C. The following are examples of character self-defining terms:

$$C'\ '\qquad\qquad C'123'\qquad\qquad C'\&\&\&\&'$$
$$C'ABC'\qquad\quad C'1*'$$

Remember that two adjacent occurrences of the apostrophe or ampersand are used to represent a single occurrence of these symbols in a character string.

The value represented by a character self-defining term is found by replacing the characters with their two-digit hexadecimal equivalents and evaluating the result. Thus,

$$C'\ ' = X'40' = 64$$

- A *hexadecimal self-defining term* consists of from one to six hexadecimal digits enclosed within apostrophes and preceded by an X. Examples of hexadecimal self-defining terms include

$$X'1' \qquad\qquad X'C1F' \qquad\qquad X'01ABC'$$

- A *binary self-defining term* consists of from one to 24 binary digits enclosed within apostrophes and preceded by a B. The following are examples of binary self-defining terms:

$$B'1' \qquad\qquad B'0010' \qquad\qquad B'1010111'$$

Binary self-defining terms have been used earlier in this text to represent the masks in the BC and BCR instructions. Actually, any self-defining term with a correct value (0 to 15) may be used to represent such a mask. For example,

```
          BCR     B'1010',14
          BCR     10,14
and       BCR     X'A',14
```

are equivalent. The binary representation was chosen because of the natural correspondence between the bits and the setting of the condition code. In practice, however, decimal terms are more commonly used to specify masks.

A *relocatable term* is a term whose value depends upon where the program of which it is a part is located in main storage. The labels of storage areas, instructions, and constants are relocatable terms. The value of a relocatable term is assigned before each execution of the program in which the term appears. This value is offset from the start of the program by some fixed amount. For example, for one execution of a program, the relocatable term

LOOP

may be assigned a value of 2110. However, for another execution of the same program, the start of the program could be offset by 100 bytes from its previous location; in this case, the value assigned would be 2210.

Expressions may be formed from self-defining and relocatable terms using arithmetic operators and parentheses. The expressions thus formed are termed either absolute or relocatable. An *absolute expression* is an expression whose value is not dependent upon the location of the program in storage. A *relocatable expression* is an expression whose value changes by n if the program of which it is a part is relocated by n bytes.

The following arithmetic symbols may be used in forming expressions from terms:

Symbol	Meaning
+	Addition
−	Subtraction
*	Multiplication
/	Division

The following rules apply to the formation of absolute expressions:

1. Each self-defining term is an absolute expression.
2. If L1 and L2 are relocatable terms, then (L1–L2) is an absolute expression.
3. If A1 and A2 are absolute expressions, then

$$(A1 + A2)$$
$$(A1*A2)$$
$$(A1 - A2)$$
and $$(A1/A2)$$

are absolute expressions.

The second rule may seem strange at first. However, consideration of the example

$$(EXIT - LOOP)$$

should lead to the conclusion that this difference remains constant regardless of the relocation factor of the program. That is, if the program is relocated, the values of EXIT and LOOP will be offset by the same amount. The following are examples of absolute expressions:

$$(((EXIT - ENTRY) + 1) + 20)$$
$$(((ADDR1 - ADDR2)/4)*X'10')$$
$$(((X'A'*B'101')/20) + 5)$$

The following rules apply to the formation of relocatable expressions:

1. Any relocatable term is a relocatable expression.
2. If A is an absolute expression and L is a relocatable expression, then

$$(A + L)$$
$$(L + A)$$
and $$(L - A)$$

are relocatable expressions.

The following are examples of relocatable expressions:

$$((START + 20) - X'13')$$
$$(LOOP - (X'ABC'/X'4'))$$
$$(EXIT - (((ADDR1 - ADDR2)/C'ABC')/X'AB'))$$

Parentheses may be omitted from expressions, and minor permutations of terms are allowed in some circumstances. The evaluation of an expression, whether fully parenthesized or not, proceeds as follows:

1. Each term is evaluated.
2. The subexpressions within parentheses are evaluated, proceeding from the innermost parentheses outward.
3. All multiplications and divisions are performed in left-to-right order; then all additions and subtractions are carried out in left-to-right order.
4. All arithmetic operations are performed on 32-bit binary numbers, and the final result is truncated to 24 bits.

A generous limit of 16 terms and five levels of parentheses is allowed in the formation of an expression.

The *DC statement*, which is used to provide constant data in storage, has the following general format:

label   DC   one or more operands

Each operand is of the form

dTmv

where   d   is the duplication factor
T   is the type
m   is the modifier (only length modifiers will be considered)
v   is the value or values

For example, in the statement

DC   5CL4'3'

5   is the duplication factor
C   is the type
L4   is the length modifier
'3'   is the value

The *duplication factor* can be specified in any one of the following ways:

- It may be omitted. In this case, a duplication factor of 1 is assumed.
- It may be a decimal self-defining term.
- It may be a positive absolute expression from which the outside parentheses have not been omitted. All labels used in this expression must be previously defined (i.e., specified earlier in the program).

The following examples illustrate the use of each form that the duplication factor can take:

```
DC        C' '
DC        3C' '
DC        (20/4 + X'A')C' '
```

If a duplication factor of 0 is used in a DC statement, execution of the state-ment generates nothing. The sole effect is to force a boundary alignment. For example, the statement

```
DC        0F'0'
```

does not cause a fullword to be generated, but merely moves the location counter ahead to the next fullword boundary.

The valid *types* that we will consider at this time are

C, X, B, F, H, A, and D

The use of each of these constant types in DC statements is discussed next, along with the value that can be associated with a DC operand.

The *length modifier* is of the form

Ln

where   n   is either a decimal self-defining term or a positive absolute expression from which the outside parentheses may not be omit-ted. (Any label used in this expression must be previously defined.)

If the length modifier is omitted, an implied length is assumed. The constant types are listed below with their respective maximum-length modifiers and implied lengths.

Constant	Maximum Length	Implied Length	Normally Aligned
C	256	As needed	On a byte
X	256	As needed	On a byte
B	256	As needed	On a byte
F	8	4	On a fullword
H	8	2	On a halfword
A	4	4	On a fullword
D	8	8	On a doubleword

The address of the label naming a DC constant is the address of the left-most byte of the first constant specified by that instruction. If no length modifier is specified in the operand, boundary alignment may occur. For example, in this instance, an F-type constant always begins on a fullword boundary. If a length modifier is specified, no boundary alignment will occur.

The value or values that can be specified with each of these constant types in an operand are as follows:

A *C-type constant* has the form

$$'string\ of\ characters'$$

Only one value may be specified in an operand. The implied length of the constant is the number of characters in the constant, and no boundary alignment is performed.

An *X-type constant* has the form

$$'string\ of\ hexadecimal\ digits'$$

Only one X-type constant may be specified in an operand. If an X-type constant contains an even number, n, of digits, the implied length of the constant is $n/2$. If the constant contains an odd number, m, of digits, a zero is affixed on the left and the implied length in this case is $(m+1)/2$. No boundary alignment occurs.

A *B-type constant* has the form

$$'string\ of\ binary\ digits'$$

Only one B-type constant may be specified in an operand. If the number of digits in a B-type constant is not an even multiple of 8, zeros are padded on the left to round the total number of digits up to an even multiple of 8. For example, the statement

$$DC \qquad B'1'$$

is equivalent to

$$DC \qquad B'00000001'$$

The implied length of a B-type constant is the number of bytes necessary to store the constant, and no boundary alignment is performed.

The *F-* and *H-type constants* can be used to generate constants that occupy fullwords and halfwords, respectively. With either type, more than one value can be specified in an operand. For example, the statement

$$DC \qquad F'1,-2,3604'$$

is valid.

An *A-type constant* can be specified by any valid absolute or relocatable expression. The value is calculated to 32 bits and then truncated to 24 bits. The implied length is 4 and the value is stored in the rightmost 24 bits of a fullword. Boundary alignment is to the next fullword boundary.

The *D-type constant* can be used to generate a constant of zero on a doubleword boundary as follows:

$$DC \qquad D'0'$$

Many uses of the D-type constant involve features of assembly language that are not covered until Chapter 10. However, the most common use is simply to reserve a doubleword of storage.

To conclude this discussion of the DC statement, we direct your attention to the fact that more than one operand can appear in a DC statement. If more than one value is specified in an operand, each value must have the same characteristics; however, different types of operands can be specified in the same DC statement. For example, the statement

$$\text{DC} \qquad \text{X}'01',\text{C}'\text{CHAR}',\text{F}'4'$$

is valid.

The *DS statement* is of the form

$$\text{label} \qquad \text{DS} \qquad \text{one or more operands}$$

With the following exceptions, the operands are of the same form as those specified for the DC statement:

1. No values need be specified for the operands.
2. The length modifier for a C- or X-type field may specify up to 65,535 bytes, rather than 256.

The DS statement generates nothing, whether or not values are specified. Its sole function is to set aside storage areas. If values are specified, they are used merely to assign implied lengths in the absence of a length modifier.

A *literal* is of the form

$$= \text{operand}$$

where the operand differs from the operand defined for the DC statement only in the following respects:

1. Unsigned decimal self-defining terms must be used to specify the duplication factor and length modifier.
2. The duplication factor must be nonzero.

Some examples of literals are

$$= \text{BL4}'1'$$
$$= \text{F}'4, -3'$$
$$= \text{CL3}'1'$$

Each label used in a program has a length attribute. This fact is usually important only in the case of labels used with DC and DS statements. The length attribute of a label used for a DC or DS statement is the value of the length modifier of the first operand or, in the absence of a length modifier, the implied length of the first operand. This is a critical fact that should be carefully noted. Following are several sample statements with their length attributes:

Statement			*Length Attribute*
FIELD1	DC	CL12'1'	12
FIELD2	DC	2CL12'1'	12
FIELD3	DC	F'0'	4
FIELD4	DS	XL3'1'	3
FIELD5	DS	(4/X'2')BL(X'A'*B'10')	20

8.2 THE AND, OR, AND EXCLUSIVE OR INSTRUCTIONS

In this section, instruction sets are introduced that can be used to perform logical operations between two fullword operands, between an immediate byte and a byte in storage, or between two fields in storage.

Some basic familiarity with the logical operators AND, OR, and EXCLUSIVE OR is required to make a discussion of these instructions meaningful. The results of performing these three logical operations on bits are summarized in Table 8-1.

Table 8-1

AND				*OR*				*EXCLUSIVE OR*		
Bit				Bit				Bit		
1	2	Result		1	2	Result		1	2	Result
0	0	0		0	0	0		0	0	0
0	1	0		0	1	1		0	1	1
1	0	0		1	0	1		1	0	1
1	1	1		1	1	1		1	1	0

The following rules should be useful:

1. When an AND operation is performed on two bits, the result is 1 only if both bits have a value of 1; otherwise, the result is 0.

2. When an OR operation is performed on two bits, the result is 0 only if both bits have a value of 0; otherwise, the result is 1.

3. When an EXCLUSIVE OR operation is performed on two bits, the result is 1 if the bits have different values; the result is 0 if both bits have the same value.

These logical operations can be extended to bit strings of any length. The result of performing a logical operation on bit strings of equal length is determined by calculating the result of performing that logical operation on each corresponding pair of bits from the two strings. This process is illustrated in the following examples:

- *Example 1.*   The AND operation.

First string	0000	0101	110101
Second string	1111	1001	011100
Result	0000	0001	010100

- *Example 2.*   The OR operation.

First string	0000	0101	110101
Second string	1111	1001	011100
Result	1111	1101	111101

- *Example 3.*   The EXCLUSIVE OR operation.

First string	0000	0101	110101
Second string	1111	1001	011100
Result	1111	1100	101001

The instructions that implement these logical operations between fullword operands are N, NR, O, OR, X, and XR. A discussion of these instructions follows.

Execution of the RX instruction

$$\text{N} \qquad \text{r,D(X,B)} \qquad\qquad (AND)$$

causes an AND operation to be performed on the fullword in the register r and the fullword in memory at the address D(X,B). The result replaces the first operand; the second operand is unaltered. If every bit in the result has a value of 0, the condition code is set to 0; otherwise, the condition code is set to 1.

The instruction

$$\text{NR} \qquad \text{r}_1\text{,r}_2 \qquad\qquad (AND\ Register)$$

is the RR counterpart of the N instruction. Execution of the NR instruction is analogous to the execution of the N instruction except that in the NR instruction the second operand is the fullword in the register r_2.

The key to most uses of the N instruction is as follows: *Any bit in the result corresponding to a bit in the second operand with a value of 0 will have a value of 0; any bit in the result corresponding to a bit in the second operand with a value of 1 will have the same value as the corresponding bit in the first operand.*

A possibly clearer, though less precise, way of stating this is as follows: *Performing an AND operation between an arbitrary bit and 0 results in a 0; performing an AND operation between an arbitrary bit and 1 leaves the value of the bit unaltered.*

Thus, execution of the instruction

$$\text{N} \qquad \text{R1,} = \text{X}'00000000'$$

will zero R1, while execution of the instruction

$$N \qquad R1, = X'FFFFFFFF'$$

will not alter the contents of R1.

The following examples illustrate uses of the AND instructions.

- *Example 1.* Assume that R1 contains an address that may or may not be on a fullword boundary. To ensure that this address is adjusted to a fullword boundary (by rounding down to the next lower fullword boundary, if necessary), it is sufficient to turn the values of the rightmost two bits of R1 to 0. (If this is not obvious, consider that the numerical value represented by any other bit in R1 is a multiple of 4.) Execution of the instruction

$$N \qquad R1, = X'FFFFFFFC'$$

will accomplish this purpose. Note that only the values of the rightmost two bits of R1 can be affected. Had it been desirable to round the address up rather than down, the following pair of instructions could have been used:

```
LA      R1,3(R1)
N       R1, = X'FFFFFFFC'
```

Analogous instructions should be used to round a binary number up or down to the nearest multiple of any other power of 2.

- *Example 2.* Occasionally it is necessary to calculate the remainder resulting from the division of a given number by a divisor that is a power of 2. In particular, suppose that the remainder resulting from the division of the number in R1 by 16 must be inserted in R0. Careful consideration of this problem should convince the reader that this remainder is the number represented by the rightmost four bits of R1. Therefore, execution of the instructions

```
L       R0, = X'0000000F'
NR      R0,R1
```

will produce the desired result.

Execution of the instruction

$$O \qquad r,D(X,B) \qquad\qquad (OR)$$

causes an OR operation to be performed on the fullwords in the register r and at the address D(X,B). The result replaces the contents of the register r; the second operand is unaltered. If the value of every bit in the result is 0, the condition code is set to 0; otherwise, the condition code is set to 1.

Execution of the instruction

$$OR \qquad r_1,r_2 \qquad\qquad (OR\ Register)$$

has an effect analogous to that produced by the execution of an O instruction except that in this case the second operand is in the register r_2.

The key to using the O instruction is as follows: *Performing an OR operation between an arbitrary bit and 0 leaves the value of the bit unaltered; performing an OR operation between an arbitrary bit and 1 results in a value of 1.*

The following simple examples illustrate uses of the OR instructions:

- *Example 1.* In the interest of conserving registers for other uses, it is sometimes desirable to use a register that otherwise may serve as a base or index register as a "flag." If such a register is used for this purpose, the right 24 bits must not be altered (these are the bits used in the computation of addresses) so as not to affect the execution of statements that use the register as a base or index register. Suppose that R12 is to be used for this purpose. The instruction

$$O \qquad R12, = X'80000000'$$

may be used to turn the leftmost bit to 1, and the instruction

$$N \qquad R12, = X'7FFFFFFF'$$

may be used to turn the leftmost bit to 0. The instruction

$$LTR \qquad R12,R12$$

may then be used to test the condition of the flag.

- *Example 2.* Suppose that R2 contains a number in the range 0 to 9. In order to contain the character representation of this integer, the rightmost byte of R2 can be changed by the instruction

$$O \qquad R2, = X'000000F0'$$

Execution of the instruction

$$X \qquad r,D(X,B) \qquad\qquad (EXCLUSIVE\ OR)$$

causes an EXCLUSIVE OR operation to be performed on the contents of the register r and the fullword at D(X,B). The result replaces the contents of the register r; the word at D(X,B) is unaltered. As with the other logical instructions, the condition code is set to 0 if all the bits in the result have a value of 0; otherwise, the condition code is set to 1.

Execution of the instruction

$$XR \qquad r_1,r_2 \qquad (EXCLUSIVE\ OR\ Register)$$

differs from that of the EXCLUSIVE OR instruction only in that the second operand is in the register r_2.

The effect of executing an EXCLUSIVE OR instruction may be summarized as follows: *Performing an EXCLUSIVE OR operation between an*

*arbitrary bit and 0 leaves the value of the bit unchanged; performing an
EXCLUSIVE OR operation between an arbitrary bit and 1 reverses the
value of the bit.*

A common use of the EXCLUSIVE OR instruction is to exchange the
contents of two registers. In particular, execution of the instructions

XR	R2,R3
XR	R3,R2
XR	R2,R3

causes the contents of R2 and R3 to be exchanged. The execution time required
by these three instructions is greater than the time required by the instructions

LR	R4,R2
LR	R2,R3
LR	R3,R4

The XR sequence does not, however, require an additional register. The
reader should convince himself that the three XR instructions do, in fact,
exchange the contents of the two registers.

The three SI instructions—NI, OI, and XI—can be used to perform logical
operations on bytes. The execution of any of these instructions will cause
the appropriate logical operation to be performed on a byte in storage, and
the immediate byte will be encoded in the instruction itself. The result replaces
the byte in storage. A description of these instructions and examples of their
uses follow.

Execution of the instruction

NI	D(B),byte	*(AND Immediate)*

will cause an AND operation to be performed on the byte in storage specified
by the first operand and the byte designated as the second operand. The
result replaces the first operand, and the second operand is unaltered. A
protection error or an addressability exception can occur. The condition code
is set as follows:

CC	*Meaning*
0	Resulting byte is 00.
1	Resulting byte is not 00.
2	—
3	—

Execution of the following two instructions is analogous to the NI except
for the logical operations involved:

OI	D(B),byte	*(OR Immediate)*
XI	D(B),byte	*(EXCLUSIVE OR Immediate)*

The keys to the use of these three instructions are:

1. An NI instruction is used to turn the values of bits to 0.
2. An OI instruction is used to turn the values of bits to 1.
3. An XI instruction is used to reverse the values of bits.

As an illustration, suppose that the one-byte field FIELD contains the value X'27'. Then, execution of the instruction

$$\text{OI} \qquad \text{FIELD,B'01001000'}$$

would alter the contents of FIELD to X'6F'; execution of the instruction

$$\text{NI} \qquad \text{FIELD,X'0F'}$$

would alter the contents of FIELD to X'07'; and execution of the instruction

$$\text{XI} \qquad \text{FIELD,X'F0'}$$

would alter the contents of FIELD to X'D7'. If these examples are not clear, the discussion of AND, OR, and EXCLUSIVE OR in this section should be carefully reviewed.

One particularly common use of NI and OI instructions is to alter the masks in branch instructions. To appreciate exactly how this is done, note that the instructions

$$\text{BC} \qquad \text{B'0000',addr}$$

and

$$\text{NOP} \qquad \text{addr}$$

are both encoded as

$$470h_I h_B h_D h_D h_D$$

where $h_I h_B h_D h_D h_D$ is the encoding of addr.

The NOP operation is an extended mnemonic that means "no operation." The RR counterpart of this NOP instruction is

$$\text{NOPR} \qquad r$$

which is encoded as

$$070h_r$$

The principal use of the NOP instruction is in generating branch instructions that can be "activated" later in the program. The following example illustrates how this is achieved:

```
LOOP       NOP      NOTFIRST
           OI       LOOP+1,X'F0'     SET BRANCH
           .
           .
           .
```

(a routine that is to be executed only once)

.
.
.

NOTFIRST . . .

In this case, the sequence of instructions between the OI instruction and NOTFIRST is executed only once. Execution of the OI instruction activates the branch so that, on any successive pass through the loop, the branch to NOTFIRST is taken. Later in the program, the branch could be deactivated by execution of the instruction

NI   LOOP + 1,X'0F'   DEACTIVATE BRANCH

Although the technique of altering branch masks is commonly employed, a growing number of people now regard it as a practice to be avoided. The basic objection is that a program containing such branch statements is frequently hard to debug and alter. A flag is clearer and therefore should normally be used.

Before we end this discussion of logical immediate instructions, one common use should be mentioned. When a packed decimal field is unpacked, the rightmost byte may contain an undesirable value due to the value for the sign. In such cases it is necessary to use an OI to make sure that the rightmost character is a printable decimal digit. Thus,

UNPK   SOCSEC(9),SSN(5)
OI   SOCSEC + 8,X'F0'

would unpack a Social Security number into a 9-character printable format.

The instructions XC, OC, and NC, which cause OR, AND, and EXCLUSIVE OR operations to be performed between two fields in storage, are used far less often than their RX, RR, and SI counterparts. In a few instances, however, they prove to be extremely useful.

Execution of the instruction

XC   D1(L,B1),D2(B2)   *(EXCLUSIVE OR)*

causes an EXCLUSIVE OR operation to be performed between the two L-byte fields at the addresses D1(B1) and D2(B2). The result replaces the first operand. The condition code is set as follows:

CC	*Meaning*
0	Resulting bytes are all 0.
1	Resulting bytes are *not* all 0.
2	—
3	—

There are two common uses of the XC instruction:

- Every byte in a field can be set to a value of 00 by performing an EXCLUSIVE OR operation between the field and itself. For example, execution of the instruction

```
XC        TABLE,TABLE
```

sets every byte of TABLE to a value of 00.

- The contents of two fields in storage can be exchanged through the use of three EXCLUSIVE OR operations. For example, execution of the sequence of instructions

```
XC        F1,F2
XC        F2,F1
XC        F1,F2
```

will cause the contents of F1 and F2 to be exchanged.

Execution of the instruction

```
OC        D1(L,B1),D2(B2)                    (OR)
```

causes an OR operation to be performed between the two operands. The result replaces the first operand. The settings of the condition code have the same meanings as for the XC instruction.

An OC instruction can be used to change the leading blanks to zeros, in a field containing numeric characters and blanks. For example, execution of the instruction

```
OC        ACCT#,=8X'F0'
```

will replace any blank in the eight-byte field ACCT# with a zero.

Execution of the instruction

```
NC        D1(L,B1),D2(B2)                    (AND)
```

causes an AND operation to be performed between the two operands. The result replaces the first operand. The settings of the condition code are the same as for XC and OC instructions.

NC instructions are used less frequently than OC and XC instructions. An example of the use of an NC instruction will be presented in Section 8.11.

8.3 THE TM INSTRUCTION

The TM instruction is an SI instruction that can be used to test the values of selected bits in a designated byte of storage. The values of the bits in the immediate byte determine which bits in the byte of storage are to be tested. Bits that correspond to a bit in the immediate byte with a value of 1 are tested, while those that correspond to a bit in the immediate byte with a value of 0 are not tested. For this reason, the immediate byte coded in a TM instruction is called a *mask*. A precise description of the TM instruction follows.

Execution of the instruction

TM   D(B),mask   (*Test under Mask*)

affects only the condition code, which is set according to the following rules:

- If every bit in the byte at the address D(B) that corresponds to a bit in the mask with a value of 1 has a value of 0, the condition code is set to 0. (The selected bits all have a value of 0.)

- If every bit in the byte at the address D(B) that corresponds to a bit in the mask with a value of 1 has a value of 1, the condition code is set to 3. (The selected bits all have a value of 1.)

- In all other cases, the condition code is set to 1.

Suppose, for example, that FLD contains X'0E'. Then, execution of the instruction

TM   FLD,B'10010000'

would set the CC to 0, since bits 0 and 3 of FLD both have a value of 0. Similarly, execution of the instruction

TM   FLD,B'10001000'

would set the CC to 1, and execution of the instruction

TM   FLD,B'00001110'

would set the CC to 3.

The set of extended mnemonics that can be used following a TM instruction are listed in Appendix B. An examination of that list will indicate that the pair of instructions

TM   WORD+3,B'00000011'
BNZ   NOTMULT4

will cause a branch to be taken if either or both of the selected bits do not have a value of 0. This condition occurs only when WORD has a value that is not a multiple of 4.

The most common use of TM instructions is for testing flag bits. This is convenient when each of several bits in a designated byte serves as a flag. For example, suppose that FLAGBYTE has been defined as

```
FLAGBYTE DC      X'00'
*   BITS    0-4    ARE UNUSED
*   BIT     5=1    END-OF-FILE HAS OCCURRED
*   BIT     6=1    INVALID ACCOUNT #
*   BIT     7=1    INVALID AMOUNT FIELD
```

Suppose further that some internal subroutine has been called to read an input card and that FLAGBYTE has been set to reflect the result of the attempted read operation. Under these conditions, the following sequence of instructions would cause a transfer of control to the appropriate routine, depending upon the settings of the flag bits:

```
TM      FLAGBYTE,B'00000100'   =1   EOF
BO      EOF
TM      FLAGBYTE,B'00000010'   =1   BAD ACCOUNT #
BO      BADACCT#
TM      FLAGBYTE,B'00000001'   =1   BAD AMOUNT
BO      BADAMNT
```

Note that the OI and NI instructions could be used to turn the flag bits on and off, respectively. For example, the instruction

```
OI      FLAGBYTE,B'00000100'
```

could be used to set the EOF indicator, and the instruction

```
NI      FLAGBYTE,B'11111110'
```

could be used to turn the BADAMNT flag off.

8.4 THE SHIFT INSTRUCTIONS

The result of performing an n-position right logical shift on a binary number containing m digits may be obtained by doing the following:

1. Remove the rightmost n digits from the original number.
2. Shift each of the remaining digits n positions to the right.
3. Place n zeros to the left of the leftmost digit of the resulting number.

For example, the process of performing a three-position, right logical shift on the number 10110001 can be illustrated as follows:

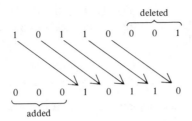

Left logical shifts are performed in a similar manner. The process of shifting 10110001 left three positions is depicted as follows:

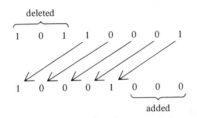

The instructions SLL and SRL perform logical shifts on the contents of a single register, whereas the instructions SLDL and SRDL perform logical shifts on the contents of an even/odd pair of registers. These four instructions are RS instructions, but the symbolic format for them differs from the format for other RS instructions. The standard symbolic format for an RS instruction is

> label   mnemonic $r_1, r_2, D(B)$

while the symbolic format for the shift instruction is

> label   mnemonic $r_1, D(B)$

In both cases, the format for the generated machine instruction is

$$h_0 h_0 h_{r1} h_{r2} \quad h_B h_D h_D h_D$$

However, when the shift instructions are encoded, h_{r2} is automatically set to 0.

Execution of the instruction

> SLL $r_1, D(B)$ *(Shift Left Single Logical)*

causes the contents of the register r_1 to be shifted left. The digits that are deleted are lost, and the condition code is not altered. The shift is an n-position logical shift, and n is calculated as follows:

1. The address $D(B)$ is calculated.
2. n is set equal to the value indicated by the rightmost six bits of the result.

This calculation is the same for all shift instructions. This means that a shift of up to 63 positions may be specified, but a single-register shift of more than 31 positions should never be used.

Execution of the instruction

$$\text{SRL} \qquad r_1, D(B) \qquad \textit{(Shift Right Single Logical)}$$

causes a right logical shift to be performed on the contents of the register r_1. In all other respects, it is analogous to the SLL instruction.

To illustrate the use of the SLL and SRL instructions, suppose that

> R1 contains 0F0F0F0F
> R2 contains 00000005

Execution of the instruction

$$\text{SLL} \qquad \text{R1,2}$$

would alter the contents of R1 to 3C3C3C3C, and execution of the instruction

$$\text{SLL} \qquad \text{R1,0(R2)}$$

would alter the contents of R1 to E1E1E1E0. Note that, in the second case, the number of positions shifted depends upon the contents of R2 (i.e., a shift of five positions would be performed). Execution of the instruction

$$\text{SRL} \qquad \text{R1,6}$$

would alter the contents of R1 to 003C3C3C.

Except that two registers participate in the shifts, execution of either of the double-register logical shift instructions is analogous to the execution of its single-register counterpart. The two registers that participate in the shift are an even-odd pair. This pair of registers is treated during the shift operation as if it were a single 64-bit register.

Execution of the instruction

$$\text{SLDL} \qquad r_1, D(B) \qquad \textit{(Shift Left Double Logical)}$$

causes the contents of the even-odd pair of registers designated by r_1 (r_1 must be even) to be shifted left.

Execution of the instruction

$$\text{SRDL} \qquad r_1 D(B) \qquad \textit{(Shift Right Double Logical)}$$

causes the contents of the even-odd pair of registers designated by r_1 to be shifted right.

The logical shift instructions are useful for positioning the bits in a register. Suppose, for example, that a payroll program using a very large table is to be written. Suppose further that each entry in the table contains three numbers:

- an employee number (4 digits)
- the number of hours worked (less than 100)
- the hourly pay rate (less than $20.00)

If a separate word were used for each number in an entry, each entry would occupy 12 bytes of storage. On the other hand, it is possible to condense all three numbers of an entry into a single word, using the following format:

> bits   0–13 = employee number
> bits   14–20 = hours worked
> bits   21–31 = pay rate

To reference the data in a single entry in the table, it would then be necessary to have a routine to isolate the numbers in separate registers. The following routine would perform this function:

```
*    ASSUME THAT R1 CONTAINS A TABLE ENTRY
          LR       R2,R1
          N        R2, = X'000007FF'
*    R2 NOW CONTAINS THE RATE
          LR       R3,R1
          SRL      R3,11     SHIFT OFF THE RATE
          N        R3, = X'0000007F'
*    R3 HAS THE HOURS
          LR       R4,R1
          SRL      R4,18
*    R4 HAS THE EMPLOYEE #
```

The following two instructions offer an alternative way to isolate the employee number:

```
          SR       R0,R0
          SLDL     R0,14
*    NOW R0 HAS THE EMPLOYEE #. NOTE THAT R1 HAS
*    BEEN SHIFTED, AS WELL AS R0.
```

In addition to the four logical shift instructions, there are four arithmetic shift instructions: SLA, SRA, SLDA, and SRDA. Although the operation of the arithmetic shifts is similar to the operation of the logical shifts, the functions for which they are normally used are quite different. The arithmetic shifts are used to achieve the effect of multiplying and dividing by powers of 2.

Execution of the instruction

> SLA r_1,D(B)   (*Shift Left Single Arithmetic*)

differs from the execution of the SLL instruction as follows:

- In an arithmetic left shift, bit 0 does not participate in the shift. If a bit that does not match the sign bit is shifted out of position 1, overflow will occur. Hence, the arithmetic shifts can never alter the sign bit.
- The condition code is set as follows:

CC	Meaning
0	Result is 0.
1	Result < 0.
2	Result > 0.
3	Overflow occurred.

The principal use of the SLA instruction is to achieve the effect of multiplication by powers of 2. Just as adding a 0 to the right of the base 10 representation of a number yields the same result as multiplying that number by 10, adding a 0 to the right of the base 2 representation of a number yields the same result as multiplying that number by 2. Thus, execution of the instruction

> SLA   R1,4

has the same effect on the contents of R1 as does the execution of the instruction

> M   R0, = F′16′

and requires less time. This technique should be applied only to powers of 2 greater than 1, since the contents of a register can be doubled in less time by adding the register to itself.

Execution of the instruction

> SRA r_1,D(B)   (*Shift Right Single Arithmetic*)

differs from the execution of the SRL instruction in the following respects:

- The bits vacated by the shift are not necessarily filled in with zeros. Instead, these bits take on the value of the sign bit. That is, zeros are filled in if the contents of the register represents a positive number, and ones are filled in if the number represented is negative. For example, the contents of R1 after execution of the instructions

> L   R1, = X′FFFFFFFF′
> SRA   R1,2

would be FFFFFFFF.

- The settings of the condition code are the same as for the SLA instruction except that overflow cannot occur.

The SRA instruction is used to achieve the effect of dividing numbers by powers of 2. For example, the result of dividing R2 by 64 is achieved by use of the instruction

$$\text{SRA} \qquad \text{R2,6}$$

When this technique is used and the number represented by the contents of the register is not a multiple of the indicated power of 2, rounding occurs. The results are always rounded down. Thus, execution of the instructions

$$\text{LA} \qquad \text{R1,22}$$
$$\text{SRA} \qquad \text{R1,2}$$

changes the contents of R1 to 00000005, while execution of the instructions

$$\text{L} \qquad \text{R1, } = F' - 22'$$
$$\text{SRA} \qquad \text{R1,2}$$

sets the contents of R1 to FFFFFFFA. This last example (involving a negative number) should be remembered since the result differs from the one that would be obtained using the Divide instruction.

The SLDA and SRDA instructions perform the same operations as the SLA and SRA instructions except that the former operations are applied to even-odd pairs of registers. These instructions are most often used to achieve the effect of multiplying and dividing 64-bit integers by powers of 2. (See Section 4.7 for routines to add, subtract, and compare 64-bit integers.)

Execution of the instruction

$$\text{SLDA} \qquad r_1\text{,D(B)} \qquad \qquad \textit{(Shift Left Double Arithmetic)}$$

causes a left arithmetic shift to be performed on the contents of the even-odd pair of registers designated by r_1. In all other details, its operation is identical to the operation of the SLA instruction.

Execution of the instruction

$$\text{SRDA} \qquad r_1\text{,D(B)} \qquad \qquad \textit{(Shift Right Double Arithmetic)}$$

causes a right arithmetic shift to be performed on the contents of the even-odd pair of registers designated by r_1. In all other respects, its operation is identical to that of the SRA instruction.

Program 8-1 concludes this section. The program reads numbers in the range 0 to 3999 and determines how many distinct numbers have been read. A table is maintained that contains 4000 one-bit entries. Initially, all bits in the table have a value of 0. As numbers are read by the program, the values of the corresponding bits in the table are changed to 1. When end-of-file is reached, the number of bits in the table with a value of 1 is determined and the answer is printed.

Program 8-1

```
        TITLE 'COUNTUP - COUNT THE NUMBER OF UNIQUE INTEGERS'
*********************************************************************
*
* THIS PROGRAM READS A STREAM OF INTEGERS, AND THEN COUNTS THE NUMBER
* OF UNIQUE VALUES THAT WERE IN THE INPUT.  AS THE VALUES ARE READ,
* BITS ARE MARKED IN A TABLE.  THE TABLE CONTAINS 32*125 BITS,
* EACH BIT CORRESPONDING TO A VALUE IN THE RANGE 0-3,999.  THE
* LOGIC OF THE PROGRAM IS AS FOLLOWS:
*
*   STEP 1.  READ THE FIRST CARD.
*
*   STEP 2.  IF EOF HAS OCCURRED, GO TO STEP 5 TO COUNT THE BITS THAT
*            WERE SET.
*
*   STEP 3.  MARK THE BIT IN THE TABLE CORRESPONDING TO THE NUMBER.
*
*   STEP 4.  READ THE NEXT CARD AND GO TO STEP 2.
*
*   STEP 5.  POSITION A POINTER TO THE FIRST WORD IN THE TABLE OF
*            BITS.
*
*   STEP 6.  IF ALL OF THE WORDS HAVE BEEN COUNTED, GO TO STEP 11.
*
*   STEP 7.  LOAD THE WORD TO BE COUNTED.
*
*   STEP 8.  IF ALL OF THE BITS HAVE BEEN COUNTED, GO TO STEP 10.
*
*   STEP 9.  FIND THE NEXT 1 BIT IN THE WORD.  COUNT IT AND RESET
*            THE BIT TO 0.  GO TO STEP 8.
*
*   STEP 10. POSITION TO THE NEXT WORD IN THE TABLE AND GO TO
*            STEP 6.
*
*   STEP 11. PRINT THE FINAL ANSWER.
*
*   STEP 12. EXIT.
*
*********************************************************************
*
COUNTUP  CSECT
         STM    R14,R12,12(R13)     STORE CALLER'S REGISTERS
         BALR   R12,0
         USING  BASEPT,R12
BASEPT   DS     0H
         LA     R14,SAVEAREA
         ST     R14,8(R13)
         ST     R13,4(R14)
         LR     R13,R14
*
***<STEP 1>    READ THE FIRST CARD
*
         XREAD  CARD,80
*
***<STEP 2>    TEST FOR END-OF-FILE
*
EOFTEST  BC     B'0100',GOCOUNT
*
```

Program 8-1 (continued)

```
***<STEP 3>    MARK THE BIT FOR THE NUMBER
*
        PACK   DWORD,CARD(6)
        CVB    R3,DWORD
*
        LA     R2,31             PUT 0000001F INTO R2
        NR     R2,R3             R2 <- REMAINDER OF #/32
        SRA    R3,5              R3 <- QUOTIENT OF #/32
        SLA    R3,2              TIMES 4 FOR DISPLACEMENT INTO TABLE
        L      R4,TABLE(R3)      R4 <- WORD WITH BIT TO MARK
        L      R5,=X'80000000'
        SRL    R5,0(R2)          POSITION BIT IN R5
        OR     R4,R5             AND MARK IT IN R4
        ST     R4,TABLE(R3)      PUT IT BACK INTO THE TABLE
*
***<STEP 4>    READ THE NEXT CARD AND GO BACK TO STEP 2.
*
READNXT XREAD  CARD,80
        B      EOFTEST
*
***<STEP 5>    SET UP TO START WITH THE FIRST WORD IN THE TABLE
*
GOCOUNT LM     R1,R4,=A(TABLE,0,1,125)
*                                R1 <- A(NEXT WORD TO COUNT)
*                                R2 <- COUNT OF BITS SET
*                                R3 <- THE CONSTANT 1
*                                R4 <- NUMBER OF WORDS TO COUNT
***<STEP 6>    TEST FOR END OF TABLE
*
TESTEND S      R4,=F'1'          DECREMENT COUNT OF WORDS LEFT
        BM     GOPRINT
*
***<STEP 7>    LOAD THE NEXT WORD TO COUNT
*
        L      R0,0(R1)
*
***<STEP 8>    MORE BITS IN THE WORD?
*
TESTFORO LTR   R5,R0
        BZ     NEXTWORD
*
***<STEP 9>    FIND THE NEXT BIT, COUNT IT, AND ZERO IT.
*
        AR     R2,R3             INCREMENT COUNT
        SLR    R5,R3             THIS INSTRUCTION AND THE NEXT
*                                ZERO THE RIGHTMOST 1 BIT IN THE
*                                REGISTER - TRY SOME EXAMPLES TO
*                                VERIFY THAT IT WORKS
        NR     R0,R5
        B      TESTFORO
*
***<STEP 10>   POSITION TO THE NEXT WORD AND GO TO STEP 6
*
NEXTWORD LA    R1,4(R1)
        B      TESTEND
*
***<STEP 11>   PRINT THE ANSWER
*
GOPRINT CVD    R2,DWORD
        MVC    ANSWER(10),=X'40206B2020206B202120'
        ED     ANSWER(10),DWORD+4
        XPRNT  CC,24
*
```

Program 8-1 (continued)

```
***<STEP 12>    EXIT
*
          L      R13,4(R13)
          LM     R14,R12,12(R13)
          BR     R14
*
          LTORG
CARD      DS     CL80             CARD INPUT AREA
SAVEAREA  DS     18F              REGISTER SAVE AREA
CC        DC     C'0THE ANSWER IS'
ANSWER    DS     CL10
DWORD     DS     D                USED FOR CONVERSIONS
TABLE     DC     125F'0'
R0        EQU    0
R1        EQU    1
R2        EQU    2
R3        EQU    3
R4        EQU    4
R5        EQU    5
R6        EQU    6
R7        EQU    7
R8        EQU    8
R9        EQU    9
R10       EQU    10
R11       EQU    11
R12       EQU    12
R13       EQU    13
R14       EQU    14
R15       EQU    15
          END    COUNTUP
```

8.5 HALFWORD INSTRUCTIONS

The IBM instruction set includes a set of instructions for manipulating 16-bit signed integers stored in halfwords. (Remember that a halfword is two contiguous bytes beginning on an even address.)

The method of encoding signed integers in 32-bit fullwords was introduced in Section 1.7. This encoding scheme, called two's complement encoding, can easily be generalized to apply to units of memory of varying size. In particular, signed integers can be encoded in halfwords as follows:

- Any number in the range 0 to $7FFF_{16}$ is represented in a halfword in its normal binary representation. Thus, the maximum number that can be represented is 32,767.

- Any number n in the range -1 to -8000_{16} is encoded by subtracting the absolute value of n from FFFF and adding 1.

Note that the sign bit (leftmost bit) of an encoded negative integer is always 1, while the sign bit of a positive number is always 0.

Halfword storage areas and constants can be generated using DS and DC statements. The only difference between the rules for halfword areas and those for fullword areas is that H should be used in place of F. Thus, the instruction

> label   DS   nH

is used to set aside a region of n halfwords ($2n$ bytes beginning on an even address), and execution of the instruction

> label   DC   nH'c'

generates n contiguous halfwords containing the constant c. In each case, if n is omitted, it is assumed to be 1. As examples of what the DC statement will generate, consider the following table:

Instruction	Generated
DC H'0'	0000
DC H'1'	0001
DC H'−1'	FFFF
DC H'−2'	FFFE
DC 2H'12'	000C000C
DC H'32767'	7FFF
DC H'−32768'	8000

Halfword literals may be used in the same manner as fullword literals. (An example is given below in the discussion of the Load Halfword instruction.)

Because the storage of halfword integers requires only half as much main storage as does the storage of fullword integers, a considerable savings in the storage requirements of a program can sometimes be achieved through their use. A limiting factor in the use of halfword integers is their range: $-32,768$ to $32,767$. This range is, however, adequate for many applications involving extensive integer tables. The halfword instructions—LH, STH, CH, AH, SH, and MH—are presented next.

Execution of the instruction

> LH   r,D(X,B)   (*Load Halfword*)

causes the contents of r to be replaced by a 32-bit representation of the number stored at the address D(X,B). Thus, after execution of the instruction, the two leftmost bytes of r will contain 0000 if the number loaded was positive or FFFF if that number was negative. The halfword operand in storage is left unchanged, and the condition code is not altered. Thus, after execution of the instruction

$$LH \qquad R1, = H' - 2'$$

the contents of R1 will be FFFFFFFE.

Execution of the instruction

$$STH \qquad r, D(X,B) \qquad\qquad (Store\ Halfword)$$

causes the halfword at D(X,B) to be replaced by a copy of the rightmost pair of bytes of r (bits 16–31). The contents of r are unchanged, and the condition code is unaltered.

Execution of the instruction

$$CH \qquad r, D(X,B) \qquad\qquad (Compare\ Halfword)$$

causes a comparison to be made between the contents of r and the halfword at D(X,B). Based on the outcome of this comparison, the condition code is set as follows:

CC	Meaning
0	The operands are equal.
1	The first operand is low.
2	The first operand is high.
3	—

There are halfword instructions—AH, SH, and MH—for performing the arithmetic operations of addition, subtraction, and multiplication. (However, there is no instruction for performing division on halfword operands.)

Execution of the instructions

$$AH \qquad r, D(X,B) \qquad\qquad (Add\ Halfword)$$

$$SH \qquad r, D(X,B) \qquad\qquad (Subtract\ Halfword)$$

is analogous to the execution of their fullword counterparts, A and S. The sole difference is that, in this case, D(X,B) refers to a halfword representation of an integer rather than a fullword representation.

The multiply halfword instruction involves a single register rather than a pair of registers as its fullword counterpart requires.

Execution of the instruction

$$MH \qquad r, D(X,B) \qquad\qquad (Multiply\ Halfword)$$

causes the contents of r and the halfword at D(X,B) to be multiplied. The result replaces the contents of r. Overflow does not cause an interrupt; hence, the programmer must assure that the result can be represented in 32 bits.

Program 8-2 illustrates the use of the halfword instructions.

Program 8-2

```
        TITLE 'HALFWORD - COUNT OCCURRENCES OF NUMBERS'
*****************************************************************************
*
* THIS PROGRAM READS IN A DECK OF CARDS, EACH OF WHICH CONTAINS
* AN INTEGER IN THE RANGE 0-9,999.  A HALFWORD COUNTER EXISTS
* FOR EACH NUMBER IN THE RANGE.  AS EACH INPUT NUMBER IS READ,
* THE CORRESPONDING COUNTER IS INCREMENTED.  AFTER ALL OF THE
* INPUT VALUES HAVE BEEN READ, THE PROGRAM PRINTS EACH COUNTER
* THAT CONTAINS A NONZERO VALUE.  THE LOGIC IS AS FOLLOWS:
*
*    STEP 1.  READ THE FIRST CARD
*
*    STEP 2.  IF EOF HAS OCCURRED, GO TO STEP 5.
*
*    STEP 3.  INCREMENT THE APPROPRIATE HALFWORD COUNTER.
*
*    STEP 4.  READ THE NEXT CARD AND GO TO STEP 2.
*
*    STEP 5.  PRINT A HEADER AND GET READY TO PROCESS ENTRIES
*             IN THE TABLE.
*
*    STEP 6.  IF ALL COUNTERS HAVE BEEN CHECKED, GO TO STEP 9.
*
*    STEP 7.  IF THE COUNTER IS NONZERO, PRINT A LINE FOR IT.
*
*    STEP 8.  POSITION TO THE NEXT COUNTER AND GO TO STEP 6.
*
*    STEP 9.  EXIT.
*
*****************************************************************************
*
HALFWORD CSECT
         STM   R14,R12,12(R13)     STORE CALLER'S REGISTERS
         BALR  R12,0
         USING BASEPT,R12
BASEPT   DS    0H
         LA    R14,SAVEAREA
         ST    R14,8(R13)
         ST    R13,4(R14)
         LR    R13,R14
*
***<STEP 1>   READ THE FIRST CARD
*
         XREAD CARD,80
*
***<STEP 2>   TEST FOR END-OF-FILE
*
EOFTEST  BC    B'0100',PRTCNTRS
```

```
*
***<STEP 3>    INCREMENT THE APPROPRIATE ACCUMULATOR
*
        PACK   DWORD,CARD(4)      PACK THE NUMBER
        CVB    R2,DWORD
        AR     R2,R2              DOUBLE THE # TO GET DISP INTO TABLE
        LH     R3,TABLE(R2)
        LA     R3,1(R3)           INCREMENT THE COUNTER
        STH    R3,TABLE(R2)       RESTORE NEW VALUE
*
***<STEP 4>    READ THE NEXT CARD
*
        XREAD CARD,80
        B      EOFTEST
*
***<STEP 5>    PRINT HEADER AND POSITION TO THE FIRST COUNTER
*
PRTCNTRS XPRNT =CL22'1 NUMBER    OCCURRENCES',22
        SR     R2,R2              R2 <- FIRST NUMBER TO CHECK
        LH     R3,=H'10000'       R3 <- # COUNTERS TO CHECK
*
***<STEP 6>    TEST FOR END OF TABLE
*
TESTEND SH     R3,=H'1'
        BM     EXIT
*
***<STEP 7>    IF THE VALUE IS > 0, PRINT IT
*
        LA     R4,0(R2,R2)        R4 <- DISP INTO TABLE FOR THE NUMBER
        LH     R5,TABLE(R4)
        LTR    R5,R5
        BZ     INCRCNT
*
        CVD    R2,DWORD
        MVC    NUMBER(7),=X'4020206B202120'
        ED     NUMBER(7),DWORD+5  EDIT IN THE NUMBER
*
        CVD    R5,DWORD
        MVC    VALUE(7),=X'4020206B202020'
        ED     VALUE(7),DWORD+5   EDIT IN # OCCURRENCES
*
        XPRNT PLINE,22
*
***<STEP 8>    GO TO NEXT COUNTER
*
INCRCNT LA     R2,1(R2)
        B      TESTEND
*
```

```
***<STEP 9>      EXIT
*
EXIT      L      R13,4(R13)
          LM     R14,R12,12(R13)
          BR     R14
*
          LTORG
DWORD     DS     D                   USED FOR CONVERSIONS
CARD      DS     CL80                INPUT AREA
SAVEAREA  DS     18F                 REGISTER SAVE AREA
PLINE     DC     C'0'
NUMBER    DS     CL7
          DC     CL5' '
VALUE     DS     CL7
          DC     CL2' '
TABLE     DC     10000H'0'           TABLE OF COUNTERS
*
R0        EQU    0
R1        EQU    1
R2        EQU    2
R3        EQU    3
R4        EQU    4
R5        EQU    5
R6        EQU    6
R7        EQU    7
R8        EQU    8
R9        EQU    9
R10       EQU    10
R11       EQU    11
R12       EQU    12
R13       EQU    13
R14       EQU    14
R15       EQU    15
          END    HALFWORD
```

8.6 THE MVCL, CLCL, AND EX INSTRUCTIONS

The MVCL and CLCL instructions are generalized versions of the MVC and CLC instructions. They are used to perform move and comparison operations on fields as long as $2^{24} - 1$.

Each of the operands of the instruction

MVCL   r1,r2   *(Move Long)*

must be an even register that is used to designate an even-odd pair of registers. Each of these register pairs specifies a field from 0 to $2^{24} - 1$ bytes in length. The rightmost three bytes of each even register specify the address of a field, and the rightmost three bytes of the odd register of each pair specify the length of the corresponding field. The contents of the field specified by r2 are moved to the field specified by r1.

If the sending field is shorter than the receiving field, a pad character represented by the leftmost byte of the odd register specified by r2 is inserted into the remaining rightmost bytes of the receiving field. If a byte is simultaneously in both the sending and receiving fields and if execution of the MVCL instruction would cause this byte to receive a new value before the original contents are moved, a condition of *destructive overlap* is said to exist. In this case, no data movement occurs. The condition code is set as follows:

CC	*Meaning*
0	The sending and receiving fields were of equal length.
1	The sending field was longer than the receiving field.
2	The receiving field was longer than the sending field.
3	A condition of destructive overlap existed.

If the movement of data actually takes place (that is, if a condition of destructive overlap does not exist), then the following occurs:

1. The even register designated by r1 is set to the address of the first byte past the end of the receiving field.
2. The odd register of the even-odd pair specified by r1 is set to 0.
3. The even register specified by r2 is set to the address of the first byte beyond the last byte moved from the sending field.
4. The odd register of the pair designated by r2 is decremented by the number of bytes transferred from the sending field.

Thus, use of the MVCL instruction offers the following advantages over use of the MVC instruction:

1. Fields of arbitrary length may be moved.
2. The lengths of the fields can be determined at execution time.
3. Padding occurs automatically.

The following examples illustrate use of the MVCL:

- *Example 1.* Suppose that R2 contains the address of a field and R3 contains the length of the field. To set each byte of the field to 00, the following code would be used:

```
        LR      R4,R2    R4 <- ADDRESS OF THE FIELD
        LR      R5,R3    R5 <- LENGTH
        LR      R6,R2    R6 MUST BE A VALID ADDRESS,
*                        BUT IT ISN'T USED
        SR      R7,R7    PAD CHARACTER AND LENGTH ARE 00
        MVCL    R4,R6    JUST PUTS THE PAD CHARACTER IN THE FIELD
```

- *Example 2.* Suppose that an integer number from one to six digits long has been moved to an area in main storage (say, DUMMY) and that a section of code must be written to move this number into PLINE so that the nonblank characters of DUMMY are left-justified in the field that begins at PLINE + 7. Suppose further that the number in question has been moved to DUMMY by means of an XDECO instruction (in this case, DUMMY is a 12-byte field, and the number is right-justified in this field) and that PLINE has been defined as

```
        PLINE    DC        CL19'0TOTAL='
```

The following segment of code represents one solution to this problem:

```
        LA      R2,DUMMY
        LA      R3,12
LOOP    CLI     0(R2),C' '    CHECK FOR THE FIRST NONBLANK
        BNE     GOTC
        LA      R2,1(R2)
        BCT     R3,LOOP
*
GOTC    O       R3,=X'40000000' PAD IS BLANK, DON'T CHANGE LENGTH
*
        LM      R4,R5,=A(PLINE+7,12)
        MVCL    R4,R2    MOVE AND PAD WITH BLANKS
*
        XPRNT   PLINE,19
```

Execution of the CLCL instruction is similar to that of the MVCL instruction except that, with the CLCL instruction, a comparison rather than a movement of data is effected.

Execution of the instruction

$$\text{CLCL} \quad r1,r2 \qquad (Compare\ Logical\ Long)$$

causes a comparison to be made between two fields in main storage. The addresses and lengths of these two fields are designated in the same manner as described for the MVCL instruction. If the fields are of unequal lengths, the pad character (represented by the leftmost byte of the odd register of the pair designated by r2) is used to extend the shorter field for purposes of comparison. (No area of storage is actually altered, but the comparison occurs as if the shorter field had been extended.) The condition code is set as follows:

CC	Meaning
0	The fields are equal.
1	The first field is low.
2	The first field is high.
3	—

The comparison occurs from left to right, one byte at a time. When two bytes match, the address (even) registers are incremented by 1 and the count (odd) registers are decremented by 1. The only exception occurs when one of the two fields has been exhausted. In this case, the bytes in the remaining field are compared to the pad character, and only the registers corresponding to this field are altered. Thus, if the two fields mismatch, the contents of the even registers of each pair can be used to determine the point of difference. Unlike the MVCL, the first and second fields used by a CLCL may overlap.

The MVCL and CLCL are useful for moving or comparing fields when the lengths must be computed at execution time. It is occasionally necessary to perform other operations, such as packing a number or scanning with a TRT, when the length of a field cannot be determined until execution time. In such cases, an EX instruction should be used.

Execution of the instruction

$$\text{EX} \qquad \text{r,D(X,B)} \qquad\qquad (Execute)$$

initiates the following sequence of events:

1. A copy of the instruction at D(X,B) is made.
2. An OR operation is performed with the second byte of this copy of the instruction and the rightmost byte of r as operands, and the result replaces the second byte of the copy of the instruction.
3. The copy of the instruction is then executed.

Neither the contents of r nor the original instruction at D(X,B) is altered. The instruction immediately following the EX instruction will be the next instruction executed, if the instruction at D(X,B) is not a branch instruction or if it is an unsuccessful branch. If the instruction at D(X,B) represents a successful branch, of course the branch is taken. The condition code is set by the instruction at D(X,B). In case r is R0, the OR operation is not performed (i.e., Step 2 is not performed).

Note that there is no restriction on the address D(X,B). The instruction referenced in an EX instruction may be located anywhere; however, it is common practice to place it with the constants at the end of the program.

The most common use of the EX instruction is to effectively insert a particular value into the second byte of the instruction it references. This is accomplished by inserting the value in the rightmost byte of the register used as the first operand of the EX instruction and then coding the referenced instruction so that the second byte of the corresponding encoded instruction contains 00. In cases where only one hexadecimal digit of the second byte is altered, only the corresponding hexadecimal digit in the referenced instruction must be 0.

To illustrate the EX, suppose that R2 contains the address of a number in zoned (or character) format and R3 contains the length of the number. Then, the following code can be used to pack the number into DWORD:

```
          SH      R3, = H'1'        R3 NOW HAS LENGTH CODE
*                                   FOR THE FIELD
          BM      ERR               BRANCH IF LENGTH WAS 0 (OR
*                                   LESS)
          EX      R3,PACKIT         PACK THE FIELD
                    .
                    .
                    .
DWORD     DS      D
PACKIT    PACK    DWORD,0(0,R2)     0 LENGTH GENERATES
*                                   0 LENGTH CODE
```

In the following sections of the text, further uses of the MVCL, CLCL, and EX will be presented.

8.7 THE TR INSTRUCTION

Occasionally it is necessary to translate the values that occur in the bytes of a given field. This translating amounts to replacing each value with a corresponding value as indicated in some fixed correspondence. As an example, suppose that a field contains the representation of a character string that is printable except that some of the alphabetic characters in the string are encoded in their lowercase representation. Since many printers do not have the capability of printing lowercase letters, it may be necessary to translate the string before printing it. The following correspondence table should be used for this translation:

original	00 01 02...80	81 82...89	8A 8B...90	91 92...99
replacement	00 01 02...80	*C1 C2...C9*	8A 8B...90	*D1 D2...D9*

	9A 9B...A1	A2 A3...A9	AA AB...FF
	9A 9B...A1	*E2 E3...E9*	AA AB...FF

The italicized sections in the illustration represent the new values with which the lowercase alphabetic character representations are to be replaced. Thus, the string C140A2A3899587 would be converted to C140E2E3C9D5C7, using the values specified in the table.

From this discussion, it should be clear that the result of translating a string is dependent upon the correspondence table used in the translation process. A correspondence table that is to be used in a translation is represented in storage by a translate table. A *translate table* is a 256-byte area in storage such that, if ff is the replacement value for aa in the represented correspondence table, then ff is the value in the byte with a displacement of aa from the beginning of the table. Thus,

table + 00   contains the replacement for 00
table + 01   contains the replacement for 01
.
.
.
table + FE   contains the replacement for FE
table + FF   contains the replacement for FF

As an illustration, the following definition of TRANTAB generates the translate table for the specific correspondence table discussed above:

```
TRANTAB    DC    X'000102030405060708090A0B0C0D0E0F'
           DC    X'101112131415161718191A1B1C1D1E1F'
           DC    X'20...
           DC    X'30...
           DC    X'40...
           DC    X'50...
           DC    X'60...
           DC    X'70...
           DC    X'80C1C2C3C4C5C6C7C8C98A8B8C8D8E8F'
           DC    X'90D1D2D3D4D5D6D7D8D99A9B9C9D9E9F'
           DC    X'A0A1E2E3E4E5E6E7E8E9AAABACADAEAF'
           DC    X'B0...
           DC    X'C0...
           DC    X'D0...
           DC    X'E0...
           DC    X'F0...
```

The TR instruction, which is used to bring about the translation of a string, has the following format:

TR $D_1(L,B_1),D_2(B_2)$ (*Translate*)

Execution of the instruction causes the field of length L at the address $D_1(B_1)$ to be translated using the translate table at the address $D_2(B_2)$. The condition code is not altered.

Thus, execution of the instruction

TR   STRING(40),TRANTAB

causes the 40 bytes of the field STRING to be altered according to the correspondence table represented by TRANTAB.

The internal subroutine presented in Program 8-3 illustrates an unusual but helpful use of the TR instruction. This subroutine can be used to convert the contents of R1 into a string that may be utilized in printing the actual hexadecimal representation of those contents. For example, if R1 contained FFFFFF1A, a call to HEXDUMP would produce C6C6C6C6C6C6F1C1. Note that the first 240 bytes of TRANTAB in the example may contain any values whatever, since every character to be translated will have F as a zone digit. Therefore, the following TR instruction and definition of TRAN-TAB are equivalent to those in the example:

<pre>
        TR   DUMMY(8),TRANTAB − C'0'
                        .
                        .
                        .

TRANTAB DC   C'0123456789ABCDEF'
</pre>

In this case, the original value of a byte in DUMMY is added to the value in TRANTAB − C'0', which always points at the desired replacement character from TRANTAB. Study this example carefully. Although the routine is short, its unusual elegance is attained through the use of several non-obvious techniques. Note that the address TRANTAB − C'0' must occur within the same CSECT as TRANTAB, or else an error will be detected by the assembler.

Program 8-3

```
        TITLE 'HEX DUMP ROUTINE'
* THE FOLLOWING ROUTINE CONVERTS THE CONTENTS OF R1 TO THE REQUIRED
* 8-CHARACTER PRINTABLE FORM.  THE RESULT IS PUT TO THE ADDRESS IN R2.
* R10 IS ASSUMED TO CONTAIN THE RETURN ADDRESS.  NO REGISTERS ARE AL-
* TERED BY THE ROUTINE.  THE LOGIC OF THE ROUTINE IS:
*
*       STEP 1.   STORE R1 INTO FWORD.
*
*       STEP 2.   UNPACK FWORD(5) INTO DUMMY(9).  THIS LEAVES THE HEX
*                 DIGITS FROM R1 IN THE NUMERIC HEX DIGITS OF THE 1ST 8
*                 BYTES OF DUMMY.  THE ZONE DIGITS FOR THESE 8 BYTES
*                 ARE ALL F.  THIS MEANS THAT THE DIGITS OF R1 HAVE ALL
*                 BEEN SPLIT INTO SEPARATE BYTES EACH WITH AN F AS THE
*                 ZONE DIGIT.  THUS, 0-9 ARE ALREADY IN PRINTABLE FORM.
*                 A-F ARE, HOWEVER, IN THE FORM FA, FB, FC, FD, FE, AND
*                 FF.
*
*       STEP 3.   TRANSLATE THE 1ST 8 BYTES OF DUMMY.  LET F0, F1, ...
*                 F9 BE TRANSLATED INTO THEMSELVES, AND LET FA, FB, FC,
*                 FD, FE, FF BE TRANSLATED INTO C1, C2, C3, C4, C5, AND
*                 C6, RESPECTIVELY.
*
*       STEP 4.   MOVE THE RESULT FROM DUMMY TO THE AREA INDICATED
*                 BY R2.
*                 EXIT BACK THRU R10.
        SPACE 3
```

Program 8-3 (continued)

```
***<STEP 1>     STORE INPUT REG INTO FWORD.
HEXDUMP   ST    R1,FWORD
***<STEP 2>     UNPACK TO ADD F ZONE DIGITS.
          UNPK  DUMMY(9),FWORD(5)   THE RIGHT BYTE IS GARBAGE IN BOTH
*                                   FWORD AND DUMMY
***<STEP 3>     TRANSLATE TO CORRECT THE ALPHABETIC DIGITS.
          TR    DUMMY(8),TRANTAB
***<STEP 4>     MOVE TO CALLER'S AREA.
          MVC   0(8,R2),DUMMY
          BR    R10               EXIT
          SPACE
FWORD     DS    F,CL1             1 WORD + 1 BYTE OF GARBAGE
DUMMY     DS    CL9
TRANTAB   DS    CL(X'F0')         THESE ARE NEVER USED
          DC    C'0123456789ABCDEF'
****** END OF HEX DUMP ROUTINE **********
```

8.8 THE TRT INSTRUCTION

The TRT instruction (Translate and Test) can be used to locate the first occurrence of a character in a string that is a member of a specified set of characters. The TRT instruction, like the TR instruction, employs a translate table. However, unlike the TR instruction, execution of the TRT instruction does not alter the string of characters specified by its first operand. The format for the TRT instruction is

$$\text{TRT} \quad D_1(L,B_1),D_2(B_2) \quad \textit{(Translate and Test)}$$

The first operand of this instruction specifies the address and length of the field to be scanned, and the second operand specifies the address of a translate table. Execution of this instruction causes each byte of the designated field to be scanned until a character is found corresponding to a value in the translate table that is not 00. If no such character is found, the condition code is set to 0. If a character corresponding to a nonzero entry in the translate table is encountered, the scan terminates and the following events occur:

1. The address of the detected character is placed in the rightmost bytes (bits 8–31) of R1. Bits 0–7 of R1 are unaltered.
2. The corresponding nonzero entry from the translate table is inserted in the rightmost byte of R2. Bits 0–23 of R2 are unaltered.
3. The condition code is set to 2 if the detected character is in the rightmost byte in the scanned field; otherwise, it is set to 1.

The following examples should help to clarify the use of the TRT instruction:

• *Example 1.* Suppose that the address of the first nonblank character in an 80-byte field called CARD is to be found. Execution of the instructions

```
        TRT    CARD(80),SCANTABL
        BC     B'1000',ALLBLANK
          .
          .
          .
SCANTABL    DC    64X'FF'
            DC    X'00'
            DC    191X'FF'
```

will cause the address of the byte in question to be inserted into the right-most three bytes of R1, and the rightmost byte of R2 will be set to FF. If every byte in CARD represents a blank, the branch to ALLBLANK is taken and neither R1 nor R2 is altered.

The ORG instruction was introduced in Section 4.6. It can be used when generating a translate table to clarify exactly which entries are being set. For example, the previous table could be generated as follows:

```
SCANTABL    DC    256X'FF'
            ORG   SCANTABL+C' '
            DC    X'00'          SKIP BLANKS
            ORG
```

- *Example 2.*   Suppose that the first blank character, rather than the first nonblank character, in CARD is to be found. Then, the following code could be used:

```
        TRT    CARD(80),SCANTABL
        BC     B'1000',NOBLANKS
          .
          .
SCANTABL    DC    256X'00'
            ORG   SCANTABL+C' '      ORG TO ENTRY FOR BLANK
            DC    X'FF'              STOP ON BLANKS
            ORG
```

- *Example 3.*   If the first occurrence of either a numeric digit or an alphabetic letter in a field called STRING is to be found, the following code could be used:

```
              SR      R2,R2                   CLEAR R2
              TRT     STRING,TRANTAB
              B       BRANCHES(R2)
BRANCHES      B       NONEFND
              B       ALPHA
              B       NUMERIC
              .
              .
              .
TRANTAB       DC      256X'00'
              ORG     TRANTAB+C'A'            ALPHAS GET X'04'
              DC      9X'04'                  A-I
              ORG     TRANTAB+C'J'
              DC      9X'04'                  J-R
              ORG     TRANTAB+C'S'
              DC      8X'04'                  S-Z
              ORG     TRANTAB+C'0'
              DC      10X'08'                 NUMERICS GET X'08'
              ORG
```

In this case, a branch to NONEFND will occur if no alphabetic or numeric characters are found; a branch to ALPHA will occur if an alphabetic character is detected; and a branch to NUMERIC will occur if a numeric digit is detected. Note in particular the use of R2 as an index into the table of branch instructions.

- *Example 4.* Suppose that the address of the first occurrence of '$' in the field beginning at the address in R3 is to be found. Suppose further that the maximum number of bytes to be searched is represented by the value in R4. The desired result may be achieved through the use of an EX instruction to insert the length code (length-1) into the second byte of a TRT instruction as follows:

```
              BCTR    R4,0                    R4 <- LENGTH CODE
              EX      R4,SCAN
              BC      B'1000',NONEFND
              .
              .
SCAN          TRT     0(0,R3),TABLE
TABLE         DC      256X'00'
              ORG     TABLE+C'$'
              DC      X'FF'                   SCAN FOR $
              ORG
```

An understanding of these examples should make the details of the external subroutine presented in Program 8-4 easy to follow. This subroutine, although reasonably short, illustrates the concepts presented in this section quite well and should be studied carefully.

286

Program 8-4

```
              TITLE 'GETNUM - EXTRACT A NUMBER FROM A FIELD'
**********************************************************************
*
* THE FOLLOWING SUBROUTINE CAN BE INVOKED TO CONVERT A ZONED
* DECIMAL NUMBER IN A FIELD (WITH POSSIBLE LEADING BLANKS,
* TRAILING BLANKS, AND SIGN) TO BINARY.  THE PARAMETER LIST IS AS
* FOLLOWS:
*
*        ADDRESS OF THE FIELD CONTAINING THE NUMBER
*        ADDRESS OF THE LENGTH OF THE FIELD
*
* IF THE CONVERSION IS SUCCESSFUL, R15 WILL BE SET TO 0, R0 WILL
* CONTAIN THE VALUE IN BINARY, AND R1 WILL POINT JUST PAST THE
* END OF THE NUMBER; ELSE, R15 WILL BE SET TO 4.
* NOTE THAT INVALID CHARACTERS THAT OCCUR BEFORE THE FIRST CHARACTER
* OF THE NUMBER  OR AFTER THE LAST DIGIT ARE IGNORED.
* THE LOGIC IS AS FOLLOWS:
*
*   STEP 1.  IF THE LENGTH IS POSITIVE, GO TO STEP 3.
*
*   STEP 2.  SET A FAILURE RETURN-CODE (4) AND GO TO STEP 13.
*
*   STEP 3.  SET A DEFAULT SIGN TO 'F' AND SCAN FOR THE FIRST
*            SIGN OR NUMERIC DIGIT IN THE FIELD.
*
*   STEP 4.  IF NO SIGN OR DIGIT IS FOUND, GO TO STEP 5.  ELSE,
*            YOU HAVE 3 CASES (+, -, OR DIGIT).  IF A
*            PLUS SIGN IS FOUND, GO TO STEP 6.  IF A MINUS SIGN
*            IS FOUND, GO TO STEP 7.  IF A NUMERIC DIGIT IS FOUND,
*            GO TO STEP 8.
*
*   STEP 5.  SET A FAILURE RETURN-CODE (4) AND GO TO STEP 13.
*
*   STEP 6.  INCREMENT THE SCAN POINTER PAST THE PLUS SIGN AND GO
*            TO STEP 8.
*
*   STEP 7.  SET THE SIGN TO 'D' (MINUS), AND INCREMENT THE POINTER
*            PAST THE SIGN.
*
*   STEP 8.  IF THE SCAN POINTER IS STILL WITHIN THE FIELD (IT
*            SHOULD POINT AT THE FIRST NUMERIC DIGIT), GO TO STEP 10.
*
*   STEP 9.  SET A FAILURE RETURN-CODE (4) AND GO TO STEP 13.
*
*   STEP 10. SCAN FOR THE END OF THE STRING OF NUMERIC DIGITS.
*            IF THERE IS AT LEAST 1 DIGIT, GO TO STEP 12.
*
*   STEP 11. SET A FAILURE RETURN-CODE (4) AND GO TO STEP 13.
*
*   STEP 12. CONVERT THE NUMBER TO BINARY AND SET THE RETURN-CODE
*            TO SUCCESS (0).
*
*   STEP 13. EXIT.
*
**********************************************************************
*
```

Program 8-4 (continued)

```
GETNUM    CSECT
          STM   R14,R12,12(R13)      SAVE CALLER'S REGISTERS
          BALR  R12,0
          USING BASEPT,R12
BASEPT    DS    0H
          LA    R14,SAVEAREA
          ST    R14,8(R13)
          ST    R13,4(R14)
          LR    R13,R14
*
          LM    R3,R4,0(R1)          R3 <- A(FIELD)
*                                    R4 <- A(LENGTH)
          L     R4,0(R4)             R4 <- LENGTH
*
***<STEP 1>  CHECK FOR INVALID LENGTH (R4 IS SET TO LENGTH CODE)
*
          SH    R4,=H'1'
          BNM   SCAN
*
***<STEP 2>  SET FAILURE RC AND EXIT
*
          LA    R15,4
          B     EXIT
*
***<STEP 3>  SCAN FOR SIGN OR NUMERIC DIGIT
*
SCAN      MVI   SIGN,X'0F'           DEFAULT SIGN IS POSITIVE
          SR    R1,R1
          SR    R2,R2
          EX    R4,SCANTRT           SCAN FOR SIGN OR DIGIT
*
***<STEP 4>  CHECK FOR NO SIGN OR DIGITS.
*
          BC    B'0110',BRANCHTB-4(R2)  GO TO CASE STRUCTURE IF HIT
*
*
***<STEP 5>  SET FAILURE RC AND EXIT
*
          LA    R15,4                SET FAILURE RC
          B     EXIT
*
BRANCHTB  B     PLUSSIGN             IF CODE IN TABLE IS 4
          B     NEGSIGN              IF CODE IN TABLE IS 8
          B     PASTSIGN             IF CODE IN TABLE IS C (DIGIT)
*
***<STEP 6>  INCREMENT SCAN POINTER PAST +
*
PLUSSIGN  LA    R1,1(R1)
          B     PASTSIGN
*
***<STEP 7>  SET MINUS SIGN AND INCREMENT SCAN POINTER
*
NEGSIGN   MVI   SIGN,X'0D'
          LA    R1,1(R1)
```

Program 8-4 (continued)

```
*
***<STEP 8>    CHECK TO MAKE SURE SCAN POINTER IS WITHIN FIELD
*
PASTSIGN LR     R5,R1              SAVE START OF DIGITS
         AR     R4,R3              R4 <- A(LAST BYTE IN FIELD)
         SR     R4,R1
         BNM    GETEND             BRANCH IF POINTER IS OK
*
***<STEP 9>    SET FAILURE RC AND EXIT
*
         LA     R15,4
         B      EXIT
*
***<STEP 10>   SCAN FOR END OF STRING OF DIGITS
*
GETEND   LA     R1,1(R4,R1)        POINT R1 JUST PAST FIELD
         EX     R4,SCANEND         SCAN FOR FIRST CHAR PAST STRING
         SR     R1,R5              R1 <- # DIGITS IN STRING
         SH     R1,=H'1'           GET LENGTH - 1
         BNM    CONVERT            BRANCH IF THERE WERE DIGITS
*
***<STEP 11>   SET FAILURE RC AND EXIT
*
         LA     R15,4
         B      EXIT
*
***<STEP 12>   CONVERT THE NUMBER TO BINARY
*
CONVERT  EX     R1,PACKNUM         PACK THE NUMBER
         NI     DWORD+7,X'F0'      SET THE SIGN
         OC     DWORD+7(1),SIGN
         CVB    R0,DWORD           R0 HAS THE VALUE
         LA     R1,1(R1,R5)        R1 POINTS JUST PAST THE FIELD
         SR     R15,R15            SET SUCCESS RETURN-CODE
*
***<STEP 13>   EXIT
*
EXIT     L      R13,4(R13)
         L      R14,12(R13)
         LM     R2,R12,28(R13)     R15, R0, & R1 KEEP THEIR VALUES
         BR     R14
*
SCANTRT  TRT    0(0,R3),TABNUM     SCAN FOR DIGIT OR SIGN
SCANEND  TRT    0(0,R5),TABEND     SCAN FOR THE FIRST NONDIGIT
PACKNUM  PACK   DWORD,0(0,R5)
*
         LTORG
*
SIGN     DS     C                  RIGHT HEX DIGIT IS SET TO SIGN
DWORD    DS     D                  FOR CONVERSION
SAVEAREA DS     18F
*
```

Program 8-4 (continued)

```
TABNUM   DC    256X'00'
         ORG   TABNUM+C'+'
         DC    X'04'
         ORG   TABNUM+C'-'
         DC    X'08'
         ORG   TABNUM+C'0'
         DC    10X'0C'
         ORG
TABEND   DC    256X'FF'
         ORG   TABEND+C'0'
         DC    10X'00'              SKIP DIGITS
         ORG
*
R0       EQU   0
R1       EQU   1
R2       EQU   2
R3       EQU   3
R4       EQU   4
R5       EQU   5
R6       EQU   6
R7       EQU   7
R8       EQU   8
R9       EQU   9
R10      EQU   10
R11      EQU   11
R12      EQU   12
R13      EQU   13
R14      EQU   14
R15      EQU   15
         END
```

8.9 THE CLM, ICM, AND STCM INSTRUCTIONS

The instructions presented in this section are not available on IBM 360 computers. They first appeared on the IBM 370s and have been a standard part of the instruction set since that time.

The CLM, ICM, and STCM are RS instructions. Each of these instructions involves an operation between two fields, the first of which is composed of selected bytes from a register and the second of which is a sequence of contiguous bytes in storage. The selection of bytes from the register is, in each case, governed by a four-bit mask. The bits in the mask correspond one-to-one with the bytes in the register. The bits in the mask that have a value of 1 designate the bytes in the register that make up the first field. As an example, execution of the instruction

$$\text{CLM} \qquad \text{R2,B'0110',KEY}$$

causes a comparison to be made between the middle two bytes in R2 and the first two bytes in the field KEY. Similarly, execution of the instruction

$$\text{CLM} \qquad \text{R2,B}'1110',\text{KEY}$$

causes a comparison between the first three bytes of R2 and the leftmost three bytes of the field KEY. Detailed descriptions of the CLM, ICM, and STCM instructions follow.

Execution of the instruction

$$\text{CLM} \qquad \text{r,m,D(B)} \qquad\qquad \textit{(Compare Logical}$$
$$\textit{Characters under Mask)}$$

causes a logical comparison to be made between two fields. In a logical comparison, the contents of the fields involved are treated as unsigned binary integers. The first of the two fields participating in the comparison is designated by the first two operands:

r   specifies a register
m   is a mask designating which bytes in r are to be included in the field

The mask m should be an absolute expression that evaluates to a value in the range 0 to 15. The length of the fields to be compared is i, where i is the number of bits with a value of 1 in the binary representation of m. The field participating in the comparison is composed of i contiguous bytes starting at the address specified by D(B). The condition code is set as follows:

CC	Meaning
0	Selected bytes are equal or the mask is 0.
1	First field is low.
2	First field is high.
3	—

For purposes of illustration, suppose that R0 contains 00AC2B40 and FIELD contains 9F013C2F. The following table gives three CLM instructions and the CC settings that would result from the execution of each of these instructions:

Instruction	Length of Comparison	Resulting CC
CLM R0,B'0000',FIELD	0	0
CLM R0,B'1010',FIELD	2	1
CLM R0,B'0111',FIELD	3	2

In the second case, the condition code is set to 1, based on the comparison of 002B with 9F01. The condition code of 2 in the third case results from the comparison of AC2B40 with 9F013C. The first case has a condition code setting of 0, because the mask is 0.

The ICM and STCM instructions are generalized versions of the IC and STC instructions. While an IC or STC instruction can be used to transfer a single byte, an ICM or STCM instruction can be used to transfer as many as four bytes under the control of a mask.

Execution of the instruction

> ICM   r,m,D(B)   (*Insert Character*
> *under Mask*)

causes zero to four bytes in main storage at the address specified by D(B) to be inserted in the register r. The four bits in the binary representation of m determine which bytes of r are to be altered. The bytes of r that correspond to bits in m with a value of 1 receive the bytes from main storage. The insertion is made from left to right. The condition code is set as follows:

CC	*Meaning*
0	All inserted bytes were 00 or the mask was 0.
1	The leftmost bit of the leftmost inserted byte was 1.
2	The leftmost bit of the leftmost inserted byte was 0 (but not all bits of the inserted bytes were 0).
3	—

Note that execution of the instruction

> ICM   r,B'1111',addr

has an effect similar to that produced by the execution of a Load instruction. However, in the case of the ICM instruction, the four bytes transferred need not be on a fullword boundary and the condition code is set.

Execution of the instruction

> STCM   r,m,D(B)   (*Store Characters*
> *under Mask*)

will cause the bytes in the register r designated by the mask m to be stored in contiguous bytes of main storage, beginning at the address specified by D(B). The condition code is unaltered.

Program 8-5 illustrates the instructions covered in this section, as well as those covered previously in this chapter.

```
          TITLE 'GETWORDS - A SUBROUTINE TO EXTRACT CHARACTER VALUES'
***********************************************************************
*
* THE PURPOSE OF THIS SUBROUTINE IS TO SCAN A STRING FOR SUBSTRINGS
* OF THE FORM
*
*    <KEYWORD>=<VALUE>
*
* WHERE <KEYWORD> CAN BE ANY WORD IN A TABLE DEFINING THE VALID
*                 KEYWORDS, AND
*
*        <VALUE>   IS A CHARACTER STRING THAT IS DELIMITED BY A BLANK
*                  OR THE END OF THE STRING BEING SCANNED.
*
* GETWORDS MUST LOCATE THESE STRINGS (WHICH MUST BE SEPARATED BY
* BLANKS).  FOR EACH SUCH STRING THE <VALUE> MUST BE MOVED INTO
* A RECEIVING FIELD, WHICH IS SPECIFIED IN THE SAME TABLE THAT
* DEFINES THE VALID KEYWORDS.  EACH ENTRY IN THE TABLE DEFINES
* A SINGLE KEYWORD AND THE FIELD THAT IS ASSIGNED THE <VALUE>
* FOR THAT KEYWORD.  THE FORMAT OF AN ENTRY IN THE KEYWORD
* TABLE IS DEFINED BY THE FOLLOWING DSECT:
*
TABENT   DSECT
KEYWORD  DS    CL10             A KEYWORD (LEFT JUSTIFIED)
RECEIVE  DS    AL3              ADDRESS OF THE RECEIVING FIELD
MAXLEN   DS    XL1              MAX. ALLOWABLE LENGTH OF THE VALUE
MINLEN   DS    XL1              MIN. ALLOWABLE LENGTH OF THE VALUE
NEXTENT  DS    0X               START OF THE NEXT ENTRY
*
* THUS, THE TABLE DEFINES THE VALID KEYWORDS AND WHERE THE VALUES
* ARE TO BE STORED.  THE ADDRESS OF THE TABLE IS PASSED AS A
* PARAMETER TO GETWORDS.  THE FORMAT OF THE RECEIVING FIELD IS
* DESCRIBED BY THE FOLLOWING DSECT:
*
RECEIVER DSECT
LENGTH   DS    XL2              LENGTH OF THE VALUE
VALUE    DS    0C               THE VALUE BEGINS HERE
*
* THE FORMAT OF THE PARAMETER LIST PASSED TO GETWORDS IS DESCRIBED
* BY THE FOLLOWING DSECT:
*
PARMS    DSECT
STRINGAD DS    A                ADDRESS OF THE STRING TO SCAN
STRNGLEN DS    A                ADDRESS OF A HALFWORD CONTAINING
*                               THE LENGTH OF THE STRING
TABLADDR DS    A                ADDRESS OF THE FIRST ENTRY IN THE
*                               KEYWORD TABLE
NUMENT   DS    A                ADDRESS OF A HALFWORD CONTAINING
*                               THE NUMBER OF ENTRIES IN THE TABLE
*
* R15 IS SET BY GETWORDS TO REFLECT SUCCESS OR FAILURE.  IF NO
* ERRORS ARE DETECTED, R15 WILL BE SET TO 0.  ELSE, IT WILL BE
* SET TO 4.  NOTE THAT THE ROUTINE STOPS SCANNING IF AN ERROR
* IS DETECTED.  IF AN ERROR IS DETECTED, R1 WILL POINT TO THE
* ERROR (AS CLOSE AS GETWORDS CAN DETERMINE).
*
*
```

Program 8-5 (continued)

```
* THE LOGIC OF GETWORDS IS AS FOLLOWS:
*
*    STEP 1.   SET THE RETURN CODE (R15) TO 0, AND R1 TO POINT AT THE
*              START OF THE STRING.
*
*    STEP 2.   IF AN ERROR HAS BEEN DETECTED, IF THERE ARE NO MORE
*              CHARACTERS LEFT TO SCAN IN THE INPUT STRING, OR IF
*              THE REMAINING CHARACTERS ARE ALL BLANKS, GO TO STEP 21.
*
*    STEP 3.   FIND THE FIRST NONBLANK CHARACTER.  IF IT OCCURS BEFORE
*              THE LAST CHARACTER IN THE STRING, GO TO STEP 5.
*
*    STEP 4.   SET R15 TO 4 (ERROR) AND LEAVE R1 POINTING TO THE LAST
*              CHARACTER IN THE STRING.  GO TO STEP 2.
*
*    STEP 5.   FIND THE FIRST '=' OR ' ' THAT OCCURS AFTER THE 1ST
*              CHARACTER IN THE WORD.  IF A BLANK OR '=' CAN BE FOUND,
*              GO TO STEP 7.
*
*    STEP 6.   SET R15 TO 4 (ERROR), SINCE THE = COULDN'T BE FOUND.
*              LEAVE R1 POINTING TO THE FIRST CHARACTER OF THE WORD,
*              AND GO TO STEP 2.
*
*    STEP 7.   IF THE CHARACTER FOUND WAS AN '=', GO TO STEP 9.
*
*    STEP 8.   SET R15 TO 4 (ERROR), SINCE THE = WAS MISSING.  LEAVE
*              R1 POINTING TO THE 1ST CHARACTER OF THE WORD, AND
*              GO TO STEP 2.
*
*    STEP 9.   INITIALIZE TO START COMPARING THE ISOLATED WORD AGAINST
*              ENTRIES IN THE KEYWORD TABLE.
*
*    STEP 10.  IF YOU'VE LOOKED AT ALL THE ENTRIES, OR IF YOU'VE FOUND
*              THE ONE THAT MATCHES, GO TO STEP 12.
*
*    STEP 11.  SET UP TO LOOK AT THE NEXT TABLE ENTRY AND GO BACK TO
*              STEP 10.
*
*    STEP 12.  IF YOU FOUND A MATCHING ENTRY, GO TO STEP 14.
*
*    STEP 13.  SET R15 TO 4 (ERROR) AND LEAVE R1 POINTING AT THE
*              '='.  GO TO STEP 2.
*
*    STEP 14.  IF THE '=' DID NOT OCCUR IN THE LAST CHARACTER OF THE
*              STRING, GO TO STEP 16.
*
*    STEP 15.  SET THE START-OF-VALUE AND PAST-VALUE POINTERS TO THE
*              FIRST CHARACTER PAST THE END OF THE STRING.  THIS WILL
*              INDICATE A NULL VALUE (WHICH MAY OR MAY NOT BE OK).  GO
*              TO STEP 18.
```

Program 8-5 (continued)

```
*
*    STEP 16. SEARCH FOR THE FIRST BLANK PAST THE '='.  IF ONE OCCURS,
*             SET THE PAST-VALUE POINTER TO IT AND GO TO STEP 18.
*
*    STEP 17. SET THE PAST-VALUE POINTER JUST PAST THE END OF THE
*             STRING.
*
*    STEP 18. CALCULATE THE LENGTH OF THE VALUE.  IF IT FALLS WITHIN
*             THE VALUES SPECIFIED IN THE KEYWORD TABLE, GO TO
*             STEP 20.
*
*    STEP 19. SET R15 TO 4 (ERROR) AND LEAVE R1 POINTING JUST PAST THE
*             VALUE.  GO TO STEP 2.
*
*    STEP 20. MOVE THE VALUE TO THE RECEIVING FIELD AND GO TO STEP 2.
*
*    STEP 21. RETURN TO THE CALLER.
*
**************************************************************************
*
GETWORDS CSECT
         STM   R14,R12,12(R13)     SAVE CALLER'S REGISTERS
         BALR  R12,0
         USING BASEPT,R12
BASEPT   DS    0H
*
         LR    R5,R1               SAVE ADDRESS OF INPUT PARAMETERS
         USING PARMS,R5
*
***<STEP 1>   INITIALIZE R15 TO 0, R1 TO START SCAN, AND R4 = LEN-1.
*
         SR    R15,R15             RC <- 0 (UNTIL WE FIND AN ERROR)
         L     R1,STRINGAD         R1 <- ADDRESS OF STRING TO SCAN
         L     R4,STRNGLEN
         LH    R4,0(R4)            R4 <- LENGTH OF STRING TO SCAN
         BCTR  R4,0                R4 <- LENGTH - 1 (LENGTH CODE)
*
***<STEP 2>   TEST FOR ERROR, END OF STRING, OR ONLY BLANKS LEFT
*
TESTEND  LTR   R15,R15             TEST FOR ERROR
         BNZ   DONE
*
         LTR   R4,R4               TEST FOR END OF STRING
         BM    DONE
*
         LR    R0,R1               SAVE ADDRESS OF START OF SCAN
         EX    R4,FINDWORD         TRT FOR THE START OF THE WORD
         BC    B'1000',DONE        BRANCH IF ONLY BLANKS LEFT
```

Program 8-5 (continued)

```
*
***<STEP 3>    IF THE HIT OCCURRED BEFORE THE LAST CHAR, GO TO STEP 5.
*
        BCTR  R4,0
        AR    R4,R0
        SR    R4,R1           R4 NOW HAS THE LENGTH-1 OF WHAT
*                             REMAINS
        BNM   FNDEQ
*
***<STEP 4>    SET R15 TO 4 AND GO BACK TO STEP 2.
*
        LA    R15,4
        B     TESTEND
*
***<STEP 5>    SCAN FOR THE FIRST '=' OR ' '.  IF FOUND, GO TO STEP 7.
*
FNDEQ   LR    R0,R1           SAVE ADDRESS OF START OF WORD
        EX    R4,EQORBLNK     SCAN FOR '=' OR ' '
        BC    B'0111',GOTCHR  BRANCH IF YOU GOT ONE
*
***<STEP 6>    SET ERROR (NO =) AND GO BACK TO STEP 2.
*
        LA    R15,4
        B     TESTEND
*
***<STEP 7>    IF IT WAS AN '=', GO TO STEP 9.
*
GOTCHR  CLI   0(R1),C'='
        BE    GOTEQ
*
***<STEP 8>    SET R15 TO 4 (MISSING =) AND GO TO STEP 2.
*
        LA    R15,4
        B     TESTEND
*
***<STEP 9>    SET UP TO SEARCH THE KEYWORD TABLE.
*
GOTEQ   SR    R1,R0
        ICM   R1,B'1000',=C' ' R1 HAS BLANK AT LEFT, LENGTH
*                              OF THE KEYWORD IN RIGHT BYTE
        STM   R0,R1,COMPREGS  SAVE FOR REPEATED COMPARES
        L     R6,TABLADDR     R6 <- ADDRESS OF FIRST ENTRY
        USING TABENT,R6
        L     R8,NUMENT
        LH    R8,0(R8)        R8 <- NUMBER OF ENTRIES
*
```

Program 8-5 (continued)

```
***<STEP 10>   IF YOU'VE RUN PAST THE END OR MATCHED, GO TO STEP 12.
*
LOOKUP    SH    R8,=H'1'          DECREMENT COUNT OF ENTRIES LEFT
          BM    EXLOOP            EXIT IF PAST THE END
          LM    R0,R3,COMPREGS    SET UP REGS TO COMPARE
          LR    R2,R6             R2 <- ADDRESS OF KEYWORD
          CLCL  R2,R0             COMPARE SCANNED WORD AGAINST KEYWORD
          BE    EXLOOP            EXIT ON MATCH
*
***<STEP 11>   POINT TO THE NEXT ENTRY AND GO BACK TO STEP 10.
*
          LA    R6,NEXTENT
          B     LOOKUP
*
***<STEP 12>   IF A MATCH OCCURRED, GO TO STEP 14.
*
EXLOOP    LTR   R8,R8
          BNM   GOTENT            BRANCH IF MATCH OCCURRED
*
***<STEP 13>   SET R15 TO 4 (INVALID WORD) AND GO TO STEP 2.
*
          L     R1,COMPREGS
          LA    R15,4
          B     TESTEND
*
***<STEP 14>   IF '=' WASN'T LAST CHARACTER, GO TO STEP 16.
*
GOTENT    LR    R1,R0
          LA    R0,1(R1)          R0 <- A(1ST CHAR PAST =)
          SH    R4,COMPREGS+6     DECREMENT BY LENGTH OF THE WORD
          BNM   FINDEND
*
***<STEP 15>   SET BOTH R1 AND R0 TO JUST PAST END.  GO TO STEP 18.
*
          LR    R1,R0
          B     CHKLEN
*
***<STEP 16>   FIND THE FIRST BLANK PAST =.  IF FOUND, GO TO STEP 18.
*
FINDEND   EX    R4,EQORBLNK       SCAN FOR AN = OR BLANK
          BC    B'1000',PASTEND   BRANCH IF NONE
          CLI   0(R1),C' '        WE'RE LOOKING FOR A BLANK
          BNE   FINDEND
          B     CHKLEN
*
***<STEP 17>   SET R1 TO POINT JUST PAST THE END OF THE STRING
*
PASTEND   LA    R1,2(R4,R1)       POINT R1 PAST STRING
*
```

Program 8-5 (continued)

```
***<STEP 18>   IF LENGTH OF VALUE IS OK, GO TO STEP 20.
*
CHKLEN    SR    R1,R0
          CLM   R1,B'0001',MAXLEN
          BH    BADLEN              BRANCH IF VALUE IS TOO LONG
          CLM   R1,B'0001',MINLEN
          BNL   VALOK
*
***<STEP 19>   SET R15 TO 4 (BAD VALUE) AND GO TO STEP 2.
*
BADLEN    LR    R1,R0               POINT R1 AT START OF VALUE
          LA    R15,4
          B     TESTEND
*
***<STEP 20>   MOVE VALUE TO RECEIVING FIELD AND GO TO STEP 2.
*
VALOK     SR    R4,R1               R4 STILL HAS LEN-1 OF REST
          ICM   R10,B'0111',RECEIVE
          USING RECEIVER,R10
          STCM  R1,B'0011',LENGTH
          LA    R10,VALUE
          DROP  R10
          LR    R11,R1              R11 NOW HAS LENGTH OF VALUE
          MVCL  R10,R0
          LR    R1,R0               R1 POINTS TO NEXT CHAR TO SCAN
          B     TESTEND
*
***<STEP 21>   EXIT
*
DONE      L     R14,12(R13)
          L     R0,20(R13)
          LM    R2,R12,28(R13)
          BR    R14                 R1 AND R15 ARE RETURNED TO CALLER
*
          LTORG
*
FINDWORD  TRT   0(0,R1),STARTAB     SCAN FOR START OF KEYWORD
EQORBLNK  TRT   1(0,R1),GETDELIM    SCAN FOR BLANK OR =
*
COMPREGS  DS    2F
          DC    A(0,10)
*
STARTAB   DC    256X'FF'            STOP ON ANYTHING BUT A BLANK
          ORG   STARTAB+C' '
          DC    X'00'
          ORG
*
GETDELIM  DC    256X'00'            STOP ON ONLY BLANK OR =
          ORG   GETDELIM+C' '
          DC    X'FF'
          ORG   GETDELIM+C'='
          DC    X'FF'
          ORG
*
```

Program 8-5 (continued)

```
R0      EQU    0
R1      EQU    1
R2      EQU    2
R3      EQU    3
R4      EQU    4
R5      EQU    5
R6      EQU    6
R7      EQU    7
R8      EQU    8
R9      EQU    9
R10     EQU    10
R11     EQU    11
R12     EQU    12
R13     EQU    13
R14     EQU    14
R15     EQU    15
        END
```

8.10 THE SPM INSTRUCTION

The reader has probably noted a certain ambiguity in the discussions concerning the effects of a fixed-point overflow condition. In particular, it was noted that an overflow may cause an error message to be generated and termination of the execution of the program to occur; however, it was also pointed out that an overflow does not necessarily have this effect. When does an overflow cause termination of the execution of a program? The answer is reasonably simple. Termination will occur if bit 36 of the Program Status Word (PSW) is 1; otherwise, execution of the program continues after the occurrence of overflow. Bit 36 is part of a segment of the PSW called the *program mask*. Bits 37–39, which form the remainder of the program mask, are used to determine what action is to be taken in other types of exceptional situations.

A natural question then is: "Can the program mask be altered?" The answer is yes. The SPM instruction is used for this purpose.

SPM   r   (Set Program Mask)

Execution of this instruction causes bits 34–39 of the current PSW to be replaced by a copy of bits 2–7 of r. Hence, the condition code as well as the program mask may be altered.

To understand the principal use of the SPM instruction, the reader should recall that execution of a BAL or BALR instruction causes a copy of the entire right half of the PSW to replace the contents of the link register. Hence, after execution of a BAL or BALR instruction, bits 2–7 of the link register contain a copy of the condition code and program mask (bits 34–39 of the PSW). Thus, if we assume that the contents of the link register have not been altered, the condition code and program mask may be restored to the values that they had before the execution of a particular BAL or BALR instruction; this restoration is done through an SPM instruction that has the link register as its operand.

A technique for altering the condition code and program mask and later restoring them to their original values can be outlined as follows:

1. Enter an instruction such as

$$\text{BALR} \qquad \text{R0,0}$$

   in the program to save the program mask and CC.
2. Enter an SPM instruction to alter the CC and program mask to any desired value.
3. Where the original values of the CC and the program mask are to be restored, enter the instruction

$$\text{SPM} \qquad \text{R0}$$

(This, of course, assumes that the contents of R0 have not been altered.)

This technique is often used when common subroutines are employed. Use of this technique allows the subroutines to be invoked with an assurance that neither the condition code nor the program mask will be altered by the call.

8.11 THE MVN, MVZ, AND MVO INSTRUCTIONS

The SRP offers a convenient way to perform shifts on packed decimal numbers. However, no such instruction existed in the IBM 360 instruction set. (The SRP first appeared on the IBM 370.) One could shift packed decimal numbers on an IBM 360 by using sequences of instructions. In this section, the MVN, MVZ, and MVO instructions are introduced, and the use of these instructions for performing shifts on packed decimal numbers is illustrated. Note, however, that these instructions are used very rarely, since the SRP offers a far better way to shift numbers. Unless you study the code written for the IBM 360, it is unlikely (but quite possible) that you will encounter these instructions.

Execution of the instruction

$$\text{MVN} \qquad \text{D1(L,B1),D2(B2)} \qquad (\textit{Move Numerics})$$

has the same effect as execution of an MVC instruction except that only the numeric digits are moved. (The right hex digit in a byte is the numeric digit.)

The zone digits in both fields remain unchanged.
    Execution of the instruction

$$\text{MVZ} \qquad \text{D1(L,B1),D2(B2)} \qquad \textit{(Move Zones)}$$

is analogous to execution of an MVN instruction. The difference in this case is that the zone digits, rather than the numeric digits, are moved.
    Execution of the instruction

$$\text{MVO} \qquad \text{D1(L1,B1),D2(L2,B2)} \qquad \textit{(Move with Offset)}$$

has the effect of moving the second operand to the field occupied by the first operand, with the digits of the second operand offset to the left in this field by four bits. This leaves the rightmost digit of the first operand unaltered. The details of this process are as follows:

1. The rightmost digit of the second operand is moved to the position occupied by the rightmost zone digit of the first operand. The remaining digits of the second operand are then successively moved to the field occupied by the first operand, proceeding from right to left.
2. The zone boundaries are reset.
3. Zeros are padded on the left if necessary to make the result L1 bytes long. If the second operand contains more digits than the L1 bytes of the first operand field will accommodate, the leftmost digits are ignored.

   The following examples should help to clarify the above discussion of the MVN, MVZ, and MVO instructions. In these examples, it is assumed that the contents of F1 are

$$01234F$$

and the contents of F2 are

$$56789D$$

- *Example 1.*   MVN   F1(3),F2
  Execution of this instruction changes the contents of F1 to 06284D. This process is pictorially depicted as follows:

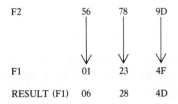

- *Example 2.* MVZ   F1(3),F2

Execution of this instruction has the following effect:

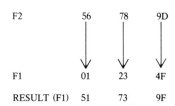

F2	56	78	9D

| F1 | 01 | 23 | 4F |
| RESULT (F1) | 51 | 73 | 9F |

- *Example 3.* MVO   F1(3),F2(2)

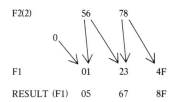

| F2(2) | 56 | 78 |

| F1 | 01 | 23 | 4F |
| RESULT (F1) | 05 | 67 | 8F |

Note here that the zero was appended to the result as a fill character (it is not just a holdover of the original contents of F1).

- *Example 4.* MVO   F1(3),F1(2)

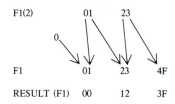

| F1(2) | 01 | 23 |

| F1 | 01 | 23 | 4F |
| RESULT (F1) | 00 | 12 | 3F |

The techniques for performing shifts on packed decimal numbers are illustrated next. For the purpose of this discussion, assume that FIELD is an eight-byte field containing a valid packed decimal number.

A shift to the right of an odd number of digits, which is equivalent to division by an odd power of 10, may be accomplished by use of an MVO instruction. Thus,

MVO   FIELD(8),FIELD(7)

has the same effect as dividing the number in FIELD by 10. If the second operand had been FIELD(6), the effect would have been a shift of three decimal digits (equivalent to division by 1000).

A shift to the right of an even number of digits may be brought about by the use of an MVN instruction. For example,

MVN   FIELD + 6(1),FIELD + 7

has the same effect as division of the number in FIELD by 100, and the result is left in FIELD(7). If the first operand had been FIELD + 5(1), the effect would have been a shift to the right of four places (equivalent to division by 10,000) and the result would have been in FIELD(6).

Shifts to the left are somewhat more complicated to achieve. A shift to the left of a single digit (the equivalent of multiplication by 10) may be accomplished by the following pair of instructions:

MVO   FIELD(8),FIELD(8)
NI   FIELD + 7,X'0F'

Shifts to the left of an odd number of digits where this number is greater than 1, can be achieved by the use of a three-instruction sequence. For example,

MVC   FIELD(7),FIELD + 1
MVO   FIELD(7),FIELD(7)
NC   FIELD + 6(2), = X'000F'

causes a shift to the left of three digits (the same as multiplication by 1000).

To perform a shift to the left of an even number of digits, a two-instruction sequence may be used. For instance, the sequence

MVC   FIELD(7),FIELD + 1
NC   FIELD + 6(2), = X'F00F'

causes a shift to the left of two digits (the equivalent of multiplication by 100).

Note that all shifts of an odd number of digits involve the use of an MVO instruction. Such shifts require a realignment of the zone boundaries, and the MVO instruction is designed to accomplish this realignment.

Exercises

1. Program 8-6 is a routine to generate random numbers. The method used is covered in "Coding the Lehmer Pseudo-random Number Generator," an article by W. H. Payne, J. R. Rabung, and T. P. Bogyo that appeared in the *Communications of the ACM*, February 1969. It is not necessary to understand the material in that article to do this assignment; what must be understood is that the routine can be invoked repeatedly to generate a sequence of random integers that are uniformly distributed in a closed interval.

Program 8-6

```
        TITLE 'RANDOM - A PSEUDO-RANDOM NUMBER GENERATOR'
**********************************************************************
*
* THE FOLLOWING RANDOM NUMBER GENERATOR RETURNS A VALUE BETWEEN
* TWO SPECIFIED VALUES.  THE PARAMETER LIST IS AS FOLLOWS:
*
*       ADDRESS OF A WORD CONTAINING THE MINIMUM ACCEPTABLE VALUE
*       ADDRESS OF A WORD CONTAINING THE MAXIMUM ACCEPTABLE VALUE
*       ADDRESS OF A WORD THAT CONTAINS THE "SEED" VALUE ON THE
*               FIRST CALL.  IT IS ALTERED BY EACH CALL, SO THAT A
*               NEW RANDOM NUMBER IS RETURNED.
*
* THE ANSWER IS RETURNED IN R0 (THIS IS A COMMON PRACTICE WHEN
* CODING ROUTINES THAT RETURN A SINGLE WORD).  R14 MUST HAVE BEEN
* SET BY A BRANCH-AND-LINK OPERATION (SINCE THE CALLER'S PROGRAM
* MASK IS ASSUMED TO BE IN R14); NORMAL LINKAGE CONDITIONS WILL
* ALWAYS CAUSE R14 TO CONTAIN THE CALLER'S PROGRAM MASK.
* THE SEED VALUE CAN BE ANYTHING ON THE FIRST CALL.  NOTE THAT
* THE ORIGINAL VALUE OF THE SEED DETERMINES THE SEQUENCE OF RANDOM
* NUMBERS THAT WILL BE PRODUCED.
*
**********************************************************************
*
RANDOM   CSECT
         STM   R14,R12,12(R13)    STORE CALLERS REGISTERS
         BALR  R12,0
         USING RANBASE,R12
RANBASE  DS    0H
*
         LM    R2,R4,0(R1)        R2 <- ADDRESS OF THE MINIMUM VALUE
*                                 R3 <- ADDRESS OF THE MAXIMUM VALUE
*                                 R4 <- ADDRESS OF X(N): X(0) IS THE
*                                       "SEED" VALUE
         L     R5,0(R3)           R5 <- MAX VALUE
         S     R5,0(R2)           R5 <- MAX VALUE - MIN VALUE
         LA    R5,1(R5)           R5 <- (MAX - MIN) + 1
         AR    R5,R5              R5 <- 2*(MAX-MIN+1)
*
         L     R1,=F'16807'       R1 <- MULTIPLIER K
         SR    R0,R0
         SPM   R0                 IGNORE OVERFLOW
         M     R0,0(R4)           K*X(N)
         SLDA  R0,1               ISOLATE Q(N)
         SRL   R1,1               ISOLATE R(N)
         AR    R1,R0              ADD Q(N) TO R(N)
         BNO   NOVERFLW
OVERFLOW SL    R1,=X'7FFFFFFF'
NOVERFLW ST    R1,0(R4)           STORE X(N+1)
*
         MR    R0,R5
         A     R0,0(R2)
*
         LM    R14,R15,12(R13)    RESTORE CALLER'S REGISTERS
         LM    R1,R12,24(R13)
         SPM   R14                RESTORE CALLER'S PROGRAM MASK
         BR    R14
         LTORG
```

Program 8-6, appropriately adapted, is to be used in this assignment. Input data for the program will consist of (1) a single card containing a positive integer X0, the starting seed value for the random number generator, followed by (2) a series of cards, each containing either a 0 or a 1 in column 1, followed (in or after column 3) by a positive integer N. If the code in column 1 is 1, the card will also contain two more numbers representing the lower and upper limits of the interval.

After setting the starting value to X0, your program should process each of the remaining cards in one of two ways, depending on the value in column 1. The program terminates at end-of-file.

If column 1 contains 0, simply generate N random numbers in the interval 1–1000 and print them, with a suitable heading, ten to a line.

If column 1 contains 1, generate random numbers in the closed interval given by the last two numbers on the card. In this case, rather than printing out the numbers as they are generated, use a distribution table to keep a count of the occurrences of each distinct value. When at least one occurrence of each of the N numbers has been generated, print out the results in a format similar to the following sample:

```
93        **
94        ***
95        ***
96        **
97        ***
98        *
99        **
100       ****
101       **
102       ***
```

The number of asterisks in each line indicates the number of occurrences of the corresponding value. Each entry in the distribution table should be a single halfword. You may assume that a table of 100 halfwords will be large enough. Note that your program can easily determine when each entry in the table contains a nonzero value, by counting the number of times that a zero value has been changed to 1. When the counter reaches the number of elements in the range, the contents of the distribution table should be displayed.

2. This exercise consists of two parts. The first part is to write an external subroutine PARSTRNG that can be called to parse a string having the following format:

<delimiters><keyword> = <value><delimiters><keyword> = <value>etc.

where   <delimiters>   means one or more blanks or commas

<keyword>   means any string of up to 11 characters that does not contain an equal sign

<value>   means a legitimate zoned decimal number of up to nine digits

For example, a valid string could be an entire card image, where the card has been punched with

RATE = 067500   PAYMENT = 102580   PRINCIPAL = 1500000

The order of the keywords on the card is not important, nor is the specific choice of keywords. For example, it should be possible to use PARSTRNG in an entirely different program, to obtain the values from a card punched as follows:

X0 = 1234   N = 200   UPPER = 99, LOWER = 0

Upon entry to the routine PARSTRNG, R1 will point to a parameter list (on a fullword boundary) containing

- 4 bytes: address of the string
- 4 bytes: address of a halfword containing the length of the string
- 4 bytes: address of a table of defined keywords
- 4 bytes: address of a halfword containing the number of entries in the table

Both the parameter list and the keyword table will have been set up by the routine that calls PARSTRNG. The keyword table will consist of one entry for each keyword that PARSTRNG should recognize as legitimate. Each entry in the table will be 16 bytes long, with the following format:

- 1 byte: length of keyword
- 11 bytes: keyword (padded on the right with blanks)
- 4 bytes: address of a fullword where PARSTRNG is to place the value associated with the keyword

To address elements of the keyword table, you should use the following DSECT:

```
$KT         DSECT
$KTLEN      DS          XL1
$KTKEY      DS          CL11
$KTPOINT    DS          A
$KTEND      DS          0F
```

It might also be convenient to DSECT the parameter list.

PARSTRNG will cause the computer to perform the following operations on the string:

1. Scan for beginning of keyword (first character that is not a comma or a blank). If all bytes in the string have been scanned, exit with a return code indicating successful completion of the parse.

2. Find end of keyword (marked by an equal sign) and calculate length of keyword.

3. Search for a matching entry in the keyword table. If none exists, exit with a return code indicating that an error occurred.

4. Obtain from the table the address of the fullword field where the value is to be placed.

5. Find the value (string of digits) assigned to the keyword in the string, calculate its length, and EXecute a PACK instruction to put the value into a doubleword. Convert the value to a fullword with a CVB and store the result in the target field.

6. Go back to Step 1.

It might be convenient to make the search of the keyword table in Step 3 a subroutine.

NOTE: A good PARSTRNG routine would normally check for errors in the input string (missing parts, invalid value, etc.). Rather than print error messages itself, it would send back a return code in R15. The register with the return code would not be restored upon exiting from PARSTRNG; on return, the calling program would test the register and print any necessary error messages.

You may assume that the string will not contain any errors and omit such checking. However, you should return an error code if a keyword cannot be found in the keyword table (perhaps 0 if no errors were detected, and 1 otherwise).

Two translate tables will probably be needed: one for finding the beginning of a keyword (first byte not containing a comma or a blank) and a second for finding the end of the value associated with the keyword (first byte that is a comma or a blank). The second table can also be used to find out where the keyword ends and its value begins, provided the equal sign has a nonzero-function byte (probably different from the one for the comma or the blank).

The second part of Exercise 2 is to write a program TEST that can be used to test PARSTRNG. This program should read cards, each containing two values. One value on each card will follow the keyword RATE=, and one will follow HOURS=. The program should invoke PARSTRNG to obtain the two values from the card and to print the product of these two numbers. For example, for the card

      HOURS=20   RATE=200

the program should print

      HOURS=20   RATE=$2.00   WAGE=$40.00

TEST should invoke PARSTRNG, as follows:

```
        L        R15, = V(PARSTRNG)
        BALR     R14,R15
          .
          .
          .
PARMLIST  DC     A(CARD,SLEN,KEYWORDS,NUMKEY)
CARD      DS     CL80
KEYWORDS  DC     X'04',CL11'RATE',A(DRATE)
          DC     X'05',CL11'HOURS',A(DHOURS)
DRATE     DS     F
DHOURS    DS     F
SLEN      DC     H'80'
NUMKEY    DC     H'2'
```

3. The Julian format of a date has the form

YY   NNN

where YY are the last two digits of the year and NNN is the number of the day in the year. Thus, the date May 31, 1975 would be represented in Julian format as

75   151

since May 31 is the 151st day of the year 1975.

In many applications, it is necessary to perform operations on dates. The basic operations normally required are as follows:

a. Convert a date from one format to another.
b. Compare two dates and determine which one occurs first.
c. Add a number of days to a date to determine the date of some future event.
d. Subtract a number of days from a date to determine the date of some past event.

In this assignment you are to program a module called DATEPROC that performs these basic operations. The three formats for dates manipulated by DATEPROC are as follows:

• A date in the Julian format will be in a three-byte packed decimal field. Thus, 75 151 would be stored as

X'75151F'

• A date can be stored in what will be referred to here as its character format. In this format, the date occupies an eight-byte field and would appear as

05/31/75

- A date can be stored in what will be referred to here as its packed decimal format. In this case, the date occupies a four-byte field and is stored as

X'0053175F'

Upon entrance to DATEPROC, R1 will contain the address of a parameter list composed of three or four words. The first word will contain the address of a four-byte field conforming to the following format:

- *2 bytes.* These two bytes indicate the type of operation DATEPROC should perform. The following values will be used:

  00 — Convert a date from one format to another.
  04 — Compare two dates.
  08 — Add a number of days to a date. In this case, the number of days will be taken from a three-byte packed decimal field.
  0C —Subtract a number of days from a date. In this case, the number of days will be taken from a three-byte packed decimal field.

- *1 byte.* This byte specifies in its rightmost two bits the format of the first date. The values are as follows:

  00 — The date is in Julian format.
  01 — The date is in character format.
  11 — The date is in packed decimal format.

Note that a single TM instruction can be used to determine the setting. The BZ, BM, and BO instructions can be used to determine the exact setting.

- *1 byte.* This byte specifies the format of the second date, using the same codes as above.

The second word in the parameter list contains the address of the first date, and the third word contains the address of the second date field. If the operation is an addition or subtraction, a fourth word will contain the address of a three-byte field containing the number of days.

If a conversion operation is requested, DATEPROC should convert the first field into the format specified for the second field. If a comparison is requested, DATEPROC should set the condition code as follows:

CC	*Meaning*
0	Dates are equal.
1	First date is less than the second date.
2	Second date is less than the first date.
3	—

If addition or subtraction is requested, the number of days should be added to or subtracted from the first date. The result should be put into the second field in the format specified for the second date.

The coding of DATEPROC will be facilitated by first coding the following six subroutines:

- CHARPDEC: a subroutine to convert a date from character format to packed decimal format
- PDECCHAR: a subroutine to convert a date from packed decimal format to character format
- PDECJUL: a subroutine to convert a date from packed decimal format to Julian format
- JULPDEC: a subroutine to convert a date from Julian format to packed decimal format
- JULADD: a subroutine to add a number of days to a date in Julian format
- JULSUB: a subroutine to subtract a number of days from a date in Julian format

4. The *Soundex* system is used to convert names into four-character codes. It has the useful property that most names that sound the same are converted to the same code. Thus, SMITH and SMYTHE are assigned the same four-character code. This is useful for applications where records must be looked up based on names. The technique was invented by Margaret K. Odell and Robert C. Russell—c.f. U.S. Patents 1261167 (1918), 1435663 (1922). The conversion is accomplished by using the following steps:

1. Keep the first letter of the name, but drop all occurrences of a, e, h, i, o, u, w, or y that occur after the first character.

2. For each character except the first, assign the character a number as follows:

$$
\begin{array}{ll}
\text{b, f, p, v} & ->1 \\
\text{c, g, j, k, q, s, x, z} & ->2 \\
\text{d, t} & ->3 \\
\text{1} & ->4 \\
\text{m, n} & ->5 \\
\text{r} & ->6
\end{array}
$$

3. If two or more letters that were adjacent in the original name (before Step 1) were assigned the same numeric value, delete all but the first.

4. If the result has less than four characters, pad on the right with zeros. If it is longer, truncate the rightmost characters.

Thus, SMYTHE would be converted as follows:

1. YHE is deleted, leaving SMT.
2. SMT gets converted to S53.
3. Since there are no identical adjacent numbers from characters that were adjacent in the original name, no characters are deleted in this step.
4. Since S53 is less than four characters, it is padded to S530.

Write a program that reads cards, each containing a last name starting in column 1. The program should print the name and the Soundex code for the name.

5. Write a subroutine called XXXXDUMP that can be invoked to print a hexadecimal display of an area in memory. The subroutine should assume that, upon entrance, R1 points to a parameter list conforming to the following format:

- *word 1:*   address of an area
- *word 2:*   address of a halfword containing the length of the area
- *word 3:*   address of a halfword containing the identifier number

XXXXDUMP should round the address of the area down to the next lowest multiple of 16 and round the ending address up to the next multiple of 16, minus 1, so that memory can be displayed in groups of 16 bytes. For example, if R1 pointed to a three-word list containing

$$000A1436$$
$$00000237$$
$$0000000A$$

then XXXXDUMP should display from address 0A1430 to 0A166F. The output produced by XXXXDUMP should conform to the following format:

```
        ID#  IS  10

0A1430      404040F5      40F1F2F3      40F0F0F0      F1F1F3F4
0A1440
              .             .             .             .
              .             .             .             .
              .             .             .             .
              .             .             .             .
```

Write a short program invoking XXXXDUMP to display several areas in memory.

6. Write three subroutines that can be used to facilitate the encoding and decoding of messages. The first subroutine, SETCODE, is used to establish the correspondence between letters in a message and the encoded form of the message. The second subroutine, ENCODE, can be called to convert a message into its encoded form, using the correspondence table established by a call to SETCODE. The third subroutine, DECODE, can be called to convert an encoded message back to its original form. Specifically, the requirements for each of the three modules are as follows:

SETCODE

Upon entrance to this subroutine, R1 will point to a parameter list in the following format:

- *word 1:* address of a fullword number of character pairs in the correspondence table used to encode the messages (Each character pair specifies an original character and the character into which it should be encoded.)
- *word 2:* address of the list of character pairs (Each two bytes in the list represent a pair.)
- *word 3:* address of a translate table to be used to encode messages
- *word 4:* address of a translate table to be used to decode messages

SETCODE must simply fill the appropriate characters into the two translate tables. For example, if AQ were a character pair, then the following should occur.

a. The entry in the position for A in the encoding table should be set to Q.
b. The entry for Q in the decoding table should be set to A.

ENCODE

Upon entrance to this subroutine, R1 will contain the address of a parameter list conforming to the following format:

- *word 1:* address of a string to encode
- *word 2:* address of a halfword containing the length of the string
- *word 3:* address of the area where the encoded string is to be constructed (Unless this is the same as the first word, the original string should not be altered.)
- *word 4:* address of the translate table to be used to encode the message

ENCODE should simply move the string to the area indicated in the third word of the parameter list and then translate it to the encoded format.

DECODE

Upon entrance to this subroutine, R1 will contain the address of a parameter list conforming to the following format:

- *word 1:* address of a string to be decoded
- *word 2:* address of a halfword containing the length of the string
- *word 3:* address of the area where the decoded string is to be constructed
- *word 4:* address of the translate table to be used to decode the string

DECODE should simply move the encoded string to the area indicated in the third word of the parameter list, and decode it back to its original contents.

To test the three subroutines, write a short program called TEST to execute the following logic:

Step 1. Read in a single card containing up to 40 character pairs. Call SET-CODE to set up the two translate tables. Note that a character pair of two blanks will have no effect, so the call to SETCODE can always specify a list of 40 character pairs.

Step 2. Read in two cards containing a message. Only the 40 characters specified in the first card may occur in the message. Print the two input cards.

Step 3. Call ENCODE to encode the message. Print the encoded message.

Step 4. Call DECODE to decode the message. Print the decoded message. Stop.

7. In many data processing applications, it is necessary to validate the contents of numeric fields. Frequently, it is necessary to determine whether a given field contains a valid number and, if the number is valid, to pack it into a designated second field.

In this exercise you are to code an external subroutine, NUMCHK, which can be called to verify the contents of a set of numeric fields. Optionally, the calling program can request that NUMCHK pack the contents of any field into a second field and check that the packed result falls within a specified range. NUMCHK may not alter the contents of any inspected field.

Upon entrance to NUMCHK, R1 will contain the address of a parameter list containing a single address, the address of the block of parameters in Table 8-2.

Table 8-2

Displacement	Length	Contents
0	4	Number of fields to check
4	28*n*	One set of parameters for each of *n* fields (28 bytes are used to specify the parameters for each field.)

Table 8-2 (continued)

Parameters for each field

0	4	Address of the field to be checked
4	4	Length of the field to check
8	1	A byte containing bit flags that specify editing options (see below)
9	1	A byte that NUMCHK will set to X′F0′ if no errors are detected, and to X′F1′ if errors are detected
10	2	Unused
12	4	Address of a receiving field (This parameter, as well as the following three parameters, is specified only if the option to pack legitimate fields is specified in the flag byte.)
16	4	Length of the receiving field
20	4	Address of a field containing the maximum legitimate value for the number (The length of the designated field is assumed to be the same as that of the receiving field.)
24	4	Address of a field containing the minimum legitimate value for the number (The length of the designated field is assumed to be the same as that of the receiving field.)

The settings of the bits in the flag byte describe the field to be verified and whether it should be packed into a receiving field. Four bits in the flag byte will be utilized. Their meanings are as follows:

bits 0,1,3,4		(Unused)
bit 2	0:	If the field is valid, pack it into the receiving field.
	1:	The number is not to be packed into a receiving field, and no check should be made to determine whether or not the number falls within specified limits.
bit 5	0:	Leading blanks are legitimate.
	1:	No leading blanks are allowed.
bit 6	0:	The field does not contain a sign. In this case, the zone digit on all nonblank bytes must be an F.
	1:	The field may contain a sign. In this case, bit 7 should be examined to determine whether the sign precedes the first numeric digit or is overpunched onto the rightmost digit.
bit 7	0:	The sign was overpunched into the rightmost byte of the field. C and F are valid plus zone digits and D is the only acceptable minus zone.

1: The optional sign should immediately precede the first numeric digit. The valid signs in this case are + and −. If the sign is omitted, the value in the field is assumed to be positive.

The scanning of a field by NUMCHK should utilize the TRT instruction twice. Two translate tables are used. The table for scanning past leading blanks is as follows:

Position	Contents
C' '	X'00'
C'+' and C'−'	X'08'
C'0'–C'9'	X'0C'
X'C0'–X'C9' and X'D0'–X'D9'	X'10'
All other positions	X'04'

The table for scanning past digits is as follows:

Position	Contents
C'0'–C'9'	X'00'
X'C0'–X'C9' and X'D0'–X'D9'	X'08'
All other positions	X'04'

The basic scanning will then be as follows:

```
          SR     R2,R2
          TRT    addr,1st table
          B      *+4(R2)
          B                      error routine—empty field
          B                      error routine—invalid 1st character
          B                      routine to check leading sign
          B                      routine to check leading blanks
          B                      a routine to check overpunched sign
OVPNCHED
                 .
                 .
          SR     R2,R2
          TRT    addr,2nd table
          B      *+4(R2)
          B                      routine to process legitimate field
          B      error routine—field contains an  invalid character
```

CHECK   routine to process trailing sign (make sure it's legal and in rightmost byte)

.

.

To test NUMCHK, use the assembler language program shown in Program 8-7.

Program 8-7

```
         TITLE 'A MODULE TO TEST NUMCHK'
*  THIS SHORT PROGRAM CAN BE USED TO TEST THE 'NUMCHK' MODULE,
*  WHICH IS CALLED TO VERIFY THE CONTENTS OF SEVERAL NUMERIC FIELDS.
*  THE LOGIC OF THE MODULE IS AS FOLLOWS:
*
*  STEP 1.   SET UP R13 AS THE BASE REGISTER.
*
*  STEP 2.   CALL 'NUMCHK' TO CHECK THE 8 FIELDS DESCRIBED IN THE
*            PARAMETER LIST.
*
*  STEP 3.   DUMP THE AREA OF CORE ALTERED BY THE CALL.
*
*  STEP 4.   EXIT.
*
*
*  FOR THE DESCRIPTION OF THE FORMAT OF THE PARAMETER LIST, SEE THE
*  DOCUMENTATION FOR THE 'NUMCHK' MODULE.
         SPACE 5
         PRINT NOGEN
TEST     CSECT
***<STEP 1>***      SAVE CALLER'S REGISTERS AND ESTABLISH R13 AS A BASE
         STM   R14,R12,12(R13)     STORE CALLERS REGISTERS
         BAL   R14,80(R15)         NOW LINK SAVE AREAS
         DS    18F                 REGISTER SAVE AREA
         ST    R14,8(R13)          STORE FORWARD LINK INTO OLD SAVE AREA
         ST    R13,4(R14)          STORE BACK LINK INTO NEW SAVE AREA
         LR    R13,R14             R13<- ADDRESS OF NEW SAVE AREA
         USING TEST+8,R13
         SPACE 2
***<STEP 2>***      CALL NUMCHK
         LA    R1,P=A(PLIST)       LOAD ADDRESS OF 1-WORD PARAMETER LIST
         L     R15,=V(NUMCHK)      NOW CALL NUMCHK
         BALR  R14,R15
         SPACE
***<STEP 3>***      DUMP OUT THE ALTERED AREAS OF CORE
         XDUMP PLIST,400           DUMP ALTERED AREAS OF CORE
         SPACE
***<STEP 4>***      EXIT
         L     R13,4(R13)          LOAD ADDRESS OF OLD SAVE AREA
         LM    R14,R12,12(R13)     RESTORE CALLER'S REGISTERS
         BR    R14                 EXIT
         SPACE
         LTORG
PLIST    DC    F'8'                TOTAL OF 8 FIELDS TO VERIFY
         DC    A(F1,7)
         DC    C'C'                FLAG1--PACK, LEADING BLANKS, LD SIGN
         DC    X'00'               ERR1
         DS    2X
         DC    A(T1,5,MAX1,MIN1)
         SPACE
         DC    A(F2,4)
```

Program 8-7 (continued)

```
        DC      C'7'                    DONT PACK, NO LEADING BLANKS, LD SIGN
        DC      X'00'
        DS      2X
        DC      A(0,0,0,0)
        SPACE
        DC      A(F3,4)
        DC      C'3'                    DONT PACK,LEADING BLANKS,LEADING SIGN
        DC      X'00'
        DS      2X
        DC      A(0,0,0,0)
        SPACE
        DC      A(F4,5)
        DC      C'3'                    DONT PACK,LEADING BLANKS,LEADING SIGN
        DC      X'00'
        DS      2X
        DC      A(0,0,0,0)
        SPACE
        DC      A(F5,3)
        DC      C'B'                    PACK,LEADING BLANKS, TRAILING SIGN
        DC      X'00'
        DS      2X
        DC      A(T5,6,MAX5,MIN5)
        SPACE
        DC      A(F6,3)
        DC      C'4'                    DONT PACK,NO LEADING BLANKS,NO SIGN
        DC      X'00'
        DS      2X
        DC      A(0,0,0,0)
        SPACE
        DC      A(F7,3)
        DC      C'C'                    PACK,LEADING BLANKS AND SIGN
        DC      X'00'
        DS      2X
        DC      A(T7,6,MAX7,MIN7)
        SPACE
        DC      A(F8,3)
        DC      C'C'                    PACK,LEADING BLANKS AND SIGN
        DC      X'00'
        DS      2X
        DC      A(T8,7,MAX8,MIN8)
        SPACE 5
F1      DC      C'  +  123'             INVALID
F2      DC      C'-12A'                 INVALID BECAUSE OF ILLEGAL RIGHT ZONE
F3      DC      C'  -24 '               VALID
F4      DC      C'     +'               INVALID
F5      DC      X'F1F2D3'               VALID
F6      DC      C'12M'                  INVALID — SIGN NOT SPECIFIED IN FLAG
F7      DC      C'  -2'                 OUT OF RANGE
F8      DC      C'+10'                  OUT OF RANGE
        SPACE 5
T1      DC      PL5'0'
T5      DC      XL6'0'
T7      DC      XL6'0'
T8      DC      XL7'0'
        SPACE 5
MAX1    DC      PL5'100'
MIN1    DC      PL5'0'
MAX5    DC      PL6'200'
MIN5    DC      PL6'-200'
MAX7    DC      PL6'10'
MIN7    DC      PL6'0'
MAX8    DC      PL7'9'
MIN8    DC      PL7'-100'
        EQUREGS
        END     TEST
```

8. Let a sentence be defined as either of the following sequences:

a. ARTICLE NOUN VERB ARTICLE NOUN
b. PRONOUN VERB ARTICLE NOUN

where   ARTICLE   is one of (the, a)
        NOUN   is one of (boy, girl, dog, lady)
        VERB   is one of (loves, hates, walks, needs)
        PRONOUN   is one of (he, she, it)

Write a program that will read a data card containing a set of words that satisfies, except for order, the definition of a sentence given above (either a or b). The program should print the words in their original order, recognize which definition has been used, arrange them into proper order, and print the sentence out with one space between each word and a period following the last word. Using definition a, there will be two articles and two nouns. Use the first one on the card as the first in your printed sentence.

Your program should contain four tables, one for each class of words. The format of entries in each table should be

* *2 bytes:* length of the word
* *10 bytes:* the word (left-justified)

Also, the number of entries in each table should be kept in a separate halfword. For example,

#ARTICLE	DC	H'2'
ARTICLES	DC	H'3',CL10'THE'
	DC	H'1',CL10'A'

would be used to define the set of valid articles. Keeping the information in tables allows the convenient addition of more words.

9. Using the definitions in Exercise 8 and the random number generator presented in Exercise 1, write a program that generates random sentences. The general technique is to use a random number generator to select one of the available options—e.g., generate randomly a 1 or a 2 that selects the sentence definition a or b. If b is selected, then randomly select one of the choices for PRONOUN, VERB, ARTICLE, and NOUN, and print the sentence. Print at least ten sentences.

10. Write two subroutines, one to convert a hexadecimal number in character format as it would appear on a card to a value in R0, and one to convert a value in R0 to the character form of the hexadecimal representation of the number. For example, the first subroutine (CHARHEX) could be used to convert

F1C1C3

on a card to 000001AC in R0, and the second subroutine (HEXCHAR) could be used to convert 000001AC in R0 to

F1C1C3

The routine HEXCHAR would be useful if one wished to display the contents of an area in storage. CHARHEX could be used to accept the hexadecimal representations of input values. The exact descriptions of the routines are as follows:

CHARHEX

Upon entrance to this subroutine, R1 will point to the address of an eight-digit hexadecimal number in character format (00000000 to FFFFFFFF). Convert the number and return the value in R0.

HEXCHAR

Upon entrance to this subroutine, R1 points to the address of an eight-byte area. The contents of R0 should be converted to character format, and the result should be put into the designated area.

To test your subroutines, write a program that can be used to add hexadecimal numbers. As input, the program should accept cards, each containing a hexadecimal number in columns 1–8 and another number in columns 9–16. The program should print a line similar to the following, for each pair of numbers:

0014A1FE   0C001A01   SUM = 0C14BBFF

11. Text processing is one of the major uses of computers. One minor technical problem in text processing is to determine where a given word can be hyphenated. That is what this assignment is about. You are to code a routine called HYPHENAT that takes the following parameter list:

- address of a "word" (a character string)
- address of a fullword containing the length of the word
- address of a fullword containing a value k that represents the minimum number of characters by which the word must be shortened
- address of a fullword set to the number of characters before the split (A value of 0 means that no split is possible. If the last character before the split is not a hyphen, it is assumed that the caller will have to append a hyphen.)

Thus,

```
LA    R1, = A(STRING,LEN,KVAL,LEFTLEN)
L     R15, = V(HYPHENAT)
BALR  R14,R15
```

.

.

.

STRING	DC	C'obtain'
LEN	DC	F'6'
KVAL	DC	F'3'
LEFTLEN	DS	F

should set LEFTLEN to 2. A variety of details must be considered:

a. Some words contain special characters or are enclosed within apostrophes. These words should not be split. For our purposes, a "breakable" word possesses the following properties:

    (1) The first character is a lowercase alphabetic character, an uppercase character, or a '('.

    (2) All other characters except the last are lowercase alphabetic characters or hyphens.

    (3) The last character is either a lowercase alphabetic character or any of the characters in the following set:

$$. \quad , \quad ; \quad : \quad) \quad ? \quad !$$

b. Some words contain hyphens. These words can be split only at the existing hyphens.

c. If a word that does not contain a hyphen is split, at least k + 1 characters must be to the right of the split (since a hyphen must be added to the left of the split).

d. There must be two characters to the left of the split.

e. There must be a vowel (a, e, i, o, or u) on each side of the split. This requirement prevents such words as "bless" from being split.

The algorithm for determining the hyphenation point is taken from *Algorithms in SNOBOL4* by James Gimpel. This book is a truly wondrous collection of algorithms. However, you should be thoroughly conversant with SNOBOL before studying the book.

    Once the word has been checked to verify that it is breakable, a check should be made to see whether there are any embedded hyphens. If there are existing hyphens, the split should occur at the rightmost hyphen such that k characters occur to the right of the hyphen. If the word contains hyphens but none has k characters to the right, the word cannot be split. If the word is breakable and contains no hyphens, the following steps should be used to locate the split point (if any):

1. Locate the range of possible split points. The leftmost possible split point is found by scanning from the left until the first vowel is found (or until

the end of the string occurs). If the first letter is a vowel, the pointer should be adjusted ahead one character (to force at least two characters to the left of a split). If a vowel is found and if $k + 1$ characters occur to the right of the resulting address, you have located the leftmost possible split point. The rightmost split point is found by scanning from the right for a vowel. The rightmost split point is such that at least $k + 1$ characters and the rightmost vowel would occur to the right of the split. Now, if the set of possible split points is nonempty (i.e., the leftmost split point $<=$ the rightmost split point), you can continue. Otherwise, the word cannot be split.

2. We start this part of the algorithm with

LC = address of the last character of the word
L   = length of the word
LS = address of the character to the left of the leftmost split point
RS = address of the character to the left of the rightmost split point

In this part of the algorithm, suffixes are examined. There are three types of suffixes (tables of all three types are given later):

- A *hyphenating suffix* is one in which a hyphen could be put in front of the suffix (if that point is between LS and RS). If the hyphenation point is to the right of RS, the suffix is "removed" and suffix checks are performed on the shortened string.

- A *neutral suffix* is one that cannot be preceded by a hyphen, but suffix checks can continue after removing the suffix.

- An *inhibiting suffix* is one that cannot be preceded by a hyphen and that terminates suffix checking (after removing the suffix).

The algorithm involves checking for suffixes and removing them until a point is reached at which no suffix matches, a hyphenation point between LS and RS is located, or an inhibiting suffix was just removed. If a hyphenation point is found, the algorithm terminates successfully. Otherwise, it will be necessary to proceed to diagram checks in the next step. To perform the suffix checking, it will be necessary to encode the different sets of suffixes. We suggest the following encoding:

```
HYPHSUFF   DC    X'4'    LENGTH OF STRING THAT FOLLOWS
           DC    C'ture'  HYPHENATING SUFFIX
*
           DC    X'9'
           DC    C'(cgst)ive'   A c,g,s, OR t FOLLOWED BY ive
*
           DC    X'A'
           DC    C'(cdmnt)ial'
```

```
*
          DC      X'3'
          DC      C'ful'
*
          DC      X'9'
          DC      C'(cgst)ian'
*
          DC      X'9'
          DC      C'(cgst)ion'
*
          DC      X'4'
          DC      C'ship'
*
          DC      X'7'
          DC      C'(ln)ess'
*
          DC      X'A'
          DC      C(cgst)ious'
*
          DC      X'D'
          DC      C'(cdglmntv)ent'
*
          DC      X'00'       END OF HYPHENATING SUFFIXES
*
NEUTSUFF  DC      X'9'        NEUTRAL SUFFIXES
          DC      C'(.;:,?!))'  ALL CHAR BETWEEN OUTERMOST PARENS
*
          DC      X'7'
          DC      C'(ai)ble'
*
          DC      X'2'
          DC      C'ly'
*
          DC      X'1'
          DC      C's'
*
          DC      X'2'
          DC      C'es'
*
          DC      X'00'       END OF NEUTRAL SUFFIXES
*
INHSUFF   DC      X'2'        INHIBITING SUFFIXES
          DC      C'ed'
```

```
*
        DC    X'7'
        DC    C'(glsv)e'
*
        DC    X'6'
        DC    C'(gq)ue'
*
        DC    X'3'
        DC    C'est'
*
        DC    X'3'
        DC    C'ing'
*
        DC    X'00'    END OF INHIBITING SUFFIXES
```

Here each of the three tables is composed of a sequence of suffix strings. Each suffix string has a one-byte length, followed by a character string of that length. The end of the sequence is marked by an entry with a length of 0. Each character string encodes a set of suffixes, as follows:

- If no parentheses occur in the string, the character string represents a single suffix.
- Where characters appear within parentheses, they represent alternatives. Thus,

$$(gq)ue$$

represents two suffixes, "gue" and "que".

You should code an external subroutine called SUFFCHK that takes as input parameters

- address of LC (the address of the end of the word)
- address of L (the length of the word)
- address of a suffix string

SUFFCHK should set R15 to 0 if and only if the suffix string matches. If the suffix string does match, SUFFCHK should also decrement both LC and L by the length of the matched suffix.

3. If the suffix checking did not succeed in locating an acceptable hyphenation point, then look for a split point using diagram checks. That is, look for adjacent characters that can be split. For each of the 26 lowercase alphabetic characters, we shall specify either of the following:

- the set of characters that could precede it and allow a split
- the set of characters that could *not* precede it and allow a split

We will use the shorter set for each letter. Each set will be represented by

- 1 one-byte length
- a character string. If the character string begins with '-', the remaining characters represent those that do not allow a split. Otherwise, the character string contains those characters that do allow a split. Further, we allow '@' to be a short representation of 'aeiou'.

With these conventions, the required diagram data can be represented as follows:

```
DIGRAMTB   DC    A(AENT)      ADDRESS OF ENTRY FOR A
           DC    A(BENT)
           DC    A(CENT)
            .
            .
           DC    A(ZENT)
*
AENT       DC    X'1',C'x'     xa CAN BE SPLIT
BENT       DC    X'2',C'-@'    A VOWEL FOLLOWED BY b CANNOT
CENT       DC    X'4',C'-@ns'
DENT       DC    X'3',C'-@r'
EENT       DC    X'1',C'x'
FENT       DC    X'2',C'-@'
GENT       DC    X'3',C'-@n'
HENT       DC    X'8,C'-@cgpstw'
IENT       DC    X'1',C'x'
JENT       DC    X'2',C'-@'
KENT       DC    X'6',C'-@clns'
LENT       DC    X'9',C'-@bcfgpty'
MENT       DC    X'3',C'-@y'
NENT       DC    X'6',C'-@gksy'
OENT       DC    X'2',C'ax'
PENT       DC    X'4',C'-@sy'
QENT       DC    X'2',C'-s'
RENT       DC    X'A',C'jklmnrsvxz'
SENT       DC    X'7',C'-@klnwy'
TENT       DC    X'6',C'-@fhsy'
UENT       DC    X'1',C'x'
VENT       DC    X'2',C'-@'
WENT       DC    X'3',C'-@s'
XENT       DC    X'2',C'-@'
YENT       DC    X'4',C'qwxy'
ZENT       DC    X'3',C'-@c'
```

You should code an external subroutine, DICHK, that takes the following parameter list:

- LC
- LS
- RS
- address of a word to be set to the address of the appropriate split point (0 if there is none)

If DICHK cannot determine a split point, HYPHENAT must return a failure.

This algorithm for hyphenation will miss a great many hyphenation points, but it will give an invalid split point in only about 1 percent of the calls, and it does not require a file (i.e., a dictionary).

This is a relatively demanding exercise. However, the result is definitely useful.

9

Macros and Conditional Assembly

9.1 SYMBOLIC PARAMETERS AND MACROS

A *macro language* is a powerful extension to a basic assembler language. This language facility provides a means for generating at assembly time a commonly used sequence of assembler-language statements as many times as required. The sequence of statements is specified, just once, in a *macro definition;* then, at any point where these statements are to be generated, a single *macro instruction* will suffice. The judicious use of macros will:

1. greatly simplify the coding of programs
2. significantly reduce the number of programming errors
3. ensure that common functions are performed by standard routines

An introduction to variable symbols and, in particular, symbolic parameters is a necessary prelude to a discussion of macros.

Variable symbols (as distinguished from ordinary symbols or labels) are symbols that can be assigned different values by either the programmer or the assembler. When assembler-language instructions are generated according to a macro definition, the variable symbols are replaced by the values that have been assigned to them. Variable symbols are of three types: symbolic parameters, system variables, and SET variables. Each of the three types of variable symbols serves a distinct function. Only the function of the symbolic parameter will be discussed in this section.

The rules of formation for variable symbols are as follows:

1. A variable symbol consists of from two to eight characters, the first of which must be an ampersand.
2. The second character must be a letter and the remaining characters, if any, must be either letters or digits.

Thus,

        &VARLEN   &GEN2
        &TABSIZE   &RIOPARM
        &SORT1   &LIST1

are all valid variable symbols.

Symbolic parameters are used in the macro definition and are assigned values by the programmer in each macro instruction that references the particular macro.

A macro definition consists of the following items in the given order:

1. A header composed solely of the operation symbol MACRO
2. A prototype statement
3. A sequence of model statements that make up the body of the macro definition
4. A trailer that is simply the operation symbol MEND

The prototype statement does not necessarily have a label; but, if it does, the label must be a symbolic parameter. The operation field must contain a symbol that is the mnemonic operation code that must appear in all macro instructions referencing the macro definition. The operand field may contain from 0 to 200 symbolic parameters, separated by commas, which serve as a vehicle for passing information to the macro. The following are examples of macro prototype statements:

```
&LABEL    EXIT
&LABEL    INVOKE &NAME
&NAME     PARSE    &LEN,&ADDR,&PARMTAB,&NUM
```

The body of the macro may contain two types of comment cards. A comment card that contains an asterisk in column 1 is reproduced with the assembler instructions generated by the macro. A comment card with a period in column 1 followed by an asterisk in column 2 is not reproduced with the instructions generated by the macro. A simple example of a macro definition follows:

```
        MACRO
&LABEL  EXIT
.*
.* THIS MACRO GENERATES THE CODE REQUIRED TO RETURN FROM A MODULE.
.* IT ASSUMES NORMAL OS LINKAGE CONVENTIONS.
.*
* NOTE THAT THIS MACRO GENERATES THE CODE TO EXIT FROM A MODULE
* WHICH HAS ESTABLISHED A SAVE AREA FOR CALLS TO LOWER LEVEL MODULES.
* IT SHOULD NOT BE USED TO EXIT FROM A LOWEST LEVEL SUBROUTINE.
&LABEL  L     R13,4(R13)         LOAD ADDRESS OF CALLER'S SAVE AREA
        LM    R14,R12,12(R13)    RESTORE CALLER'S REGISTERS
        BR    R14
        MEND
```

A macro instruction may have any valid label or it may have no label. The operation field must contain the mnemonic operation code of a macro definition and the operand field may contain from 0 to 200 operands, separated by commas. These positional parameters replace the symbolic parameters in the macro definition when the code corresponding to a particular macro instruction is generated. As an example, the macro instruction

> LEAVE   EXIT

can be utilized to reference the previous macro definition. In this case, the sequence of generated code would be

```
* NOTE THAT THIS MACRO GENERATES THE CODE TO EXIT FROM A MODULE
* WHICH HAS ESTABLISHED A SAVE AREA FOR CALLS TO LOWER LEVEL MODULES.
* IT SHOULD NOT BE USED TO EXIT FROM A LOWEST LEVEL SUBROUTINE.
LEAVE    L      R13,4(R13)        LOAD BACK POINTER
         LM     R14,R12,12(R13)   RESTORE CALLER'S REGS
         BR     R14               EXIT
```

Note that the symbolic parameter &LABEL in the macro definition is replaced by the label LEAVE from the macro instruction in the generated code. If the macro instruction had included no label, &LABEL would have been replaced by the null string. Also note that the comments following the instructions are reproduced in the generated code, as are the comment cards with an asterisk in column 1, but that the comment cards beginning with .* are not reproduced.

As a second example, consider the following macro, which could be used to generate calls to external subroutines:

```
         MACRO
&LABEL   INVOKE   &NAME
&LABEL   L        R15,=V(&NAME)
         BALR     R14,R15
         MEND
```

In this case the macro instruction

> INVOKE   SUBRTN

would cause the following code to be generated:

```
         L        R15,=V(SUBRTN)
         BALR     R14,R15
```

Here the symbolic parameter &NAME in the macro definition is replaced by the operand SUBRTN from the operand field of the macro instruction. The symbolic parameter &LABEL is replaced by the null string, because the macro instruction did not have a label.

When macro definitions are included in a source program, the macro definitions must precede all assembler-language statements in the program. However, a title card and comment cards may precede the macro definitions. In the program listing produced by the assembler, each macro instruction is followed by the assembler-language statements generated from the macro. Of course, the object module produced by the assembler corresponds to the code in this listing.

An important concept must be grasped: When the assembler processes a macro instruction, assembler-language code is generated according to the specifications inherent in the macro definition. Object code is generated only when the assembler processes assembler-language instructions. To understand how source decks containing macro definitions and instructions are processed, it is useful to think of the assembler as containing two distinct programs: a macro processor and an assembler code processor. Then, the actual processing can be visualized as occurring according to the steps depicted in Figure 9-1.

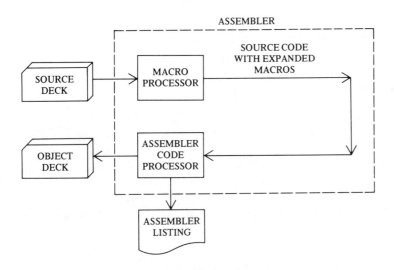

Figure 9-1

Program 9-1 is the listing of a source deck that includes the macro definitions illustrated in the examples in this section.

```
          MACRO
&LABEL    EXIT
.*
.* THIS MACRO GENERATES THE CODE REQUIRED TO RETURN FROM A MODULE.
.* IT ASSUMES NORMAL OS LINKAGE CONVENTIONS.
.*
 * NOTE THAT THIS MACRO GENERATES THE CODE TO EXIT FROM A MODULE
 * WHICH HAS ESTABLISHED A SAVE AREA FOR CALLS TO LOWER LEVEL MODULES.
 * IT SHOULD NOT BE USED TO EXIT FROM A LOWEST LEVEL SUBROUTINE.
&LABEL    L      R13,4(R13)          LOAD ADDRESS OF CALLER'S SAVE AREA
          LM     R14,R12,12(R13)     RESTORE CALLER'S REGISTERS
          BR     R14
          MEND
          MACRO
&LABEL    INVOKE &NAME
.*
.* THIS MACRO CAN BE USED TO INVOKE AN EXTERNAL ROUTINE.  THE NAME
.* OF THE ROUTINE TO BE CALLED SHOULD BE GIVEN AS THE FIRST OPERAND.
.*
&LABEL    L      R15,=V(&NAME)       LOAD ADDRESS OF ROUTINE TO CALL
          BALR   R14,R15             CALL THE ROUTINE
          MEND
MAIN      CSECT
          STM    R14,R12,12(R13)     STORE CALLER'S REGISTERS
          BAL    R14,80(R15)         NOW SET UP R13 AS THE BASE
          DS     18F                 REGISTER SAVE AREA
          ST     R13,4(R14)          STORE BACK POINTER
          ST     R14,8(R13)          STORE FORWARD POINTER
          LR     R13,R14             R13 IS THE BASE REGISTER
          USING  MAIN+8,R13
          LM     R2,R3,=A(TABLE,10)  LOAD PARAMETERS FOR CALL TO 'SORT'
          INVOKE SORT                CALL THE ROUTINE SORT
LEAVE     EXIT
          LTORG
TABLE     DC     F'4,-10,9,43,32,-8,12,0,1,64'
CARD      DS     CL80                INPUT CARD AREA
R2        EQU    2
R3        EQU    3
R12       EQU    12
R13       EQU    13
R14       EQU    14
R15       EQU    15
          END
```

Program 9-2 is a copy of the assembler listing generated by this source deck. Note that, in the assembler listing, each statement generated by a macro instruction is distinguished by a plus sign appearing to its left. These listings should be studied carefully, along with the material in this section, before proceeding.

9.2 CONDITIONAL ASSEMBLY

The conditional assembly instructions provide a facility for altering the sequence in which source program statements are processed by the assembler. They in fact provide the means for instructing the assembler to branch and loop among such statements in much the same way as the computer branches and loops among statements in an executable program. Although conditional assembly statements can be used in other portions of a source

Program 9-2

LCC	OBJECT CODE	ADDR1	ADDR2	STMT	SOURCE STATEMENT
				1	MACRO
				2	&LABEL EXIT
				3	.*
				4	.* THIS MACRO GENERATES THE CODE REQUIRED TO RETURN FROM A MODULE.
				5	.* IT ASSUMES NORMAL OS LINKAGE CONVENTIONS.
				6	.*
				7	* NOTE THAT THIS MACRO GENERATES THE CODE TO EXIT FROM A MODULE
				8	* WHICH HAS ESTABLISHED A SAVE AREA FOR CALLS TO LOWER LEVEL MODULES.
				9	* IT SHOULD NOT BE USED TO EXIT FROM A LOWEST LEVEL SUBROUTINE.
				10	&LABEL L R13,4(R13) LOAD ADDRESS OF CALLER'S SAVE AREA
				11	LM R14,R12,12(R13) RESTORE CALLER'S REGISTERS
				12	BR R14
				13	MEND
				14	MACRO
				15	&LABEL INVOKE &NAME
				16	.*
				17	.* THIS MACRO CAN BE USED TO INVOKE AN EXTERNAL ROUTINE. THE NAME
				18	.* OF THE ROUTINE TO BE CALLED SHOULD BE GIVEN AS THE FIRST OPERAND.
				19	.*
				20	&LABEL L R15,=V(&NAME) LOAD ADDRESS OF ROUTINE TO CALL
				21	BALR R14,R15 CALL THE ROUTINE
				22	MEND
000000				23	MAIN CSECT
000000	90EC D00C		0000C	24	STM R14,R12,12(R13) STORE CALLER'S REGISTERS
000004	45EF 0050		00050	25	BAL R14,80(R15) NOW SET UP R13 AS THE BASE
000008				26	DS 18F REGISTER SAVE AREA
000050	50DE 0004		00004	27	ST R13,4(R14) STORE BACK POINTER
000054	50ED 0008		00008	28	ST R14,8(R13) STORE FORWARD POINTER
000058	18DE			29	LR R13,R14
				30	USING MAIN+8,R13 R13 IS THE BASE REGISTER
00005A	9823 D068		00070	31	LM R2,R3,=A(TABLE,10) LOAD PARAMETERS FOR CALL TO 'SORT'
				32	INVOKE SORT CALL THE ROUTINE SORT
00005E	58F0 D070		00078	33+	L R15,=V(SORT) LOAD ADDRESS OF ROUTINE TO CALL
000062	05EF			34+	BALR R14,R15 CALL THE ROUTINE
				35	LEAVE EXIT
				36+	* NOTE THAT THIS MACRO GENERATES THE CODE TO EXIT FROM A MODULE
				37+	* WHICH HAS ESTABLISHED A SAVE AREA FOR CALLS TO LOWER LEVEL MODULES.
				38+	* IT SHOULD NOT BE USED TO EXIT FROM A LOWEST LEVEL SUBROUTINE.
000064	58DD 0004		00004	39+	LEAVE L R13,4(R13) LOAD ADDRESS OF CALLER'S SAVE AREA
000068	98EC D00C		0000C	40+	LM R14,R12,12(R13) RESTORE CALLER'S REGISTERS
00006C	07FE			41+	BR R14
000070				42	LTORG
000070	0000007C 0000000A			43	=A(TABLE,10)
000078	00000000			44	=V(SORT)
00007C	0000D004 FFFFFFF6			45	TABLE DC F'4,-10,9,43,32,-8,12,0,1,64'
0000A4				46	CARD DS CL80 INPUT CARD AREA
000002				47	R2 EQU 2
000003				48	R3 EQU 3
0000C				49	R12 EQU 12
0000D				50	R13 EQU 13
0000E				51	R14 EQU 14
0000F				52	R15 EQU 15
				53	END

program, only their use in macro definitions, which is far more common, will be discussed in this section.

Several definitions must be given before proceeding to the discussion of conditional assembly. For the purposes of the discussion in this section, an *arithmetic expression* is an expression that can be formed from

• self-defining terms
• the operators $+$, $-$, $*$, and $/$
• variable symbols
• parentheses to indicate grouping

A *logical expression*, for the present purpose, is one of the following:

• A 0 or a 1 with or without enclosing parentheses
• Two arithmetic expressions separated by a relational operator and enclosed within parentheses. The valid relational operators are

EQ	equal
NE	not equal
LT	less than
GT	greater than
LE	less than or equal
GE	greater than or equal

When such a logical expression is evaluated, 1 is assigned as the value if the two expressions stand in the given relation; otherwise, 0 is assigned as the value.

• A character string of from 0 to 255 characters enclosed within apostrophes, and a symbolic parameter enclosed within apostrophes, separated by a relational operator, and enclosed within parentheses. When an expression of this type is evaluated, the character string is compared to the character value assigned to the symbolic parameter and, if these two strings satisfy the given relation, 1 is assigned as the value; otherwise, 0 is assigned as the value.

A more inclusive definition of a logical expression will be given in Section 9.3.

A *sequence symbol* is any symbol formed according to the following rules:

• A sequence symbol consists of from two to eight characters, the first of which must be a period.
• The second character must be a letter, and the remaining characters, if any, must be letters or digits.

Sequence symbols are used in statement name fields and are the only names that can be used in the operand fields of the conditional-assembly branch instructions.

The AIF instruction is the conditional-assembly, conditional-branch instruction. This instruction has the following format:

> sequence symbol　AIF　(logical expression) sequence symbol

The identifying sequence symbol is optional. When the assembler processes this instruction, the logical expression in the operand field is evaluated. If the value of this expression is 1, a branch is taken to the statement named by the sequence symbol in the operand field. Otherwise, the statement immediately following the AIF instruction is processed by the assembler.

The AGO instruction is the conditional-assembly, unconditional-branch instruction. The format for this instruction is

> sequence symbol　AGO　sequence symbol

As in the case of the AIF instruction, the name field is optional. When the assembler processes this instruction, an unconditional branch is taken to the statement named by the sequence symbol in the operand field.

The ANOP instruction provides a means for branching to statements that have symbols or variable symbols in their name fields. This is a necessary facility, since the statements referenced in the operand fields of AIF and AGO statements must be named by sequence symbols. The format for this instruction is

> sequence symbol　ANOP

When a branch is taken to an ANOP instruction, the effect is the same as when the branch is taken to the statement immediately following the ANOP instruction.

It is important to remember that the AIF, AGO, and ANOP instructions cause no code to be generated. The sole function of these instructions is to conditionally alter the sequence in which the assembler processes source-program or macro-definition statements.

The following example illustrates the use of the AIF, AGO, and ANOP instructions and sequence symbols:

```
        MACRO
&LABEL  ROUND &WAY,&REG
.* THIS MACRO GENERATES THE CODE REQUIRED TO ROUND THE ADDRESS IN
.* THE REGISTER &REG TO A FULLWORD BOUNDARY.  THE VALUE IS ROUNDED
.* UP IF &WAY IS UP, AND DOWN IF &WAY IS DOWN.
        AIF     ('&WAY' EQ 'UP').UP
        AIF     ('&WAY' NE 'DOWN').END
&LABEL  N       &REG,=X'FFFFFFFC'
        AGO     .END
.UP     ANOP
&LABEL  LA      &REG,3(&REG)
        N       &REG,=X'FFFFFFFC'
.END    MEND
```

If this macro definition were referenced by the macro instruction

ALIGN   ROUND UP,2

the following code would be generated:

ALIGN   LA   2,3(2)
N   2, = X′FFFFFFFC′

In this case, the first AIF instruction in the macro definition causes a branch to the ANOP instruction with the sequence symbol .UP in its name field. Since the ANOP serves only to establish a branch point, the code corresponding to the two following model statements is then generated. Note that the AIF, AGO, and ANOP instructions cause no code to be generated, but simply determine the sequence in which the macro processor processes the statements in the macro definition. Also note the use of the sequence symbol .END as a name for the MEND statement.

The following alternative definition of the ROUND macro is less cumbersome than the previous one.

```
        MACRO
&LABEL  ROUND &WAY,&REG
.* THIS MACRO GENERATES THE CODE REQUIRED TO ROUND THE ADDRESS IN
.* THE REGISTER &REG TO A FULLWORD BOUNDARY.  THE VALUE IS ROUNDED
.* UP IF &WAY IS UP, AND DOWN IF &WAY IS DOWN.
&LABEL  DS    0H                    GENERATE A LABEL
        AIF   ('&WAY' EQ 'DOWN').AND
        AIF   ('&WAY' NE 'UP').END
        LA    &REG,3(&REG)
.AND    N     &REG,=X'FFFFFFFC'
.END    MEND
```

Parameters can be omitted in the operand field of a macro instruction, provided that the commas separating the parameters are appropriately placed to indicate which parameters have been omitted. Two adjacent commas in the operand field indicate the omission of a parameter in the interior of the list. A leading comma and a final comma indicate omission of a parameter at the beginning and end of a list, respectively. If a parameter is omitted, the corresponding symbolic parameter is assigned the null string as a value.

A symbolic parameter in a model statement of a macro definition can be immediately preceded or followed by other characters or another symbolic parameter. When this occurs, the other characters or those assigned to the other symbolic parameter are combined with the characters assigned to the symbolic parameter in question. Such a combining of characters is called *concatenation*. There is just one restriction: If a symbolic parameter is to be combined with a character string that begins with a letter, a left parenthesis, or a period, then a period must be inserted immediately following the symbolic parameter. A symbolic parameter followed by a period is simply replaced by the value assigned to the symbolic parameter. Hence, excessive use of periods in such cases can do no harm.

The following example should serve to illustrate some of the ideas in the preceding discussion:

```
          MACRO
&LABEL    BHLE    &REG1,&REG2,&HIGH,&LOW,&EQ
.* THIS MACRO MAY BE USED TO COMPARE THE VALUE IN &REG1 WITH THE
.* VALUE IN &REG2 AND EFFECT A BRANCH TO &HIGH, &LOW, OR &EQ
.* DEPENDING UPON THE VALUES IN THE REGISTERS.  ANY COMBINATION
.* OF THE PARAMETERS &HIGH, &LOW, AND &EQ MAY BE OMITTED.
&LABEL    CR      R&REG1,R&REG2
          AIF     ('&HIGH' EQ '').LOW
          BH      &HIGH
.LOW      AIF     ('&LOW' EQ '').EQ
          BL      &LOW
.EQ       AIF     ('&EQ' EQ '').END
          BE      &EQ
.END      MEND
```

If the macro BHLE is referenced by the macro instruction

      COMPARE   BHLE   3,4,,LOWVAL,EQVAL

the following code is generated:

      COMPARE   CR   R3,R4
                     BL   LOWVAL
                     BE   EQVAL

Note that the R&REG1 in the operand field of the CR instruction has been replaced by R3. This is an example of concatenation. Note also that, in the first AIF instruction, &HIGH has been compared to the null string (indicated by adjacent apostrophes) and, since the parameter corresponding to &HIGH was omitted, the branch to .LOW was taken.

The reader should by now be quite familiar with symbolic parameters and the way that values are assigned to this type of variable symbol. Here a second type of variable symbol, the system variable symbol, will be introduced. System variable symbols are automatically assigned values by the assembler. In this section, only &SYSNDX will be covered.

The system variable symbol &SYSNDX provides the means for creating unique names for any number of statements that can be generated from the same model statement. This is accomplished by concatenating &SYSNDX with other characters in the name field of a model statement. Then, when the macro in which the model statement appears is invoked, these characters and the value assigned by the system to &SYSNDX become the label of the statement generated from that model statement.

The value assigned to &SYSNDX by the system is a four-digit number. When the first macro instruction in a program is encountered, &SYSNDX is assigned a value of 0001. Then, as each subsequent macro instruction is encountered, the value of &SYSNDX is incremented by 1.

The following example illustrates how &SYSNDX can be used:

```
          MACRO
&LABEL    INVOKE &NAME
.* THE INVOKE MACRO CAN BE USED TO GENERATE A CALL TO THE MODULE
.* DESIGNATED BY THE SINGLE PARAMETER.  BOTH REGISTER 14 AND
.* REGISTER 15 ARE AUTOMATICALLY RESTORED TO THEIR ORIGINAL VALUES
.* AFTER THE CALL.
&LABEL    STM    R14,R15,IN&SYSNDX
          L      R15,=V(&NAME)
          BALR   R14,R15
          LM     R14,R15,IN&SYSNDX
          B      LV&SYSNDX
IN&SYSNDX DS     2F
LV&SYSNDX DS     0H
          MEND
```

If the macro INVOKE were referenced somewhere in the program by the macro instruction

INVOKE   READ

and if this were the twenty-third macro instruction to be processed, the following code would be generated:

	STM	R14,R15,IN0023
	L	R15, = V(READ)
	BALR	R14,R15
	LM	R14,R15,IN0023
	B	LV0023
IN0023	DS	2F
LV0023	DS	0H

It is important to note that no other macro instruction in the program that references the macro INVOKE would cause the same labels to be generated.

The assembler listing in Program 9-3 illustrates the use of a macro called ARRIVE.

Exercises

1. It is occasionally necessary to move more than 256 bytes of data from one field to another. Commonly, the length of the move cannot be determined until execution time. With an IBM 370, you can simply use the MVCL instruction to perform the required operation. No such instruction exists on an IBM 360, however. Code a macro BIGMVC that can be invoked to execute long moves on an IBM 360. The first two operands of BIGMVC should specify

Program 9-3

```
LOC   OBJECT CODE   ADDR1 ADDR2   STMT   SOURCE STATEMENT

                                   1     &LABEL  MACRO
                                   2     &LABEL  EXIT
                                   3     .*
                                   4     .* THIS MACRO GENERATES THE CODE REQUIRED TO RETURN FROM A MODULE.
                                   5     .* IT ASSUMES NORMAL OS LINKAGE CONVENTIONS.
                                   6     .*
                                   7     .* NOTE THAT THIS MACRO GENERATES THE CODE TO EXIT FROM A MODULE
                                   8     .* WHICH HAS ESTABLISHED A SAVE AREA FOR CALLS TO LOWER LEVEL MODULES.
                                   9     .* IT SHOULD NOT BE USED TO EXIT FROM A LOWEST LEVEL SUBROUTINE.
                                  10     &LABEL  L     R13,4(R13)        LOAD ADDRESS OF CALLER'S SAVE AREA
                                  11             LM    R14,R12,12(R13)   RESTORE CALLER'S REGISTERS
                                  12             BR    R14
                                  13             MEND
                                  14             MACRO
                                  15     &LABEL  INVOKE &NAME
                                  16     .*
                                  17     .* THIS MACRO CAN BE USED TO INVOKE AN EXTERNAL ROUTINE. THE NAME
                                  18     .* OF THE ROUTINE TO BE CALLED SHOULD BE GIVEN AS THE FIRST OPERAND.
                                  19     .*
                                  20     &LABEL  L     R15,=V(&NAME)     LOAD ADDRESS OF ROUTINE TO CALL
                                  21             BALR  R14,R15           CALL THE ROUTINE
                                  22             MEND
                                  23             MACRO
                                  24     &NAME   ARRIVE &BR
                                  25     .*
                                  26     .* THIS MACRO CAN BE INVOKED TO ESTABLISH A CSECT, SET
                                  27     .* UP A SAVE AREA, AND INITIALIZE A BASE REGISTER. THE
                                  28     .* SINGLE OPERAND SPECIFIES THE BASE REGISTER.
                                  29     .* THE REGISTER NUMBER MUST BE SPECIFIED AS A NUMERIC VALUE; FOR
                                  30     .* EXAMPLE BR12 SHOULD BE SPECIFIED AS 12.
                                  31     .*
                                  32     &NAME   CSECT
                                  33             STM   R14,R12,12(R13)   SAVE CALLER'S REGISTERS
                                  34             AIF   (&BR EQ 13).BASE13 BRANCH IF R13 IS TO BE THE BASE
                                  35             BALR  R&BR,0            SET UP THE BASE REGISTER
                                  36             USING *,R&BR
                                  37             LA    R14,SAVE&SYSNDX   R14 <- ADDRESS OF THE SAVE AREA
                                  38             B     ST&SYSNDX         BRANCH AROUND THE SAVE AREA
                                  39             AGO   .NOT13
                                  40     .BASE13 BAL   R14,80(R15)       R14 <- ADDRESS OF THE SAVE AREA
                                  41     .NOT13  ANOP
                                  42     SAVE&SYSNDX DS 18F              REGISTER SAVE AREA
                                  43             SPACE
                                  44     ST&SYSNDX ST R13,4(R14)        SET BACK LINK IN THE SAVE AREA
                                  45             ST    R14,8(R13)        SET THE FORWARD POINTER
                                  46             LR    R13,R14           R13 IS THE BASE
                                  47             AIF   (&BR NE 13).END
                                  48             USING SAVE&SYSNDX,R13
                                  49     .END    MEND
```

Program 9-3 (continued)

```
LOC    OBJECT CODE         ADDR1 ADDR2  STMT   SOURCE STATEMENT

                                        51  *  THIS SIMPLE PROGRAM ILLUSTRATES THE USE OF MACROS.  IT SIMPLY

                                        52  *  CALLS A SUBROUTINE TO SORT A TABLE.  TWO MACROS ARE USED,
                                        53  *  ONE TO GENERATE THE CALL TO SORT AND ONE TO GENERATE THE
                                        54  *  INSTRUCTIONS TO CAUSE AN EXIT FROM THE PROGRAM.

000000                                  55  MAIN      ARRIVE 13
000000                                  56+ MAIN      CSECT
000000 90EC D00C              0000C     57+           STM  R14,R12,12(R13)      SAVE CALLER'S REGISTERS
000004 45EF 0050              00050     58+           BAL  R14,80(R15)          R14 <- ADDRESS OF THE SAVE AREA
000008                                  59+ SAVE0001  DS   18F                  REGISTER SAVE AREA

000050 50DE 0004              0004      61+ STO001    ST   R13,4(R14)           SET BACK LINK IN THE SAVE AREA
000054 50ED 0008              0008      62+           ST   R14,8(R13)           SET THE FORWARD POINTER
000058 18DE                             63+           LR   R13,R14              R13 IS THE BASE
                                        64+           USING SAVE0001,R13
00005A 9823 D068              0070      65            LM   R2,R3,=A(TABLE,10)   LOAD PARAMETERS FOR CALL TO 'SORT'
                                        66            INVOKE SORT               CALL THE ROUTINE SORT
00005E 58F0 D070              0078      67+           L    R15,=V(SORT)         LOAD ADDRESS OF ROUTINE TO CALL
000062 05EF                             68+           BALR R14,R15              CALL THE ROUTINE
                                        69  LEAVE     EXIT
                                        70+ *  NOTE THAT THIS MACRO GENERATES THE CODE TO EXIT FROM A MODULE
                                        71+ *  WHICH HAS ESTABLISHED A SAVE AREA FOR CALLS TO LOWER LEVEL MODULES.
                                        72+ *  IT SHOULD NOT BE USED TO EXIT FROM A LOWEST LEVEL SUBROUTINE.
000064 58DD 0004              0004      73+ LEAVE     L    R13,4(R13)           LOAD ADDRESS OF CALLER'S SAVE AREA
000068 98EC D00C              0000C     74+           LM   R14,R12,12(R13)      RESTORE CALLER'S REGISTERS
00006C 07FE                             75+           BR   R14
                                        76            LTORG
000070 0000007C0000000A                 77                 =A(TABLE,10)
000078 00000000                         78                 =V(SORT)
00007C 00000004FFFFFFF6                 79  TABLE     DC   F'4,-10,9,43,32,-8,12,0,1,64'
0000A4                                  80  CARD      DS   CL80                 INPUT CARD AREA
                                        81  R2        EQU  2
                             00003      82  R3        EQU  3
                             0000C      83  R12       EQU  12
                             0000D      84  R13       EQU  13
                             0000E      85  R14       EQU  14
                             0000F      86  R15       EQU  15
                                        87            END
```

the addresses of the receiving and sending fields, respectively. The third operand should specify a register containing the number of bytes to be moved. For example,

```
MOVE      BIGMVC      FIELD1,FIELD2,R8
```

should generate something similar to

```
MOVE        STM      R14,R1,SAVR0023
            LR       R0,R8
            LA       R14,FIELD1
            LA       R15,FIELD2
            LA       R1,255
LP0023      CR       R0,R1
            BH       *+8
            LR       R1,R0
            BCTR     R1,0
            EX       R1,MOV0023
            LA       R14,1(R1,R14)
            LA       R15,1(R1,R15)
            SH       R0,=H'256'
            BP       LP0023
            LM       R14,R1,SAVR0023
            B        SAVR0023+16
MOV0023     MVC      0(0,R14),0(R15)
SAVR0023    DS       4F
```

2. In Section 4.7, routines were given to add, subtract, or compare two-word, fixed-point integers. Write the macros to generate the appropriate code. The prototype instructions should be as follows:

```
&LABEL    ADDL       &DWD1,&DWD2
&LABEL    SUBL       &DWD1,&DWD2
&LABEL    COMPL      &DWD1,&DWD2
```

Thus,

```
ADDL              NUM1,NUM2
```

should generate something similar to

```
STM      R0,R1,SAVR0004
LM       R0,R1,NUM1
AL       R1,NUM2+4
BC       B'1100',*+8
A        R0,=F'1'
A        R0,NUM2
STM      R0,R1,NUM1
```

```
            LM      R0,R1,SAVR0004
            B       SAVR0004+8
SAVR0004    DS      2F
```

3. In Exercise 1 following Section 8.11, you were asked to code an external subroutine that could be invoked to generate random numbers. Write a macro, RANGEN, that can be invoked to generate a call to the random number generator. The prototype statement of RANGEN should be

&NAME   RANGEN   &UPPER,&LOWER,&XVALUE

where &UPPER is the address of a one-word field containing the upper bound

&LOWER is the address of a one-word field containing the lower bound

&XVALUE is an optional parameter giving the address of a word that should be used to reset the XVALUE field

Thus,

RANGEN   UP,LOW.

should generate something similar to

```
            STM     R14,R15,SAVR0010
            L       R15,=V(RANDOM)
            LA      R1,PLST0010
            BALR    R14,R15
            LM      R14,R15,SAVR0010
            B       NXT0010
SAVR0010    DS      2F
PLST0010    DC      A(UP)
            DC      X'80'
            DC      AL3(LOW)
NXT0010     DS      0H
```

4. Write a macro called INCR that can be used to increment a fullword in memory. The prototype of INCR should be

&LABEL   INCR   &ADDR,&INCR

where &ADDR is the address of the word in storage

&INCR is a decimal number specifying the increment

The code generated by the macro might destroy the contents of R0.

9.3 ARITHMETIC SET SYMBOLS

SET symbols constitute the third type of variable symbols that can be used in macro definitions. SET symbols are classified as arithmetic, binary, or character, depending upon the nature of the values that can be assigned to them. As in the case of system variables, each SET symbol is assigned an initial value by the macro processor. However, unlike system variables or symbolic parameters, the values assigned to SET symbols can be altered during the expansion of a macro instruction.

SET symbols are of two types, *local* and *global*. A local SET symbol is assigned an initial value every time that a macro instruction references a macro definition containing an occurrence of that SET symbol. If several macro definitions contain occurrences of the same local SET symbol, these occurrences are treated as distinct SET symbols. Thus, if &VAR were a local SET symbol occurring in two separate macro definitions, it would be processed as if these occurrences had been given different names in the two macro definitions. On the other hand, global SET symbols are initialized just once— the first time that a macro definition containing an occurrence of the given symbol is invoked. Thus, the use of global SET symbols allows values to be passed between the different macro instructions occurring in a program. A detailed example of this technique will be presented later in this section. Only the arithmetic SET symbols will be discussed further in this section. Detailed discussions of the binary and character SET symbols are deferred to Sections 9.4 and 9.5, respectively.

The following instructions can be used to define and to alter the values of arithmetic SET symbols:

1. One or more statements of the form

> GBLA   symbol1,symbol2, . . .

must be used in a macro definition to declare all of the global arithmetic SET symbols occurring in that definition. This statement or statements should immediately follow the prototype statement in the macro definition. The first time that a macro definition containing an occurrence of a GBLA statement defining a given global arithmetic SET symbol is invoked, a value of 0 is assigned to that SET symbol. On any subsequent invocation of this macro definition (or other macro definitions containing an occurrence of a GBLA statement defining the SET symbol under discussion), the value last assigned to that SET symbol is unaltered.

2. One or more statements of the form

> LCLA   symbol1,symbol2, . . .

must be used in a macro definition to declare all of the local arithmetic SET symbols occurring in that definition. This statement or statements should immediately follow the declarations of global SET symbols, if any. If no global SET symbols are declared in the macro definition, then the statements declaring the local symbols must immediately follow the prototype statement. Every time that the macro processor processes an LCLA statement, the value of each local arithmetic symbol defined in that statement is initialized to 0.

3. Statements of the form

> symbol   SETA   arithmetic-expression

can be used to assign the value represented by arithmetic-expression to a global or local arithmetic SET symbol. Integer values in the range -2^{31} to $2^{31} - 1$ are allowable. For example, the statement

> &RANGE   SETA   (&VALUE*16)/X'A'

could be used to assign a value to the arithmetic SET symbol &RANGE. Because SETA statements are used to assign values to arithmetic SET symbols, these symbols themselves are sometimes called SETA symbols.

The following example illustrates how local SETA symbols can be used in a macro definition:

```
        MACRO
        EQUREGS
        LCLA  &REG
.*
.*  THIS MACRO CAN BE INVOKED TO GENERATE THE SIXTEEN REGISTER EQUATES
.*  REQUIRED TO REFERENCE REGISTERS AS R0, R1, R2, ...
.*
.LOOP   ANOP
R&REG   EQU   &REG
&REG    SETA  &REG+1
        AIF   (&REG LE 15).LOOP
        MEND
```

Since &REG has been declared to be a local SETA symbol, its value is initialized to 0 each time the macro EQUREGS is invoked. Therefore,

> R0   EQU   0

is, inevitably, the first statement generated in the expansion of this macro. The SETA statement causes &REG to be incremented by 1 each time the loop is executed, and a branch to .LOOP occurs in case all 16 EQUates have not been generated.

A somewhat more complex example is required to illustrate the use of global SETA symbols. The two macros COUNT and GENTAB in Program 9-4 provide the programmer with a convenient means of keeping a count of how many times any given section of code in a program is executed.

Program 9-4

```
        MACRO
&LABEL   COUNT  &ENTRY
         GBLA   &MAX
         LCLA   &DISP
.*
.* THIS MACRO CAN BE INVOKED TO ADD 1 TO THE ENTRY IN 'COUNTERS' GIVEN
.* BY THE ONLY OPERAND.  THE USES OF THE VARIABLE SYMBOLS ARE AS
.* FOLLOWS:
.*
.*       &ENTRY     GIVES THE NUMBER OF THE ENTRY IN THE TABLE.  THIS
.*                  ENTRY WILL BE INCREMENTED BY 1.  THE ENTRIES IN THE
.*                  TABLE ARE NUMBERED STARTING WITH 1.
.*
.*       &MAX       IS SET TO THE MAXIMUM ENTRY REFERENCED SO FAR BY A
.*                  COUNT MACRO.  IT WILL BE USED BY GENTAB TO
.*                  DETERMINE HOW MANY ENTRIES SHOULD BE IN 'COUNTERS'.
.*
.*       &DISP      IS SET TO THE DISPLACEMENT INTO 'COUNTERS' OF THE
.*                  REFERENCED 5-BYTE ENTRY.
.*
         AIF    (&MAX GE &ENTRY).GETDISP
.* NOW &MAX IS RESET, SINCE &ENTRY IS THE HIGHEST NUMBERED ENTRY
.* REFERENCED SO FAR.
&MAX       SETA &ENTRY
.GETDISP ANOP
.* &DISP IS NOW SET TO THE DISPLACEMENT INTO 'COUNTERS' REQUIRED TO
.* REFERENCE THE DESIGNATED ENTRY.
&DISP    SETA   (&ENTRY-1)*5
&LABEL   AP     COUNTERS+&DISP.(5),=P'1'  INCREMENT THE COUNTER
         MEND
         MACRO
         GENTAB
         GBLA   &MAX
.* THIS MACRO SIMPLY GENERATES A TABLE OF 5-BYTE PACKED DECIMAL
.* COUNTERS.  THE NAME OF THE TABLE IS 'COUNTERS', AND IT WILL CONTAIN
.* &MAX ENTRIES.
COUNTERS DC     &MAX.PL5'0'         TABLE OF COUNTERS
         MEND
```

When these macros are included in a program, a macro instruction of the form

      name   COUNT n

will cause 1 to be added to the Nth counter in a table of counters each time it is executed; a macro instruction of the form

          GENTAB

causes a table called COUNTERS to be generated at the end of the program along with the constants. The following sequence of code illustrates the use of these macros:

```
      LOOP      .
                .
                .

                .
                BE        ROUT2
      ROUT1     COUNT     1
                .

                .

                .
                B         LOOP
      ROUT2     COUNT     2
                .

                .

                .
                B         LOOP
      END       XDUMP     COUNTERS,10
                .

                .

                .
                LTORG
                GENTAB
                END
```

A careful study of the macros will indicate that, if the preceding sequence of code were executed, the XDUMP instruction would display the table COUNTERS in such a way that (1) the first entry would indicate the number of times that ROUT1 was executed and (2) the second entry would indicate the number of times that ROUT2 was executed.

Note how the global SETA symbol is used to pass a value from the COUNT macro instructions to the GENTAB macro. For the variable &MAX to be set properly to the number of entries required in the table COUNTERS, the occurrence of the GENTAB macro instruction in a program must follow all occurrences of macro instructions invoking the COUNT macro.

Program 9-5 presents a simple program, along with the output produced, as an illustration of exactly what code is produced by the COUNT and GENTAB macros.

Although it may not be readily apparent to the reader, the COUNT and GENTAB macros can be quite useful. For example, in complex routines that must be coded as efficiently as possible, these macros could be used to determine which sections of code are executed most frequently. The information thus obtained could then be utilized in deciding which constants should be kept in registers. The capacity to make such decisions correctly can sometimes radically reduce the execution time required by a complex routine.

Program 9-5

BALANCE-AN ILLUSTRATION OF THE COUNT AND GENTAB MACRUS

LOC	OBJECT CODE	ADDR1	ADDR2	STMT	SOURCE STATEMENT
				52	* THIS SIMPLE PROGRAM ILLUSTRATES THE USE OF THE COUNT AND
				53	* GENTAB MACRUS. IT READS CARDS REPRESENTING CHECKS AND DEPOSITS
				54	* AGAINST A BANK ACCOUNT AND CALCULATES THE RESULTING BALANCE.
				55	* IN THE CODE THE AMOUNT OF A DEPOSIT IS COMPLEMENTED AND THEN
				56	* PROCESSED IN THE SAME MANNER AS THAT OF A CHECK. IF THERE
				57	* WERE ACTUALLY MORE DEPOSITS THAN CHECKS, IT WOULD BE FASTER
				58	* TO COMPLEMENT THE CHECKS. TO TEST WHICH ACTUALLY OCCURS
				59	* MORE, TWO COUNT MACRO INSTRUCTIONS ARE USED.
				60	*
				61	*
000000				62	BALANCE CSECT
				63	*
				64	* <STEP 1> SAVE REGISTERS AND ESTABLISH THE BASE REGISTER
000000	90EC D00C			65	STM R14,R12,12(R13) SAVE ORIGINAL CONTENTS OF REGISTERS
000004	18CF			66	LR R12,R15 R12 WILL BE THE BASE REGISTER
000000				67	USING BALANCE,R12
				68	EQUREGS
000000				69	R0 EQU 0
000001				70	R1 EQU 1
000002				71	R2 EQU 2
000003				72	R3 EQU 3
000004				73	R4 EQU 4
000005				74	R5 EQU 5
000006				75	R6 EQU 6
000007				76	R7 EQU 7
000008				77	R8 EQU 8
000009				78	R9 EQU 9
00000A				79	R10 EQU 10
00000B				80	R11 EQU 11
00000C				81	R12 EQU 12
00000D				82	R13 EQU 13
00000E				83	R14 EQU 14
00000F				84	R15 EQU 15
				85	*
				86	* <STEP 2> ZERO THE ACCUMULATOR
				87	*
				88	*
				89	* <STEP 3> READ IN A CARD. ON EOF GO TO STEP 6.
				90	*
0C0006	1B22			91	LOOP SR R2,R2 R2 ACCUMULATES THE BALANCE
0C0008	E000 C053 0050	00053	00032	92	XREAD CARD,80 READ A CHECK OR DEPOSIT CARD
00000E	4740 C032	00032		93	BC B'0100',EOF BRANCH ON END-OF-FILE
				94	*
000012	5330 C054	00054		95	XDECI R3,CARD+1 GET THE AMOUNT
				96	*
				97	* <STEP 4> IF IT'S A DEPOSIT, COMPLEMENT THE AMOUNT.
				98	*
				99	*
000016	95C3 C053	00053		100	CLI CARD,C'C' C => A CHECK; ELSE, IT'S A DEPOSIT
				101	*
				102	* THE NEXT FEW INSTRUCTIONS CAUSE THE AMOUNT TO BE COMPLEMENTED
				103	* IF THE CARD REPRESENTED A DEPOSIT. THIS IS MORE EFFICIENT
				104	* THAN COMPLEMENTING THE CHECKS, ASSUMING THAT MORE CHECKS ARE
				105	* PROCESSED THAN DEPOSITS. THIS ASSUMPTION CAN BE TESTED WITH
				106	* THE COUNT MACRO. IF THE 1ST COUNTER IS MORE THAN HALF OF THE

Program 9-5 (continued)

```
BALANCE-AN ILLUSTRATION OF THE COUNT AND GENTAB MACROS

LOC  OBJECT CODE    ADDR1 ADDR2  STMT  SOURCE STATEMENT
                                  107 * SECOND, THEN THE CODE IS INEFFICIENT.
                                  108 *
00001A 4780 C026           00026  109        BE    DONTCOMP    BRANCH IF IT WAS A CHECK
00001E 1333                       110        LCR   R3,R3       COMPLEMENT A DEPOSIT
                                  111 *
                                  112        COUNT 1
0C0020 FA40 C049 C048 00049 00048 113+       AP    COUNTERS+0(5),=P'1'    INCREMENT THE COUNTER
                                  114+*
                                  115 *
                                  116 ***<STEP 5>  SUBTRACT THE AMOUNT FROM THE ACCUMULATOR AND GO BACK.
                                  117 *
0C0026 FA40 C04E C048 0004E 00048 118  DONTCOMP COUNT 2
                                  119+DONTCOMP AP   COUNTERS+5(5),=P'1'   INCREMENT THE COUNTER
                                  120 *
0C002C 1B23                       121        SR    R2,R3       ACCUMULATE THE BALANCE
0C002E 47F0 C008           00008  122        B     LOOP
                                  123 *
                                  124 ***<STEP 6>  PRINT THE FINAL ANSWER AND EXIT.
000032 5220 C0AB           000AB  125  EOF   XDECO R2,OUTVAL   PRINT THE BALANCE
000036 E020 C0A3 0014 000A3       126        XPRNT ANSWER,20
                                  127 *
0C003C E060 C049 0008 00049       128        XDUMP COUNTERS,8
                                  129 *
000042 98EC D00C           0000C  130        LM    R14,R12,12(R13)  RESTORE ORIGINAL CONTENTS OF THE REGS
000046 07FE                       131        BR    R14         EXIT
                                  132 *
                                  133 *
000048 1C                         134        LTORG
                                  135        =P'1'
                                  136 *
000049 000000000C000000           137  GENTAB
                                  138+COUNTERS DC   2PL5'0'     TABLE OF COUNTERS
                                  139 *
0C0053 F0                         140  CARD  DS    CL80        READ CARDS INTO HERE
0C00A3 F0                         141  ANSWER DC   C'0'         CARRIAGE CONTROL
0000A4 C1D5E2E6C5D97E             142        DC    C'ANSWER='   BALANCE IS PUT HERE
0000AB                            143  OUTVAL DS   CL12
                                  144        END   BALANCE

*** NO STATEMENTS FLAGGED - NO WARNINGS, NO ERRORS

*** DYNAMIC CORE AREA USED: LOW: 5884 HIGH: 624 LEAVING: 59028 FREE BYTES. AVERAGE: 44 BYTES/STMT ***

*** ASSEMBLY TIME =  0.676 SECS,  214 STATEMENTS/SEC ***

*** PROGRAM EXECUTION BEGINNING - ANY OUTPUT BEFORE EXECUTION TIME MESSAGE IS PRODUCED BY USER PROGRAM ***

ANSWER=   3306

BEGIN XSNAP - CALL  1 AT D0000042 USER STORAGE

                         CORE ADDRESSES SPECIFIED-      000049 TO 000051
000040  00089BEC DD0C07FE 1C00000O 00200000  0000BCC3 F2F4F040 40404040 40404040   *....................C240   *
```

9.4 BINARY SET SYMBOLS

The binary SET symbols are SET symbols that can be assigned a value of only 0 or 1. The statements used to define binary SET symbols and to assign values to these symbols are as follows:

1. A statement or statements of the form

   GBLB   symbol1,symbol2, . . .

   must be used in a macro definition to declare all of the global binary SET symbols that occur in that definition. Although the order within the sequence of statements declaring global SET symbols in a macro definition is not critical, the sequence of all such statements should immediately follow the prototype statement. As in the case of the global SETA symbols, a global binary SET symbol is initialized to a value of 0 just once—the first time a macro definition containing a GBLB statement that contains an occurrence of that particular symbol is invoked.

2. A statement or statements of the form

   LCLB   symbol1,symbol2, . . .

   must be used to declare all of the local binary SET symbols occurring in a macro definition.

3. Statements of the form

   symbol   SETB   logical-expression

   can be used to alter the values assigned to binary SET symbols. Here, logical-expression includes the class of logical expressions defined in Section 9.2; in addition, a binary SET symbol enclosed within parentheses is also considered to be a logical expression. Thus, the two statements

   &BSYM   SETB   ('&WAY' EQ 'DOWN')

   and

   &BSYM   SETB   (&SYM2)

   are both valid if it is assumed that &SYM2 is a binary SET symbol. Just as the arithmetic SET symbols are sometimes referred to as SETA symbols, the binary SET symbols are often referred to as SETB symbols.

The expanded class of logical expressions introduced in item 3 above can also be used in conjunction with AIF statements. For example, the statement

AIF   (&BSYM).SEQSYM

causes a branch to .SEQSYM only when &BSYM has an assigned value of 1.

Global SETB symbols are used far more frequently than local SETB symbols, and in the vast majority of cases these symbols perform a similar function. To illustrate the function for which these symbols are most commonly used, we shall reconsider the macro EQUREGS introduced in the last section. Suppose that a subroutine containing a macro instruction to invoke EQUREGS has been coded. Then, if a calling routine that also contains a macro instruction to invoke EQUREGS is assembled along with this subroutine, two occurrences of the sequence of instructions

```
R0        EQU      0
R1        EQU      1
          .
          .
          .
R15       EQU      15
```

would be generated. Suppose also that there are occasions when it would be desirable to assemble the subroutine by itself. Then, if the macro instruction to invoke EQUREGS were removed from the subroutine, errors would occur. The following version of EQUREGS could be used to overcome this difficulty:

```
          MACRO
          EQUREGS
          GBLB   &EQUREGS
          LCLA   &REG
.*
.* THIS MACRO CAN BE INVOKED TO GENERATE THE SIXTEEN REGISTER EQUATES
.* REQUIRED TO REFERENCE REGISTERS AS R0, R1, R2, ...
.*
.* IF MORE THAN 1 EQUREGS OCCUR IN THE SAME PROGRAM,
.* THERE WILL STILL BE ONLY 1 SET OF EQUATES GENERATED
.* (&EQUREGS=1 -> ONE SET OF EQUATES HAS BEEN
.* GENERATED).
.*
          AIF    (&EQUREGS).END
&EQUREGS  SETB   1
.LOOP     ANOP
R&REG     EQU    &REG
&REG      SETA   &REG+1
          AIF    (&REG LE 15).LOOP
.END      MEND
```

Program 9-6 illustrates the implementation of a similar technique to increase the flexibility of the COUNT and GENTAB macros introduced in Section 9.3.

Program 9-6

```
          MACRO
&LABEL    COUNT   &ENTRY
          GBLA    &MAX
          GBLB    &COUNT
          LCLA    &DISP
.*
.* THIS MACRO CAN BE INVOKED TO ADD 1 TO THE ENTRY IN 'COUNTERS' GIVEN
.* BY THE ONLY OPERAND.  THE USES OF THE VARIABLE SYMBOLS ARE AS
.* FOLLOWS:
.*
.*        &ENTRY      GIVES THE NUMBER OF THE ENTRY IN THE TABLE.  THIS
.*                    ENTRY WILL BE INCREMENTED BY 1.  THE ENTRIES IN THE
.*                    TABLE ARE NUMBERED STARTING WITH 1.
.*
.*        &MAX        IS SET TO THE MAXIMUM ENTRY REFERENCED SO FAR BY A
.*                    COUNT MACRO.  IT WILL BE USED BY GENTAB TO
.*                    DETERMINE HOW MANY ENTRIES SHOULD BE IN 'COUNTERS'.
.*
.*        &DISP       IS SET TO THE DISPLACEMENT INTO 'COUNTERS' OF THE
.*                    REFERENCED 5-BYTE ENTRY.
.*
.*        &COUNT      CAN BE SET TO 1 TO SUPPRESS GENERATION
.*                    OF ANYTHING BUT A LABEL.
.*                    THE SETTING OF &COUNT CAN BE ALTERED WITH
.*                    THE SETCNT MACRO.
.*
          AIF     (&MAX GE &ENTRY).GETDISP
.* NOW &MAX IS RESET, SINCE &ENTRY IS THE HIGHEST NUMBERED ENTRY
.* REFERENCED SO FAR.
&MAX      SETA    &ENTRY
.GETDISP  ANOP
.* &DISP IS NOW SET TO THE DISPLACEMENT INTO 'COUNTERS' REQUIRED TO
.* REFERENCE THE DESIGNATED ENTRY.
&DISP     SETA    (&ENTRY-1)*5
&LABEL    DS      0H   GENERATE THE LABEL
          AIF     (&COUNT).END
          AP      COUNTERS+&DISP.(5),=P'1'   INCREMENT THE COUNTER
.END      MEND
          MACRO
          GENTAB
          GBLA    &MAX
          GBLB    &COUNT
.* THIS MACRO SIMPLY GENERATES A TABLE OF 5-BYTE PACKED DECIMAL
.* COUNTERS.  THE NAME OF THE TABLE IS 'COUNTERS', AND IT WILL CONTAIN
.* &MAX ENTRIES.  IF &COUNT HAS BEEN SET TO 1, GENERATION
.* OF THE TABLE WILL BE SUPPRESSED.
          AIF     (&COUNT).END
COUNTERS  DC      &MAX.PL5'0'           TABLE OF COUNTERS
.END      MEND
```

In this case, the code necessary to define the table and to increment the counters is generated only when &COUNT has a value of 0. This would allow the counting facility to be turned on or off in a program without the necessity of adding or removing a large number of statements. The following macro SETCNT could, in fact, be used to set the variable &COUNT:

```
          MACRO
          SETCNT  &ONOFF
          GBLB    &COUNT
.*
.* THIS MACRO CAN BE USED TO CONTROL THE GENERATION OF CODE BY THE
.* COUNT AND GENTAB MACROS BY ALTERING THE SETTING OF &COUNT.
.*
.*    &ONOFF = ON MEANS THAT &COUNT WILL BE SET TO 0.
.*
.*    &ONOFF = OFF MEANS THAT &COUNT WILL BE SET TO 1.
.*
.*    &ONOFF = ANY OTHER VALUE WILL HAVE NO EFFECT.
.*
          AIF     ('&ONOFF' NE 'ON').TRYOFF
&COUNT    SETB    0
          AGO     .END
.TRYOFF   AIF     ('&ONOFF' NE 'OFF').END
&COUNT    SETB    1
.END      MEND
```

Thus, the macro instruction

         LOOP   COUNT 4

will cause the instructions

         LOOP   DS   0H
                    AP   COUNTERS + 15(5), = P′1′

to be generated if &COUNT has a value of 0. However, only the instruction

         LOOP   DS   0H

is generated if the macro instruction

                    SETCNT OFF

is inserted at the start of the program.

9.5 CHARACTER SET SYMBOLS

Character SET symbols are SET symbols that can be assigned character strings of from zero to eight characters in length as values. Because the way in which the GBLC and LCLC statements function is so similar to the way in which the global and local declaration statements discussed in Sections 9.3 and 9.4 function, no detailed discussion of these statements should be necessary. It must be noted, however, that the values of character SET symbols are initialized to the null string—rather than to 0, as is the case with arithmetic and binary SET symbols. On the other hand, an understanding of how the SETC statement can be used requires some knowledge of what constitutes a character expression.

A character expression can be formed by enclosing within apostrophes any of the following:

- a character string
- a variable symbol immediately followed by a period
- a concatenation of the preceding two

The character string to which a character expression of this form evaluates is determined by replacing each variable symbol in the expression, along with its associated period, with the value assigned to that variable symbol and removing the enclosing apostrophes. For example, if &SYM1 has an assigned value of AB% and &SYM2 has an assigned value of REG, the character expression

$$\text{'AZ.\&SYM1.C\&SYM2.'}$$

evaluates to the character string

$$\text{AZ.AB\%CREG}$$

A substring of a character expression can be specified by placing two arithmetic expressions, separated by a comma and enclosed within parentheses, immediately following the character expression. The substring thus specified can be determined by the following method:

1. Evaluate the character expression and the two arithmetic expressions.
2. The result of evaluating the first arithmetic expression indicates which character in the character string is the first character of the substring.
3. The result of evaluating the second arithmetic expression specifies the length of the substring.

Thus, the substring specification

$$\text{'ABCDEF'(2,2)}$$

evaluates to BC. Similarly, if &VAR has an assigned value of 2 and &STR has an assigned value of ABCD, then the substring specification

$$\text{'\&STR.\%'(2,\&VAR*2)}$$

will evaluate to BCD%.

A substring specification is a character expression, and more complex character expressions may be formed from sequences of character expressions by separating the individual expressions in the sequences by periods. For example, the character expression

$$\text{'AB'.'CD'.'EFG'(1,2).'G'}$$

evaluates to ABCDEFG.

The SETC instruction has the format

      symbol   SETC   character-expression

The value assigned to the SETC symbol is determined by evaluating the character expression. If the result of this evaluation is a string of more than eight characters in length, only the leftmost eight characters are assigned as a value to the SETC symbol.

Before the next macro example is presented, one more detail must be considered. Each macro instruction operand has certain attributes associated with it. One of these attributes, the *count attribute*, is the number of symbols in the operand. This attribute can be referenced by

$$K'\&sym$$

where &sym is the symbolic parameter corresponding to the appropriate operand. For example, the prototype statement of the macro presented in Program 9-7 is

&LABEL GET# &FIELD

If the macro instruction

GET# F1(4)

were issued, K'&FIELD would be assigned a value of 5, since there are five symbols in F1(4). The count attribute of a symbolic parameter can be used in the composition of arithmetic expressions.

The following macro, GET#, can be used to generate a call to the GET-NUM subroutine presented in Section 8.8. In this case, a two-word parameter list must be generated by the macro. The information from which the list is generated is extracted from the single operand of the GET# macro. For example, if the macro instruction

GET# F1(4)

were coded, the parameter list generated for the call to GETNUM would be

DC A(F1,*+4)
   A(4)

The definition of GET# is as shown in Program 9-7.

9.6 THE MNOTE AND MEXIT INSTRUCTIONS

The two instructions introduced in this section, MNOTE and MEXIT, can be used only in macro definitions.

The MNOTE instruction is used to generate an error message in an assembler listing. It is normally good practice to utilize this statement wherever error checks are made in macro definitions. The most common format for the MNOTE instruction is

Program 9-7

```
        MACRO
&LABEL  GET#    &FIELD
        LCLC    &ADDR,&LEN,&SUF
        LCLA    &SCANNER
.*
.* THIS MACRO CAN BE USED TO GENERATE A CALL TO 'GETNUM', THE MODULE
.* PRESENTED IN CHAPTER 8.  THE PARAMETER LIST FOR 'GETNUM' IS AS
.* FOLLOWS:
.*
.*      ADDRESS OF A FIELD CONTAINING A NUMBER
.*      ADDRESS OF A WORD CONTAINING THE LENGTH OF THE FIELD
.*
.* THE MEANINGS OF THE VARIABLE SYMBOLS USED BY GET# ARE:
.*
.*      &FIELD      SHOULD BE THE LABEL OF A FIELD IMMEDIATELY
.*                  FOLLOWED BY THE LENGTH IN PARENTHESES.  FOR
.*                  EXAMPLE, F1(7) WOULD SPECIFIY THAT THE NUMBER
.*                  IS IN F1, WHICH IS A 7-BYTE FIELD.
.*
.*      &ADDR       IS SET TO THE SUBSTRING OF &FIELD THAT CONTAINS
.*                  THE NAME OF THE FIELD
.*
.*      &LEN        IS SET TO THE LENGTH OF THE FIELD
.*
.*      &SUF        IS SET TO THE VALUE OF &SYSNDX.  THIS ALLOWS
.*                  THE PROGRAMMER TO AVOID THE USE OF NAMES SUCH
.*                  AS TABL&SYSNDX, WHICH IS OVER 8 CHARACTERS LONG
.*
.*      &SCANNER    IS USED TO INDEX THE CHARACTER IN &FIELD THAT
.*                  IS CURRENTLY BEING SCANNED
.*
.* BRANCH TO .END IF &FIELD WAS ASSIGNED TOO FEW CHARACTERS
        AIF     (K'&FIELD LT 4).END
.* START SCANNING THE CHARACTERS IN &FIELD, STARTING WITH THE 2ND
&SCANNER SETA   2
.* THE FOLLOWING LOOP SCANS FOR THE LEFT PARENTHESIS IN &FIELD
.TESTL  AIF     ('&FIELD'(&SCANNER,1) EQ '(').GOTLEFT
        AIF     (&SCANNER EQ K'&FIELD-1).END
.* THE PRECEDING BRANCH IS TAKEN ONLY IF &FIELD IS INVALID
&SCANNER SETA   &SCANNER+1
        AGO     .TESTL
.GOTLEFT ANOP
&ADDR   SETC    '&FIELD'(1,&SCANNER-1)
        AIF     ('&FIELD'(K'&FIELD,1) NE ')').END
.* THE PRECEDING BRANCH IS TAKEN ONLY IF THE RIGHT PARAN IS MISSING
&LEN    SETC    '&FIELD'(&SCANNER+1,K'&FIELD-&SCANNER-1)
&SUF    SETC    '&SYSNDX'
&LABEL  ST      R14,SAVE&SUF
        LA      R1,PLST&SUF
        L       R15,=V(GETNUM)
        BALR    R14,R15
        L       R14,SAVE&SUF        RESTORE R14 (ONLY R0, R1, AND
*                                   R15 ARE ALTERED)
        B       SAVE&SUF.+4
PLST&SUF DC     A(&ADDR.,*+4)
        DC      A(&LEN.)            THIS WORD CONTAINS THE LENGTH
SAVE&SUF DS     F                   R14 IS SAVED HERE
.END    MEND
```

MNOTE   'error message'

Execution of this instruction will cause the error message to be displayed in the assembler listing.

Optionally, the user can assign a severity code to the error through use of the format

MNOTE   code,'error message'

The severity code, which will in this case be printed along with the error message, can be given an integer value in the range 0 to 255. If this code is omitted, a severity code of 1 is assigned by the assembler.

The MEXIT instruction can be used to terminate the processing of a macro definition. As an illustration, the sequence of code

```
        MACRO
          .
          .
          .
        MNOTE    '***MISSING OPERAND***'
        MEXIT
```

could be used rather than the sequence

```
        MACRO
          .
          .
          .
        MNOTE    '***MISSING OPERAND***'
        AGO     .END
          .
          .
          .
.END    MEND
```

Here the advantage is that, in the first sequence of code, an exit is made from the macro instruction immediately upon encountering the MEXIT instruction. In the second case, the assembler, having encountered the AGO instruction, must scan ahead for an instruction with a label .END. A significant time savings can be effected through the judicious use of MEXIT statements.

A rewritten version of the GET# macro is presented in Program 9-8 as an illustration of how the MEXIT and MNOTE instructions should be used.

Program 9-8

```
        MACRO
&LABEL  GET#   &FIELD
        LCLC   &ADDR,&LEN,&SUF
        LCLA   &SCANNER
.*
.* THIS MACRO CAN BE USED TO GENERATE A CALL TO 'GETNUM', THE MODULE
.* PRESENTED IN CHAPTER 8.  THE PARAMETER LIST FOR 'GETNUM' IS AS
.* FOLLOWS:
.*
.*        ADDRESS OF A FIELD CONTAINING A NUMBER
.*        ADDRESS OF A WORD CONTAINING THE LENGTH OF THE FIELD
.*
.* THE MEANINGS OF THE VARIABLE SYMBOLS USED BY GET# ARE:
.*
.*        &FIELD    SHOULD BE THE LABEL OF A FIELD IMMEDIATELY
.*                  FOLLOWED BY THE LENGTH IN PARENTHESES.  FOR
.*                  EXAMPLE, F1(7) WOULD SPECIFIY THAT THE NUMBER
.*                  IS IN F1, WHICH IS A 7-BYTE FIELD.
.*
.*        &ADDR     IS SET TO THE SUBSTRING OF &FIELD THAT CONTAINS
.*                  THE NAME OF THE FIELD
.*
.*        &LEN      IS SET TO THE LENGTH OF THE FIELD
.*
.*        &SUF      IS SET TO THE VALUE OF &SYSNDX.  THIS ALLOWS
.*                  THE PROGRAMMER TO AVOID THE USE OF NAMES SUCH
.*                  AS TABL&SYSNDX, WHICH IS OVER 8 CHARACTERS LONG
.*
.*        &SCANNER  IS USED TO INDEX THE CHARACTER IN &FIELD THAT
.*                  IS CURRENTLY BEING SCANNED
.*
.* BRANCH TO .END IF &FIELD WAS ASSIGNED TOO FEW CHARACTERS
        AIF    (K'&FIELD LT 4).END
.* START SCANNING THE CHARACTERS IN &FIELD, STARTING WITH THE 2ND
&SCANNER SETA  2
.* THE FOLLOWING LOOP SCANS FOR THE LEFT PARENTHESIS IN &FIELD
.TESTL  AIF    ('&FIELD'(&SCANNER,1) EQ '(').GOTLEFT
        AIF    (&SCANNER NE K'&FIELD-1).TRYNXT
.* AT THIS POINT AN ERROR HAS BEEN DETECTED; THERE WAS NO LEFT PAREN.
        MNOTE  '*** MISSING LEFT PARENTHESIS ***'
        MEXIT
.TRYNXT ANOP
&SCANNER SETA  &SCANNER+1
        AGO    .TESTL
.GOTLEFT ANOP
&ADDR   SETC   '&FIELD'(1,&SCANNER-1)
        AIF    ('&FIELD'(K'&FIELD,1) EQ ')').GOTRGHT
.* AT THIS POINT AN ERROR HAS BEEN DETECTED; THE LAST CHARACTER
.* IS NOT A RIGHT PARENTHESIS.
        MNOTE  '*** MISSING RIGHT PARENTHESIS ***'
        MEXIT
```

Program 9-8 (continued)

```
.GOTRGHT ANOP
.* THE PRECEDING BRANCH IS TAKEN ONLY IF THE RIGHT PARAN IS MISSING
&LEN     SETC  '&FIELD'(&SCANNER+1,K'&FIELD-&SCANNER-1)
&SUF     SETC  '&SYSNDX'
&LABEL   ST    R14,SAVE&SUF
         LA    R1,PLST&SUF
         L     R15,=V(GETNUM)
         BALR  R14,R15
         L     R14,SAVE&SUF     RESTORE R14 (ONLY RO, R1, AND
*                               R15 ARE ALTERED)
         B     SAVE&SUF.+4
PLST&SUF DC    A(&ADDR.,*+4)
         DC    A(&LEN.)         THIS WORD CONTAINS THE LENGTH
SAVE&SUF DS    F                R14 IS SAVED HERE
.END     MEND
```

9.7 OPERAND SUBLISTS

Any single operand in a macro instruction can itself contain a list of operands. To achieve this, the list of operands must be written in the form of a sublist; that is, the elements in the list must be separated by commas and enclosed within parentheses. For example,

INVOKE SORT,(TABLE,20),2

is a macro instruction with three operands. The second operand is a sublist containing two elements. A discussion of the techniques used in processing operand sublists follows.

To motivate this discussion, the INVOKE macro introduced in Section 9.2 will be reconsidered. The version of INVOKE presented there can be used to generate a call to a subroutine. Now, consider the problem of recoding INVOKE in such a way that it could also be used to generate the parameter list to be passed to the subroutine that it invokes. There is no convenient general way to do this without utilizing sublists, because the number of parameters to be included in the parameter list varies with the module to be called.

However, if sublists are used, the prototype statement for INVOKE could be

&LABEL   INVOKE &NAME,&PARMS,&NUM

where &PARMS can be assigned any sublist of parameters as its value and &NUM can be assigned a numeric value indicating the number of parameters in this sublist.

To reference an individual element in a sublist, a subscript is used with the symbolic parameter that corresponds to the sublist. For example, the second element of the sublist assigned to &PARMS is referenced by

&PARMS(2)

Although the subscript can be represented by more complex arithmetic expressions, an integer or a variable symbol is normally used for this purpose.

The version of INVOKE in Program 9-9 can be used to generate both a parameter list and the code required to call any module that may be needed.

Program 9-9

```
          MACRO
&LABEL    INVOKE &NAME,&PARMS,&NUM
          LCLA   &ELEMENT
.*
.* THIS VERSION OF THE INVOKE MACRO WILL NOT ONLY GENERATE A CALL TO
.* THE DESIRED MODULE; IT WILL GENERATE THE PARAMETER LIST FOR THE CALL
.* AS WELL.  THE MEANINGS OF THE VARIABLE SYMBOLS ARE:
.*
.*        &NAME     IS THE NAME OF THE MODULE WHICH IS TO BE CALLED.
.*
.*        &PARMS    GIVES THE PARAMETERS TO BE PUT IN THE PARAMETER
.*                  LIST.  *** NOTE *** THIS IS A SUBLIST OPERAND.
.*
.*        &NUM      GIVES THE NUMBER OF ELEMENTS IN THE SUBLIST
.*                  ASSIGNED TO &PARMS.
.*
.*        &ELEMENT  INDEXES THE ELEMENTS IN &PARMS AS THE PARAMETER
.*                  LIST IS BEING GENERATED.
.*
&LABEL    STM    R14,R15,IN&SYSNDX   STORE ALTERED REGISTERS
          L      R15,=V(&NAME.)      LOAD ADDRESS OF MODULE TO CALL
          AIF    ('&PARMS' EQ '').NOPARM1
*** NOTE THAT THE VALUE IN R1 IS DESTROYED BY THE CALL
          LA     R1,PLST&SYSNDX
.NOPARM1  BALR   R14,R15             CALL THE MODULE
          LM     R14,R15,IN&SYSNDX   RESTORE ALTERED REGISTERS
          B      LV&SYSNDX           BRANCH PAST STORAGE AREAS
IN&SYSNDX DS     2F                  STORE R14 AND R15 HERE
          AIF    ('&PARMS' EQ '').NOPARM2
.* NOW GENERATE THE PARAMETER LIST
PLST&SYSNDX DS 0A                    PARAMETER LIST
.GENLOOP  ANOP
&ELEMENT  SETA   &ELEMENT+1
          DC     A(&PARMS(&ELEMENT).)
          AIF    (&ELEMENT LT &NUM).GENLOOP
.NOPARM2  ANOP
LV&SYSNDX DS     0H
          MEND
```

In Section 9.5, it was pointed out that the operands in macro instructions are assigned certain attributes and the count attribute was discussed. Another attribute, the *number attribute*, can be referenced to obtain the number of elements in an operand sublist. The number attribute is referenced by using

N'&operand

where &operand is the symbolic parameter corresponding to the operand sublist. Thus, if the macro instruction

INVOKE   SORT,(TABLE,20),2

were issued, N'&PARM would be assigned a value of 2. This eliminates the need for the third symbolic parameter in the prototype statement of INVOKE. That statement could be replaced by the statement

&LABEL   INVOKE &NAME,&PARMS

and the statement

AIF   (&ELEMENT LT &NUM).GENLOOP

could be replaced by the statement

AIF   (&ELEMENT LT N'&PARMS).GENLOOP

In most cases, it is much more convenient to access the number attribute of an operand than to burden the programmer with filling in an additional operand, a task that can only lead to unnecessary mistakes.

&SYSLIST is a system variable that, like &SYSNDX, will prove to be quite useful. When a macro definition is processed, &SYSLIST is treated as if it were a symbolic parameter corresponding to an operand sublist, the elements of which are all of the operands in the macro instruction that invoked the macro. Thus, &SYSLIST(1) would refer to the first operand in the macro instruction, &SYSLIST(2) to the second, and so forth. If one of the operands is a sublist, double subscripts can be used with &SYSLIST to reference any individual element of the sublist. For example, if the macro instruction

TRANTAB   TRTAB X'00',(X'04',C' ')

were issued, &SYSLIST(2,2) in the macro definition would refer to C' '. The macro definition in Program 9-10 illustrates the use of &SYSLIST. The macro TRTAB can be used to generate a translate table.

9.8 KEYWORD MACRO DEFINITIONS

It is occasionally desirable to code a macro definition that involves parameters, some of which may be omitted or assume default values during most expansions of the macro. In such instances, keyword macro definitions should be used. A keyword macro definition is written in the same way as any other macro definition except that the operands in the prototype statement are different and &SYSLIST cannot be used in these definitions. The operands in the prototype statement are formed by immediately following a symbolic

Program 9-10

```
           MACRO
&TNAME     TRTAB
           LCLA  &PTR
.*
.* THE TRTAB MACRO CAN BE USED TO GENERATE A TRANSLATE TABLE.  THE
.* VARIABLE &TNAME WILL BE ASSIGNED AS THE NAME OF THE GENERATED
.* TABLE.  ALL OPERANDS ARE REFERENCED AS ELEMENTS OF &SYSLIST.
.* THE FIRST OPERAND GIVES THE DEFAULT CHARACTER TO BE ASSIGNED
.* TO ALL POSITIONS IN THE TABLE WHICH ARE NOT SPECIFIED IN LATER
.* OPERANDS.  ALL FOLLOWING OPERANDS ARE OF ONE OF THE TWO
.* FOLLOWING FORMS:
.*
.*     (<CHAR>,<POS>)             IN THIS CASE <CHAR> SHOULD BE PUT
.*                                IN THE POSITION OF THE TABLE GIVEN
.*                                BY <POS>.
.*
.*     (<CHAR>,<START>,<END>)     IN THIS CASE <CHAR> SHOULD BE PUT
.*                                INTO ALL POSITIONS OF THE TABLE
.*                                FROM <START> TO <END>.
.*
.* FOR EXAMPLE
.*
.*TAB       TRTAB X'00',(X'04',C'0',C'9'),(X'08',C' ')
.*
.* WOULD CAUSE A TABLE TO BE GENERATED WITH 04 IN THE POSITIONS
.* CORRESPONDING TO THE 10 NUMERIC DIGITS, 08 IN THE POSITION FOR
.* A BLANK, AND 00 IN ALL THE REMAINING POSITIONS.
.*
.* THE VARIABLE &PTR IS USED TO INDEX THE ELEMENTS OF &SYSLIST.
.*
           AIF   ('&TNAME' EQ '').ERR
           AIF   (N'&SYSLIST GE 2).OK
.ERR       MNOTE '*** TOO FEW OPERANDS ***'
           MEXIT
.OK        ANOP
&TNAME     DC    256&SYSLIST(1)
&PTR       SETA  1
.LOOP      ANOP
&PTR       SETA  &PTR+1
           ORG   &TNAME.+&SYSLIST(&PTR,2)
           AIF   (N'&SYSLIST(&PTR) EQ 2).JUSTTWO
           DC    (&SYSLIST(&PTR,3)-&SYSLIST(&PTR,2)+1)&SYSLIST(&PTR,1)
           AIF   (&PTR LT N'&SYSLIST).LOOP
           AGO   .TABDONE
.* THE FOLLOWING SECTION IS PROCESSED FOR TWO ELEMENT OPERANDS.
.JUSTTWO DC    &SYSLIST(&PTR,1)
           AIF   (&PTR LT N'&SYSLIST).LOOP
.TABDONE ORG
           MEND
```

parameter with an equals sign that is, optionally, immediately followed by a default value. For example, the statement

&LABEL   ARRIVE   &REGS = NO,&BR = , &CSECT = NO,&SAVE = NO

is a valid prototype statement for a keyword macro definition. When a keyword macro instruction is written, the operands in this instruction can occur in any order. These operands consist of symbolic parameters, with the ampersands omitted, followed immediately by an equal sign that is, in turn, followed by a value. For example,

ARRIVE BR = 10,REGS = YES

is a valid keyword macro instruction. If this macro instruction were issued, &BR would be assigned 10 as its value, &REGS would be assigned YES as a value, and &CSECT and &SAVE would both be assigned their default value NO.

Three distinct advantages may be gained through the use of keyword macro definitions:

1. There is no need for the programmer to remember the order of the operands.
2. If operands are omitted, no specific actions are required (such as adding commas to indicate where the omissions occur).
3. Default values can be specified.

The first two advantages are significant only for macros that require more than a few operands.

The definition of the ARRIVE macro presented in Program 9-11 illustrates how a keyword macro definition should be coded. One interesting aspect of this macro is that the macro EQUREGS is invoked in the definition of ARRIVE. This use of a macro instruction in a macro definition is perfectly legal. This feature of the macro language allows a programmer to create hierarchies of more and more powerful macro definitions.

Exercises

1. If you are programming on an IBM 370, you have the SRP instruction to shift packed decimal fields. However, on an IBM 360, short routines of the sort described in Section 8.11 are normally used.

a. Write a macro RSHIFT with the prototype

&LABEL   RSHIFT &FIELD,&NUM

where &FIELD   is a label followed by the length enclosed within parentheses
       &NUM   is the number of positions that the field should be shifted to the right

For example,

RSHIFT F1(7),1

should generate

MVO   F1(7),F1(6)

Program 9-11

```
          MACRO
&LABEL    ARRIVE &REGS=NO,&BR=,&CSECT=YES,&SAVE=YES
.*
.* THE ARRIVE MACRO GENERATES THE CODE REQUIRED TO ENTER A MODULE,
.* SET UP A BASE REGISTER, AND (OPTIONALLY) SET UP A SAVE AREA.
.* THE PARAMETERS ARE ALL KEYWORDS AND HAVE THE FOLLOWING
.* MEANINGS:
.*
.*        &REGS        - NO → DO NOT GENERATE REGISTER EQUATES.
.*                       YES → GENERATE REGISTER EQUATES.
.*
.*        &BR          - GIVES THE REGISTER TO BE SET UP AS THE BASE
.*                       REGISTER.
.*
.*        &CSECT       - YES → GENERATE A CSECT STATEMENT.
.*                       NO → DO NOT GENERATE A CSECT STATEMENT.
.*
.*        &SAVE        - YES → GENERATE A SAVE AREA
.*                       NO → THIS IS A LOWEST LEVEL SUBROUTINE, SO
.*                             DON'T GENERATE A SAVE AREA.
.*
          AIF    ('&REGS' EQ 'NO').NOREGS
          AIF    ('&REGS' NE 'YES').ERR1
          EQUREGS
.NOREGS   AIF    ('&CSECT' EQ 'NO').NOTCS
          AIF    ('&CSECT' NE 'YES').ERR2
&LABEL    CSECT
          STM    R14,R12,12(R13)     STORE CALLER'S REGS
.COMMON   AIF    ('&SAVE' EQ 'NO').NOSAVE
          AIF    ('&SAVE' NE 'YES').ERR3
          AIF    ('&BR' NE 'R13').NBR13
          BAL    R14,80(R15)
          USING  *,R13
          DS     18F                 REGISTER SAVEAREA
          ST     R14,8(R13)          SET UP LINKS
          ST     R13,4(R14)
          LR     R13,R14
          MEXIT
.NOTCS    USING  *,R15
.* NOTE THAT IT IS ASSUMED THAT R15 CONTAINS THE ADDRESS OF THE
.* ENTRY POINT.
&LABEL    STM    R14,R12,12(R13)     STORE CALLER'S REGS
          AGO    .COMMON
.NOSAVE   AIF    ('&BR' EQ 'R13').ERR4
.SETBASE  BALR   &BR,R0
          USING  *,&BR
          MEXIT
.NBR13    BAL    R14,80(R15)
          DS     18F                 REGISTER SAVEAREA
          ST     R14,8(R13)          SET UP LINKS
          ST     R13,4(R14)
          LR     R13,R14
          AGO    .SETBASE
.ERR1     MNOTE '*** BAD REGS PARAMETER ***'
          MEXIT
.ERR2     MNOTE '*** BAD CSECT PARAMETER ***'
          MEXIT
.ERR3     MNOTE '*** BAD SAVE PARAMETER ***'
          MEXIT
.ERR4     MNOTE '*** INVALID USE OF R13 ***'
          MEND
```

b. Write a macro LSHIFT that can be used to generate the code required to shift a packed decimal field to the left. The prototype statement should be

&LABEL   LSHIFT &FIELD,&NUM

where the operands are identical to those of RSHIFT.

2.

a. Modify COUNT and GENTAB so that the table COUNTERS contains the number of entries in the first word of the table.

b. Write a macro with the following prototype statement:

&NAME   TPRNT   &TABLE

The macro should generate a call to the subroutine TABPRINT, passing a parameter list containing only the address of the table to be displayed. TABPRINT should produce the following output:

THE TABLE CONTAINS n ENTRIES

COUNTER1 = c1
COUNTER2 = c2
.
.
.
COUNTERn = cn

Thus,

TPRNT   COUNTERS

would cause the entries in COUNTERS to be printed. The macro may cause only registers R14, R15, and R1 to be altered.

c. Do the same as in Exercise 2b, but save and restore the values in R14, R15, and R1.

3. In Exercise 2 at the end of Section 9.2 you were asked to write three macros—ADDL, SUBL, and COMPL—which could be used to manipulate 64-bit fixed-point integers. Rewrite them so that both of the following are true:

a. The first time one of the macros occurs in a program, a short internal subroutine is generated, as well as a call to the subroutine.

b. On all subsequent occurrences, only the instructions required to call the subroutine are generated.

For example, suppose that

ADDL   NUM1,NUM2

were the first occurrence of ADDL in a program. Then

```
        * NOTE THAT NEITHER R1, R2, R14, NOR R15 MAY BE
        * USED AS A BASE REGISTER.
                STM     R14,R2,SAV0005
                LM      R14,R15, = A(NUM1,NUM2)
                BAL     R2,ADDLRT
                LM      R14,R2,SAV0005
                B       SAV0005 + 20
ADDLRT          LM      R0,R1,0(R14)
                AL      R1,4(R15)
                BC      B'1100',* + 8
                A       R0, = F'1'
                A       R0,0(R15)
                STM     R0,R1,0(R14)
                BR      R2
SAV0005         DS      5F
```

should be generated. If

```
ADD2        ADDL        NUM3,NUM4
```

were to occur later in the same program,

```
        * NOTE THAT NEITHER R1, R2, R14, NOR R15 MAY BE
        * USED AS A BASE REGISTER.
                STM     R14,R2,SAV0008
                LM      R14,R15, = A(NUM1,NUM2)
                BAL     R2,ADDLRT
                LM      R14,R2,SAV0008
                B       SAV0008 + 20
SAV0008         DS      5F
```

should be generated.

4. Write a macro called PARSE that can be used to call the subroutine PARSTRNG described in Exercise 2 at the end of Section 8.11. The prototype for PARSE should be

```
&LABEL      PARSE       &STRING,&KWORDS
```

where &STRING   is a label followed by a length and is used to define the address and length of the string to be scanned

      &KWORDS is a sublist operand with two elements per keyword to be scanned for: (1) the keyword and (2) the address of the doubleword into which the value should be packed.

Thus,

PARSE   CARD(80),(TIME,DTIME, RATE,DRATE)

should generate something similar to

```
         *  NOTE THAT R14, R15, R0, and R1 ARE ALTERED.
         *  THE ERROR CODE WILL BE RETURNED IN R0.
                    L       R15, = V(PARSTRNG)
                    LA      R1,PLST0028
                    BALR    R14,R15
                    B       NXT0028
         PLST0028   DC      A(CARD)
                    DC      A(SLN0028)
                    DC      A(*+8)
                    DC      A(KNM0028)
                    DC      FL1'4',CL11'TIME',A(DTIME)
                    DC      FL1'4',CL11'RATE',A(DRATE)
         SLN0028    DC      H'80'
         KNM0028    DC      H'2'
         NXT0028    DS      0H
```

5. In Exercise 1 at the end of Section 9.2, you were asked to code a macro BIGMVC that could be used to move a field of arbitrary length in situations where the length was not known at assembly time. Now write a macro called BMVC that can be used to move a field of arbitrary, but known, length. For example,

```
         MOVE      BMVC    FIELD1(494),FIELD2
```

should generate

```
         MOVE      MVC     FIELD1(256),FIELD2
                   MVC     FIELD1+256(238),FIELD2+256
```

6. In this exercise you are to write four macros. Three will be used by the fourth, $CALL, which can be used to generate a call to an external subroutine. The definition of $CALL is as follows:

```
         &LABEL    $CALL    &MOD,&LIST,&SAVE = NO
```

where   &MOD   is the name of the module to be invoked
        &LIST   specifies the contents of the parameter list (and is described
                below)

&SAVE   is a keyword parameter. NO means R0, R1, R14, and R15 may be altered. YES means R0, R1, R14, and R15 must be stored and restored if they are altered. If &LIST is specified (i.e., if it is nonnull), all four registers should be stored and restored. If &LIST is omitted, only R14 and R15 should be saved.

&LIST will be of the form

$$(<P1>,<P2>, \ldots ,<Pn>)$$

where <Pi> can be any of the following:

a. a register in parentheses
b. an address suitable for use in an RX instruction (such as an LA) preceded by an asterisk
c. a value that can be generated by an address constant (A-con)

For example, if &LIST is

$$(WORD,(R14),*10(R1),20)$$

the parameter list will eventually be composed of

• the address of WORD (generated by an A-con)
• the value from register 14
• the address generated by LA   r,10(R1)
• the value 20 (generated by an A-con)

Thus,

```
        GENCALL  $CALL    MYMOD,(WORD,(R14),*10(R1),20)
```

should generate

```
GENCALL  DS      0H
         ST      R14,PLST0023+4
         LA      R0,10(R1)
         ST      R0,PLST0023+8
         LA      R1,PLST0023
         L       R15,=V(MYMOD)
         BALR    R14,R15
         B       NXT0023
PLST0023 DS      0A
         DS      A(WORD)
         DS      A
         DS      A
         DC      A(20)
NXT0023  DS      0H
```

Note the following:

a. If SAVE = YES had been specified, then R0,R1,R14, and R15 would have to have been saved and restored. (This would also require generating a four-word area to save them.)

b. The values in &LIST that are registers in parentheses should be stored before the RX-type addresses. This allows (R0) as an element in the list.

c. Values that can be generated as A-cons should be generated in the parameter list.

d. &SYSNDX should be used to create unique labels.

The coding of $CALL will be significantly simplified if the following three macros are coded first:

&LABEL   RRPARM &ADDR,&LIST

where   &ADDR   is the label of the parameter list
        &LIST   is the same as for $CALL

RRPARM should just generate the ST instructions for those elements of &LIST that are registers in parentheses. For example,

RRPARM PLIST,((R0),TWO,10,(R14),(R15))

should generate

```
ST        R0,PLIST + 0
ST        R14,PLIST + 12
ST        R15,PLIST + 16
```

Thus, RRPARM could be invoked by $CALL in the form

RRPARM   PLST&SYSNDX,&LIST

to generate the required ST instructions to fill in the parameter list.

&LABEL   RXPARM &ADDR,&LIST

RXPARM is similar to RRPARM except that it should generate the LA-ST pairs required for those elements of &LIST beginning with an asterisk. Thus,

RGEN   RXPARM MYLIST,(WORD,*DSTART,*4(R1))

should generate

```
RGEN        DS        0H
            LA        R0,DSTART
            ST        R0,MYLIST + 4
```

```
              LA        R0,4(R1)
              ST        R0,MYLIST + 8
```

```
&LABEL    PGEN      &LIST
```

This macro should generate the parameter list described by &LIST. All A-con entries should be DC'ed in, while all RR and RX entries should be DS'ed in. Thus,

```
    PLIST         PGEN      (WORD,*DSTART,*4(R1))
```

should generate

```
    PLIST         DS        0A
                  DC        A(WORD)
                  DS        A
                  DS        A
```

To see exactly how these four macros are related, examine the definition of $CALL in Program 9-12.

Program 9-12

```
              MACRO
&LABEL    $CALL    &MOD,&LIST
.*
.* THIS SIMPLIFIED VERSION OF $CALL DOES NOT
.* ALLOW THE 'SAVE=' OPERAND.  IT SIMPLY
.* GENERATES A CALL TO &MOD, PASSING
.* THE PARAMETER LIST DETERMINED BY
.* &LIST.  NO CHECK IS MADE TO SEE IF
.* &LIST IS OMITTED, WHICH SHOULD BE
.* INCLUDED IN THE READER'S VERSION OF
.* $CALL.  THE MEANING OF THE OPERANDS ARE
.* AS FOLLOWS:
.*
.*     &MOD <=  THE NAME OF THE EXTERNAL
.*              SUBROUTINE TO BE INVOKED.
.*
.*     &LIST <= A LIST OF VALUES TO MAKE
.*              UP THE PARAMETER LIST
.*              PASSED TO &MOD.   EACH
.*              ELEMENT CAN BE
.*
.*                 A.  A VALID EXPRESSION
.*                     TO BE USED IN AN
.*                     A-TYPE CONSTANT.
.*
.*                 B.  A VALID RX-TYPE
.*                     ADDRESS PRECEDED BY
.*                     AN *.
.*
.*                 C.  A REGISTER ENCLOSED BY
.*                     PARENTHESIS.
```

Program 9-12 (continued)

```
.*
.* REGISTERS R0, R1, R14, AND R15, ARE ALTERED.
&LABEL    DS    0H                    GENERATE THE LABEL
          RRPARM PLST&SYSNDX,&LIST
.*
.* THE PRECEDING CALL GENERATES THE INSTRUCTIONS TO STORE THE REGISTERS
.* INTO THE PARAMETER LIST.
.*
          RXPARM PLST&SYSNDX,&LIST
.*
.* THE PRECEDING CALL GENERATES THE INSTRUCTIONS TO STORE THE RX-TYPE
.* ADDRESSES INTO THE PARAMETER LIST.
.*
          L     R15,=V(&MOD.)
          LA    R1,PLST&SYSNDX        LOAD ADDR. OF PARAMETERS
          BALR  R14,R15               CALL THE SUBROUTINE
          B     NXT&SYSNDX
PLST&SYSNDX PGEN &LIST
NXT&SYSNDX DS   0H                    GENERATE LABEL FOR CONTINUATION POINT
          MEND
```

7. In Exercise 3 at the end of Section 8.11 you were asked to code a subroutine called DATEPROC to perform manipulations on dates. Write a macro called DATES with the following prototype statement:

&LABEL   DATES   &OPER,&DATE1,&DATE2,&DAYS

where &OPER can be any of the following:

a. CONVERT (meaning that a conversion is desired)
b. COMPARE (meaning that a comparison is desired)
c. ADD (meaning that an addition is desired)
d. SUBTRACT (meaning that a subtraction is desired)

and where &DATE1 is (type,address): type can be JUL, CHAR or PDEC and address is the label of a field containing the date

&DATE2 is (type,address): the meanings are the same as for &DATE1

&DAYS gives the address of a three-byte field containing a number of days to be added or subtracted from the first date (This operand is optional.)

DATES should generate the appropriate parameter list and invoke DATEPROC to perform the desired operation. No registers should be altered (i.e., DATES should store and restore the contents of R14, R15, R0, and R1).

9.9 ADDITIONAL USES
OF CONDITIONAL ASSEMBLY

Although the techniques of conditional assembly are most frequently used in macro definitions, these techniques can also be used in programs that do not utilize macros. The following statements can all be used outside macro definitions:

GBLA	LCLA	SETA	AIF
GBLB	LCLB	SETB	AGO
GBLC	LCLC	SETC	ANOP

The intelligent employment of these statements enables a programmer to create programs that are more easily debugged, maintained, and altered.

There are two uses of conditional assembly that very frequently occur in the *open code* (the code outside macro definitions) of a program. The most common of these involves the setting of critical parameters through the use of SETA symbols. For example, suppose that a program is to perform the following simple tasks:

• Read a list of integers into a table.
• Print the integers that have been read.
• Sort the integers in the table into ascending order.
• Print the sorted list of integers.

Clearly, the size of the table limits the number of integers that can be used as input. No matter what size is chosen, it may very well have to be altered later (downward for use on small computers or upward if the program is to be transferred to a larger machine). To facilitate such alterations, the table could be declared as

```
                    macro definitions
              LCLA  &TSIZE
    *&TSIZE SHOULD BE SET TO THE MAXIMUM
    *NUMBER OF INTEGERS TO BE SORTED.
    &TSIZE       SETA        500
    SORTPROG     CSECT
                  .
                  .
                  .
    TABLE        DS          &TSIZE.F
                  .
                  .
                  .
                 END         SORTPROG
```

The declaration statement must immediately follow the macro definitions, but the SETA statement could occur anywhere in the program. If all critical parameters are set in the beginning of a program, it will not be necessary to search through the entire listing when alterations must be made.

The second most common use of conditional assembly in open code involves the use of SETB symbols to control the generation of debugging statements. In very large projects, the task of detecting the causes of errors can be incredibly complex. Statements that cause the contents of critical storage locations to be printed for inspection should be included at critical points in all modules. At a minimum, each module should contain statements that cause the values of all incoming variables and returned values to be displayed. Rather than removing these debugging statements once the modules have been partially debugged (modules are seldom completely debugged), the following scheme should be used:

```
                    macro definitions
                    LCLB       &DEBUG
&DEBUG              SETB       1
                     .
                     .
                     .
                    AIF        (&DEBUG).SKIP1
                    debugging statements
.SKIP1              ANOP
                     .
                     .
                     .
                    AIF        (&DEBUG).SKIP2
                    debugging statements
.SKIP2              ANOP
                     .
                     .
                     .
                    END
```

In this case, if a need arises for generating the debugging statements at a later date, the SETB statement can be removed and the program reassembled.

10

Floating-Point Arithmetic

10.1 INTRODUCTION

The floating-point instruction set is used primarily for performing scientific calculations. These instructions allow the manipulation of numbers in a far wider range of magnitudes than do the binary or decimal instructions. In addition, the clerical work involved in keeping track of the decimal point is automatically handled by the computer.

The scheme for representing floating-point numbers is based on the familiar scientific notation that is taught in high school physics and chemistry classes. In this notation, numbers are represented as a fraction times a power of 10. The fraction is sometimes called the *mantissa* and the exponent of 10 is called the *characteristic*. For example, 421,000 could be expressed in scientific notation as

$$.421 \times 10^6$$

and .00421 could be expressed as

$$.421 \times 10^{-2}$$

It should be pointed out that

$$.0421 \times 10^7$$

represents the same decimal number as

$$.421 \times 10^6$$

If the first digit of the fraction is nonzero, the number representation is said to be normalized.

This scheme for representing numbers is certainly not dependent upon the number base. For example, the hexadecimal number 4AEF could be represented as

$$.4AEF \times 16^4$$

Since the computers we are discussing are, in some sense, hexadecimal machines, this last example more accurately reflects how a floating-point number would be represented in the computer.

There are two formats in which floating-point data may be represented. The short (or single-precision) format occupies 32 bits, while the long (or double-precision) format occupies 64 bits. Four floating-point registers are provided for use with data in either the short or long format. The instructions are in either RR or RX format. Load, Store, Compare, Add, Subtract, Multiply, Divide, and sign control instructions are available for use with operands in either the long or short format.

10.2 FLOATING-POINT NUMBER REPRESENTATIONS

In computer memory, a short-format, floating-point data item occupies a fullword, while the long format requires a doubleword. These formats are:

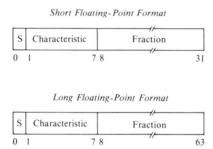

where   S   is a binary sign bit (The sign bit is 0 for a positive number and 1 for a negative number.)

and where, if it is assumed that the number is in hexadecimal scientific notation, then the following are true:

- Characteristic is a seven-bit representation of the exponent of 16. The characteristic is in excess 64 notation. The decimal number represented by these seven bits can range from 0 to 127. The actual characteristic is obtained by subtracting 64 from this number.

- Fraction is a binary representation of the fraction.

In both the long and short formats, a characteristic in the range -64 to 63 can be represented. The short format allows for six hexadecimal digits in the fraction, while the long format allows for 14 digits. The maximum range of decimal numbers that can be represented in either format is approximately

$$5.4 \times 10^{-79} \text{ to } 7.2 \times 10^{75}$$

The following examples of corresponding representations of numbers should help clarify these concepts.

Short Format	Scientific Notation
1. C3478100	$-.478100 \times 16^3$
2. 43478100	$.478100 \times 16^3$
3. 85130101	$-.130101 \times 16^{-59}$
4. C5130101	$-.130101 \times 16^5$

In the first example, the binary expansion of the first two hexadecimal digits is

$$1100 \quad 0011$$

The first binary digit is 1, indicating a negative number. The second binary digit is also 1, thus ensuring that the characteristic will be nonnegative. The magnitude of the representation of the characteristic in bits 1 through 7 is 67. Thus, the actual characteristic is

$$67 - 64 = +3$$

In the second example, the binary expansion of the first two hexadecimal digits is

$$0100 \quad 0011$$

The first digit is 0, indicating a positive sign. The second digit is 1, again ensuring that the characteristic will be nonnegative. The characteristic is again determined to be

$$67 - 64 = +3$$

In the third example, the binary expansion of the first two hexadecimal digits is

$$1000 \quad 0101$$

The 1 in the first bit indicates a negative number. The 0 in the second bit position indicates a characteristic representation less than 64; hence the actual characteristic will be negative. The characteristic is calculated to be

$$5 - 64 = -59$$

It should be noted that, if the first hexadecimal digit in a floating-point data item is greater than 7, a negative number is indicated, and if the second binary digit is not 1, a negative characteristic is indicated. The second binary bit is called the *bias bit*.

Exercises

1. Represent the following hexadecimal numbers as short-format, floating-point numbers.

a. $FE6.478 \times 16^3$
b. $64.21A6 \times 16^{-4}$
c. $AE.1234 \times 16^{-43}$
d. $.BCDEFA \times 16^{14}$
e. $.1234AE \times 16^{63}$

2. Represent the following hexadecimal numbers as long-format, floating-point numbers.

a. $1234.56789ABCDE \times 16^{14}$
b. $AE.CBDF12345F1B \times 16^{-23}$
c. $.000AECBDF12345 \times 16^3$
d. $.123456789ABCDE \times 16^{-72}$
e. $123456789.ABCDE \times 16^{-9}$

3. Convert the following short-format, floating-point numbers to hexadecimal numbers in scientific notation.

a. C5478100
b. 46478100
c. 8A123456
d. C7ABCDEF
e. 6FCDEF01

4. Convert the following long-format, floating-point numbers to hexadecimal numbers in scientific notation.

a. C5478100 ABCDEF01
b. 46478100 12345678
c. 8A123456 F12345BC
d. C7ABCDEF 01234567
e. 6FCDEF01 FEDCBA98

10.3 E- AND D-TYPE DC AND DS STATEMENTS

E- and D-type DC statements are used to generate floating-point constants in the short and long format, respectively. Provided that no length modifier is specified, an E-type DC statement forces alignment to a fullword boundary, and a D-type DC statement forces alignment to a doubleword boundary. In either case, the constant is written as a decimal number. The decimal point and sign are optional.

The constant may be followed by a decimal exponent of the form

$$En$$

where n is a signed or unsigned decimal number. The number is adjusted by shifting the decimal point (assumed to follow the last digit, if not specified) to the right or left the number of places indicated by the decimal exponent. The number is then converted to the appropriate floating-point format. The floating-point number is normalized to retain the maximum number of significant digits. Since the result is normalized, any padding of zeros or truncation of excess digits occurs on the right.

The following are valid floating-point DC statements with their corresponding generated values:

Statement	*Generated Result*	
DC E'6'	41600000	
DC D'3.1416'	413243FE5C91D14E	
DC E'-1234.567E5'	C775BCCC	
DC D'567.89E-4'	3FE89B951C5C5719	
DC D'31416E-4'	413243FE5C91D14E	
DC 2D'1.27'	411451EB851EB852	411451EB851EB852

Note that multiple constants can be used in an operand and that duplication factors are allowed.

E- and D-type DS statements are used to define storage areas for floating-point numbers. Boundary alignment is forced as in the case of the corresponding DC statements. Values may be specified in the operand field but, of course, no constants are generated.

10.4 CONVERSIONS BETWEEN DECIMAL AND FLOATING-POINT NUMBERS

The following brief discussion of conversion algorithms should allow the reader to verify the generated results shown in Section 10.3. Algorithms for converting between decimal and hexadecimal integers were given in Chapter 1. For this reason, here we will deal only with the conversion of fractions.

The following algorithm can be used to convert a hexadecimal fraction to a decimal fraction:

Step 1. Express the hexadecimal fraction as an integer times a power of 16.
Step 2. Convert the resulting integer to a decimal integer.

Step 3. Multiply this decimal integer by the power of 16 in the representation resulting from Step 1.

For example, consider $.4ABC_{16}$.

1. $.4ABC = 4ABC \times 16^{-4}$
2. $4ABC = 19{,}132$
3. $19{,}132 \times 16^{-4} = 19{,}132/65{,}536 = .2919$

Exercise

Convert the following hexadecimal numbers to decimal numbers.

a. ACE.1234
b. 12.09AC
c. .FEDC
d. .0987
e. .0099

The following algorithm can be used to convert a decimal fraction to a hexadecimal fraction.

Step 1. Multiply the decimal fraction by 16, and convert the resulting integer part of the result to a hexadecimal digit. (This is the next digit of the hexadecimal fraction that is sought.)

Step 2. If enough digits have been generated, stop. Otherwise, take the fraction part of the result and go to Step 1.

For example, consider .2919.

1. $.2919 \times 16 = \boxed{4}$ .6704
2. $.6704 \times 16 = \boxed{10}$ .7264
3. $.7264 \times 16 = \boxed{11}$ .6224
4. $.6224 \times 16 = \boxed{9}$ .9584

Therefore, $.2919 \approx .4AB9_{16}$.

The error results from the fact that only four fractional digits were carried in the intermediate calculations. Check the result, using six fractional digits in the intermediate calculations, and round the result.

Exercise

Convert the following decimal numbers to hexadecimal numbers.

a. 9876.3456
b. .9876
c. .0099

d. 123.7654

e. 9999.9987

10.5 NORMALIZATION
AND FLOATING-POINT REGISTERS

As mentioned in Section 10.1, if the high-order fraction digit of a floating-point data item is nonzero, the number is said to be normalized. In any other case, the data item is said to be unnormalized. It should be noted that the leftmost three binary bits of a normalized floating-point fraction could be zeros.

An unnormalized floating-point number is normalized as follows:

1. The fraction is shifted, one hexadecimal digit at a time, until the high-order digit is nonzero.
2. The characteristic is reduced by the number of digits that the fraction was shifted.

The initial operands in a floating-point arithmetic operation need not be normalized. However, except in the case of the unnormalized Add and Subtract instructions, the final result is normalized, since normalization is performed on the intermediate result to produce the final result. This is called *postnormalization.*

Only the algorithms for performing multiplication and division cause the operands to be normalized before performing the arithmetic operation. This is called *prenormalization.*

A floating-point data item with a zero fraction cannot be normalized. In this case, the characteristic is unchanged when normalization is called for.

A floating-point number with a zero characteristic, a zero fraction, and a positive sign is called a *true zero* number.

Four registers are provided solely for use in performing floating-point operations. These registers, each 64 bits in length, are numbered 0, 2, 4, and 6. For the remainder of this discussion, the floating-point registers will be referred to as FPR0, FPR2, FPR4, and FPR6, respectively.

A complete dual set of floating-point instructions exists for short- and long-format operands. When short-format instructions are performed, all operands must be in short format and, with the exception of multiplication, only the leftmost 32 bits of the registers participate. The results are in short format. In the case of multiplication, the result occupies the full 64 bits of the participating result register and is in long format. When long-format instructions are performed, all operands and results are in the 64-bit long format.

10.6 THE FLOATING-POINT LOAD AND STORE INSTRUCTIONS

The mnemonics for the floating-point instructions should be transparent, if the conventions for naming these instructions are understood. These conventions are as follows:

1. The first letter or two of the mnemonic is the standard mnemonic for the function to be performed by the instruction (for example, L for Load, A for Add, M for Multiply, ST for Store).
2. The letter following the function mnemonic indicates whether the operands of the instruction are in short or long format. E or U indicates short operands, and D or W indicates long operands.
3. If the instruction is of the RR type, an R is appended to the mnemonic to indicate this.

One exception to these rules is that a new function mnemonic, H, is introduced. H indicates a special type of divide function, Halve, which is the equivalent of division by 2.

With the above conventions in mind, the reader should easily guess the results of execution of the Load instructions LE, LER, LD, LDR, LTER and LTDR.

LE	r,D(X,B)	*(Load Short)*

Execution of this instruction causes a copy of the fullword at the address specified by D(X,B) to replace the leftmost (high-order) 32 bits of the floating-point register specified by r. The low-order 32 bits of r are unaltered.

LER	r1,r2	*(Load Register Short)*

Execution of this instruction causes a copy of the 32 high-order bits of the register specified by r2 to replace the 32 high-order bits of r1. The contents of r2 and the 32 low-order bits of r1 are unaltered.

LD	r,D(X,B)	*(Load Long)*
LDR	r1,r2	*(Load Register Long)*

Execution of either of these instructions causes the entire 64 bits of the first operand to be replaced by a copy of the second operand. The second operand of the LD instruction must be aligned on a doubleword boundary.

LTER	r1,r2	*(Load and Test Register Short)*
LTDR	r1,r2	*(Load and Test Register Long)*

Execution of the first of these two instructions causes the 32 high-order bits of r1 to be replaced by a copy of the 32 high-order bits of r2. Execution of the second instruction causes the entire 64 bits of r1 to be replaced by a copy of the 64 bits of r2. In either case, the condition code is set as follows:

CC	Meaning
0	Result fraction is 0.
1	Result < 0.
2	Result > 0.
3	—

The two Store instructions are STE and STD:

STE	r,D(X,B)	(Store Short)
STD	r,D(X,B)	(Store Long)

Execution of the first instruction causes a copy of the 32 high-order bits of r to replace the fullword specified by D(X,B). Execution of the second instruction causes a copy of the entire 64 bits of r to replace the doubleword specified by D(X,B).

10.7 THE FLOATING-POINT ADD, SUBTRACT, AND COMPARE INSTRUCTIONS

In the case of the Add, Subtract, Compare, Halve, and Multiply instructions, all intermediate calculations are performed using one more digit than the six (in short format) or 14 (in long format) in the operands and final result. This additional digit, called the *guard digit,* increases the accuracy of the final result.

The instructions for addition and subtraction of short-format operands (AE, AER, SE, and SER) cause only the high-order 32 bits of the result operand to be altered, while the corresponding instructions for long-format operands (AD, ADR, SD, and SDR) alter the entire 64 bits of the result register. Each Add and Subtract instruction causes the condition code to be set as follows:

CC	Meaning
0	Result fraction is 0.
1	Result < 0.
2	Result > 0.
3	—

The short-format Add instructions are AE and AER:

AE	r,D(X,B)	(Add Short)
AER	r1,r2	(Add Register Short)

Execution of either of these instructions causes copies of both operands to be moved to special unaddressable work areas. A guard digit, initially zero, is kept with each copy. The guard digit may be thought of as an additional low-order hexadecimal digit appended to the right of the number representation. The operand with the smaller characteristic is right shifted one digit at a time, increasing the characteristic by 1 for each shift, until the characteristics agree. The digits shifted off the right successively replace the guard digit; so when the alignment is complete, the guard digit contains the last digit shifted out of the affected operand. Addition is then performed on the fractions of the operands, and the result is normalized. If normalization results in a left shift of at least one digit, the guard digit becomes part of the final result. Additional digits created on the right by the left shift are padded with zeros. This intermediate result then replaces the 32 high-order bits of the first operand.

The long format Add instructions are AD and ADR:

AD	r,D(X,B)	*(Add Long)*
ADR	r1,r2	*(Add Register Long)*

Execution of these instructions is the same as in the case of the corresponding short-format instructions except that, in this case, 64 bits are involved rather than 32. A guard digit is again retained in all intermediate calculations.

The floating-point Subtract instructions are SE, SER, SD, and SDR:

SE	r,D(X,B)	*(Subtract Short)*
SER	r1,r2	*(Subtract Register Short)*
SD	r,D(X,B)	*(Subtract Long)*
SDR	r1,r2	*(Subtract Register Long)*

Execution of each of these instructions causes copies of both operands to be placed in work areas. The sign of the working copy of the second operand is reversed. Addition is then performed in the same manner as for the corresponding add operation. The short-format Subtract instructions alter only the 32 high-order bits of the first operand.

The floating-point Compare instructions are CE, CER, CD, and CDR:

CE	r,D(X,B)	*(Compare Short)*
CER	r1,r2	*(Compare Register Short)*
CD	r,D(X,B)	*(Compare Long)*
CDR	r1,r2	*(Compare Register Long)*

The operations performed by each of these instructions are the same as those performed by the corresponding Subtract instructions except that, in this case, neither operand is altered. The condition code is set just as for the

Subtract instructions but, for the Compare instructions, the interpretation is as follows:

CC	Meaning
0	Operands are equal.
1	First operand is low.
2	First operand is high.
3	—

It should be pointed out that a Compare Short instruction involving two operands with values such as

$$4400 \quad 0C00$$

and

$$41C0 \quad 00BB$$

will set the condition code to 0. This occurs because right shifting of the operand with the smaller characteristic will cause the rightmost two digits to be lost. The remaining digits of the two operands (including the guard digit) are then identical.

10.8 THE FLOATING-POINT MULTIPLY, DIVIDE, AND HALVE INSTRUCTIONS

Dual sets of RR and RX instructions are provided for the multiplication and division of short- and long-format, floating-point operands.

The instructions for multiplication of short-format operands are

ME	r,D(X,B)	(*Multiply Short*)

and

MER	r1,r2	(*Multiply Register Short*)

The corresponding instructions for long-format operands are

MD	r,D(X,B)	(*Multiply Long*)

and

MDR	r1,r2	(*Multiply Register Long*)

The algorithm governing the execution of these instructions can be described as follows:

Step 1. Copies of the two operands are normalized (by prenormalization) in work areas. With short operands, prenormalization affects only the 32 high-order bits of the operands.

Step 2. The sign of the result is determined in accordance with the rules of algebra. This amounts to performing an EXCLUSIVE OR operation on the sign bits of the two operands.

Step 3. The characteristic of the result is determined. This is equivalent to adding the characteristics of the operands and then subtracting the bias quantity (40_{16}).

Step 4. Multiplication of the fractions of the normalized operands is performed with the following results:

     a. In the case of short operands, the six-hexadecimal-digit fractions of the operands are multiplied, yielding a 12-hexadecimal-digit result. Since the contents of the entire result register will be replaced by the final result, the rightmost two hexadecimal digits of that register will be hexadecimal zeros.

     b. In the case of long operands, the 14-hexadecimal-digit fractions of the operands are multiplied, yielding a 28-digit result. This result is truncated to 15 digits (including the guard digit).

Step 5. The intermediate result determined by Steps 1–4 is then normalized (this could result in, at most, a shift of one digit to the left) to create the final result, which replaces the contents of the result register. The second operand is not altered by these operations.

The following examples should help to clarify these concepts.

- *Example 1.* Suppose that FPR2 contains 43003000 00000000 and FLOAT1 contains 43453211 23450032. Then, execution of the instruction

         ME   2,FLOAT1

can be described as follows:

1. Prenormalization results in

         FPR2:   41300000   00000000
         FLOAT1:43453211   23450032

2. The sign of the result is determined as

         0 (EXCLUSIVE OR) 0 = 0

3. The characteristic of the result is determined as

         41 + 43 − 40 = 44

4. Multiplication of the normalized operands yields

         0CF963   30000000

5. Postnormalization yields the final result

         43CF9633   00000000

- *Example 2.* Assume the same original contents of FPR2 and FLOAT1 as in Example 1. Then, execution of the instruction

    MD   2,FLOAT1

is as follows:

(The first three steps are exactly as described in Example 1.)

4. Multiplication of the fractions and subsequent truncation yields

    0CF963   369CF009   6

5. Postnormalization yields the final result

    43CF9633   69CF0096

Note that the guard digit participates in the final result in Example 2. We should emphasize that only the first 32 bits of the operands are affected in the prenormalization process, in operations on short operands.

  The instructions for division of short-format operands are

    DE   r,D(X,B)   *(Divide Short)*

and

    DER   r1,r2   *(Divide Register Short)*

  The corresponding instructions for long-format operands are

    DD   r,D(X,B)   *(Divide Long)*

and

    DDR   r1,r2   *(Divide Register Long)*

Execution of these instructions is as follows:

Step 1. Copies of the two operands are prenormalized in work areas.

Step 2. The sign of the result is determined in the same manner as in the corresponding multiply operation.

Step 3. The characteristic of the result is determined by subtracting the characteristic of the normalized second operand from the characteristic of the normalized first operand and adding 40_{16}.

Step 4. Division of the fraction of the first operand by the fraction of the second operand is performed, and the result becomes the fraction of the intermediate quotient. No remainder is retained. In the case of short-operand instructions, only six hexadecimal digits of the fractions participate in this operation.

Step 5. Postnormalization of the intermediate result is never necessary. A shift to the right of one hexadecimal digit and corresponding adjustment of the characteristic, however, may be necessary to arrive at the final result.

  The following examples illustrate the operation of the Divide instructions.

• *Example 1.* Suppose that FPR2 contains 42080000 23456789 and FLOAT1 contains 420C0000 00000000. Then, execution of the instruction

DE   2,FLOAT1

proceeds as follows:

1. Prenormalization of the operands yields

      FPR2   :   41800000   23456789
      FLOAT1:   41C00000   00000000

2. The sign is determined by

      0 (EXCLUSIVE OR) 0 = 0

3. The characteristic is determined by

      41 − 41 + 40 = 40

4. Division of the fractions yields

      800000 / C00000 = AAAAAA

5. No shift is necessary, so the final result is

      40AAAAAA

- *Example 2.*   Suppose that FPR4 contains 41600000 00000000 and FPR6 contains 41400000 00000000. Then execution of the instruction

      DDR   4,6

   is as follows:

1. No prenormalization is necessary.
2. The sign is determined by

      0 (EXCLUSIVE OR) 0 = 0

3. The characteristic is determined by

      41 − 41 + 40 = 40
4. Division of the fractions yields

      600000   00000000 / 400000   00000000 = 1800000   00000000

   The 1 in the result represents a carry digit.
5. A right shift of one digit and an increase of 1 in the exponent yields the final result

      41180000   00000000

The Halve instructions HER and HDR cause the contents of the second operand to be divided by 2, and this result replaces the contents of the first operand.

HER	r1,r2
HDR	r1,r2

Execution of these instructions yields the same result as would be obtained by regular division by a constant 2.

10.9 SIGN CONTROL

The floating-point instruction set provides dual sets of RR instructions for performing load complement, load negative, and load positive operations. These instructions are:

LCER	r1,r2	(*Load Complement Short*)
LCDR	r1,r2	(*Load Complement Long*)
LNER	r1,r2	(*Load Negative Short*)
LNDR	r1,r2	(*Load Negative Long*)
LPER	r1,r2	(*Load Positive Short*)
LPDR	r1,r2	(*Load Positive Long*)

Execution of each of these instructions replaces the first operand with the result obtained by adjusting the sign bit of the second operand appropriately. These adjustments are made as follows:

1. For the Load Complement instructions, an EXCLUSIVE OR operation is performed on the sign bit of the second operand and a 1.
2. For the Load Negative instructions, an OR operation is performed on the sign bit of the second operand and a 1.
3. For the Load Positive instructions, an AND operation is performed on the sign bit of the second operand and a 0.

10.10 UNNORMALIZED ADD AND SUBTRACT INSTRUCTIONS

Dual sets of RR and RX instructions for performing unnormalized addition and subtraction operations are provided. These instructions are:

AU	r,D(X,B)	(*Add Unnormalized Short*)
AUR	r1,r2	(*Add Register Unnormalized Short*)
AW	r,D(X,B)	(*Add Unnormalized Long*)
AWR	r1,r2	(*Add Register Unnormalized Long*)

SU	r,D(X,B)	(*Subtract Unnormalized Short*)
SUR	r1,r2	(*Subtract Register Unnormalized Short*)
SW	r,D(X,B)	(*Subtract Unnormalized Long*)
SWR	r1,r2	(*Subtract Register Unnormalized Long*)

Execution of each of these instructions is the same as execution of the corresponding normal instruction except that no postnormalization is performed.

The principal reason for including these instructions in the floating-point package is to implement schemes to record the significance of digits in results of sequences of floating-point operations. Two factors, however, severely limit the utility of these instructions for this purpose:

1. Since the computations are done in hexadecimal arithmetic, the loss of decimal digits would, at best, be measured rather crudely.

2. The multiply and divide operations force complete prenormalization of the operands. The inclusion of these operations in any sequence of floating-point operations would, therefore, make it almost impossible to keep track of significance with any accuracy.

Other schemes have been developed to record the significance of digits, but these are beyond the scope of this book.

10.11 EXTENDED-PRECISION ARITHMETIC AND ROUNDING

The set of instructions discussed in this section includes the five extended-precision arithmetic instructions that utilize 28-digit operand or result formats. In addition, two Load instructions that can be utilized to round from longer to shorter formats are included. One of these instructions rounds an extended-precision operand to long format, and the other rounds a long-format operand to short format.

An extended-precision, floating-point number consists of two long-precision, floating-point numbers in consecutive registers. Only the register pairs FPR0, FPR2 and FPR4, FPR6 can be used to represent extended-precision, floating-point numbers. The long floating-point number in the first register of the pair is called the *high-order part* and the long floating-point number in the second register of the pair is called the *low-order part* of the extended-precision number. The sign and characteristic of the high-order part are taken as the sign and characteristic of the extended-precision number. The extended-precision format is illustrated as follows:

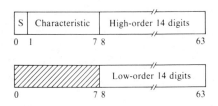

If the high-order part is normalized, the extended-precision number is considered to be normalized. The sign and characteristic of the low-order part are ignored.

When extended-precision results are calculated, the sign of the low-order part of the result is made to match the sign of the high-order part; the characteristic of the low-order part is made to be 14 less than the characteristic of the high-order part, provided that the high-order characteristic is at least 14. If subtracting 14 from the high-order characteristic results in a negative number, then the characteristic of the low-order part is made 128 larger than its correct value.

The AXR, SXR, and MXR instructions constitute the entire set of instructions that operate on two extended operands and produce extended-precision results. In each case, the results produced are postnormalized. No facility is provided for division of extended-precision operands.

> AXR r1,r2 *(Add Extended)*

Execution of this instruction is analogous to that of the Add Short or Add Long instructions except that, in this case, 28 digits of the operands are involved and adjustments are made on the low-order sign and characteristic, as explained previously.

> SXR r1,r2 *(Subtract Extended)*

Execution of this instruction is analogous to execution of the Add Extended instruction except that, in this case, the sign of the second operand is reversed before the addition is performed.

> MXR r1,r2 *(Multiply Extended)*

Execution of this instruction is analogous to that of the MER and MDR instructions except that, of course, 28 digits of the operands are involved. The sign and exponent of the low-order part of the result are adjusted as in the case of the AXR and SXR instructions.

The following Multiply instructions operate on two long-precision operands to produce extended-precision results:

> MXD r,D(X,B) *(Multiply Long to Extended)*
>
> MXDR r1,r2 *(Multiply Register Long to Extended)*

Execution of either of these instructions causes the normalized product of the long second operand and the long first operand to be generated. This product then replaces the contents of the specified result register and the next-higher addressed register. The sign, characteristic, and high-order 14 digits of the product fraction replace the first operand. The 14 low-order digits of the product fraction replace bit positions 8–63 of the next-higher addressed register. The sign bit of this register is made to match the sign bit of the result register. The characteristic of the low-order register is adjusted to 14 less than the high-order characteristic if the high-order is at least 14; otherwise, the low-order characteristic is made 128 greater than its correct value. If either or both operand fractions are zero, both parts of the result are made true zero. The condition code is not altered.

The instructions for rounding operands are

	LRER	r1,r2	*(Load Rounded Short/Long)*
and	LRDR	r1,r2	*(Load Rounded Long/Extended)*

Execution of either of these instructions causes the second operand to be rounded to the short format, and the result replaces the first operand. The second operand is not altered unless the two operands are the same. In the case of the LRER instruction, rounding is accomplished by adding 1 to the contents of bit position 32 of the second operand and propagating the carry to the left. In the case of the LRDR instruction, rounding depends on the contents of bit position 8 of the low-order part of the second operand: If the contents of this bit position is 1, 1 is added to bit position 63 of the result register and the carry is propagated to the left. In either case, rounding could result in a carry out of the high-order digit position of the result fraction. If this occurs, the result fraction is shifted one digit to the right and the characteristic is increased by 1. The condition code is not altered by the execution of these instructions.

10.12 FLOATING-POINT ARITHMETIC EXCEPTIONS

Seven types of errors can occur with the use of floating-point instructions. Of these, three should be familiar to and predictable by the reader. These are operation, addressing, and protection exceptions. The four other types of exceptions are peculiar to the floating-point instruction set. These are the exponent overflow, exponent underflow, significance, and floating-point divide exceptions. A brief description of each of these seven exceptions is given in this section. Refer to the IBM 370 *Principles of Operations Manual* for complete details.

- *Operation.* If an attempt to execute a floating-point instruction is made on a system that does not support the floating-point package, this error will occur.
- *Addressing.* If an operand specifies an address that is outside the address range of the particular system, this type of exception will occur.
- *Protection.* This type of exception will occur if an attempt is made to address a storage area that has not been allocated to the program being executed.
- *Exponent Overflow.* This type of exception will occur if the result of a floating-point Add, Subtract, Multiply, or Divide instruction has a characteristic exceeding 127 and if the result fraction is not zero.
- *Exponent Underflow.* This error will occur if the characteristic of the result of a floating-point Add, Subtract, Multiply, Divide, or Halve instruction is less than zero.
- *Significance.* This exception will occur if the result fraction of a floating-point Add or Subtract instruction is zero.
- *Floating-Point Divide.* This exception will occur if division by a floating-point number with a zero fraction is attempted.

10.13 THE INPUT AND OUTPUT OF FLOATING-POINT NUMBERS

No instructions are provided for converting floating-point numbers from external format to internal format and vice versa. This lack presents a formidable obstacle to the use of floating-point instructions. Various routines have been developed for doing these conversions; however, a discussion of such routines is beyond the scope of this text.

A simple, if somewhat unusual, technique to facilitate the full use of the floating-point instruction set follows. This technique takes advantage of an IBM ANS COBOL extension that does provide the means for converting between internal and external formats. The COBOL subroutine FLETOI can be used to convert floating-point numbers from external to internal format, and FLITOE can be used to convert from internal to external format. These two routines are listed in Program 10-1.

Program 10-1

```
PP 5734-CB2 V4 RELEASE 1.5 10NOV77        IBM OS AMERICAN NATIONAL STANDARD COBOL


     1


00001         IDENTIFICATION DIVISION.
00002         PROGRAM-ID. FLETOI.
00003
00004       * THIS SHORT COBOL SUBROUTINE IS USED TO CONVERT A NUMBER IN
00005       * FLOATING POINT EXTERNAL FORMAT INTO INTERNAL FORMAT.
00006
00007         ENVIRONMENT DIVISION.
00008         CONFIGURATION SECTION.
00009         SOURCE-COMPUTER. IBM-370.
00010         OBJECT-COMPUTER. IBM-370.
00011         DATA DIVISION.
00012         LINKAGE SECTION.
00013
00014         01   EXT-FLOAT   PIC +.9(16)E+99.
00015         01   INT-FLOAT   USAGE IS COMP-2.
00016
00017         PROCEDURE DIVISION USING EXT-FLOAT INT-FLOAT.
00018
00019             MOVE EXT-FLOAT TO INT-FLOAT.
00020             GOBACK.

PP 5734-CB2 V4 RELEASE 1.5 10NOV77        IBM OS AMERICAN NATIONAL STANDARD COBOL


     1


00001         IDENTIFICATION DIVISION.
00002         PROGRAM-ID. FLITOE.
00003
00004       * THIS SHORT COBOL SUBROUTINE IS USED TO CONVERT A NUMBER IN
00005       * FLOATING POINT INTERNAL FORMAT INTO EXTERNAL FORMAT.
00006
00007         ENVIRONMENT DIVISION.
00008         CONFIGURATION SECTION.
00009         SOURCE-COMPUTER. IBM-370.
00010         OBJECT-COMPUTER. IBM-370.
00011         DATA DIVISION.
00012         LINKAGE SECTION.
00013
00014         01   INT-FLOAT   USAGE IS COMP-2.
00015         01   EXT-FLOAT   PIC +.9(16)E+99.
00016
00017         PROCEDURE DIVISION USING INT-FLOAT EXT-FLOAT.
00018
00019             MOVE INT-FLOAT TO EXT-FLOAT.
00020             GOBACK.
```

Program 10-2, FLOATEX, illustrates the use of the double-precision, floating-point instructions, as well as the calls to FLETOI and FLITOE.

To understand how Program 10-2 was prepared for execution, the reader should refer to the discussion in Sections 6.1 and 6.2. The COBOL subroutines were separately compiled into two object modules. Then, the assembler program FLOATEX was assembled, producing a third object module. The three modules were then combined to produce the executable program in memory.

Program 10-2

```
LOC      OBJECT CODE   ADDR1 ADDR2  STMT   SOURCE STATEMENT

                                     2            PRINT NOGEN
                                     3     *****************************************************************
                                     4     *
                                     5     *  THIS PROGRAM ILLUSTRATES THE USE OF FLOATING POINT NUMBERS, AS WELL
                                     6     *  AS HOW TO INVOKE COBOL SUBROUTINES FROM ASSEMBLER.  IT PERFORMS
                                     7     *  THE FOLLOWING STEPS:
                                     8     *
                                     9     *    STEP 1.  READ IN A CARD WITH 2 DOUBLE-PRECISION NUMBERS (CALL
                                    10     *             THEM A AND B).  THE NUMBERS ARE IN THE EXTERNAL
                                    11     *             FLOATING POINT FORMAT DESCRIBED IN THE COBOL LANGUAGE
                                    12     *             REFERENCE MANUAL.
                                    13     *
                                    14     *    STEP 2.  INVOKE THE COBOL SUBROUTINE 'FLETOI' TO CONVERT THE
                                    15     *             NUMBERS INTO INTERNAL FLOATING POINT FORMAT.  THIS
                                    16     *             REQUIRES
                                    17     *
                                    18     *                 A)  A CALL TO 'ILBOSTPO' TO INITIALIZE THE
                                    19     *                     COBOL ENVIRONMENT,
                                    20     *
                                    21     *                 B)  CALLING 'FLETOI' TWICE (ONCE TO CONVERT
                                    22     *                     A AND ONCE TO CONVERT B)
                                    23     *
                                    24     *    STEP 3.  XDUMP OUT A AND B.
                                    25     *
                                    26     *    STEP 4.  COMPUTE A+B, A-B, A*B, A/B, AND HALF(A).
                                    27     *
                                    28     *    STEP 5.  XDUMP OUT THE VALUES.
                                    29     *
                                    30     *    STEP 6.  CALL 'FLITOE' 5 TIMES TO CONVERT THE VALUES TO
                                    31     *             PRINTABLE FORMAT (EXTERNAL FLOATING POINT).
                                    32     *
                                    33     *    STEP 7.  PRINT THE RESULT.
                                    34     *
                                    35     *    STEP 8.  EXIT.
                                    36     *****************************************************************
                                    37     *
000000                              38     FLOATEX  CSECT
000000  90EC D00C            0000C  39              STM    R14,R12,12(R13)          SAVE CALLER'S REGISTERS
000004  05C0                       40              BALR   R12,0
                             00006  41              USING  BASEPT,R12
000006                              42     BASEPT   DS     0H
                                    43     *
000006  18ED                       44              LR     R14,R13
000008  41D0 C25E           00264  45              LA     R13,SAVEAREA
00000C  50DE 0008           00008  46              ST     R13,8(R14)
000010  50ED 0004           00004  47              ST     R14,4(R13)
                                    48     *
                                    49     ***<STEP 1>  READ THE CARD WITH A AND B.
                                    50     *
000014                              51              XREAD  CARD
00003A                              61              XPRNT  CARD-1,81                 ECHO OUT THE CONTENTS OF THE CARD
                                    71     *
                                    72     ***<STEP 2>  CONVERT A AND B TO INTERNAL FORMAT.
```

Program 10-2 (continued)

```
                FLOATING POINT EXAMPLE

    LOC    OBJECT CODE   ADDR1  ADDR2   STMT   SOURCE STATEMENT

                                         73   *
00005E  58F0  C252               00258   74         L     R15,=V(ILBOSTPO)
000062  05EF                              75         BALR  R14,R15              INITIALIZE COBOL ENVIRONMENT
                                         76   *
000064  4110  C21A       00220           77         LA    R1,=A(EXTA,INTA)
000068  58F0  C256       0025C           78         L     R15,=V(FLETOI)
00006C  05EF                              79         BALR  R14,R15              CONVERT A TO INTERNAL FORMAT
                                         80   *
00006E  4110  C222       00228           81         LA    R1,=A(EXTB,INTB)
000072  58F0  C256       0025C           82         L     R15,=V(FLETOI)
000076  05EF                              83         BALR  R14,R15              CONVERT B TO INTERNAL FORMAT
                                         84   *
                                         85   ***<STEP 3>   XDUMP THE CONVERTED VALUES
                                         86   *
000078                                   87         XDUMP INTA,16
                                        104   *
                                        105   ***<STEP 4>   COMPUTE A+B, A-B, A*B, A/B, AND HALF(A)
                                        106   *
0000FA  6800  C2FA       00300          107         LD    FPR0,INTA
0000FE  6A00  C302       00308          108         AD    FPR0,INTB
000102  6000  C30A       00310          109         STD   FPR0,SUM             CALCULATE A + B
                                        110   *
000106  6800  C2FA       00300          111         LD    FPR0,INTA
00010A  6B00  C302       00308          112         SD    FPR0,INTB
00010E  6000  C318       00318          113         STD   FPR0,DIFF            CALCULATE A - B
                                        114   *
000112  6800  C2FA       00300          115         LD    FPR0,INTA
000116  6C00  C302       00308          116         MD    FPR0,INTB
00011A  6000  C320       00320          117         STD   FPR0,PRODUCT         CALCULATE A * B
                                        118   *
00011E  6800  C2FA       00300          119         LD    FPR0,INTA
000122  6D00  C302       00308          120         DD    FPR0,INTB
000126  6000  C328       00328          121         STD   FPR0,QUOTIENT        CALCULATE A / B
                                        122   *
00012A  6800  C2FA       00300          123         LD    FPR0,INTA
00012E  2400                            124         HDR   FPR0,FPR0
000130  6000  C32A       00330          125         STD   FPR0,HALFA           CALCULATE HALF(A)
                                        126   *
                                        127   ***<STEP 5>   XDUMP RESULTS
                                        128   *
000134                                  129         XDUMP SUM,40
                                        146   *
                                        147   ***<STEP 6>   CONVERT TO EXTERNAL FORMATS
                                        148   *
0001B6  4110  C22A       00230          149         LA    R1,=A(SUM,EXTSUM)
0001BA  58F0  C25A       00260          150         L     R15,=V(FLITOE)
0001BE  05EF                            151         BALR  R14,R15
                                        152   *
0001C0  4110  C232       00238          153         LA    R1,=A(DIFF,EXTDIFF)
0001C4  58F0  C25A       00260          154         L     R15,=V(FLITOE)
0001C8  05EF                            155         BALR  R14,R15
                                        156   *
0001CA  4110  C23A       00240          157         LA    R1,=A(PRODUCT,EXTPROD)
```

Program 10-2 (continued)

FLOATING POINT EXAMPLE

```
LOC     OBJECT CODE     ADDR1  ADDR2    STMT   SOURCE STATEMENT

0001CE  58F0 C25A              00260    158           L     R15,=V(FLITOE)
0001D2  05EF                            159           BALR  R14,R15
                                        160    *
0001D4  4110 C242             00248     161           LA    R1,=A(QUOTIENT,EXTQUOT)
0001D8  58F0 C25A             00260     162           L     R15,=V(FLITOE)
0001DC  05EF                            163           BALR  R14,R15
                                        164    *
0001DE  4110 C24A             00250     165           LA    R1,=A(HALFA,EXTHALFA)
0001E2  58F0 C25A             00260     166           L     R15,=V(FLITOE)
0001E6  05EF                            167           BALR  R14,R15
                                        168    *
                                        169    ***<STEP 7>   PRINT THE RESULTS
                                        170    *
0001E8                                  171           XPRNT PLINE,133
                                        181    *
                                        182    ***<STEP 8>   EXIT
                                        183    *
00020E  58DD 0004             00004     184           L     R13,4(R13)
000212  98EC 1BFF             0000C     185           LM    R14,R12,12(R13)
000216  1BFF                            186           SR    R15,R15          SET RETURN CODE TO 0
000218  07FE                            187           BR    R14              RETURN TO THE SYSTEM
                                        188    *
000220                                  189           LTORG
000220  000002AD00000300                190                 =A(EXTA,INTA)
000228  000002C400000308                191                 =A(EXTB,INTB)
000230  0000031000000339                192                 =A(SUM,EXTSUM)
000238  0000031800000351                193                 =A(DIFF,EXTDIFF)
000240  0000032000000369                194                 =A(PRODUCT,EXTPROD)
000248  0000032800000381                195                 =A(QUOTIEN,EXTQUOT)
000250  0000033000000399                196                 =A(HALFA,EXTHALFA)
000258  00000000                        197                 =V(ILBOSTP0)
00025C  00000000                        198                 =V(FLETOI)
000260  00000000                        199                 =V(FLITOE)
                                        200    *
000264                                  201    SAVEAREA  DS   18F            REGISTER SAVE AREA
0002AC  40                              202              DC   C' '
0002AD                           002AD  203    CARD      DS   CL80           READ INPUT CARD INTO HERE
0002FD                                  204              ORG  CARD
0002AD                           002C4  205    EXTA      DS   CL22
0002C3                                  206              ORG  CARD+23
0002C4                           002FD  207    EXTB      DS   CL22
0002DA                                  208              ORG
000300                                  209    INTA      DS   D              A IN INTERNAL FORMAT
000308                                  210    INTB      DS   D              B IN INTERNAL FORMAT
                                        211    *
000310                                  212    SUM       DS   D              A + B
000318                                  213    DIFF      DS   D              A - B
000320                                  214    PRODUCT   DS   D              A * B
000328                                  215    QUOTIENT  DS   D              A / B
000330                                  216    HALFA     DS   D              HALF(A)
                                        217    *
000338  404040404040404040             00339  218    PLINE     DC   CL133' '
0003BD                                  219              ORG  PLINE+1
```

```
FLOATING POINT EXAMPLE

LOC     OBJECT CODE   ADDR1  ADDR2   STMT  SOURCE STATEMENT
000339                              220   EXTSUM   DS    CL22
00034F                       00351  221            ORG   PLINE+25
000351                              222   EXTDIFF  DS    CL22
000367                       00369  223            ORG   PLINE+49
000369                              224   EXTPROD  DS    CL22
00037F                       00381  225            ORG   PLINE+73
000381                              226   EXTQUOT  DS    CL22
000397                       00399  227            ORG   PLINE+97
000399                              228   EXTHALFA DS    CL22
0003AF                       003BD  229            ORG
                                    230   *
00000                               231   R0       EQU   0
00001                               232   R1       EQU   1
00002                               233   R2       EQU   2
00003                               234   R3       EQU   3
00004                               235   R4       EQU   4
00005                               236   R5       EQU   5
00006                               237   R6       EQU   6
00007                               238   R7       EQU   7
00008                               239   R8       EQU   8
00009                               240   R9       EQU   9
0000A                               241   R10      EQU   10
0000B                               242   R11      EQU   11
0000C                               243   R12      EQU   12
0000D                               244   R13      EQU   13
0000E                               245   R14      EQU   14
0000F                               246   R15      EQU   15
                                    247   *
00000                               248   FPR0     EQU   0
00002                               249   FPR2     EQU   2
00004                               250   FPR4     EQU   4
00006                               251   FPR6     EQU   6
                                    252            END   FLOATEX

000000

+.1234567890123456E+05   -.9876543210654321E-01

BEGIN XSNAP - CALL   1 AT 40316148 USER STORAGE

        CORE ADDRESSES SPECIFIED-     3163C8  TO 3163D8
3163C0  40404040 40777777 443039AD CC78A7A4  C01948B0 FCDF7720 77777777 77777777  *................................*

BEGIN XSNAP - CALL   2 AT 60316204 USER STORAGE

        CORE ADDRESSES SPECIFIED-     3163D8  TO 316400
3163C0  40404040 40777777 443039AD CC78A7A4  C01948B0 FCDF7720 44303994 83C7AAC4  *....G..............G.D*
3163E0  443039C7 1529A483 C34C3538 923A6A5A  C51E847F FB5A07AC 44181CD6 E63C53D2  *...G.....C.......E.........OW..K*

+.1234558013580244E+05   +.1234577766666665E+05   -.1219326311329064E+04   -.1249999886515661E+06   +.6172839450617277E+04
```

11

Debugging a Program

11.1 INTRODUCTION

Once a program has been coded, it must still be tested. Any errors (commonly called "bugs") must be detected and corrected. The object is to eventually produce a program that consistently performs as desired. A few simple principles can be used to minimize the effort required to "debug" a program.

Principle 1. Before a program is submitted for its first test, it should be listed and carefully deskchecked.

It seems to be extremely difficult for beginners to accept this principle. There is a strong tendency to believe that it is faster to "let the machine find the errors." Understanding that this is categorically wrong is a major step toward good debugging skills.

The reasons for deskchecking a program carefully before submitting it for execution are as follows:

- If the program is very long, several errors are normally detected during the deskcheck. The time spent checking the program is usually much less than the time that would have been spent tracking down the errors individually.

- The time spent reviewing the program can also be used to determine which verifications must be made to ensure the accuracy of the results. This topic will be covered in Section 11.2.

Note that saving machine time is not a major reason for deskchecking: The main reason is to save your time.

It is normally a very good practice to have someone else deskcheck (or "walk through") your code before continuing. In a classroom environment, this will depend on the rules established by your instructor. However, most good, experienced programmers regularly deskcheck each other's code.

11.2 VERIFICATION TECHNIQUES

As the program is being deskchecked, it should be examined in light of the following principle:

Principle 2. A program should be broken up into sections of code that perform separate functions. (Frequently, these are subroutines, but sometimes a single routine can also be broken into sections.) Determine how to verify that each section is performing its function correctly, and add the required statements.

For example, suppose that SORTTAB is a program to read in a table of integers, sort the table, and print the sorted values. The program can immediately be broken into three major sections:

• the section that reads in a table of integers
• the section that sorts the table
• the section that prints the table

The last two sections might be further subdivided into smaller sections.

To verify that the section to read in the table works correctly, it is necessary to display the contents of the table. Supposing that the number of entries in the table is kept in a register, the contents of that register must be displayed as well.

Assuming that the section to read the table has executed properly, the results of the sort can be verified by again displaying the contents of the table. Finally, the output of the print routine can be checked by examining the values that are actually printed.

Now, before submitting the program for its first debugging run, the extra statements should be added:

```
SORTTAB      CSECT
             read  logic
                .
                .
                .

             XDUMP                       ** ADDED **
             XDUMP TABLE,100             ** ADDED **
                .
                .
                .

             sort  logic
                .
                .
                .

             XDUMP TABLE,100             ** ADDED **
```

.
.

                  print logic
.
.
                  BR R14
       TABLE   DS 25F
.
.
.

                  END SORTTAB

The addition of these extra statements will make the output of the run much more useful by allowing you to determine which routines executed properly and, normally, to isolate an error to a single routine.

Before continuing, it seems appropriate to discuss the format of the output produced by XDUMPs. Consider the following output, which might have been produced by the first two XDUMPS:

```
BEGIN XSNAP - CALL     1 AT D0000034 USER REGISTERS

  REGS 0-7      F4F4F4F4     00000048     00000013    F4F4F4F4     00000004     0000001B    000000EC    F4F4F4F4
  REGS 8-15     F4F4F4F4     F4F4F4F4     F4F4F4F4    F4F4F4F4     F4F4F4F4     00000110    FFFE7960    00000000


BEGIN XSNAP - CALL     2 AT D000003A USER STORAGE

                        CORE ADDRESSES SPECIFIED-      0000AC TO 000110
  0000A0    F5F5F5F5 F5F5F5F5 F5F5F5F5 00000006    00000002 00000000 00000013 F5F5F5F5   *555555555555..............5555*
  0000C0    F5F5F5F5 F5F5F5F5 F5F5F5F5 F5F5F5F5    F5F5F5F5 F5F5F5F5 F5F5F5F5 F5F5F5F5   *5555555555555555555555555555555*
  LINES    0000E0-0000E0    SAME AS ABOVE
  000100    F5F5F5F5 F5F5F5F5 F5F5F5F5 F5F5F5F5    F5F5F5F5 00000000 F5F5F5F5 F5F5F5F5   *5555555555555555555555....55555555*
```

Note the following features:

• XDUMP output always begins with a line of the form

       BEGIN XSNAP = CALL   n AT mmaaaaaa USER type

   where   n   is an integer that increases by 1 for each XDUMP
                      output
           mmaaaaaa   is the rightmost four bytes of the PSW (i.e., aaaaaa
                      gives the address in the program of the first instruc-
                      tion past the XDUMP that produced the output)
           type   is REGISTERS or STORAGE, depending on which
                      format of the XDUMP produced the output

The aaaaaa is normally the most useful information. It allows you to locate quickly the XDUMP that produced the output. For example, the first XDUMP above has an address of 000034. This means that 34 is the address of the first statement past the XDUMP that displayed the registers.

- The first XDUMP has no operands. This causes the registers to be displayed. Registers 0 through 7 appear on one line, and registers 8 through 15 appear on the next line. Thus, by looking at the output, you should be able to verify that register 4 contained 00000004 at the time of the dump.
- The second XDUMP displays an area in memory. The line

CORE ADDRESSES SPECIFIED — 0000AC TO 000110

gives the range of addresses to be displayed. Each line of the display contains the address of the first byte displayed on the line, 32 bytes of memory in hexadecimal format, and finally the same 32 bytes in character format. ("Unprintable" characters are printed as periods.) Thus,

Address	Hexadecimal output of 32 bytes	Character output
0000A0	F5F5F5F5 F5F5F5F5 F5F5F5F5 00000006 00000002 00000000 00000013 F5F5F5F5	.55555555555...............5555.

The reader should now be able to see that the word at that address contains 00000006. Note that the display prints only complete 32-byte lines and that each line begins with an address that is a multiple of 32 (20_{16}). This can cause confusion, so the reader should make sure that the format is intelligible. (To test yourself, find the contents of the byte at address BB. The answer is 13.)

Most of the debugging time spent on assignments from this text should be spent deskchecking, inserting XDUMPS to verify results, and carefully checking the produced output.

One more principle relating to verification must be covered:

Principle 3. If a program is large enough to contain several routines, test the routines separately.

To illustrate this principle, consider the SORTTAB program. One reasonable way to write such a program is as follows:

1. Write the section that reads in the table of integers. Run this short program, XDUMPing the completed table to verify that everything is working properly.
2. While you are debugging the read routine, code the sort and print routines.
3. Combine the read and sort routines and test them together, XDUMPing the sorted table to verify the sort. At the same time, you can combine the read and print routines (without the sort) to begin debugging the print routine.

There are several benefits to this approach:

- Most errors are easy to locate, since only a small amount of untested code is used in each run.

- Debugging can begin earlier. This makes the process less vulnerable to unforeseen disasters (such as computer breakdown).

- It is easier to make an accurate estimate of progress. If all the program is coded but none of it has been debugged, it is hard to say when the program will be finished. On the other hand, if three-fourths of the routines are coded and half are debugged, there is some basis for projecting the time required to complete the project.

11.3 WORKING FROM A DUMP

When a program ends abnormally due to an error, a "dump" is produced. Program 11-1 on page 400 gives an example of an ASSIST dump.

In this section, the basic technique for locating an error from information in a dump will be covered. We have chosen a relatively simple program to illustrate how a dump should be approached. Please read through the source listing before continuing. Note that the line numbers on the left would not normally appear—we have included them for the purpose of this discussion. You may very well have spotted the bug. If so, do not let that distract you from the goal of learning how to extract information from a dump.

A great deal could be said about the art of reading dumps. However, following just a few basic principles will usually make the task of locating bugs quite straightforward.

Principle 4. Find out exactly what caused the abnormal termination.

To do this, perform the following tasks:

1. Determine the type of error that caused termination. This is done by examining the first line of the dump (line 97). In this dump

    COMPLETION CODE   SYSTEM = 0C7   DATA

    appears. There is a manual that lists the meanings of all completion codes. For the dumps that you encounter with the assignments in this text, however, DATA conveys all the relevant information. Here, a data exception caused termination.

2. Determine the exact instruction that caused the error. In our example, this can also be determined from line 97. The right word of the PSW contains the address of the instruction following the one where the error occurred. Thus, since the address is 00001A, the error occurred while executing the ST instruction shown on line 48. (The left column of the source listing gives the location of the instruction.) ASSIST also provides a convenient instruction trace (lines 98–109). The last ten executed instructions are given, and the instruction that caused the error is labeled.

Program 11-1

2   $JOB

PAGE   1

```
      LOC    OBJECT CODE    ADDR1 ADDR2  STMT   SOURCE STATEMENT
  4                                        STMT   SOURCE STATEMENT
  5                                          1  * THIS PROGRAM READS IN A SET OF INTEGERS INTO A TABLE AND XDUMPS
  6                                          2  * IT.  AS THE VALUES ARE READ THEY ARE ACCUMULATED.  AT THE END
  7                                          3  * THE SUM OF THE TABLE ENTRIES IS PRINTED.  THE LOGIC IS
  8                                          4  *
  9                                          5  * STEP 1.  SET COUNT OF TABLE ENTRIES TO 0, SUM OF TABLE ENTRIES
 10                                          6  *          TO 0, AND INITIALIZE A POINTER TO POINT TO THE FIRST
 11                                          7  *          TABLE ENTRY.
 12                                          8  *
 13                                          9  * STEP 2.  READ THE FIRST CARD.
 14                                         10  *
 15                                         11  * STEP 3.  IF EOF HAS OCCURRED, GO TO STEP 6  TO XDUMP THE TABLE
 16                                         12  *          AND PRINT THE SUM OF THE ENTRIES.
 17                                         13  *
 18                                         14  * STEP 4.  STORE THE NUMBER INTO THE TABLE, INCREMENT THE COUNT OF
 19                                         15  *          TABLE ENTRIES, AND ADD THE NUMBER TO THE SUM.
 20                                         16  *
 21                                         17  * STEP 5.  READ THE NEXT CARD AND GO TO STEP 3.
 22                                         18  *
 23                                         19  * STEP 6.  XDUMP THE COUNT OF THE TABLE ENTRIES AND THE TABLE.
 24                                         20  *          THEN PRINT THE SUM OF THE ENTRIES.
 25                                         21  *
 26                                         22  * STEP 7.  EXIT.
 27                                         23  *
 28  000000                                 24  DUMPEX   CSECT
 29  000000                                 25           USING DUMPEX,R15
 30                                         26  *
 31                                         27  ***<STEP 1>  SET COUNT AND SUM TO 0.   POINT TO 1ST TABLE ENTRY.
 32                                         28  *
 33  000000 1B44                            29           SR    R4,R4            SET COUNT TO 0
 34  000002 1B55                            30           SR    R5,R5            SET SUM TO 0
 35  000004 4160 F0AC           000AC       31           LA    R6,TABLE         POINT TO 1ST TABLE ENTRY
 36                                         32  *
 37                                         33  ***<STEP 2>  READ THE FIRST CARD
 38                                         34  *
 39  000008 E000 F046 0050  00046           35           XREAD CARD,80
 40                                         36  *
 41                                         37  ***<STEP 3>  IF EOF HAS OCCURRED, GO TO STEP 6.
 42                                         38  *
 43  00000E 4740 F02E           0002E       39  LOOP     BC    B'0100',EOF      BRANCH ON EOF
 44                                         40  *
 45                                         41  ***<STEP 4>  ADD ENTRY TO TABLE, INCR COUNT, AND ADD TO SUM
 46                                         42  *
 47  000012 5320 F046           00046       43           XDECI R2,CARD          R2 HAS NEXT ENTRY
 48  000016 5026 0000           00000       44           ST    R2,0(R6)         STORE INTO THE TABLE
 49  00001A 4166 0004           00004       45           LA    R6,4(R6)         POINT TO NEXT ENTRY
 50  00001E 4144 0001           00001       46           LA    R4,1(R4)         INCR COUNT
 51  000022 1AF2                            47           AR    15,R2            ACCUMULATE THE SUM
 52                                         48  *
 53                                         49  ***<STEP 5>  READ THE NEXT CARD AND GO BACK TO STEP 3
 54                                         50  *
 55  000024 E000 F046 0050  00046           51           XREAD CARD,80
```

Program 11-1 (continued)

```
        LOC     OBJECT CODE     ADDR1 ADDR2   STMT   SOURCE STATEMENT
 56
 57   00002A   47F0 F00E              0000E     52          B     LOOP
 58                                             53   *
 59                                             54   ***<STEP 6>    XDUMP THE TABLE AND PRINT THE SUM
 60                                             55   *
 61   00002E   E160 0000 0000   00000           56   EOF    XDUMP
 62   000034   E060 F0AC 0064   000AC           57          XDUMP TABLE,100      R4 HAD THE COUNT IN THE 1ST XDUMP
 63   00003A   5250 F0A0                         58          XDECO R5,SUM
 64   00003E   E020 F096 0016   00096           59          XPRNT ANS,22         PRINT THE SUM
 65   000044   07FE                              60          BR    R14           EXIT
 66                                             61   *
 67   000046                                    62   CARD   DS    CL80           CARD IO AREA
 68   000096   F05C5C5C40E2E4D4                 63   ANS    DC    C'0*** SUM ='
 69   0000A0                                    64   SUM    DS    CL12
 70   0000AC                                    65   TABLE  DS    25F
 71                                             66          LTORG
 72   000000                                    67   R0     EQU   0
 73   000001                                    68   R1     EQU   1
 74   000002                                    69   R2     EQU   2
 75   000003                                    70   R3     EQU   3
 76   000004                                    71   R4     EQU   4
 77   000005                                    72   R5     EQU   5
 78   000006                                    73   R6     EQU   6
 79   000007                                    74   R7     EQU   7
 80   000008                                    75   R8     EQU   8
 81   000009                                    76   R9     EQU   9
 82   00000A                                    77   R10    EQU   10
 83   00000B                                    78   R11    EQU   11
 84   00000C                                    79   R12    EQU   12
 85   00000D                                    80   R13    EQU   13
 86   00000E                                    81   R14    EQU   14
 87   00000F                                    82   R15    EQU   15
 88                                             83          END   DUMPEX
 89

 90   *** NO  STATEMENTS FLAGGED - NO   WARNINGS,   NO   ERRORS
 91   *** DYNAMIC CORE AREA USED:  LOW:  2468 HIGH:  576 LEAVING:  99356 FREE BYTES. AVERAGE:  36 BYTES/STMT ***
 92   *** ASSEMBLY TIME = 0.049 SECS,  1714 STATEMENTS/SEC ***

 93   *** PROGRAM EXECUTION BEGINNING - ANY OUTPUT BEFORE EXECUTION TIME MESSAGE IS PRODUCED BY USER PROGRAM ***

 94   *** EXECUTION TIME = 0.000 SECS.    13 INSTRUCTIONS EXECUTED -    13000 INSTRUCTIONS/SEC ***

 95   *** FIRST CARD NOT READ: 0

 96   ASSIST COMPLETION DUMP

 97   PSW AT ABEND FFC50007 C000001A     COMPLETION CODE    SYSTEM = 0C7 DATA

 98   ** TRACE OF INSTRUCTIONS JUST BEFORE TERMINATION: PSW BITS SHOWN ARE THOSE BEFORE CORRESPONDING INSTRUCTION DECODED ***

 99   IM LOCATION    INSTRUCTION :   IM = PSW BITS 32-39(ILC,CC,MASK) BEFORE INSTRUCTION EXECUTED AT PROGRAM LOCATION SHOWN

100   00   000008    E000 F046 0050
```

Program 11-1 (continued)

```
101   C0   00000E     4740 F02E
102   80   000012     5320 F046
103   A0   000016     5026 0000
104   A0   00001A     4166 0004
105   A0   00001E     4144 0001
106   A0   000022     1AF2
107   60   000024     E000 F046 0050
108   C0   00002A     47F0 F00E
109   80   000014     F046 5026 0000   <-- LAST INSTRUCTION DONE - PROBABLE CAUSE OF TERMINATION
110

111  ** TRACE OF LAST 10 BRANCH INSTRUCTIONS EXECUTED: PSW BITS SHOWN ARE THOSE BEFORE CORRESPONDING INSTRUCTION DECODED ***
112   IM LOCATION   INSTRUCTION :   IM = PSW BITS 32-39(ILC,CC,MASK) BEFORE INSTRUCTION EXECUTED AT PROGRAM LOCATION SHOWN
113   00   00002A     47F0 F00E

114   REGS 0-7    F4F4F4F4  00000047  00000006  F4F4F4F4  00000001  00000000  000000B0  F4F4F4F4
115   REGS 8-15   F4F4F4F4  F4F4F4F4  F4F4F4F4  F4F4F4F4  F4F4F4F4  00000110  FFFE7960  00000006
116   FLTR 0-6    F4F4F4F4F4F4F4F4   F4F4F4F4F4F4F4F4   F4F4F4F4F4F4F4F4   F4F4F4F4F4F4F4F4

117   USER STORAGE

                     CORE ADDRESSES SPECIFIED-           000000  TO 000258
118   000000   1B441B55 4160F0AC E000F046 00504740 F0253320 F0465026 00044144            *............0....0....0......*
119   000020   00011AF2 E000F046 00504740 F00EE160 00000000 E060F0AC 00645250 F0AE0020   *....2..0....C0......0.....0...*
120   000040   F0960016 07EF640  F2404040 40404040 40404040 40404040 40404040 40404040   *0.....6....2..................*
121   000060   40404040 40404040 40404040 40404040 40404040 40404040 40404040 40404040   *..............................*
122   000080   40404040 40404040 40404040 40404040 40404040 40404040 E4D4407E            *.............UM.*
123   0000A0   F5F5F5F5 F5F5F5F5 F5F5F5F5 F5F5F5F5 F5F5F5F5 F5F5F5F5 00000006            *555555555555...5555555*
124   0000C0   F5F5F5F5 F5F5F5F5 F5F5F5F5 F5F5F5F5 F5F5F5F5 F5F5F5F5                      *5555555555555555555555*
125   LINES    0000E0-0000E0    SAME AS ABOVE
126   000100   F5F5F5F5 F5F5F5F5 F5F5F5F5 F5F5F5F5 00000000                              *5555555555555...555555555*
127   000120   F5F5F5F5 F5F5F5F5 F5F5F5F5 F5F5F5F5 F5F5F5F5 F5F5F5F5 F5F5F5F5 F5F5F5F5    *5555555555555555555555555555*
128   LINES    000140-000220    SAME AS ABOVE
129

130
131  *** TOTAL RUN TIME UNDER ASSIST =        0.083  SECS***
```

Note the discrepancy! Lines 108 and 109 show that the branch instruction at line 58

B   LOOP

caused a branch to location 000014 (not to location 00000E, as was intended). All this may seem confusing. Do not let this disturb you—just continue gathering information, always asking: "How could this have happened?" Never assume that it could not have happened, that "the machine broke."

3. Verify that the program has not been altered in memory (by storing values over instructions). At this point, we are mostly concerned with the instructions in the area of 000012-000022. Lines 119 through 129 display the contents of memory at the time of the error. Since the format is the same as that used by an XDUMP, you should be able to compare the contents of 000012-000022 with the source listing. (The object code is shown in the second, third, and fourth columns of the source listing.) Verify that the instructions have not been altered.

4. It is sometimes interesting to look at the contents of data areas. In our example, it might be useful to examine the contents of CARD and TABLE. (Do this as an exercise in locating memory locations.) The registers at the time of the error appear in lines 114–115. (The floating-point registers, which are seldom of interest, appear in line 116.) Registers 2, 4, 5, and 6 all have some bearing on this problem. Check their contents and determine whether they contain "expected" values.

At this point, after analyzing the state of the machine when the error occurred, a new principle must be applied.

Principle 5. Isolate the error. Determine which section of code produced unexpected, erroneous results.

The example that we are considering is so short that this principle really does not apply. In a longer program, however, it is extremely important. Too often a student will simply peruse page after page of code, hoping that the error will become apparent. If the verification of output is not adequate to isolate the error, carefully add more verification logic and resubmit the program.

Finally, after isolating the section of code that produced the error, use the following principle:

Principle 6. Ask yourself: "What could have caused the error?" Work backward from the error.

This is the "detective" part of debugging. In this example, the procedure might go as follows:

a. We know that

    B   LOOP

caused a branch to location 000014. The actual branch was not altered. This can occur only if the address that was computed resulted in 000014.

b. The address in the branch instruction is F00E (14 bytes past the address in R15). Since this gave the wrong value, R15 must not be set properly.

c. Since R15 was set properly when the program was entered (by assumption), the program must have altered R15. Now we have the bug. The program should not have altered R15, but it did. By looking through the code, you will see in line 51

    AR   15,R2

R15 is altered. (The "15" should be "R5.") The bug was probably caused by a typing error.

With more experience in debugging, the error could have been detected more quickly. Useful rules, such as

If the PSW (location of the next instruction) does not point at a valid instruction or points at a quite unexpected location, check to see whether the program in memory was altered or a base register was altered

will eventually become part of your debugging repertoire.

11.4 SUMMARY

Being able to debug a program is a skill required of any programmer. A good way to develop the ability to debug a program rapidly is to study the six principles and consistently apply them.

Principle 1.   Before a program is submitted for its first test, it should be listed and carefully deskchecked.

Principle 2.   A program should be broken up into sections of code that perform separate functions. (Frequently, these are subroutines, but sometimes a single routine can also be broken into sections.) Determine how to verify that each section is performing its function correctly, and add the required statements.

Principle 3.   If a program is large enough to contain several routines, test the routines separately.

Principle 4.   Find out exactly what caused the abnormal termination.

Principle 5.   Isolate the error. Determine which section of code produced unexpected, erroneous results.

Principle 6. Ask yourself: "What could have caused the error?" Work backward from the error.

Finally, after locating each troublesome bug, reevaluate your attack on the error. Determine whether you approached it methodically or wasted time and effort. Try to synthesize your experience into general rules. Learn from your errors so that you can avoid repeating them.

12

Structured Programming

12.1 INTRODUCTION

Since the first edition of this text was written, a number of advances have been made in programming methodology. In particular, the advantages of structured programming techniques have become widely recognized. For this reason, most of the examples in the preceding chapters have been replaced with structured programs. In this chapter, the techniques for creating structured programs are presented in detail.

As programming problems become larger and more complex, correct solutions are increasingly difficult to produce. More care is required at the design stage to ensure that the program will produce satisfactory results. All routines and subroutines must be designed so that they will work together correctly and simply.

Each programming task poses a unique set of problems, but the following design criteria apply to every program:

- *Clarity.* The logic of the program should be easy to understand.
- *Modularity.* A program should be broken down functionally into subroutines that interact with each other. It is possible to understand large programs only if they are designed in this way.
- *Ease of modification.* Very few programs survive for long without some changes. Programs should be designed so that modifications can be easily made.
- *Correctness.* An algorithm that has been designed with simplicity as a goal will be easier to verify. In such cases, coding the program should be a routine chore.

Structured programming techniques have been designed and adopted to aid in satisfying these criteria.

The germ of the idea of structured programming came from a paper presented in 1964 to the International Colloquium on Algebraic Linguistics and Automata Theory in Israel. In this paper, Corrado Böhm and Guiseppe Jacopini proved that any programming logic can be expressed using sequential processes and only two control structures.

The first large-scale application of structured programming techniques to a commercial setting took place from 1969 to 1972—the highly publicized "New York Times Project," carried out by the IBM Corporation. The remarkable success of this project and the publicity it received led to general acceptance of structured programming techniques by the mid-1970s.

Pseudo-code came into vogue as a notation for presenting program logic, along with the general acceptance of structured programming techniques. In this section and Sections 12.2 and 12.3, pseudo-code is introduced by displaying the logic of some simple constructs and programs in pseudo-code, as well as in flowcharts.

Before considering an example, we shall present a definition of *structured logic*. The meaning and significance of structured logic will become apparent as the examples in the rest of this chapter are examined. A *basic block of code* is a sequence of assembler instructions that is executed from top to bottom. It can contain calls to subroutines, but it cannot include branches. A *structured block of code* can be defined as follows:

1. A basic block of code is a structured block of code.
2. If **block a** and **block b** are both structured blocks of code, then the structure representing **block a** followed by **block b** is a structured block of code. Such a structure is called a *sequence structure*.
3. If **block a** and **block b** are both structured blocks of code and if **cond** is a condition, the structure that causes **cond** to be tested and **block a** or **block b** to be selected on the basis of that test is a structured block of code. Such a structure is called an *if-then-else structure*. Either **block a** or **block b**, but not both, may be vacuous.
4. If **block a** is a structured block of code and if **cond** is a condition, the structure that causes **block a** to be executed repeatedly until **cond** is true is a structured block of code. Such a structure is called a *do-while structure*.

A *structured program* is one that can be formed by repeated application of these four rules. Figure 12-1 and the corresponding pseudo-code illustrate the logic of a structured program.

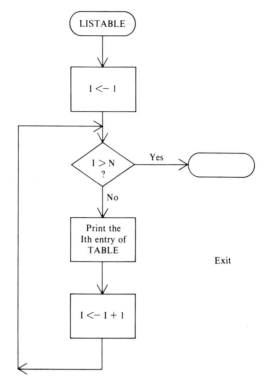

Figure 12-1

PSEUDO-CODE

LISTABLE: Proc(TABLE,N)
    I <− 1
    Do while (I <= N)
        Print the Ith entry of TABLE
        I <− I + 1
    Enddo
Endproc

   Study the flowchart to make sure that you understand the logic. The algorithm prints the N entries in TABLE. I is used as a subscript. Now the pseudo-code should be decipherable:

a.   LISTABLE: Proc(TABLE,N)
           .
           .
           .

      Endproc

indicates a module called LISTABLE with two input parameters (TABLE and N). The logic will be described in detail between Proc and Endproc.

b. The individual steps in the pseudo-code correspond to boxes in the flowchart.

c. The loop is presented as

> Do while (condition)
> .
> .
> .
> Enddo

which means that the steps between Do and Enddo are to be repeated until the condition is not true. To visually set off the body of the loop, we indent it.

In the following sections of this chapter, the rules for constructing accept-able patterns of logic will be considered. For now, a basic grasp of flowcharts and pseudo-code will suffice.

12.2 LOOPS—THE DO-WHILE CONSTRUCT

The structure of the loop in Figure 12-1 can be generalized. Consider the problem of processing the elements of an ordered set, as shown in Figure 12-2 on page 410.

In Figure 12-1, the ordered set was the set of entries in TABLE. Thus, in Figure 12-2,

1. "Set up to access the first element" means "set I to 1."
2. "Has the entire set been processed?" means "check to see whether I is greater than N."
3. "Process one element" means "print the Ith element."
4. "Set up to access the next element" means "add 1 to I."

Now consider the problem of listing a deck of cards, as shown in Figure 12-3 on page 410. Note that the pattern of logic is identical to that exhibited in Figure 12.2.

Now we will examine the logic of a program to read in a set of test scores (one per card) and calculate the average of the scores. Before continuing, write a flowchart to describe the algorithm.

The pseudo-code (which hopefully matches your flowchart) for the problem is as follows:

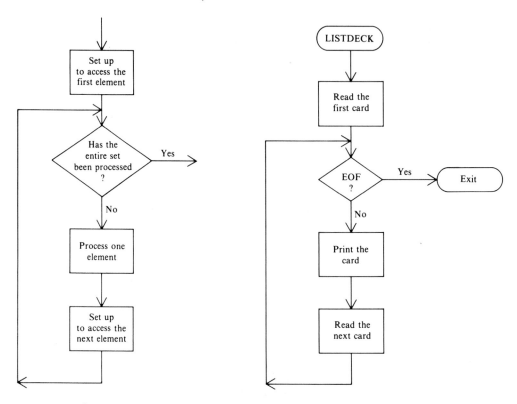

Figure 12-2   **Figure 12-3**

```
TESTAVG: PROC
      SUM <- 0
      NUM <- 0
      Read the first card
      Do while (EOF has not occurred)
           add the test score to SUM
           NUM <- NUM + 1
           Read the next card
      Enddo
      AVG <- SUM/NUM
      Print AVG
Endproc
```

You might have added a line to print each value or a check to see whether
EOF occurred on the first read. What is important is that your loop be
similar to the one above. That is, it should have a structure as shown in
Figure 12-4.

The pattern of logic that occurs in each of these loops is one of the fundamental patterns of logic. Most loops can be thought of as following this pattern. All loops can be made to conform to the structure of Figure 12-5. This is the pattern represented by the "do-while" construct in pseudo-code. In a structured program, all loops must conform to this pattern.

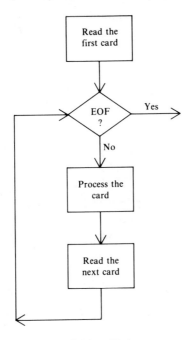

Figure 12-4

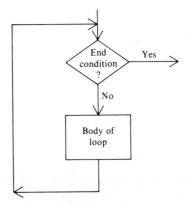

Figure 12-5

12.3 PROCESSING ALTERNATIVES— THE IF CONSTRUCT

At certain points in an algorithm it is necessary to break the logic into alternatives. In this case, the "if <cond> then <code-1> else <code-2>" construct should be used. (See Figure 12-6.)

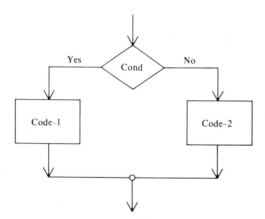

Figure 12-6

PSEUDO-CODE—IF

```
If (cond)
      code-1
else
      code-2
Endif
```

To illustrate this pattern, consider Figure 12-7, an algorithm to find the largest integer in a table of N numbers.

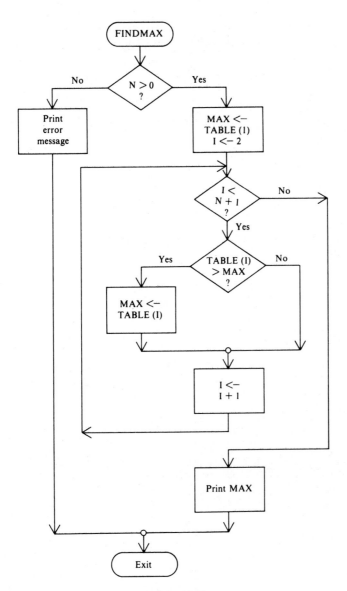

Figure 12-7

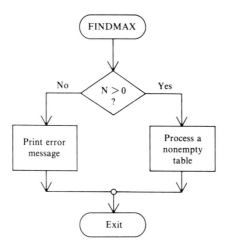

Figure 12-8

The structure of FINDMAX can be visualized as in Figure 12-8, where "process a nonempty table" is as in Figure 12-9.

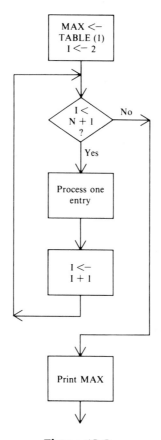

Figure 12-9

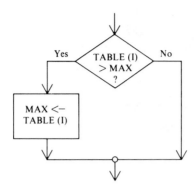

Figure 12-10

In Figure 12-10, "process one entry" is valid, even though one alternative contains no code. The pseudo-code for FINDMAX would be as follows:

```
FINDMAX: Proc(TABLE,N)
    If (N <= 0)
        Print error message
    else
        MAX <- TABLE(1)
        I <- 2
        Do while (I < N + 1)
            If (TABLE(I) > MAX)
                MAX <- TABLE(I)
            Endif
            I <- I + 1
        Enddo
        Print MAX
    Endif
Endproc
```

Note the exact correspondence between the flowchart and the pseudo-code.

Occasionally, there will be more than two alternatives. This is called a *case analysis* and is depicted as in Figure 12-11.

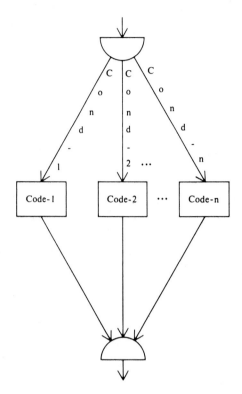

Figure 12-11

The pseudo-code for this logic is

       If
    Cond(cond-1)
        code-1

    Cond(cond-2)
        code-2
    .
    .
    .

    Cond(cond-n)
        code-n

       Endif

Here it is assumed that at least one of the conditions will be true. For convenience, the last condition may be given as

       Cond Else
        Code

To illustrate this type of structure, suppose that a program to balance a checkbook processes three types of transactions:

• checks
• deposits
• automatic deductions and service charges

Each transaction contains a code (C, D or A) to identify the type of transaction. In this case, the logic might appear as in Figure 12-12.

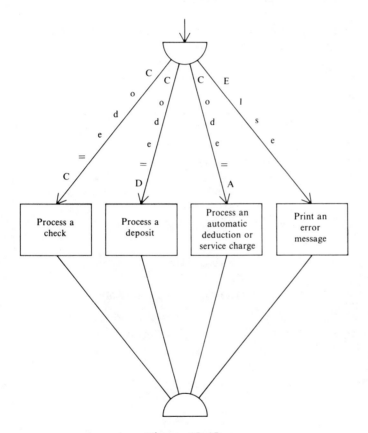

Figure 12-12

PSEUDO-CODE

> If
> Cond (code = C)
> > Process a check
> Cond (code = D)
> > Process a deposit

```
Cond (code = A)
        Process an automatic deduction or service charge
Cond Else
        Print an error message
Endif
```

12.4 HOW TO FORMULATE AN ALGORITHM—STEPWISE REFINEMENT

Once the requirements of a program are well understood, the programmer faces the problem of formulating an appropriate algorithm. The technique of stepwise refinement imposes a discipline that allows the programmer to methodically reach a correct, well-structured solution. In this section, we will describe this approach and illustrate its use in a typical program.

The logic of most programs is quite complex. To attack such a problem, it is necessary to break it into subproblems. This is really the key to the design of good logic—the ability to break up a problem into the correct subproblems. The algorithm must be broken up into a few major subfunctions so that, if you think of the subfunctions as subroutines, the algorithm is short and clear. The algorithm should, of course, be constructed using the do-while logic for each loop and the if-then-else logic whenever alternative processing is required.

Once the main routine is properly completed, each subroutine can be attacked using the same approach:

1. Define the subfunctions that allow the task to be broken into a few basic components.
2. Using the defined subfunctions, compose the logic of the algorithm, using the do-while and if-then-else constructs.

To illustrate this technique, we will reconsider a problem presented in Chapter 4: Formulate the logic for a program to produce "class lists" for each class being taught in a given school. The input to the program is assumed to be a set of cards punched to conform to the following format:

Card Column	Contents
1–4	Department offering the course
5–8	Course number
9–18	Last name of student
19–28	First name of student
29–80	(Unused)

It is further assumed that this card file has been sorted into ascending order, based on the first 28 columns. The program is to produce a class list for each class, which includes the total number of students registered in the class.

This problem represents a general category of data processing programs called *reports*. Although this program will be relatively simple, the basic logic is typical of most reports.

First, note the function of the report—to produce a set of class lists. It is useful to think of the input as a sequence of groups, each group containing the cards for one class. The function of the program is to process a sequence of groups, producing a class list for each group. If a subroutine is used to process a single group (producing one class list), then the rest of the logic will become manageable. (See Figure 12-13.)

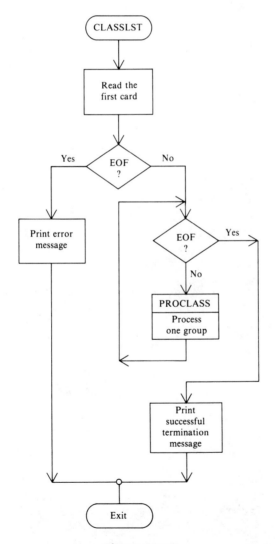

Figure 12-13

Note that the logic depicted in Figure 12-13 is essentially the same as that used to list a deck of cards, with an additional check to ensure that the input file is not empty. The first card must be read before calling PROCLASS, since PROCLASS must always read through the first card of the next group. (This is nontrivial—make sure that you understand.)

The flowchart for CLASSLST is simple and comprehensible. It is properly structured using the if-then-else and do-while patterns. It may be necessary to make some minor modifications later, but at this point it seems correct.

Now the logic for PROCLASS can be considered. If you think about it, there are three basic pieces of logic, as shown in Figure 12-14.

1. Initialization involves
   - saving the department and course number from the first card (which was already read)
   - setting the count of students in the list to zero
   - printing the page headers on the first page of the class list

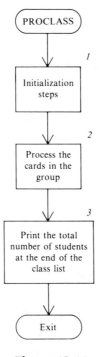

Figure 12-14

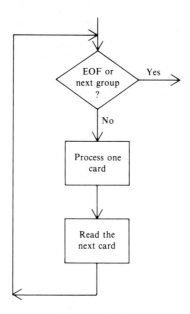

Figure 12-15

2. Processing the cards involves printing the data from each card in the current group and stopping as soon as the first card from the next group is encountered (or when EOF occurs).

3. The only total in this report is the number of students in the class.

You must admit that the resulting logic is simple! The first block can be expanded to three, one for each initialization step. It is not necessary to implement each block as a separate subroutine. A single block can be replaced by several if doing so does not make the logic overly complex. However, the overall flowchart should always fit on a single page.

The second block processes a sequence of cards (those in the group). This logic should be familiar to you by now. (See Figure 12-15.)

"Process one card" simply means

- build a print line
- call PRINTSP1 to print it after single-spacing (unless it is time to skip to the next page)
- increment the count of students

After expanding PROCLASS, the logic shown in Figure 12-16 results.

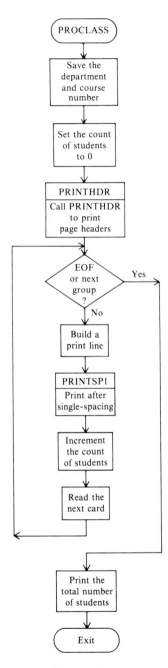

Figure 12-16

PRINTHDR actually contains only trivial logic—print the headers and set the LINECTR to 5. (LINECTR will always contain the line number of the next line on the page.) PRINTSP1 is only slightly more complex. (See Figure 12-17.)

A "rough draft" of the logic for the program is now complete. We achieved this by continually deferring problems, to keep the logic of each routine simple. This is important: It is the only way to consistently compose correct algorithms.

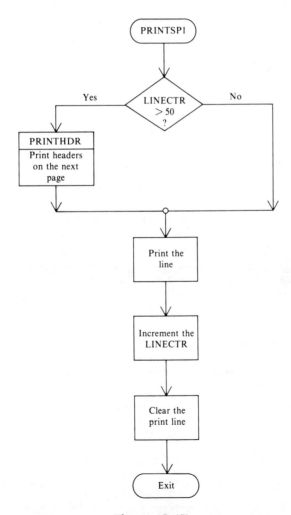

Figure 12-17

Our final version of the logic has only two slight modifications:

- A subroutine was created to read cards and set an end-of-file flag.
- We decided that the main routine should initially clear the print line. Then the print line will be cleared immediately after each line is printed.

12.5 A STRUCTURED PROGRAM WITH PSEUDO-CODE

The documentation of a structured program is more naturally accomplished with pseudo-code than with step algorithms. Programs 12-1 and 12-2 implement the CLASSLST and PROCLASS algorithms from Section 12.4.

Program 12-1

```
***********************************************************************
*
* CLASSLST: PROGRAM
*
* (1) CALL READCARD TO READ THE FIRST CARD AND SET EOFFLAG TO Y
*          IF END-OF-FILE IS DETECTED
*
*      IF (EOF OCCURRED - NO CARDS IN THE INPUT FILE)
*
* (2)      PRINT AN ERROR MESSAGE (EMPTY INPUT FILE)
*
*      ELSE
*
* (3)      CLEAR THE PRINT LINE. FROM NOW ON IT IS CLEARED AFTER EACH
*             LINE IS PRINTED.
*
*          DO WHILE (EOF HAS NOT YET OCCURRED)
*
* (4)          CALL PROCLASS TO PROCESS THE CARDS FOR ONE CLASS LIST
*                 (AND TO READ THE 1ST CARD FOR THE NEXT LIST)
*
*          ENDDO
*
* (5)      PRINT A "SUCCESSFUL TERMINATION" MESSAGE
*
*      ENDIF
*
*    ENDPROG
*
***********************************************************************
*
CLASSLST CSECT
         LR    R12,R15               SET UP R12 AS THE BASE REGISTER
         USING CLASSLST,R12
*
         BAL   R11,READCARD          READ THE 1ST CARD            (1)
*
         CLI   EOFFLAG,C'Y'
         BNE   CLEARLN               BRANCH IF EOF WAS NOT DETECTED
*
         XPRNT =C'1*** NO INPUT ***',17                          (2)
         B     EXIT
*
CLEARLN  MVI   PRNTLINE,C' '         CLEAR THE PRINT LINE        (3)
         MVC   PRNTLINE+1(132),PRNTLINE
```

Program 12-1 (continued)

```
*
PROCLOOP CLI    EOFFLAG,C'Y'      CONTINUE LOOPING UNTIL EOF
         BE     PRINTEND
*
         BAL    R11,PROCLASS      PRINT 1 CLASS LIST              (4)
*
         B      PROCLOOP
*
PRINTEND XPRNT  =C'1*** SUCCESSFUL TERMINATION ***',31           (5)
*
EXIT     BR     R14               LEAVE THE PROGRAM
*
```

Program 12-2

```
**********************************************************************
*
* PROCLASS PRODUCES 1 CLASS LIST.  WHEN IT COMPLETES, EITHER
* EOF HAS OCCURRED (EOFFLAG WILL BE Y) OR THE FIRST CARD FOR THE
* NEXT CLASS LIST HAS BEEN READ.  THE LOGIC IS AS FOLLOWS:
*
* PROCLASS: PROC
*
*  (1)     SAVE THE DEPARTMENT AND COURSE FOR THIS LIST
*
*  (2)     SET THE COUNT OF THE STUDENTS IN THE LIST TO 0
*
*  (3)     CALL PRINTHDR TO PRINT THE HEADERS FOR THE FIRST PAGE OF
*              THE CLASS LIST
*
*          DO WHILE (EOF HAS NOT OCCURRED AND THE CURRENT CARD IS FOR
*                    THE CLASS LIST THAT WE ARE PRINTING)
*
*  (4)         BUILD A PRINT LINE FROM DATA ON THE CARD
*
*  (5)         CALL PRINTSP1 TO PRINT AFTER SPACING 1 (HEADERS
*                  WILL BE PRINTED IF THE NEXT LINE ON THE PAGE
*                  IS GREATER THAN 50)
*
*  (6)         ADD 1 TO THE COUNT OF STUDENTS IN THE LIST
*
*  (7)         CALL READCARD TO READ THE NEXT CARD AND SET EOFFLAG
*
*          ENDDO
*
*  (8)     PRINT THE TOTAL NUMBER OF STUDENTS IN THE CLASS LIST
*
*     ENDPROC
*
**********************************************************************
*
PROCLASS STM    R14,R12,PRCLSAVE+12 SAVE CALLER'S REGISTERS
*
         MVC    CURRKEY,CARD      SAVE THE KEY (DEPT,COURSE)    (1)
*
         SR     R2,R2             SET COUNT OF STUDENTS IN THE  (2)
*                                 LIST TO 0
*
         BAL    R11,PRINTHDR      PRINT THE PAGE HEADERS        (3)
*
         CLI    EOFFLAG,C'Y'      END LOOP ON EOF OR NEW KEY
         BE     PRINTTOT
         CLC    CURRKEY,CARD
         BNE    PRINTTOT          MISMATCH MEANS NEW KEY
*
```

Program 12-2 (continued)

```
         MVC    DEPTOUT,DEPTIN          NOW MOVE DATA FIELDS           (4)
         MVC    COURSOUT,COURSIN        THE PRINT LINE
         MVC    LNAMEOUT,LNAMEIN
         MVC    FNAMEOUT,FNAMEIN
*
         BAL    R11,PRINTSP1            PRINT THE LINE (AND HEADERS,   (5)
*                                       IF NECESSARY)
*
         LA     R2,1(R2)                ADD 1 TO COUNT OF STUDENTS     (6)
*
         BAL    R11,READCARD            TRY TO READ THE NEXT CARD      (7)
*
         B      PROCLOOP
*
PRINTTOT XDECO  R2,PRNTLINE+25          PUT TOTAL INTO PRINT LINE      (8)
         MVC    PRNTLINE+7(18),=C'TOTAL # STUDENTS ='
         MVI    PRNTLINE,C'0'           SET CARRIAGE CONTROL FOR
*                                       DOUBLE-SPACE
         XPRNT  PRNTLINE,133            PRINT LAST LINE FOR LIST
         MVI    PRNTLINE,C' '           CLEAR THE PRINT LINE
         MVC    PRNTLINE+1(132),PRNTLINE
*
         LM     R14,R12,PRCLSAVE+12 RESTORE CALLER'S REGISTERS
         BR     R11
*
PRCLSAVE DS     18F                     REGISTER SAVE AREA
*
```

There are many documentation styles. We feel that the following features are significant:

- The pseudo-code should never contain "go to step n." All loops should follow the do-while pattern, and all alternatives should follow the if-then-else (or case analysis) pattern.

- The instructions that implement the pseudo-code should faithfully implement the described logic. In Programs 12-1 and 12-2, we number the English descriptions in the pseudo-code and use these numbers as comments in the actual code. This usage allows the reader to locate a section of code rapidly.

12.6 WRITING STRUCTURED PROGRAMS USING MACROS TO IMPLEMENT THE STRUCTURES

A variety of macro libraries have been developed to support structured programming. Appendix F contains the listings of one such library. These macros were developed by Dave Carpenter, Naiping Lee, and Gene Petrie at Northern Illinois University. They use features that are not supported by ASSIST's macro processor; they are intended for use with any standard assembler supplied by IBM (or any compatible assembler).

An example will help to clarify the use of such macros. The following

```
                IF (LTR,R15,R15,M)
*
                L       R2, = F' − 1'
*
                ELSE
*
                SR      R2,R2
*
                ENDIF
```

generates code equivalent to

```
                LTR       R15,R15
                BNM       POS
                L         R1, = F' − 1'
                B         NEXTINS
POS             SR        R2,R2
NEXTINS         EQU       *
```

Note the clarity that is achieved by using the macros and a few interspersed comment cards.

The IF, ELSE and ENDIF macros generate the testing and branch instructions required to support alternatives. These can be coded as follows:

```
            IF condition
*
                code to execute if the condition is true
*
            ELSE
*
                code to execute if the condition is false
*
            ENDIF
```

or as

```
            IF condition
*
                code to execute if the condition is true
*
            ENDIF
```

The condition can take several forms. A basic condition can be one of the following:

1. *A branch mask.* Thus

```
        IF (M)
            LPR  R4,R4
        ENDIF
```

    is equivalent to

```
            BNM      NEXTINS
            LPR      R4,R4
NEXTINS     EQU      *
```

2. *A comparison.* Here the condition is specified as a list with four components:

    (comparison mnemonic,first operand,operator,second operand)

    The valid comparison operators are

```
        EQ      NE
        LT      LE
        GT      GE
```

    Thus,

```
        IF (C,R4,GT, = 'F'10')
            SR  R4,R4
        ENDIF
```

    is equivalent to

```
            C        R4, = F'10'
            BNH      NEXTINS
            SR       R4,R4
NEXTINS     EQU      *
```

3. *A noncomparison instruction.* Here the condition is specified as

    (instruction mnemonic,first operand,second operand,branch mask)

    Thus,

```
        IF (SH,R2, = H'1',NM)
            LA R3,80(R3)
        ENDIF
```

    is equivalent to

```
            SH       R2, = H'1'
            BM       NEXTINS
            LA       R3,80(R3)
NEXTINS     EQU      *
```

A "complex" condition can be formed using the AND and OR parameters. For example,

        IF (C,R4,GE, = F'90),AND,(C,R4,LE, = F'100')
            code
        ENDIF

causes the code to be executed if R4 contains a value in the range 90 to 100.

        IF (CLI,ERRFLAG,EQ,C'T'),OR,(LTR,R6,R6,M)
            code
        ENDIF

causes the code to be executed if the ERRFLAG is T or if R6 contains a negative value. Similarly,

        IF (CLC,RC,EQ, = F'0'),AND,(SH,R4, = H'1',NM),AND,(LTR,R7,R7,P)
            code
        ENDIF

causes the code to be executed only when all three conditions are true.

Since a condition is composed of a list of macro operands, parentheses cannot be used to force a desired grouping. Thus,

        IF (cond-1,AND,(cond-2,OR,cond-3))

is not legal. To force this grouping

        IF cond-1,ANDIF,cond-2,OR,cond-3

would be used. The ANDIF and ORIF parameters are provided to give the effect of enclosing the remaining parameters within parentheses. Although the programmer does not have the freedom to use parentheses arbitrarily, in practice the constraint is seldom noticed.

Finally, if a case analysis is desired, the following pattern can be used:

            IF
            COND cond-1
                code to be executed if cond-1 is true
        *
            COND cond-2
                code to be executed if cond-2 is true
        *
            .
            .
            .
            COND cond-n
                code to be executed if cond-n is true
            ENDIF

Here one of the conditions is assumed to be true. (If none is, an abnormal termination results.) For convenience,

    COND ELSE

can be used as the last condition. For example,

```
IF
COND (CLI,TRANCD,EQ,C'A'),OR,(CLI,TRANCD,EQ,C'X')
    code-1
COND (CLI,TRANCD,EQ,C'D')
    code-2
COND (CLI,TRANCD,EQ,C'E')
    code-3
COND ELSE
    code-4
ENDIF
```

selects one of four sections of code, based on the value in TRANCD.

Looping can be achieved by using DO and ENDDO instead of IF and ENDIF. For example,

```
LA      R6,50
DO WHILE,(SH,R6, = H'1',NM)
    code
ENDDO
```

executes the code 50 times. Similarly,

```
DO WHILE,(LTR,R7,R7,P),AND,(CLI,ERRFLAG,EQ,C'F')
    code
ENDDO
```

loops while both basic conditions are true.

The following versions of CLASSLST and PROCLASS in Programs 12-3 and 12-4 illustrate use of the macros.

Program 12-3

```
************************************************************************
*
* CLASSLST: PROGRAM
*
* (1) CALL READCARD TO READ THE FIRST CARD AND SET EOFFLAG TO Y
*         IF END-OF-FILE IS DETECTED
*
*      IF (EOF OCCURRED - NO CARDS IN THE INPUT FILE)
*
* (2)      PRINT AN ERROR MESSAGE (EMPTY INPUT FILE)
*
*      ELSE
*
* (3)      CLEAR THE PRINT LINE. FROM NOW ON IT IS CLEARED AFTER EACH
*            LINE IS PRINTED.
*
*          DO WHILE (EOF HAS NOT YET OCCURRED)
*
* (4)          CALL PROCLASS TO PROCESS THE CARDS FOR ONE CLASS LIST
*                (AND TO READ THE 1ST CARD FOR THE NEXT LIST)
*
*          ENDDO
*
* (5)      PRINT A "SUCCESSFUL TERMINATION" MESSAGE
*
*      ENDIF
*
*    ENDPROG
*
************************************************************************
*
CLASSLST CSECT
         LR    R12,R15             SET UP R12 AS THE BASE REGISTER
         USING CLASSLST,R12
*
         BAL   R11,READCARD        READ THE 1ST CARD              (1)
*
         IF (CLI,EOFFLAG,EQ,C'Y')  IF EOF OCCURRED
*
           XPRNT =C'1*** NO INPUT ***',17                        (2)
*
         ELSE
*
           MVI   PRNTLINE,C' '     CLEAR THE PRINT LINE          (3)
           MVC   PRNTLINE+1(132),PRNTLINE
*
           DO WHILE,(CLI,EOFFLAG,NE,C'Y')  WHILE NOT EOF
*
             BAL   R11,PROCLASS       PRINT 1 CLASS LIST         (4)
*
           ENDDO
*
           XPRNT =C'1*** SUCCESSFUL TERMINATION ***',31          (5)
*
         ENDIF
*
         BR    R14                 LEAVE THE PROGRAM
*
```

```
**********************************************************************
*
* PROCLASS PRODUCES 1 CLASS LIST.  WHEN IT COMPLETES, EITHER
* EOF HAS OCCURRED (EOFFLAG WILL BE Y) OR THE FIRST CARD FOR THE
* NEXT CLASS LIST HAS BEEN READ.  THE LOGIC IS AS FOLLOWS:
*
* PROCLASS: PROC
*
*  (1)      SAVE THE DEPARTMENT AND COURSE FOR THIS LIST
*
*  (2)      SET THE COUNT OF THE STUDENTS IN THE LIST TO 0
*
*  (3)      CALL PRINTHDR TO PRINT THE HEADERS FOR THE FIRST PAGE OF
*              THE CLASS LIST
*
*           DO WHILE (EOF HAS NOT OCCURRED AND THE CURRENT CARD IS FOR
*                     THE CLASS LIST THAT WE ARE PRINTING)
*
*  (4)          BUILD A PRINT LINE FROM DATA ON THE CARD
*
*  (5)          CALL PRINTSP1 TO PRINT AFTER SPACING 1 (HEADERS
*                  WILL BE PRINTED IF THE NEXT LINE ON THE PAGE
*                  IS GREATER THAN 50)
*
*  (6)          ADD 1 TO THE COUNT OF STUDENTS IN THE LIST
*
*  (7)          CALL READCARD TO READ THE NEXT CARD AND SET EOFFLAG
*
*           ENDDO
*
*  (8)      PRINT THE TOTAL NUMBER OF STUDENTS IN THE CLASS LIST
*
*      ENDPROC
*
*
**********************************************************************
*
PROCLASS STM   R14,R12,PRCLSAVE+12 SAVE CALLER'S REGISTERS
*
         MVC   CURRKEY,CARD         SAVE THE KEY (DEPT,COURSE)   (1)
*
         SR    R2,R2                SET COUNT OF STUDENTS IN THE (2)
*                                   LIST TO 0
*
         BAL   R11,PRINTHDR         PRINT THE PAGE HEADERS       (3)
*
         DO WHILE,(CLI,EOFFLAG,NE,C'Y'),AND,(CLC,CURRKEY,EQ,CARD)
*
             MVC   DEPTOUT,DEPTIN    NOW MOVE DATA FIELDS        (4)
             MVC   COURSOUT,COURSIN  THE PRINT LINE
             MVC   LNAMEOUT,LNAMEIN
             MVC   FNAMEOUT,FNAMEIN
*
             BAL   R11,PRINTSP1      PRINT THE LINE (AND HEADERS, (5)
*                                    IF NECESSARY)
*
             LA    R2,1(R2)          ADD 1 TO COUNT OF STUDENTS   (6)
*
             BAL   R11,READCARD      TRY TO READ THE NEXT CARD    (7)
*
         ENDDO
*
         XDECO R2,PRNTLINE+25        PUT TOTAL INTO PRINT LINE    (8)
         MVC   PRNTLINE+7(18),=C'TOTAL # STUDENTS ='
         MVI   PRNTLINE,C'0'         SET CARRIAGE CONTROL FOR
*                                    DOUBLE-SPACE
         XPRNT PRNTLINE,133          PRINT LAST LINE FOR LIST
         MVI   PRNTLINE,C' '         CLEAR THE PRINT LINE
         MVC   PRNTLINE+1(132),PRNTLINE
*
         LM    R14,R12,PRCLSAVE+12 RESTORE CALLER'S REGISTERS
         BR    R11
*
PRCLSAVE DS    18F                  REGISTER SAVE AREA
*
```

Appendix A

Illustration of Subroutines

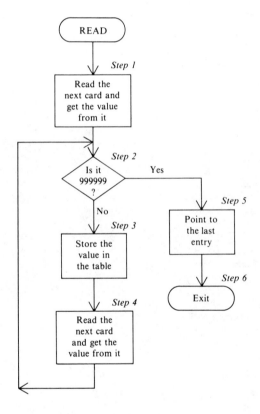

Figure A-1

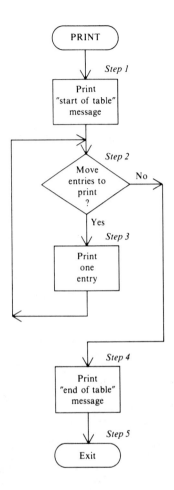

Figure A-2

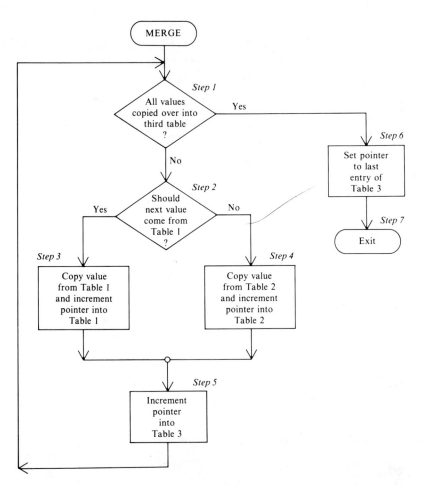

Figure A-3

Program A-1

```
*******************************************************************************
*
* THIS PROGRAM ILLUSTRATES THE USE OF SUBROUTINES.  THE PROGRAM
*
*        1) READS A SET OF NUMBERS INTO 'TABLE1'.  IT IS
*           ASSUMED THAT THE INPUT VALUES HAVE BEEN SORTED INTO
*           ASCENDING ORDER.
*
*        2) PRINTS OUT THE NUMBERS IN 'TABLE1'.
*
*        3) READS IN A SECOND SET OF NUMBERS INTO 'TABLE2'.
*
*        4) PRINTS OUT THE NUMBERS IN 'TABLE2'.
*
*        5) MERGES THE NUMBERS IN THE TWO TABLES INTO 'TABLE3'.
*
*        6) PRINTS OUT THE NUMBERS IN 'TABLE3'.
*
* THE LOGIC OF THE PROGRAM IS AS FOLLOWS:
*
*        STEP 1.  CALL 'READ' TO READ IN THE FIRST TABLE.  THIS WILL
*                 REQUIRE PASSING TO 'READ' THE ADDRESS OF THE TABLE
*                 TO FILL.  THE 'READ' ROUTINE WILL RETURN THE ADDRESS
*                 OF THE LAST ENTRY, WHICH IS STORED IN 'ENDT1'.
*
*        STEP 2.  CALL 'PRINT' TO PRINT OUT THE VALUES IN 'TABLE1'.
*
*        STEP 3.  CALL 'READ' TO READ IN THE VALUES FOR 'TABLE2', AND
*                 SAVE THE ADDRESS OF THE LAST ENTRY IN 'ENDT2'.
*
*        STEP 4.  CALL 'PRINT' TO DISPLAY THE VALUES IN 'TABLE2'.
*
*        STEP 5.  CALL 'MERGE' TO MERGE THE VALUES IN 'TABLE1' AND
*                 'TABLE2' INTO 'TABLE3'.
*
*        STEP 6.  CALL 'PRINT' TO DISPLAY THE VALUES IN 'TABLE3'.
*
*        STEP 7.  EXIT.
*
*******************************************************************************
*
MAINPROG CSECT
         USING MAINPROG,R15
*
***<STEP 1>  · READ IN THE VALUES FOR 'TABLE1'.
*
         LA   R2,TABLE1           R2 IS USED TO PASS THE ADDRESS OF
*                                 WHERE THE VALUES ARE TO BE STORED
         BAL  R10,READ            READ IN 'TABLE1'
         ST   R3,ENDT1            SAVE THE ADDRESS OF THE LAST VALUE
*
***<STEP 2>  PRINT OUT THE VALUES IN 'TABLE1'.
*
         BAL  R10,PRINT           R2 MUST HAVE ADDRESS OF 'TABLE1' AND
*                                 R3 MUST HAVE ADDRESS OF LAST ENTRY
```

Program A-1 (continued)

```
*
***<STEP 3>     READ IN THE VALUES FOR 'TABLE2'.
*
        LA      R2,TABLE2          POINT TO THE SECOND TABLE
        BAL     R10,READ           READ IN THE VALUES
        ST      R3,ENDT2           SAVE ADDRESS OF LAST ENTRY
*
***<STEP 4>     PRINT OUT THE VALUES IN 'TABLE2'.
*
        BAL     R10,PRINT
*
***<STEP 5>     NOW MERGE THE TWO TABLES INTO 'TABLE3'.
*
        LA      R2,TABLE1          R2 <- ADDRESS OF FIRST TABLE
        LA      R3,TABLE2          R3 <- ADDRESS OF SECOND TABLE
        LA      R4,TABLE3          R4 <- ADDRESS OF TABLE TO BUILD
*
        L       R5,ENDT1           R5 <- ADDRESS OF LAST ENTRY IN TABLE1
        L       R6,ENDT2           R6 <- ADDRESS OF LAST ENTRY IN TABLE2
*
        BAL     R10,MERGE          NOW MERGE THE TWO TABLES
*
***<STEP 6>     PRINT OUT THE CONTENTS OF 'TABLE3'.
*
        LA      R2,TABLE3
        LR      R3,R7              'MERGE' PUT ADDRESS OF LAST ENTRY
*                                  INTO R7
        BAL     R10,PRINT          NOW PRINT THE MERGED TABLE
*
***<STEP 7>     EXIT.
*
        BR      R14
*
************************************************************************
*
*             STORAGE AREAS FOR THE MAIN ROUTINE
*
************************************************************************
*
        LTORG
ENDT1   DS      F                  ADDRESS OF LAST ENTRY IN TABLE1
ENDT2   DS      F                  ADDRESS OF LAST ENTRY IN TABLE2
TABLE1  DS      50F                BUILD THE FIRST TABLE HERE
TABLE2  DS      50F                AND THE SECOND TABLE HERE
TABLE3  DS      100F               AND THE MERGED TABLE HERE
************************************************************************
*
*                   READ ROUTINE
*
* THIS IS THE READ ROUTINE.  WHEN IT IS ENTERED, R2 CONTAINS THE
* ADDRESS OF THE TABLE TO BE FILLED.  EACH DATA CARD CONTAINS ONE
* NUMBER. END OF THE TABLE IS DESIGNATED BY A CARD CONTAINING
* 999999.  UPON EXITING, R3 CONTAINS THE ADDRESS OF THE LAST ENTRY
* OF THE TABLE.  NO OTHER REGISTERS ARE ALTERED.  R10 IS THE LINK
* REGISTER.
*
```

Program A-1 (continued)

```
*
* THE LOGIC IS AS FOLLOWS:
*
*         STEP 1.   READ THE NEXT CARD AND GET THE VALUE OFF IT.
*
*         STEP 2.   IF THE VALUE ON THE CARD IS 999999, GO TO STEP 5.
*
*         STEP 3.   STORE THE VALUE INTO THE TABLE BEING BUILT.
*                   INCREMENT THE POINTER TO WHERE THE NEXT VALUE GOES.
*
*         STEP 4.   READ THE NEXT CARD, GET THE VALUE OFF IT, AND GO
*                   BACK TO STEP 2.
*
*         STEP 5.   SET R3 TO POINT TO THE LAST ENTRY.
*
*         STEP 6.   EXIT.
*
**************************************************************************
*
READ      STM   R4,R2,READSAVE      SAVE ALL REGS EXCEPT R3
***<STEP 1>      READ THE NEXT CARD AND GET THE VALUE OFF IT.
*
          XREAD CARD,80             IT IS ASSUMED THAT THERE IS A CARD
          XDECI R4,CARD             AND THAT THE NUMBER IS VALID
*
***<STEP 2>      TEST FOR END OF LOOP (VALUE OF 999999).
*
READLOOP  C     R4,=F'999999'
          BE    SETLAST             BRANCH IF END OF INPUT VALUES
*
***<STEP 3>      STORE VALUE INTO TABLE AND INCREMENT NEXT ENTRY POINTER.
*
          ST    R4,0(R2)            STORE ENTRY
          LA    R2,4(R2)            POINT TO NEXT ENTRY
*
***<STEP 4>      READ THE NEXT CARD, GET VALUE, AND GO TO STEP 2.
*
          XREAD CARD,80             READ THE CARD
          XDECI 4,CARD              AND GET THE VALUE
          B     READLOOP
*
***<STEP 5>      SET POINTER TO LAST ENTRY.
*
SETLAST   LR    R3,R2               R2 HAS ADDRESS OF "NEXT ENTRY"
          S     R3,=F'4'            R3 NOW POINTS TO LAST ENTRY
*
***<STEP 6>      RETURN TO CALLER.
*
          LM    R4,R2,READSAVE      RESTORE ALL REGISTERS BUT R3
          BR    R10                 AND RETURN
*
          LTORG
*
CARD      DS    CL80                CARD INPUT AREA
*
READSAVE  DS    15F                 ROOM FOR ALL REGISTERS, EXCEPT R3
```

Program A-1 (continued)

```
*
*
*****************************************************************
*
*                   PRINT ROUTINE
*
* THIS ROUTINE PRINTS OUT THE VALUES IN THE TABLE POINTED TO BY
* R2.  R3 MUST CONTAIN THE ADDRESS OF THE LAST ENTRY IN THE TABLE.
* R10 IS THE LINK REGISTER.  ENTRIES ARE PRINTED OUT 1 PER LINE.
* NO REGISTERS ARE ALTERED BY A CALL TO THIS ROUTINE.
* THE LOGIC IS AS FOLLOWS:
*
*       STEP 1.  PRINT A HEADING.
*
*       STEP 2.  IF ALL OF THE ENTRIES HAVE BEEN PRINTED, GO
*                TO STEP 4.
*
*       STEP 3.  PRINT ONE ENTRY, INCREMENT POINTER TO NEXT ENTRY,
*                AND GO BACK TO STEP 2.
*
*       STEP 4.  PRINT "END OF TABLE" MESSAGE.
*
*       STEP 5.  EXIT.
*
*****************************************************************
*
PRINT     STM   R0,R15,PRINTSAV    SAVE ALL OF THE REGISTERS
*
***<STEP 1>     PRINT A HEADING.
*
          XPRNT =C'0*** START OF TABLE ***',23
*
***<STEP 2>     CHECK FOR END OF TABLE.
*
PRINTLP   CR    R2,R3               COMPARE CURRENT AGAINST LAST
          BH    PRINTEND            BRANCH IF PAST LAST ENTRY
*
***<STEP 3>     PRINT ONE ENTRY AND GO BACK TO STEP 2.
*
          L     R4,0(R2)            GET A VALUE FROM THE TABLE
          XDECO R4,OUTVAL           CONVERT TO PRINTABLE FORMAT
          XPRNT PRNTLINE,13         PRINT IT
*
          LA    R2,4(R2)            INCREMENT POINTER TO NEXT ENTRY
          B     PRINTLP
*
***<STEP 4>     PRINT "END OF TABLE" MESSAGE.
*
PRINTEND  XPRNT =C'0*** END OF TABLE ***',21
*
***<STEP 5>     EXIT.
*
          LM    R0,R15,PRINTSAV     RESTORE ALL REGISTERS
          BR    R10                 EXIT
```

Program A-1 (continued)

```
*
         LTORG
*
PRNTLINE DC    C' '               CARRIAGE CONTROL
OUTVAL   DS    CL12               OUTPUT THE VALUES HERE
*
PRINTSAV DS    16F                SAVE REGISTERS HERE
*
*************************************************************************
*
*                     MERGE ROUTINE
*
* THIS ROUTINE MERGES THE TWO SORTED TABLES INTO A THIRD TABLE.  UPON
* ENTRANCE
*
*         R2 = ADDRESS OF FIRST TABLE
*         R3 = ADDRESS OF SECOND TABLE
*         R4 = ADDRESS OF THIRD TABLE
*         R5 = ADDRESS OF LAST ENTRY IN FIRST TABLE
*         R6 = ADDRESS OF LAST ENTRY IN SECOND TABLE
*
* THE ROUTINE WILL SET R7 TO THE ADDRESS OF THE LAST ENTRY IN THE
* THIRD TABLE, WHICH IS PRODUCED BY MERGING THE FIRST TWO TABLES.
* R10 IS THE LINK REGISTER.  ONLY R7 IS ALTERED BY A CALL TO THIS
* ROUTINE.
*
* THE LOGIC IS AS FOLLOWS:
*
*         STEP 1.  IF ALL VALUES FROM BOTH TABLES ARE IN THE THIRD
*                  TABLE, GO TO STEP 6.
*
*         STEP 2.  IF (ALL VALUES IN TABLE2 ARE ALREADY IN TABLE3 OR
*                     (SOME VALUES IN TABLE1 HAVE NOT YET BEEN
*                     MOVED AND THE NEXT ONE FROM TABLE1 IS LESS
*                     THAN THE NEXT ONE FROM TABLE2)), GO TO STEP 3.
*                     ELSE, GO TO STEP 4.
*
*         STEP 3.  MOVE A VALUE FROM TABLE1 TO TABLE3, UPDATING THE
*                  POINTER TO THE NEXT ENTRY IN TABLE1.  GO TO STEP 5.
*
*         STEP 4.  MOVE A VALUE FROM TABLE2 TO TABLE3, UPDATING THE
*                  POINTER TO THE NEXT ENTRY IN TABLE2.
*
*         STEP 5.  UPDATE THE POINTER TO THE NEXT ENTRY IN TABLE3 AND
*                  GO BACK TO STEP 1.
*
*         STEP 6.  SET R7 TO POINT TO THE LAST ENTRY IN TABLE3.
*
*         STEP 7.  EXIT.
*
*************************************************************************
*
MERGE    STM   R8,R6,MERGESAV    SAVE ALL REGS, EXCEPT R7
*
***<STEP 1>    BRANCH TO STEP 6, IF ALL ENTRIES HAVE BEEN MOVED.
*
MERGELP  CR    R2,R5
         BNH   SOMELEFT          BRANCH IF NOT ALL OF TABLE1 HAS
*                                BEEN MOVED
         CR    R3,R6
         BH    POINTR7           BRANCH IF ALL ENTRIES HAVE BEEN
*                                MOVED TO TABLE3
```

Program A-1 (continued)

```
*
***<STEP 2>    FIGURE OUT WHICH TABLE THE NEXT ENTRY COMES FROM.
*
SOMELEFT CR    R3,R6
         BH    FROMT1            BRANCH IF TABLE2 EXHAUSTED
*
         CR    R2,R5
         BH    FROMT2            BRANCH IF TABLE1 EXHAUSTED
*
         L     R8,0(R2)          R8 <- NEXT ENTRY FROM TABLE1
         C     R8,0(R3)
         BH    FROMT2            BRANCH IF T1'S ENTRY IS HIGH
*
***<STEP 3>    MOVE ENTRY FROM TABLE1 TO TABLE3.
*
FROMT1   L     R8,0(R2)          LOAD ENTRY FROM TABLE1
         ST    R8,0(R4)          STORE INTO TABLE3
         LA    R2,4(R2)          INCREMENT POINTER INTO TABLE1
         B     INCRT3            GO INCREMENT TABLE3'S POINTER
*
***<STEP 4>    MOVE ENTRY FROM TABLE2 TO TABLE3.
*
FROMT2   L     R8,0(R3)          LOAD ENTRY FROM TABLE2
         ST    R8,0(R4)          AND PUT IT INTO TABLE3
         LA    R3,4(R3)          INCREMENT POINTER INTO TABLE2
*
***<STEP 5>    INCREMENT TABLE3'S POINTER AND GO BACK TO STEP 1.
*
INCRT3   LA    R4,4(R4)          INCREMENT POINTER TO NEXT ENTRY
*                                FOR TABLE3
         B     MERGELP
*
***<STEP 6>    POINT R7 AT LAST ENTRY IN TABLE3.
*
POINTR7  LR    R7,R4             R4 POINTS JUST PAST LAST ENTRY
         S     R7,=F'4'          NOW R7 POINTS AT LAST ENTRY
*
***<STEP 7>    EXIT.
*
         LM    R8,R6,MERGESAV    RESTORE ALL REGISTERS BUT R7
         BR    R10               AND RETURN
*
MERGESAV DS    15F               REGISTER SAVEAREA
         LTORG

R0       EQU   0
R1       EQU   1
R2       EQU   2
R3       EQU   3
R4       EQU   4
R5       EQU   5
R6       EQU   6
R7       EQU   7
R8       EQU   8
R9       EQU   9
R10      EQU   10
R11      EQU   11
R12      EQU   12
R13      EQU   13
R14      EQU   14
R15      EQU   15
         END   MAINPROG
```

Table of Extended Mnemonics

Extended Mnemonic		Meaning	Corresponding BC or BCR Instruction	
B	address	Branch Unconditional	BC	B'1111',address
BR	r	Branch Unconditional	BCR	B'1111',r
NOP	address	No Operation	BC	B'0000',address
NOPR	r	No Operation	BCR	B'0000',r

Used after Comparison Instructions

BH	address	Branch on High	BC	B'0010',address
BL	address	Branch on Low	BC	B'0100',address
BE	address	Branch on Equal	BC	B'1000',address
BNH	address	Branch on Not High	BC	B'1101',address
BNL	address	Branch on Not Low	BC	B'1011',address
BNE	address	Branch on Not Equal	BC	B'0111',address

Used after Arithmetic Instructions

BO	address	Branch on Overflow	BC	B'0001',address
BP	address	Branch on Plus	BC	B'0010',address
BM	address	Branch on Minus	BC	B'0100',address
BZ	address	Branch on Zero	BC	B'1000',address
BNO	address	Branch on Not Overflow	BC	B'1110',address
BNP	address	Branch on Not Plus	BC	B'1101',address
BNM	address	Branch on Not Minus	BC	B'1011',address
BNZ	address	Branch on Not Zero	BC	B'0111',address

Used after Test under Mask Instructions

BO	address	Branch If Ones	BC	B'0001',address
BM	address	Branch If Mixed	BC	B'0100',address
BZ	address	Branch If Zeros	BC	B'1000',address
BNO	address	Branch If Not All Ones	BC	B'1110',address
BNM	address	Branch If Not Mixed	BC	B'1011',address
BNZ	address	Branch If Not All Zeros	BC	B'0111',address

Appendix C

Converting Hexadecimal to Punched Card Codes

You will find the following tables particularly useful. However, all this information and much more is contained in the System/370 Reference Summary, published by IBM.

CHARACTER-TO-HEXADECIMAL CONVERSIONS

Hexa-decimal	Character	Punched Card Code	Hexa-decimal	Character	Punched Card Code
00		12-0-1-8-9	15		11-5-9
01		12-1-9	16		11-6-9
02		12-2-9	17		11-7-9
03		12-3-9	18		11-8-9
04		12-4-9	19		11-1-8-9
05		12-5-9	1A		11-2-8-9
06		12-6-9	1B		11-3-8-9
07		12-7-9	1C		11-4-8-9
08		12-8-9	1D		11-5-8-9
09		12-1-8-9	1E		11-6-8-9
0A		12-2-8-9	1F		11-7-8-9
0B		12-3-8-9	20		11-0-1-8-9
0C		12-4-8-9	21		0-1-9
0D		12-5-8-9	22		0-2-9
0E		12-6-8-9	23		0-3-9
0F		12-7-8-9	24		0-4-9
10		12-11-1-8-9	25		0-5-9
11		11-1-9	26		0-6-9
12		11-2-9	27		0-7-9
13		11-3-9	28		0-8-9
14		11-4-9	29		0-1-8-9

Hexa-decimal	Character	Punched Card Code	Hexa-decimal	Character	Punched Card Code
2A		0-2-8-9	58		12-11-8-9
2B		0-3-8-9	59		11-1-8
2C		0-4-8-9	5A	!	11-2-8
2D		0-5-8-9	5B	$	11-3-8
2E		0-6-8-9	5C	*	11-4-8
2F		0-7-8-9	5D	)	11-5-8
30		12-11-0-1-8-9	5E	;	11-6-8
31		1-9	5F	¬	11-7-8
32		2-9	60	-	11
33		3-9	61	/	0-1
34		4-9	62		11-0-2-9
35		5-9	63		11-0-3-9
36		6-9	64		11-0-4-9
37		7-9	65		11-0-5-9
38		8-9	66		11-0-6-9
39		1-8-9	67		11-0-7-9
3A		2-8-9	68		11-0-8-9
3B		3-8-9	69		0-1-8
3C		4-8-9	6A	¦	12-11
3D		5-8-9	6B	,	0-3-8
3E		6-8-9	6C	%	0-4-8
3F		7-8-9	6D	—	0-5-8
40		no punches	6E	>	0-6-8
41		12-0-1-9	6F	?	0-7-8
42		12-0-2-9	70		12-11-0
43		12-0-3-9	71		12-11-0-1-9
44		12-0-4-9	72		12-11-0-2-9
45		12-0-5-9	73		12-11-0-3-9
46		12-0-6-9	74		12-11-0-4-9
47		12-0-7-9	75		12-11-0-5-9
48		12-0-8-9	76		12-11-0-6-9
49		12-1-8	77		12-11-0-7-9
4A	¢	12-2-8	78		12-11-0-8-9
4B	•	12-3-8	79	`	1-8
4C	<	12-4-8	7A	:	2-8
4D	(	12-5-8	7B	#	3-8
4E	+	12-6-8	7C	@	4-8
4F	|	12-7-8	7D	'	5-8
50	&	12	7E	=	6-8
51		12-11-1-9	7F	"	7-8
52		12-11-2-9	80		12-0-1-8
53		12-11-3-9	81	a	12-0-1
54		12-11-4-9	82	b	12-0-2
55		12-11-5-9	83	c	12-0-3
56		12-11-6-9	84	d	12-0-4
57		12-11-7-9	85	e	12-0-5

Hexa-decimal	Character	Punched Card Code	Hexa-decimal	Character	Punched Card Code
86	f	12-0-6	B4		12-11-0-4
87	g	12-0-7	B5		12-11-0-5
88	h	12-0-8	B6		12-11-0-6
89	i	12-0-9	B7		12-11-0-7
8A		12-0-2-8	B8		12-11-0-8
8B		12-0-3-8	B9		12-11-0-9
8C		12-0-4-8	BA		12-11-0-2-8
8D		12-0-5-8	BB		12-11-0-3-8
8E		12-0-6-8	BC		12-11-0-4-8
8F		12-0-7-8	BD		12-11-0-5-8
90		12-11-1-8	BE		12-11-0-6-8
91	j	12-11-1	BF		12-11-0-7-8
92	k	12-11-2	C0	{	12-0
93	l	12-11-3	C1	A	12-1
94	m	12-11-4	C2	B	12-2
95	n	12-11-5	C3	C	12-3
96	o	12-11-6	C4	D	12-4
97	p	12-11-7	C5	E	12-5
98	q	12-11-8	C6	F	12-6
99	r	12-11-9	C7	G	12-7
9A		12-11-2-8	C8	H	12-8
9B		12-11-3-8	C9	I	12-9
9C		12-11-4-8	CA		12-0-2-8-9
9D		12-11-5-8	CB		12-0-3-8-9
9E		12-11-6-8	CC	∽	12-0-4-8-9
9F		12-11-7-8	CD		12-0-5-8-9
A0		11-0-1-8	CE	Ч	12-0-6-8-9
A1	~	11-0-1	CF		12-0-7-8-9
A2	s	11-0-2	D0	}	11-0
A3	t	11-0-3	D1	J	11-1
A4	u	11-0-4	D2	K	11-2
A5	v	11-0-5	D3	L	11-3
A6	w	11-0-6	D4	M	11-4
A7	x	11-0-7	D5	N	11-5
A8	y	11-0-8	D6	O	11-6
A9	z	11-0-9	D7	P	11-7
AA		11-0-2-8	D8	Q	11-8
AB		11-0-3-8	D9	R	11-9
AC		11-0-4-8	DA		12-11-2-8-9
AD		11-0-5-8	DB		12-11-3-8-9
AE		11-0-6-8	DC		12-11-4-8-9
AF		11-0-7-8	DD		12-11-5-8-9
B0		12-11-0-1-8	DE		12-11-6-8-9
B1		12-11-0-1	DF		12-11-7-8-9
B2		12-11-0-2	E0	\	0-2-8
B3		12-11-0-3	E1		11-0-1-9

Hexa-decimal	Character	Punched Card Code
E2	S	0-2
E3	T	0-3
E4	U	0-4
E5	V	0-5
E6	W	0-6
E7	X	0-7
E8	Y	0-8
E9	Z	0-9
EA		11-0-2-8-9
EB		11-0-3-8-9
EC	⊢	11-0-4-8-9
ED		11-0-5-8-9
EE		11-0-6-8-9
EF		11-0-7-8-9
F0	0	0
F1	1	1
F2	2	2
F3	3	3
F4	4	4
F5	5	5
F6	6	6
F7	7	7
F8	8	8
F9	9	9
FA	|	12-11-0-2-8-9
FB		12-11-0-3-8-9
FC		12-11-0-4-8-9
FD		12-11-0-5-8-9
FE		12-11-0-6-8-9
FF		12-11-0-7-8-9

OP CODES OF COMMONLY USED INSTRUCTIONS

Name	Mnemonic	OP Code
Add	AR	1A
Add	A	5A
Add Decimal	AP	FA
Add Halfword	AH	4A
Add Logical	ALR	1E
Add Logical	AL	5E
AND	NR	14
AND	N	54
AND	NI	94
AND	NC	D4
Branch and Link	BALR	05
Branch and Link	BAL	45
Branch on Condition	BCR	07
Branch on Condition	BC	47
Branch on Count	BCTR	06
Branch on Count	BCT	46
Branch on Index High	BXH	86
Branch on Index Low or Equal	BXLE	87
Compare	CR	19
Compare	C	59
Compare Decimal	CP	F9
Compare Halfword	CH	49
Compare Logical	CLR	15
Compare Logical	CL	55
Compare Logical	CLC	D5
Compare Logical	CLI	95
Compare Logical Characters under Mask	CLM	BD
Compare Logical Long	CLCL	0F
Convert to Binary	CVB	4F
Convert to Decimal	CVD	4E
Divide	DR	1D
Divide	D	5D
Divide Decimal	DP	FD
Edit	ED	DE
Edit and Mark	EDMK	DF
Exclusive OR	XR	17
Exclusive OR	X	57
Exclusive OR	XI	97
Exclusive OR	XC	D7

Name	Mnemonic	OP Code
Execute	EX	44
Insert Character	IC	43
Insert Characters under Mask	ICM	BF
Load	LR	18
Load	L	58
Load Address	LA	41
Load and Test	LTR	12
Load Complement	LCR	13
Load Halfword	LH	48
Load Multiple	LM	98
Load Negative	LNR	11
Load Positive	LPR	10
Load PSW	LPSW	82
Move	MVI	92
Move	MVC	D2
Move Long	MVCL	0E
Move Numerics	MVN	D1
Move with Offset	MVO	F1
Move Zones	MVZ	D3
Multiply	MR	1C
Multiply	M	5C
Multiply Decimal	MP	FC
Multiply Halfword	MH	4C
OR	OR	16
OR	O	56
OR	OI	96
OR	OC	D6
Pack	PACK	F2
Set Program Mask	SPM	04
Shift and Round Decimal	SRP	F0
Shift Left Double	SLDA	8F
Shift Left Double Logical	SLDL	8D
Shift Left Single	SLA	8B
Shift Left Single Logical	SLL	89
Shift Right Double	SRDA	8E
Shift Right Double Logical	SRDL	8C
Shift Right Single	SRA	8A
Shift Right Single Logical	SRL	88
Store	ST	50
Store Character	STC	42
Store Characters under Mask	STCM	BE
Store Halfword	STH	40
Store Multiple	STM	90

Name	Mnemonic	OP Code
Subtract	SR	1B
Subtract	S	5B
Subtract Decimal	SP	FB
Subtract Halfword	SH	4B
Subtract Logical	SLR	1F
Subtract Logical	SL	5F
Supervisor Call	SVC	0A
Test under Mask	TM	91
Translate	TR	DC
Translate and Test	TRT	DD
Unpack	UNPK	F3
Zero and Add Decimal	ZAP	F8

POWERS OF 16

16^n						n
					1	0
					16	1
					256	2
				4	096	3
				65	536	4
			1	048	576	5
			16	777	216	6
			268	435	456	7
		4	294	967	296	8
		68	719	476	736	9
	1	099	511	627	776	10
	17	592	186	044	416	11
	281	474	976	710	656	12
4	503	599	627	370	496	13
72	057	594	037	927	936	14
1	152	921	504	606	846	976	15

POWERS OF 2

2^n			n
		512	9
	1	024	10
	2	048	11
	4	096	12
	8	192	13
	16	384	14
	32	768	15
	65	536	16
	131	072	17
	262	144	18
	524	288	19
1	048	576	20
2	097	152	21
4	194	304	22
8	388	608	23
16	777	216	24

FORMAT OF THE PROGRAM STATUS WORD (PSW)

The PSW is composed of 64 bits, which are used as follows:

Bits	Use
0–7	System mask (used to mask interrupts)
8–11	Memory protection key
12–15	Status bits. The most significant for our purposes are:
	14 indicates whether or not the machine is in the wait state
	15 indicates whether the machine is in supervisor or problem state
16–31	Interruption code. Information concerning the cause of an interrupt is stored here when the old PSW is stored.
32–33	Instruction length code. Normally, this is set to the number of halfwords in the last instruction decoded.
34–35	Condition code
36–39	Program mask
	36 A value of 1 will cause an interrupt on fixed-point overflow.
	37 A value of 1 will cause an interrupt on decimal overflow.
	38 A value of 1 will cause an interrupt on exponent underflow.
	39 A value of 1 will cause an interrupt on a significance exception.
40–63	Address of next instruction

Appendix D

Errors and Their Causes

This appendix contains a short discussion of the common causes of the following types of errors:

- Addressing exception
- Data exception
- Decimal-overflow exception
- Decimal-divide exception
- Fixed-point overflow exception
- Fixed-point divide exception
- Operation exception
- Protection exception
- Specification exception

The comments here on each type of error are not comprehensive. The reader should consult the IBM *Principles of Operation Manual* for more details. A table summarizing the errors that can occur during the execution of each type of instruction is included at the end of this appendix.

1. *Addressing exception.* This error results when an attempt is made to reference an address outside the limits of the actual memory. For example, if R1 contained 00A2FC04 and the highest address of an actual word of memory were 07FFFC, then

      L   2,0(1)

would cause an addressing exception. The usual cause of this error is inadvertent destruction of the contents of a base or index register (or failure to initialize a base or index register properly). For example, if the following routine were used to initialize all entries in a table to the value 100000, an addressing exception might occur.

```
                    LA          2,TABLE
                    SR          3,3
                    L           4, = F'100000'
                    L           5,NUMENT
        *
        LOOP        ST          4,0(4,2)
                    LA          3,4(3)
                    BCT         5,LOOP
                     .
                     .
                     .
        NUMENT      DC          F'100'              # OF ENTRIES
```

In this case, a keypunch error was probably responsible for

```
        LOOP        ST          4,0(4,2)
```

which should have been

```
        LOOP        ST          4,0(3,2)
```

Since the address of TABLE would be offset by 100000, the result might well be an address beyond the limits of the memory of the machine.

2. *Data exception.* This error is normally caused by an attempt to manipulate a field that is expected to contain a valid packed-decimal number but actually contains something else. For example, if

$$01*23$$

were the first five characters on a card, then

```
        XREAD       CARD,80
        PACK        INVAL(4),CARD(5)
        AP          TOTAL, INVAL(4)
```

would result in a data exception. In this case, the PACK would leave 0001C23F in INVAL. Since this is not a valid packed-decimal value, the attempt to add it to TOTAL will result in an error.

3. *Decimal-overflow exception.* A decimal overflow is usually the result of performing a decimal arithmetic instruction when the result cannot be represented in the receiving field. For example, if an input card contained

$$996$$

in the first three columns, then

```
        XREAD   CARD,80
        PACK    TESTAVG(2),CARD(3)
        AP      TESTAVG(2), = P'5'
        MVO     RESULT,TESTAVG(1)
* THE LAST 2 INST. ARE DESIGNED
* TO ROUND THE SCORE TO THE NEAREST
* VALUE IN THE RANGE 0–99
        .
        .
        .
TESTAVG DS      PL2
RESULT  DC      PL2'0'
```

would result in an overflow (since 996 + 5 = 1001, which cannot be represented in a two-byte field).

4. *Decimal-divide exception.*   This error occurs on a DP when the quotient is too large to be represented in the allotted space or when an attempt is made to divide by zero. For example, if NUMIND contained 002C and TOTAL contained 00200C, then

```
        DP      TOTAL,NUMIND
```

would cause a decimal-divide exception (since 100 cannot be represented in one byte—the length of the quotient).

5. *Fixed-point overflow exception.*   This error occurs when the result of an arithmetic operation cannot be represented in a 32-bit word. For example, if R1 contained 80000000, then

```
        LPR     2,1
```

would cause an error. (The machine cannot complement the smallest negative value.) Similarly,

```
        S       1, = F'10'
```

will cause an error, since the result is less than the smallest number that can be represented in one word.

6. *Fixed-point divide exception.*   This error is most often caused by an attempt to divide by 0. However, it can also result when the quotient cannot be represented in 32 bits; normally, this would be caused by failure to clear the even register of the pair. For example,

```
        L       3,TOTAL
        D       2,NUM
```

could cause an error. (R2 should be zeroed first to assure the correct result.) Another cause of a fixed-point divide exception is an attempt to convert a large decimal number to binary with a CVB. For example, if NUM contained 123456789012345F, then

CVB   0,NUM

would result in an error (since the result cannot be represented in one word).

7. *Operation exception.* This error results from an attempt to execute a value in memory that does not represent a valid instruction. There are several common causes:

a. If a constant is included in the middle of a routine, an operation error normally results. For example,

```
            L      0,RESULT
            A      0, = F'1'
            ST     0,RESULT
RESULT      DS     F
            B      RETURN
```

will probably cause an operation exception, since the left byte of the result will probably be 00, which is an invalid operation code.

b. If a section of a program is altered during execution, an operation exception can result. For example, if the following code were executed, an operation exception would result:

```
*  INITIALIZE TABLE
            LM     0,3, = A(0, TABLE,4, TABLE + 400)
ZEROIT      ST     0,0(1)
            BXLE   1,2,ZEROIT
            B      GO
TABLE       DS     100F
*
GO          LA     1,TABLE
                    .
                    .
                    .
```

Here, the instruction at GO would be altered to 00000000 before being executed.

c. If a branch address is incorrect, an operation exception often results. Thus, if

BC   B'1111',14

were used rather than

```
        BCR      B'1111',14
```

an operation exception might result (if the value at location 14 were not a valid instruction).

8. *Protection exception.* This error is caused by the execution of an instruction that accesses or alters an area in memory outside the limits of the program. Normally, such an error results from an unexpected value in either an index or a base register. If such an error occurs, do the following:

   - Look in memory to make sure that the instruction causing the error matches the generated code in the assembler listing. (The instruction might have been altered during execution.)
   - Look at the generated base and index registers. (If you failed to drop a register, these registers might not be what you expected.)

   These two steps should at least allow you to detect rapidly which register contains the incorrect value.

9. *Specification exception.* By far the most common cause of a specification exception is a failure to observe a boundary alignment. This can result from a simple error such as:

```
        L           1, STARTVAL
        .
        .
        .
WORD1   DS          F
HEADER  DC          C'0***PAGE HEADER***'
*
STARTVAL DS         CL4
```

Here STARTVAL is not on a fullword boundary, so a specification error will result. More frequently, however, specification exceptions are caused by an unexpected value in an index register. In this case, as with protection and addressing exceptions, you can determine which register is invalid by examining the instruction in memory and the contents of the appropriate registers.

ERRORS OCCURRING DURING EXECUTION OF SPECIFIC INSTRUCTIONS

The meanings of the column headers are as follows:

A	Addressing exception	FD	Fixed-point divide exception
D	Data exception	FO	Fixed-point overflow exception
DO	Decimal-overflow exception	P	Protection exception
DD	Decimal-divide exception	S	Specification exception

Mnemonic	A	D	DO	DD	FD	FO	P	S
A	X				X		X	X
AH	X				X		X	X
AL	X						X	X
ALR								
AP	X	X	X				X	
AR						X		
BAL								
BALR								
BC								
BCR								
BCT								
BCTR								
BXH								
BXLE								
C	X						X	X
CH	X						X	X
CL	X						X	X
CLC	X						X	
CLCL	X						X	X
CLI	X						X	
CLM	X						X	
CLR								
CP	X	X					X	
CR								
CVB	X	X				X	X	X
CVD	X						X	X
D	X					X	X	X
DP	X	X		X			X	X
DR						X		X
ED	X	X					X	
EDMK	X	X					X	
EX	X						X	X
IC	X						X	

Mnemonic	A	D	DO	DD	FD	FO	P	S
ICM	X						X	
L	X						X	X
LA								
LCR					X			
LH	X						X	X
LM	X						X	X
LNR								
LPR					X			
LR								
LTR								
M	X						X	X
MH	X						X	X
MP	X	X					X	X
MR								X
MVC	X						X	
MVCL	X						X	X
MVI	X						X	
MVN	X						X	
MVO	X						X	
MVZ	X						X	
N	X						X	X
NC	X						X	
NI	X						X	
NR								
O	X						X	X
OC	X						X	
OI	X						X	
OR								
PACK	X						X	
S	X				X		X	X
SH	X				X		X	X
SL	X						X	X
SLA					X			
SLDA					X			X
SLDL								X
SLL								
SLR								
SP	X	X	X				X	
SPM								
SR					X			
SRA								
SRDA								X

Mnemonic	A	D	DO	DD	FD	FO	P	S
SRDL								X
SRL								
SRP	X	X	X				X	
ST	X						X	X
STC	X						X	
STCM	X						X	
STH	X						X	X
STM	X						X	X
TM	X						X	
TR	X						X	
TRT	X						X	
UNPK	X						X	
X	X						X	X
XC	X						X	
XI	X						X	
XR								
ZAP	X	X	X				X	

Appendix **E**

Interrupts and the Supervisor

INTERRUPTS

The Supervisor is a program that is kept permanently in main storage. The function of this program is to provide a variety of services to user application programs and to handle unusual conditions that could cause the processing of an application program to be temporarily suspended. Since the Supervisor and any application program constitute two distinct programs, processing in the central processing unit (CPU) alternates between the two. The CPU is said to be in the *supervisor state* when the Supervisor is being executed and in the *problem state* when an application program is being executed.

Electronic circuitry, known as the automatic interrupt system, transfers control from an application program to the Supervisor. Such a transfer of control is termed an *interrupt*. Before discussing the precise nature of an interrupt, several preliminary details must be covered.

First, recall that the PSW (Program Status Word) contains pertinent status information about a program, including

- the address of the next instruction to be executed
- the condition code
- the program mask

Some of the other status information contained in the PSW will be covered later in this appendix. However, for the moment it is critical to remember that the PSW keeps track of the next instruction to be executed. Transfer of control to the Supervisor is effected through a complete change of the PSW.

Another background detail is that the Supervisor resides in low storage; that is, it starts at the address 000000. An application program can begin anywhere beyond the end of the Supervisor. This results in the following general picture of main storage:

000000	Supervisor
	User programs
	Unused

There are five types of interrupts on an IBM System/360: I/O, program, external, machine-check, and supervisor-call. (The Sytem/370 includes a sixth type of interrupt. However, its function is well beyond the scope of this discussion.) Of these interrupts, the first four notify the Supervisor of a specific condition that requires action, while the fifth is initiated by the application program to request a service from the Supervisor. Corresponding to each of the five types of interrupts are two doublewords at fixed memory locations. One doubleword of each of these pairs is provided for the storage of an "old" PSW, and the other contains a "new" PSW. The following diagram indicates the locations of these doublewords:

000018	External old PSW
000020	Supervisor-call old PSW
000028	Program old PSW
000030	Machine-check old PSW
000038	I/O old PSW
000058	External new PSW
000060	Supervisor-call new PSW
000068	Program new PSW
000070	Machine-check new PSW
000078	I/O new PSW
	⋮

Now we can describe the exact sequence of events that occurs when one of the conditions causing an interrupt is encountered. Assume that a condition that will cause one of the five types of interrupts has arisen. Then, the automatic interrupt system performs the following actions:

- The current PSW is stored in the location reserved for the old PSW for that particular type of interrupt.
- The doubleword stored in the location that contains the new PSW for that type of interrupt is loaded as the current PSW.

As an example, suppose that a condition that causes an external interrupt has been encountered. Then,

- The current PSW is stored in the doubleword at 000018, the area marked external old PSW.
- The doubleword at 000058, the area marked external new PSW, becomes the current PSW.

The next instruction address contained in the new PSW, which is activated as a result of the interrupt, is the address of a routine that processes the conditions that may have caused the interrupt. This routine is a part of the Supervisor; hence, control of the CPU has been effectively transferred to the Supervisor, as a result of the interrupt.

If control is to be returned to the application program after the condition that caused the interrupt has been processed, this can be accomplished by making the old PSW (stored as a result of the interrupt) the current PSW again. This would result in the resumption of the processing of the application program at the point where the interrupt occurred. The LPSW (Load PSW) instruction is provided for this purpose. This is one of a class of "privileged" instructions that only the Supervisor can issue. Privileged instructions will be covered more thoroughly later in this appendix.

A partial list of the conditions that can cause each type of interrupt is as follows:

1. An external interrupt is most often generated by a hardware device called a timer. The timer can be set to generate an interrupt after any predetermined time interval. This allows control to be passed to the Supervisor from a program that has exceeded its time limit, perhaps because it is in an infinite loop.

2. A supervisor-call interrupt is generated when an application program issues an

        SVC   n   (*Supervisor-Call*)

   instruction. The operand n is a nonnegative integer that is stored in the old PSW when the interrupt occurs. A supervisor-call is issued whenever it is necessary to call upon the Supervisor to perform some service. The integer n stored in the old PSW determines what service is to be performed.

3. A program interrupt occurs when an error is detected in an application program. This allows control to be passed to the Supervisor so that a dump can be generated or another required task can be performed. This

type of interrupt includes addressing, protection, etc.

4. A machine-check interrupt indicates a hardware failure.

5. An I/O interrupt signifies that an I/O operation has been completed. This will be covered in more detail later in this appendix.

The following example illustrates how a user might request a service from the Supervisor (such as determining the time or the correct date) and how the Supervisor would honor such a request:

1. The user's program issues an SVC instruction, causing a supervisor-call interrupt. As a result, the current PSW is stored in the doubleword at 000020 and a new PSW is taken from the doubleword at 000060.

2. The address specified in the PSW taken from the doubleword at 000060 is the address of a routine that will do the following:

   a. Save the old PSW (from 000020) and the user's registers.
   b. Determine what service the user wants by examining the operand of the SVC instruction. (Remember, this operand is available in the PSW at 000020.)
   c. Perform the requested service.
   d. Restore the user's registers (except those that can be used to return an answer).
   e. Issue an LPSW instruction to reload the user's PSW. (This causes control to be returned to the user's program.)

3. Processing of the user's program resumes immediately following the SVC instruction.

STORAGE PROTECTION

At the beginning of this appendix, we indicated that when instructions in the Supervisor are being executed, the CPU is normally in the supervisor state, and when instructions in an application program are being executed, the CPU is in the problem state. Bit 15 of the PSW indicates which state the CPU is in at any given time. If this bit is 0, the CPU is in the supervisor state; if it is 1, the CPU is in the problem state. The sole difference between these two states is that the previously mentioned class of privileged instructions can be executed only when the CPU is in the supervisor state.

The process by which the CPU is correctly switched between the supervisor and problem states is quite simple. The PSW initially assigned to any application program has a 1 in bit 15. If an interrupt occurs, the new PSW loaded to transfer control to the Supervisor has a value of 0 in bit 15, and thus the CPU is automatically switched to the supervisor state. For the Supervisor to return control to an application program, an LPSW must be issued to load the old PSW associated with that program. This old PSW, of course, contains a 1 in bit 15, and so the CPU is switched back to the problem state with the execution of this instruction.

The previous discussion should make it clear that the user must depend on the Supervisor to perform any service that requires the use of privileged instructions. One such service provided by the Supervisor is storage protection.

The main storage of an IBM 360/370 is divided into 2K (or 2,048-byte) blocks. A five-bit protection key is associated with each block of storage. This key can be altered only by the execution of the privileged instruction SSK (Set Storage Key). The current PSW contains a four-bit protection key. Whenever the execution of an instruction in any program would alter an area in storage, the protection key in the PSW is matched against the four high-order bits of the protection key for that block of storage. If these keys do not match, a protection exception (a particular type of program interrupt) occurs. This protection against alteration is called *store protection*.

A block may be protected against being read as well as against being altered. Such protection is called *store and fetch protection*. If the fifth bit (the low-order bit) of the protection key for a block is 0, the block is protected against alteration only. If this bit is 1, the block is protected against read requests as well as alteration.

The above discussion requires one amendment: If the protection key in the PSW is 0000, no matches against storage protection keys are performed. A PSW with a protection key of 0000 should be current only when the CPU is in the supervisor state. Hence, the Supervisor, and the Supervisor alone, is executed under a protection key of 0000.

Storage protection is essential to the maintenance of the role of the Supervisor. To illustrate this, suppose that storage protection did not exist. Then, a user could write a program that would do the following:

1. Alter the areas in storage where the new PSWs for interrupts are stored. (This could be done so as to change the next instruction addresses in these PSWs to addresses of instructions in the user program.)

2. Generate an interrupt.

This interrupt would transfer control back to the user program, rather than to an interrupt routine in the Supervisor. Furthermore, the user program would now be executed with the CPU in the supervisor state. Thus, the user would gain unrestricted use of the machine. Sections of the Supervisor could be wiped out, and general chaos could result.

It should, at this point, be clear to the reader that, through the combined effects of storage protection and the distinction between the problem and supervisor states, the role of the Supervisor is rigidly maintained.

In the simplest situation, when the Supervisor and only one application program are in storage, the sole function of storage protection is to protect the Supervisor against errors in the application program. This, however, is not the normal situation. Since the execution of a program must frequently be suspended to await the completion of I/O operations, it is often desirable to allow several application programs to reside in storage simultaneously. Then, when the execution of one program must be suspended, control can be turned over to another program for a time. This is called *multiprogramming*, and it is practiced extensively on most large computers.

In a multiprogramming environment, storage protection must secure each program from errors that can occur in the others. To provide this protection, the Supervisor is programmed to perform the following functions:

- When a program is loaded into storage, an unused protection key must be found and assigned to all the storage blocks to be used by that program. Since the Supervisor operates with the key 0000, the keys 0001 through 1111 (15 in all) are available for assignment to application programs.

- When execution of a program is terminated, the protection key and storage blocks used by that program must be freed for reallocation.

Storage protection is controlled by the Supervisor through the use of two privileged instructions. The SSK (Set Storage Key) instruction allows the five-bit key on any block to be set to any value, and the ISK (Insert Storage Key) instruction allows the storage key for a storage block to be retrieved for examination. These instructions, as well as the other privileged instructions, will never be used unless a programmer is actually working on the coding of a Supervisor. However, a rudimentary understanding of their functions should give the reader some insight into the interaction that takes place between the Supervisor and application programs.

I/O OPERATIONS

A brief, general discussion of what is involved in an I/O operation is presented in this section. The fact that these operations often require time intervals equivalent to the execution of thousands of instructions presents problems that should be understood. The interested reader is urged to consult the IBM System/360 or System/370 Principles of Operation Manual for further details about I/O operations.

As a prelude to this discussion, it will be necessary to distinguish between some of the major hardware subsystems of an IBM System/360/370. For this purpose, Figure E-1 depicts the basic machine broken down into a central processing unit (CPU), main storage, channels, control units, and specific devices.

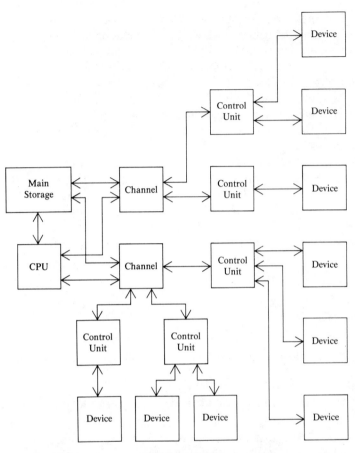

Figure E-1

The execution of application programs and the Supervisor takes place in the CPU. The channels are themselves small computers that supervise I/O operations. The fact that channels are separate computers makes it possible for a channel and a CPU to operate simultaneously on different tasks. Thus, the processing of user programs can take place in the CPU while the channels are managing the transfer of data to and from I/O devices through the control units. This potential for overlapping instruction processing and I/O processing is very important. It is the responsibility of the Supervisor to utilize this capability while managing I/O requests from application programs. Some details of how this is accomplished are presented next.

A channel, like any other computer, executes programs. Such a program—called a *channel program*—must be constructed in main storage before any request to initiate an I/O operation is issued. The instructions in a channel program are called *channel command words* (CCWs). Each CCW occupies one doubleword of storage. A channel program, then, is a sequence of CCWs that must be executed by the channel to cause an I/O operation to be performed. For example, a channel program for a print operation might consist of two CCWs—one to cause the printer to skip to the top of the next page and another to cause a line to be printed.

The format and rules for the construction of CCWs can be found in the IBM *Principles of Operation Manual*. Since the types of operations that can be performed vary with each I/O device, it is necessary to consult the manual giving the physical characteristics of a particular device before attempting to write a channel program to initiate an I/O operation on that device.

To initiate an I/O operation (that is, to actually communicate to a channel that a task is to be performed), the following three steps must be taken:

1. A channel program must be constructed in an area in main storage.
2. The word at address 000048, known as the *channel address word* (CAW), must be set up such that the following are true:
   a. Bits 0–3 contain a protection key. This key will be matched against the key of any main storage block involved in a transfer of data during the I/O operation.
   b. Bits 4–7 are 0000.
   c. Bits 8–31 contain the address of the channel program to be initiated.
3. A Start I/O (SIO) instruction must be issued. This instruction has an operand that must contain the information required to designate the particular channel and I/O device to perform the operations specified in the channel program.

The first step is usually performed by the user program or by a routine written by a systems programmer and called by the user program. The next two steps must be performed by the Supervisor because

- the CAW is in a main storage block that is protected from the user program
- the SIO instruction is a privileged instruction

When the SIO instruction is issued, the information required to initiate the operation is passed to the channel. Execution of this instruction causes the condition code to be set to reflect whether initiation of the operation was successful. The initiation will not be successful if, for some reason, the device is unavailable. If the I/O operation has been initiated, the CPU can be utilized to perform any appropriate action, and an overlap between CPU and channel activity will occur.

As an example, an operation to read a card could be initiated as follows:

1. The user program creates a channel program that will cause one card to be read and the data to be stored in a specified area of main storage.

2. The user program issues an SVC instruction with the appropriate operand to pass control to the I/O handling routine in the Supervisor. It is the responsibility of this routine to start the I/O request and then pass control back to the user program.

3. The Supervisor routine takes the address of the channel program (from a previously agreed-upon register) and the protection key (from the old PSW) and fills in the CAW.

4. The Supervisor routine issues an SIO instruction specifying the correct channel and device.

Suppose that an I/O operation has been initiated through a particular channel. When this operation is completed (successfully or otherwise), it is the responsibility of the channel involved to communicate this fact to the Supervisor. This is accomplished through the generation of an I/O interrupt with the following effects.

- A change in PSWs occurs, just as it would with any interrupt.
- Status information is stored in the doubleword at location 000040, the channel status word (CSW). This information reflects whether the I/O operation was successful.

The routine in the Supervisor that processes I/O interrupts is responsible for passing the status information back to the user program that made the request.

The question of what use will be made of the CPU while an I/O operation is in progress remains unanswered. There are, essentially, three alternatives:

1. If execution of the active user program can be continued while the I/O operation is being performed, control can be passed back to this program via the old PSW. Then, when the I/O interrupt is initiated by the channel, the Supervisor will post a flag in the user program to indicate that the I/O operation has been completed.

2. In a multiprogramming environment, the Supervisor may pass control to another user program.

3. If neither of these alternatives is possible, the Supervisor can load a PSW with a 1 in bit 14. This puts the CPU into the "wait" state (as opposed to the normal "running" state). The CPU will then sit idle until a new PSW goes into effect. This will occur with the next interrupt, which could be the I/O interrupt from the channel.

Appendix F

Listing of Structured Programming Macros

```
         MACRO
         COND
.*************************************************************************
.*                                                                      *
.* MACRO:      COND--ATTACH CONDITION TO AN "IF" OR "DO" MACRO.          *
.*                                                                      *
.* FUNCTION:   TO GENERATE AN INSTRUCTION SET WHICH WILL TEST THE        *
.*             CONDITION SPECIFIED BY THE USER.                          *
.*                                                                      *
.* PARAMETERS: CODED AS A LIST OF INSTRUCTIONS AND LOGICAL OPERANDS      *
.*             AS FOLLOWS:                                               *
.*                                                                      *
.*             (INSTRUCTION),LOGICAL-OPERATOR,(INSTRUCTION),ETC...       *
.*                                                                      *
.*             THE LOGICAL OPERATORS ARE AND, OR, ANDIF, AND ORIF.       *
.*                                                                      *
.*             ALSO CAN BE CODED AS "ELSE" WHICH CAN ONLY BE CODED       *
.*             WITHIN AN "IF" MACRO AS LAST OF ALL COND'S WITHIN THE     *
.*             "IF" AND MUST NOT BE THE ONLY COND.  IF THE USER DOES     *
.*             NOT USE "COND  ELSE" WITHIN AN "IF" AND NONE OF THE       *
.*             COND'S CODED ARE SATISFIED, THE ROUTINE WILL ABEND.       *
.*                                                                      *
.* XREF:       MACROS USED--CPARSE                                       *
.*             MODULES CALLED--NONE                                      *
.*                                                                      *
.* AUTHOR:     DAVID T. CARPENTER.                                       *
.*                                                                      *
.* DATE:       10 OCTOBER 1976.                                          *
.*                                                                      *
.* SEE THE "NIU STRUCTURE MACROS"  WRITEUP FOR FURTHER DOCUMENTATION.    *
.*                                                                      *
.*************************************************************************
```

```
            GBLA    &LVLPTR             LEVEL OF MACRO INVOCATION
            GBLA    &CONDEX(50)         STACK OF COND SEQUENCE LABELS
            GBLA    &DOIFEX(50)         STACK OF UNIQUE LABELS PER LEVEL
            GBLB    &ELSE(50)           INDICATOR OF ELSE PROCESSED AT LEVEL
            GBLB    &EXCODE(50)         TYPE OF MACRO AT GIVEN LEVEL
            GBLB    &ERRFLAG            INTERMACRO ERROR INDICATOR
            GBLB    &FIRSTC             INDICATOR OF FIRST $COND PROCESSED
&ERRFLAG    SETB    0                   SET &ERRFLAG=OFF
            AIF     (&EXCODE(&LVLPTR) EQ 1).FORIF IF "IF"-->.FORIF
            AIF     ('&SYSLIST(1)' NE 'ELSE').CHKERR  IF "ELSE" NOT PARM
&ERRFLAG    SETB    1                   SET &ERRFLAG=ON
            MNOTE   12,'*** USE OF ELSE PARM ON COND WITHIN DO ILLEGAL ***'
            AGO     .CHKERR             GO TO CHKERR
.FORIF      ANOP
            AIF     (&ELSE(&LVLPTR) EQ 0).NOELSE   IF NO ELSE YET-->.NOELSE
            MNOTE   12,'*** PREVIOUS COND ELSE MUST BE LAST OF CONDS ***'
            AGO     .CHKERR             GO TO .CHKERR
.NOELSE     ANOP
            AIF     ('&SYSLIST(1)' NE 'ELSE').CHKERR IF NOT ELSE -->.CHKERR
            AIF     (&FIRSTC EQ 1).BADELSE  IF ELSE IS FIRST $COND-->BADELS
&ELSE(&LVLPTR) SETB 1                   SET THE ELSE FLAG ON AT THAT LEVEL
            AGO     .CHKERR             GO TO .CHKERR
.BADELSE    ANOP
&ERRFLAG    SETB    1                   SET THE &ERRFLAG=ON
            MNOTE   12,'*** COND ELSE AS FIRST COND IS ILLEGAL ***'
.CHKERR     ANOP
            AIF     (&ERRFLAG EQ 1).CHKC  IF &ERRFLAG=ON, GO TO CHKC
            AIF     (&FIRSTC EQ 1).SETC   IF THIS IS THE FIRST $COND-->.SETC
            BC      15,@#EX&DOIFEX(&LVLPTR) BRANCH TO ENDIF OR DO
            EXLBL   COND                GENERATE BRANCH LABEL FROM LAST COND
            AGO     .CHKELSE            GO TO .CHKELSE
.SETC       ANOP
&FIRSTC     SETB    0                   INDICATE FIRST $COND PROCESSED
.CHKELSE    ANOP
            AIF     (&ELSE(&LVLPTR) EQ 1).NOMORE IF PARM IS ELSE-->.NOMORE
            AIF     (N'&SYSLIST EQ 1).ISSIMP CHECK FOR SINGLE CONDITION
            CPARSE  &SYSLIST(1),&SYSLIST(2),&SYSLIST(3),&SYSLIST(4),&SYSLIX
            ST(5),&SYSLIST(6),&SYSLIST(7),&SYSLIST(8),&SYSLIST(9),&SX
            YSLIST(10),&SYSLIST(11),&SYSLIST(12),&SYSLIST(13),&SYSLIX
            ST(14),&SYSLIST(15),&SYSLIST(16),&SYSLIST(17),&SYSLIST(1X
            8),&SYSLIST(19),&SYSLIST(20),&SYSLIST(21),&SYSLIST(22),&X
            SYSLIST(23),&SYSLIST(24),&SYSLIST(25)
            AGO     .NOMORE             GO TO .NOMORE
.ISSIMP     ANOP
            GENCODE &SYSLIST(1),@#EX&CONDEX(&LVLPTR),NOT
            AGO     .NOMORE
.CHKC       ANOP
            AIF     (&FIRSTC EQ 0).NOMORE  IF &FIRSTC NOT ON-->.NOMORE
&FIRSTC     SETB    0                   ELSE SET IT OFF
.NOMORE     ANOP
            MEND
```

```
          MACRO
          CPARSE
.*  ********************************************************************
.*
.*    MACRO:      'CPARSE'
.*
.*    FUNCTION:   TO GENERATE TESTING AND BRANCHING CODE IMPLEMENTING
.*                THE 'COND' MACRO.
.*
.*    OPERANDS:   BEGINNING AND ENDING WITH SIMPLE CONDITIONS, THE
.*                OPERAND LIST CONSISTS OF SIMPLE CONDITIONS AND
.*                LOGICAL OPERATORS APPEARING IN TURNS.
.*                FOR FULL INFORMATION ABOUT SIMPLE CONDITIONS AND
.*                LOGICAL OPERATIONS, CONSULT 'CODING OF CONDITIONS'
.*                IN USER'S MANUAL.
.*
.*    XREF:       MACROS USED - 'GENCODE'
.*
.*    AUTHOR:     NAIPING LEE.
.*
.*    DATE:       24 OCT 1976
.*
.*  ********************************************************************
.*
          GBLB  &ERRFLAG            FLAG WHEN ON, MEANS ERROR OCCURRED
          GBLA  &LVLPTR            PTR TO CURRENT LEVEL
          GBLA  &CONDEX(50)        STACK CONTAINING LABEL SUFFIX OFNEXT -
                                   COND SEGMENT
          GBLA  &N1                SUFFIX # TO DISTINGUISH 'LO' LABEL
          GBLA  &N2                SUFFIX # TO DISTINGUISH 'NH' LABEL
          GBLA  &N3                SUFFIX # TO DISTINGUISH 'HO' LABEL
          GBLA  &N4                SUFFIX # TO DISTINGUISH 'CD' LABEL
          LCLB  &LOFLAG            FLAG, WHEN ON, INDICATES PREVIOUS   -
                                   LOGICAL OPR IS 'AND'
          LCLB  &NHFLAG            FLAG, WHEN ON, INDICATES OR IN      -
                                   CURRENT LOW LEVEL
          LCLB  &HOFLAG            FLAG, WHEN ON, LAST HIGH LEVEL IS   -
                                   'ENDIF'
          LCLB  &ENDFLAG           FLAG, WHEN ON, INDICATES END OF PARMS
          LCLA  &CNTR              POINTER TO CPARSE PARM BEING PROCESSD
          LCLA  &LOSTPTR           STACK PTR OF &LOSTACK
          LCLA  &LOSTACK(6)        STACK OF LO LABELS EQU NEXT HO
          LCLA  &NHSTPTR           STACK PTR OF &NHSTACK
          LCLA  &NHSTACK(6)        STACK OF NH LABELS EQU NEXT CD
.*
&CNTR     SETA  1                  POINT CNTR TO 1ST PARAMETER
.*
.QUITEST  AIF   (&ERRFLAG).CPREXIT    IF ERRFLAG OR
          AIF   (NOT &ENDFLAG).CHKCNTR   ENDFLAG IS ON
.CPREXIT  MEXIT                         THEN MEXIT
.*
.CHKCNTR  AIF   ('&SYSLIST(&CNTR)' EQ '').EVEN#P  BRANCH ON EVEN# PARMS
          AIF   ('&SYSLIST(&CNTR+1)' EQ '').NULL  BRANCH TO PROPERLY PROC
          AIF   ('&SYSLIST(&CNTR+1)' EQ 'AND').AND    PARMS ACCORDING TO
          AIF   ('&SYSLIST(&CNTR+1)' EQ 'OR').OR      TYPE OF CURRENT
          AIF   ('&SYSLIST(&CNTR+1)' EQ 'ANDIF').ANDIF   LOGICAL OPR
          AIF   ('&SYSLIST(&CNTR+1)' EQ 'ORIF').ORIF
          AGO   .OTHER
```

```
.*
.AND      GENCODE &SYSLIST(&CNTR),@#LO&N1,NOT  GENERATE TESTING CODE
          AIF    (&ERRFLAG).INCNTR            SKIP ON ANY ERROR
&LOFLAG   SETB   1                            INDICATE PREVIOUS LOGICAL OPR IS 'AND
          AGO    .INCNTR                      GO TO STEP 10
.*
.OR       GENCODE &SYSLIST(&CNTR),@#NH&N2  GENERATE TESTING CODE
          AIF    (&ERRFLAG).INCNTR            SKIP ON ANY ERROR
.*
          AIF    (NOT &LOFLAG).SETF2  BRANCH IF NO LO LABEL TO BE GENED
@#LO&N1   EQU    *
&N1       SETA   &N1+1                UPDATE LO SUFFEX # N1
&LOFLAG   SETB   0                    TURN OFF LOFLAG
.*
.SETF2    ANOP
&NHFLAG   SETB   1                    TURN ON NHFLAG
          AGO    .INCNTR              GO TO STEP 10
.*
.ANDIF    GENCODE &SYSLIST(&CNTR),@#HO&N3,NOT  GENERATE TESTING CODE
          AIF    (&ERRFLAG).INCNTR              SKIP ON ANY ERROR
.*
          AIF    (NOT &LOFLAG).AF2TEST  BRANCH IF NO LO LABEL TO BE GENED
&LOSTPTR  SETA   &LOSTPTR+1            INCREMENT LO STACK PTR BY 1
&LOSTACK(&LOSTPTR)   SETA   &N1       STACK LO LABEL SUFFIX # TO BE GENED
&N1       SETA   &N1+1                UPDATE LO SUFFEX # N1
&LOFLAG   SETB   0                    TURN OFF LOFLAG
.*
.AF2TEST  AIF    (NOT &NHFLAG).SETF3  BRANCH IF NO NH LABEL TO BE GENED
@#NH&N2   EQU    *
&N2       SETA   &N2+1                UPDATE NH SUFFIX # N2
&NHFLAG   SETB   0                    TURN OFF NHFLAG
.*
.SETF3    ANOP
&HOFLAG   SETB   1                    TURN ON HOFALG
          AGO    .INCNTR              GO TO STEP 10
.*
.ORIF     GENCODE &SYSLIST(&CNTR),@#CD&N4  GENERATE TESTING CODE
          AIF    (&ERRFLAG).INCNTR   SKIP ON ANY ERROR
.*
          AIF    (NOT &LOFLAG).OF2TEST  BRANCH IF NO LO LABEL TO BE GENED
@#LO&N1   EQU    *
&N1       SETA   &N1+1                UPDATE LO SUFFEX # N1
&LOFLAG   SETB   0                    TURN OFF LOFLAG
.*
.OF2TEST  AIF    (NOT &NHFLAG).OF3TEST  BRANCH IF NO NH LABEL TO BE GENED
&NHSTPTR  SETA   &NHSTPTR+1           INCREMENT NH STACK PTR BY 1
&NHSTACK(&NHSTPTR)   SETA   &N2       STACK NH LABEL SUFFIX # TO BE GENED
&N2       SETA   &N2+1                UPDATE NH SUFFIX # N2
&NHFLAG   SETB   0                    TURN OFF NHFLAG
.*
.OF3TEST  AIF    (NOT &HOFLAG).INCNTR  BRANCH IF NO HO LABEL TO GENED
.OFLOLP   AIF    (&LOSTPTR EQ 0).OFGENHO BRANCH ON END OF STACKED LOLABEL
@#LO&LOSTACK(&LOSTPTR)   EQU    *
&LOSTPTR  SETA   &LOSTPTR-1            DECREMENT STACK POINTER BY 1
          AGO    .OFLOLP              LOOP BACK TO TEST
```

```
.OFGENHO ANOP
@#HO&N3  EQU    *
&N3      SETA   &N3+1              UPDATE HO LABEL SUFFIX # N3
&HOFLAG  SETB   0                  TURN OFF HOFLAG
         AGO    .INCNTR            GO TO STEP 10
.*
.NULL    GENCODE &SYSLIST(&CNTR),@#EX&CONDEX(&LVLPTR),NOT
         AIF    (&ERRFLAG).INCNTR    SKIP ON ANY ERROR
.*
         AIF    (NOT &LOFLAG).NF2TEST  BRANCH IF NO LO LABEL TO BE GENED
&LOSTPTR SETA   &LOSTPTR+1         INCREMENT LO STACK PTR BY 1
&LOSTACK(&LOSTPTR) SETA   &N1      STACK LO LABEL SUFFIX # TO BE GENED
&N1      SETA   &N1+1              UPDATE LO SUFFEX # N1
&LOFLAG  SETB   0                  TURN OFF LOFLAG
&HOFLAG  SETB   1                  TRUN ON HOFLAG
.*
.NF2TEST AIF    (NOT &NHFLAG).NF3TEST  BRANCH ON NO NH LABEL TO BE GENED
&NHSTPTR SETA   &NHSTPTR+1         INCREMENT NH STACK PTR BY 1
&NHSTACK(&NHSTPTR) SETA   &N2      STACK NH LABEL SUFFIX # TO BE GENED
&N2      SETA   &N2+1              UPDATE NH SUFFIX # N2
&NHFLAG  SETB   0                  TURN OFF NHFLAG
.*
.NF3TEST AIF    (NOT &HOFLAG).NHLOOP
         B      *+8
.NLOLOOP AIF    (&LOSTPTR EQ 0).NGENHO BRANCH ON END OF STACKED LO LABEL
@#LO&LOSTACK(&LOSTPTR)   EQU    *
&LOSTPTR SETA   &LOSTPTR-1         DECREMENT STACK POINTER BY 1
         AGO    .NLOLOOP           LOOP BACK TO TEST
.NGENHO  ANOP
@#HO&N3  B      @#EX&CONDEX(&LVLPTR)
&N3      SETA   &N3+1              UPDATE HO LABEL SUFFIX # N3
&HOFLAG  SETB   0                  TURN OFF HOFLAG
.*
.NHLOOP  AIF    (&NHSTPTR EQ 0).GENCD BRANCH ON END OF STACKED NH LABELS
@#NH&NHSTACK(&NHSTPTR)   EQU    *
&NHSTPTR SETA   &NHSTPTR-1         DECREMENT STACK POINTER BY 1
         AGO    .NHLOOP            LOOP BACK TO TEST
.GENCD   ANOP
@#CD&N4  EQU    *
&N4      SETA   &N4+1              UPDATE CD LABEL SUFFIX # N4
&ENDFLAG SETB   1                  INDICATE END OF PROCESSING
         AGO    .INCNTR            GO TO STEP 10
.*
.OTHER   MNOTE  12,'*** ERROR: INVALID LOGICAL OPERATER OCCURRED AFTER P-
         ARM &CNTR ***'
&ERRFLAG SETB   1                  SET ON ERROR FLAG
         AGO    .INCNTR            GO TO STEP 10
.*
.EVEN#P  MNOTE  12,'*** ERROR: UNBALANCED (EVEN) NUMBER OF PARAMETERS **-
         *'
&ERRFLAG SETB   1                  SET ON ERROR FLAG
.*
.INCNTR  ANOP
&CNTR    SETA   &CNTR+2            UPDATE PTR TO CURRENT PARMS
         AGO    .QUITEST           GO TO STEP 2
         MEND
```

```
         MACRO
         DO      &WHILE=
.*********************************************************************
.*                                                                   *
.*  MACRO:  DO                                                       *
.*                                                                   *
.*  FUNCTION:  THE DO MACRO FORMS THE INITIAL DELIMITER FOR A        *
.*     DO-COND-ENDDO MACRO SEQUENCE.  IT PERFORMS THE STACK INITIAL- *
.*     IZATION FUNCTIONS FOR THE SEQUENCE AND GENERATES AN END LABEL.*
.*     IN ORDER TO ACCOMMODATE THE CODING FORMAT FOR THE IBM CONCEPT *
.*     14 MACROS, ANY ARGUMENTS CODED WITH THE DO MACRO ARE PASSED   *
.*     TO A GENERATED COND.                                          *
.*                                                                   *
.*  PARAMETERS:                                                      *
.*                                                                   *
.*     &WHILE=  A CONDITION IS CODED WITH THIS PARAMETER WHICH IS    *
.*              PASSED TO A GENERATED COND.                          *
.*                                                                   *
.*  XREF:  MACROS USED - PUSHNEST, EXLBL.                            *
.*                                                                   *
.*********************************************************************
         GBLB   &FIRSTC            FLAG INDICATING START OF SEQUENCE
         AIF    (&FIRSTC EQ 0).DOK IF NOT ON PROCEED NORMALLY
         MNOTE 12,'***ERROR: DO OCCURS IMMEDIATELY AFTER DO OR IF***'
         AGO    .END
.DOK     ANOP
&FIRSTC  SETB   1                  TURN ON &FIRSTC
         PUSHNEST DO               INITIALIZE STACKS
         EXLBL DOIF                GENERATE THE DO LABEL
         AIF    (N'&SYSLIST EQ 0 AND '&WHILE' EQ '').END IF NO ARGS EXIT
         AIF    ('&WHILE' EQ '').MULTARG  MULTIPLE ARGS GIVEN
         COND   &WHILE             PASS ARGS TO COND
         AGO    .END               THEN LEAVE
.MULTARG COND &SYSLIST(2),&SYSLIST(3),&SYSLIST(4),&SYSLIST(5),         X
               &SYSLIST(6),&SYSLIST(7),&SYSLIST(8),&SYSLIST(9),        X
               &SYSLIST(10),&SYSLIST(11),&SYSLIST(12),&SYSLIST(13),    X
               &SYSLIST(14),&SYSLIST(15),&SYSLIST(16),&SYSLIST(17),    X
               &SYSLIST(18),&SYSLIST(19),&SYSLIST(20),&SYSLIST(21),    X
               &SYSLIST(22),&SYSLIST(23),&SYSLIST(24),&SYSLIST(25),    X
               &SYSLIST(26)
.END     MEND



         MACRO
         ELSE
.*********************************************************************
.*                                                                   *
.*  MACRO:  ELSE                                                     *
.*                                                                   *
.*  FUNCTION - ELSE ACCOMMODATES THE CODING FORMAT OF THE            *
.*             IBM CONCEPT-14 IF-ELSE-ENDIF MACRO FORMAT.            *
.*                                                                   *
.*********************************************************************
         COND ELSE
         MEND
```

```
          MACRO
          ENDDO
.***********************************************************************
.*                                                                    *
.*  MACRO:  ENDDO                                                      *
.*                                                                    *
.*  FUNCTION:  THE ENDDO MACRO FORMS THE ENDING DELIMITER FOR A       *
.*     DO-COND-ENDDO MACRO SEQUENCE.  IT GENERATES AN END LABEL       *
.*     AND DECREMENTS THE STACKS POINTER, CLEARING THE STACKS FOR     *
.*     THIS SEQUENCE.                                                 *
.*                                                                    *
.*  PARAMETERS:  NONE.                                                *
.*                                                                    *
.*  XREF:  MACROS USED - EXLBL.                                       *
.*                                                                    *
.***********************************************************************
          GBLB    &EXCODE(50)         THE STACK FOR $IF OR $DO ID
          GBLA    &LVLPTR             THE STACKS INDEX
          GBLA    &DOIFEX(50)         THE $DO OR $IF END LABEL STACK
          GBLB    &FIRSTC             INDICATOR OF SEQUENCE START
          AIF     (&LVLPTR GT 0).CHKF  CHECK INVALID STACK LEVEL
          MNOTE   12,'***ERROR: UNMATCHED ENDDO***'
          AGO     .END
.CHKF     AIF     (&FIRSTC EQ 0).EOK  IF NOT ON PROCEED NORMALLY
          MNOTE   12,'***ERROR: ENDDO IMMEDIATELY FOLLOWS DO OR IF***'
&FIRSTC   SETB    0                   TURN OFF &FIRSTC
          AGO     .DECR
.EOK      B       @#EX&DOIFEX(&LVLPTR)  BRANCH BACK TO $DO
          EXLBL   COND                GENERATE END LABEL
          AIF     (&EXCODE(&LVLPTR) EQ 0).DECR  CHECK INVALID MATCH
          MNOTE   12,'***ERROR: ENDDO PAIRED WITH IF***'
.DECR     ANOP
&LVLPTR   SETA    &LVLPTR-1           DECREMENT STACKS INDEX
.END      MEND


          MACRO
          ENDIF
.***********************************************************************
.*                                                                    *
.*  MACRO:  ENDIF                                                      *
.*                                                                    *
.*  FUNCTION:  ENDIF FORMS THE ENDING DELIMITER FOR A IF-COND-ENDIF   *
.*     MACRO SEQUENCE.  IT GENERATES END LABELS AND A CON-            *
.*     DITIONAL ABEND INSTRUCTION DEPENDING ON THE &ELSE FLAG,        *
.*     WHICH INDICATES THE PRESENCE OF A PRECEDING COND WITH AN       *
.*     ELSE ARGUMENT.  IN ADDITION, THE &ARGS FLAG INDICATES TO       *
.*     ENDIF WHETHER THE IBM CONCEPT-14 FORMAT IS BEING UTILIZED,     *
.*     WHICH ALSO SUPPRESSES THE ABEND GENERATION.  LASTLY, THE       *
.*     ENDIF MACRO DECREMENTS THE STACKS POINTER TO CLEAR THE         *
.*     STACKS FOR THIS SEQUENCE.                                      *
.*                                                                    *
.*  PARAMETERS:  NONE.                                                *
.*                                                                    *
.*  XREF:  MACROS USED - EXLBL                                        *
.*                                                                    *
.***********************************************************************
```

```
          GBLB  &FIRSTC              FLAG TO DETECT START OF SEQUENCE
          GBLB  &ELSE(50)            STACK TO DETECT $COND ELSE PRESENCE
          GBLB  &ARGS(50)            INDICATES SIMPLE IF-ELSE-ENDIF STRUC
          GBLB  &EXCODE(50)          THE STACK FOR $IF OR $DO ID
          GBLA  &LVLPTR              THE STACKS INDEX
          GBLA  &DOIFEX(50)          THE $DO OR $IF END LABEL STACK
          AIF   (&LVLPTR GT 0).CHKF  CHECK INVALID STACK LEVEL
          MNOTE 12,'***ERROR: UNMATCHED ENDIF***'
          AGO   .END
.CHKF     AIF   (&FIRSTC EQ 0).CHKNXT IF NOT ON, PROCEED NORMALLY
          MNOTE 12,'***ERROR: ENDIF IMMEDIATELY FOLLOWS IF OR DO***'
&FIRSTC   SETB  0                    TURN OFF &FIRSTC
          AGO   .DEC
.CHKNXT   AIF   (&ELSE(&LVLPTR) EQ 1).ABCOM  DONT GENERATE ABEND
          AIF   (&ARGS(&LVLPTR) EQ 0).ABND   THEN GENERATE ABEND
          EXLBL COND                 GENERATE LABEL
          AGO   .ABCOM               BRANCH TO GET LABEL
.ABND     B     @#EX&DOIFEX(&LVLPTR)  BRANCH AROUND ABEND
          EXLBL COND                 GENERATE LABEL
          ABEND 50,DUMP
.ABCOM    AIF   (&EXCODE(&LVLPTR) EQ 1).DECR  THEN MATCH OK
          MNOTE 12,'***ERROR: ENDIF PAIRED WITH DO***'
.DECR     EXLBL DOIF                 GENERATE ENDIF LABEL
&ELSE(&LVLPTR) SETB  0               TURN &ELSE OFF
&ARGS(&LVLPTR) SETB  0               TURN OFF &ARGS
.DEC      ANOP
&LVLPTR   SETA  &LVLPTR-1            DECREMENT STACKS INDEX
.END      MEND
```

```
          MACRO
          EXLBL &TYPE
.*****************************************************************
.*                                                              *
.*  MACRO:  EXLBL                                               *
.*                                                              *
.*  FUNCTION:  THE EXLBL MACRO IS AN INTERNALLY INVOKED SUPPORT *
.*     MACRO.  IT PERFORMS THE OPERATION OF CONDITIONALLY GENERATING *
.*     TWO DIFFERENT TYPES OF END LABELS DEPENDING ON THE ARGUMENT *
.*     &TYPE.                                                   *
.*                                                              *
.*  PARAMETERS:                                                 *
.*                                                              *
.*     &TYPE  INDICATES THE TYPE OF INVOCATION:                 *
.*            DOIF - CAUSES THE GENERATION OF A LABEL FROM THE DOIFEX *
.*               STACK, WHICH IS THE LABEL ASSOCIATED WITH THE ENDIF *
.*               OR DO MACROS.                                  *
.*            COND - CAUSES THE GENERATION OF A LABEL FROM THE CONDEX *
.*               STACK WHICH IS PART OF THE SEQUENCE OF LABELS   *
.*               CARRIED BETWEEN CONDS.  AFTER GENERATION A NEW  *
.*               UNIQUE LABEL IS PLACED ON THE STACK.           *
.*                                                              *
.*****************************************************************
```

```
          GBLA    &EXGEN                 THE LABEL COUNTER
          GBLA    &LVLPTR                INDEX INTO THE STACKS
          GBLA    &DOIFEX(50)            STACK FOR $ENDIF AND $DO LABELS
          GBLA    &CONDEX(50)            STACK FOR $COND END LABELS
          GBLB    &EXCODE(50)            STACK FOR $DO OR $IF TYPE INDICATORS
          AIF     ('&TYPE' NE 'DOIF').GENLBL  THEN WANT CONDEX LABEL
@#EX&DOIFEX(&LVLPTR) EQU  *
          AGO     .END                   LEAVE
.GENLBL ANOP
@#EX&CONDEX(&LVLPTR) EQU  *
&CONDEX(&LVLPTR) SETA &EXGEN             PLACE VALUE OF &EXGEN ON &CONDEX
&EXGEN    SETA    &EXGEN+1               INCREMENT &EXGEN BY 1
.END      MEND


          MACRO
          GENCODE &INST,&LBL,&TYPE
.***************************************************************************
.*                                                                        *
.* MACRO:      GENCODE--GENERATE INSTRUCTION OF COND PARAMETER LIST.       *
.*                                                                        *
.* FUNCTION:   TO PARSE THE INSTRUCTION SUBLIST PASSED AND GENERATE        *
.*             THE PROPER CONDITIONAL BRANCH ACCORDING TO PARAMETERS       *
.*             PASSED.                                                     *
.*                                                                        *
.* PARAMETERS:                                                            *
.*                                                                        *
.*         &INST   THE INSTRUCTION SUBLIST (EXACT ALLOWABLE FORMS          *
.*                 SPECIFIED IN THE "NIU STRUCTURED MACROS" WRITEUP).      *
.*                                                                        *
.*         &LBL    LABEL TO BE ATTACHED TO THE CONDITIONAL BRANCH.         *
.*                                                                        *
.*         &TYPE   IS EQUAL TO "NOT" WHEN CODED; SPECIFIES THAT BRANCH     *
.*                 TO BE TAKEN IF SPECIFIED CONDITION IS NOT TRUE.         *
.*                                                                        *
.* XREF:       MACROS USED--GETCC                                         *
.*             MODULES CALLED--NONE                                       *
.*                                                                        *
.* AUTHOR:     DAVID T. CARPENTER.                                        *
.*                                                                        *
.* DATE:       10 OCTOBER 1976.                                           *
.*                                                                        *
.* SEE THE "NIU STRUCTURE MACROS"  WRITEUP FOR FURTHER DOCUMENTATION.     *
.*                                                                        *
.***************************************************************************
          GBLB    &ERRFLAG               INTERMACRO ERROR FLAG
          GBLB    &LBLFLAG               FLAG INDICATES USER MNEMONIC
          GBLA    &CCVAL                 RETURNED CC VALUE FROM GETCC
          LCLA    &CCLOC                 LOCATION OF CONDITION IN SUBSTRING
          AIF     (N'&INST EQ 1).ISCC   IF SUBLTRING OF ONE-->.ISCC
          AIF     ('&INST(1)'(1,1) EQ 'C').ISCOMP IF INST COMPARE-->ISCOMP
          AIF     (N'&INST NE 5).CHKFOUR IF NOT 3-OP-->CHKFOUR
          &INST(1) &INST(2),&INST(3),&INST(4)
&CCLOC    SETA    5                      CONDITION IS 5TH OF SUBSTRING
          AGO     .CHKERR                GO TO .CHKERR
.CHKFOUR ANOP
          AIF     (N'&INST NE 4).CHKTRI  IF NOT 2-OP-->CHKTRI
          &INST(1) &INST(2),&INST(3)
```

```
&CCLOC    SETA   4                     CONDITION IS 4TH IN SUBSTRING
          AGO    .CHKERR               GO TO .CHKERR
.CHKTRI   ANOP
          AIF    (N'&INST NE 3).BADLIST  IF NOT 1-OP-->BADLIST
          &INST(1) &INST(2)
&CCLOC    SETA   3                     CONDITION IS 3RD IN SUBSTRING
          AGO    .CHKERR               GO TO .CHKERR
.BADLIST  ANOP
          MNOTE  12,'*** IMPROPER NON-COMPARE SUBLIST ***'
&ERRFLAG  SETB   1                     SET &ERRFLAG=ON
          AGO    .CHKERR               GO TO .CHKERR
.ISCOMP   ANOP
          AIF    (N'&INST NE 5).CHEKFOR  IF NOT 3-OP-->CHEKFOR
          &INST(1) &INST(2),&INST(3),&INST(5)
&CCLOC    SETA   4                     CONDITION IS 4TH IN SUBSTRING
          AGO    .CHKERR               GO TO .CHKERR
.CHEKFOR  ANOP
          AIF    (N'&INST NE 4).BADLST  IF NOT 2-OP-->BADLST
          &INST(1) &INST(2),&INST(4)
&CCLOC    SETA   3                     CONDITION IS 3RD IN SUBSTRING
          AGO    .CHKERR               GO TO .CHKERR
.BADLST   ANOP
          MNOTE  12,'*** IMPROPER COMPARE SUBLIST ***'
&ERRFLAG  SETB   1                     SET &ERRFLAG=ON
          AGO    .CHKERR               GO TO .CHKERR
.ISCC     ANOP
&CCLOC    SETA   1                     CONDITION IS THE SUBSTRING
.CHKERR   ANOP
          AIF    (&ERRFLAG EQ 1).ISERR  IF ERROR-->ISERR
          GETCC  &INST(&CCLOC)         CONVERT AND CHECK CONDITION VALUE
          AIF    (&LBLFLAG EQ 1).ISLBL  IF USER MEM-->ISLBL
          AIF    ('&TYPE' EQ 'NOT').GENNOT  IF A 'NOT'-->GENNOT
          BC     &CCVAL,&LBL
          MEXIT
.GENNOT   ANOP
          BC     15-&CCVAL,&LBL
          MEXIT
.ISLBL    ANOP
&LBLFLAG  SETB   0                     SET &LBLFLAG OFF
          AIF    ('&TYPE' EQ 'NOT').GENNLBL
          BC     &INST(&CCLOC),&LBL
          MEXIT
.GENNLBL  ANOP
          BC     15-&INST(&CCLOC),&LBL
          MEXIT
.ISERR    ANOP
          MEND
```

```
          MACRO
          GETCC &COND
.*****************************************************************
.*                                                              *
.* MACRO:     GETCC--RETURN PROPER CC VALUE TO CALLING MACRO.    *
.*                                                              *
.* FUNCTION:  TO VERIFY AND TRANSLATE IF NECESSARY THE SPECIFIED *
.*            USER CONDITION.                                    *
.*                                                              *
.* PARAMETERS:                                                  *
.*                                                              *
.*        &COND   THE SYMBOL SPECIFYING THE USER CONDITION THAT IS *
.*                TO BE VERIFIED AND TRANSLATED.                 *
.*                                                              *
.* XREF:      MACROS USED--NONE                                 *
.*            MODULES CALLED--NONE                              *
.*                                                              *
.* AUTHOR:    DAVID T. CARPENTER.                               *
.*                                                              *
.* DATE:      10 OCTOBER 1976.                                  *
.*                                                              *
.* SEE THE "NIU STRUCTURE MACROS"  WRITEUP FOR FURTHER DOCUMENTATION. *
.*                                                              *
.*****************************************************************
          GBLA  &CCVAL
          GBLB  &LBLFLAG              FLAG INDICATES USER MNEMONIC
          LCLC  &LWK1
          AIF   ('&COND'(1,1) LT '0' OR '&COND'(1,1) GT '9').NOTNUM
          AIF   (K'&COND GT 2).NUMERR
          AIF   (K'&COND EQ 1).NUMOK
          AIF   ('&COND'(1,2) GE '10' AND '&COND'(1,2) LE '15').NUMOK
.NUMERR   ANOP
          MNOTE 12,'*** INVALID NUMERIC CONDITION ***'
          MEXIT
.NUMOK    ANOP
&CCVAL    SETA  &COND
          MEXIT
.NOTNUM   AIF   (K'&COND NE 1).TWOCHAR
&LWK1     SETC  '&COND'
          AGO   .CALCC
.TWOCHAR  AIF   (K'&COND NE 2).INVCOND
          AIF   ('&COND'(1,1) NE 'N').OTHERMN
&LWK1     SETC  '&COND'(2,1)
          AGO   .CALCC
.OTHERMN  AIF   ('&COND' EQ 'EQ').BC8
          AIF   ('&COND' EQ 'LT').BC4
          AIF   ('&COND' NE 'LE').TRYGT
&CCVAL    SETA  13
          MEXIT
.TRYGT    AIF   ('&COND' EQ 'GT').BC2
          AIF   ('&COND' NE 'GE').INVCOND
&CCVAL    SETA  11
          MEXIT
.CALCC    AIF   ('&LWK1' NE '0').TRYH
&CCVAL    SETA  1
          AGO   .TSTN
.TRYH     AIF   ('&LWK1' EQ 'P' OR '&LWK1' EQ 'H').BC2
          AIF   ('&LWK1' EQ 'L' OR '&LWK1' EQ 'M').BC4
```

```
                AIF ('&LWK1' EQ 'E' OR '&LWK1' EQ 'Z').BC8
                     AGO   .INVCOND
.BC8            ANOP
&CCVAL          SETA 8
                     AGO   .TSTN
.BC4            ANOP
&CCVAL          SETA 4
                     AGO   .TSTN
.BC2            ANOP
&CCVAL          SETA 2
.TSTN           AIF  ('&COND'(1,1) NE 'N').DONE
&CCVAL              SETA 15-&CCVAL
.DONE           MEXIT
.INVCOND ANOP
&LBLFLAG SETB   1                        INDICATE USER MNEMONIC
                MEND




                MACRO
                IF
.*****************************************************************
.*                                                              *
.*  MACRO:  IF                                                  *
.*                                                              *
.*  FUNCTION:  THE IF MACRO FORMS THE BEGINNING DELIMITER FOR A *
.*     STRUCTURED IF-COND-ENDIF MACRO SEQUENCE.  IT PERFORMS THE*
.*     INITIAL STACK PROCESSING FOR THE SEQUENCE.  IN ADDITION, IN*
.*     ORDER TO ACCOMMODATE THE CODING FORMAT FOR THE IBM CONCEPT-14 *
.*     MACROS, ANY ARGUMENTS CODED WITH THE IF MACRO ARE PASSED TO *
.*     A GENERATED COND.  A FLAG, &ARGS, IS ALSO SET TO INDICATE *
.*     THIS CONDTION.                                           *
.*                                                              *
.*  PARAMETERS:  ARGUMENTS MAY BE PASSED THROUGH &SYSLIST.      *
.*                                                              *
.*  XREF:  MACROS USED - PUSHNEST.                              *
.*                                                              *
.*****************************************************************
        GBLB   &FIRSTC              FLAG TO SIGNAL START OF SEQUENCE
        GBLB   &ARGS(50)            INDICATES SIMPLE IF-ELSE-ENDIF STRUC
        GBLA   &LVLPTR              THE STACKS INDEX
        AIF    (&FIRSTC EQ 0).TURNON IF NOT PROCEED NORMALLY
        MNOTE 12,'***ERROR: IF IMMEDIATELY FOLLOWS IF OR DO***'
        AGO   .END                 LEAVE
.TURNON  ANOP
&FIRSTC  SETB  1                    TURN ON &FIRSTC
        PUSHNEST IF                 INITIALIZE STACKS
        AIF    (N'&SYSLIST EQ 0).END IF NO ARGS, EXIT
&ARGS(&LVLPTR) SETB  1              TURN ON &ARGS FLAG
        COND  &SYSLIST(1),&SYSLIST(2),&SYSLIST(3),&SYSLIST(4),        X
              &SYSLIST(5),&SYSLIST(6),&SYSLIST(7),&SYSLIST(8),        X
              &SYSLIST(9),&SYSLIST(10),&SYSLIST(11),&SYSLIST(12),     X
              &SYSLIST(13),&SYSLIST(14),&SYSLIST(15),&SYSLIST(16),    X
              &SYSLIST(17),&SYSLIST(18),&SYSLIST(19),&SYSLIST(20),    X
              &SYSLIST(21),&SYSLIST(22),&SYSLIST(23),&SYSLIST(24),    X
              &SYSLIST(25)
.END     MEND
```

```
          MACRO
          PUSHNEST &TYPE
.**********************************************************************
.*                                                                    *
.*   MACRO:  PUSHNEST                                                  *
.*                                                                    *
.*   FUNCTION:  THE PUSHNEST MACRO IS AN INTERNALLY INVOKED SUPPORT    *
.*        MACRO WHICH PERFORMS THE INITIAL LABEL STACKING OPERATIONS   *
.*        NECESSARY TO ESTABLISH AN IF-COND-ENDIF OR A DO-COND-ENDDO   *
.*        SEQUENCE.  THIS INCLUDES STACKING A UNIQUE DOIF END LABEL    *
.*        FOR THE ENDIF OR DO MACROS, AND STACKING A LABEL TO BE USED  *
.*        BY THE INTERVENING CONDS.  THE TYPE CODE (IF OR DO) IS ALSO  *
.*        STACKED TO ALLOW SUBSEQUENT MACRO COMPATIBILITY CHECKING     *
.*        DURING ENDIF OR ENDDO PROCESSING.                            *
.*                                                                    *
.*   PARAMETERS:                                                       *
.*                                                                    *
.*      &TYPE  INDICATES THE TYPE OF INVOCATION.  CAN BE ONE OF THE    *
.*             FOLLOWING:                                              *
.*             IF - PUSHNEST INVOKED FROM IF MACRO.                    *
.*             DO - PUSHNEST INVOKED FROM DO MACRO.                    *
.*                                                                    *
.**********************************************************************
          GBLA  &EXGEN                THE LABEL COUNTER
          GBLA  &LVLPTR               THE STACKS INDEX
          GBLA  &CONDEX(50)           THE &COND LABEL STACK
          GBLA  &DOIFEX(50)           THE $DO OR $ENDIF END LABEL STACK
          GBLB  &EXCODE(50)           STACK OF MACRO TYPE CODES:
.*                                       0 = $DO
.*                                       1 = $IF
          AIF   (&LVLPTR LT 50).ADDSTK  IF NOT FULL PROCEED NORMALLY
          MNOTE 12,'***ERROR: NESTING LEVEL EXCEEDS CAPACITY***'
          AGO   .END
.ADDSTK  ANOP
&LVLPTR  SETA  &LVLPTR+1               INCREMENT &LVLPTR FOR NEXT ENTRY
&DOIFEX(&LVLPTR) SETA  &EXGEN          PUT &EXGEN COUNTER VALUE ON &DOIFEX
&CONDEX(&LVLPTR) SETA  &EXGEN+1        PUT NEXT &EXGEN ON &CONDEX
&EXGEN   SETA  &EXGEN+2                SET UP NEXT UNIQUE VALUE
          AIF   ('&TYPE' EQ 'IF').IFCALL   IF NOT IF PROCESS DO
&EXCODE(&LVLPTR) SETB  0               PUT DO CODE ON &EXCODE
          AGO   .END
.IFCALL  ANOP
&EXCODE(&LVLPTR) SETB  1               PUT IF CODE VALUE ON &EXCODE
.END     MEND
```

WHBrn

TAVINERYcp

Order#

3022689 1 7

"les tima keep"

be llevasin plitrade

Tonopan 336
Will 378
Elon 347
Last 378
Dulles 357
Sweet 385

Petro
347
Rem 378
El paso 378
Weather 374
SFA 369.

1/24/14

mumbolissa

Appendix G

Answers to
Nonprogramming Exercises

Chapter 1 Number Systems and Computer Storage

1.2 Binary- or Hexadecimal-to-Decimal Conversion

a. 3	c. 30	e. 7	g. 375
b. 23	d. 59	f. 15	h. 7

a. 15	c. 3026	e. 3311	g. 241
b. 161	d. 4096	f. 239	h. 294

1.3 Decimal-to-Binary or -Hexadecimal Conversion

1. a. 7C	b. 2A	c. FA0	d. 1B0

2. a. 01111100	b. 00101010	c. 111110100000	d. 000110110000

1.4 Conversions between Binary and Hexadecimal Representations

1. a. 1110   c. 1011100101110110   e. 1111111110101011
   b. 0001000011001101 d. 0100001000010000   f. 1010101111001101

2. a. 16F   b. 155   c. A   d. F1   e. 5EF   f. BCE2

1.5 Addition and Subtraction of Binary and Hexadecimal Numbers

1. a. 100011	b. 1011010	c. 101100	
2. a. 10100	b. 1000	c. 11111	
3. a. 12D7C	b. 9C4F	c. 185D	d. 2DC3
4. a. 6484	b. 250F	c. 4F1F	d. 1520

1.7 Binary Representation of Integer Numbers

a. 00000001	c. FFFFFFFF	e. 000020DC
b. 000000F8	d. FFFFFFF6	f. FFFFDF24

1.8 Overflow

a. no   b. no   c. yes   d. no   e. yes   f. yes   g. no

1.9 General-Purpose Registers and Relative Addressing

1. a. valid, 0001E0
   b. valid, 08ACD8
   c. valid, 00005C
   d. not in the form D(B)
   e. valid, 000012
   f. valid, 000012
   g. not in the form D(B)
   h. not in the form D(B)

2. a. valid, 08ABD0
   b. valid, 00008C
   c. valid, 000002
   d. valid, 000059
   e. valid, 000059
   f. not valid
   g. valid, 8AB9D
   h. valid, 8AB9D

Chapter 2   Basic Concepts

2.2 RR Instructions

1. a. 1A1F   b. 1B2A   c. 1AE3   d. 1B00   e. 1AFE

2. a. LR   2,0   c. SR   12,12
   b. AR   15,14   d. LR   3,4

3.

	R0	R1	R6
a.	not changed	not changed	001A2F0B
b.	not changed	not changed	FFE5EAE4
c.	not changed	FFFFBC0B	not changed
d.	not changed	FFFF882D	not changed
e.	not changed	00000000	not changed

2.3 RX Instructions

1. a. 58F32000   c. 58F20000   e. 58F00018
   b. 58F02000   d. 502ED014   f. 50680004

2. a.   L   0,12(1,5)   d.   L   4,4(5,14)
   b.   ST   1,4   e.   ST   2,12(3,13)
   c.   L   1,28(1,8)

3. a. 000ABC20   b. 000C1F21—error   c. 000C1F30
   d. 0016DB21—error

2.7 The XREAD and XDECI Instructions

1. 5C 5C F1 F2 F2 C1 F3   2. 5B 7C 7B E7 E9

2.8 The XPRINT and XDECO Instructions

>   C1 40 40 40 40
>   C1 C1
>   C2 40 C2 40 C2 40
>   F1 7D
>   50 F0
>   5B 5B E6 D6

2.10 Multiplication and Division

	R0	R1	R2	R3
a.	not changed	not changed	FFFFFFFF	FFFFFFFC
b.	FFFFFFFF	FFFFFFFD	not changed	not changed
c.	not changed	not changed	00000000	00000010
d.	not changed	not changed	00000000	0000000C
e.	FFFFFFFF	FFFFFFF6	not changed	not changed
f.	00000000	00000002	not changed	not changed
g.	not changed	not changed	00000000	00000028
h.	not changed	not changed	FFFFFFFF	FFFFFFF8

	R1	R2	R3	R4	R5
a.	not changed	00000002	00000006	not changed	not changed
b.	not changed	00000000	FFFFFFEC	not changed	not changed
c.	not changed	00000014	00000000	not changed	not changed
d.	not changed	not changed	not changed	00000000	FFFFFFB0
e.	not changed	00000000	FFFFFFFB	not changed	not changed
f.	not changed	00000006	00000001	not changed	not changed
g.	not changed	not changed	not changed	00000000	0000003C
h.	not changed	not changed	not changed	FFFFFFFE	FFFFFFEF

Chapter 3 Looping, Subroutines, and More Instructions

3.3 The BXLE and BXH Instructions

1. a. 12 b. 8 c. 2^{31} d. 4 e. 5 f. 5 g. 6

Chapter 5 Decimal Arithmetic

5.2 The PACK and UNPK Instructions

1. 00 01 2F
2. BA
3. 00 01 23 4F
4. 00 BD FE
5. F1 F2 F3
6. F0 F0 F2 C6
7. FC FD FE
8. F0 F0 F0 D4

5.3 The Decimal Instructions AP, SP, and ZAP

1. 01 23 3C
2. 01 23 5C
3. 02 1C
4. 00 10 0D
5. 00 08 0D
6. 00 00 00 0C

5.4 The Decimal Instructions MP, DP, and CP

1. 00 08 0C
2. 00 11 7D
3. 00 30 00 0C

4. 2C 00 0C
5. 40 2C 0D
6. 00 5C 00 0C

5.6 The ED Instruction

		Resulting Pattern Value											*Character String*
	40	F1	F2	F3									_123
1.	40	40	40	40									____
2.	40	40	F1	F2									_12
3.	40	F1	F2	F3									_123
4.	40	40	40	F0									__0
5.	40	40	F1	F2									_12
6.	5C	F1	F2	F3									*123
7.	5C	5C	5C	F0									***0
8.	5C	5C	F1	F2									**12
9.	40	F1	4B	F2	F3								_1.23
10.	40	40	40	40	40								____
11.	40	40	40	F1	F2								__12
12.	40	F1	4B	F2	F3								_1.23
13.	40	40	4B	F0	F0								__.00
14.	40	40	4B	F1	F2								__.12
15.	40	F1	F2	6B	F3	F4	F5	4B	F6	F7			_12,345.67
16.	40	40	40	40	40	40	F1	4B	F2	F3			_____1.23
17.	40	40	40	40	40	40	40	4B	F0	F0			_____.00
18.	40	F1	F2	6B	F3	F4	F5	4B	F6	F7	40	40	40	_12,345.67___
19.	40	40	40	40	40	40	F1	4B	F2	F3	40	40	40	_____1.23___
20.	40	40	40	40	40	40	40	4B	F0	F0	40	40	40	_____.00___
21.	40	40	40	40	40	F1	F2	4B	F3	F4	40	C3	D9	_____12.34_CR

5.7   The SRP Instruction

1. 40 00 0C
2. 01 30 0D
3. 00 00 00 3C
4. 00 00 1C

5. 00 02 7C
6. 00 16 80 0C
7. 00 00 00 0C

Chapter 10   Floating-Point Arithmetic

10.2   Floating-Point Number Representations

1. a. 46FE6478
   b. 3E6421A6
   c. 17AE1234

   d. 4EBCDEFA
   e. 7F1234AE

2. a. 52123456789ABCDE
   b. 2BAECBDF12345F1B
   c. 43000AECBDF12345

   d. not possible
   e. 40123456789ABCDE

3. a. $-.478100 * 16^5$
   b. $.478100 * 16^6$
   c. $-.123456 * 16^{-54}$

   d. $-.ABCDEF * 16^7$
   e. $.CDEF01 * 16^{47}$

4. a. $-.478100ABCDEF01 * 16^5$
   b. $.47810012345678 * 16^6$
   c. $-.123456F12345BC * 16^{-54}$

   d. $-.ABCDEF01234567 * 16^7$
   e. $.CDEF01FEDCBA98 * 16^{47}$

10.4   Conversions between Decimal and Floating-Point Numbers

Hexadecimal to Decimal
a. 2766.07110596
b. 18.037781
c. .99554443

d. .03721619
e. .00233459

Decimal to Hexadecimal
a. 2694.5879
b. .FCD3
c. .0288

d. 76.C3F1
e. 270F.FFAA

Index